Tsong Khapa's
Speech of Gold in the
Essence of True Eloquence

Princeton Library of Asian Translations

Tsong Khapa's Speech of Gold in the *Essence of True Eloquence*

Reason and Enlightenment in the Central Philosophy of Tibet

TRANSLATED WITH AN INTRODUCTION BY
Robert A. F. Thurman

Princeton University Press
Princeton, New Jersey

Published by Princeton University Press,
41 William Street, Princeton, New Jersey 08540
In the United Kingdom: Princeton University Press,
Guildford, Surrey

Library of Congress Cataloging in Publication Data
will be found on the last printed page of this book

ISBN 691-07285-x

Publication of this book has been aided by a grant from
The Whitney Darrow Publication Reserve fund of
Princeton University Press

This book has been composed in Linotron Sabon
Clothbound editions of Princeton University Press books
are printed on acid-free paper, and binding materials
are chosen for strength and durability

Printed in the United States of America by
Princeton University Press, Princeton, New Jersey

This book is dedicated to
the late Geshe Ngawang Wangyal (1901-1983),
founder of the Lamaist Buddhist Monastery of America,
teacher of unerring wisdom and inconceivable kindness.

CONTENTS

List of Illustrations ix

Foreword *by His Holiness the Dalai Lama* xi

Preface xiii

Note xvii

Introduction 1

I. *Reverence to the Guru, Manjughosha!* 3
II. *Shambhu, Meghavahana, Hiranyagarbha* 9
III. *I bow devoted to Maitreya and Manjughosha* 18
IV. *I bow my head to the feet of Nagarjuna and Asanga* 21
V. *Respectfully I bow to those Master Scholars* 33
VI. *Many who did not realize That* 49
VII. *But I have seen It quite precisely* 63
VIII. *You who aspire to Peerless Philosophy* 89

The Short *Essence of True Eloquence* 175

The Great *Essence of True Eloquence* 185

Prologue 187
I. Statements from the *Elucidation of Intention* 191
II. Explanations of the Scripture's Statements 209
III. The Essential Centrist Message 253
IV. Explanations of the Followers of the Savior Nagarjuna 265
V. The Dialecticist Elucidation of the Holy Intention 288
VI. Avoidance of Contradiction between the (Dialecticist) System and the Scriptures 345
VII. The Chief Reason for Negation of Ultimate Status 364

Glossary of Technical Terms 387

List of Abbreviations 401

Bibliography of Principal Sources 407

Index 421

LIST OF ILLUSTRATIONS

(following p. 22)

1. Tsong Khapa and main disciples receiving mystic revelation from Manjushri. Detail of Illustration 11.
2. Manjughosha Kumarabhuta, the supernal Bodhisattva in his role as mystic inspirer of Centrist philosophers. Detail of th'anka, collection of Office of Tibet, New York.
3. Shakyamuni Buddha. Detail of th'anka, collection of Office of Tibet, New York.
4. Maitreya Bodhisattva, the future Buddha in his Tushita heaven mansion, in his role as inspirer of the "magnificent deeds" lineage of Buddhist philosophers. Detail of th'anka, collection of Office of Tibet, New York.

(following p. 190)

5. Nagarjuna. Detail of th'anka, collection of Office of Tibet, New York.
6. Aryasanga. Detail of th'anka, collection of Office of Tibet, New York.
7. Aryadeva. Detail of th'anka, collection of Office of Tibet, New York.
8. Vasubandhu. Detail of th'anka, collection of Office of Tibet, New York.
9. Dignaga. Detail of th'anka, collection of Office of Tibet, New York.
10. Dharmakirti. Detail of th'anka, collection of Office of Tibet, New York.
11. Tsong Khapa, founder of dGa-ldan school of Tibetan Buddhism, and scenes from his life. Th'anka, collection of The Newark Museum (11.707).
12. Icon of "refuge assembly." Th'anka, collection of Mead Art Museum, Amherst College, gift of George L. Hamilton.

THE DALAI LAMA

THEKCHEN CHOLING
MACLEOD GANJ 176216
KANGRA DISTRICT
HIMACHAL PRADESH

FOREWORD

I am very happy that Tsong Khapa's masterpiece of Tibetan Buddhist philosophy, the *Legs bShad sNying po*, has been translated into English, and can now be studied by Western philosophers and practitioners of Buddhism. It has long been one of my favorite works, and I hope that others will appreciate its deep thought and lucid insights as we have for centuries in Tibet. It has always been considered by our most learned scholars an extremely profound and difficult work, and I know Dr. Thurman has struggled with it for more than ten years, as well as questioning me and a number of Tibetan scholars about the many difficult points. Beyond the difficulty of understanding, there is the problem of getting the right terminology in English for our complicated Tibetan technical terms. It may perhaps take decades for the full transmission of the Central Way philosophy into modern philosophical circles, just as we Tibetans labored for many centuries to master the deep thought of the Ornaments of Indians such as Nagarjuna and Asanga. I am confident that Dr. Thurman has made a good beginning with this translation, and that the clear light of Tsong Khapa's philosophical genius will shine forth from these pages to kindle a spark of recognition in the minds of free thinkers in the west. The spirit of open, critical inquiry that descends from Shakyamuni Buddha through spiritual teachers such as Tsong Khapa to us is one of the most precious parts of mankind's common heritage. But to benefit human beings, it must be used by individual thinkers who are concerned with understanding the true nature of the self and of the world. The deepest insights are not recommended to us just because they spring from one particular tradition or another, eastern or western. As Shakyamuni himself said, "Just as the goldsmith gets his gold, first testing by melting, cutting, and rubbing, the wise accept my teachings after full examination, and not just out of devotion to me." So I urge you neither to accept nor reject these teachings of the Central Way tradition just because they are Buddhist, but to work with them, melting them in your deep thoughts, cutting them with critical analysis, and rubbing them against the touchstone of your own experience. I have found them to be true gold, and shall be pleased if others discover their benefit as well.

June 4, 1981

PREFACE

I offer this work on the "Speech of Gold" of the great Tsong Khapa in the hope that the always imperfect filter of translation will not discolor it beyond the recognition of those who seek the "complete clarity" that is the goal of live philosophy, the complete clarity of "perfect enlightenment." The great *Essence of True Eloquence* itself, the translation of which is the ground and heart of this book, has been called "Tsong Khapa's iron bow." Extremely hard to understand in Tibetan, how much harder to translate it and expound it. Yet here I find I have done just that; may Manjushri protect me!

Shakyamuni Buddha was averse to teaching his most profound message, lest it be seriously misunderstood. Nagarjuna warned that a misunderstood absolute emptiness is like a wrongly held snake, highly dangerous when its medicine of relativism is taken as the poison of nihilism. Yet Tsong Khapa and his successors became more and more open about teaching absolute emptiness over the last five centuries. Today it seems dangerous not to teach it widely. Perhaps the evolution of civilizations has brought us to a brink where confrontation with the absolute is no longer a responsibility or privilege of an elite, but a vital necessity for all. Our power over matter has become rather godlike, indeed. If our understanding of reality and ourselves does not correspond, we will surely make this world a hell. It is too cowardly to blame it on God, Buddha, Brahma, the Tao, the Random Universe, or whatever else. And it is a poor gamble to bank on nothingness—"what does it matter?—in hope of automatic anaesthesia beyond individual or planetary death. However difficult it may seem, we must each take responsibility for our own absolute, examine what we think it is, how we came to that perspective, if it withstands critical analysis, and how it affects our actions. So we are vitally concerned to undertake the struggle for this Everest peak of Tibetan thought on the absolute, this *Essence of True Eloquence*.

I have spent some effort in its introduction, setting up a base camp for your expedition, describing the terrain of the tradition within which Tsong Khapa taught, giving an inventory of the best modern equipment from contemporary thought, demonstrating training exercises, showing various routes of ascent, and warning of dangerous chasms. The actual assault is up to each person. Each must release the intellect, to experience the triumph for himself or herself.

The late Venerable Geshe Wangyal first urged me to translate this book. He himself had memorized it during his "graduate studies" at Drepung Monastic University near Lhasa. He recited it in the Great Assembly and defended his understanding before the most learned and enlightened teachers. That was in the 1930s. He then went to Wu Tai Shan in China and meditated on it for some years. When he emerged into the world, he began to teach himself English. By the workings of *karma* or history, he eventually migrated to New Jersey, where I met him and studied with him at the first Lamaist Buddhist Monastery of America. Seven years later, he started me off on the *Essence of True Eloquence*.

In between, at Harvard, Professor Daniel H. H. Ingalls patiently grounded me in the broad and beautiful land of Sanskrit, and my gratitude for his generous brilliance grows ever deeper as the years go by. Professor Masatoshi Nagatomi taught me Buddhological scholarship, with its dedication to impartiality and its concern for precision of detail as well as depth of insight. I am always grateful for his tireless good humor, his subtlety of understanding, and his skillful kindness. Beginning the *Essence* in 1970, I went to India to consult other teachers. Dr. V. V. Gokhale gave great help in understanding the Svatantrikas, or "Dogmaticists" as I have called them. It was a privilege to witness a mind at work that could freely move back and forth between Tibetan and Sanskrit, never losing sight of the philosophical issues. He is a living example of the great Indian Pandita, as if himself an incarnation of the genius of Bhavaviveka.

In Dharamsala, I was blessed with the delight of hard-working conversations with His Holiness the Fourteenth Dalai Lama of Tibet, or as he calls himself, the Buddhist monk-scholar Tenzin Gyatso. When, after the shock of meeting again after six years, he heard which book I was undertaking to translate, he seemed a bit concerned for me. I mentioned Geshe Wangyal's instigation and showed him the very rough draft I had already produced at Deya on Mallorca, from an edition of the text His Holiness himself had given me long before. Suddenly, he laughed in his sunny way, called for his own hand-annotated copy, and stunned his secretaries by throwing his schedule to the winds. He started at once to run through the text, giving me the corrections and variants he had collected through his own extensive study. This continued for a number of sessions, and was an immeasurable help. He would stop at certain passages, explaining the kernel or pointing out a knot for reflection, mentioning related works and commentaries that would help me with the unraveling of the deep meanings. Most of all, he shared with me his own deep love for this challenging and illuminating work. Words cannot express my gratitude for his generosity and kindness, and my admiration for his oceanic genius.

Subsequently, I had the good fortune to work through the dPal 'Byor Lhun Grub commentary with the Venerable Tara Rinpoche, then abbot of the Gyuto Monastery in Dalhousie. Through his insight, erudition, and skill in explanation, I was able to produce a workable second draft, although there were certain sections I still could not crack, especially those on the distinctive specialties of the Dialecticists (*Prāsaṅgika*).

When I returned to America at the end of 1971, Geshe Wangyal conferred upon me the all-important "personal textual transmission" (*lung*). In the Tibetan tradition, it is believed that the oral transmission of such central teachings must be preserved unbroken, and that the seeds of eventual understanding are planted by hearing the text read through or recited by a teacher who has himself heard it from another, and so back in an unbroken line to the origin of the teaching; in this case Tsong Khapa and, according to the tradition, Manjushri himself. At the time of this transmission, the teacher begins by telling the student the line of teachers through whom it has come. And so I must list and express my deepest thanks to all these teachers. First of all of course is Manjushri, the Bodhisattva of Transcendent Wisdom, whose vow is to appear everywhere throughout the universes to stimulate inquiry into the profound teaching of the absolute reality of emptiness. Then there is Tsong Khapa (1357-1419). From him the line leads (with some uncertainty at the beginning due to the large number of his enlightened disciples) through mKhas Grub rJe (1385-1438), Ba-so Chos-kyi rGyal-mtshan (1402-1473), Grub-chen Chos-kyi rDo-rje (late 15th century), rGyal-ba dbEn-sa-ba (1505-1566), Sangs-rgyas Ye-shes (1525-1591), Pan-chen bLo-bzang Chos-kyi rGyal-mtshan (1570-1662), rDo-rje 'Dzin-pa dKon-mchog rGyal-mtshan (1612-1687), 'Jam-dbyangs bZhad-pa Ngag-dbang brTson-'grus (1648-1721), Khri-chen bLo-bzang bsTan-pai Nyi-ma (1689-1746), lCang-kya Rol-pai rDo-rje (1717-1786), Thu'u-bkvan bLo-bzang Chos-kyi Nyi-ma (1737-1802), dKon-mchog 'Jigs-med dbAng-po (1728-1791), Gun-thang 'Jam-dbyangs bsTan-pai sGron-me (1762-1823), dbAl-mang dKon-mchog rGyal-mtshan (19th century), rTsa-bai bLa-ma rTa-mgrin bLo-bzang rTa-dbyangs (1867-1937), and Geshe sByin-pa of the sGo-mang College of Drepung, who transmitted it to the venerable Geshe Wangyal. The remarkable lives of these philosopher-saints of Tibet and Mongolia are stories for another occasion. Here I avow my deep appreciation of their genius, effort, and compassion, in keeping alive this clear stream of critical philosophy. I must also render my heartfelt thanks to the Venerable Tshanshab Serkhong Rinpoche, who conferred upon me a "mystic" (*nye brgyud*) textual transmission, which he received from his father, also Serkhong Rinpoche, who in Tibet received the transmission as a mystic revelation directly from Tsong Khapa. In August 1981, Serkhong Rinpoche (in his late sixties) recited the entire book from memory in four hours as I followed the text.

I must also thank my fellow Buddhologists, Professors Jeffrey Hopkins and David S. Ruegg, each of whom separately taught me through their important translations and studies, as well as in a number of helpful conversations, much that I had missed in the vast literature of Tibetan thought. And I have a great sense of gratitude to another colleague and kindred spirit, the late philosopher Ludwig Wittgenstein, whom I never was privileged to meet, but whose courageous breakthroughs and lucid insights provided me with the key concepts with which to bring Dialectical Centrism to life in the modern universe of philosophical discourse. I also thank my students over the last years at Amherst College and the American Institute of Buddhist Studies, who struggled with the evolving versions of the translation of the *Essence*, helping me with their questions and insights to see more and more of the further dimensions of its subtleties. Special thanks to Joseph Loizzo, whose brilliant *summa* essay on the *Essence* in relation to Nietzsche and Wittgenstein encouraged me greatly; first that it could be understood by a sharp and honest western thinker, and second that the Central Way is more than ever relevant to current philosophy.

Words of thanks to my wife, Nena von Schlebrugge, are completely inadequate for her unfailing, patient, critical support of this seemingly interminable project. Without her inspiration, this work would never have been completed.

Among institutions, thanks are due to the American Institute of Indian Studies for sending me twice to India, in 1970-1971 and in 1979-1980; to Amherst College and the American Institute of Buddhist Studies for assistance in preparation of the manuscript; to the *Journal of the American Academy of Religion*, *Philosophy East and West*, and *Tibet Journal*, for graciously allowing me to use portions of essays published in them; and to Margaret Case and the staff of the Princeton University Press for seeing the work through the publication process.

I must end where I began, with a special homage to the late Venerable Geshe Wangyal, as this work has only been possible because of his infinite kindness and consummate skill as a teacher. He led me into the heart of the Tibetan language and gave me the keys to this *Essence of True Eloquence*. A simple, unassuming man, he preferred to tend the flowers in his garden in the gentle hills near the Delaware, shunning a highly merited acclaim in the forums of philosophy in Tibet, India, or America.

But he was the most profound philosophical genius I have encountered, from the little bit I was able to recognize. And he exemplified for me the central fact that philosophy is no mere word game, but is the ground of life, transformation, sheer joy; tolerance in little things and selfless effort in the bigger ones. His daytime garden was lush and beautiful in recent days, with roses and peonies and bright orange tiger lilies, and he was never happier than when he carefully watered them in the cool of the late afternoon. But for me his most wonderful garden is ever, to borrow Tsong Khapa's exquisite metaphor, the "night-lily garden of the treatises of Nagarjuna," wherein the white night-blooming *kunda*-lilies are our "eyes of intellect," which, after much patient tending and watering with the nectar of open teaching, may bloom in the silvery rays of the moon of Chandrakirti's and Tsong Khapa's elucidations. And so it is by the kindness of this Guru, one and the same as Manjushri to me, that the "darkness of the extremist heart" has begun to be dispelled, the "constellations of confusing teachings" to be eclipsed, and my mind feels some "relief at last!" As a small gesture to repay such unrepayable kindness, I now offer in the golden light of dawn this inevitably imperfect study and translation, in the hope that others may find benefit and joy in Tsong Khapa's overview of the liberating Central Way.

Amherst, Massachusetts
May 18, 1981
Chitra Full Moon, Iron Bird Year
Amended on Geshe Wangyal's Nirvana,
January 29, 1983

NOTE

In transliteration of Sanskrit words, I have followed the standard conventions in the italicized occurrences in parentheses and footnotes, but have departed from this in the English text, omitting diacritical vowel marks, using sh for ś, sh for ṣ, and ch for c. For the Tibetan alphabet I have adopted the following English letters: k, kh, g, ng, c (also ch in English text), ch, j, ny, t, th, d, n, p, ph, b, m, ts, tsh, dz, w, zh, z, ' (initial, but not for base of attached vowel signs i, u, e, o) and a (final) y, r, l, sh, s, h, a. For most Tibetan names I have kept in the unsounded pre-initial letters, capitalizing the first sounded initial consonant. Tsong Khapa's name I anglicize.

Italicized section headings in the Introduction are lines from Tsong Khapa's own introductory verses in the great *Essence*, printed in continuum at the beginning of the translation. The Introduction may be read as a study in itself, but it is framed on Tsong Khapa's verses, and is intended to give readers from a cultural universe different from that of his original readers a good vantage from which to plunge into the *Essence*.

INTRODUCTION

I

Reverence to the Guru, Manjughosha!

So I begin,[1] joining Tsong Khapa in paying homage to the "Eternal Youth of Dulcet Voice," Manjughosha Kumarabhuta, the great spiritual hero who raises up the shining golden sword of transcendent wisdom in all universes where living beings seek the real meaning of their existence and need the liberating path of philosophy.

According to the belief of Universal Vehicle Buddhists, Manjushri became a perfectly enlightened Buddha many aeons ago in another universe. However, one manifestation of his special skill in liberative technique is to emanate as a bodhisattva in all those universes where Supreme Buddhas dwell. He always asks them to teach living beings, divine as well as human, the wondrous message of the Profound, the Ultimate Reality, the Transcendent, often called "Selflessness," "Emptiness," "Signlessness," or "Wishlessness." In his most common icon, Manjushri appears as a princely youth of sixteen years, saffron-gold in hue, radiant, holding a text of the *Transcendent Wisdom Scripture* in his left hand, and a flame-tipped sword—the two-edged, razor-sharp sword of critical wisdom—upraised in his right hand. The light from the tip of the sword floods the intellects of all present in the assembly, clearing away the darkness of confusion that has enshrouded them since beginningless time. He is called "Lord of the Word" *Vāgiśvara*, and also "Sole Father of all Victors" (*Sarvajinapitā*), the Prince Consort of the Supreme Queen, Transcendent Wisdom, *Prajñāpāramitā*, the Mother of All Buddhas.

As spiritual Father, it is fitting that he be the patron divinity of literature, the Word used consciously as tool of liberation, a sharp sword that cuts away the tangle of misknowledge that traps humans and gods in the automatic habit patterns of cyclic living. Thoreau echoed this symbolism when he called this transvalued word "our father tongue, a reserved and select expression, too significant to be heard by the ear, which we must be born again in order to speak."[2] It may surprise some,

[1] Each of the sections of this introductory essay is headed by a line or lines in italics, which are drawn from the opening verses of the *Essence of True Eloquence*, the main work under consideration. Although the introduction thus attempts to follow the pattern of introduction used by Tsong Khapa himself, his brief lines have exploded into a long essay, due to the enormous differences in historical context, presupposed knowledge, and assumed attitudes, between his readers in the early fifteenth century and us today.

[2] H. D. Thoreau, *Walden and Other Writings*, edited by J. W. Krutch (New York: Bantam, 1977), p. 180.

who have heard that words cause confusion and that the "mystic sages" seek to transcend words to commune with the "inexpressible beyond," to see how great is the veneration accorded the Word in the Buddhist tradition. Tsong Khapa himself wrote, the very morning of his highest enlightenment, that "Of all deeds, the deeds of speech are supreme; hence, it is for them that the wise commemorate a Buddha!"[3] And Manjushri, as god of the Word, is the universal icon of the liberative power of the Word. Thus he is invoked at the beginning of all works of philosophy in the Buddhist tradition.

For what is of value in a work of philosophy? Is it the amount of information given in displays of erudition, the density of thought of the writer, the completeness of schematization of reality, or the acuity of critical penetration? It is all of these, of course, but what is that underlying criterion that itself makes them all worthwhile? Is it not the exact degree to which the work conveys "Truth"? And is not "Truth," after all, not merely "right" as opposed to "wrong," but rather "that which makes one free"? "Love of Wisdom" is fundamentally liberative. It is a love of that faculty of genius that comes to apprehend truth, in truth embraces freedom, and then flows out to liberate the genius of others. There are only two kinds of words, those that breed misknowledge and thereby increase bondage, and those that open to wisdom and thereby liberate. The engine of language never idles, as Wittgenstein observed, and so even this here now is leading either to bondage or liberation. It is to aspire, invoke, and ensure the latter that I, too, as a translator and elucidator of the central way philosophy in our times and culture, pay homage to my innermost guru. May the radiance of his intelligence and the music of his eloquence illuminate my mind and energize my speech.

The heart of this work is the gift of the great Tsong Khapa (1357-1419), and is not originally mine, although any work of genuine translation places the responsibility for understanding on the translator, or "public eye" (*lokacakṣu*),[4] as he is called in Indo-Tibetan traditions. And even Tsong Khapa, as great a genius as he was, owes this *Essence of True Eloquence* to Manjushri's supernal activities.

The story goes, as we shall see in greater detail, that Tsong Khapa was greatly discouraged at the prospect of writing his most advanced philosophical works, the first being the transcendent insight (*vipaśyana*) section of his *Stages of the Path of Enlightenment*.[5] The reason for his discouragement was not the difficulty of the work, for he could cope

[3] See the short *Essence of True Eloquence*, below.

[4] Tib. *lo-tsva-ba*. The Skt. *loka* means "people" or "society," as well as "world," like the Greek *cosmos*.

[5] LRC.

very well with even these extreme subtleties and profundities, but rather his sense that few if any of his contemporaries and successors would be able to benefit by his efforts. He felt that his genius was almost extraterrestrial, and that it would be fruitless to impose his teachings on mere mortals (a feeling Shakyamuni Buddha is said also to have experienced after his enlightenment). But Manjushri appeared to Tsong Khapa and demanded to know what the procrastination was all about. When Tsong Khapa complained about his sense of being a misunderstood genius, the bodhisattva scathingly challenged his ability to count the geniuses in the world, in those times or in the future, and then gave his assurance that many would indeed benefit, beyond Tsong Khapa's fondest imaginings. This verbal assurance was reinforced by a continuous vision Tsong Khapa had from that moment, while working on the book, of the formulae of the twenty emptinesses from the *Transcendent Wisdom Scriptures* written in three-dimensional translucent silver letters in the sky all around him.[6] A few years later, when he wrote the second book, the *Essence* now before us, in conjunction with his master commentary on Nagarjuna's *Wisdom*, the vision returned for several months, but that time in letters of pure gold. I will return to this story in the biography below.

I make no claim to such a vision. And if the original author felt diffident about the work's usefulness in his times, how much more should I be discouraged by the enormity of the task of making these insights available to a modern audience! Indeed, the question must be faced, just what is the audience of this book?

First, the *Essence of True Eloquence* is a work of "philosophy," and hence a communication to "philosophers" in the true sense of the title, as "lovers of wisdom, whose wisdom is their love." But where are today's philosophers to be found? Too many have almost forgotten that Science and Technology are mere children, that ageless Father Philo and Mother Sophia still must worry about their notions and their adventures. Thus neglecting the parents, these philosophers become enthralled by the willful children. Their "philosophy" becomes a mere "handmaiden" of "Science," and is hard-pressed even to cope with rambunctious Technology. They take comfort in assuming the role of technicians of language and other conceptual systems, servicing the theoretical software of the empirical experimenters, whose work they assume to be *really* important

[6] There are numerous lists of the four, sixteen, eighteen, and twenty emptinesses. The usual emptinesses are those of 1) the internal, 2) the external, 3) both internal and external, 4) emptiness, 5) the ultimate, 6) the created, 7) the uncreated, 8) eternity, 9) non-rejection, 10) the universal, 11) nature, 12) all things, 13) intrinsic identity, 14) non-apprehension, 15) phenomena, 16) nothingness, 17) both things and nothings, 18) intrinsic reality, 19) intrinsically real nothingness, and 20) infinity.

as directly affecting "physical reality." They constantly proclaim the "end of philosophy," or the "end of metaphysics," and devote much care to the history of this now obsolete pursuit. In fact, metaphysical thought is still very much in charge of the prevalent world view. It seems at an end only because it has become stuck on materialism, it has conceded final, "objective" reality to the "given data" of the senses. In short, it has become dogmatic and, like other dogmatisms before it, it has little patience with heresies. In particular, it has eviscerated itself by completely devaluing the power and importance of the mind, losing sight of the role the understanding plays in the actual construction of "reality." It has therefore ruled out in principle its own power, the power of philosophy, to transform life, either individual or social.

On the other side are the existentialist, humanistic philosophers, who decry the sterility of the technicians' approach, and position themselves somewhere among the poets and theologians. Still, all too often they also take the "massive facticity"[7] of the "given" for granted, and do not fully take responsibility for their imaginative construction of reality. They tend to defend metaphysics as an art form, avoiding the critical insights of the materialists, whom they rightly consider as having gone too far, as having lost sight of the whole enterprise. In response, these "essentialist" philosophers tend to lose their moorings in metaphysical flights of imagination, unleashing torrents of terminology.

In the spirit of Manjushri, I would urge that philosophers hampered by either tendency, materialistic or romantic, no matter how diffident they may have become about the critical central role and liberative power of philosophy, might find a new encouragement and inspiration from the "light of the East," if only they could break free of certain tacit presuppositions imposed on them by the conventional wisdom of our culture. In my concern to open the door for them to appreciate central way thought (which I will call "Centrism"),[8] I see the main obstructive presuppositions shared by most modern philosophers to be: a sense of the superiority, rational and cultural, of the "West"; a sense of the intrinsic progressivity of history; a sense of the intrinsic value of originality; and a sense of the fundamental non-perfectability of human understanding. These four presuppositions prevent them even from seeking in this book that which they would find interesting and helpful in their current phil-

[7] Phrase from Peter Berger's *Social Construction of Reality* (New York: Doubleday, 1967).

[8] I have broken a translator's convention here, as most call the *Madhyamaka* "The Middle Way," and leave *Mādhyamika*, the name for the school, untranslated, although all tacitly accept it as the "central philosophy" of Buddhism. All such choices are basically conventional, and I have chosen to modify this convention in order to get a sound English name for the school.

osophical malaises, for which the theories of emptiness and relativity are more than ever the needed medicines.

In another cultural universe, this *Essence of Eloquence* is a major document in the great river of teachings known as the Buddha Dharma. It is thus of great importance to all practitioners of Buddhism, especially those concerned with transcendent wisdom. The type of inquiry and intensity cultivated by this book is appropriate to the practice of transcendent insight, the advanced meditation of selflessness. But where are today's real practitioners of Buddhism to be found? Most of today's practitioners of Buddhism suffer from a variety of entrenched notions against the intellect and its role and power as a vehicle of liberation. They consider their duty to be the cultivation of a supposed "pure experience" free of concepts, unwitting of the fact that the conceptual aggregate (*saṃjñāskandha*) is always operative to determine any state of consciousness. This is particularly tragic for many "meditators," since by *conceptually* choosing to eschew concepts, they lose the flexibility of conceptual adaptation, and become stuck with whatever range of concepts their habit of mind deems comfortable. This dooms them as modern persons to the grievous error of taking the nihilistic reification of the metaphysical nothingness underlying materialist culture to be the emptiness or selflessness that is ultimate reality. And this tends to make them morally defenseless against the dictates of various secular agencies. Practitioners from the remaining Asian traditionalistic Buddhist societies, on the other hand, most often fasten on some simple faith, stuck in an image of themselves as incapable of taking the responsibility of understanding the nature of reality on their own.

Thus blocked in their access to the royal road of central way philosophy, the main obstructive presuppositions Buddhist practitioners hold are: 1) a sense of the religious and cultural superiority of the "East"; 2) a sense of the inexorable degeneracy of the process of history; 3) a sense of the intrinsic value of traditionality, especially as supporting the cultivation of quietistic states of withdrawal; and 4) a sense of the vast difference between their own state of "ignorance" and the "enlightenment" of the Buddhas and bodhisattvas. As a result, these practitioners consider the expression "Buddhist philosophy" a contradiction in terms, which view prevents them from engaging with this *Essence* as a vital path of practice, the critical contemplation of the analytic insights of intuitive wisdom.

I have had some experience in argument against these presuppositions of both modern philosophers and Buddhist practitioners, but I have no space here to engage in this at length. So I will assume that those who open this book and reach this page already have transcended these forms of conventional wisdom. I shall trust that they intend to explore the most useful philosophical and scientific teachings from "West" or East"; that they face the fact that history is not predetermined as inevitably progress or degeneration, and so take responsibility for creating progress, whether it seems feasible or not; that they realize that there is an age-old "tradition of originality," the enlightenment traditions that have flourished in all cultures. And most importantly, I shall trust that they suspend dogmatic prejudgment of the issue of the perfectability of human understanding, having realized the arbitrariness of either theistic or materialistic insistence on a fundamental imperfection in human genius, either dogma or "fact" arising as a philosophical or "scientific" buttress of authoritarian social structure, in ancient and modern cases, respectively.

I close this elucidation of the import of saluting Manjushri at the outset of the work by welcoming these readers to the *Essence*. May that incisive, irrepressible Youth that is the genius of each of them help them on their way, and remove all obstacles from their journeys to its profoundness and its beauty!

II

Shambhu, Meghavahana, Hiranyagarbha,
Anangapati, Damodara, and the other (gods),
All puffed up with self-infatuation
They roar their lordship o'er the worlds;
And yet before the vision of His body,
They dim like fireflies in the sun!
Then down they bow their sparkling diadems
In reverence to the lotuses of His feet!
I pay homage to that Lord of Sages,
The God of all the gods!

It is remarkable how the first words of this great work reveal its quintessence. Tsong Khapa opens this, his magnum opus in philosophy, with a brilliant flash of poetic imagery, flooding the mind of the sensitive reader with the scintillating glare of the naked sun. Since the context is philosophical, and the reader ventures into this work out of interest in the nature and structure of knowledge and ultimate reality, this sun symbolizes the sun of transcendent wisdom. Tsong Khapa is signaling forcefully that this is a work written not out of perplexity, but out of a vivid and precise vision of the ultimate condition and specific constitution of reality, and out of a joyous generosity to share his vision, energizing our intellects to transcend our self-imposed limitations.

But this is traditional in Buddhist philosophy—indeed, is that which distinguishes it from other philosophical traditions throughout the world. For Buddhist philosophy is founded on a sense of the unlimited potential of the intelligence, that is, on the insight that we can successfully attain knowledge of *everything* we need to know, becoming "perfectly enlightened" (*saṃbuddha*), "omniscient" (*sarvajña*), and "transcendently realized" (*tathāgata*); and on its corollary that many human beings have already done so and have subsequently given guidance. Thus Buddhist thought differs from most theological systems, which presuppose that the human capacity for knowledge is limited, that only gods can be perfectly enlightened or omniscient, and that therefore certainty can only arise from dogmatic authority, from the recordings of the utterances of these gods in sacred texts. It also distinguishes it from the philosophies of skeptics, nihilists, atheists, and materialists, who, although they are eager to be critical and eschew theological dogmatism, unwittingly presuppose dogmatically the impossibility of perfect enlightenment, certain only that they must always remain uncertain about ultimate questions, that all humans have always been so uncertain, and that any who claimed otherwise were deluded or pretending. Recent western philosophy is particularly characterized by this tendency, manifested most clearly by its ceding to "science" the quest of reality, to psychology the examination of knowing, and to theology or sociology the determination of values. Its a priori exclusion of even the possibility of solutions has led to the disastrous fragmentation of knowledge we now experience.

Against the theological dogmatists, Buddhist philosophy is critical of their restriction of omniscience to superhuman beings and affirms the transcendent potential of humans. Against the philosophical sophists, Buddhist philosophy is critical of their dogmatic insistence that all certainty is merely dogmatic and that omniscience is utterly impossible, and affirms that a rigorously honest confrontation with actual experience does afford an ultimately certain insight into its reality and function.

Shakyamuni, the recent historical perfect Buddha in "Supreme Emanation Body" (*paramanirmānakāya*) form, is thus represented by Tsong Khapa as expressing even in physical form the awesome balance, stability, and brilliant intensity of the radiance of the full power of the liberated intelligence in its compassionate manifestation to encourage others. He is shown in triumph over a scene in which the gods themselves, the most powerful, immense, and clever individual beings imaginable, literally bursting with pride and blustering with a rather rational self-esteem are brought up short in their tracks. For down on a tiny planet filled with insignificant humans, a Single Being irresistibly attracts their attention, fascinating them with the beauty of his body and the poignancy of his deeds. He draws them helplessly into the vortex of his own direct experience of the dimensionless emptiness that is the very fabric of all realities. With their supernormal perceptions, they do not perceive him merely as one being but as a cloud of beings pervasive even in the very atoms of which their own many bodies are constituted; and as this dawns on them, their self-assurance of hugeness and brightness melts away as they feel engulfed in the immensity of infinity, the dimensionless immeasurability of absolute voidness. They become like fireflies in the sun, eclipsed and dazzled by the Lord Buddha. Yet, after their initial anger and terror melt away, they feel protected by the adamantine intensity of the ultimate-reality awareness in his balanced presence, and illuminated by the cheerful radiance of his unfailing concern for the welfare of sentient beings, themselves included. Then joyously and humbly, they prostrate themselves before the undeniable refuge of his axial centrality and warm omnipresence.

Why does Tsong Khapa pick such a terrific and challenging icon for his introductory verse in this work on the supreme subtleties of philosophy? Surely, a more gentle or more intellectual salutation would have sufficed. It will help to glance at the salutatory verses of some of the other major treatises of the tradition, to see how the Buddha is presented in relation to the fundamental accomplishments of the particular works. This will put this verse and the accomplishment of the present work in sharper focus.

Nagarjuna begins his own fundamental work on the central way, the book called simply *Wisdom* (*Prajñā*), with a more obviously philosophical verse of salutation.

> I praise that perfect Buddha,
> The Supreme Philosopher,
> Who taught us relativity;
> Free of cessation and creation,
> Without annihilation and permanence,
> With no coming and no going,
> Not a unity, nor a plurality,
> Fabrications quieted, the supreme bliss![9]

This creates a poetic icon of the Buddha suitable for the homage of philosophers, as well as conveying the central teaching of the central way, the teaching of relativity (*pratītyasamutpāda*), or, as it can be translated in a metaphysical rather than a critical context, "dependent origination." The great central way Master here salutes Shakyamuni as the foremost

[9] MMK, I: 1-2. *anirodham-anutpādam-anucchedam-aśāśvataṃ anekārtham-anānārtham-anāgamam-anirgamaṃ // yaḥ pratītyasamutpādaṃ prapañcopaśamaṃ śivaṃ / deśayāmāsa saṃbuddhastaṃ vande vādatāṃ varaṃ //*

of philosophers, primarily as a master of illuminating speech, and indicates the unsurpassability of the Teacher's achievement and its communication. The salutation exemplifies the traditional Buddhist philosophical grounding in the perfect enlightenment of all the Buddhas represented in our history by Shakyamuni. The reader of the twenty-seven chapters on transcendent *Wisdom* that follow has at the outset this description of the goal of his own study as well as of the source of the teaching and warrant of its efficacy. Tsong Khapa himself adopts a similar tone when writing his own master commentary on the *Wisdom*, his *Ocean of Reason*, which work is closely connected to our *Essence*. For the *Essence* was written in its entirety while he was in the middle of the commentary on the first chapter of the *Wisdom*, as he realized that a separate work was needed to resolve the subtle points without digressing too widely from his fundamental text. In the *Ocean*, he opens simply:

> May that Victor e'er protect us!
> He who taught that natural emptiness equals relativity,
> For which the sages of the perfect universes
> Praise him as crown jewel of philosophers![10]

Here the epithet "Victor" (*Jina*) echoes the triumphal note sounded in the *Essence*, and the royal brilliance of a Buddha is conveyed in the "crown jewel" metaphor. But the heart of the salutation is the acknowledgement of a Buddha's teaching that emptiness and relativity are equivalent, which Tsong Khapa celebrates below as the essential message of the liberative doctrine. For this insight is the very ground and basis of a Buddha's achievement, his consummation of his personal goal in the permanent peace of absolute, transcendent wisdom, and his public manifestation of supreme benefit, bringing understanding and security to the world by teaching all beings the reality of their condition.

Nor is this understanding of relativity a mere passive or "mystic" insight, opening the door into a solipsistic neglect of others and the world of causation. Rather, just like the modern scientific theory of relativity, which enabled human beings to tear apart the very atoms of the planet, the insight of relativity is rational, critical, and realistic, and leads to the development of the supreme energy of the universe, which the Buddha called "great compassion," rather than "nuclear energy," or "gravitation," or "electro-magnetism." This "strong force" is symbolized by the double-helix-like Vajra, the diamond thunderbolt scepter of great compassion.

[10] RG, v.1. *gang zhig gsungs pas smra bai gtsug rgyan zhes / rab 'byams zhing gi mkhas pas rab bsngags pa / rang bzhin stong pa rten 'byung don nyid du / gsung bai rgyal ba de yis rtag skyong zhig //.*

Maitreyanatha opens his great work, *Analysis of the Jewel Matrix*, with a more Buddhological tone, nonetheless quite philosophical in impact:

> I bow to him who attained Buddhahood,
> Peaceful, without beginning, middle, or end;
> And who from his realization taught the path,
> Fearless and firm, to enlighten the unawake;
> And who holds the supreme sword of wisdom
> And wields the thunderbolt of compassion,
> Cutting through all the weeds of suffering,
> Smashing the great barrier of perplexity,
> Buried deep in the jungle of various views.[11]

This image is appropriate to the title of the work, evoking an expedition into jungle wilderness and the discovery of the treasures of an ancient civilization whose lost cities are deeply overgrown in impenetrable tangles. This salutation occupies a middle point between Nagarjuna's and Tsong Khapa's. It indicates, by "without beginning," etc., the absolutely transcendent nature of Buddhahood, but then goes on to describe in detail its dynamic function, whereby the Buddha works to liberate living beings, delivering them from their entrapment in the tangle of false views and perplexities. It is for their elaboration of this aspect of great compassion that Maitreyanatha and his great champion, Aryasanga, are celebrated, whereas Nagarjuna is reknowned for his elucidation of the aspect of wisdom; *Wisdom* is the actual title of his major work.

Another descendant in the line from Asanga and Vasubandhu, one who took the same enlightenment deep into the philosophical territory of logic and epistemology, was the great Dignaga, the "All-Conquering Elephant," whose most important work begins with another remarkable verse of salutation:

> I bow to the Teacher, the Blissful, the Savior,
> Who wills the good of all, personifying reason. . . .[12]

These five epithets of the Buddha form the framework for the Buddhological chapter of Dharmakirti's *Treatise*, which is inspired especially by the famous "reason personified" (*pramānabhūta*), which describes the Buddha's very being as made of reason. A Buddha's knowledge and

[11] RGV, I, v. 4. *yo buddhatvam-anādimadhyanidhanaṃ śāntaṃ vibuddhaḥ svayaṃ, buddhvā ca-abudha-bodhanārtham-abhayaṃ mārgaṃ dideśa dhruvaṃ / tasmai jñānakṛpāsi-vajravaradhṛg duḥkhāñkuraikacchide nānādṛg gahanopagūdhavimati-prakārabhettre namaḥ //.*

[12] PS, I, v. 1ab. *pramāṇabhūtāya jagaddhitaiṣiṇe prānamyā śāstre sugatāya tāyine //.*

compassion both are emphasized, and the claim is made that reason perfected *is* enlightenment, contrary to the conventional dualism that would have the transcendent gained only at the sacrifice of reason. Thus, Dignaga's empiricist revolution in epistemology and logic is integrated into the liberative technique of the path to enlightenment.

Let us now return to the fundamental accomplishment of this *Essence*, revealed by the dramatic opening icon. We saw that Nagarjuna's salutation celebrated the Buddha's philosophical teaching on the profound, the nature of ultimate reality, as did Tsong Khapa's own super-commentary on that work. Maitreyanatha's salutation celebrated the Teacher from the point of view of his perfection of wisdom and compassion, and his manifestation of the magnificent path of the far-reaching deeds of the career of the bodhisattva. Dignaga, while following closely that spirit, added the epistemologically apt characterization of "reason personified" to the Buddha's myriad manifestations. Each of these salutations thus pictures the Buddha in a way appropriate to the fundamental tasks of the work. In a sense, if a work of Buddhist philosophy is something like a *samadhi*, a sustained and penetrating contemplation of certain pathways of thought and insight, the first picture of the Buddha stands as the icon of the contemplation. The *samadhi* of the *Essence*, the contemplative state in which the work is written and must be read, is the state of the supreme triumph of human genius. The false pride that arises from egocentric knowledge, the *hubris* that led to the downfall of many a Western hero, is attributed to the gods themselves, the powerful overlords of the universe, whose magnitude and energy have transcended the merely planetary scale. They are mentioned, one by one, as floating beyond the universes in the infinite field of space. I take them also as representing the major trends of thought that purport to grasp the essence of the reality of the world.

No commentator remarks on the mention of these Indian gods, except to identify them. But, in a work such as this, it would be amiss to assume that they were randomly selected. I propose an interpretation that can show how each stands as emblematic of a particular trend of egocentrist philosophical thought, so many of which proliferated in the fertile minds of the thinkers of India.

There is Shiva, Shambhu, the blissful yogi whose bliss arises from his consort Uma; he is the original "exact scientist," the patron of the grammarians, the Naiyayikas, and the Vaisheshikas, who were the ancient Indian equivalent of our linguists, logicians, and physicists. Their schools were based on Panini's *Vyākaraṇasūtra*, Gautama's *Nyāyasūtra*, and Kanada's *Vaiśeṣikasūtra*. It is Shiva whose blazing third eye penetrates the structure of material quanta, and who turns the material universe back into the state of dissolution through the ultimate thermonuclear explosion. The fire of his eye flares out in pure supernovas, as he disregards the petty humanoid configurations of mere matter that appear and disappear with the shifting galaxies. His callousness seems hard-headed realism to him, and he might argue that, after all, all things are merely substantial quanta, which are never lost, but only transformed. The essence of his view is an extreme confidence in his own precise grasp of the substance of the universe, in his knowledge of the ultimate categories, and in his perception of the ultimate particulars, the indivisible particles that are the stuff of everything. From him come the Nyaya school of logic and epistemology, and the Vaisheshika school of metaphysical science, as well as the science of linguistics perfected by Panini, who received Shiva's gift of the algebraic formulae with which all linguistic transformations can be expressed most elegantly and precisely.

Next, there is Indra, Meghavahana "who rides upon the clouds," the king of the gods of the Vedic pantheon who presides over the functions of life on earth; bringing thunder, lightning, and rain, which make growth possible; bringing victory over enemies; protecting against the demons and the titans. He symbolizes the violent manipulation of nature by human beings, hence the force of civilization. As an ecstatic war god, when he is offered great draughts of *soma* elixir, he forgets who he is or what is the planet and becomes himself the whole universe in a completely psychedelic expansion of self to cosmic dimensions. He is only controlled and tempered by the Vedic ritual, and therefore from him proceeds the school of the Mimamsa, the technicians of ancient Indian society who knew how to tinker with nature by means of magic chants, offerings, and ceremonious oblations. Their school, based on Jaimini's *Mīmāṃsāsūtra*, understands the universe as a giant machine whose vast energies are modulated and directed by the control panel of the fire altar. Hence, all solemn ritual actions performed on this panel have great power and efficacy. This school is also substantivistic, but more moralistic and theological in tenor than the Nyaya-Vaisheshika, since it tries to preserve in the new terms of discourse of each period of Indian history the basic sense of the universe first put forth in the Brahmanas, the ritual and speculative texts associated with the Vedas.

Third, in the center of this pantheon of five, there is the great "Creator" Brahma, Hiranyagarbha the golden egg, who epitomizes the energy of life and light and growth, whose body is constituted by the fifty sacred seed syllables of the divine language of perfection (*saṃskṛta*), and who *is* actually all things and beings. They have only to realize their oneness with him to be released from the illusion of multiplicity and the sufferings it entails, to *become* the Being that they *are*, as Shvetaketu is told again and again in the *Great Solitude Teaching (Bṛhadāraṇyaka upaniṣad)*, "THAT ART THOU!" Brahma is not at all destructive, unlike Shiva and Indra, who are capable of great destruction and violence, but is the essence of creativity. This supreme creativity is somewhat out of control, however, in that Brahma is irresponsible for his dreams, spinning out universes right and left on great clouds of golden energy in which beings are born, live, suffer, and die when the destroyers come around to keep the balance. Those elite intellectuals who can participate in Brahma's vision and see the universe as a vision of gold can float in the four Brahma realms of immeasurable love, compassion, joy, and equanimity. They have no foresight about the inevitable cycle of action and reaction, of karmic evolution. But the cycle shatters their dream and re-immerses them in the illusion of plurality, and they recognize too late the illusiveness of unity as well. From Brahma comes the school of Vedanta, sometimes called the "Later Technicians" (*Uttaramīmāṃsā*), who follow Badarayana, author of the *Brahmasūtras*, and eventually Shankara, Ramanuja, and Madhva, who expound the monistic nature of the universe in a highly refined "mystic" theology.

Fourth, there is the Indian Cupid, known as Kama, "passion," or Anangapati, the "Bodiless Lord," from the incident in which Shiva incinerates him for trying to sneak up on his meditation to shoot him with the flower arrows of love, so that the yogi-god would fall in love with Uma. Kama is the patron of the Charvakas, materialists in the mundane as well as the philosophical sense, the Indian hedonists, who coined the aphorism "eat, drink, and be merry, for tomorrow we may die!" centuries before Epicurus. Westerners are surprised to hear of the great libertines of the ancient Indian metropolises, who enjoyed mercantile fortunes built on the China-India-Alexandria trade. These were India's own hard-headed pragmatists, who resolutely maintained a skeptical attitude toward mind and all unseen phenomena, and even denied the validity of inference, accepting only the evidence of their senses. Their school was important in Indian philosophy. Like Buddhism, it was denied Brahminically "orthodox" status due to its denial of the validity of the Vedas. It was resolutely atheistic, and utterly skeptical about the efficacy of the rituals.

The Charvakas were the targets of much criticism by the Buddhists as well as by the Brahmins. Both considered that a person who did not believe in future life, did not accept responsibility for his own acts or fear their consequences beyond the present lifetime, would be a moral monster, unaccountable to society, except as constrained by brute force. Fittingly, Charvaka thought decisively influenced the main writers in the field of political economy, the *Arthaśāstra* literature, the most famous text being that of Kautilya, in which they taught a ruthless pragmatism that Max Weber admitted "out-Machiavellied Machiavelli."[13]

The interesting point about these Indian materialistic hedonists is their "modernity," in that their complex of views is very similar to that of many nineteenth-century thinkers. Modern philosophers, intellectual historians, and sociologists of knowledge like to think that the "modern constellation of consciousness" is unique to our time and to the "West,"[14] but the existence and statements of the Charvaka are evidence to the contrary. The chilling implication of their similarity is that, if the other Indian schools were right in fearing the radical materialist for his moral unaccountability, then we have every reason to fear the worst in the apocalyptic vein. For the first time in history, Charvaka-type materialists are in control of the planet's destiny, not only in the persons of the rulers and managers of the avowedly "dialectically materialist" societies, but also in the persons of most of the rest of us brought up on Darwin, Marx, Freud, and Newton, that is, in a popular culture that has not yet realized the implications of the theory of relativity and the uncertainty principle. And this does much to explain the *après moi, le déluge* mentality that lets our managers store nerve gas in leaky containers, throw plutonium wastes in the sea or in pools in the woods, pollute the air and water, use up the ozone layer, finish off the petroleum reserves, and invest billions yearly in sterile engines of destruction. It is up to future generations to look after themselves, they seem to say, something to restore the planet's earth, water, fire, and air. It is indeed fitting that Kama, the patron of the ancient counterparts of these hedonistic egotists, became Mara the tempter, the prime challenger of the Buddha, the equivalent of the Mediterranean Satan.

Finally, Tsong Khapa mentions the god Vishnu, Damodara the "Broad-bellied" Preserver, the all-pervasive god of stability and duration who grew more and more powerful in medieval India, until, with his mythology of "ten incarnations" (*daśāvatāra*), he became the cosmic progenitor, the world savior, the demon-slayer, the Lord Krishna, the Teacher Buddha, and the final apocalyptic redeemer Kalki, the next and final incarnation to come. Especially in his form of Krishna, featured in the *Bhagavadgīta*, the *Bhagavatapurāṇa*, and numerous medieval devotional works, Vishnu became the monotheistic devotional God par excellence, the icon not only for millions of pious believers, but also for numerous philosophical schools whose goal was union with the ultimate reality as personified in the godhead of Krishna. Thus, the theistic Samkhya-yoga

[13] M. Weber, *The Religion of India* (New York: Free Press, 1958).

[14] See P. Berger, B. Berger, and T. Luckmann, *The Homeless Mind* (New York, Doubleday, 1974).

schools, based on Kapila's *Sāṃkhyā Kārikās* and Patanjali's *Yogasūtra*, developed conceptual and psycho-physiological yogic technologies to achieve union with God as Ishvara or Krishna. The basic dualism of the Samkhya set the stage for the eventual merging of the little personal soul with the great oversoul of the god, although in most forms of the soteriology there was a hierarchical difference maintained between even the saved devotee and the god, just as in the heaven of Dante the individuality and subordination of the human devotee is preserved even in a state of grace. The goal of these theistic schools could only be salvation, as there was no hope in principle of perfect union with God, no sharing of His Omniscient Knowledge.

By thus associating the five gods that Tsong Khapa mentions with the major trends of egocentrist Indian philosophy, the picture of Buddha's triumph emerges as an icon of the potential for the liberation of the whole range of thinkers from the egocentrist's predicament, in its many diverse forms, through Buddhist philosophy. The Nyaya, Vaisheshika, Vaiyakarana, Mimamsa, Vedanta, Charvaka, Samkhya, and Yoga schools are all represented by their patron deities. The nature of Indian thought being as it is, of course, there is considerable overlapping and inter-relationship at different times and areas. And, in a way, these schools represent most of the main trends of any substantivist, egocentrist philosophical tradition in any culture. We may label the followers of these schools as logicalists, atomists, conceptualists, mechanists, monistic mentalists, materialistic skeptics, and theistic dualists, respectively. Thus the five gods that confront the Buddha in Shakyamuni's form in our icon represent the major possibilities of thought of that time, and so the verse is the perfect icon of the overwhelming of egocentrist dogmatism by the critical penetration of transcendent insight.[15]

Now this triumph would not be complete if there were only a conquest by force of insight, if the deities themselves were merely held in check by the intellectual power of the Buddha. The egocentrist, no matter how fixed, also seeks the bliss of complete liberation. He feels, at first encounter, a shock of losing all hold on his sense of greatness, feeling his pride and sense of self dwindle to nothing before the immensity, impred-

[15] In relating each deity to a school or group of schools, I make no claim that all members of those schools exclusively worshiped that one deity. The actual history and the relations of religious beliefs to philosophical tenets and systems are much more complex and varied. Yet these sketches of the outlines of the schools, the feelings of their followers, and the attributes of the different deities conveniently serve to indicate vividly the pluralism of Indian thought to the non-Indologist. And I think Tsong Khapa had such associations in mind in picking the particular group of deities to mention. Though he was Tibetan, he was quite familiar with the attributes and myths of the various Indian deities through his knowledge of Tantric literature.

icability, and ungraspability of the Buddha, who stands for the evolutionary perfection of life itself. But then there is a sense of great relief, a bliss of release from the burden of maintaining a whole world, a pleasure of transcending the Atlas pose at the core of egocentrism. From this relief received from the Buddha's grace in presenting himself to these beings as inevitably greater than they—by being himself in union with the absolute while still unconditionally embracing them, by being liberated and transcendent while remaining aware, sensitive, and vulnerable to the pulse of life—from this relief the gods willingly and happily prostrate themselves before their own God. The Buddha's Body of Truth (*Dharmakāya*), from which his Body of Beatitude (*Saṃbhogakāya*) of Infinite Light (*Amitābha*) and Infinite Life (*Amitāyus*), and his Body of Emanation (*Nirmāṇakāya*) are indivisible, is the "God beyond the gods" (*Devātideva*).[16]

This is the samadhi of the *Essence*, then, a heroic, triumphal, adamantine breaking through all perplexities of egocentrism, a penetrating insight that opens beyond entrapment in cyclic systems and structures into a beatific universe of freedom. Therefrom spontaneously emerges an expansive sensitivity to the unfortunate predicament of the innumerable living beings still laboring under the delusions of a frozen selfhood, crushed between the iron mountains of birth and death, in little lives of uninterrupted problems, not even coming to any final end. And the healing energy for these sorrows rises like a brilliant sun, the blazing heat and light of wisdom that thaws and illuminates all living beings. Tsong Khapa himself in writing this *Essence* feels this way, and he is signaling to us that we should put our minds to what follows in a spirit of confidence that reason can open for us the door to liberation, really and finally, so that our study of even these difficult subtleties will be for us a liberation, not merely a drudgery of intellectual circlings of thought. This opening flash of sunlight intimates to us the vision of the golden energy in which his words were wrought.

III

I bow devoted to Maitreya and Manjughosha,
Vast oceans, treasuries of jewels of eloquence,
Rippling with mighty waves of enlightened deeds,
Hard to fathom in their depths of wisdom,
Hard to measure in their great expanse of love!

[16] The three Bodies of Buddhahood are most fully elaborated in the works of Maitreyanatha and Asanga, especially MSA and RGV.

Manjughosha, or Manjushri, has already been introduced, saluted at the outset as the patron of the philosophy of the profound, path of the wisdom of selflessness. Maitreya is the "Regent" of Shakyamuni in the Tushita heaven, where the Buddha sojourned as Shvetaketu, "White Banner," at the midpoint of his descent from the highest heaven, Akanishtha, into the world of human beings on the planet earth.[17] Maitreya will continue that regency until such time as evolution brings our world to the point of readiness to receive his mission. According to legends,[18] this will be many years in the future, when the human lifespan has increased again to many thousands of years, and when the planet will be entirely dominated by a benevolent "Wheel-Turning" Sovereign named Shankha. Maitreya will be born the son of a Brahmin priest, unlike the Kshatriya warrior Shakyamuni, and will renounce the world and attain enlightenment in a single day, not requiring six long years, as did Shakyamuni. His teaching will not deviate from that of previous Buddhas, except for an interesting tradition that he will not teach any esoteric Tantras. This is sometimes considered a drawback to his mission, especially by those who know of the extraordinary efficacy and beauty of the Tantric teachings and treasure them above all others. But they overlook, I think, the basic likelihood that Maitreya's ministry will in general be more, not less, effective than Shakyamuni's. This improvement, of course, does not show any difference in the perfection of liberative technique of the two Buddhas, but rather a difference in the evolutionary stage of the human beings on the planet. Shakyamuni taught at a time of violence and widespread militarism, and had to turn the martial qualities of toughness, asceticism, and determination toward the pursuit of enlightenment. Thus,

[17] The Universal Vehicle legend is that the Buddha dwells in Beatific Body form in the Pure Lands of the Akanishtha region along with the tenth-stage bodhisattvas. Thence they emanate the Supreme Emanation Bodies (*Paramanirmāṇakāya*) to human universes to liberate living beings there. The magnificence of the conception lies in the fact that their highest consecration into full Buddhahood comes not in their enjoyment of Pure Land Beatitude, the bliss of universality, but in their emergence into individual Supreme Emanation Body forms, performing the twelve exemplary deeds of perfect Buddhas. The first of these is to stop in Tushita Heaven, fourth up in the desire realm above the human world. There, they teach the gods of that realm, some of them bodhisattvas, and survey the particular planet and its history and the evolutionary state of its population. Shakyamuni was known as Shvetaketu in his last Tushita incarnation, and he crowned Maitreya as the bodhisattva who would succeed him reigning there and watching over the earth's destiny, until Maitreya himself would emanate as a Supreme Incarnation a hundred thousand years hence. Part of his caretaking involves appearing ahead of time in this world, to keep humans moving in the right evolutionary direction, so to speak, as in the case of Saint Asanga and many others.

[18] There are many scriptures, mostly in the Universal Vehicle canon but also in the Individual Vehicle canon, that tell of Maitreya's activities, his presence and teaching in Tushita, and the particulars of his eventual descent onto the earth and human history. See P. Demieville's essay, "Maitreya l'inspirateur," in *Bulletin de l'École Française de l'Extrême-Orient*, 44:19, pp. 376-398.

he was born himself a warrior, and his name means "Ascetic of the Shakya" (warrior clan). Maitreya's name is derived from *maitrī*, "love" related to *mātr* "mother," and *mitra* "friend". The world in his time will be politically centralized, and therefore the warrior class and its martial virtues will be obsolete. Thus he will be born among the intellectuals, the religious Brahmins; his teaching will bring the gentler emotions to the fore, and he will not need to reserve the more advanced techniques for cultivating the emotions known as "Tantras" for an esoteric elite but can teach them publicly with the integration of Sutra and Tantra. Thus, that his teaching lacks a separate Tantra might be a quality of its excellence, and not a sign of incompleteness.

Maitreya also often figures among the great bodhisattvas in the assemblies gathered around Shakyamuni to listen to his teaching of the Universal Vehicle discourses. He and Manjushri are often paired there in dialogues, or in alternating interlocution of the Buddha. Whereas the Individual Vehicle scriptures are collected by Ananda, Shariputra, and so forth, the Universal Vehicle Scriptures are collected by Maitreya, Manjushri, and Vajrapani. Furthermore, although presently considered to reside in Tushita heaven, he does not fail to work through miraculous means in this world to help living beings mature toward his eventual Buddha-mission. It is considered (especially in the Tibetan tradition, with the Chinese and Japanese agreeing in general, although differing in particulars), that Maitreya authored five great treatises, using saint Asanga as a scribe, that serve as the basis of the idealistic school of Universal Vehicle philosophy, the Experientialist (*Yogācāra*), or Idealist (*Vijñānavāda*) school.

One of the most common icons in Tibet is called the "refuge field,"[19] which presents the Buddha Shakyamuni in the center of a host of Indian, Tibetan, and supernatural teachers. To Shakyamuni's left is Manjushri, at the head of the lineage of the "profound view" stage of the path of enlightenment, and to his right is Maitreya, at the head of the lineage of the "magnificent deeds" stage of the path of enlightenment. Beneath Manjushri sit Nagarjuna and Aryadeva, at the head of the historical teachers who maintained the unbroken succession of this tradition of critical philosophy. Beneath Maitreya sit Asanga and Vasubandhu at the head of the succession of ethically oriented philosophers. The Buddha in the center of this icon represents the unification of both these lineages, so no ultimate dichotomy is intended by the separation of the two. There are, however, different persons on different stages of the path at different times, and different teachings are elaborated for their benefit that emphasize either wisdom or compassion.

[19] See the example of "refuge field," illustration 12, with Tsong Khapa in center.

The team of Maitreya and Manjushri, heading the two main branches of the great tree of this philosophical tradition, assure that the balance never goes too far in either direction, either toward the sentimental and mystical extreme that Maitreya himself favors, as recorded in the Universal Vehicle scriptures, or toward the cold and skeptical extreme that Manjushri might seem to manifest in his single-minded pursuit of the transcendent wisdom of selflessness. Indeed, it may be that Berkeley and Hegel and Heidegger and so on will someday be claimed by Europe as representatives of the Maitreya lineage of magnificence, as Hume and Kant and Nietzsche and Wittgenstein and so on may be claimed to represent the Manjushri lineage of the profound. I do myself so perceive them, especially since this *Essence of Eloquence* would not be intelligible and could not even have been translated in our far-western culture, were it not for their extraordinary works and profound teachings. They should be included in the refuge-field icon we are constructing under which to read this *Essence*. It must be remembered, of course, that this division into two lineages is only for emphasis and for dealing with differing tendencies and different times, and there is no essential conflict between critical reason and reasonable faith. The balance between the two is necessary to maintain the central way that leads to and, apparently, from enlightenment.

IV

I bow my head to the feet of Nagarjuna and Asanga,
Who pioneered the ways for Champions of philosophy,
With two interpretations of Sugata's sacred discourse,
And made that superb doctrine of that Victor
Shine like sunlight throughout the triple world!

Coming to the human plane, we encounter the two "Great-Charioted Ones" (*Mahāratha*), or "Champions" in the battle of philosophy against misknowledge, those founders of the branches of Universal Vehicle philosophy who fashioned systems to serve as vehicles for later thinkers and practitioners to ride upon. The metaphor is interesting, in that the Mahayana itself is a "universal vehicle," that is, a mode of transport that takes everyone to the destination of freedom and enlightenment. The two great masters, then, are those who furnished a method of coming to a profound and extensive understanding of that Vehicle, in a sense enabling beings to use it in the proper manner. They are thus like "drivers" of the Vehicle; with them holding the reins, the Vehicle moves swiftly and unerringly to its goal. In another sense, the struggle with misknowledge and the sufferings of birth, sickness, decay, and death is like a battle, and the Universal Vehicle a war-chariot. The two are thus "Great Champions," leading to victory in the war on misknowledge.

1. Nagarjuna

Nagarjuna's life is aglow with legends. He has been properly "demythologized" by "modern" scholarship, and his exploits over the centuries have been broken into the separate careers of three different Nagarjunas, one living around the time of the origin of the Universal Vehicle, one living in the second century (the "philosopher"), and one living in the 8th or 9th century C.E. (so late because of the modern preconception about the lateness of the Tantra system).[20] Be this as it may, I will render the legendary account, since the mythic Nagarjuna is the one Tsong Khapa has in mind when he refers to him as "Champion" (*Mahāratha*), "Holy Father" (*Āryapitā*), "Savior" (*Nātha*), or "Great Master" (*Mahācārya*), one whose philosophical profundity is integrated indivisibly with his religious sanctity, and even with the magical prowess of his enlightened compassion.

Chandrakirti himself (ca. seventh century C.E.) shows his vision of his master Nagarjuna at the beginning of his famous work, *Lucid Exposition*, likening him to his namesake the *nāgas*, or great sea-dragons, and to Arjuna, the archer-hero.

> I bow to that Nagarjuna,
> Who lives to dispel the dwelling in extremism,
> Being born in the ocean of the genius of the Buddhas,
> Who compassionately taught from his own realization
> The profundities of the treasury of Holy Dharma;
> The blaze of whose insight is kindled by opinions of opponents,
> And burns away the darkness from their minds;
> Matchless in intuition, the showers of arrows of his words
> Win him the glory of sovereignty over the three realms
> Of this world of disciples including the gods,
> And completely conquer the enemy army of cyclic life.[21]

[20] Modern scholars have much debated the "historicity" of Nagarjuna. The tradition has him live for five hundred sixty years, due to his alchemical prowess, and hails him as a great Tantricist as well as a philosopher and an alchemist. Modern scholars therefore consider there to have been at least three different famous Nagarjunas.

[21] The Sanskrit of these verses is found PPMMV, p. 1. *yo antadvayāvāsavidhūtavāsaḥ saṃbuddhadhīsāgaralabdhajanma / saddharmatoyasya gambhīrabhāvaṃ yathānubuddhaṃ krpāyā jagāda // yasya darśanatejāṃsi paravādimatendhanaṃ / dahantyadyāpi lokasya manasāni tamāṃsi ca // yasya asamajñānavacaḥśaraughā nighnanti niḥśeṣabhāvā-*

1. Tsong Khapa and main disciples receiving mystic revelation from Manjushri.

2. Manjughosha Kumarabhuta, the supernal Bodhisattva in his role as mystic inspirer of Centrist philosophers.

3. Shakyamuni Buddha.

4. Maitreya Bodhisattva, the future Buddha in his Tushita heaven mansion, in his role as inspirer of the "magnificent deeds" lineage of Buddhist philosophers.

According to legend,[22] Nagarjuna was in his former life the Licchavi youth Priyadarshana, who figured as one of the members of the assembly at Vimalakirti's house in Vaishali, during the Buddha's own time. There he pronounced a version of the teaching of non-duality, quite remarkable considering his later career, concerning the non-duality of form and emptiness, and he witnessed Vimalakirti's famous silence and attained the tolerance of inconceivability.[23] Shakyamuni himself prophesied that, four hundred years after his Nirvana, a mendicant would appear in the south of India who would spread his central way teaching far and wide, and then go on to the Sukhavati pure land; and that he would be called "Naga."[24] It seems that Nagarjuna was born in south India, in a town called Vidarbha, in a Brahmin family. His parents were, of course, delighted with him, but an astrologer predicted that he would definitely die before his seventh year was finished. So, during his seventh year, his parents released him to enter the mendicant order of the Buddhists. He wandered from teacher to teacher, until he came to the great monastery in the Ganges plain, Nalanda, where he met his main teacher, Rahulabhadra, known esoterically as the Adept Saraha. The boy was ordained as the monk Shriman, and soon he became a master of the Buddhist teaching, as well as an adept at medicine and alchemy. His fame as a teacher spread so widely that he attracted several *nāgas*, mythic dragon-like beings from the depths of the ocean, whose magic powers included the ability to assume human form when visiting among humans. When

---

risenaṃ / tridhāturājyaśriyam adadhāna vineyalokasya sadevakasya // nāgārjunāya pranipatya tasmai.

[22] Principal sources for the legendary accounts of the great philosophers of Buddhist India that follow are N. Roerich, trans., *The Blue Annals* (Delhi: Motilal Banarsidass, 1976); Bu-ston, *History of Buddhism*, translated by E. Obermiller (Heidelberg, 1931-1932); A. Chattopadhyaya and L. Chimpa, *Tāranātha's History of Buddhism in India* (Simla: Indian Institute of Advanced Study, 1970); and the Tibetan *Garland of Perfect Gems, Biographies of the Succession Gurus of the Path of Enlightenment Teachings* (Dharamsala block print; two chapters translated by G. Mullin (with L. Tsonawa), *Lives of the Six Ornaments* (Mundgod: Drepung Monastery Press, Dreloma, 1979-1980).

[23] Tsong Khapa (RG, p. 4) notes a statement from the *Golden Light Scripture* that identifies the Licchavi bodhisattva Priyadarshana as the former life of Nagarjuna. This fits very intriguingly with that bodhisattva's pronouncement on nonduality in the famous chapter nine of the *Vimalakīrti*. "The Bodhisattva Priyadarshana declared, 'Form itself is empty. Emptiness does not result from the destruction of form, but the nature of form is itself emptiness. Therefore, to speak of emptiness on the one hand, and of form, or of sensation, or of intellect, or of motivation, or of consciousness on the other—is entirely dualistic. Consciousness itself is emptiness. Emptiness does not result from the destruction of consciousness, but the nature of consciousness is itself emptiness. Such understanding of the five compulsive aggregates and the knowledge of them as such by means of intuitive wisdom is the entrance into nonduality' " (Thurman, R. A. F., "*Holy Teaching of Vimalakīrti* (University Park; Penn State University Press, 1977), p. 75.

[24] Tsong Khapa (RG, pp. 3ff.) quotes the LAS, the *Golden Light*, the *Mahāmegha*, the *Mañjuśrīmūlakalpa*, and the *Mahāḍuṇḍubhi* Scriptures.

Shriman recognized them, they acknowledged themselves as *nāgas* from the ocean kingdom. They then told him of the great treasury of scriptures they had kept there from the Buddha's time, among which were the *100,000 Verse Transcendent Wisdom Scripture*, the *100,000 Verse Garland Scripture*, and the *Jewel Heap Scripture*.[25] Shriman accepted their invitation to visit, and spent fifty years in the *nāga* kingdom, whence he eventually returned bringing numerous scriptures of the Universal Vehicle, which was all but unknown in India at that time—just as Shakyamuni had prophesied.

From this he became known as "Nagarjuna," "one who has achieved [his goal] with the aid of the dragons," and he published numerous scriptures of the Universal Vehicle, which spread throughout the land. He also fashioned the main teachings of these scriptures into a systematic philosophical vehicle, the "central way" (*madhyamaka*), or "Centrist" system, for the benefit of his colleagues and disciples, who found the oceanic teaching of the Universal Vehicle overwhelming, and who had become hardened into substantivistic habits of thought due to an overly realistic understanding of reality.

Although his own interest was unwaveringly existential and transformative, he wished to liberate beings from the traps of views and false notions that kept them from realizing their true potential. He was no sophist delighting in argument for argument's sake, yet he did not hesitate to enter the most abstruse and technical system of thought with his critical and penetrative vision. In Buddhist thought of his day, the refined science of the Abhidharma (itself merely a systematization of the Buddha's critique of the naive realists) had ossified into a more subtle form of realism, a kind of reductionistic pluralism that took an atomistic form with the Vaibhashikas, the "Analysts," and a nominalistic form with the Sautrantikas, the "Traditionists." These philosophers had analyzed the universe, categorizing mind and mental phenomena together with form and matter, and including uncreated noumena such as space and the various types of cessations or Nirvanas along with created phenomena, into a fixed number of categories, the most popular number being seventy-five, but with some schools having up to one hundred and eight. The basic idea was that the illusion of combination was the cause of the sufferings of life, and that if you could separate things analytically back into their primary components, you could control them, lay them to rest, become free of their effects. Especially since you would then discover that there was no permanent stuff of any sort, including no self and no unchanging individuality, your sense of alienated self would become transformed into the cessation, the bliss of Nirvana. Thus, the goal of the contemplative

[25] *Prajñāpāramitā*, *Avataṃsaka*, and *Ratnakūta Sūtras*.

monastic philosopher—and this philosophy was very much the province of a professional elite, not usually the province of the layman—was to use his critical wisdom (*prajñā*) defined as the "analysis of things" (*dharmapravicaya*) literally to "see his way through ordinary reality" and attain liberation. He would then come to understand that his ordinary reality was merely established by his own conceptual and perceptual habits, its apparent inevitability merely illusory, and this understanding would bring him the peace he sought.

The problem with this system was that it was not immune to the reificatory mental habits that plague people and philosophers everywhere. Thus, their at first extraordinary reality in which the transcendent noumenon of Nirvana reduced the everyday world to a mere cocoon to be escaped as soon as possible became reconstituted as an ordinary reality of an extreme spiritualistic dualism, in which a "real samsara" filled with "real phenomena" stood on one side, and a real noumenal Nirvana, a resting place without remainder, stood on the other. This reality was of course rather cold—if not totally frozen—depreciative of the world and the other people in it, and it naturally led one to seek permanent association with the transcendent to the exclusion of the transcended. It became escapist. That is to say, the naive realism with which all living beings build up their worlds had here been transposed by the early systematizers of the Abhidharma into a conceptual scheme that preserved the remarkable and transformative new spiritual dimension of the transcendent, but still lacked the final cure for the self-destructive habit of naive realism itself.

This cure had been taught from the very beginning by the Buddha, of course, but it was a message that was hard for simple country folk to assimilate, with their unquestioning acceptance of culturally inculcated realities, as it so went against the grain of their habits of thought and experience. So, as the Buddha himself had said, it took the culture some centuries of "pluralization of the life world" (in Berger's phrase) before they could come to grips with the constructed nature of reality. By Nagarjuna's time, apparently, enough people were ready for his teaching to have considerable impact.[26]

Thus, Nagarjuna, like Kant against the rationalists of medieval theology, and like Wittgenstein against the logical atomists, had to wield the sword of analysis against the Analysts, non-Buddhist as well as Buddhist; he had to level a complete critique against their absolutisms, either spiritualistic dualism or atomistic pluralism. This he did in a series of

26 "Pluralization of the life-world" comes from Berger et al.'s *Homeless Mind*. For an interesting comparison between the Abhidharmikas and western logical atomists, such as Russell, see C. Gudmunsen, *Wittgenstein and Buddhism* (London: Allen & Unwin, 1979).

works, whose critical thought patterns are effective for releasing us from almost any trap of dogmatism. His main works are known as the *Sixfold Canon of Philosophy* (*rigs tshogs drug*), including the major treatises called *Wisdom* (PM), the *Rebuttal of Objections* (VV), the *Finely Woven* (VP), the *Philosophical Sixty* (YṢ), the *Emptiness Seventy* (ŚS), and the *Jewel Garland* (RA). These works have stood largely unrefuted for the duration, now almost two thousand years, of the constant battles of Indian philosophy. A number of writers have made deprecatory comments about Nagarjuna's central way, calling him a "no-good nihilist," and other names, but no one has taken up his position point by point and rejected it in a cogent and persuasive manner. Indeed, even the great Asanga, who later found Nagarjuna's system to be too negativistic and warned people away from it, offering them the gentler Experientialist system, did not criticize it in detail. And the great Brahmin philosopher Shankaracarya tacitly admitted its unassailability by merely dismissing Nagarjuna as unworthy of consideration, after having just leveled a Nagarjunian critique against every other opponent in the field.[27]

The central gist of the Universal Vehicle and therefore of Nagarjuna's own philosophy is the spirit of enlightenment of love and compassion for all living beings. Although Shakyamuni Buddha had taught in the same spirit, the love aspect of his teaching was not so easily put into practice as the wisdom aspect, especially by the monastic community, and therefore its importance waned and the Universal Vehicle was forgotten. However, after four centuries, in the first century B.C.E., the civilized world was ripe for mass religious movements that stressed the solidarity of brotherhood and universal love and compassion in place of the older militaristic values of hierarchy, fatherhood, and tribal distinctiveness. The time was ripe for the Universal Vehicle. According to the legend, the great stream of love and compassion was brought up out of the *nāga* kingdom deep in the ocean onto the shores of India, and from there in a few centuries it spread throughout central Asia into China and eventually even into Tibet, Japan, and Mongolia. It is interesting that, at about the same time, Jesus brought another great stream of love and compassion to the West, whence in a few centuries it spread West into Europe and North Africa, and eventually even to Russia, Scandinavia, and Britain.

After his first round of teaching the Universal Vehicle and the Centrist philosophy, Nagarjuna again went off with the *nāgas* to the northern land, Uttarakuru, where the wild maize grows abundantly, and the people

[27] See G. Thibault, *The Vedāntasūtras of Bādārāyana*, translated with Shankara's commentary, (New York: Dover, 1968), I: 344ff.

are rich in cattle and game and live long and peaceful lives like gods. He spent two hundred fifty years there, before returning to India with a new batch of scriptures from the *nāga* libraries, the Idealist scriptures such as the *Elucidation of the Intention* and the *Mission to Lanka*,[28] which were of great influence in inspiring Aryasanga's philosophy. During this third sojourn in India, Nagarjuna also began to teach more openly the esoteric Tantras that, in the traditional view, he had been practicing in secret all along, as he had received them from the Great Brahmin Saraha, his early teacher. He composed the *Five Stages of the Perfection Stage of the Esoteric Communion* and other important Tantric commentaries, systematizing what later became known as the Arya Lineage of the Esoteric Communion Tantra (*Guhyasamāja*).[29]

Because of his youthful mastery of alchemy, this legendary Nagarjuna had the power of longevity, never eating coarse food, but subsisting on a magic pill he took daily, staying longer and longer to continue his work of benefiting living beings. He had a royal friend, King Antivahana, sometimes called Udayi, of the Shatavahana dynasty of south central India, whom he kept alive with him, to fund his projects of building monuments, monasteries, libraries, universities, hospitals, and welfare houses. But, as the legend concludes, the king's son finally became impatient, wanting his own turn at the throne, so he went to Nagarjuna and asked him for his head, calling upon him to live up to the bodhisattva ideal of transcendent generosity. Nagarjuna took this opportunity to conclude his work for the time, remembered a time when he had once killed some bugs by being in too much of a hurry to get some kusha grass for his meditation mat, and so handed the prince a blade of kusha grass and let him cut off his head. When the head rolled to the floor, it did not bleed but turned, along with the trunk, to alabaster, and spoke out clearly to the prince: "Now my head has left my body, but it will not be destroyed and later they will rejoin, when it is time for me to speak out again and bring the central way between the extremisms of absolutism and nihilism back to prominence in the world!"

Nagarjuna is also counted as a patriarch in the succession of "wordless

[28] SN and LAS.

[29] Even though I have said I am giving the "legendary" account, historically minded colleagues are no doubt appalled by the extravagance of the Indian hagiographic imagination. In my forthcoming work on Nagarjuna's Tantric writings, I argue that evidence internal to the texts supports the traditional claim that one person wrote both the philosophical and Tantric books. As we cannot accept the longevity this entails under our present system of dating the emergence of Tantrism, we should revise that patchwork of inferences. We date from the rare mention of texts or from their translation into Chinese and Tibetan, whereas the Tantrics themselves claim that they prevented these teachings from being published in any form for seven centuries, the better to preserve their secrecy.

enlightenment" teaching that descended from Shakyamuni to Bodhidharma and thence through the several major Ch'an and Zen lineages. The eloquent Nagarjuna, who wrote many books himself, discovered many more, and did more than almost anyone to spread the Universal Vehicle scriptures throughout the world, is claimed as a pivot of the "scriptureless tradition" of direct enlightenment through "Mind-Seal Transmission!"

2. Asanga

Asanga's dates are no better known than those of Nagarjuna, although his hagiographers had him live a mere one hundred fifty years, from approximately 300 C.E. to 450 C.E. Legend has it that his mother was a Buddhist nun who despaired of the state of Buddhism in the India of that time, and decided to renounce her nunhood to bear sons who would renew its energies. First, from a warrior father, she gave birth to Asanga; then from a Brahmin, Vasubandhu; and third, from a merchant, a son called Virinchavatsa. Asanga was first a member of the Vatsiputriya branch of the Sarvastivada school, and became a great teacher of the Individual Vehicle. He then heard of the Universal Vehicle teaching, and became interested in the teaching of great compassion and transcendent wisdom. Here he recognized the saving doctrine that could bring Indian Buddhism into its glory. He received initiation into the *Māyājāla Tantra*, and then set forth to contemplate great compassion, seeking to enlist the mystic aid of the supernal bodhisattva Maitreyanatha. He reasoned that, since the teaching of Shakyamuni Buddha was so poorly understood and practiced throughout the land, the future Buddha, believed to reside in the Tushita heaven, should be requested to make an anticipatory visit to the planet to revive the Dharma.

Leaving his home monastery in Takshashila, near present-day Peshawar, Asanga meditated on compassion and on the invocation of the bodhisattva Maitreya for twelve long years. At last, frustrated by failure, he abandoned the quest. His faith and his sense of self-worth utterly shattered, he wandered forth from the cave a broken man. He stopped near the first town at the sight of an old female dog who was suffering terribly from a suppurating wound in her hindquarters. He became absorbed involuntarily in the relatively simple task of trying to help at least this one sentient being. If only he could bring even temporary relief to one other being, perhaps his life would have served some purpose. As he was about to clean her wound, he noticed her live flesh was already crawling with maggots, so he could not help her without harming them.

After a moment's thought, he took a jagged shard and cut a piece of flesh from his own meagre thigh, shrunken by his long asceticism, and placed it on the ground next to the dog. He resolved to pick off the maggots one by one and place them on the fresh flesh. Unable to grasp them with his fingers, he put out his tongue to lick them off. As he neared the foul-smelling dog, he felt overwhelmed by revulsion, and, closing his eyes, had to force himself to go through the operation. Suddenly there was a kind of electronic explosion in front of his face, and as he started back and opened his eyes, he beheld the bodhisattva Maitreya standing before him, radiant, enhaloed in a rainbow aura. Overwhelmed with faith and joy, he prostrated himself at the Lord's feet over and over again. Finally, recovering his composure, he ventured to question Maitreya as to why he had been so long in responding. Maitreya replied that he had always been right with him, but that, as Asanga himself had persistently been caught up in self-involvement and had not yet generated great compassion, he had been unable to see him. After all, Maitreya is the incarnation of love (*maitrī*), and only those with great compassion can perceive love, even when it is right before them. Asanga was not convinced by this explanation, so Maitreya shrunk himself into a small globe of light and permitted Asanga to carry him through the town to show him to the populace. Asanga, heedless of his gaunt appearance and even his mangled thigh, did as he was told and ran joyfully through the town proclaiming the advent of the future Buddha. The townspeople looked wonderingly at what they saw as a crazed yogi from a cave, bleeding and tattered, running around with a contemptible, sick dog on his shoulder shouting about the future Buddha. Finally they drove him from the town.

The bodhisattva, however, used his supernatural power to take Asanga with him to the Tushita heaven, where he instructed him in the Universal Vehicle doctrines. He received then and there, in the altered time frame of that heaven, five important texts, known subsequently as the "Five Teachings of Maitreya": the *Ornament of Realizations (Abhisamayālaṃkāra)*, the *Ornament of the Universal Vehicle Scriptures* (*Mahāyānasūtrālaṃkāra*), the *Analysis of the Jewel Matrix* (*Ratnagotravibhāga*), the *Discrimination between Center and Extremes* (*Madhyāntavibhāga*), and the *Discrimination between Phenomenon and Noumenon* (*Dharmadharmatāvibhaṅga*).[30]

[30] Hereafter AA, MSA, RGV, MAV, and DDV. Modern scholars have debated the issue of Asanga and Maitreyanatha for over fifty years. The supernaturalism of the traditional account runs counter to the penchant for "demythologizing," what Demiéville called *la manie historiciste*. Further, the Chinese and Tibetan traditions differ as to who wrote which books, who lived when, and so forth. The Chinese accounts even differ with each other on some points. Is Maitreyanatha an historical person? Is he a religious fiction? Is he

Asanga brought these five books back to earth with him, and built a new monastery at the sacred grove Veluvana, in Magadha. A circle formed around him to learn the new synthesis of the Universal Vehicle teachings. He was at first unable to explain fully some of the more abstruse doctrines of the new idealistic system that Maitreyanatha taught, so he persuaded the bodhisattva to come down in person to the great lecture hall of the monastery during the nights, where, invisible to all but Asanga, the bodhisattva would directly teach his own doctrines. In time, Asanga went on to write a compendium of the new teachings, a massive and comprehensive synthesis of Buddhist doctrines and practices known as *The Stages of Yoga Practice (Yogācārabhūmi)*, as well as five analytic commentaries on that work. Toward the end of his life, Asanga wrote a commentary on the *Jewel Matrix* that affirmed his own Centrist viewpoint, according to the Tibetan tradition, as his elaboration of the Idealist system had been in terms of the needs of the disciples of his day, and not really an expression of his own final understanding.

At the time of Asanga, Nagarjuna's teachings had spread in India for about two hundred years. The Individual Vehicle Abhidharma teachings were widely studied and practiced. The Kushan dynasties had had their day, their power had waned, and the vacuum had not yet been filled by the Guptas, who were not to come to power until the end of the fourth century. It was a time of uncertainty and creativity in Indian civilization, and a prescient thinker might well have foreseen a resurgence of Indian nationalistic feeling, and wished to formulate Buddhist thought in such a way as to enable it to take its place near the center of the coming "classical" culture. The major forms of Buddhist thought then available were not suited to fulfill that function. Individual Vehicle monasticism with its refined psychological scholasticism, and central way critical thought with its razor-sharp dialectic, both were too remote from the needs of the rising middle classes, having little explicit emphasis on social philosophy, little devotionalism or ritualism to involve the masses, and few connections with the Brahminical culture other than critical opposition. The Universal Vehicle scriptures were still well ensconced in the popular imagination of the southern kingdoms that enjoyed the prosperity and peace inherited from the Shatavahana dynasty that had supported Nagarjuna. But on the intellectual level, the philosophy of Nagarjuna was

Asanga's mystic inspirer? Does his teaching represent the influence of Iranian or Greek ideas in Indian religion? It has been a fertile issue, indeed. See J. Takakusu, "Life of Vasubandhu," *Toung-Pao*, V (1904), 271-293; S. Levi, "Maitreya le consolateur," *Mélanges Linossier*, III, 369-384; E. Obermiller, "Sublime Science of Maitreya," *Acta Orientalia*, IX (1932); G. Tucci, *On Some Aspects of the Doctrines of Maitreya(natha) and Asanga* (Calcutta: University of Calcutta Press, 1944); E. Frauwallner, *On the Date of the Buddhist Master of the Law Vasubandhu*, Rome: Serie Orientale Roma III, 1951.

too abstruse and difficult for many educated middle-class thinkers, its uncompromising central doctrine of emptiness too easily confused with a nihilism sanctioning complete withdrawal from social concerns. In sum, a new synthesis of Brahminical culture and the Universal Vehicle scriptures was required, a synthesis that could make Buddhism accessible as a lay religion, with philosophical appeal for the educated elite. There was no departure from the spirit of Nagarjuna's own breakthroughs in epistemology and metaphysics, as well as his practical systematization of the trove of scriptures he discovered. It was rather a matter of shifting the emphasis from the profound aspect, the teaching of the absolute reality, to the magnificent aspect, the elaboration of the far-reaching paths of bodhisattva practices, including the magnificent panorama of the activities of the supernal bodhisattvas in the far-flung Buddha-lands throughout the universes of the multiverse. This was Asanga's mission, and it was in executing this mission that he received the supernatural aid of the bodhisattva Maitreyanatha.

The new philosophy relates to the Nagarjunian system much as Hegel relates to Kant, to make an analogy that will make it understandable to modern thinkers (but bearing in mind that it is only an analogy). Kant's great sword of critical reason began the work of cutting away the confusions of both absolutist rationalists and nihilistic skeptics of his day, and released the energies of critical reason needed for the task of acknowledging the real transcendentality of the transcendent, thereby freeing the realm of practical reason for truly empirical investigation. Upon this foundation, Hegel built up a more positive philosophical system that reintroduced the transcendental into the workings of the relative, but no longer in a mechanistic or naive way. Kant's greatness lay in his thrust toward freedom from both rationalistic complacency and skeptical despair. Hegel's lay in his courageous exploration of the possibilities of reinvesting that freedom in vistas of harmonious structures of living, of society, and of history.

Similarly, Nagarjuna, having discovered the Universal Vehicle scriptures, wherein transcendent freedom and immanent involvement were explicitly stated by the Buddha, related that most profound teaching to the doctrines of the Abhidharmists. In their rigid scholasticism, they had banished the absolute into a neat set of categories, off with space, somewhere "beyond" the formless realms of trance. Nagarjuna rightfully exploded this rationalistic dualism by leveling his "critique of pure reason," as it were, which de-reified the absolute and returned it to its place as the very fabric of the ineluctable relativity of the conventional world. His philosophical tool par excellence came from the Universal Vehicle scriptures, namely the doctrine of the two realities (*satyadvaya*), the absolute and the conventional, or ultimate and superficial. These two are only superficially opposite; ultimately they are the same. The absolute is equated with transcendent wisdom (*prajñāpāramitā*), and the superficial with great compassion (*mahākaruṇā*). Thus, the most throughgoing transcendentalism, instead of robbing the relative world of value, emerged to reinforce the relative commitment to great compassion, in its quest to benefit living beings and transform their world into a pure land of enlightenment.

The difficulty of this teaching for Asanga's purposes was that the two-edged sword cut so devastatingly through all pretensions of the conceptual mind that it left lesser minds feeling as if they had no ground to stand on. Indeed, the stance of the *Transcendent Wisdom Scripture* itself was that the ground of the bodhisattva is groundlessness. So, Asanga, to provide a more solid footing, came up with a system of scriptural hermeneutics that could reconcile a less insecure stance with the scriptural basis. He discovered the key he needed in the *Elucidation of the Intention Scripture*, with its theory of the "three wheels of Dharma," and its theory of the "three realities." This enabled him to provide the ground he felt people needed, and that ground he located in the mind.

The three wheels of Dharma doctrine was a way to elaborate the new doctrine without giving up allegiance to the *Transcendent Wisdom Scripture*, the Mother of All Buddhas. Thus, in the first wheel of Dharma, said Shakyamuni in the *Elucidation of the Intention*, the Buddha took for granted the apparent reality of both "samsara" and "nirvana," the wheel of the four holy truths. In the second wheel of Dharma, he taught the teaching of *Transcendent Wisdom*, stressing the universal emptiness of all things, to remove the disciples' attachment to existence, and introducing them to ultimate non-existence. Finally, in the third wheel of Dharma, he taught the existence of some things and the non-existence of other things, for those disciples of sharp discrimination. This third wheel of Dharma taught the three-reality theory, as a refinement of the basic two-reality theory taught in the second wheel, adding a central "relative reality" to serve as a ground of both the absolute and the superficial. Tsong Khapa elaborates this fully at the beginning of the *Essence* below.[31]

Maitreyanatha and Asanga, in emphasizing the paths of the bodhisattva, the magnificent deeds of great compassion and universal love that move the universe and bring sentient beings to perfection in the course of evolution, thus provided the religious ground on which the Universal Vehicle became accessible to the nascent "classical culture" of India, the culture that was coming to flower in the Gupta era with its

[31] See the great *Essence*, Ch. I.

great artists, poets, playwrights, and religious and philosophical geniuses. Just as Augustine of Hippo forged a new universe of discourse out of classical Greco-Roman culture and Christian spiritual vision (at about the same time), so Asanga followed Maitreyanatha's inspiration and made the Universal Vehicle literarily, philosophically, and religiously available to the classical Indian culture, bringing the Buddhist teaching out of the rarefied monastic atmosphere in which it had existed from its beginnings into the mainstream of the society.

So Tsong Khapa salutes these two Great Champions of humankind's battle against misknowledge, and thanks them for ensuring that the sunlight of the Victor's teaching still shines brightly in the minds of thoughtful people. We shall soon see whether, as the works of Nagarjuna and Asanga are properly translated into modern languages, that same sun will dawn again today.

V

Respectfully I bow to those Master Scholars,
Best Heralds of the non-decline of Buddha's Teaching,
Who upheld those two systems of the Champions,
And opened the eyes of millions of geniuses—
To the ornaments of the Holy Land of India,
Aryadeva, brave Buddhapalita, Bhavya, Chandrakirti,
Vasubandhu, Sthiramati, Dignaga, and Dharmakirti!

One of the modern prejudices about Indian philosophy is that it is not true philosophy, because it is so involved with religious concerns, and hence too dogmatic. Yet here Tsong Khapa praises the great masters of Buddhist India as "master scholars," and appreciates them for opening the eyes of "geniuses," that is, for their feats of scholarship and intellectual lucidity, not for religious piety. Within Indian philosophy, Indologists have followed Brahmin writers in taking "Bauddha" thought as one of the "heterodox" systems, a "negativist" system, due to the fact that the Buddhists did not affirm the Vedas and Upanishads, repudiated the caste system, and did not worship the national gods. But the Buddhist critical, anti-authoritarian, individualistic, and rationalistic approach is exactly what is meant by "philosophy," that is, an unprejudiced quest of truth. And therefore the Buddhist thinkers, far from being peripheral to the mainstream, were the main figures in Indian philosophy from approximately 500 B.C.E. to 1000 C.E.

First there is Shakyamuni Buddha himself, who is the most famous and influential of all the great figures of the Shramanic period, which includes the Upanishadic sages as well as the Jain Viras, the Charvaka materialists, and so on. Second, there are the great Elders, beginning with Shariputra and including the great Nagasena and many others like him, as the monastic communities refined and developed the scientific physics, ethics, and psychology of the Abhidharma "matrices" (*Mātrka*) of human knowledge. The style of systematic liberative education that they cultivated clearly influenced the whole development in the lay Brahmin community of the "Sutra" system employed in linguistics, medicine, logic, theology, and philosophy.

Thus, this period contains most of the Brahmin Sutra writers, who were stimulated by the success of the Buddhist monastic academies to formulate their own "matrices" for their "orthodox" styles of thought: that is, Jaimini's *Mīmāṃsāsūtra*, Badarayana's *Brahmasūtra*, Kapila's *Saṃkhyākārikā*, Patanjali's *Yogasūtra*, Kanada's *Vaiśeṣikasūtra*, and Gotama's *Nyāyasūtra* were probably worked out during this period, about 400 B.C.E. to 200 C.E., although the actual texts were codified by commentators somewhat later.

Third, there are Nagarjuna, Maitreya-Asanga, and their many colleagues in related fields, who shattered the insularity of the monastic universe and opened up the first great universities in India early in the first millennium. Their philosophical edifice accommodated the whole society, built on the foundation of the nondualist metaphysics of Nagarjuna's *Wisdom* and Maitreya's *Five Books*. The Universal Vehicle scriptures were rediscovered and promulgated at the popular level, the Buddha's story and evolutionary background were told in a new type of mass literature and drama (by Ashvaghosha and Aryashura, for example), and a newly humanistic political ethics was promoted (by Nagarjuna in his *Precious Garland*; Aryadeva in the *Four Hundred*; Maitreya in the *Ornament of Universal Vehicle Scriptures*). A new popular art arose, presenting the transcendent and exalted in forms suitable for the devotion of the masses, who found in Amitabha and in his sons, the great bodhisattvas such as Avalokiteshvara, sustaining hope in the outreaching dynamism of great compassion. This movement was completed by Aryasanga, who synthesized its great depth and magnificence into a form thoroughly connected to the national character. After his time, from about 500 C.E., the Brahmin philosophers emerged in a creative dialogue with the Buddhist "master scholars."

Thus, the pioneering activity of the Buddhist Champions provided the undergirding of the Brahmin elaboration of mass culture through the codification of the *Mahābhārata*, including the syncretic *Gīta*, the development of the great *kavyas*, the dramas of Kalidasa and others, and the broad cultural synthesis of the Gupta dynasty. In short, the "classical

Hindu" culture was formed, and clearly could be described as the synthesis between Brahmin traditional particularism and Buddhist radical universalism, the confluence of Brahmana and Shramana that has come to be called Hinduism.[32]

The brilliant elaboration of this great classical synthesis over the next centuries culminated in the baroque magnificence of the post-Gupta dynasties in Bihar and the Pala dynasty of Bengal. The leading figures of the philosophical development of these times are the "Great Ornaments" listed above. Their lives are legendary, both in the sense of being somewhat fantastic in tenor and in the sense of providing models for thousands of outstanding thinkers and creative artists who flourished in this most sophisticated era of Indian history. They were participants in the mainstream of the pluralistic culture, stimulating the greatest Hindu philosophers, who themselves rose to prominence in their brilliant efforts to answer the Buddhist challenge, seeking to match its sophistication of thought, while tempering the radical nature of its results in order to incorporate them within the hierarchical tradition of Brahmin culture. Prashastapada, Gaudapada, Uddyotakara, Prabhakara, Kumarila, Shankara, Vacaspatimisra, and so forth, all of them worked in direct interaction with Buddhist thought, in the intellectual and contemplative atmosphere emanating from the Buddhist universities from the fifth to the tenth centuries C.E. They developed their "Six Philosophical Visions" (*darśana*) in clear parallel to the Buddhist refinement of the "Four Philosophies" (*siddhānta*). It was surely their intellectual contest that spurred

[32] Medieval Brahmin scholars such as Madhva (1199-1276) and modern Brahmin followers of the neo-Hindu revival led by Swami Vivekananda, such as Dr. Radhakrishnan, present a very different version of Indian intellectual history. They seem determined to avert their gaze from the Buddhist, or more inclusively, Shramanic (including Jainas and Ajivakas, etc.) contribution to Hindu culture. For example, Professor Raju writes that the Buddhist tendency in thought was only a passing phase, a momentary diversion from the mainstream of Indian philosophy; and on the same page of his book, in a table of dates of major philosophers, there is a gap of one thousand years between the Brahminical Sutra writers (c. 400 B.C.E.) to Kumarila (c. 600 C.E.)! (P. T. Raju, *Philosophical Traditions of India*, London: Allen & Unwin, 1971, pp. 30-33.) This curious blind spot in historical perspective can only be explained by the low-caste (which means ritually unclean) connotation of "Buddhism" for these highly educated and intelligent men. In fact, it is no accident that it is the Buddhist thought of India that has long been of worldwide interest in both ancient and modern times. I therefore dwell on these accounts of the Buddhist thinkers in the hope that modern Indian intellectuals may come themselves to rediscover and lay claim to these gems of their intellectual history, emulating the generous salutation by Professor D. N. Shastri, who opened his fine book, *Critique of Indian Realism* (Agra: Agra University Press, 1964), by saluting the Master Dignaga—about whom he learned from the great Russian scholar Stcherbatski, as Dignaga was hardly known by the modern pandits of India. The modern Indian historian of Buddhism who has done most to redress this distortion of perspective is Professor L. M. Joshi, whose *Studies in the Buddhistic Culture of India* (Delhi: Motilal Banarsidass, 1980), is a milestone.

both traditions to ever greater heights of creativity. Let us now review the mythic stories of the "master scholars" who were the vital forces on the Buddhist side of this tradition.

1. Aryadeva

Aryadeva was born as the son of the king of Shri Lanka in about the third century C.E., miraculously appearing in a lotus in the garden, according to legend. Although placed on the throne at an early age, he felt dissatisfied with royal life and soon renounced his role in society and wandered off to South India to study the Dharma, taking ordination from the great teacher Nagarjuna himself. He soon became the master's foremost disciple, even surpassing his master in some respects, as conveyed in the legends of his Tantric *persona*, Karnaripa. This is only startling if we fail to recognize the basic anti-authoritarian and progressive stance of Buddhism, even in those ancient times.

The most famous story about Aryadeva is his debate with the great Pandit Matrcheta, later known as Aryashura according to Tibetan sources, though not by modern scholars.[33] This Matrcheta was a Shaivite, a great logician as well as a great sorcerer, and no one could withstand him in disputation. Eventually he conquered the monastic university of Nalanda, as in those days a school had to defend its philosophical positions against all comers if it was to retain its endowment and control over its curriculum. He was lording it over all the monks, forcibly converting them to his own theism and making them participate in his chosen rites. The monks were desperate and secretly performed a ceremony to the Dharma-Protector Mahakala, the Terrible One. They wrote a plea for help on a piece of paper and placed it on the altar, and, legend has it, a crow flew out of the Mahakala image and carried the message off toward the south. Whatever the source, Nagarjuna did hear of the plight of his colleagues, but did not feel like going himself. Aryadeva volunteered to go, but first Nagarjuna tested him by arguing the positions Matrcheta would be likely to take. He argued these so forcibly, he eventually enraged Aryadeva, who dropped all deference and, attacking the master with all his force, succeeded in toppling his arguments. Nagarjuna was delighted that Aryadeva had so forgotten himself in the heat of debate that he had taken his own teacher for a theist. He pronounced him capable of winning the victory over Matrcheta. He warned Aryadeva that he would have to

[33] See A. K. Warder, *Indian Buddhism*, (Delhi: Motilal Banarsidass, 1970), pp. 389ff; A. Chattopadhyaya and L. Chimpa, *Taranatha's History of Buddhism*, p. 132.

make a sacrifice on the way, but that if he did not regret it, it would be restored to him.

Sure enough, a beggar came to Aryadeva as he traveled through the forest to the north, and asked him for the gift of one of his eyes. The bodhisattva gave it unhesitatingly, pulling it from its socket, and proceeded on his way. He could not restrain his curiosity, however, and when he looked back he saw that the beggar, unable to implant the eye in his own head, was furiously pounding it to bits on a tree stump. Aryadeva felt a twinge of regret at this total waste, and therefore, it is said, his eye was never restored. For this reason, he is also known as Kanadeva, the One-Eyed Lord. He continued to Nalanda, and met his opponent.

The account of their contest is amusing. When Matrcheta first noticed Aryadeva, he said, "Where has this extra shaved head come from?" Aryadeva replied, "It has come from this neck!" clapping himself on the back of the neck. Matrcheta took note that a worthy adversary had arrived. Another time, Aryadeva went down to the Ganges riverbank with Matrcheta and his followers. When they were performing ritual ablutions, Aryadeva entered the water holding a golden pot filled with excrement, officiously washing the outside of it. Matrcheta said, "Why wash the outside if the inside is filled with excrement?" Aryadeva said, "How can you purify your bodies with Ganges water on the outside when the inside is full of defilements?" Another time, Matrcheta stood in a doorway and asked, "Am I going out or coming in?" Aryadeva said, "That depends on your motivation." Matrcheta then held up a bird in his hand, "Am I going to kill this bird or not?" Aryadeva replied, "That depends on your compassion." Later Matrcheta was performing an ancestral sacrifice at the fire altar, and Aryadeva came there with some dry kusha grass and began sprinkling it with water. Matrcheta asked, "What are you doing?" Aryadeva said, "I am watering a withered tree on Shri Parvata." "How can you water a tree there by sprinkling water here?" "Then how can you offer food to your long-dead, far-away ancestors by burning it up here?" When the debate itself began, Aryadeva put a bag of excrement on Matrcheta's parasol to keep away Shiva, threw oil on the magic slate where the god would write the arguments, manifested a cat to kill Shiva's parrot-emanation who would whisper Matrcheta the answers, and made obscene gestures at Parvati to prevent her from coaching his opponent. Matrcheta said, "How dare you challenge me, with your one eye, to debate?" Aryadeva replied, "Ishvara with his three eyes cannot see the nature of reality, but I see it very clearly with my one. Why then should I not defeat you?" And Aryadeva won.

After his defeat, Matrcheta was so mortified he flew off into space.

Aryadeva followed him and saved his life by warning him at the last minute that he would die if he left the atmosphere. Thus tamed, the pandit returned with Aryadeva. Aryadeva shut him up in the library, where he began to read the Buddhist literature. Finally, Matrcheta came upon a prophecy of himself, how he was defeated by Aryadeva, and how he became a great teacher of the Universal Vehicle tradition. He was so amazed that he became a sincere student of the Buddha Dharma, and eventually one of its greatest writers.

It is interesting that Aryadeva, like Nagarjuna, is claimed as a patriarch by the Ch'an/Zen school of the Far East, whose version of his defeat of the theist stands in interesting parallel to the Indo-Tibetan one:

> In Kanadeva's day, the heretics impounded the drum and bell in the Buddhist community temple in a purge. At this time the honorable Kanadeva knew that the Buddhist teaching was in trouble, so he made use of his supernatural powers to ascend the bell tower and ring the bell, for he wanted to drive out the heretics. Soon one of the heretics called out, "Who is up in the tower ringing the bell?" Kanadeva said, "A deva." The heretic asked, "Who is the deva?" Kanadeva said, "I." The heretic said, "Who is 'I'?" Kanadeva said, " 'You' is a dog." The heretic asked, "Who is the dog?" Kanadeva said, "The dog is you." After seven go-rounds like this, the heretic realized he was beaten, so he submitted and himself opened the door of the bell tower, whereupon Kanadeva came down from the tower holding the red flag (the convention for the victor). The heretic said, "Why do you not follow?" Kanadeva said, "Why do you not precede?" The heretic said, "You're a knave." Kanadeva said, "You're a free man!"[34]

Aryadeva's principal works often explicitly apply the Centrist critique to the various Brahmin schools of thought, whereas Nagarjuna had mainly confined himself to refuting the Individual Vehicle Abhidharma masters. Aryadeva's greatest work of critical philosophy was the *Experientialist Four Hundred*,[35] which begins with a systematic arrangement of the Universal Vehicle path, and continues with a devastating critique of all the extremist ideologies existent in India during his time. His major work in the Tantric field, the *Lamp of Concentrated Practice*, is remarkable for its lucidity and comprehensiveness.[36] In spite of the modern insistence that there was no Tantra in his time, the Indo-Tibetan tradition itself is unanimous that the same Aryadeva wrote both philosophic and yogic

[34] T. and J. C. Cleary, *Blue Cliff Record*, p. 89.

[35] CŚ.

[36] *Cāryāmelāpakapradīpa*, considered by modern scholars to be written by Aryadeva the Second, as the *Pañcakrama* is considered to be written by Nagarjuna the Third!

works, quite in keeping with Indian tradition, wherein any philosopher worth the name is inevitably a master yogi.

2. Buddhapalita

Buddhapalita was born of a Brahmin family in approximately 470 C.E. in the Tambala region of south India, in a town called Prasannamula, and studied under Master Sangharakshita, who was himself a disciple of Nagamitra, according to some traditions. The legendary tradition would make him a direct disciple of Nagarjuna, as well as a mystic who achieved communication with the supernal bodhisattva Manjushri. His great achievement was the elucidation of Nagarjuna's *Wisdom*,[37] and his commentary became the foundational work for the Dialecticist interpretation of the Centrist philosophy (*Prāsaṅgikamādhyamika*). In elucidating Nagarjuna's critiques, he avoided putting forth formal syllogisms in a dogmatic manner, preferring to use consequential inferences in a dialectical manner to demonstrate the inherent contradictions in the opponent's positions. Tsong Khapa always felt deeply his debt to this great master, as it was while reading Buddhapalita's book that he attained his highest enlightenment experience. There is a Tibetan tradition that holds Buddhapalita to be the reincarnation of the Licchavi Vimalakirti, famous wise layman of the Buddha's time. Buddhapalita was also considered an adept (*siddha*), and to have passed away to the realm of the Mystic Sages (*Vidyādhara*) around 550 C.E.

3. Bhavaviveka

Bhavaviveka (also Bhavya) was a younger contemporary of Buddhapalita, apparently born in Andhra, near Dhanyakataka, around 500 C.E., not far from the center of Buddhist learning in the south of India. He was evidently of Brahmin lineage, as witnessed by the mastery of Brahminical philosophical systems displayed in his voluminous work of comparative ideologies, the *Heart of the Central Way* and its commentary *Blaze of Argument*.[38] This is one of the earliest systematic works on the "history of philosophy" in the world, wherein he studies the Individual Vehicle, the Idealists, the Centrists, the Mimamsaka, the Nyaya, the Vaisheshika, the Vedanta, and the Samkhya, as well as other lesser schools of the time. He traveled to the Magadha area of north India to visit the great teacher Dharmapala, who, like Shankara later, died very young, but Dharmapala

[37] BMMV.
[38] MH and TJ.

was in retreat at Bodhgaya and refused to debate with Bhavya. Bhavya returned to the south, where he studied the great commentary of Devasharma, *Sītābhyudaya*[39] *(White Exaltation)*, with full approval, and the works of Buddhapalita, which he found too radical and unsystematic for his taste. In his commentary on the *Wisdom*, the *Lamp of Wisdom*,[40] he found fault with Buddhapalita at every turn, especially from the point of view of methodology. He elaborated the method of proving the Centrist position with positive, private, dogmaticist syllogisms, thus becoming the source of the Dogmaticist Centrist school (*Svātantrikamādhyamika*).[41] After Chandrakirti and the refinement of the Dialecticist Centrism, and especially after its transplantation into Tibet after Atisha, Bhavaviveka came to be the butt of ridicule as the example par excellence of a self-contradictory Centrist. Chandrakirti himself may have been somewhat responsible for this by employing some strong language and humorous teasing in his critique of Bhavya's critique of Buddhapalita's elucidation of Nagarjuna's critique of the Samkhya position on production. Chandra said, "Master Bhavya likes to show off his expertise in logic!" and so forth. But most of his critique is serious, taking Bhavya seriously, and there is no suggestion that he thinks Bhavya ridiculous. Tsong Khapa himself is very critical of the Dogmaticist Centrist position, and refutes Bhavya on certain points incisively. However, he makes a point of accepting many of Bhavya's definitions and insights on other matters as authoritative, of saluting him in this introduction, and of praising him on his deep knowledge of many issues.

4. Chandrakirti

Chandrakirti was also from south India, born probably in the latter part of the sixth century C.E. in a place called Samanta, according to Tibetan sources. He was ordained and studied under Buddhapalita's disciple Kamalabuddhi. After becoming an expert himself, he went to Nalanda in the north, and eventually became abbot. At the time, the ruling post-Gupta monarch was somewhat opposed to Buddhist scholars, and so they were restricting their teaching activities to the monastic university proper. Chandrakirti changed that, and began again to teach the Universal Vehicle and the Centrist philosophy widely. He had a famous debate that lasted for seven years with the master grammarian and Idealist

[39] This work is lost, though Tsong Khapa mentions it as the model for Bhavya's own commentary on the *Wisdom*, the PrPr.

[40] PrPr.

[41] For the English terms I use for Svatantrika and Prasangika, see the great *Essence*, Ch. V. n. 98.

philosopher, Chandragomin, who, it was later revealed, managed to stand up to Chandrakirti only through daily consultations with the Bodhisattva Avalokiteshvara, through a famous statue standing in a courtyard at the monastery. When Chandrakirti complained to the bodhisattva that he was showing favoritism, he was told, "You don't need me, you have Manjushri helping you! So I just thought to help this fellow along a little."

According to the Tibetan tradition, Chandrakirti was the "ultimate" disciple of Nagarjuna himself, at the end of the latter's long life, to whom he taught his "ultimate" teaching, that of the uncreated. Whatever this may mean historically, it indicates a sense of Chandrakirti's destiny as elucidator of the essence of Nagarjuna's message, as does his mystic connection with Manjushri. Other legendary events of his life are that he milked the picture of a cow to feed the monks of Nalanda during a famine; rode a stone lion to frighten away a barbarian Turkish army that was threatening the monastery; and survived a forest fire while meditating in retreat, his rescuers finding him in the middle of an unburnt circle on his grass mat, saying, "My master Nagarjuna burnt entirely the fuel of phenomena with the fire of the uncreated; my abbot has done so, and I have done so; so how can the phenomenal fire burn me?" Many other such signs are recounted. A final interesting story about him was his interaction with Avalokiteshvara, after he discovered that the bodhisattva had been helping his adversary Chandragomin in the debate. Avalokiteshvara said that he was always there to help everyone, but that people couldn't see him. Chandra carried him around town on his head, but most people saw nothing: some saw a dead dog, and one prostitute saw a foot of the Lord Avalokiteshvara, whereby she instantly attained numerous powers. It is interesting that a story so similar to the legend of Saint Asanga should be attached to this paragon of the deep wisdom lineage. Chandrakirti's greatest works were his *Introduction to the Middle Way*,[42] his commentary on Nagarjuna's *Wisdom*, the *Lucid Exposition*,[43] and his commentary on the *Perfection Stage Five Stages* of Nagarjuna, the *Luminous Lamp*.[44] These latter two are known as the sun and moon, lighting up the worlds of Sutra and Tantra, respectively. The Tibetans consider him also to be one of the "Eighty-four Adepts."

5. Vasubandhu

After much scholarly discussion, there is as yet no unanimity about the dates of Vasubandhu, due both to the complexities arising from the

[42] MA.
[43] PPMMV.
[44] Again, supposed to be written by Chandrakirti the Second.

differences between the Chinese and Tibetan histories, and the fact that there probably really were two well-known Vasubandhus.[45] Our Vasubandhu the Great, author of the great *Treasury*, the *Twenty*, and the *Thirty*,[46] as well as numerous commentaries on works of Asanga and Maitreya and on Universal Vehicle scriptures, was the younger brother of Asanga, at first a great scholar of Individual Vehicle philosophies, and, after his conversion by Asanga, a great teacher of Universal Vehicle thought, especially the Idealist school. His dates can be given as ca. 385-480 C.E. His mother, Prakashashila, bore him by a Brahmin father one year after Asanga's ordination as a Buddhist monk. She charged him sternly to devote himself to Buddhism, so he was ordained at Nalanda around 400 C.E. He traveled to Kashmir and studied the Abhidharma extensively under the great master Samghabhadra, becoming so proficient in the subtleties of the Individual Vehicle Analytical schools that legend has it he was not allowed to leave the country, lest that area lose its monopoly on expertise in the Abhidharma. He managed to outwit his captors, however, and made his way to Nalanda. There he flourished as a teacher of Abhidharma, displaying his remarkable critical and expositional skill in drafting the *Treasury of Abhidharma*, one of the great works of world philosophy. In its verses he presents the Analysts' version of the Abhidharma, using an ambiguous exclamation "Indeed!" (*kila*, emphatic or ironic) to set them up for the refutation he presents in the commentary, from the Traditionists' perspective. His subtle way of going about his critique was occasioned by his reluctance to offend his teacher, Samghabhadra, an Analyst. In spite of his reverence, his independent critical thinking could not rest content with the Analysts' somewhat dogmatic method of presenting reality in a rigid set of categories supposed to correspond to objective reality. To this Vasubandhu preferred the Traditionists' more nominalistic understanding of the program of analytic wisdom.

After this, he chanced to read through Asanga's massive work, *Stages of Yoga Practice*,[47] a compendium of Individual and Universal Vehicle teachings presented as an independent, synthetic treatise. Taranatha reports that he remarked, "Alas! Though Asanga meditated for twelve years in the forest, instead of attaining success in his meditation he has composed a work like an elephant's load!" Hearing of this, Asanga decided it was time to open his brother's eyes to the Universal Vehicle. He pretended to be near death and called for his brother to visit him. Vasubandhu came, and Asanga commissioned two monks to recite for

[45] See references above, n. 30.
[46] AK, Vim., and Trim.
[47] YBh.

him the two scriptures, the *Teaching of Akshayamati* and the *Ten Stages*, from the *Heap of Jewels* and the *Garland* collections, respectively.[48] From the first, Vasubandhu was forced to concede the superiority of the Universal Vehicle in philosophical theory, and from the second, he became inspired by its glory in terms of extensive practice. He began to feel remorse about having previously denigrated the Universal Vehicle. He felt so bad that he wished to cut out his tongue. Asanga is said to have instructed him that he should rather turn his tongue to the benefit of living beings by teaching far and wide the Universal Vehicle doctrine. He then set himself to memorize the entire *Heap of Jewels* (forty-nine scriptures) and *Garland* collections, on top of numerous Individual Vehicle scriptures. He also recited a number of wisdom-spells (*dhāraṇī*), at least according to the Tibetans, becoming proficient in Tantric meditation as well as Universal Vehicle philosophy. When he converted to the Universal Vehicle, it is said that about five hundred of his formerly Individualist disciples converted him. From then until the Nirvana of Asanga, he spent most of his time learning and reciting scriptures. There is a legend that he used to spend a fortnight of each year soaking in a tub of sesame oil reciting the *Transcendent Wisdom Scriptures* and other works. During that time he would complete as many scriptures as an ordinary person might recite throughout a whole year.

After Asanga had passed on, Vasubandhu became the abbot of Nalanda, and worked twenty hours a day, teaching and ordaining monks in the morning, teaching Universal Vehicle philosophy during the afternoon, sometimes for twelve hours at a stretch, and dividing the night between a short sleep and periods of meditation. He stayed mostly in Magadha, but his impact was enormous in spreading the system of monastic education throughout India, and he personally made triumphal teaching journeys into Bengal and Orissa. Taranatha records the tradition that he founded six hundred fifty-four schools during his tenure as abbot of Nalanda. His teaching was particularly appealing since he combined overwhelming expertise in the Individual Vehicle teachings with inspired enthusiasm for the Universal Vehicle. Thus he was able to teach the numerous Buddhist monks in terms familiar to them. He taught the Universal Vehicle teaching in integration with the Individual Vehicle. His collected writings on Universalist subjects are traditionally given as fifty scriptural commentaries and eight original treatises, but Taranatha makes the point that he also wrote important commentaries on the treatises of his brother, which formed a third voluminous category. He also converted numerous Brahmins to Buddhism, persuading them through his lucid

[48] AMN, DBS; *Ratnakūta*, and *Avataṃsaka Sūtras*.

argumentation and sincerity of purpose. At the end of his life, he visited Nepal to teach there. In that Himalayan country, he was distressed by the condition of the Dharma, and was particularly disturbed by the Nepali monks who worked their own fields, having adapted to the non-Indian situation in that way. Vasubandhu died in Nepal at an age of almost one hundred years. The Tibetans revere him as a "Second Victor." His *Treasury of Abhidharma*, combined with Asanga's *Abhidharma Synthesis*,[49] forms the basis of their "science curriculum"; his commentaries on the Maitreya and Asanga works are regularly studied in their Transcendent Wisdom curriculum, and his *Twenty Verses* and *Thirty Verses* are important in their hermeneutical studies.[50]

6. Sthiramati

Legend has it that Sthiramati's just previous life was that of a dove who lived in the rafters of the residence where Vasubandhu memorized and recited scriptures and spells after his conversion by Asanga. Dying as a dove, he was reborn as the son of a merchant in the south, in a place whose name is reconstructed as Dandakaranya. From youth he began to ask for Vasubandhu, the master of Magadha, so he was sent to him as a disciple at the age of seven. He was then said to have obtained the tutelage of the goddess Tara: one day he refused to eat his beans because her stone statue would not accept his offering of a portion, and he wept bitterly; the statue is said thereupon to have blessed him and taken the beans, and after that his studies became effortless and he soon mastered all the scriptures and treatises. He became the leader of the Order after Master Vasubandhu passed on, and is credited, along with the great Gunamati, with opening a monastic university in Vallabhi in western India, under the Maitraka kings in Kathiawar, which became the Nalanda of the west. He wrote numerous subcommentaries on Vasubandhu's treatises, as well as a number of treatises of his own.

7. Dignaga

Dignaga was born in Simhavaktra, near Kanchi in the south, around the beginning of the fifth century. He was ordained under a master of the Vatsiputriya school of the Individual Vehicle, Nagadatta, who was also

[49] AS.

[50] Tib. *mNgon pa*, *Phar phyin*, and *Drang nges*, respectively, three of the important branches of study in the Tibetan philosophical curriculum.

renowned for his knowledge of the Brahminical philosophical traditions, the Nyaya, Vaisheshika, Samkhya, and Mimamsa. The Vatsiputriyas asserted a special theory of self, claiming that there was such a self, but that it was inexpressible—reminiscent of the later claims of the Uttaramimamsa, or Vedanta school. In his quest for this self, Dignaga was said to have meditated naked with all the windows open by day and with lamps and fires burning at night to find the "inexpressible self," only to report his failure to do so to his teacher. His teacher took this as an indirect criticism, and so he sent Dignaga away to study elsewhere.

Tradition has it that Dignaga studied with Vasubandhu at Nalanda, which may mean that he became the student of Sthiramati or another of Vasubandhu's successors, when the school was still energetic with the recent impact of the great master. At any rate, Dignaga mastered all the scriptures of Individual and Universal Vehicles, as well as all the important treatises. He even practiced Tantric meditation, and is said to have obtained the special mystic gift of frequent visitation and revelations directly from Manjushri himself. He retired to Orissa for forest meditation for some years, but returned to Nalanda to defend the monastery from learned Brahmin challengers who were skilled in logic and epistemology. Dignaga became famous by defeating the great Brahmin logician, Sudurjaya, converting him and his numerous disciples. But rather than stay on as leader of the school, he preferred to return to Orissa and his contemplative life. After some time, he resolved to write a *Synthesis of Validating Cognition*,[51] to put forward a reliable system of epistemology and logic, built out of a critique of the various methods prevalent in philosophical circles of the day. On a rock outside his cave hermitage, he first wrote the extraordinary verse of salutation that we have discussed above:

> I bow to the Teacher, the Blissful, the Savior,
> Who wills the good of all, personifying reason!
> To expound validating cognition, I gather here
> A synthesis of all my fragmentary treatises.[52]

When he wrote this, it is said, the earth quaked, a dazzling light burst forth, and thunder rolled in the clear sky. A Brahmin ascetic called Krishnamuni observed all this, and he came to the cave while Dignaga was out on alms-rounds, and erased the verse. Dignaga wrote it again; again it was erased. The third time Dignaga left an additional note, "This is an important verse, so please don't erase it just for fun. If you disagree

[51] PS.
[52] RGV, I, v. 4.

with it, you are only wiping out the chalk and not the idea. You should show yourself, and we'll debate." Krishnamuni was waiting for him when he returned this time. They debated, and Dignaga defeated him three times. He said, "Now you have lost! You must embrace the Buddha Dharma!" Instead, Krishnamuni became furious, creating magical flames that burned down the hermitage and almost killed Dignaga. Dignaga became depressed, feeling that if he could not help this one highly intelligent Brahmin, what would be the use of writing his *Synthesis*? He threw his chalk up in the air, saying, "When it falls down, I will give up the spirit of universal enlightenment!" Suddenly, Manjushri appeared and caught the chalk in the air. "Don't do this, my son! Your intelligence will deteriorate if you seek personal peace alone in the Individual Vehicle. None of the Brahmin pandits will ever harm your treatise. I'll be your spiritual friend until you reach the stage yourself. And in the future, your treatise will become the sole eye of all living beings!" Thus encouraged, Dignaga continued the work. This *Synthesis* of his has been continuously studied, along with its important elaborations by Dharmakirti, from then until modern times, at first widely in India, and subsequently in Tibet and Mongolia. Recently, it has begun to exert influence in Japan and the West, initially through the work of the Russian translator and philosopher, Theodor Stcherbatski.[53]

After finishing the work, Dignaga began to travel around Orissa, debating and converting Brahmins and Individual Vehicle monks, eventually gaining the patronage of the king. He then rebuilt sixteen monasteries, which had been founded earlier but had been neglected and had fallen into disrepair. He was also renowned as a Tantric adept, and performed numerous miracles, as well as enjoying many mystic *samadhis* and experiences due to the special blessings of Manjushri.

As Stcherbatski himself so eloquently and accurately pointed out, Dignaga's pivotal accomplishment was the critical separation of the realms of sense and reason. All previous Indian formal systems of logic had failed to overcome the reificatory habit-pattern of projecting human concepts into perceptual reality, and hence always fell short of true empiricism. Shakyamuni Buddha, Nagarjuna, and many others had of course personally transcended this, and had devastatingly criticized naive realism. It was left to Dignaga, however, to elaborate this crucial insight of the absolute unconstructedness of pure experience in epistemological terms, critically isolating the omnipresent world-constructive activity of the imagination—thereby anticipating Hume—yet subtly understanding the role of conceptualizing imagination and language in the process of

[53] BL, I and II; Stcherbatsky used Dharmakirti's NB as his main source.

construction itself—thus anticipating Kant and Wittgenstein. So his achievement is significant not only in the context of Buddhism or of Indian thought, but must be appreciated as a major landmark in the history of world philosophy.[54]

8. Dharmakirti

Dharmakirti was born of a high Brahmin family in Tirumalai in the Chudamani kingdom of Tamilnadu, in about 580 C.E. Until sixteen he was trained in the Brahminical traditional lore, excelling all his classmates from the earliest age. After that, he read some Buddhist scriptures and became so enthusiastic he changed his dress to the Buddhist style. The Brahmins were annoyed by this and drove him away. So he went to Nalanda and studied extensively under Master Dharmapala. He then went to Master Ishvarasena, a direct disciple of Dignaga, and studied the *Synthesis*, in the understanding of which he almost immediately surpassed his teacher. The teacher was delighted, and commissioned him to write a new commentary on the work. He also studied the *Heruka Tantra*, and is said to have attained the vision and blessing of Shri Heruka. He then composed his major philosophical work, the *Treatise on Validating Cognition*,[55] ostensibly a commentary on the *Synthesis*, but actually more like an independent treatise on the subject, which brings Dignaga's insight to the fullest degree of subtlety and profundity. It stands today as perhaps the greatest work on logic and epistemology in Indian philosophical history, leaving its impact on all schools of thought. He wrote six other works, two of them abridgments of the *Treatise*, and four other treatises on separate issues: on logic, debate, theory of relations, and solipsism.[56] He also wrote Tantric commentaries, literary criticism, and even excellent erotic poetry.

The legends of his debates with numerous non-Buddhist Brahmins are delightfully colorful. He wished to learn the Brahmin ideas thoroughly, as the story goes, so he went to the estate of the great Mimamsaka philosopher Kumarila, and served him as student and servant for a number of years, pretending not to be a Buddhist. After a year or two, he had mastered all the doctrines of this master, getting the secret points through the family, though the master himself also liked him a great deal for his prodigious intellect. He then left, went to a nearby city, and began

[54] BL, I.
[55] PV.
[56] *Pramāṇaviniścaya, Nyāyabindu, Hetubindu, Vādanyāya, Saṃbandhaparīkṣa, Saṃtānāntarasiddhi.*

his missionary work by nailing up a challenge to all comers for debate. He began to defeat everyone from all schools, ultimately even Kumarila himself, though he did not claim anyone's life, as was previously the custom in that region. Instead, he converted the Brahmins to Buddhism, built many new schools and temples, and traveled far and wide. Taranatha's account even records that he encountered the great Shankaracharya three times, defeating him every time, although he could win his conversion only in the third debate in the third lifetime. The first two times Shankara lost, he drowned himself in the Ganges rather than become a Buddhist, vowing to reincarnate as the son of one of his disciples in order to return to the contest anew. Finally, the third reincarnation was converted to Buddhism after the debate, and Dharmakirti's mission was proclaimed a success from Kashmir to Tamilnadu.[57] Dharmakirti died after establishing a new school and temple in Kalinga, and a stupa was erected to enshrine the crystal ball that miraculously appeared as the residue of his pyre. He was said to have been a contemporary of King Songzen Gambo (Srong-btsan sGam-po, r. 627-651), who began the process of importing Buddhism into Tibet.

Whatever the truth of the legends about his activity, which are obversely mirrored in the Hindu legends about Shankaracharya, he seems to have been connected with a great flourishing of Buddhism during the seventh century. This gave its institutions the momentum needed for their continued vitality right up to the Turkish invasions of the tenth through twelfth centuries, when their devastation was completed. Through the tremendous impact of these "Great Ornaments" of India, the Brahminical philosophies and religious schools incorporated much of the essential import of the Buddhist Dharma. But once the great universities were gone, there was no more social loophole in the caste system, no way for the low-caste person to achieve education and high status, and no more of that ferment of new ideas that requires ideological openness and social mobility. Hence, under the Muslim rulers, the Brahminical conservatism and hierarchicalism of the medieval period set in, to last until the twentieth century without any serious challenge. And the philosophy of this period is marked by a trend toward doctrinal conservatism and dogmatism, most creativity being channeled into technical and theological refinements. Indeed, it was not long before the *bhakti* conservatives, Ramanuja (twelfth century C.E.) and Madhva (thirteenth century C.E.), threw out even Shankara's Vedantic nondualism as a vestige of Universal Vehicle Buddhism, calling Shankara himself a "crypto-Buddhist," and reinstated theistic "dualistic nondualism," or just plain dualism, as the

[57] A. Chattopadhyaya and Chimpa, *Taranatha's History of Buddhism in India*, pp. 233-37.

orthodox understanding of the Vedanta. In logic and epistemology, the New Nyaya school after Gangesha (twelfth to thirteenth century) wound itself tightly in a tangle of subtleties, reducing its extreme realism to formalism, among the most intricate ever developed anywhere. Indian philosophy is perhaps only just beginning to awaken now, with the rediscovery of its own ancient "tradition of originality."

The first phase of this awakening has come from Swami Vivekananda and other great figures of the neo-Hindu renaissance, with the bringing of Shankara back into international prominence. The second phase, now beginning, may well arise from Indian philosophers' taking inspiration from the "Great Ornaments," whose major works are being restored from the treasuries long preserved in Tibet.[58]

VI

There have been many who did not realize That Place,
Although they strived, were not lowly in accomplishments
From direct experience, were learned in the Doctrine,
And even dedicated themselves to the path of philosophy!

Now Tsong Khapa wishes to give his own reason for writing the *Essence*, having saluted the authors of the many profound and crucial works that elaborate the philosophies of the Great Champions. Immediately he brings up the transcendental matter, "That Place," the exalted stage of unexcelled perfect enlightenment, including phenomenal omniscience as well as noumenal omniscience.[59] He calls it "Place" since it is, finally, only a perfectly Enlightened One who really knows where he is, both in ultimate actuality and in relative coordinates on various levels.

In this verse Tsong Khapa refers to his predecessors and some contemporaries in Tibet, as those "who did not realize That Place." He then proceeds to praise them for what they did accomplish, to indicate that his critical concern on this occasion is very specific, lest it be thought that his purpose is merely polemical or sectarian. He is critical of these predecessors for their not having attained Buddhahood, perfect enlightenment. He does not challenge their genuine attainment of bodhisattvahood, of high stages of enlightenment, of great erudition, and he is ap-

[58] The work in Shantiniketan, Nalanda, Delhi University, Andhra, and Madras is beginning this process. The most significant recent development is the Indian Goverment project in Saranath, at the Central Institute for Higher Tibetan Studies, under the Venerable Samdong Rinpoche, to translate the major lost Indian works from the Tibetan canon back into modern scholarly Sanskrit.

[59] Tib. *ji snyed mkhyen pai ye shes, ji lta mkhyen pai ye shes.*

preciative of their works of genius. Implicit in this critique is his claim of his own perfect enlightenment, which seems startling perhaps to some, may stir others to indignation, but which is in fact well precedented in the Enlightenment Tradition.

Shakyamuni, in certain contexts, did not hesitate to profess his own perfect understanding. The Great Champions and Supreme Ornaments did not always veil their own achievements, but acknowledged them at times in order to give their disciples confidence that their teachings had validity, and that the disciples too could reach the highest attainment. But their claim of authority is quite different from a prophetic claim of divine mission or a dogmatic claim of perfect orthodoxy, and they should not be confused. This claim of perfect enlightenment occurs within the context of a teaching that often insists "There is no enlightenment, no attainment of enlightenment, and no non-attainment either!" Therefore the claim is made not to enforce submissive obedience or orthodoxy, but to demand the full deployment of the disciples' or hearers' or readers' own critical insight and transformative energies. It is made within a context where "Truth" is not a matter of divine edict or dogmatic formulae, but a matter of each individual's potential genius, personal experience, and individual responsibility. But we will return to this in the next section. Now we consider Tsong Khapa's predecessors and the course of Buddhist thought in Tibet.

The commentators on this verse of Tsong Khapa's prologue state that he intends Dol-bu-pa Shes-rab rGyal-mtshan (1292-1361) by "not lowly in accomplishments," rNgog Lo-tsva-ba bLo-ldan Shes-rab (1059-1109), Sakya Pandita Kun-dga rGyal-mtshan (1182-1251), and Bu-ston Rinchen-grub (1290-1364), by "learned in the Doctrine," and Phya-pa Chos-kyi Seng-ge (1109-1169) and others by "dedicated themselves to the path of philosophy." This is no doubt accurate, and the works of these masters on the profound view are often indirectly referred to by Tsong Khapa during the course of his elucidations in the *Essence*. However, it is important to recognize that these figures were only the most influential writers in a six-hundred-year tradition of the Tibetan understanding of the deepest teaching of ultimate reality of emptiness. They stand, therefore, as representatives of a number of philosophical tendencies that must be understood and then transcended to reach the most profound experience. Hence other figures must be discussed to trace the evolution of the Tibetan understanding of emptiness that culminates with Tsong Khapa's experience at Ol Kha in 1398, during his fortieth year of age.

Let us summarize briefly the main currents of Universal Vehicle thought and realization that flowed in India from the time of Nagarjuna's *Wisdom* (ca. second century C.E.) to the time of Shantarakshita (ca. 740-810) and Kamalashila (ca. 760-815) (in Tibet ca. 790-815 C.E.). Nagarjuna unveiled the full critical thrust of the central way in the context of liberating the Individualist Scientists (*Hīnayāna-abhidharmika*) from their overly realistic self-enclosure in the analytical categories of Analyst thought. He also spent some effort to free the Brahmin logicians and metaphysicians from their more naively realistic postures, but concentrated his critiques on the liberation of the Buddhist realists. Aryadeva came next and focused his attention on Brahmin opponents, although he reinforced and supplemented Nagarjuna's critique of Individual Vehicle realism. Then Asanga and Vasubandhu emerged during the formation of Gupta "classical civilization" and refined the central way, adding a more positive Idealistic thrust to make it more accessible to the optimistic and syncretic spirit of the age. Dignaga soon followed to unfold the impact of their breakthrough in logical and epistemological realms of discourse, for the benefit of the Brahmin and Individual Vehicle philosophers who were flourishing during the sixth century.

Buddhapalita, working in the south at approximately the same time, renewed Nagarjuna's most radical critical method, hewing away all pretensions of systematization with the sword of critical wisdom to keep the central way free of the overgrowth of dogmatism. Soon after, Bhavaviveka, fearing that Buddhapalita's uncompromising critique would lead too many too easily into a nihilistic skepticism, returned to the syncretistic mode by incorporating the rigor of the formalized logic refined by Dignaga into the methodology of the central way. On the other side he resisted the overly absolutistic approach of the Idealists, and criticized them for having come too close to the absolutist tendencies of the Advaitavedanta, which was just then gaining momentum under the Universalists' impetus. From the turn of the eighth century, Dharmakirti penetrated the Brahmin philosophical realm even further by unpacking the system of Dignaga to a far greater degree of refinement for the benefit of both Buddhist and Brahmin thinkers. And Chandrakirti emerged to vindicate the radical thrust of Buddhapalita's interpretation of the liberative technique of Nagarjuna and Aryadeva, critically reopening the Dialecticist central way by clearing away any overlays of the other thinkers, his sharpest surgery employed on the excessive formalism of Bhavaviveka to liberate him from his most subtle form of dogmatism.

Finally, at the end of the eighth century, the great master and disciple, Shantarakshita and Kamalashila, capped the entire process with a masterful synthesis of all the preceding trends, elaborating an Idealistic-Dogmaticist-Centrist way that incorporated the psychological sophistication of the Idealists and the logical subtlety and formal rigor of the Dogmaticists. They did not directly challenge the Dialecticist radicality of the

Buddhapalita-Chandrakirti current, leaving it unchallenged for those who might require it, yet finding the Dogmaticist approach more useful in their own teachings. This may well have been related to the fact that the vital need of further elaboration of the central way in India had declined, and their main field of work lay in the newly opened areas of Nepal and Tibet.

In the same vein, the next great representative of the Dialecticist trend, Atisha Dipamkara Shrijnana (982-1054), did not address himself in any extetnsive literary way to the refinement and critique of Shantarakshita's school, concerned as he was with the revival of the practice of compassion in India and the establishment of the Buddha Dharma on a firm footing in Tibet. Indeed, he left this task in the realm of subtle philosophical thought to Tsong Khapa, as we shall see below.[60]

From the above summary, it can be seen that the first Tibetan exposure to the profound philosophy of ultimate reality came through the Idealistic Dogmaticist Centrist thought of Shantarakshita and Kamalashila, as expounded principally in their *Ornament of the Central Way* and *Central Way Illumination*, respectively.[61] In the Idealistic Dogmaticist section of the translation below, Tsong Khapa himself deals lucidly with the main outlines of their methodology.[62] Here, we need to get the feel of this philosophical position, and trace some of its implications in practice, in order to understand subsequent Tibetan philosophical evolution. First, as can be understood from the other name of the Idealists, the Experientialists (*Yogācāra*), their philosophical tendency is highly soteriological. The quest of the profound is subsumed within the religious enterprise of transformation, as also evidenced by the term for the lineage of Idealistic teachers: the "magnificent practice lineage" (*udārācāraparaṃpara*).[63] This suited very well the needs of the early Tibetan Buddhists, in that their immediate concern was not the subtle questions of Indian philosophy, but rather the ethical transformation of a rough frontier society and the psychological transformation of themselves as individuals. Second, the Dogmaticists, with their concern for methodology and logic, placed a high value on clear thinking, on engaging in the critical quest for the profound ultimate reality in a context of rigorous precision of thought and extensive philosophical education. Bhavaviveka, as mentioned above, had initiated the genre of comprehensive, critical histories of philosophy, as known to him, with his *Blaze of Argument*. Shantarakshita went further in his encyclopedic compendium of philosophic

[60] A. Chattopadhyaya, *Atiśa and Tibet* (Calcutta: R. D. Press, 1967).
[61] MAlam and MAlok.
[62] See the great *Essence*, Ch. IV.
[63] Tib. *rgya chen spyod pai brgyud*.

reasoning in his day, the *Compendium of Principles*.[64] And in his work of setting up an educational system in a country newly emerged into literacy and critical awareness, his stress on principles of rigorous logical thought and comparative philosophy was very helpful. A strong anti-intellectual trend spearheaded by the Chinese Ch'an teacher, Hoshang Mahayana, began rapidly to gain ground during this very same time. In response, Kamalashila drew on his wide scholarship and lucid philosophical command of Buddhist doctrine to refute the Hoshang and keep the Tibetans on the path of an education that integrated the general Buddhistic humanism and promotion of ethical civilization with the special transformative goal of the attainment of individual enlightenment.[65]

The strengths of this school in soteriology, ethics, and education helped the Tibetan assimilation of Buddhism, whereas a too radical insistence on Dialecticist Centrist transcendentalism and the subtleties of conventionalism would probably have led many undeveloped people into a naive skepticism, the ensuing nihilism in ethics, and anti-intellectualism in education, which had been observed as the dangers of the central way since Nagarjuna's time (as today). On the other side, the weakness of this school lies in its Dogmaticist tendency to orthodoxy and hence inflexibility in adapting to changing social and individual needs. If it had not been for Padma Sambhava, for instance, who, as a Tantric master of the Unexcelled Yoga Tantra, was operating from its Dialecticist Centrist philosophical base,[66] the charismatic and transformative power of the Dogmaticist masters would have been inadequate to the situation in Tibet, and the whole monastic, educational work could not have begun. Further, the form of Buddhism elaborated at the new monasteries remained aloof from the mass of the Tibetan people, and aligned itself mainly with the dynastic state, so that when royal patronage was withdrawn during the next century, the institutions were vulnerable, and were temporarily destroyed. In short, the Dogmaticists' philosophical rigidity and orthodoxy and their intellectual penchant for hierarchy made them prone to align themselves with Tibetan political and cultural hierarchies, and greatly reduced their effectiveness in transforming the land and the masses of its people. The Tibetan Tantrics prior to Tsong Khapa, represented by the great Milarepa (1040-1123), naturally inclined to the Dialecticist central

[64] TS.

[65] For accounts of their famous debate organized by the Tibetan king Khri-srong lDe-btsan (754-797), see G. Tucci, *Minor Buddhist Texts* (Rome: Serie Orientale Roma, 1958); P. Demiéville, *Le Concile de Lhasa* (Paris: École des Hautes Études, 1963).

[66] For the deeds of Padmasambhava, see W. Y. Evans-Wentz, *Tibetan Book of the Great Liberation* (London: Oxford, 1968). For the connection between the Prasangikamadhyamika view and the Anuttara-Yogatantra practice, see Tsong-ka-pa (J. Hopkins, trans.), *Tantra in Tibet* (London: Allen & Unwin, 1978).

way, reaching it directly through the teachings associated with Unexcelled Yoga, and without educational access to the extensive philosophical literature and its subtleties. They often found the elitist monastic communities of scholars and hierarchs incompatible with their experiential and transcendentalistic understanding, hence chose to live outside, among the people.[67] Of course, after a few generations, the successors of these charismatic saints also tended to form new seats, to align themselves with the hierarchy, and thus to lessen the direct contact with human reality so cherished by their founding masters.

To pick up the philosophical thread again, the main view formally expressed in the literature of early Tibetan Buddhism was Idealistic Dogmaticist Centrism. The works of Chandrakirti and Buddhapalita were not translated well, and Shantideva's work was mainly valued for its sublime presentation of the bodhisattva ethic.[68] When the new period began, the translator Rin-chen bZang-po (958-1055) followed the Dogmaticist Centrist tendencies of the *Ornament of Realizations* and its commentarial literature, and although he met Atisha toward the end of his long life, the latter communicated to him mainly in terms of the Tantras.

It is with the work of rNgog Lo-tsva-ba bLo-ldan Shes-rab (1059-1109) that the works of Chandrakirti entered the literature of Tibetan philosophy. rNgog-lo translated innumerable works, among them Chandrakirti's *Lucid Exposition* and *Introduction to the Middle Way*, as well as Asanga's commentary on Maitreya's *Jewel Matrix*, considered by Tibetans to show Asanga's own Dialecticist Centrist point of view.[69] rNgog-lo further wrote his own independent treatises on the central way, in the form of commentaries on Nagarjuna's *Wisdom* and on Maitreya's *Jewel Matrix* and in the "transcendent insight" (*lhag mthong*) sections of his *Stages of the Path* works, which he wrote under the influence of the Kadampas.[70]

This is the reason that Tsong Khapa alludes to rNgog-lo in the above verse, as the latter was the first to attempt to understand the Chandra-Bhavya controversy and the Dialecticist-Dogmaticist distinction in the Centrist philosophical path to enlightenment. rNgog-lo's difficulty in

[67] For the life of Milarepa, see L. Lhalungpa, *Life of Milarepa* (New York: Dutton, 1977).

[68] The *Bodhicaryāvatāra*, known for its sublime poetry of altruism, but also for its remarkably profound ninth chapter, which presents emptiness according to the Dialecticist method. The best translation is by S. Batchelor, *Shantideva: Guide to the Bodhisattva's Way of Life* (Dharamsala: Library of Tibetan Works and Archives, 1979).

[69] PPMMV, MA, RGVV.

[70] None of these independent works of rNgog-lo seems to have survived the recent holocaust in Tibet, during which numerous Tibetan extra-canonical texts were destroyed by invading troops and "cultural revolutionaries."

interpreting the fine points of the Dialecticist Centrist position, hence his obstacle in complete realization of "That Place," had to do with his notion of the way word and concept relate to ultimate truth. He held the Dogmaticist-Centrist position in general, according to subsequent authorities, but his main error was not one for which Bhavaviveka could be held responsible. He held that ultimate reality was beyond the sphere of word and concept, therefore utterly lacking in any sort of characteristic whatsoever, and therefore not an object of knowledge at all. This strikingly Kantian position was completely different from that held by Bhavaviveka, who was accused by Chandrakirti of giving ultimate reality too much accessibility to discursive reasoning, on a supremely subtle level. rNgog-lo's position seems rather to resemble a distorted version of the Dialecticist Centrist's insistence on the radical transcendentality of the ultimate, expressed in the classical texts of Nagarjuna and Aryadeva, that the Centrist should hold no "thesis" or "philosophical position" (*pakṣa*) at all. Tsong Khapa discusses the misunderstanding of this radical position as nihilistic skepticism.[71]

rNgog-lo seems to hold, like Kant, to the total transcendentality of the ultimately real, beyond cognitive experience, while yet maintaining a practical Dogmaticist method of philosophy in the realm of relative reality, replete with an Idealistic soteriology employing the notion of "primordial Buddha-nature" as the ultimate, inexpressibly inherent in all living beings. Once the link between sharp critical reasoning and the ultimate reality is broken in this way, however, philosophy has only a dubious role in the path to enlightenment, as intellect and experience have become ultimately separated. It is for this that Tsong Khapa refutes this interpretation of the inexpressibility, unconceptualizability, and uncognizability of the absolute, toward the end of the *Essence*.[72] In quick preview, although word, concept, and intellect cannot *encompass* the ultimate, as the well-known epithets, "inexpressible," and so on indicate, that does not mean that they cannot *reach* the ultimate, bring the philosopher to the point of nonconceptual realization, as it were. If they could not even reach that point, there is an awkward picture of a gap and a leap—but how would one know where to leap?—or the equally awkward nihilistic denial that there is any such thing as the ultimate. In short, the philosopher is left floundering, to elaborate all manner of extravagant conventionalities, uncontrolled by any ultimate meaningfulness. rNgog-lo did not provide any helpful suggestions at this point, and his special theory indicates he was misled himself. Indeed, it is re-

[71] See the great *Essence*, Ch. V, Section 2C.

[72] See Introduction, VIII, 1 and 4, and great *Essence*, Ch. VII.

corded that the great Kadampa Master Shar-ba-pa (eleventh to twelfth centuries) expressed reservations when he used rNgog-lo's translations of the *Supreme Tantra* and of central way texts, and asked the translator Pha-tshab to work with the Indian Jayananda to retranslate or correct them.[73] Thus, Tsong Khapa is following the tradition of Atisha's direct disciples in finding fault with rNgog-lo's understanding.

Before going on, it is important to realize how specific and at what a high level this discernment of shortcomings is. The foremost disciple of rNgog-lo, Gro-lung-pa bLo-gros 'Byung-gnas (twelfth century), also a master of the early Kadampa, wrote the version of the "Stages of the Path," the *bsTan-rim-chen-mo*,[74] that Tsong Khapa most preferred, after Atisha's own *Lamp of the Path of Enlightenment*.[75] So Tsong Khapa appreciated much that was of benefit descending from the great translation work of rNgog-lo-tsva-ba.

One of the disciples of Gro-lung-pa was the famous logician, Phya-ba Chos-kyi Seng-ge (1109-1169), who also studied the central way with rGya-dmar-pa Byang-chub-grags, another Idealist Dogmaticist Centrist of the old school, revived from Kashmir. Phya-pa was especially famous for his systematization of validating cognitions, basing himself on the works of Dignaga and Dharmakirti. As the abbot of gSang-phu monastery, he had eight great disciples, known as the "Lions of Logic," who set the standard for training in logic and epistemology for all the later schools. Phya-pa was too good in logic to agree with rNgog-lo's notion of the verbal and conceptual inaccessibility of the ultimate, and he understood very well that the ultimate was precisely the absolute negation that is the emptiness of truth, hence accessible to word and concept.[76] However, in reacting thus against rNgog's extreme cognitive dualism, he went too far in the other direction, positing that the absolute is absolutely established, beginning the move, later taken to extremes by Dol-bu-pa, of transcendentalist absolutism. This is a dangerous error to make, according to the Dialecticist Centrists, because if the absolute is taken to be too absolute, then the relative ends up being repudiated, self-annihi-

[73] N. Roerich, *The Blue Annals* (Delhi: Motilal Banarsidass, 1976), p. 272. This remarkable native history of Tibetan Buddhism, written by 'Gos Lotsawa in 1478, is the source of most of the historical and anecdotal information below on the various Tibetan scholars and teachers.

[74] Tsong Khapa first read this influential work when he was visiting the Nyingma-Kadampa master Nam-mkha rGyal-mtshan at Lho-brag, and was deeply impressed by it. It thus formed part of his inspiration to write his own masterpiece, the *Great Stages of the Path of Enlightenment* (LRC). Unfortunately, Gro-lung-pa's work seems to have been lost.

[75] Atisha's *Bodhipathāpradīpa*; see Chattopadhyaya, *Atisha and Tibet*, and A. Wayman, *Calming the Mind and Discerning the Real* (New York: Columbia University Press, 1978).

[76] See D. S. Ruegg, *La Théorie du tathàgatagarbha et du gotra* (Paris: École Française de l'Extrême-Orient, 1969), p. 302n.

lative wisdom is cultivated exclusively, and the ultimate concern of great compassion is deprived of drive and field of play. Moreover, it contradicts extensive textual evidence for the non-absoluteness of the absolute, as in the *Transcendent Wisdom* themes of the "emptiness of emptiness," the "emptiness of the uncreated," and the "emptiness of the absolute." Another feature of Phya-pa's feeling was his apparently strong dislike for Chandrakirti, whom he was said to have vehemently opposed. Although there is little direct evidence as to the details of Phya-pa's thought, it may be surmised from his fondness for logic and formal thought-systems that he found the logical conventionalism so powerfully presented by Chandrakirti in *Lucid Exposition I* and *Introduction VI* extremely distasteful. Even in recent times, great critical scholars such as Stcherbatski and Murti were misled by this famous chapter into thinking that the Centrists were "metaphysical absolutists" who repudiated all forms of logic whatsoever, along with the meaningfulness of all language.[77] So Phya-pa can hardly be blamed for taking offense at Chandrakirti's demolition of Bhavaviveka's logically formal Centrism.

In parallel to the case of rNgog-lo, although Phya-pa's own view is found wanting, his work on logic is highly appreciated by Tsong Khapa and his successors, and the Centrist works of his greatest disciple, gTsang-nag-pa brTson-'grus Seng-ge are said to be the best expositions of the Dialecticist thought of Chandrakirti of that time. That gTsang-nag-pa himself felt quite free to disagree fundamentally with his own master in this regard, while carrying on his teachings of logic, is indicative of the spirit of free thought preserved in the Tibetan monastic academies, in continuation of the Indian tradition—contrary to modern notions of the slavish traditionalism of Tibetan scholars. Another Tibetan innovation probably begun by these masters and continued by Tsong Khapa was the use of the dialectical (*prasaṅga*) type of argumentation even in logical or ethical philosophical realms, instead of the formal, positive syllogisms that were traditional in India. This gave the Tibetan tradition a greater flexibility and analytic brilliance, as argumentation was much more wide-ranging and less cumbersome. These qualities were also helped by the extreme conciseness of the Tibetan language.

The next great figure in the particular context of "realization of That Place" is the Sakya (*Sa-skya*) Pandita Kun-dga rGyal-mtshan (1182-1251). His monumental scholarship and deep insight in matters religious and philosophical earned him an important place in many of the lineages of teaching most treasured by Tsong Khapa. It is important to stress how

[77] See T. Stcherbatski, *The Conception of Buddhist Nirvana* (Leningrad: USSR Academy of Science, 1927); T. R. V. Murti, *The Central Philosophy of Buddhism* (London: Allen & Unwin, 1955).

highly Tsong Khapa revered this master, so that it may be abundantly clear that the critique of his ultimate view was purely on the philosophical plane. And, lest the Sakya Pandita's ultimate realization seem to be called into question inappropriately, it must be borne in mind from the beginning that his important work in the central way, influential in his school and throughout Tibet, was the *Analysis of the Three Vows (sDom-gsum-rab-dbye)*, a compendium of Buddhist thought written while he was still quite young. It is therefore not certain what view he came to with maturity. Upon his supreme enlightenment experience at age forty-one, Tsong Khapa himself repudiated the profound view expounded in his own youthful work, the *Golden Rosary*, completed at thirty-one, letting stand much else of value on other subjects in the work.

The Sakya Pandita, as he is popularly known, is believed to have been himself an incarnation of Manjushri.[78] It was said that he spontaneously spoke Sanskrit while still a child, causing his mother a fright when she could not understand him, and that by his teens he had mastered all the teachings of his school. He then continued to study widely under a variety of masters, learning logic from a disciple of Phya-pa, sTsegs dbAng-phyug Seng-ge; learning Abhidharmic science directly from Vasubandhu in a series of dreams while still eighteen years of age; and learning Centrist thought from mTshur-ston gZhon-nu Seng-ge of Nyang-stod. He also mastered all the traditional fine arts, being especially proficient in poetic composition; his *Elegant Sayings* became enduring models of the bon mot in Tibet. He was also a great missionary, leaving his comfortable throne for the wilds of Mongolia and China, where he began the process of taming the Mongols, who had just founded the Yuan Empire in China and were at the height of their power. Due to the patronage of the Yuan, he was given temporal authority in Tibet, and thus began the pattern of monastic rule there. Due to this altruistic activity, Tibet was spared the depredations of the Jenghizid Mongols and enjoyed a century of peace, with the energetic educational and religious progress it made possible.

In philosophy, he began the critique of some Tibetan distortions of the profound view, rejecting the beginnings of the Jo-nang-pa absolutism, which is discussed more fully below. He also rejected the tendency to relegate the logical and epistemological teachings to the plane of mundane knowledge, and he clearly linked the understanding of the thought of Dignaga and Dharmakirti with the path of liberation, although Tsong Khapa's recording of the contemporary view that logic was of no use for liberation shows that such discrimination still persisted. His short-

[78] The source for this biographical summary of Sakya Pandita is K. Sangpo, *Biographical Dictionary of Tibet and Tibetan Buddhism* (Dharamsala: Library of Tibetan Works and Archives, 1979), X: 137ff.

coming, from Tsong Khapa's point of view, was that he still held the Dogmaticist Centrist position originating with Shantarakshita, failing to appreciate fully the contribution of Chandrakirti, hence failing to grasp the subtleties of Chandrakirti's rejection of the private object and the private reason. But we shall postpone extensive discussion of this crucial point.

This same kind of shortcoming is found in the great master of Zhva-lu, Bu-ston Rin-chen-grub (1290-1364), who was one of the teachers to whom Tsong Khapa was most indebted, although he never met him personally.[79] Bu-ston was intellectually closely related to the Sakyas, revering especially the Sakya Pandita, whose views on Idealistic Dogmaticist Centrism he followed closely. But Bu-ston remained independent from all the other Buddhist sects of his day, having his own patrons in the princes of Zhva-lu, who ruled one of the thirteen principalities into which the Mongol governor had divided Tibet's administration, under the spiritual hegemony of the Sakyas. Bu-ston was a prodigious writer on all subjects, as well as an historian and encyclopedist of astonishing ability. His collection of the vast Indo-Tibetan commentarial literature into the *bsTan-'gyur*, in parallel to the scriptural collection, the *bKa-'gyur*, was one of the great scholarly achievements of the time. In a sense, it made possible Tsong Khapa's wide-ranging critical scholarship, which drew on the entire literature, by creating the bibliographic resources. In the field of Tantra, Bu-ston was an adept especially in the *Esoteric Communion* and *Wheel of Time*[80] traditions, and Tsong Khapa ranked him as an important ancestor in these lineages, enjoying visionary meetings with him on a number of occasions. Nevertheless, Tsong Khapa found him lacking in the area of the profound view of emptiness, as Bu-ston still adhered to the old line of the Idealist Dogmaticist Centrists, with their syncretism, scholarship, and yet subtle vestige of naive realism.

The only line of scholars preceding Tsong Khapa that he felt was definitely wrong-headed and extremely misleading was that of the Jonang-pa school. Although the Sakyapas, Nyingmapas, and Zhvalupas all tended to the Dogmaticist view it was never made official by any of them, and there was always room for individuals to transcend the private object, or conventional intrinsic identifiability, and attain the open reality of the Dialecticist Centrists, available from the works of Chandrakirti. In fact, one of Tsong Khapa's main teachers, Red-mda-ba gZhon-nu bLo-gros (1349-1412), had independently come to adopt the Dialecticist Centrist position, while remaining an honored master in the Sakyapa school. In

[79] For the life of Bu-ston, see D. S. Ruegg, *Life of Bu Ston Rin Po Che* (Rome: ISMEO, 1966).

[80] *Guhyasamāja* and *Kālacakra*.

those days, philosophical matters were not important in sectarian identity, and sectarian conflict usually arose from political involvements and sometimes from matters of religious practice. The philosophical subtleties involved here in the rarefied atmosphere of central way thought, although making all the difference for the individuals holding the various views and attaining the realizations, were not important enough to lead to conflict among whole monasteries or schools.

The Jo-nang-pa position was different. Again and again in the *Essence*, Tsong Khapa, never mentioning names, takes to task the view that absolute reality is absolutely established, and that therefore "emptiness" is a concrete emptiness that is the absolute devoid of the relative. In the *Essence*, concerned with pure philosophy and not with tracing the ethical impact of different metaphysical views, the powerful implications of such a position are not spelled out. But they are, of course, that the entire Universal Vehicle concern with great compassion is defeated, if there is an absolute into which the enlightened sage enters, leaving behind the illusory relative world and its suffering beings. In fact, such absolutism is refuted by all the Buddhist schools of thought, even those of the Individual Vehicle, when it appears in the guise of Vedantic monism. There, the absolute Brahman is absolutely absolute, the relative world is merely *māyā*—"illusion," not just "like illusion"—and the enlightened person, or even Brahma himself, need not concern himself about the suffering of the illusion-beings. Ethically, of course, this legitimates the static class hierarchy of Brahminical India, providing no motivation for world-transforming great compassion.

Dol-bu-pa Shes-rab rGyal-mtshan (1292-1361) was the first of the abbots of the Jo-mo-nang monastery to codify textually their special philosophical view in his famous *Ocean of Definitive Meaning*,[81] and he wrote several other treatises in this vein, as well as commentaries on the *Supreme Tantra* and on the *Transcendent Wisdom Hundred Thousand*. It is said that he erected a great stupa at the monastery, and on the day of its dedication, the "absolute absolute" view became experientially manifest to him, and he perceived his teaching flowing out from the great stupa in an oceanic stream; hence the title of his treatise. His principal sources seem to have been the *Wheel of Time Tantra*, the *Jewel Matrix* and the idealistic scriptures most quoted by it, and the *Elucidation of the Intention Scripture*, the "hermeneutical" scripture par excellence.[82]

Before outlining his view, it is necessary to show that even this scholar, whose view is so strongly criticized, was highly respected by Tsong Khapa

[81] Tib. *Nges Don rGya mTsho*, also called *Ri Chos Nges Don rGya mTsho*.
[82] Roerich, *Blue Annals*, pp. 776-77.

as transmitter of the *Wheel of Time Tantra*, a teaching and methodology he supremely treasured. This lineage issued from the Kashmiri master Somanatha, who taught it to, among others, the great yogi Yumo Mi-bskyod rDo-rje, who was the first, it is said, to have the experience of the "radically other emptiness." However, he did not put this in the form of a treatise, and the teaching stayed in the form of oral transmission for several centuries, although it was well enough known to receive critical treatment from the pen of Sakya Pandita, among others. The lineage of the principal transmission of Mi-bskyod rDo-rje's teachings includes gSer-sdings-pa gZhon-nu Od and his son Chos-sku Od-zer, who are worshiped by Tsong Khapa as spiritual ancestors in his *Esoteric Communion* and *Wheel of Time* writings. The teaching came finally to Kun-spangs Thugs-rje brTson-'grus (1243-1313), a charismatic ascetic and great teacher who founded the Jo-mo-nang monastery. The third abbot of that monastery was Dol-bu-pa, whose *Wheel of Time* teaching was equaled by none, except for Bu-ston himself. Thus, Tsong Khapa praises his many accomplishments in all sincerity, while finding his philosophical view seriously defective. Bu-ston had already taken issue with the view, particularly on the score of its version of the "Buddha-essence" (*tathāgatagarbha*).[83]

In brief, Dol-bu-pa's idea was as follows: 'Emptiness' is the true nature of reality. It is a radically "other" reality, other than the world of illusion. Itself, it is not empty, but absolutely established. It is not "empty in itself" (*rang stong*). In the world of living beings it manifests as a permanent, unchanging, and stable self of all beings, whose illusory incidental defilements have only to be removed for the individual to perceive his real self as this absolute. In particular, this revelation is granted in the scriptures of Shakyamuni's third turning of the wheel of Dharma, given at the end of his life, especially the *Elucidation of the Intention*. In that scripture, the three natures (imagined, relative, and perfect), are to be understood as follows: the imagined and the relative are two ways of characterizing the illusory reality, and the absolute perfect is attained by realizing that it itself is empty of both the relative and the imagined. It is an "other" emptiness, an "alternative reality," an "absolute other," and it is empty of the alien relative and imagined realities of things and persons.

Since Tsong Khapa himself begins his *Essence* with the interpretation of the *Elucidation*, it is better to leave the refutation of this view to him. It is particularly interesting, though, that one of the chief prior antagonists

[83] Ruegg clearly shows this in his two fine works, the *Théorie* and the *Traité du Tathāgatagarbha de Bu Ston Rin Chen Grub* (Paris: Ecole Française de 'Extreme-Orient, 1973), especially pp. 3-6, 122ff.

(*pūrvapakṣa*) of Tsong Khapa's interpretation of the central way should be a type of absolutist, since there are quite a number of scholars even today who still consider that the central way itself is fundamentally an absolutism. In fact, as we shall see again and again, the Centrists themselves, whether Dogmaticist or Dialecticist, take absolutism as one of the chief extremisms, the other being, of course, the dreadful skeptical nihilism.

In sum, Tsong Khapa feels the need to write the *Essence*, since, from the perspective opened for him that morning in the hermitage at Ol Kha, all his predecessors in Tibet (at least those who had written influential treatises) had failed to recognize the ultimately liberative benefit of the Dialecticist Centrist vision of reality. He finds rNgog-lo, Phya-pa, and Dol-bu-pa especially misleading, each in his own way, and he finds fault in otherwise eminent teachers, such as Sakya Pandita and Bu-ston, although we might also add others in their schools, as well as the great Nyingma, kLong-chen Dri-med Od-zer (1308-1363), whose masterful "Great Perfection" synthesis of all Buddhist teachings still preserves the Idealist Dogmaticist Centrism of Shantarakshita and Kamalashila.

And as for the Great Seal teaching of the Kagyupas, Tsong Khapa seems to share the view of the great master Shar-ba-pa of the Kadampas that it expresses the view of the *King of Samadhis Scripture*, and therefore should not be criticized, but that to practice it without its refined elaboration by the lucid Chandrakirti was educationally undesirable for those whose path lay through the intellect. Tsong Khapa does not, of course, include great yogis such as Milarepa and Ras-chung-pa in his critique, in that their paths took them to the profound in a very direct, nonphilosophically elaborated way. They were not scholastically trained, and hence did not require the critical sophistication of the philosophy of Chandrakirti. Tsong Khapa had nothing but the highest praise for their realizations, and had no need to criticize anything about them, since they did not write any treatises on the central way.

Tsong Khapa's own central way verbal transmission lineage (*lung-gi-brgyud-pa*) is given in his *Lineage Record*, as follows:[84] In India, he counts Nagarjuna, Aryadeva, Buddhapalita, and Bhavaviveka, and he considers that Chandrakirti studied directly with all four of these masters. From Chandrakirti he includes Vidyakokila, Saraha, Hasumati, and Kanakavarma, the latter having worked in Tibet as a translator during the time of Atisha. Then sPa-tshab Nyi-ma Grags (twelfth century), the great translator, whose verions of Chandrakirti's important texts were done with the assistance of Atisha's greatest disciples, transmitted the central

[84] This list of the lineage of the verbal transmission (*lung*) of the central way teaching comes from Tsong Khapa's *gSan Yig*, TKSB (*bKra-shis Lhun-po* edition), vol. ka, f. 30b.

way authority to three abbots of rMa-bya Monastery, near Sa-skya: Byang-chub Ye-shes, brTson-grus Seng-ge (a defector from the school of Phya-pa), and Shakya Seng-ge. From him, it came down through the fourteenth century via Kun-mkhyen mChims, sKyo-ston-pa, rGyang-ro Pan-chen, dPal-ldan mChims, and finally Rin-po-che Kun-rgyal, with mention in between of mTshur gZhon-nu Seng-ge, mKhan-chen Zhang-pa, sLob-dpon dGe-'bar, dbU-tshad-pa Od-zer-grub, and Mog-lo bZang-po, the latter three contemporaries of Bu-ston. There is very little information about these latter figures, except that they were learned teachers in the monasteries of gTsang where Tsong Khapa studied so extensively.

In spite of receiving all these textual lineages, however, and in spite of his extensive study with Red-mda-ba, Tsong Khapa's own enlightenment in the profound represents something completely new, which is expressed in his claim of receiving the teaching directly from the supernal Bodhisattva Manjushri, going over the heads, as it were, of all the previous Tibetans.

But lest we think Tsong Khapa was devoid of respect for the accomplishments of his great predecessors, this section fittingly closes with his verses from his early work, the *Golden Rosary.*

> Here, where even the great ranges of white peaks,
> Unbroken in all directions, dimming the brilliance of Kailash,
> Were obscured by the thick fog of misknowledge,
> The magically incarnate Translators, Pandits, Kings, and Ministers
> Made supreme efforts to make clear the path of liberation
> For all beings. By accurate translation of word and meaning
> Of the statements of the Buddha, and of the elucidations
> Of the Sages, masters in discernment of their meaning,
> They thus established this Land of Snows
> As the field of worship by the world's crowns, including gods—
> My mind takes refuge in them with great faith forever![85]

VII

> *But I have seen It quite precisely,*
> *By grace of my Guru, Savior Manjughosha,*
> *And I am going to explain it with great love!*

What does Tsong Khapa claim here? It must come as a shock for those who think of Buddhist "selflessness" as "egolessness," for this is no

[85] *Legs bshad gser 'phreng,* opening verses.

vanished ego speaking here, but a conventional sense of self, secure in the clarity of perfected understanding of the uttermost subtleties of philosophical exploration of the nature of reality. And this is not merely an academic matter, for, once again, "philosophy" in the Buddhist sense is not a matter of mere intellect, although intellectual genius is cultivated to the fullest. The Buddhist view is that the ultimate resolution of intellectual difficulties is simultaneous with the ultimately transformative experience of unexcelled perfect enlightenment. Therefore, Tsong Khapa is indeed claiming perfect Buddhahood in this passage. But then, we object, where are his thirty-two major and eighty minor auspicious signs and marks of the superhuman? We may recall that "Buddhahood" represents perfection of the body as well as perfection of the mind, and here we are in the realm of wisdom of the mind, and so the claim is of the Buddha-mind of perfected genius of mundane and transcendental understanding. The hagiographic tradition is well established that Tsong Khapa attains physical evolutionary perfection in Buddhahood in the third lifetime after this Tibetan life, after a stint in Tushita and a life in the world as a universal monarch. So even the most enthusiastic biographer makes no claim of physical Buddhahood for him. But Buddhahood in the subtle realm and the transcendent realm of wisdom is being claimed, so that is what we must reflect upon.

In this introductory context, this means that he writes from the complete disappearance of perplexities that Wittgenstein stated to be the goal of the philosopher. This means that it is possible for us, the students of his thought, to achieve the same, if we can understand it and follow its imperative to the confrontation with reality. It does not mean that he now can give us "the answer," in the sense of some scheme or system that encompasses all reality and that we merely need to adopt to be enlightened. Enough has already been said about the non-dogmatic nature of central way philosophy. Rather it is a matter of hanging onto the high trapeze of his thought for it to swing us out beyond our habitual image of ourselves as perplexed non-geniuses into the free flight of the wisdom that we all possess. This can be seen more fully as we read his treatise, wherein each section tends to end with a question, with an elusive passage that throws the reader into a process of reevaluation of what he thinks, of what has been said elsewhere, an intensity of inquiry that impels us to our own investigative breakthroughs. The claim also serves as the reason for the treatise in the first place, for here finally is a model of the examination of these deepest, most elusive questions, a model that can be relied upon. When we become confused, uncertain in our reading, we must therefore push ourselves first to think more deeply, and cannot easily sit back and find the fault in the writer or the text. However, that there may be faults is always an open question, too, as this is only a claim, after all, and we are not asked to believe it at face value.

Only the enlightened can really recognize enlightenment, it is said. But does it not transform the enterprise of study and inquiry to carry it on in the context that the result of penetration is transformative experience? If we understand this investigation, we will transform our understanding of everything. We will be transformed in our perceptions, thoughts, and responses. If we have not been transformed, we have not understood. This understanding, in other words, is not intellectually responsible if it remains merely intellectual. The claim strips from us the habitual excuse that "after all we are only human, humans a priori are imperfect and cannot understand everything, very few even rank as geniuses, and philosophical thought is nice for those who have the time and patience, but 'real' experience is the only school for personal growth." No, the author claims, "I have seen It quite precisely!" And there seems to be strong evidence from his contemporaries, deeds, and writings that he did attain a thorough enlightenment through the sucessful completion of this inquiry into the nature of reality. He then, out of love for beings caught in the network of perplexities, made a ladder available for their climb out of the materials he employed, refined, and strengthened by his own meditations and realizations. We thus must engage in the climb with a fundamental openness about the result. Constricting armor of habit peeled away, we are open for the encounter with the sharp sword blade of the liberative Word of the Father Tongue, a refined language that exudes awareness and is expert in the conventionalities of Mother Tongues, but transcends habitual acceptance of them: hence it can transform them and can inspire their users to transform themselves through understanding.

Now this new enlightenment of Tsong Khapa he credits to the grace of Manjughosha, the Bodhisattva of Transcendent Wisdom whom we met above at the beginning. The only way to explain this extraordinary, rather mystical than philosophical, assertion is briefly to recount Tsong Khapa's life, at least in its educational and philosophical aspects. For the fuller details of his life history, a number of other works can be consulted.[86]

Tsong Khapa was born in 1357, in the Tsong-kha valley of Amdo province in northeast Tibet, in an area populated by a diverse amalgam of peoples, a kind of crossroads between Tibet, Mongolia, and China. His fame spread even as a baby, due to the miraculous events associated

[86] For fuller treatments of the biography of Tsong Khapa, see R. Kaschewsky, *Das Leben des Lamaistischen Heiligen Tsongkhapa Blo-Bzang-Grags-pa* (Wiesbaden: Otto Harrassowitz, 1971); R. Thurman, ed., *Life and Teachings of Tsong Khapa* (Dharamsala: Library of Tibetan Works and Archives, 1981).

with his birth. Whatever the historical reality underlying the colorful legends, something must have happened to attract the great Kadampa teacher, Chos-rje Don-grub Rin-chen, who came all the way from bDe-ba-can monastery in sNye-thang to ask the family for the boy to become his disciple. According to the story, the Chos-rje had been prepared for the extraordinary boy by a prophecy given him by his clairvoyant yogi teacher, the Siddha bLo-bzang Grags-pa, who asked that Tsong Khapa be given his name, which was done. Tsong Khapa left home to live with Don-grub Rin-chen at the age of three, and exhibited extreme precocity at once, learning to read and write on seeing the Tibetan alphabet a single time. He spent thirteen years with this master, memorizing all the major textbooks of philosophical and meditational teachings, and learning the oral teachings of the Kadampas, as well as entering the important Unexcelled Yoga Tantra mandalas, performing their retreat meditations, and performing their meditative rites every day. He describes his own life in his autobiographical poem, *Destiny Fulfilled*,[87] which serves as a good framework to show the dimensions of his education and practice.

> First I sought out often extensive learning,
> Then all teachings dawned as transformative precepts;
> Finally I practiced all day and all night,
> Completely dedicated to spread the Teachings!

His quest of extensive learning took him to central and southern Tibet at the age of sixteen, where he studied under more than fifty of the most learned teachers of the land, representatives of all the schools flourishing at the time. His initial emphasis was on the *Five Treatises of Maitreya*. In his own words:

> If the lamp of true learning does not illumine
> The darkness that hides the ground of ethical choice,
> You cannot know even the path, not to mention
> Entrance into the supreme city of liberation!
> Thus, not satisfied with rough ideas and partialities,
> I studied closely all the books of Maitreya, Dharma-Lord.

This emphasis on Maitreya's *Ornament of the Universal Vehicle Scriptures, Jewel Matrix, Ornament of Realizations, Discrimination between Center and Extremes*, and *Discrimination between Phenomenon and Noumenon* followed the Kadampa use of these texts and their various commentaries to give the student the widest possible sense of Buddho-

[87] Tib. *mDun Legs Ma*. For the full translation of this poem, see Thurman, *Life and Teachings of Tsong Khapa*.

logical thought, synthesizing as they do all the ethical, meditational/psychological, and philosophical teachings of the Universal Vehicle. Tsong Khapa learned them all by heart, a total of several thousand long verses, and studied all the commentaries with their controversial investigations into the deeper meanings. That he was not content with general ideas or sectarian orthodoxies is explicitly mentioned. We should note that much in these texts concerns meditational experience, as they contain elaborate psychologies of altered states of consciousness, and so their study includes sustained meditation practice, as well as learning and inquiry. He next concentrated on the logical and epistemological teachings of Dignaga and Dharmakirti, memorizing their several thousand verses and devouring their vast commentarial literature, as well as learning the methods of using the analytic techniques in forensic debate in the great schools of the Sakyas and Kagyus.

> Especially for an egocentric person, the sole door
> For determining the exact reality of things
> Is the text on valid reasoning; so, laboriously,
> I studied its crucial points again and again.

He indicates his agreement with the insight of the Sakya Pandita and Bu-ston that logic is essential to enlightenment, not merely a branch a mundane knowledge. By "egocentric" (*arvāgdarśana*), he means the ordinary person, who is immersed unself-consciously in his own subjective perspective, and hence requires a rigorous training in logic and epistemology to acquire the flexibility of view that incorporates enough objectivity to transcend habitual subjectivity and gain a deeper insight. The academic training in formal debate, inherited from the great Indian monastic universities and refined in Tibet over centuries, is an extraordinary technique in ego-broadening. The student has to defend his viewpoint before a number of antagonists, advancing different reasonings in rapid succession, and often the view he must defend is not his own at all. There are no loose arguments and no room for face-saving casuistry, as the strict rules of content and format are enforced by skilled judges. Emotions may run extremely high, and therefore one is forced to learn to maintain clarity and objectivity amid the intense heat of conviction and sting of ridicule. Graduation from such training, begun at an early age, gives tremendous intellectual agility and a philosophical suppleness that enables the inquirer to see any question from many different perspectives. This ability is then brought to bear on essential questions of ethics, in *Transcendent Wisdom* studies, and on ultimate questions of metaphysics in central way thought, which Tsong Khapa next addresses.

I had already struggled with the Sutra and Tantra texts,
And I was practicing and teaching the impact of the profound,
When I realized that my view had not progressed far beyond
The view that has learned nothing and knows nothing at all.
So then I studied thoroughly all the essential keys
That bring out the authentic view, which I found
On the path of subtle philosophy that probes the profound,
Especially opened up in the texts of Nagarjuna;
And I resolved all perplexities completely.

His record of his studies here moves into central way thought, in which he reveals that, even after having published an important treatise, the *Golden Rosary*, which elucidates the *Ornament of Realizations* literature interconnected with the other Maitreya books, having been extensively taught the methodology of logic, having mastered textually the central way literature, and being already considered a prodigy as a teacher in his own right, he discovered that he had been taking the easy interpretation of the central way, that it is merely a matter of complete dialectical skepticism. One just refutes all views, dismisses the meaningfulness of language, and presumes that as long as one remains devoid of any conviction, holding no view, knowing nothing, and achieving the forgetting of all learning, then one is solidly in the central way, in the "silence of the sages." (It is interesting how much this sounds like most modern interpretations of the central way!) Fortunately, Tsong Khapa came to understand—just how we will see below— that this was merely skeptical nihilism, and so he turned in a vital, yogic way again to the intensive study of the central way texts, until his perplexities were fully resolved.

The poem then records his scholarship in the literature of the Tantras, which is noteworthy in that modern interpreters have considered the Tantras mainly a matter of mysticism and meditation; the latter is to be sure, extremely important in all phases of Buddhist education. But the Tantras themselves have an enormous literature concerning their methodology and aesthetic psychology, which literature can easily absorb lifetimes of concentrated study. Tsong Khapa did not enter these studies without encountering some problems with his contemporaries. Although there were certain great individuals, such as the Kagyu, Sakya, and Nyingma hierarchs, or Bu-ston himself, who were equally masters of exoteric philosophical studies and of esoteric Tantric studies, the prevailing view in Tibet at that time was that the two were mutually exclusive paths. Those proficient in scholarship were highly suspicious of the wild men of Tantric yoga, the mad yogis and ascetic saints, and the ascetic saints tended to be contemptuous of the "book-learning" of the scholars, whom they considered merely erudite and quite unenlightened. Archetypes of these two points of view were, on the scholastic side, 'Brom-ston-pa of the Kadampas, who himself was deeply versed in Tantra, but felt that it should remain esoteric and so for the most part discouraged his disciples from studying it. And on the Tantric side, Milarepa was plagued with the pettiness and jealousy of those who were self-inflated because of their intellectual learning, and so developed an aversion to scholarship and even monasticism, although he commissioned one of his greatest disciples, Gampopa, to enshrine his yogic teachings within an educational monastic tradition. And Tsong Khapa had to proclaim his independence from his major teacher, the Sakya Red-mda-ba, who strongly disapproved Tsong Khapa's fervor for Tantric studies and practice.

But Tsong Khapa was determined, having already practiced much under Don-grub Rin-chen in his youth, and having recognized how philosophical insights reach a practical consummation in the aesthetic and yogic contemplations of the Tantras. And so he plunged in with energetic thoroughness. His poem records the apparent dilemma, as well as his own sense of it.

> It is said that "there are two vehicles
> For the journey to perfect enlightenment,
> The Transcendence Vehicle and the deep Vajra Vehicle;
> And the secret Tantras are very much superior
> To the Vehicle of the Transcendences!"
> This is as well-known as the sun and moon.
> Yet there are those, pompous with pretense of wisdom,
> Who verbally assert the truth of that saying,
> Yet make no inquiry into the Vehicle of the Profound.
> If such as they are supposed to be intelligent,
> Who else could ever be thought stupid?
> Alas! It is amazing that any should repudiate
> Such an unexcelled path, so hard to come across!
> So I entered that deep treasury of twin accomplishments,
> The Vajra Vehicle, supreme vehicle of the Victors,
> More rare even than the Buddhas themselves;
> And I worked hard at it, and studied it afar.

His main human teachers in Tantric studies were, after his boyhood teacher, Rin-chen rDo-rje of Sakya, who taught him the *Hevajra*,[88] sPyan-snga Rinpoche of 'Bri-gung, a Kagyupa seat of the Phag-mo-gru, who taught him all the teachings from Milarepa; Bo-dong Phyogs-las rNam-

[88] See D. L. Snellgrove, *The Hevajra Tantra* (London: Oxford, 1959).

rgyal of Jo-nang, who taught him the *Wheel of Time*; Khyung-po Lhas-pa and Chos-kyi dPal-pa, both disciples of Bu-ston, who taught him *Esoteric Communion*,[89] *Supreme Bliss*,[90] and more on the *Wheel of Time*.

To return to the poem, it lists the main Action, Practice, and Yoga Tantras Tsong Khapa studied, mainly the *Ultimate Contemplation*, the *Realization of Vairocana*, and the *Compendium of Principles*,[91] in each class, respectively, and then lists the Unexcelled Yoga Tantras.

> Among the fourth class Unexcelled Yoga Tantras,
> I studied the Root Tantras and Explanatory Tantras
> Of the Father Tantra, the *Glorious Esoteric Communion*,
> Renowned as sun and moon among the Indian sages:
> And of the Yogini Tantras such as the *Supreme Bliss* and the *Hevajra*,
> And of the *Wheel of Time*, Tantra of the Champions,
> Whose method differs from all other Sutras and Tantras,
> Along with its commentary, the *Immaculate Light*.[92]

It is interesting that he does not mention the *Vajrabhairava Tantra*, which was centrally important in his lifelong practice, as he was initiated into it by Don-grub Rin-chen first of all. It is most closely related to Manjushri, and his own writings on it were extremely important for his successors. It perhaps reflects the rigorous secrecy that is maintained with regard to this Tantra by its line of practitioners. And perhaps he felt that, from a scholarly point of view, mention of the important *Esoteric Communion* was sufficient to represent the Father Tantras. Further, it should not be thought that by "Transcendence Vehicle" only the *Transcendent Wisdom Scriptures* are intended. In dividing the Universal Vehicle into "Transcendence" and "Vajra" Vehicles, he designates practices according to all the Universal Vehicle scriptures, which set forth the entire panoply of the Bodhisattva's exoteric career right up to Buddhahood over three incalculable eons of evolution, and practices according to the Tantric scriptures, which set forth the Bodhisattva's esoteric accelerated meditational path as a mystic Vajrasattva. Finally, he praises the *Wheel of Time* as the pinnacle of Buddhist thought and practice, distinct from all other exoteric and esoteric teachings, with its positive philosophy of history and its supremely sophisticated contemplative science.[93]

[89] See A. Wayman, *Yoga of the Guhyasamājatantra* (Delhi: Motilal Banarsidass, 1980).

[90] See S. Tsuda, *The Samvarodaya Tantra* (Tokyo:Hokuseido, 1977).

[91] The *Dhyānottara*, *Vairocanābhisaṃbodhi*, and *Tattvasaṃgraha*.

[92] The *Vimalaprabhā*, main commentary on the *Wheel of Time (Kālacakra) Tantra*.

[93] For details of Tsong Khapa's Tantric contributions, see my forthcoming *The Vajra Hero*, a study of the life-style and yoga of the Great Adepts of the Unexcelled Yoga Tantras, based on Nagarjuna's *Five Stages (Pañcakrama)* and Tsong Khapa's super-commentary on it, the *Extremely Brilliant Lamp (Rab-tu-gsal-bai-sgron-me)*.

The main point is that Tsong Khapa's pursuit of extensive learning included an encyclopedic knowledge and thorough practice of the Tantras, which he felt to be the essential complement of his philosophical studies, and not a contradictory alternative. And this determination to harmonize all the apparent contradictions in the vast Dharma of the Buddha fits very well with the original inspiration of the great Atisha, whose famous "Four-Square Path" made a deep impression on Tsong Khapa. He frames the whole beginning of his masterpiece, the *Great Stages of the Path of Enlightenment*[94] around it. Atisha's saying was as follows:

> All scriptures should be realized free of contradictions,
> And their teachings emerge as transformative precepts.
> Then, the Buddha's intention is easily understood,
> And the pitfall of abandoning the Dharma is avoided.

Indeed, this imperative not to cast out any of the liberative Dharma of the Buddha is powerfully operative in the *Essence* below, wherein the entire diversity of philosophies that constitutes the Buddhist literature is reconciled, and a complex hermeneutical scheme, even a hermeneutic of hermeneutics, is developed to organize them into a ladder of philosophical development. One does climb above lower rungs, yet each is essential to the viability of the whole ladder.

Now we turn to the realm of his inner growth, which he records in his poem as the "dawning of the teachings as transformative precepts."

> With a firm, intense, and enduring faith in Manjushri,
> Best banisher of darkness from the disciple's mind,
> I prayed that all teachings dawn as transformative precepts,
> And applied myself to all the required conditions.

From his youthful initiation when he was seven years old into the Yamantaka practice by Don-grub Rin-chen, Tsong Khapa was inwardly propitiating Manjushri. Manjushri is the ultimate reality intuitive wisdom (*dharmadhātujñāna*), and his terrific form, Yamantaka Vajra Bhairava, the "Vajra Seraph, Destroyer of Death," is the incarnation of critical genius in its most adamantine form. The ordinary world of naive realism

[94] LRC. This work integrates all the major practices of the Individual and Universal Vehicles, up to the beginning of the esoteric Tantras, into a single path from beginning to end. It represents a kind of capstone of a tradition begun with Nagarjuna's *Scripture Synthesis*, including works by Asanga, Shantideva, Chandrakirti, Atisha, and earlier Tibetan writers. See Wayman, *Calming the Mind*, Introduction. The Tibetan of Atisha's famous formula is: */ bstan pa thams cad 'gal med rtogs pa dang / gsung rab thams cad gdams ngag tu 'char ba dang / / rgyal bai dgongs pa bde legs tu rnyed pa dang / / de nas chos spangs gyang sa chen poi las byed bsrungs /.*

is summed up as "death," and this genius transcends it to reach the realm of the "deathless," enlightenment. Thus, in the midst of all the extensive educational training outlined above, an inner process of total dedication to transcendent wisdom was intensely maintained. It was not until he was forty-one, however, that this process would come to experiental fruition, as recounted below. Meanwhile, his poem alludes to some landmark experiences during the intervening years.

> Working in that way, I found a special certainty
> In the stages of the path of enlightenment,
> The tradition come down from Nagarjuna and Asanga,
> And the *Transcendent Wisdom*, best book on the profound,
> Dawned for me as a transformative precept.

Tsong Khapa had studied the *Transcendent Wisdom* and the related *Maitreya Books* under Don-grub Rin-chen, but his most intense period of concentration on these subjects came between his seventeenth and nineteenth years, from 1374 to 1376, when he studied at sNye-thang, the shrine of Atisha's remains, under the Kadampa scholar, bKra-shis Seng-ge and his colleagues. He was particularly impressed by the Sakyapa commentary composed by 'Jam-skya Nam-mkha dPal, a teacher of Buston, and the Jo-nang commentary composed by Nya-dpon dPal, whom he later met. He also studied further the *Maitreya Books* under the master 'Jam-rin-pa. He quickly became known as a prodigy in his mastery of these texts, and was often called upon to teach others, though still of such a tender age. Then, an extraordinary thing happened to him at nineteen, when he was participating in a ceremony of recitation of the *Transcendent Wisdom Scripture* at the sKyor-mo-lung monastery. In the words of mKhas-grub's *Biography*:

> He began to join the recitation from memory, when suddenly he fell into a trance oriented toward the import of the "non-identifiability of all things." The movements of the monks and the words they were chanting went completely unnoticed by him, as he had terminated all fluctuation of thought, and he remained in one-pointed concentration on the natural incomprehensibility of emptiness and appearance. The other monks concluded their chanting, had their tea, and departed, while he, oblivious, effortlessly maintained his absorption.[95]

It is recorded that he remained thus transfixed throughout the night, and, when he was brought out of it in the morning by concerned monks, he had some moments of confusion, trying to remember who, what,

[95] TKSB, ka, f. 14b1-6; Thurman, trans., *Haven of Faith*, pp. 29-30.

where he was, although soon he was feeling joyous and mentally active as usual. Several years after this, he was pronounced a qualified master of the *Transcendent Wisdom* literature, and he began the composition of the *Golden Rosary*, a critical study of the entire field that is still used as a textbook today in Tibet, although he himself, after his final experience years later, was dissatisfied with its expression of the profound import. At that time, rGyal-tshab Dar-ma Rin-chen wrote a further work, improving on those points under his instruction, the *Ornament of the Essence of Exposition*.[96] His experience on this occasion is instructive to us today, in that the achievement of such a deep contemplative trance would seem to most modern students of altered states of realization a goal in itself. However, although this was an important experience for his development, it was not considered a consummation at all, but rather a preliminary attainment of concentrative stability, honing the mind for further study, and not to be clung to as any sort of ultimate for fear of losing the razor's edge of nonduality between emptiness and appearance, between peace and activity.

From his twenty-second year, while working intermittently on the *Golden Rosary*, he went to Mal-gro Lha-lung monastery, and entered into intensive study of Dharmakirti's *Treatise on Validating Cognition* under the Sakyapa master, bSod-nams Grags-pa. Except for his lessons, he maintained a close meditation retreat on the text, particularly absorbed in the study of the commentary by the Sakya Pandita, called the *Treasury of Validating Cognition*.[97] This period is described in his own poem.

> In this northern land, many speak out in unison,
> Whether they have studied the logical texts or not,
> "There is no stage of practice of the enlightenment-path
> In the *Synthesis* or *Seven Branch Texts* of *Validating Cognition*."
> But one should take as authoritative the direct revelation
> Granted by Manjushri to Dignaga, saying explicitly
> "This book will in future become the eye for all beings!"
> Thus seeing that the above view was absolutely wrong,
> Especially investigating deeply the methods therein,
> I developed a deep-seated conviction
> About the import of the dedication of the *Synthesis*;
> That the Lord, as personification of reason,
> Is authoritative for the seeker of liberation,
> Due to his [unerring description] of evolution and cessation,
> And therefore his teaching is the only haven

[96] *rNam bshad snying poi rgyan*, GTSB, vol. kha.
[97] The famous *Tshad mai mdzod*.

For those who would be free. And I found a special joy
In getting clear all keys of the paths of both vehicles,
By studying them in combination on the path of reason.

And mKhas-grub's *Biography* describes his experience:

> Because of his insight into the section of the second chapter of the *Treatise* that expounds the arrangement of the path, he was swept up involuntarily by an intense and immeasurable faith in the scheme and method of reasoning of Dharmakirti. And during his stay there that autumn, the mere sight of a volume of the *Treatise on Validating Cognition* would cause the hairs on the back of his neck to stand up with the intensity of his faith, and invariably he could not hold back his tears.[98]

The key to the inclusion of the study of logic in the mainstream of the path of enlightenment lay in the opening verse of Dignaga's *Synthesis of Validating Cognition*, quoted above, which is beautifully unpacked in the "Personification of Reason" chapter of Dharmakirti's *Treatise*. The essential idea is that the Buddha is not to be followed as a teacher because of any dogmatic claim to authority, but rather because his teaching appeals to reason, to the cultivated common sense of the practitioner. Hence, the Buddha's authority is based on his attainment, whereby he became the very personification of rationality. This stems from the original celebration of Buddha as the "discoverer of causality," discussed above, and represents Dignaga and Dharmakirti's elaboration of this key insight in the universe of discourse of Indian logic and epistemology. The aim, even in this instance where the procedure is purely scientific and objective, is still unwaveringly soteriological. Tsong Khapa himself cleaves to this complementarity of reason and faith, with reason occupying the ultimate authority in impeccably scientific fashion, in the *Essence* below, where he states this explicitly at the very beginning. And yet here, contrary to our Western presuppositions concerning the incompatibility of reason and faith, we see tears of faith and joy flowing from insight in the course of study of some of the hardest-headed logical thinking in world philosophical literature.

For the next eleven years, Tsong Khapa traveled from monastic college to monastic college, studying and teaching all the important subjects and texts, and working on his *Golden Rosary* as well. His main teacher of this period was the Sakyapa, Red-mda-ba gZhon-nu bLo-gros (1349-1412), who was expert in all fields of philosophic study, having himself adopted the Dialecticist Centrist view of Chandrakirti. Red-mda-ba was

[98] TKSB, ka, f.17a6-b3; Thurman, *Haven of Faith*, p. 39.

also Tsong Khapa's close friend, and sometimes learned from Tsong Khapa, depending on the subject. This was a period of widening and deepening for Tsong Khapa, especially in his appreciation of the magnificence and vastness of the bodhisattva path. It was also the period in which he began to discern the underlying pattern of a comprehensive path of practice, integrating all the diverse practices of all the vehicles into a single vehicle for enlightenment.

> Then through the hard, methodical work of connecting
> The *Bodhisattva Stages* and the *Ornament of Universal Scriptures*,
> All the treatises of the Invincible Dharma Lord,
> And those following them, dawned as transformative precepts. . . .
> Especially, depending on the *Synthesis of Educations*,[99]
> Which grants certainty on all essentials of the path
> By ordering profound and magnificent scriptures in stages,
> I saw clearly as stages of practice the many meanings
> Of Nagarjuna's superior texts, such as *Scripture Synthesis*.[100]

All these works are essential sources for his *Great Stages of the Path of Enlightenment*, which he considered the full elucidation of the integrative synthesis of the teachings achieved by Atisha in his *Lamp of the Path of Enlightenment*,[101] and which has stood as one of the monuments of Tibetan literature ever since, serving as the most useful manual of practice for Tibetans of all walks. Tsong Khapa had experienced a visionary meeting with Atisha at the age of seven, and his sense of mission was closely connected with the revitalization of the pure stream of comprehensive teaching introduced by Atisha over three centuries earlier. This was preserved in the practice of the Kadampas and in their educational systems and techniques, which were adopted by all the other schools without exception as the textual groundwork underlying their otherwise distinctive religious orientations.

Also, in this period, Tsong Khapa read exhaustively all the Tantric literature, relying mainly on Buddhaguhya's important commentaries on the *Supreme Meditation*, *Vairocana Realization*, and *Compendium of Principles*, for the three lower Tantra classes.[102] And his deep dedi-

[99] Shantideva's *Śikṣasamuccaya.*

[100] *Sūtrasamuccaya.*

[101] Atisha's *Bodhipathāpradīpa*; see Wayman, *Calming the Mind*, pp. 9-14; Chattopadhyaya, *Atisha and Tibet.*

[102] Kriya, Carya, and Yoga Tantra classes. Buddhaguhya's commentaries on the *Dhyānottara*, the *Vairocanābhisaṃbodhi*, and the *Tattvasaṃgraha* were considered the best works for the study of these three classes of Tantras, and he relied on them in his *Great Stages of the Path of Esoteric Tantra.* See abridgment of that work in Wayman and Lessing, *Mkhas-grub-rje's Fundamentals of the Buddhist Tantras* (The Hague: Mouton, 1968).

cation to the *Glorious Esoteric Communion* and the highest Tantras in general is worth observing in his poem.

The ultimate of all eloquent teachings of the Sage
Is the glorious Unexcelled Yoga Tantra.
And among them the most unutterably profound
Is the King of Tantras, the *Glorious Esoteric Communion.*
The supreme philosopher Nagarjuna said about it
That "the essentials of the path of the *Root Tantra*
Are sealed therein by the six limits and the four ways,
And thus they must be understood by the Guru's precepts
In accordance with the *Explanatory Tantras.*"[103]
Holding that fact as crucial, I deeply inquired
Into all subtleties of the Holy Tradition of the *Communion,*
The ultimate secret instructions in the *Five Stages,*[104]
The *Lamp of Concentrated Practice,*[105] the *Stages of Array,*[106] etc.
Relying on their bright illumination of the *Root Tantra,*
Combining the five great *Explanatory Tantras,*
I practiced with enormous efforts.
With practice I discovered all the essentials
Of the *Communion*'s two stages in general,
And especially the essentials of the perfection stage. . . .
By the power of that, essential imports of many Tantras,
Such as *Supreme Bliss*, *Hevajra*, and *Wheel of Time*,
Dawned in my mind as transformative precepts.

He considered, in accordance with the later Indian tradition, that the Tantras were also taught by the Buddha, in hermetic secrecy, even more secretly than he taught the Universal Vehicle, which also was reserved for certain audiences. Tsong Khapa also considered, again following the Indians, that the very same Nagarjuna, teacher first of medicine and alchemy, and later of the central way discipline, was the teacher of the holy tradition of the *Esoteric Communion*, author of the *Five Stages* manual of practice of the perfection stage of Unexcelled Yoga Tantra,

103 The five explanatory Tantras of the *Guhyasamāja* are traditionally considered the *Tantrottara* (Eighteenth Chapter of the *Guhya Samāja Tantra* itself), the *Vyavasthānakrama*, the *Caturdevīpariprcchā*, the *Vajramāla*, and the *Saṃdhivyākaraṇa*. See A. Wayman, *Yoga of the Guhyasamājatantra*, pp. 84-89, where he mentions the possible inclusion of the *Vajrajñānasamuccaya* in place of the *Vyavasthānakrama*.

104 Nagarjuna's *Pañcakrama*; see L. de la Vallee Poussin, *Receuil de Travaux*, 16me fascicule, *Pañcakrama* (Gand: Université de Gand, 1896), for Skt.; see also my forthcoming work, *The Vajra Hero*.

105 Above, n. 36.

106 *Vyavasthānakrama*.

and teacher of a number of other Tantric methods.[107] From this, we can see how extensive was Tsong Khapa's study of the Tantric literature, how he fit it into his great synthesis, and how committed he was to the extremely difficult and totally demanding yoga of the perfection stage. That stage is unquestionably the most advanced practice in the whole Buddhist repertoire, involving unflinching experimentation with one's own deepest biological processes, instincts, one's own death, between-state transitions, and rebirth. And Tsong Khapa did not shrink from these challenging practices.

Throughout the poem we have been using runs a refrain repeated between the verses:

> Thinking this over, how well my destiny was fulfilled!
> Thank You so very much, O Holy Wisdom-Treasure!

"Wisdom-Treasure" (*mkhyen-pai gter*) is a name of Manjushri, and the direct form of address indicates the startling fact that Tsong Khapa considered the supernal bodhisattva to be present before him as he reflected and wrote the poem. It was well known to Tsong Khapa's contemporaries that he had attained the constant vision of Manjushri, who appeared to him frequently and informally, teaching him, guiding him, now and then teasing him in an altogether unsupernal manner. The story of this vision is connected with Tsong Khapa's relationship with the remarkable Lama Umapa (dbU-ma-pa), whom he met when he was thirty-three, in Rong in the province of gTsang, where Umapa came to study Chandrakirti's *Introduction to the Central Way* with Tsong Khapa. The biographies do not give dramatic detail of their first meeting, but it must have been remarkable. Umapa was originally an illiterate cowherd who was suddenly smitten with a vision of Manjushri, which he subsequently cultivated and eventually experienced all the time. He had then, under Manjushri's direction, studied and practiced under various teachers, and had rapidly gained numerous realizations. But he was not a great scholar like Tsong Khapa and Red-mda-ba, who were in Rong together on a teaching tour. What must all Tsong Khapa's colleagues and students have thought when the respected scholar and teacher suddenly took up with the odd mystic, forsook his academic pursuits, and eventually wandered off to the retreat caves that were always nearby in Tibet? It is recorded that it was about this time that Tsong Khapa disagreed with Red-mda-ba about his irresistible urge to study the Tantras, as Tsong Khapa was turning more and more to that pursuit. It is clear that Red-mda-ba looked askance upon Tsong Khapa's involvement with Umapa at first, and Tsong

[107] See above, nn. 20, 29.

Khapa's own courage, integrity, and determination were obviously required for this change of course.

For the account of the early studies with Manjushri, we have the standard version in mKhas- grub's *Secret Biography*.[108] This account of his encounters with Manjushri can be seen to reveal his innermost process of thought and development. It is not important whether we interpret these experiences as mystical encounters with a genuine spiritual being or whether we consider them visions through which Tsong Khapa brought out his own deepest feelings. In any case, this is the account of the process of the deepest inspiration which led him ultimately to be able to create the *Essence*, pouring his complete enlightenment experience into philosophical expression.

> His [Tsong Khapa's] history before he met the Lama Umapa is described in the ordinary biography. As for Lama Umapa himself . . . from his very early childhood, when he was a cowherd in Amdo, inside his body, directly from his heart, he heard the sound of the mantra A RA BA TSA NA. Whenever it happened, the hairs all over his body would tingle, and it would seem to him as if he had no control at all over his mind. Once, when it happened, he fainted. When he awoke, he saw the holy Manjushri plainly before him, the color of his body being dark blue. Subsequently, receiving the Tantric permission and blessing from a qualified guru, he made intense efforts in propitiation and meditation. Finally . . . he became constantly aware of Manjushri's verbal and physical presence. When rJe Rinpoche [Tsong Khapa] met him in gTsang Rong, Lama Umapa would serve as interpreter for him to question the holy Manjushri on religious matters. Especially since the Holy Father and Son [Nagarjuna and Aryadeva] had declared that one cannot find the life of the path without seeking the central way view, that even if one does seek it it is extremely hard to find, and that the pitfalls and disadvantages of misapprehending it are greater than [those of] misapprehending other things . . . rJe Rinpoche mainly asked His Holiness questions concerning the profound view at this time. "Is this view of mine Dialecticist? Or Dogmaticist?" The Holy Lord declared [through Umapa], "It is neither!" At that time, there was no philosophical position at all in the mind of rJe Rinpoche, his mind was just resting easy in the view of not allowing the holding of anything.[109]

We should note that this diagnosis was given after twenty years of concentrated study with the best teachers in Tibet on the part of an

[108] *gSang bai rnam thar*, TKSB, ka; Thurman, "Golden Speech," PhD. dissertation, Harvard University, 1972; pp. 175ff.

[109] TKSB, ka, ff.2b2-3a3.

undoubtedly great genius, who had also exerted himself uninterruptedly in deep meditation on the nature of reality. This is what is meant by "the profound view is hard to find!" It also provides a clue as to why many may feel that the intellectual pursuit of the path of philosophy cannot produce transformative change. It is not that it is not transformative, it is just that it must be continued until the very end, until complete clarity is reached. Luckily for Tsong Khapa, Manjushri would not settle for his academic self-image as a bona fide Dialecticist, and gave him no such confirmation. Crestfallen, no doubt, Tsong Khapa continued to question through his "medium."

> When he questioned, debated, and analyzed further in regard to the view, the holy Manjughosha repeatedly declared, "You should never allow yourself to cling to preference for either the appearance side or the empty side. But you must take special consideration of the appearance side."[110]

This is an extremely important point. Once the basic thrust of emptiness is acknowledged, the deepest subtleties do not concern the absolute nature. Rather, the most difficult points concern the superficial, relative, or apparent reality. This will become abundantly clear below in the *Essence*, in the Dialecticist sections concerning the "presentation of conventional reality," where the Dogmaticists' subtle vestigial naive realism asserts itself, blocking their full encounter with reality. And it is in this enterprise, in carrying out this precept of Manjushri's, that Tsong Khapa precedes Wittgenstein by centuries in the exquisite and liberative understanding of the surface, the "bed-rock of the conventional," as the latter put it, in all its nearness and beauty and yet maddening elusiveness. After this, Umapa had to visit eastern Tibet for a while, and so Tsong Khapa went to Khyung-po Lhas-pa, the Tantric heir of Bu-ston, and received from him a veritable feast of teachings, consecrations, and blessings in the various Tantras, especially the *Esoteric Communion*. After two years, Umapa returned, and the two went into retreat in dGa-gdong to pursue studies with Manjushri, as well as to wait out a war for control of Tibet incurred by the Phag-mo-gru in the process of consolidating their power.

> Later, when they were settled in dGa-gdong, many such statements were made. In essence, the Holy Lord was very emphatic in refuting any attitude that holds the supreme central way view to be the nihilistic view that repudiates evolutionary causality, with no place to ground one's own scheme of things, no holding of anything at all, with no

[110] TKSB, ka, f.3a4.

ground for conventional validating cognition, only presenting things according to sheer illusion to go along with others.[111]

This particular error occurred often in the tradition, for example in the case of rNgog Lotsawa, as mentioned above, arising from a misinterpretation of Nagarjuna's and Aryadeva's statements to the effect that "they assert no position" (*pakṣa*) or thesis of their own.

During these sessions of inquiry, debate, and analysis, sometimes the Holy Lord taught the concentrated seeds of the precise discernment of the distinctions between the Dogmaticists and the Dialecticists, concerning the self as held by the two self-habits, naive unconscious and intellectual, the approximate and precise criteria for the rational negatees involved, the criterion for the realization of the authentic view, and the procedure whereby the technique of this Dialecticist's view establishes the superficial reality, and so forth. And sometimes he taught the concentrated essentials of the path common to philosophy and Tantra, of the specially extraordinary actuality, sequence, and definitions of the five stages of the *Glorious Esoteric Communion*. Finally, rJe Rinpoche said, "there are some things I still do not understand." The Lord replied, "See that you do not forget them. Write them down. Petition the Guru and the Tutelary Deity, making them indivisible, and perform the rites of propitiation. Make the proper efforts of purification and accumulation of merit. Do not be easily satisfied in the practice of your precise and concentrated reflections, having rationally analyzed the meaning of the treatises. Inquire correctly and continually. When the time comes, conditioned by my planting of these seeds, a correct understanding will suddenly arise." [Tsong Khapa persisted,] "I have intense desire to understand the systems of the Holy Father and Son in the central way and also in the *Glorious Esoteric Communion*. Who is the best teacher in Tibet for this research?"

"There is no one superior to Red-mda-ba. However, there cannot arise in you an understanding that is complete and totally decisive. Were I to teach you, with Umapa as interpreter, it would be somewhat better, but it seems he soon has to go back to Amdo. Therefore, from now on, you should resort to solitude, refraining from giving teachings [to others], and practice concentratedly as I told you before. Make the proper effort to cultivate your understandings and so forth, and before long, you will discover their meaning."

rJe Rinpoche further asked, "There are no limits to the statements concerning which keys of the teaching and which treatises are reliable

[111] TKSB, f.3a5ff. See the great *Essence*, Ch. III.

for investigation. Among the expert Indian pandits, there are some whose treatises cannot be accepted as completely error-free. Nevertheless, might it not be correct to accept Chandrakirti as completely error-free in his elucidation of the intention of the holy Nagarjuna?"

"Chandrakirti . . . took rebirth intentionally in this field in order to illuminate the essence of the teaching, the system of holy Nagarjuna. He makes not even the slightest mistake, either in the context of Tantric methodology or in that of philosophy, and should definitely be accepted as the sole ground of belief."

. . . rJe himself was still inclined to study and teach a little, and Lama Umapa agreed, so they urged Manjughosha, "Being still quite young, with good knowledge and intentions, if I were to learn and teach still more, it would be very helpful to the doctrine. And . . . if I were to withdraw from activity, people would criticize me. Thus, would it not be permitted for me to study and teach a little more?"

"You do not know what is helpful to people, nor to the doctrine. When people criticize you, cultivate your patience. If you do not meditate in solitude, your life will not last very long, and your usefulness will be no more than apparent. It is right for you to withdraw from activity."

Therefore the two meditated at skyid-shod dGa-gdong, with no other companions. They had separate quarters, only meeting when they partook of tea, etc. During the tea, Umapa serving as interpreter, rJe Rinpoche received many instructions from the Holy Lord, and asked him many questions. Then, he learned from Umapa the concentrations in serenity given by the Holy Lord, and began to meditate with them. But the same day, he thought that it was more important to pray to the Holy Lord himself and perform propitiations. He asked the Lama, who said that it must be so. Thus, day and night, he performed the propitiations, praying to the Lama and the Holy Lord, making them indivisible [in his mind]. Before many days had passed, he saw a perfectly round, beautiful, deep-blue shape, of a size appropriate to the center of a mandala, as if exquisitely painted, of extreme clarity, whose edges were laced with a rainbow of five-colored light-rays. In the blue center, he clearly beheld Manjughosha A-ra-ba-tsa-na himself, the color of saffron, sitting in the vajra posture, his appearance such that one never tired of looking at him. Without being told, Umapa rightly said at tea, "You seem to have had the vision of his body!" rJe Rinpoche has said, "From that time always until now, whenever I wish, with a certain amount of prayer, such a vision of his body normally will clearly appear." Then rJe Rinpoche, Umapa [still] serving as interpreter, received from the Holy Lord Manjughosha himself the four consecrations of meditation, the permissions, and the blessings, of Manjughosha Ekavira, Anuttaramanjughosha, and the outer, inner, and secret Dharmapalas, [known as various forms of] Yama Dharmaraja. While the Holy Lord was bestowing the permission of Ekavira, he was there in the form of Ekavira himself, and when he gave them the consecration for inner and secret attainments, he, as Ekavira, instantaneously transformed himself into the male-female in embrace. When he gave the permission of the Dharmapala, he was immediately transformed into Bhagavan Vajra Bhairava, . . . and so forth. He displayed many such wonderful emanations.

Afterwards, [rJe Rinpoche] heard the rituals of propitiation and the stages of cultivation of comprehension from Umapa, who had heard them from the Holy Lord himself. Thereafter, he made up his mind to strive for attainment. Escorting Umapa on his way to Amdo, he visited Lhasa, and [Umapa said to him, at parting], "Now then, teacher and student will not meet again for some time. Pray to the Holy Lord here in this blessed place, and you might receive some instruction, integrating all the keys of practice."

He assembled offerings on the southern balcony under the golden eaves of the Lhasa [cathedral] and prayed intensely. The Holy Lord appeared and uttered some verses that contained in concentrated form the keys of practice, and rJe Rinpoche wrote them down directly, in the order they were spoken.[112]

The poem, the *Secret Biography Invocation* by 'Jam-dbyangs Chos-rje bKra-shis dPal-ldan, gives this account also, in eulogy form.

O Holy Lord of phenomenal existence,
You directly perceived Manjushri,
Bodhisattva of the wisdom of emptiness,
Seated in a radiant aura as blue
As the color of a perfect sapphire. . . .
From this time onward, O Exalted One,
Whenever you desired you could invoke
Manjushri, Treasure of Stainless Wisdom,
And constantly listen to the teachings
Of both the Sutric *Transcendent Wisdom*
And the Tantric *Esoteric Communion*.[113]

The story goes that from this time, Tsong Khapa experienced himself as directly under the tutelage of the supernal bodhisattva, who counseled

[112] TKSB, ka, ff.3a6-6a5.

[113] TKSB, ka, 2aff. See Thurman, *Life and Teachings of Tsong Khapa*, for complete poem, translated by Glenn H. Mullin, pp. 47-55.

him in practical actions as well as in spiritual matters. In the winter of 1392-1393, he followed Manjushri's instructions to withdraw from the academic activity of teaching and learning and to concentrate on solitary meditation, retiring to Bya-bral hermitage with eight carefully picked disciples who also wished to take a long retreat. He began there a series of thirty-five sets of one hundred thousand prostrations, one to each of the thirty-five "Buddhas of confession," offered hundreds of thousands of offering mandalas of the universe, and recited millions of purificatory mantras.[114] He also studied intensively the central texts on interpretable and definitive meaning, as well as the *Esoteric Communion* texts, concentrating on the achievement of the Illusion Body, the third stage of the five stages of the perfection stage. He was very much inspired during this time by the example of the Bodhisattva Sudhana of the *Garland Scripture*, which he read repeatedly between meditations, especially reciting the famous *Vows of Samantabhadra.*[115] In 1394, continuing this retreat, they moved to Ol Kha. During this period they all, but especially he, experienced numerous visions of the deities they were propitiating: the thirty-five Buddhas one by one, Tara, Ushnishavijaya, Sarasvati, all the great Bodhisattvas; and numerous historical figures from the profound, magnificent, and practice lineages: Nagarjuna and his followers, Asanga and his, and Vajradhara and the many Indian adepts such as Saraha and his followers. He had one vision of Manjushri that was particularly striking, wherein the bodhisattva's sword of wisdom extended from his own heart, the tip touching Tsong Khapa's heart, and the rainbow-colored nectar of the five wisdoms flowed down the sword from heart to heart. He received the prediction of his own future physical Buddhahood as the Buddha Simhanada ("Lion's Roar") in the universe Adbhutavyuha ("Miraculous Array").

This retreat was a time of great blessing and numerous visions and insights, but still the deepest experience had not ripened to fruition. However, in 1395, they decided to break the retreat to descend to the

[114] Concerning this retreat, the arduousness of his practice can be glimpsed by making a little calculation of what is involved in doing thirty-five sets of one hundred thousand prostrations, each being the equivalent of a combined deep-knee-bend and push-up. By my rough estimate, at a rate of ten per minute, six hundred per hour, six thousand per ten-hour day, he would complete these sets in slightly less than six hundred days! Since he had three or four years of retreat, we can lessen the pace, to allow time for the hundreds of thousands of "Hundred-syllable Vajrasattva Mantras" he recited, the numerous offering mandalas performed, the numerous sadhanas contemplated. Still, he must have reached a razor's edge of physical, volitional, and mental keenness during this time.

[115] This famous prayer occurs at the end of the *Gaṇḍavyūha* section of the *Avataṃsaka Sūtra*, where it was taught to the Bodhisattva Sudhana by Samantabhadra himself. It was much beloved for millennia in all Universal Vehicle Buddhist countries. For translations of the prayer, see G.C.C. Chang's *Buddhist Teaching of Totality* (University Park: Pennsylvania State University Press, 1977), pp. 32-34, 188-196; G. H. Mullin et al., *Garland of Prayers* (Dharamsala: Library of Tibetan Works and Archives, 1980), my translation.

'Dzing-ji temple near Ol Kha, to refurbish and rededicate the famous and especially sacred image of the future Buddha Maitreya that had been erected there centuries ago by Gar-mi Yon-tan gYu-drung, but had fallen into disrepair in recent years. Donors and artists gathered spontaneously from all over the area, and the temple was made even more beautiful than before, the whole event becoming a mass meditation due to the powerful charismatic energy generated by Tsong Khapa and his eight companions from their arduous ascetic retreat. When the dedications were performed, it was said that the sun delayed its setting so the ceremonies could be completed, all present perceived numerous Buddhas and bodhisattvas in the sky, and saints from all over Tibet experienced visions of the great event.

For the next three years, the nine companions continued in semi-retreat, moving down to Lho-brag at the invitation of mKhan-chen Nam-mkhai rGyal-mtshan, a venerable Nyingmapa master, also deeply educated in the Kadampa tradition, who was considered an incarnation of Vajrapani. He and Tsong Khapa would teach each other numerous teachings, he perceiving Tsong Khapa as Manjushri when Tsong Khapa would teach, and Tsong Khapa perceiving him as Vajrapani when he would teach. Luckily, Vajrapani dissuaded the companions from going on pilgrimage to the Buddhist Holy Land in India. So they returned to central Tibet, going for a final year of retreat in 1397 at the hermitage near Ol Kha known as O-de-gung-rgyal. Tsong Khapa again returned to concentrated study of the central way, rereading the Buddhapalita commentary on Nagarjuna's *Wisdom* once again.[116]

Finally, in 1398, the long years of effort came to fruition. The seed planted by Manjushri produced its flower. One night in the late spring of 1398, Tsong Khapa dreamed that he was in a heavenly realm, probably the Tushita heaven where Maitreya dwells surrounded by the great masters of earth's history, according to tradition. He was sitting on the fringe of a gathering of Nagarjuna, Aryadeva, Buddhapalita, Bhavaviveka, and Chandrakirti, who were lucidly discussing the uttermost subtleties of the central way, to his great delight. At one point, Buddhapalita, whom he recognized for his dark bluish complexion and unusually tall stature, arose from the conversation; holding a Sanskrit volume in his hand, he approached Tsong Khapa smiling radiantly, and touched him on the head with the book in the gesture of blessing. Tsong Khapa awoke at this, filled with bliss, and, in the predawn light, opened his own Tibetan copy of the Buddhapalita commentary to the page he had been reading the day before. His finger traced the words at the beginning of the eight-

[116] BMMV.

eenth chapter, "it is an imperative consequence that the self is not the same as the aggregates, and the self is not different from the aggregates. . . ." At that instant, the perfect realization of the central way arose within him effortlessly—the essential keys of the dialecticist view, the criteria of the logical negatee, and so on—all with profound certitude. All his "sign-habit-orientations" dissolved, and all his perplexities about the import of ultimate Thatness disappeared. He said later that his view of the world changed radically, that it had been exactly upside down before, and that the authentic view was precisely the opposite from what he had expected.

In a very real sense, this moment in 1398 can be understood as the end of Tsong Khapa's life-story in ordinary time. The subsequent events of the final twenty one years of his physical life are merely the unfolding of the tremendous impact of his realization throughout Tibet and the world. For, when a single heart opens into Buddhahood, the entire universe of living beings is included with it. And it is characteristic of him, and of his renewal of the transformative commitment of the path of philosophy embodied in the *Essence*, that his eyes were on a text at the very moment, not half-shut in transic absorption. Immediately afterward, as the sun rose on that day of 1398, he wrote the *Essence of True Eloquence* (the concise version), called "Praise of Shakyamuni for his Teaching of Relativity," translated below as *Praise for Relativity*.[117] Again, he did not lounge in bliss in his total enlightenment; he poured forth his wisdom for others in a hymn of gratitude to the teaching that made it possible.

The subsequent deeds of his life were his teachings, his spontaneous response to the great stir that awoke in Tibet from his epoch-making insight. They are traditionally enumerated as the "four major deeds." The first had already been accomplished, in fact: the refurbishing of the 'Dzing-ji Maitreya, in 1395, although the great festival he held there at Tibetan New Year of 1400 consummated it by drawing the whole of Tibet into the auspicious event, with its great promise for a glorious future with the coming of Buddha Maitreya. The second was the great teaching of the *Discipline* (*Vinaya*), the monastic Rule, that took place in gNam-rtse ldeng, in the cathedral of Byang-chub Ye-shes, where he and Red-mda-ba and the great Rinpoche Lotsawa sKyabs-mchog dPal-bzang-po spent several months going over the entire *Discipline* literature with thousands of monks from all schools. This was very significant, in that by this he affirmed the importance of the Individual Vehicle and the monastic Order as the foundation of the Dharma, its root, and the source

[117] See the short *Essence*.

of its successful practice, even though the advanced practitioner may enter the Universal Vehicle and the perilous yoga of the Vajra Vehicle. The *Discipline* was thus renewed as the basis of Tsong Khapa's integrative synthesis of the teachings.

The third great deed was his establishment of the Great Prayer Festival in Lhasa in 1409. This was an unusual act for a great intellectual, and shows the far-reaching social concern of Tsong Khapa. By this time, over ten years since his "Great Enlightenment," numerous patrons had been moved by the great waves of charisma to come forward to honor him, including the Ming Emperor Yung Lo, who had sent an embassy loaded with gifts, hoping to invite Tsong Khapa to be honored at his court. The master declined the invitation, which was another historical first in relations between Tibetan lamas and Chinese emperors. Most great teachers by this time would have built a special seat of their own, a new monastery to serve as focus for their movement. Tsong Khapa had consistently refused such offers, preferring to stay in existing monasteries, letting them be refurbished for his disciples as their numbers grew. But by this time, pressure was building on him to establish a new seat of his own. Before letting this take place, he decided instead to devote all the wealth now at his disposal to a great popular festival to be held in the city of Lhasa, focused at the ancient cathedral built by Srong-btsan sGam-po, the Jo Khang, wherein the most sacred image of Shakyamuni in Tibet was enshrined, the Jo-bo Chen-po.

This socially far-reaching move seems to have been designed to diminish the Tibetan tendency to sectarianism, which was the religious institutions' continuation of the age-old Tibetan political regionalism, and could have been predicted to intensify still further as the various monastic orders became ever more powerful and entrenched economically and socially. For the festival established a tradition whereby all Tibetan Buddhists of all orders would come to Lhasa at the Tibetan New Year, and spend two weeks until the full moon of that late winter/early spring month commemorating the fortnight of miracles enacted by Shakyamuni before the kings and people of India at Shravasti. It created two weeks of "liminality," in Turner's word,[118] when people could rise above their sectarian identities and affirm a universally shared participation in the miracle of enlightenment. So Tsong Khapa gave everything he had to the support of this great festival, and he was joined by all the powers of the land as well as by the Chinese emperor and other neighboring kings. The festival was held amid a host of auspicious apparitions as a national renewal. Tsong Khapa himself offered to the Jo-bo image beau-

[118] Victor Turner, *The Ritual Process* (Ithaca: Cornell University Press, 1977).

tifully wrought adornments of gold and gems, to symbolize the heavenly glory of the Beatific Body Buddha in the aura of Shakyamuni, formally a Supreme Emanation Body Buddha. The festival was held, with one or two interruptions during times of unrest, from 1409 until 1959, since which time it has been held in Dharamsala, India, at the seat of the present Dalai Lama.

The fourth great deed grew out of the Great Festival outpouring. Tsong Khapa's disciples and patrons now insisted that they build a special monastery in celebration of his great achievement. Tsong Khapa himself had been wishing to construct architecturally the mandalas of the major Unexcelled Yoga Tantra Buddha Deities, *Esoteric Communion* with thirty-two deities, *Supreme Bliss* with sixty-two, *Vajrabhairava* with thirteen deities. Such mandalas should only be built in a private enclosure, as access to them has to be restricted to those properly prepared persons who have been initiated into the practices or who are ready to be. Therefore, he assented to the building of the new monastery, on Nomad Mountain (*'Brog Ri-bo-che*), and called it Ganden (*dGa-ldan*), the Tibetan name of Maitreya's Tushita heaven. The monastery was completed and dedicated in 1410, the special halls for the mandalas were built in 1415, and the mandalas themselves erected and the images of the deities installed in 1417, during Tsong Khapa's sixtieth year—the same Bird year as his birth, according to the sixty-year Tibetan time cycle. These images were constructed by the finest artists in Tibet, under Tsong Khapa's personal visionary direction, with the finest gems and gold and silver, over the gold-bronze basic bodies. It is one of the great tragedies of recent cultural history that they all disappeared, along with every stone of Ganden monastery, during the frenzy of the cultural revolution under the Chinese occupation of Tibet.

Tsong Khapa taught very extensively during these last years, sometimes almost day and night. He passed into Nirvana in a miraculous manner, his body assuming the form of a sixteen-year-old Manjushri, according to all the hagiographies. His impact on Tibet was enormous; and through the Tibetan interaction with China and Mongolia (some of his successors were gurus of Manchu emperors), his influence spread to Buddhists there. Just recently, with the Tibetan diaspora since the Chinese invasion, his influence has become international. Further details of his life can be learned from my forthcoming *Biography*.[119]

Finally, in relation to his explanation "from great love" of the philosophical basis of his enlightenment, there are two further accounts to

[119] Expanding my *Haven of Faith* translation, I am in the process of translating the *rNam thar chen mo* of rGyal dbang Chos rje (NTC); Tib. text, Saranath: Elegant Sayings Press, 1968.

give concerning the composition of his central way works. First, the concise *Essence of True Eloquence* was written on the very morning of his enlightenment, as recounted above. Then, in 1402, he was invited to Rva-greng, the monastery originally founded by 'Brom-ston-pa, and was requested to write a comprehensive *Stages of the Path of Enlightenment*, fulfilling the intention of Atisha's *Lamp*. Many auspicious visions and signs occurred, and he quickly wrote the first two-thirds of the work. When he came to the final section, that on the central way, where he had to go for the first time in independent writing into the subtleties of the Dogmaticist-Dialecticist controversy in order to elucidate the practice of the transcendent insight, which inquires into the ultimate reality of selflessness, he became disheartened, and put aside the work. It was not difficult for him to write it, he said, as the matter was quite clear to him. We must remember that in his tradition, masters did not write to discover truth themselves; this they did in their deep studies and meditations. They only wrote "out of love" for others, to benefit them by providing them a doorway to their own realizations. And here, as I mentioned in the very beginning, Tsong Khapa became doubtful that very many people could follow his thought. What was the use of writing down such subtleties, when so few could benefit from them? I have already mentioned how Manjushri exhorted him to carry on anyway, and that it would have a moderate benefit. He then granted Tsong Khapa the continuous vision of the twenty emptinesses from the *Transcendent Wisdom Hundred Thousand* in three-dimensional silver Devanagari letters in the sky all around him. And sometimes these silver letters would occur in shadow on the page before him as he wrote.[120]

Then, in the winter of 1407, at the Sera Chos-sdings monastery, he was requested to write a comprehensive critical commentary on Nagarjuna's *Wisdom*, which he began there and quickly accomplished. He found, however, that he had no room to elucidate the full range of hermeneutical questions that came up between the Idealist, Dogmaticist, and Dialecticist schools. His main task was to elucidate Nagarjuna's work, and he had to stay close to the basic text. So, in the winter of 1407-1408, he sneaked out of the monastery at night with two companions, in order to avoid being followed by a crowd of disciples, and sealed himself up in the hermitage at Rakha Rock, to write the great *Essence of True Eloquence, Distinguishing the Interpretable and Definitive Meanings of the Teachings of the Victor*, the main work translated below. During the months of work on this, the twenty emptinesses again surrounded him, this time in golden Devanagari letters. And, as he says

[120] NTC, p. 268.

in his conclusion, he relied throughout the work on the blessed Manjushri, sitting in the center of the lotus of his heart.[121]

It turned out to be fortunate that he had escaped in secrecy, because an embassy from the chinese emperor, Yung Lo of the Ming, arrived at Sera early that year to see him. After his other disciples finally tracked him down with a messenger, he still kept the ambassador waiting several more months, while he finished the book. It is also said in the biographies that during the composition he would often discuss the issues and questions directly with Manjushri, and only write down a section after such thorough deliberation had been concluded. However we understand that, the atmosphere of the work is certainly that of a deep, penetratingly thoughtful inquiry into each of the questions, whose greatest gift is perhaps that the conclusions seem to open the mind out into further, more intensive deliberations, instead of closing thought off with an "answer," although many irksome questions of great difficulty are clearly settled.

In conclusion, it has always puzzled me that the voluminous writings of Tsong Khapa are not included among his "four major deeds," as mentioned above. Perhaps it may be that they are considered the natural outflow of perfect enlightenment, an indivisible part of the person himself. After all, a "person" in Buddhist usage consists of body, speech, and mind, and this *is* Tsong Khapa's speech, perhaps the most precious part of his person, in that his love extends through it to all those who encounter it in the course of their own quests for enlightenment. And it is "golden speech," as good as the proverbially golden silence, in that it transcends the silvery speech of persuasion that leads us to another's view, and inspires us directly to open our hearts and minds to the flowering of our own realizations.

VIII

You who aspire to Peerless Philosophy,
Listen with reverence,
With the critical discrimination that realizes
The Thatness of the Teaching!

1. Peerless Philosophy

By Peerless Philosophy, Tsong Khapa means the realm of a perfectly enlightened Buddha. He or she is one who has reached the conclusion

[121] NTC, pp. 285-86.

of the path of transformation through critical wisdom that has long been known in the west as "philosophy," the love of wisdom. Modern translators who render a common Buddhist expression for ultimate truth as "beyond the realm of the philosophers" (*atītatarkikagocara*) seriously mistranslate the Sanskrit. *Tarkika*, means "sophist," or "dogmatist," not "philosopher," that is, one who argues for the love either of argument or of dogma, not one who inquires into things for the love of wisdom. Just as Socrates distinguishes between sophists who made a living out of showing off their skill in argument and philosophers who lived to discover the liberating truth, the Buddhists always distinguished between the yogi of wisdom (*jñānayogin*) and the sophist who merely argued for fame and patronage, criticizing and tricking others without speaking up for anything himself, or the dogmatist who argued without staking his own view on the outcome of the debate.

If we grant that the inquirer into the nature of reality, who embarks on the yoga of the *Essence* is a philosopher, what kind of philosopher is he or she? We may distinguish here, thanks to the breakthrough of that modern incarnation of Manjushri, Ludwig Wittgenstein (1889-1951), two kinds of philosophers: those who adopt the "egocentrist approach" and those who adopt the "non-egocentrist approach." We might align these two categories loosely with "constructive" and "critical" philosophy, in keeping with the basic emphases of the two approaches.

In their formulation of the crucial "private language argument," generated by Wittgenstein's insights in his *Philosophical Investigations*,[122] Saunders and Henze define the two types of philosophers:

> The series of problems [that is, physical world, perception, self, and so on, relating to the private language question] . . . may be said to constitute the *egocentric predicament*: the predicament of one who begins "from his own case" and attempts to analyze and justify his system of beliefs and attitudes. . . . This is the predicament of "how to get out," how to move justifiably from one's own experiential data to the existence of an external world. . . . If the egocentric predicament be taken as a legitimate problem, then the response to this problem will constitute one or another of the strands composing what we have called the egocentric outlook. This is the outlook of one who begins at home, with the private object (with his own private experiential data), and attempts, in one way or another, to "go abroad." . . . If, on the other hand, the egocentric predicament be viewed as an illegitimate problem, a pseudo-problem, then the response to this "problem" will be to repudiate the egocentric viewpoint. This is the response

[122] L. Wittgenstein, *Philosophical Investigations*, translated by G. Anscombe (New York: Macmillan, 1953).

of one who "begins abroad," who begins in the public rather than in the private domain, and attempts in one way or another to understand both of these domains. It is the response of one who holds that only via public standards of justification can our system of beliefs be warranted and understood. This sort of philosopher turns away from the logically private language, rejects the private object, in his effort to accomplish the latter task.[123]

This formulation is particularly striking since although it aims to describe the modern private language debate, it could equally well be applied to the ancient Brahmin-Buddhist debate, or to the much more subtle intra-Buddhist debate between the Dialecticists and all the other schools, from Dogmaticists on down. The terms used by Saunders and Henze, "philosophical egocentrist" and "philosophical non-egocentrist," are precisely adequate to translate the Sanskrit *ātmavādin* (lit. "self-advocate") and *anātmavādin* (lit. "selflessness-advocate"). This most central Indian philosophical dichotomy persists at the subtlest levels in a running debate among non-egocentrists over presence or absence of "intrinsic reality" (*svabhāva*), "intrinsic identity" (*svalakṣaṇa*), and finally "dogmaticist privacy" (*svātantrya*). Once struck by this parallel between ancient Indian and modern western "egocentrists" and "non-egocentrists," we naturally become interested in the arguments used by both sides in the ancient period, considering the longevity of the issue in India and Tibet, and its relative newness in the West.

In general, modern philosophers have failed to appreciate the richness of the Buddhist critical non-egocentrist tradition due to their unwarranted prejudice that Buddhist thought is "mysticism," that is, antiphilosophical or aphilosophical. This prejudice has only been intensified by those contemporary "mystics" who have pointed to the young Wittgenstein's famous statement about silence in the *Tractatus* as evidence of his similarity to the imagined "silent sages of the East." [124] In actuality, the vast majority of "mystics," or non-rationalists, both Eastern and Western, has

[123] J. T. Saunders and D. F. Henze, *The Private Language Problem: A Philosophical Dialogue* (New York), 1976, p. 11. An earlier version of the rest of this subsection appeared as an article in *Philosophy East and West* 30, July 1980, and is included here with some modifications, by their kind permission.

[124] L. Wittgenstein, *Tractatus Logico-Philosophicus* (New York: Humanities Press, 1961): p. 74, "That whereof one cannot speak, thereof one must be silent." This famous phrase of Wittgenstein has led many to compare him with Zen masters and mystics in general. Although I grant that both recognize the limitations of language in the attempt to encompass ultimate reality, I argue that most comparisons have missed the point in both cases. "Mystic silence" is a referential silence that itself pretends to encompass reality as a reified ineffable "beyond," whereas enlightened silence is simply restraint of speech in certain contexts wherein speech would be mistaken as ultimately authoritarian. See Thurman, *Holy Teaching of Vimalakīrti* (University Park: Pennsylvania State University Press, 1977), pp. 59, 77, and Ch. IX n. 15.

usually belonged to the egocentrist camp, at least tacitly if not formally. Recourse to mysticism is a typical aspect of being stuck in the egocentric predicament. The mature Wittgenstein refutes his own earlier view,[125] and clearly exposes the tremendous amount of mysticism involved in the uncritical use of ordinary language, especially by the egocentrist philosophers. He humorously points to our predilection to reify things by constructing realities out of concepts, substances out of substantives, revealing the common notion of "naming as, so to speak, an occult process . . . and . . . when the philosopher tries to bring out *the* relation between name and thing by staring at an object in front of him and repeating a name or even the word 'this.' . . . And *here* we may fancy naming to be some remarkable act of mind, as it were an inner baptism of an object."[126] An egocentric philosopher, when yet unwilling to surrender his reified notions as mere imaginative constructions, quite typically resorts to "ineffability," "inexpressibility," and so forth, making a virtue of his inability to find intrinsic objectivities or to acknowledge their absence.

On the other hand, the mainstream Buddhist philosophers were typically non-egocentrist and critical, not mystical, in approach. The famous doctrine of "two realities" (*satyadvaya*), the absolute (*paramārtha*) and the superficial (*saṃvṛti*) or conventional (*vyāvahārika*) is not at all mystical but is rather an effective technical device for analyzing out the "queer," "occult," "mysterious," hence absolutistic element, so as to clear up the realm of experience, causality, and action. The doctrine properly puts the "absolute" in its place as a conceptual limiting case, which frees the conventional world, the space of living, from absolutism and its problems. The fundamental insight is that egocentrist absolutisms, ranging from the unconscious and perceptual to the theoretical and ideological, all categorized under the rubric "misknowledge" (*avidya*), cause all evils and problems. Thus, in the Buddhist tradition, philosophical analysis is seen as the way to treat the prevalent forms of "misknowledge"

[125] In *Philosophical Investigations*, paragraph 374, Wittgenstein says: "The great difficulty here is not to represent the matter as if there were something one *couldn't* do. As if there really were an object, from which I derive its description, but I were unable to shew it to anyone." If we apply this penetrating remark to "silence," we can see how referential silence, the above silence of the *Tractatus*, presumes and portends an "object," an "ultimate object" that we "cannot express," but from which we can derive a description; this description consists of portentous silence, which is perceived as pointing to the ineffable ultimate and which invariably makes the hearer, in his immediate relative situation, feel absolutely removed from the ultimate. The non-mystical, non-authoritarian, critical philosopher, such as the later Wittgenstein and Tsong Khapa, recognizes silence as itself a "use of language," and hence regards it as no more intrinsically portentous than any other use of language, although he takes care with it as being no less portentous, either.

[126] *Philosophical Investigations*, 143.

by applying criticism to the conceptual knots of the day. The level of sophistication of the application varied according to the sophistication of the philosophical knots, resulting in the Analysts' "critical metaphysics" to treat naive realism, the Traditionists' "critical nominalism" to treat the metaphysicians, the Idealists' "critical idealism" to treat the nominalists, and finally the "critical relativism" of the Centrists to treat all of them. The high point in this philosophical refinement process was reached by Chandrakirti in the sixth century, who entered into the refutation of dogmaticist privacy in order to treat the perplexities of his colleague Bhavaviveka and his followers, who as relativist critics of others' absolutisms, stumbled and inadvertently let a subtle form of absolutism creep back into their philosophic methodology. This refutation, as preserved in Chandra's *Lucid Exposition*, Chapter I, served as the basis of a philosophical discussion that went on for more than three centuries in India. It then came down to the present day preserved in the lively traditions of the Tibetan philosophical training colleges.

These subtleties could not even be translated intelligibly into Euro-American philosophical discourse, were it not for the consummation of the enterprise of critical philosophy reached by Wittgenstein. The overthrow of dogmaticist privacy in his mature works provides for the first time in Western philosophy a texture of inquiry suitable to parallel that of Tsong Khapa. Therefore it is necessary to sketch the parallels between him and Tsong Khapa in more detail, to bring out the philosophical relevance of the *Essence* below.

One of the remarkable things about Wittgenstein was his great courage, his ability to make a radical change in his thinking and publicly repudiate his earlier statements. In the *Philosophical Investigations*, he mentions his earlier attempt to find an absolutistic peg in reality on which to hang language through meaning, and he then repudiates it: "What lies behind the idea that names really signify simples? . . . [then quoting Plato,] 'what exists in its own right has to be . . . named without any other determination . . . its name is all it has.' . . . Both Russell's 'individuals' and my 'objects' [*Tractatus*] were such primary elements. . . . [However] it makes no sense at all to speak absolutely of 'the simple parts of a chair'."[127] Tsong Khapa in the *Essence* describes the habitual mode of intellectual reification in parallel terms, calling that "essence" in things that anchors their names "intrinsic identity," indispensable for the egocentrist, impossible for the non-egocentrist:

> What sort of mental habit holds things to be intrinsically identifiable? . . . the philosophers . . . investigate the meaning of the conventional

[127] Ibid., 46-47.

expression "person" in such uses as this "this person performed this action and experienced this result," by such analysis as "is the 'person' the very same thing as 'his' own aggregates? Or is 'he' something different from them?" When they discover whichever possibility, either sameness or difference [to be the case], it gives them a basis for establishing that "person," and they are then able to establish his accumulation of evolutionary action, and so forth. If they do not find [any such basis], they are unable to establish [either "person" or his "actions," etc.]. Hence they cannot rest content with the mere use of the expression "person." Thus, such establishment of "person" through analytic investigation into the referent of the conventional expression "person" is the establishment of person as having intrinsically identifiable status.[128]

Now, Wittgenstein had been one of the foremost investigators into the referents of names, looking for the essences in objects they hooked onto, but, unlike the egocentrist philosophers, he had not pretended to come up with anything solid, nor did he solidify the absence of that solidity into a real nothing. Thus he was able to return to the surface as a non-egocentrist, appreciating the conventionality of the expression, working with that. Further, he was able to isolate the mental habit that had caused him the whole problem, revealing the egocentrist's dependence on the "private object," internally designated by means of the "private language."

He mentions the "private language" explicitly: "a language in which a person could write down or give vocal expression to his inner experience—his feelings, moods, and the rest—for his private use?—Well, can't we do so in our ordinary language?—But that is not what I mean. The individual words of this language are to refer to what can only be known to the person speaking; to his immediate private sensations. So another person cannot understand the language."[129] It is clear he does not mean simply the private use of language, the internal enunciation of the usual public means of communication. Rather, he imagines a *logically private* language, a language in principle unique to the individual who invents and employs it; in Centrist terms, an absolutely private, not a conventionally private language. But why does Wittgenstein bother to imagine such a thing? He does so as that is the best way to make explicit the unconscious assumptions of "reality," "massiveness," "absoluteness," "facticity," "objectivity," and so on, that we habitually impose upon our perceptions. Thus, logical privacy is the inevitable absurd con-

[128] See the great *Essence*, Ch. V, 1.
[129] *Philosophical Investigations*, 243.

sequence (*prasaṅga*) forced upon the philosophical egocentrist, as he tries to give an account of his absolute "given," "simple," "first," "individual," "essence," "self," and so on, that is, the prime element constitutive of reality, self-evident, irreducible, and indispensable to the coherence of his world. The egocentrist is indeed so strongly attached to his groundedness on this supposed solid basis that he perceives any challenge as mere nihilistic skepticism. Thus he is best approached by the non-egocentrist (for whom things' very non-solidity itself is their actual workability), by demonstrating the absurdity of his absolutism either through such means as Wittgenstein's hyperbolic imaginings of private language or through the Centrists' dialecticist consequences. These are brought into play on this same level of subtlety in Chandrakirti's refutation of dogmaticist logical privacy, manifested by Bhavya in his adherence to private dogmaticist reasons based on the private, irreducible, intrinsically identifiable empirical object.[130] But before elucidating the actual refutations of privacy, ancient and modern, let us develop a partial typology of philosophical egocentrism and non-egocentrism.

The outlook of philosophical egocentrism is characterized by an avid grasp of the "given," a sort of "private object." self-evident and indubitable, the substance of all order, whether it be used to justify materialism, skeptical nihilism, phenomenalism, positivism, idealism, or any other form of ancient or modern absolutism. The egocentrist does employ critical methods in dealing with predecessors and adversaries, but once he feels he has found the "essence," he proceeds constructively, systematizing reality deductively according to discovered "laws," "principles," and so forth. This essence then becomes the foundation of practical life in social reality, and any relativistic account of language, meaning, morals, and so on, is dismissed as anarchistic and nihilistic. He is absolutistic even in empirical matters. Finally, he considers philosophy a constructive activity, an elaboration of formal structures of truth, beauty, and goodness. Hence his contribution is always dated, useful in the period as a temple and perhaps later as a museum, an edifice that stands quite apart from the person himself.

In contrast, the non-egocentrist outlook is essentially critical of all givens, not by taking as "given" the essential unreliability of everything, as does the absolutistic skeptic, but by never being satisfied with any supposedly analysis-proof element, and by sustaining the critical process itself as a valid mode of thought, cultivating a high tolerance of less than absolute security. The non-egocentrist's attitude toward the empirical is thoroughly relativistic and conventionalistic. Having found that life goes

[130] See the great *Essence*, Ch. V, 2c.

on even without any irreducible element, he works flexibly with what is consensually established, and yet does not abdicate the task of refining the consensus. He considers philosophy itself a therapeutic process, rather than a constructive metascience. Rather than building up grand solutions, he dissolves problems critically, finding the inconsistencies in the terms of the questions. He perceives perplexity, "misknowledge," a disease, and the clarity and insight afforded by critical analysis a cure. His philosophy tends to be less dated, less systematic, and more informal than the egocentrist's, since his refinement of thought, intensity of insight, and attention to self-transformation render his philosophizing more accessible to perplexed thinkers of later eras.

How do Wittgenstein and the Buddhist non-egocentrists fit into this typology? It will readily be granted that the mature Wittgenstein was primarily critical in approach, and the Buddhists were well known for their critical attitude toward the "given" as naively accepted in all their host cultures. *Vipaśyana*, or transcendent insight, is the main type of Universal Vehicle meditation, and *prajña*, critical wisdom, is glossed as *dharmapravicaya*, literally, the "analysis of things," symbolized as a sword that cuts through the knot of perplexity. And the similarity of the actual texture of critical analysis of the two types of non-egocentrist is striking. First, Wittgenstein:

> Again, does my visual image of this tree, of this chair, consist of parts? And what are its simple component parts? Multi-coloredness is one kind of complexity; another is, for example, that of a broken outline composed of straight bits. And a curve can be said to be composed of an ascending and a descending segment. . . . But isn't a chessboard, for instance, obviously and absolutely composite? —You are probably thinking of the composition out of thirty-two white and thirty-two black squares. But could we not say, for instance, that it was composed of the colors black and white and the schema of the squares? And if there are quite different ways of looking at it, do you still want to say that the chessboard is absolutely composite? . . . (Is the color of a square on a chessboard simple, or does it consist of pure white and pure yellow? And is white simple, or does it consist of the colors of the rainbow?)[131]

He applies the same type of analysis to his feelings as to objects:

> "At that moment I hated him"—What happened here? Didn't it consist in thoughts, feelings, and actions? And if I were to rehearse that moment to myself, I should assume a particular expression, think of certain

[131] *Philosophical Investigations*, 47.

> happenings, breathe in a certain way, arouse certain feelings in myself.[132]

and even to himself analyzing himself:

> Here we have a case of introspection, not unlike that from which William James got the idea that the "self" consisted mainly of "peculiar motions in the head and in between the head and the throat." And James' introspection showed not the meaning of the word "self" (so far as it means something like "person," "human being," "he himself," "I myself"), nor any analysis of any such thing, but the state of a philosopher's attention when he says the word "self" to himself and tries to analyze its meaning. (And a good deal could be learned from this.)[133]

Examples from the Buddhist philosophical literature are abundant. In the *Essence*, Tsong Khapa runs through the critical techniques of his predecessors, in this case Kamalashila:

> The absolute status of anything is refuted by showing first of all, in the face of no matter what assertion of Buddhist or non-Buddhist scholar, the impossibility of an indivisible, a thing without a multiplicity of parts such as periods of time, parts of physical objects, or aspects of cognitive objects. Then one demonstrates that, whereas conventional objects may exist as unitary things while established as composed of many parts, as far as absolute status is concerned, there are inevitable inconsistencies. If part and whole are absolutely different, there can be no connection between them, and if part and whole are absolutely the same, then the whole becomes a multiplicity. . . . [To give an actual line of argument] "to refute [absolute] production of one thing from another, the cause is first restricted to being either permanent or impermanent, and production from a permanent thing is refuted. Then, production from an impermanent thing is restricted to being either sequential or simultaneous, and production from a simultaneous cause is refuted. Then, a sequential cause is restricted to being either destroyed or undestroyed (in producing its effect), and production from a destroyed cause is refuted. Then production from a previously undestroyed cause is restricted to being either obstructed or unobstructed, and production from an obstructed cause is refuted." The refutation thus far is rather easy. "Then, production from an unobstructed cause is restricted to being either wholly unobstructed

[132] Ibid., 642.
[133] Ibid., 413.

or partially unobstructed; then, in the former case, there must be a confusion of two things occurring at different times, an atom and [its aggregative effects such as] a molecule must be confused as a single object, [the causal atoms] being wholly unobstructed; or else, in the latter case, as [the cause, the indivisible, etc.] would have parts, production would be a superficial [production, no longer absolute]."[134]

Here the opponent, like the interlocutor in the *Investigations* passage, is a philosophical absolutist, a substantivist, who is "bewitched by language" into perceiving things to be absolutely true, "really real" before him. The Wittgensteinian and Centrist non-egocentrist critical analyses intend to force him to look deeper into things and processes by examining his account of them, to try to find the essence assumed to correspond to the name, the "metaphysical real," the "simple," the "indivisible." The absolutist's failure to find any such analysis-resistant essence is the first step on the road to liberation of his intelligence from the spell of language. The century- and culture-spanning similarity of therapeutic technique is startling.

Relativism or conventionalism about the empirical, which focuses primarily on language, is a central component of the non-egocentrist outlook, the key to the non-egocentrist's avoidance of nihilistic skepticism and absolutist mysticism. The egocentrist tends to engage in one or the other of these alternatives when his critical analysis goes further than usual and he sees through his previously accepted "givens," such as "self," "matter," "object," or "sense-contents," and so on, and he feels his universe crumble. And even if he never reaches such a frontier, he perceives the non-egocentrist as courting chaos, and typically accuses him of nihilism. Wittgenstein responds to the charge:

> Not at all. It is not a *something*, but not a *nothing* either! The conclusion was only that a nothing would serve just as well as a something about which nothing could be said. We have only rejected the grammar which tries to force itself on us here. The paradox disappears only if we make a radical break with the idea that language always functions in one way.[135]

He goes still further in response to another challenge:

> Where does our investigation get its importance from, since it seems only to destroy everything interesting, that is, all that is great and important? (As it were all the buildings, leaving behind only bits of

[134] See the great *Essence*, Ch. IV, Section II.
[135] *Philosophical Investigations*, 304.

stone and rubble.) What we are destroying is nothing but houses of cards and we are clearing up the ground of language on which they stand.[136]

Thus it is precisely the reaffirmation of language, free of any supposed absolute substratum, as a practical, conventional process, an ordinary activity of human beings, a "form of life" that sets the non-egocentrist analytic philosopher apart from the skeptic. The skeptic indeed transfers his instinctual absolutism to "nothing," making the mistake of thinking that lack of absolute basis is no basis at all, lack of absolute process is no process at all, lack of absolutistic, privately grounded language is no language at all, lack of mathematically perfect logic is no logic at all, and so on. Wittgenstein is most explicit about the sheer conventionality of language, as in the following group of statements:

> The point here is not that our sense-impressions can lie, but that we understand their language. (And this language, like any other, is founded on convention.)[137]
>
> One objects: "So you are saying that human agreement decides what is true and what is false?" —It is what human beings *say* that is true and false; and they agree in the *language* they use. That is not agreement in opinions but in form of life.[138]
>
> Here we strike rock bottom, that is, we have come down to conventions.[139]
>
> When philosophers use a word—"knowledge," "being," "object," "I," "proposition," "name"—and try to grasp the *essence* of the thing, one must always ask oneself: is the word ever actually used in this way in the language-game which is its original home. What *we* do is to bring words back from their metaphysical to their everyday use.[140]
>
> The meaning of a word is its use in the language.[141]
>
> When I talk about language (words, sentences, etc.) I must speak the language of everyday. Is this language somehow too coarse and material for what we want to say? *Then how is another one to be constructed?*[142] A main source of our failure to understand is that we do

[136] Ibid., 118.
[137] Ibid., 355.
[138] Ibid., 241.
[139] L. Wittgenstein, *The Blue and Brown Books* (New York: Harper and Row, 1958), p. 24.
[140] *Philosophical Investigations*, 116.
[141] Ibid., 43.
[142] Ibid., 120.

> not *command a clear view* of the use of our words.[143] Philosophy may in no way interfere with the actual use of language; it can in the end only describe it. For it cannot give it any foundation either. It leaves everything as it is.[144]
>
> *Essence* is expressed by grammar.[145]
>
> Grammar tells what kind of object anything is. (Theology as grammar.)[146]

And finally, to ward off the temptation to feel disappointed with settling for conventionality, aware of the depth of absolutistic thought-patterns:

> The great difficulty here is not to represent the matter as if there were something one *couldn't* do. As if there really were an object, from which I derive its description, but I were unable to show it to anyone.
> —And the best I can propose is that we should yield to the temptation to use this picture, but then investigate how the *application* of the picture goes.[147]

The Dialecticist counterpart of this conventionalism can be most clearly seen in the *Essence* below on Chandra's critique of Bhavya's use of the "head of Rahu, body of pestle" examples as justification for employing the expression "hardness is the intrinsic identity of earth" as a conventionally acceptable expression.[148] (Rahu is a mythological demon who is all head and no body; a pestle is all body and no head; so "head" and "Rahu" and "body" and "pestle" refer to the same things, as do "hardness" and "earth.") Chandra states:

> Moreover, this example is incorrect because the expressions "pestle" and "Rahu" do exist among mundane conventions, established without analysis, and do apply to their referents body and head [respectively], just like the conventional designation "person."

Tsong Khapa here comments:

> It is correct, according to conventions of social communication, for a speaker to dispel the doubt of a listener with the expressions "pestle" and "Rahu" since the latter has formed the notions of "body" and "head" from hearing the corresponding words and is wondering "whose body?" and "whose head?" The speaker thus wishes to eliminate the

[143] Ibid., 122.
[144] Ibid., 124.
[145] Ibid., 371.
[146] Ibid., 373.
[147] Ibid., 374.
[148] See the great *Essence*, Ch. V, Section 1, for following quotes.

possibility of reference to any body other than that of the pestle or to any head other than that of Rahu. However, this example does not correspond to the case of the expression "hardness is the intrinsic identity of earth," there being no earth which is not hard, and hence no need to dispel any such doubt.

The main target of the critique is the notion of "intrinsic identity," which would not occur to the ordinary hearer. "Hardness of earth" might fit with the example, but there is no room for notions of "intrinsic identity"—the hearer would not wonder "whose intrinsic identity?" but only "whose hardness?"

Chandra again returns to the attack, saying that conventionally "body" and "pestle" and "head" and "Rahu" are different, hence the example cannot illustrate a supposed case of essential nondifference. But then, rejoins the substantivist (Bhavya), when one investigates the referents of the expressions, they prove to be the same thing. Chandra then succinctly states his conventionalism about language:

> If you propose that the example is indeed applicable since [pestle and Rahu] are proved to be nothing other than body and head, since only the latter can be apprehended, I say that is not so; for, in the usage of social conventions, such a sort of analysis [as that seeking essential identity, etc.] is not employed, and further, the things of the world are existent [only insofar] as unexamined critically.

Chandra states that once one looks analytically for "head," "Rahu," "body," "pestle," or anything else, nothing can be found to withstand analysis, but still those things are there when unanalytically accepted. He pursues this idea then with a key concept:

> Although analytically there is no self apart from form, etc., from the social superficial (*lokasaṃvṛtyā*) point of view such [a self] has its existence dependent on the aggregates.

Conventionally, even the abhorrent [to the non-egocentrist] "self" is reinstated, as "part of the grammar" of mundane communication. And thus the feared nihilism, which the absolutist imagines lurks at the end of the analysis that seeks a self and cannot find anything, is avoided through the reaffirmation of the mutually dependent, social, conventional, nonanalytic existence of self. And, Chandra finally shows his awareness of how such nihilism cannot be avoided by any means other than such thoroughgoing conventionalism, saying: "otherwise, the superficial [reality] would no longer be the superficial and would either lack validity entirely or would become [ultimate] reality." Thus, no "simple" analysis-resistant referential base can be found to anchor the conventional, which is precisely why it works as sheer conventionality, free of extremisms of absolutism and nihilism.

It should be noted that Chandra's opponent in this is by no means a naive absolutist, but is only trying to uphold the "intrinsic identity" of things *conventionally*, having already, as he thinks, ruled it out *absolutely*. Chandra's thrust is thus to show the incompatibility of the concepts of "conventionality" and "intrinsicality." Finally, to forestall any misunderstanding about the sort of analysis that can be involved in calling the conventional "nonanalytic," Tsong Khapa comments (with intriguing implications for Wittgenstein's "everyday" use of language, even philosophically):

> We might suppose here, as the mundane person engages in a great deal of analysis—"Is it happening or not?" or "Is it produced or not?"—that it must be improper to reply to such inquiries "It happens" or "It is produced." However, this type of [conventional] inquiry and the above analytic method [seeking absolute referential bases] are utterly different. The mundane person is not inquiring into coming and going through analysis into the meaning of the use of the conventional expressions "comer," "goer," "coming," and "going," out of dissatisfaction with [the fact that they are] merely conventional usages. He is rather making unreflective inquiry into the unreflective usage of the expressions "coming" and "going."

The mature Wittgenstein's refusal to pretend to a system, his insistence on ordinary language (which so frustrated logical absolutists such as Russell), gains support when juxtaposed to Chandra's view of language, conceptual analysis, and philosophical investigation as conventional procedures, programs that function on the surface, the superficial level. Indeed, how could language, logic, and understanding exclude themselves from the universal relativity that permeates all causal processes?

Finally, the philosophical non-egocentrist's attitude toward philosophy as therapy is attested in Wittgenstein's writings, as in the following famous passages:

> For the clarity we are aiming at is indeed *complete* clarity. But this simply means that the philosophical problems should *completely* disappear. The real discovery is the one that makes me capable of stopping doing philosophy when I want to. —The one that gives philosophy peace, so that it is no longer tormented by questions that bring itself into question. —Instead, we now demonstrate a method, by examples; and the series of examples can be broken off. —Problems

> are solved [difficulties eliminated], not a *single* problem. There is not *a* philosophical method, though there are indeed methods, like different therapies.[149]

> The philosopher's treatment of a question is like the treatment of an illness.[150]

> What is your aim in philosophy? —To shew the fly the way out of the fly-bottle.[151]

What seemed irreverence to some of his contemporaries is perfectly in accord with the Centrist tradition. For educated Buddhists see philosophy as a means of liberation from the suffering of the misknowledge-governed life-cycle, and the Centrist seeks escape from the prison of egocentrist views and egocentric instinctual habits through the therapeutic use of critical wisdom. And how strikingly Wittgenstein's call for "complete clarity" and "peace" echoes Nagarjuna's salute of relativity taught by the Buddha as the "supreme bliss of the quiescence of perplexities."

At this point we must go further into the question of logical dogmaticist privacy, as this is the crux of the connection we have established between Dialecticist Centrism and Wittgenstein. I feel I must make this available to the reader, because it was only with the help of Wittgenstein and his insight into this most subtle of subtleties, as Tsong Khapa calls it, that I myself was able to get clear these profound sections of the *Essence*,[152] not to speak of translating them. And although it is important to work up to them on the ladder of the earlier sections of the *Essence* itself, it is suitable for this introduction to deal in detail with the Gordian knot of the book. Once it is untied, the other sections can be more easily sorted out. Furthermore, the many readers, either from the Western philosophical side or the Buddhist experiential side, who are still predisposed to dismiss the bridge built by Tsong Khapa between philosophy and realization, intellect and experience, and so on, will find this the point of greatest resistance and thus of deepest penetration. So let us proceed with the refutation of dogmaticist logical privacy.

Tsong Khapa introduces the refutation as follows:

> In general, the two masters [Buddhapalita and Chandrakirti] took as the ultimate in profound and subtle reasonings both those reasonings proving the perfect viability of all systems such as causality in the

[149] *Philosophical Investigations*, 133.
[150] Ibid., 255.
[151] Ibid., 309.
[152] That is, the sections refuting the private reason and the private object in the *Essence*, Ch. V, Section 2C.

absence of the intrinsic reality that is negated as intrinsic identifiability even conventionally, and (those reasonings) negating that negatee (of intrinsic identifiability) by the very reason of relativity, asserted clearly to be the relativity of all things, transcendental and non-transcendental. Moreover, they took this refutation of dogmaticist privacy as the most subtle among them.[153]

Thus the refutation of dogmaticist privacy is stated to be a form of the negation of intrinsic identity, at the final level of subtlety. "Intrinsic identity," as we have seen, is the egocentrist's designative base, the essentialist or substantivist private object, necessary for private reference and language. Such a basis is formally accepted by Bhavaviveka, though he refutes the *ultimate* status of intrinsic identity. However, it is his *conventional* insistence on intrinsic identity that reveals his subtle substantivism, which Chandra treats through his critique in terms of philosophical methodology.

The word I have rendered in the above passage as "dogmaticist privacy" is the Tibetan *rang rgyud*, which renders the Sanskrit *svātantrya*, previously rendered in this context by Stcherbatski as "independence," and by Hopkins as "autonomy."[154] Mention of the Tibetan as well as the Sanskrit here is important, since it was mainly in Tibet that followers of Chandra's thought elaborated this question in great detail. The usual Tibetan translation for Sanskrit *svātantrya* (adjectivally, *svatantra*) is *rang dbang*, which is also the normal Tibetan expression for "independent," meaning literally "self-powered," opposed to "other-powered" (*gzhan dbang*, *paratantra*). Why then, in this crucial philosophical context, a context that generated centuries of discussion and volumes of commentary and rigorous analysis, did the Tibetan translators and scholars use *rang rgyud*, which literally means "own-continuum," translating back into Sanskrit in most contexts as *svasaṃtāna*, often "own personality" or even "own mind"? To be sure, Tsong Khapa himself glosses *rang rgyud* with *rang dbang* (just as Saunders and Henze gloss "private language" as a language whose words are "conceptually *independent* of publicly observable phenomena"), but that does not alter the fact that he and his colleagues persisted in using *rang rgyud*, talking of the *rang rgyud* problem, which would not have been necessary if *rang rgyud* were identical with *rang dbang* in all of its contexts. Looking at these, we note that *rang rgyud* is used nominally, as direct object of *'gog pa*, to negate, and *sgrub pa*, to establish. "Independence" here, although not wrong, is

[153] Ibid.

[154] See Stcherbatski, *Buddhist Logic, Vol. II* (New York: Dover, 1972); P. J. Hopkins, *Meditations on Emptiness* (Ann Arbor: Xerox University, Microfilms, 1972).

too vague, used for the crude Individualist notion of "independent self" (*rang dbang can gyi bdag*), and does not specifically connect to the philosophical issues of extreme subtlety involved here. *Rang rgyud* is used adjectivally with "reason" (*hetu*), "mark" (*liṅga*), "thesis" (*pratijña*), "position" or "subject" (*pakṣa*), "probandum" (*sādhya*), "syllogism" (*anumāna*), and "validating cognition" (*pramāṇa*), all of which are essentially linguistic phenomena, although it is never to my knowledge used with "language" (*bhāṣya*). In all of these cases, its linguistic opposite is not "dependent" (*paratantra*), but "public" (*paraprasiddha*, literally, "other-acknowledged") reason, thesis, and so on. Finally, it crops up in the name of Bhavaviveka's Centrist school, Dogmaticist (*Svātantrika*), the "school of those who use private dogmaticism," as opposed to Chandra's Dialecticist (*Prāsaṅgika*), the "school of those who use the dialectical consequences" (*prasaṅga*) of their opponent's absolutisms, the most public form of philosophical approach. Thus, the former are aptly called the "Dogmaticist Centrists," in contrast to the "Dialecticist Centrists." (I call them "Dogmaticists" rather than "Dogmatists" in that their dogmatism is only conventional, being their unwitting resurrection of intrinsic identity in the form of dogmaticist privacy as the basis of conventional objectivity and of language used rigorously in philosophical arguments.)

Tsong Khapa, in typical Tibetan philosophic style, first cites the Indian Jayananda's attack on the private reason and then goes on to reject it as the wrong approach.[155]

> In this regard, a certain pandit argues, "the private reason would be appropriate if there were substantiation by validating cognition of both reason and the invariable concomitance proving the probandum; but it is not appropriate, such not being the case. For it is wrong to assert that a reason can be authoritatively substantiated for both protagonist and antagonist, since the protagonist does not know what is established by validating cognition for the antagonist, as he cannot know the details of the other's thoughts either by perception or inference, nor does he know what is established by validating cognition for himself, as it is always possible his judgment is in error." —[But we respond that] this [approach] is utterly wrong; for, if such were the case, it would also be inappropriate to refute [an antagonist with a public syllogism] based on his own assertions; for one could not know that antagonist's position, not knowing his thoughts, and one's own refutation by advancing his fallacies could be wrong, as it would always be possible that one's judgment about those fallacies could be mistaken.

[155] See the great *Essence*, Ch. V, Section 2C.

This false start on the refutation of dogmaticist privacy is strikingly reminiscent of Saunders and Henze's formulation of the opening "prong" of the assault on the private language, where the possibility of a private language is challenged on grounds of the unreliability of subjective memory impressions which are not independently checkable or substantiable. But, just like Jayananda's, this attack is not conclusive, since the criterial demand itself is too stringent, and the antagonist is able to throw the same doubt back at public discourse—"you think you can check public impressions based on others' testimony, etc., but couldn't you hear them wrong?"—and so forth.[156] The Wittgensteinian is then required to come back stressing the *conventional* acceptability of public substantiation and so on, which corresponds with Tsong Khapa's procedure.

Tsong Khapa elucidates Chandra's assault on a typical private syllogism of Bhavaviveka. This passage in the *Lucid Exposition* I is considered the locus classicus of the refutation of dogmaticist privacy. Bhavaviveka is arguing against a naive absolutist of the Samkhya school, who believes that an effect preexists in its cause. Bhavya argues: "internal sense-media (such as eye-consciousness) are not self-produced absolutely; because they exist, just like consciousness itself." The reason that this syllogism is private is that it is based, for Bhavaviveka himself and for his antagonist, according to him, on their respective private objects. Bhavaviveka considers that each has a private perception of the subject of the syllogism (eye-consciousness, etc.), the reason employed (its existence), and the concomitance perceived in the example. These are named in the argument and understood by each through each object's *conventional intrinsic identity*, which Bhavaviveka maintains consistently to be indispensable for conventional functionality. The Samkhya himself is much more grossly absolutistic, believing that inner phenomena such as eye-consciousness are absolutely existent, self-produced, and so on. And this is why Bhavaviveka feels it necessary to qualify his argument, adding "absolutely" (*paramārthataḥ*), which Chandra seizes upon as evidence of his subtle absolutization of the conventional. Chandra attacks as follows:

> Your use of the thesis-qualification "absolutely" is unnecessary from your own standpoint, since you do not accept self-production even superficially . . . (If you maintain that) it relates to others' standpoints, it would be better to refute heterodox (opponents) without any such qualifications, since outsiders muddle the two realities and should be refuted in terms of both. Further, since it is inappropriate to refute the claim of self-production in mundane conventional terms, it is inappropriate to employ such qualifications in that context; for the mundane person assents to mere arisal of an effect from a cause without

[156] Saunders and Henze, *The Private Language*, pp. 218ff.

> any analytic inquiry into whether it is produced from self or other, etc. Again, if it is the case that you wish to refute even the superficial production of the eye, etc., which your opponent believes to be absolute, this then entails with respect to yourself the thesis-fault of subjectlessness, or the reason-fault of groundlessness, since you yourself do not accept eye, etc., as absolutely existent.[157]

Chandra here basically challenges Bhavya to give an account of his supposed privately based dogmaticist discourse, asking him how he can find any common ground of discussion with his antagonist, since each exists in a private, logically inaccessible world of private objects, and so on. Sensing these difficulties, Bhavya sidesteps the necessity of the qualification "absolutely," and instead tries to show his argument's conventional viability, arguing for the accessibility of a general subject of the syllogism, mere eye-consciousness, and so on, disregarding all qualifications. He gives the plausible example of the argument between the Buddhist Analyst and the Brahminical Vaisheshika about the status of sound, which proceeds on the basis of the general subject "mere sound" not qualified as either "etheric sound" (unacceptable to Analyst) or "material sound" (unacceptable to Vaisheshika). This, Bhavya argues, evades the thesis-fault of subjectlessness, restores a "bare datum" as the logically private object, in principle accessible to both parties as the basis of the private dogmaticist syllogism.

This apparently reasonable tack proves calamitous for Bhavya, as it enables Chandra to expose his subtle absolutism, his commitment to a private object as the objectively real basis of perception, hence of justification, language, even causality. Tsong Khapa paraphrases Chandra's argument here:

> It is inappropriate to posit mere eye, etc., disregarding qualifications in light of the two realities, as subjects of the syllogism proving the absence of the self-production of eye, etc.; because (according to your own system), the validating cognition that encounters that subject is a cognition unmistaken about the intrinsic reality of eye, etc.; and because, as unmistaken cognition does not mistake intrinsic reality, the object it encounters cannot be an erroneous object that falsely appears to have intrinsic identifiability when actually it does not.

Chandra argues that Bhavya cannot have a "mere object," general and unqualified, and still uphold his private dogmaticism, since according to that even a "bare datum" can only exist if encountered by a validating

[157] This and following quotes from the *Essence* are found in Ch. V, Section 2C. Skt. original of Chandra's argument, PPMMV, pp. 8ff.; quoted below in the great *Essence*, Ch. V, nn. 133-38.

cognition that must not mistake the object's intrinsic identity. Such a bare datum thus must be absolutely real even to be *there* for an absolutist who requires its certification by a private, unmistaken, validating cognition. Tsong Khapa clarifies this point:

> In a philosophical system that claims that whatever exists, exists by virtue of its own objectivity, a [cognition] that errs in its perception of intrinsic identifiability cannot be represented as discovering its proper object. Any sort of validating cognition, either conceptual or nonconceptual, must be unmistaken about the intrinsic identity of its validated object, whether perceptual or conceptual. Thus, a validating cognition must derive its validity from *an object that, not being merely a conventional, nominal designation, has intrinsic objectivity or intrinsic reality as its own actual condition*. And this is just what [Bhavya's] own system claims. [Italics added.]

The refutation here comes down to the hyperbolically isolated, presumed private object, just as it does in the modern one. The Dialecticist probes the roots of the Dogmaticist's apparently innocent methodological formalism and discovers the last vestige of the naive realism of egocentrist misknowledge, the conventionally intrinsically identifiable private object. The resonance of Saunders and Henze's description of the private "experiential-datum" needed to anchor the term in private language is obvious.

> [A private language is] a language, each word of which refers to experiential data, although each of these words is conceptually independent of publicly observable phenomena. (When we say that an experiential-datum term, "E," is *conceptually independent* of publicly observable phenomena, we mean this: the existence of an E neither entails nor is entailed by the existence of any publicly observable phenomena; nor is it part of the meaning of "E" that publicly observable phenomena provide evidence for the existence of an E.)[158]

To recapitulate, Bhavya tries to reestablish his private syllogism by employing a mere general (that is, publicly observable and ostensible) object as a basis of discussion, thus tacitly acknowledging the publicness of objects, subjects, syllogisms, language, and so on. But this he cannot rightly do in the framework of his system, which posits *intrinsic*, not merely conventional, objectivity to genuine phenomena, hence cannot tolerate their mere relativity and superficiality. And Chandra holds him to his own basic outlook without letting him pay lip-service to conventionality, saying, as it were, your "bare datum" must be absolute, in-

[158] Saunders and Henze, *The Private Language*, pp. 6-7.

trinsically identifiable and hence privately cognizable and substantiable, if only for you to perceive it at all, since for you nothing can even exist even conventionally unless it is thus established.

Chandra then follows this point with a refutation of Bhavya's example itself, pointing out its inapplicability. Chandra agrees that the Analyst and the Vaisheshika each can point out a "mere sound" to argue about, since both tacitly share a sense of the perceptual objectivity, the private "givenness" of the object, its "thereness," as it were. However, as Tsong Khapa paraphrases:

> The case is different when the advocate of the emptiness of intrinsic reality proves to the advocate of nonemptiness of intrinsic reality that eye, etc., are not self-produced. For not only can they not discover any objective existence or even any objective non-existence, but also they cannot point out to each other "such a thing as 'this' we both encounter as the actual thing to use as subject of our argument."[159]

This is perhaps the most subtle point to grasp, either in the Wittgensteinian or in the Dialecticist context, because of our innate perceptual absolutism, reinforced by culture through language, but the attainment of the accomplished non-egocentrist philosopher comes down even to this. In looking for an object to use as subject of a syllogism, the non-egocentrist (that is, advocate of emptiness) cannot find anything whatsoever, when he looks with truth-determinant analysis at objects supposed to have cognitively objective status, according to the egocentrist (nonemptiness advocate). Of course, conventionally all sorts of unanalyzed objects are right there without having to be looked for—relative, designatively dependent, publicly observable, and so forth—easily accessible to the nonanalytic attitude of everyday. However, when he adopts the attitude which is called "philosophical cognition analytic of ultimacy" (*don dam dpyod pai rigs ses*), closely related to the "holy spacelike samadhi intuition," which he does when advocating emptiness to the absolutist in the attempt to cure the latter's absolutistic illness, he cannot find any single thing that is intrinsically identifiable, privately cognizable, ostensively definable or even perceptually accessible. Under this analysis, both public and private disappear, as they can only exist in mutual dependence. And only such an appreciation of the transformative power of analytic insight, its close relation to samadhic intuition of emptiness, can ever make clear the otherwise cryptic statement of Wittgenstein:

> "But when I imagine something, or even actually *see* objects, I have *got* something which my neighbor has not!" —I understand you. You want to look about you and say: "at any rate, only I have got

[159] See the great *Essence*, Ch. V, Section 2C.

THIS!" What are these words for? They serve no purpose. —Can one not add: "there is here no question of a 'seeing' and therefore none of a 'having'—nor of a subject, nor therefore of 'I' either"? Might I not ask: in what sense have you *got* what you are talking about and saying that only you have got it? Do you possess it? YOU DO NOT EVEN SEE IT! And this too is clear: if as a matter of logic you exclude other people's having something, it loses its sense to say that you have it. [Small capitals added.][160]

Here again we find Wittgenstein leveling the clincher at his opponent, preceding what Saunders and Henze call the "ascription argument," namely, that no "private" object, perception, or language can exist without the public notion of "person," which thus vitiates the logical privacy of them. As they put it, "the traditionist (just like Dogmaticist) cannot treat the notions of 'I' and 'my experience' as logically primitive with respect to the notions of 'he' and 'his experience' because one who does not possess the latter notions lacks the former notions as well."[161] This argument topples the traditionist's adherence to the private language, enables Wittgenstein to exclaim to his absolutist interlocutor "*You do not even see it!*" and enables Chandra to demolish Bhavya's sense of the plausibility even of his example, as the two parties in the supposed private dogmaticist argument cannot find as "this" either any objective existence or any objective nonexistence! Thus the non-egocentrist, Wittgenstein, and Chandra all end up on the same point, from which proceed their non-egocentrist methodologies. The non-egocentrist does not try to employ private syllogisms, reasons, and so forth, since antagonist and protagonist are so apart there is no ground of discussion established in any satisfactory manner, but rather makes his own analytic, critical attitude available to his antagonist dialectically, leading the latter through the logical ramifications of the latter's own position that end up with absurd consequences. The antagonist thus is able to see the awkwardness of his original position and gracefully abandon it.

As Wittgenstein proposed, the non-egocentrist should "yield to the temptation to use this [absolutist's] picture [of the world], but then investigate how the *application* of the picture goes."[162] And, as we see him now, thus confirmed by the more systematized Dialecticist methodology, it is obvious why Wittgenstein refused to appear too systematic or formal in his mature investigations, why he adopted an inner dialogue form, and why many of his points are made through asking obviously unan-

160 *Philosophical Investigations*, 398.
161 Saunders and Henze, *The Private Language*, p. 139.
162 *Philosophical Investigations*, 374.

swerable questions. Indeed, it is amazing how he managed, all alone as he was, not knowing that he was in fact a luminary of the "anti-dogmaticist tradition," to apply to European absolutism the same critique earlier applied to Indian absolutism by the proponents of the central way!

There are far-reaching implications for philosophy in this remarkable fact that Wittgenstein and his successors came so close to the Dialecticist tradition, without knowing anything about them directly, simply from pursuing the deepest questions of philosophy in a rigorously critical way, and in spite of the enormous temporal and cultural differences involved. After all, many philosophers who overlook Buddhist thought and dismiss its philosophical importance greatly respect Wittgenstein. Yet, the critical insight he achieved and cultivated on his own was already highly developed and systematically cultivated in a great tradition with many thousands of members in India, Tibet, Mongolia, China, and Japan. One aspect of our first "western renaissance" was our discovery of the hidden treasures of Greek thought. Our second renaissance may now well come from our discovery of the even greater treasures of Asian thought. We should make a special effort to make our own the heritage of the non-egocentrist, critical tradition of the central way, which was born from liberation from cultural conditioning at the deepest levels, perceptual as well as ideological. It is thus free for the using, as it never belonged to any race, culture, or even linguistic tradition, but only to those of whatever tradition who dare to question what is authoritatively told to them and even what seems natural and self-evident before them. For these demand the surpassing peace that comes with the eradication of perplexity, and so are dedicated to the Peerless Philosophy.

2. Listen with Reverence

The longer title of the *Essence* is the *Discrimination between the Interpretable and Definitive Meanings of the Teachings of the Jina*. The categories "interpretable meaning" (*neyārtha*) and "definitive meaning" (*nītārtha*) are the key terms in the hermeneutical thought of the Buddhist tradition. When Tsong Khapa urges us to "listen with reverence," he reminds us not only that his *Essence* flows from Manjushri, from Tsong Khapa's own merger with Manjushri in the highest individual realization, but also that this *Essence* grants us accessibility to a sacred spiritual tradition, as well as to the ultimate sacredness of our own eventual enlightenments. In this section, we will take a broad look at the central hermeneutical concern of the *Essence*, how it relates to the several millennia of Buddhist hermeneutics, and how the various systems explored in the *Essence* resolve the dilemma.[163]

In all the Buddhist traditions, faith is but a way to wisdom, doctrines but prescriptions for practices, and thus scripture has less authority than reason. It should not be surprising therefore that hermeneutics, the science of interpretation of sacred doctrine (*saddharma*), should be central in the methodology of enlightenment.

According to the tradition, Gautama, the Shakyamuni Buddha, attained unexcelled perfect enlightenment during his thirty-fifth year, in about 529 B.C.E., and spent the next half-century teaching the thousands of persons coming from all over India as well as from foreign lands, who sought his wisdom. The single aim of all his teaching was to evoke enlightenment in living beings. The methods he used toward this end were as various as are living beings themselves. It would not have served his purpose to preach a single message dogmatically. Rather, he exercised what is known as his "skill in liberative technique" (*upāya-kauśalya*), which is defined as including supernormal powers and knowledge such as clairvoyance about the past experience, present inclinations, and future destiny of disciples; but most importantly including an unimpeded eloquence in "turning the wheel of the Dharma," or instructing disciples in the nature of the supreme reality.

A Buddha's pedagogic versatility is well illustrated in a famous parable in the *Lotus Sutra* about a man with many children who are playing in a burning house. At first they will not listen to his warnings, as they are too absorbed in their play, so he changes his tack and instead tells them he has some marvelous toys for them outside and they should come and see. Knowing what each one likes, he tells some he has deer-carts for them, some he has horse-carts, and some bullock-carts. Out they rush pell-mell, only to discover that after all the man has only bullock-carts for them to ride in. At the cost of a slight disappointment, they all escape the burning house.

In the Individual Vehicle discourses, the Buddha speaks of real suffering and its real cessation, and urges his hearers to abandon the one by attaining the other. He rejects any form of speculation that does not directly contribute to this goal. In the *Transcendent Wisdom* discourses, he rejects the previous teaching, saying it was intended for those persons too narrow-minded to conceive of the magnificent aims of the Universal Vehicle, in order to focus them on personal development and so broaden

[163] Much of this subsection appeared in an earlier version in the *Journal of the American Academy of Religion*, XLVI (January 1978), 19-39, under the title "Buddhist Hermeneutics," and is included here in modified form with their permission.

them to undertake eventually the more universal path of the bodhisattva. He teaches that suffering and its cessation are ultimately empty or unreal, although empirically real, and that their ultimate unreality must be understood in order to transcend empirical suffering. In the *Elucidation of the Intention* discourses, he disclaims the ultimate validity of both of the former teachings, giving a new instruction that purports to steer a middle course between the naive realism of the first type of instruction and the apparently nihilistic skepticism of the second type. Finally, in the *Mission to Lanka*, he disclaims the *Elucidation of Intention* type of discourse, saying he only resorted to it to render the picture of the ultimate reality less terrifying to the neophyte, to avoid either frightening him or letting him misconstrue it as nihilism.[164] And there are yet other hermeneutical schemes put forth by the Teacher himself in his various discourses.

Now, all of these have scriptural status, all of them are spoken by the Buddha, the "Teacher of Men and Gods." And yet they appear to contradict one another. How is one to decide these questions? To reject completely as false any teaching of the Buddha is traditionally a grave sin, known as "abandonment of the Teaching." And yet a practitioner must settle on one method, technique, or discipline. One can hardly set out to win liberation and enlightenment, or even to live properly in an ethical sense, until one has decided which of these teachings is right, and what ways lead to their realization. Thus, it is clear that the hermeneutical enterprise in this tradition is an essential part of practice on whatever level, an essential vehicle on the way of enlightenment. Since the various scriptural passages are contradictory on the surface, scriptural authority alone will not fully settle the hermeneutical questions, since the scriptures themselves are in a sense the basis of discussion. In the final analysis, rationality (*yukti*), inference (*anumāna*), or philosophical logic (*nyāya*) become the highest authority (*pramāṇa*) for deciding which scriptural passage is ultimately valid.[165]

Most commentaries on the *Essence* place it in the context of the four traditional hermeneutical strategies called the "Four Reliances," which are as follows:

a. rely on the teaching, not the teacher('s authority);
b. rely on the meaning, not the letter;
c. rely on the definitive meaning, not the interpretable one;
d. rely on (non-conceptual) wisdom, not on (dualistic) cognition.[166]

[164] Thurman, *Life and Teachings of Tsong Khapa*, pp. 150ff.

[165] See the great *Essence*, Prologue.

[166] These four reliances are common in Universal Vehicle texts. The earliest instance of their mention and detailed analysis is in Asanga's *Bodhisattva Stages*, where they are given in Skt., BBh, (Dutt, *Bodhisattva-bhumi*, pp. 175-76). There are some variations from the

a. Rely on the Teaching, not the Teacher

Tradition has it that the first words of the Buddha upon his enlightenment bespoke an outlook of pedagogical pessimism, to say the least: "Deep, peaceful, undefiled, luminous, and uncreated—I have found a Truth, like nectar of immortality! Though I teach it to them, no one will understand it—better I should stay alone in the forest in silence!"[167] If we took him literally here, we should be most surprised to see how much he actually talked to how many people. So how are we to interpret his words? How are we to understand the fact that his culminatory experience of supreme enlightenment appears not to have filled him with zeal to lead others thereunto? As we have discussed above, his enlightenment is not a revelation accorded him by any external agency or supreme being, but is rather the spontaneous flow of his own attainment of unexcelled perfect enlightenment as to the ultimate actuality of all things. Hence, his authority derives not from his investiture with a mission to save living beings, but rather from his own personification of full knowledge of reality. And his very first instruction to his fellows comes in his abstention from proclaiming any dogmatic truth, but indicating by indirection that the truth must be realized by each alone, that one cannot install another in enlightenment, that mere authority is not the vehicle to enlightenment.

Of course, he was not allowed to take his ease in the forest for very long; he was stirred, tradition has it, by his own great compassion, as stated in the *Questions of Rashtrapala*: "Living beings wander [from life to life] by their not knowing the way of voidness, peace, and uncreatedness–impelled by his great compassion for them [a Buddha] turns them [toward it] with the methods of his liberative techniques and with hundreds of philosophical reasons."[168] This verse makes several points. First, it is compassion that motivates a Buddha's teaching activity; he feels sympathetic about the troubles of living beings, he wishes they could feel at ease, as he does. Second, he does not see himself as installing them in liberation, but sees himself as turning them in the right direction. The progress is up to them. Third, he does not try only one way, but tirelessly invents different reasons and methods to help different beings.

Of all his liberative techniques, however, his teachings are most effec-

---

final Tibetan tradition, in order and terminology, though the thrust is the same. BBh pairs: *bhāṣitasyārtha . . . na vyañjanābhisaṃskārārtha; yukti . . . na pudgala; nītārtha . . . na neyārtha; bhāvanāmayena adhigamajñāna . . . na śrutacintāvijñānamātrakena.* Mvy pairs: *artha . . . na vyañjana; dharma . . . na pudgala; jñāna . . . na vijñāna; nītārthasūtra . . . na neyārthasūtra.*

[167] Skt. from *Lalitavistara* (Vaidya ed.), p. 286: *gambhīra śanto virajaḥ prabhāsvaraḥ prāptomi dharmo hyamṛto 'saṃskrtaḥ / deśeya cāhaṃ na parasyajane yannuna tuṣṇī pavane vaseyaṃ /.*

[168] See the great *Essence*, Prologue, n. 8.

tive. As Matrcheta wrote, "Buddhas do not purify sins with water, nor heal by laying on of hands, nor transmit their knowledge into others' minds; by teaching ultimate reality, they lead to liberation."[169] Now the verbal teachings of the Buddha, called the Holy Dharma (*Saddharma*), were collected after his final liberation in three collections (called three "baskets," *tripiṭaka*): "Discipline" (*Vinaya*), "Discourse" (*Sūtra*), and "Pure Science" (*Abhidharma*) collections. The third collection, the *Abhidharma*, consists of scientific texts that do not claim direct authorship of the Buddha. They are rather the systematic analyses of the major topics and categories employed by the Buddha in his Discourses, composed by the major disciples, with the Buddha's authorization. And yet these texts enjoy the same scriptural status as do those that record the actual sayings of the Buddha. Furthermore, if we note their correspondence with categories of practice, the "Three Educations" (*triśikṣa*) of Morality, Mind, and Wisdom, it can be seen that in some respects the *Abhidharma* collection is superior to the *Sūtra* collection. The latter merely records sermons given in the context of personal interviews, whereas the former represents the concentrated quintessence of all those sermons. Hence, the prefix "*abhi-*," which means "super-," is attached to Dharma as "doctrine," giving "Super-Doctrine." Certainly the early monastic schools devoted most of their energy to the study of the Abhidharma, considering it the elite teaching of greatest practical value. And it is the Abhidharma that contains the earliest forms of the hermeneutical concepts that we encounter in the *Essence*.

In sum, the first Reliance alerts us to the fact that Buddha's Dharma claims to stand on its own philosophical cogency, and does not require a personal authoritarianism for its legitimation. We are reminded of the famous goldsmith verse:

> O Bhikshus! Just as a goldsmith gets his gold,
> First testing by melting, cutting, and rubbing,
> Sages accept my teachings after full examination,
> And not just out of devotion [to me].[170]

b. Rely on the Meaning, Not the Letter

The three educations exactly correspond to the three collections, constituting the "practical Dharma" (*adhigamadharma*), whereas the latter constitute the "verbal Dharma" (*āgamadharma*). The point is that the essence of the teachings lies in the practice of them. This is a point that

[169] Famous verse from Matrcheta's *Praise of the Praiseworthy*.
[170] See the great *Essence*, Prologue, n.12.

is generally understood about Buddhism, at least conceptually, and we need not elaborate here. Important to note in this regard, however, is that again in the threefold classification, it is wisdom (*prajña*), here in its Abhidharmic meaning of analytic discernment of realities (*dharma-pravicaya*), that is preeminent, rather than meditation or ethical behavior, although all three are of course needed in combination. In the special context of the *Essence*, it is wisdom that is reached through the practice of hermeneutics. Finally, note that wisdom, presented as the culmination of the intellectual enterprise, as the perfection of analytic reason, the ultimate refinement of discriminative awareness, is considered a practice, considered to be experiential and realizational. Thus, again we see that there is no dichotomy between intellect and experience, the rational and the mystical, and so forth. Enlightenment as wisdom is perfected as the culmination of the most refined rational inquiry, not at the cost of reason.

c. Rely on Definitive Meaning, Not Interpretable Meaning

This brings us to the main subject of the *Essence*, for granted that the meaning is more important than the mere letter, how is the meaning to be decided? What kind of meaning is to be accepted? Here we are in the realm of hermeneutical strategies. It will be instructive to look at Buddhist hermeneutical strategies other than those covered by Tsong Khapa, to put the *Essence* in perspective.

The obvious and most simplistic approach to this question of interpretability and definitiveness is found in the Individualist Abhidharma tradition, where "definitive meaning" is defined as "meaning acceptable as literally expressed" (*yathārutavaśena jñatavyārthaṃ*), and "interpretable meaning" as "meaning acceptable after interpretation" (*niddhāretva grahitavyārthaṃ*).[171] Thus the two can be aligned merely with explicit and implicit teaching, that is, teachings wherein a teacher directly states his point, as opposed to those in which a teacher hints at his point, perhaps because his disciple is not ready for the explicit statement, or perhaps because the impact will be greater when indirectly approached. This interpretation of the two categories has been prevalent in Western scholarship to date, and most Buddhologists translate the terms simply as "implicit" and "explicit" meanings. Indeed, in the Abhidharma context these terms will do, but we shall see that they do not suffice in the Universal Vehicle context. A final point about this type of scheme is that it has no historical dimension. That is to say, a Buddha might switch from interpretable meaning statement to definitive meaning statement in

[171] De la Valée Poussin, *L'Abhidharmakośa de Vasubandhu*, V: 246 n. 2.

the same discourse, depending upon the context, and thus one would not necessarily consider the entire discourse to be interpretable in meaning or vice versa. This is a general characteristic of hermeneutical strategies that depend upon content rather than context.

Another strategy is set forth in the *Elucidation of the Intention*. This scripture was highly regarded by Asanga, as mentioned above, and he founded the hermeneutical strategy of the Idealist school upon it. The strategy is that known as the Three Wheels of Dharma (a Buddha's teaching is metaphorically called a "turning of the wheel of Dharma").

The "first wheel" is the Individual Vehicle teaching, explicating the truth of suffering of the samsaric life-cycle, and the truth of its cessation in Nirvana, and so on. It presupposes the truth-status of things, both mundane and transcendental, and hence is suitable for the realistically minded. The "second wheel" is the "Transcendent Wisdom" type of Universal Vehicle teaching, explicating the fundamental truthlessness of persons and things, which is called their absolute emptiness. It aims to free its disciples from attachments and ignorance, but can be dangerous if taken too literally and interpreted nihilistically. Therefore, the "third wheel" is the supreme one, being the teaching of the *Elucidation of the Intention* itself, known as the "subtly discriminative" type of Universal Vehicle teaching.

What are the "fine distinctions" drawn in the third wheel that make it "subtly discriminative"?

At stake primarily is the interpretation of the frequent statements of the Buddha in the Universal Vehicle Scriptures to the effect that all things are empty, often phrased as straight negations: that is, "there is no form, no feeling, no Buddha, no enlightenment, no non-enlightenment" and so forth. The Centrists supply the qualifier "ultimately" in all texts other than the *Transcendent Wisdom Hundred Thousand*, where the qualifier is in the text. But for the Idealists, Buddha considered this insufficient, and hence devised a scheme known as the "three natures" (*trilakṣaṇa*). Things have three natures, an imaginatively constructed (*parikalpita*) nature, a relative (*paratantra*) nature, and a perfect, or absolute (*pariniṣpanna*) nature. When all things are said to be "empty of intrinsic reality," this only applies to them in their imaginatively constructed nature; they continue to exist as relative things, and their ineffable relativity devoid of conceptual construction is their absolute nature. Thus, the insertion of the relative category between the conceptual (*parikalpita*) and the absolute (*pariniṣpanna*) insulates the practitioner against nihilism.

The following diagram illustrates the relation of the three natures or realities with the Centrist two-reality theory. Using this hermeneutical

Centrist *Two Realities*	*Idealist* *Three Natures*
superficial (*saṃvṛti*) conventional (*vyāvahārika*) reality (*satya*)	imaginatively constructed (*parikalpita*) nature (*lakṣaṇa*)
	relative nature (*paratantra lakṣaṇa*)
profound (*saṃvṛta*) ultimate (*pāramārthika*) reality (*satya*)	perfect (*parinispanna*) nature (*lakṣaṇa*)

scheme, the disciple of the third wheel can follow exactly what is said and attain the highest goal, free of the dangers of naive realism or nihilism, and thus this teaching is definitive in meaning.

This scheme of the *Elucidation of Intention*, fundamental for the Idealists, is both historical (as relating to Buddha's biography) and philosophical (as relating to the content of the teaching). It seems to present a rather logical progression from the elementary to the advanced. Tsong Khapa points out[172] that it treats the interpretability of the first two wheels differently, since the first wheel is plainly misleading as it stands, since things are not intrinsically real as they appear, and hence it must be justified purely as pedagogic technique. Thus, in teaching that wheel, the Buddha expounds the analysis of the elements of internal and external reality in order to convey the message of personal selflessness, leaving intact for the time the disciples' false notions concerning the truth-status of such objects. On the other hand, the second wheel is much closer to the definitive teaching, since it does not actually assume any naive realism about external objects, but only falls short of definitiveness by failing to demonstrate explicitly precisely how things are empty. However, when the distinctions brought out in the third wheel are understood, the second wheel can be understood in the light of its intention, and then has great value in practice, once one is safe from the danger of a nihilistic extremism. As Tsong Khapa says: "Thus [this Idealist system] states the *Mother Scripture* to be interpretable, not because its meaning is the indiscriminate ultimate unreality of all things, but because it requires further explanation, as it is not fit to be literally accepted, hence is not definitive as it is."[173]

Although this system is far more elaborate than the Individualist her-

[172] See the great *Essence*, Ch. II, Section 3.
[173] See the great *Essence*, Ch. II, Section 3.

meneutic given above, the literal acceptability or unacceptability of a scripture still seems to be the basic criterion for its interpretability or definitiveness. Indeed, the Idealist thinkers still did invoke scriptural authority for the establishment of literally definitive scriptures. They give three types of literally definitive scriptures: those that so establish themselves, those that are so established by another scripture, and those established both by themselves and by others, exemplified by the *Mission to Lanka* and the *Elucidation* itself, by the *Transcendent Wisdom Eight Thousand*, and by the *Transcendent Wisdom Eighteen Thousand*, respectively.

There are two main criticisms of this Idealist hermeneutic. First, mere literal acceptability is an inadequate criterion of definitiveness, since there are varieties of interpretability—some involve symbolism, some involve intention, some involve context, some merely involve restoring abbreviated expressions, and so forth. Hence the criterion is too rigid and simplistic to cope with the intricacies of the teachings. Second, for all its claims to fine analytic discrimination, three-nature theory and all, this hermeneutical strategy is still itself scripturally justified—it is, after all, the scheme set forth in the *Elucidation of Intention Scripture*. No abstract rational rule or criterion to distinguish between scriptural claims is disclosed, and hence the obvious circularity of invoking a scripture's own claim of definitiveness as proof of its own definitiveness. The great Centrists, especially Chandrakirti and Tsong Khapa, level these criticisms at the Idealist hermeneutic before setting forth their own strategies. But before we take these up, we should consider briefly the Chinese tradition, to put the Tibetan tradition in perspective.

Although Leon Hurvitz makes no mention of the fact in his important study of Chih I (538-597),[174] the first Chinese scholar to work on hermeneutics, the *Elucidation of Intention* was well known in China before his time, having been translated during the fifth century by both Gunabhadra and Bodhiruci.[175] It is almost certain that the ten schools mentioned by Chih I as preceding him in elaborating hermeneutical strategies were influenced by this scripture, as their main categories, "sign-doctrine" and "signless doctrine," correspond precisely to the *Elucidation* characterization of the first two wheels, respectively. However, according to Hurvitz, the *Mission to Lanka* and the *Great Final Nirvana* were the most important scriptural sources for the Chinese hermeneuticians, which discipline they called "doctrinal analysis."[176] Most important for Chih I was the parable of the five stages of milk in the *Great Final Nirvana*:

[174] L. Hurvitz, *Chih I* (Brussels: Institut Belge des Hautes Etudes Chinoises, 1962).

[175] Nanjio, *Catalogue of the Buddhist Tripitaka* (Oxford: Clarendon Press, 1883), 49 and 68, respectively.

[176] Hurvitz, *Chih I*, pp. 214ff.

> It is just as from a cow one extracts milk, from milk one extracts cream, from cream butter, from butter clarified butter, and from clarified butter the essence of clarified butter. The essence is the best of these. If anyone take it, his ailments shall all be cleared away, and all medicines that are shall enter his system. Good Sir! The Buddha is also like this. From the Buddha are extracted the twelve kinds of scriptures, from them are extracted the [Universal Vehicle] scriptures, from the [Universal Vehicle] scriptures are extracted the Expansive [*Vaipulya*] scriptures, from the Expansive scriptures is extracted the *Transcendent Wisdom*, and from the *Transcendent Wisdom* is extracted the *Great Final Nirvana*.[177]

Chih I's doctrine of the five periods follows this scriptural theme almost exactly, with the differences that Chih I reverses the order of numbers one and two, taking the general "scriptures" as the *Garland Scripture*, and that he includes the *Lotus Scripture* in the final category, which he takes to be supreme, as teaching the eternality of Buddhahood, the universality of Buddha-nature, and the happiness and bliss of Nirvana. Of course, the *Garland Scripture*, according to Chih I, has already conveyed this message from the moment of the Buddha's enlightenment, but only a very few were able to realize its meaning at that time.

Although this scheme, like the theory of the three wheels of Dharma in the *Elucidation*, is historical in using the Buddha's biography as framework, Chih I's analysis of it is somewhat more sophisticated. First, although each period is dominated by the teaching it is associated with, the other teachings may be given to some disciples during any of the periods, as the Buddha's capacities are ever adaptable to the pedagogical necessities. Second, Chih I coordinates the context-classification with a methodological classification, known as the "Four Methods of Conversion," which consist of: 1) the sudden teaching, which corresponds to the first period of the *Garland Scripture*, and which conveys instantaneous enlightenment to those with the necessary ability; 2) the gradual teaching, corresponding to the second through fourth periods, giving the stages of progress of Individualist and Universalist disciples; 3) the secret indeterminate teaching, which is Buddha's method of teaching a number of different disciples, unaware of each other, different teachings simultaneously; and 4) the express indeterminate teaching, which is Buddha's method of doing the same to different disciples in the same assembly. The two latter methods are practiced in the first four periods. Finally, Chih I also coordinates the historical context and the methodological scheme with a content scheme, known as the "Four Principles of Con-

[177] Ibid., p. 217 (terminology slightly modified).

version," namely: 1) the storehouse teaching, or the Individual Vehicle; 2) the Pervasive (Transitional) teaching, including the central way and general analysis counteractive to Individualist notions; 3) the Separate (Discriminate) teaching, which consists of Idealism; and 4) the Round teaching, which consists of the teaching of the ultimate nonduality of the world of common experience with the ultimate reality, the Body of Truth, the containment of infinity in an atom, of eternity in an instant, and so on. We may again note here that the first three principles correspond quite precisely to the three wheels of Dharma of the *Elucidation of the Intention*.

This latter classification of Chih I is further refined by Fa Tsang (643-720),[178] who pays less heed to the historical approach, although he does not contest it. He puts the last four of Chih I's categories into his first three, adds a new one that is a scriptureless, meditational school, later identified with Ch'an or Zen, and places his own beloved *Garland Scripture* with its miraculous view of reality at the very top. Fa Tsang was one of the greatest philosophers of all of Chinese philosophy, and his elaboration of a hermeneutic is extremely refined and detailed, dealing as it does with most of the major problems of the tradition. These schemes can perhaps best be conveyed in Table A.

In general, the Chinese tradition was basically scripture-oriented, as relatively few of the Indian technical treatises were translated into Chinese. Thus, although the hermeneutical strategies were extremely refined in some respects, the Chinese philosophers still based their work finally on a particular scripture: Chih I on the *Lotus*, Fa Tsang on the *Garland*, others on the *Pure Land*. The main thrust of their hermeneutics was to place their favorite scripture at the apex of a doctrinal pyramid. In contrast, of course, the Ch'an school eschewed the whole enterprise, purporting to cast aside ultimately all scriptures—although this is perhaps one of the most important of all hermeneutical strategies, certainly em-

[178] For Fa Tsang's hermeneutic, see Chang, *Buddhist Teaching of Totality*. I must mention an interesting coincidence, in connection with the hermeneutical thought of the great Chinese masters such as Chih I and Fa Tsang. In 1972, I entitled my doctoral dissertation on Tsong Khapa and his *Essences, "Golden Speech,"* for reasons I will elaborate further in the final section of this study. Dr. Neal Donner, in his doctoral dissertation on Chih I's *Mo-ho-chih-kuan* (*Extensive Serenity and Insight*), mentions that Chih I considered himself a teacher in the "Golden Mouth" (Chin. 金口 jin ko) lineage, inherited successively from Shakyamuni. This I learned upon reading that dissertation in 1977, and was delighted to find such even coincidental support for my intuitive choice of title. I would not go so far as to speculate on any direct historical connection between Chih I and Tsong Khapa, rather suggesting that they both are strongly inspired by the *Elucidation of Intention Scripture*, from which they make different moves, Chih I in the direction of the *Lotus*, Tsong Khapa in the direction of the *Questions of Akshayamati* and its recommended rationalism.

TABLE A. Scripture-Based Hermeneutical Schemes

Three Wheels of Dharma from the Elucidation of Intention	*Chih I's T'ien T'ai*		*Fa Tsang's Hua Yen*
	Historical	*Philosophical*	
1. Individual Vehicle, at Deer Park, for disciples, realistic, on Four Holy Truths.	1. *Garland Sutra*, at Bodhi tree for three weeks; sudden teaching.	1. Storehouse teaching (Individual Vehicle)	1. Individual Vehicle
2. Universal Vehicle, *Transcendent Wisdom*, at Vulture Peak, for Bodhisattvas, emptiness, signlessness, interpretable to avoid nihilism.	2. Individual Vehicle, twelve years; gradual teaching.	2. Pervasive teaching (Central Way)	2. Preliminary Universal Vehicle (including Chih I's historical Nos. 3 and 4).
3. Universal Vehicle, *Elucidation of Intention*, at Vaishali and in heaven, for bodhisattvas, three natures, fine distinctions, definitive in meaning, etc.	3. General Universal Vehicle to correct Individual Vehicle narrowness, eight years, gradual teaching.	3. Discriminate teaching (Idealism)	3. Final Universal Vehicle (including Chih I's No. 5, i.e., *Lotus Sutra* and *Mahāparinirvāṇa*).
	4. *Transcendent Wisdom*, twenty-two years, on emptiness; gradual teaching; secret and express indeterminate teachings in 1 through 4.	4. Round teaching (*Lotus Sutra*, etc.)	4. Instantaneous Enlightenment; Scriptureless school, later identified with Ch'an.
	5. *Lotus Sutra*, for eight years; *Mahāparinirvāṇa* for twenty-four hours, supreme teaching of universal enlightenment; sudden teaching again.		5. Round Doctrine of the *Garland Scripture*; one in one, all in all, one in all, all in one, etc.

inently rational, and perhaps closest in China to the Dialecticist Centrist practice.

The hermeneutical strategies of the Centrists of India and Tibet are mainly content-oriented. They too depart from a scriptural basis, though one with a difference. The study of these masters is the core of Tsong Khapa's *Essence*, and his own position fits into their tradition. In the *Teaching of Akshayamati Scripture* there is the following famous passage:

> Which scriptures are definitive in meaning? Which are interpretable? Those teaching superficial realities are interpretable in meaning. Those teaching ultimate realities are definitive in meaning. Those teaching various words and letters are interpretable. Those teaching the profound, the difficult to see, and the difficult to understand, are definitive. Those introducing the path are interpretable. Those introducing the goal are definitive. Those scriptures that teach as if there were a lord in the lordless, using such expressions as "self," "living being," "life," "soul," "creature," "person," "human," "man," "agent," "experiencer," etc., are interpretable. And those scriptures that teach the doors of liberation, the emptiness of things, their signlessness, wishlessness, inactivity, non-production, non-occurrence, living-beinglessness, lifelessness, personlessness, and lordlessness, and so on, are definitive in meaning. You should rely on the latter, not the former.[179]

Here we note a new hermeneutical strategy whose essence is the alignment of the categories of interpretable and definitive with the epistemological and ontological polarities superficial/ultimate or relative/absolute, that is, the two realities. This is a departure from the equation of the Idealists, namely, interpretable/definitive–implicit/explicit, since now a nonexplicit teaching that concerns itself with the ultimate reality is definitive in meaning, whether or not it requires some verbal interpretation due to its indirectness, figurativeness, or laconicness. On the other hand, a completely explicit statement that concerns itself with some superficial, mundane state of affairs is interpretable in meaning, even if it can be understood literally as it is, since it fails to communicate the ultimate condition of that state of affairs. For example, a statement such as "there is no Buddha," which often occurs in the *Transcendent Wisdom Scriptures*, is definitive in meaning. For its meaning, that in terms of ultimate reality there is no such thing as even a Buddha, concerns the ultimate condition of a Buddha, even though it requires the verbal interpretation of supplying the phrase "in the ultimate," since it does not mean that there is no such thing as a Buddha in the relative, superficial, conventional, and mundane realm. Indeed, such statements are often

[179] See the great *Essence*, Ch. III n. 2.

made by the Buddha himself, and obviously on the relative level he is making the statement, and thus has to be there. To give an example of the second type, the statement "the sprout is born from the seed" is interpretable in meaning, even though it is true on the relative, conventional level, since it fails to communicate the ultimate condition of the sprout and the seed, neither of which exist ultimately, although the sentence seems to affirm the hearer's false assumption that both do indeed have objective existence.

The philosophically minded will here object that there appears to be a lack of parity at work in the analysis of the statements. After all, the latter statement can be interpreted by supplying the qualification "conventionally" (just as we have supplied the qualification "ultimately" in the first case), which would then make the statement definitive in meaning, whereas the former statement could be said to be assuming the "reality" of a Buddha in the course of denying it. The source of this objection is the erroneous idea that there should be parity between the two realities, the relative and the absolute. In fact, the absolute takes precedence over the relative, not intrinsically or ontologically, as it were, since the "two" realities are precisely presented as a conceptual dichotomy, but epistemologically, since the mind's orientation toward the absolute is more beneficial and liberating than is its orientation toward the relative, which after all is the creation of misknowledge. Thus, the statement "there is no Buddha" contains the negation of the truth-status of a Buddha, and points to his ultimate status which is truthlessness, or realitylessness, or emptiness. The directionality of our cognition here is correct and does not need further correction, even though a word might be supplied here and there, since it aims at the absolute, as it were, aimed by an absolute negation. On the other hand, the statement "the sprout is born from the seed" confirms our habitual instinctual reification of the intrinsic reality of sprout, seed, production, and so on, and brings us no closer to the ultimate; hence the directionality of our cognition is wrong. We are confirmed in our "naive realism" about persons and things, in our habitual clinging to their apparent objectivity, and although the interpretive correction with the supplied qualification "conventionally" may give us pause by having us think "ah, that means not ultimately," this is secondary, and the statement remains interpretable according to this hermeneutical scheme.

In this system, the "interpretation" involved in "interpretable meaning" does not mean any sort of trivial verbal interpretation or qualification, but only that type of interpretation that brings out the ultimate relevance, meaning, reality of things. And the only type of verbal statement that does not require such interpretation is that which is absolutely negative, an "absolute negation" in the logical sense of a strict negation of its negatee without establishing or implying anything else. To apply this scheme to the three wheels of Dharma, the middle wheel of Dharma, that of the *Transcendent Wisdom*, is seen to be the most definitive, although the third and even the first contain some statements that can be accepted as definitive. Such flexibility is there because on this interpretation, the subject matter—the concern, superficial or ultimate—is all-important. This, Tsong Khapa states, is the position of Nagarjuna and Chandrakirti, among others.

Not all Centrists were agreed on the precise ramifications of this principle, of course. Of the two main subschools, the Dogmaticist and the Dialecticist, the former drew back from the rigorously critical position of the latter and attempted to syncretize the Centrist system with either the Traditionist system or the Idealist system. Thus Shantarakshita and Kamalashila took the interesting position that in a strong sense both the second and third wheels of Dharma were definitive in meaning.[180] Indeed, Kamalashila states that it is the *Elucidation of Intention* interpretation of the *Transcendent Wisdom* message of pure negation that brings out its definitive meaning. For, he reasons, the *Transcendent Wisdom* negations are often laconic, failing to mention the qualification "ultimately," and the *Elucidation of Intention* type of interpretation through the three-nature theory enables us to remember the constant need to assume the qualifier "ultimately" as understood. Thus, a nihilistic skepticism, or "repudiation" (*apavāda*), is avoided by negating the literalness of the negations, and a naive realism, or "reification" (*samāropa*), is avoided by negating the truth-status of the relative. On this latter point, he differs from the Idealists, who believe the relative nature to be ultimately real, as distinct from the imagined nature, which is unreal. The type of "reality" involved here is called by the Idealists "intrinsic identifiability" (*svalakṣaṇasiddhatvaṃ*), and is distinguished from "objective reality" (*svarūpasiddhatvaṃ*). Kamalashila reorganizes somewhat these different types of reality status by denying the ultimacy of the relative and perfect natures, that is, seeing the relative/absolute formula as a conceptual, mentally constructed dichotomy, while affirming the intrinsic identifiability of both of them on the conventional level, as he thinks this necessary to avoid the extremism of repudiation (*apavāda*), of nihilistic skepticism. Thus, not only does he use the *Elucidation of Intention* to interpret the *Transcendent Wisdom* in order to discover the latter's definitiveness (that is, not to prove its interpretability as did the Idealists), but he also uses subtle logical reasoning to interpret the *Elucidation of*

[180] See the great *Essence*, Ch. IV, Section II.

Intention itself, taking the emptiness of imaginatively constructed things, defined as "identity-unreality," to mean that the relative and the perfect lack ultimacy, instead of to mean that the relative and the perfect gain their ultimacy when distinguished from the ultimately unreal imaginatively constructed, which is how the Idealist takes it, and is what is explicitly said in the *Elucidation* itself. In essence, the Idealist Dogmaticist tactic is to reconcile Idealism with Centrism by accepting the three-nature theory as conventionally, not ultimately, valid.

Chandrakirti, perhaps the greatest of the Indian Dialecticist philosophers, was dissatisfied with any such attempt of the Dogmaticists. He considered the *Teaching of Akshayamati* statement to mean just what it said, that only statements concerning the ultimate are definitive, and that all statements concerning any aspect of the superficial, conventional, social, relative reality are interpretable. Thus, the whole interpretive scheme of the three natures is unacceptable to him and is itself interpretable, and he will not allow any intrinsic identifiability in the relative at all.

d. Rely on (Nonconceptual) Wisdom, Not on (Dualistic) Consciousness

The fourth step of the Buddhist hermeneutical movement expresses an unswerving dedication to practice. Thus, even after having discerned the definitive meaning of the scriptures as consisting of an absolute negation of the truth-status, intrinsic reality, selfhood, and so on, of all things, relative and absolute, having discerned it with a critical consciousness that is called "intellectual wisdom" (*cintāmayīprajña*), one still has not concluded the hermeneutical enterprise. In fact, it cannot be concluded until enlightenment is attained, until intellectual wisdom concerning the ultimate has been combined with one-pointed concentration, which combination leads to the holy knowledge of the spacelike equipoise (*ākāsavatsamahitajñāna*), the meditative wisdom (*bhāvanāmayīprajña*), the nondual intuition. Thus, even though one has reached a profound intellectual knowledge of the definitive meaning of the scriptures, one must go on cultivating this knowledge until it permeates one's deeper layers of consciousness. Of the utmost significance is the fact that at no point is the intellectual study merely cast aside. On the contrary, reason is pushed to its utmost and held there by the cultivated power of concentration (*samādhi*).

To rephrase this in hermeneutical terms, we must remember that the hermeneutical rule that the definitive teaching is that which concerns the ultimate is itself a teaching concerning the superficial. It is a teaching concerning teachings, it is not itself a pure negation pointing to the ultimate reality. Thus, although Chandra aligns himself with it, he does not base his position on it as dogmatic authority. Authority for him is reason, and reason is consummated only in enlightenment.

To make this point in another way, although conceptual, analytic wisdom is absolutely indispensable to attain a correct cognition of ultimate reality through an accurate understanding of the absolute negations that are definitive in meaning, it will not produce the experiential transformation called "Enlightenment," unexcelled and perfect, unless it is combined with a systematically cultivated one-pointedness of mind. Ultimate reality eludes encompassment in any concept, no matter how hallowed, and hence the hermeneutician would betray his avocation if he were to rest forever on the intellectual plane, no matter how refined his understanding. Thus, the Buddhist hermeneutical tradition is a tradition of realization, devoid of any dichotomy between intellect and intuition. Authority here gives way to intellect, yet never lets intellect rest in itself, as it were, but pushes it toward a transformative nondual experience.

It is remarkable how this hermeneutic of the Dialectical Centrist tradition (that is, the alignment of interpretable and definitive with the conventional and ultimate realities, respectively), coming as it does as the culmination of a philosophical development of many centuries, as the supreme refinement of the critical analysis that leaves no dogmatic attitude unscathed, uses such rigorous reasoning to affirm the unswerving practicality at the heart of the tradition. It is further worth noting, contra notions of Zen as "nonrational mysticism," that this hermeneutic is identical in an exact manner with the principal strategy of the Ch'an/Zen tradition, even though that school is rightly called by Fa Tsang, as mentioned above, the "scriptureless school." For although the Centrists may seem at first glance to be based on the *Transcendent Wisdom*, the "Mother of All Buddhas," what finally does it mean to be "based on" a scripture that constantly repeats the litany, "There is no Buddha, no Dharma, no attainment, no attainer, no ground, no ungrounded . . ." and so on? As Vimalakirti says to Manjushri: "Manjushri, when something is baseless, how can it have any root? Therefore, all things stand on the root which is baseless."[181] Thus, to stand on the *Transcendent Wisdom* is to stand ultimately on groundlessness, that is, to belong to the "scriptureless school." As for the important citation above from the *Teaching of Akshayamati*, this is of course a scriptural passage and is taken by the Centrists as authoritative, yet if we follow the sense of it, it self-destructs as dogma, stating that teachings about teachings, which include its own herme-

[181] Thurman, *Vimalakīrti*, p. 58.

neutical statements, are *all* interpretable in meaning, and that only teachings about absolute, ultimate reality, that is, pure negations such as "all things are empty of intrinsic reality," and so on, are definitive in meaning. Finally, when we examine these two traditions, Centrism and Zen, in the light of the above taxonomy of hermeneutical strategies, they emerge as not at all "mystical," as scholars have so commonly misinterpreted them, but as rationalistic, non-authoritarian, and experientially pragmatic, whereas the various types of scripture-based traditions emerge as "mystical" insofar as they remain dogmatically attached to sacred authority in the final analysis.

Nagarjuna, in the climactic chapter of his *Wisdom*, in which he analyzes the concept of "Nirvana" and finally equates Nirvana and samsara, anticipates the objections of those who will consider him to have made some authoritarian statement about Nirvana by listing a version of the "Fourteen Unpronounced Verdicts"[182] of the Buddha and concluding with the following extraordinary verse: "The quiescence of all perceptions and fabrications, that is the Highest Bliss! No doctrine at all was ever taught by any Buddha to anyone."[183] Instead of settling for the usual platitude about Nagarjuna's alleged "mysticism" here, we can clearly see this hermeneutically as his steadfast refusal to allow any verbal formula to be misconstrued as authoritarian dogma.

Precisely the same point is made forcefully by the great Ch'an Master Pai Chang (720-814) to his disciple Nan Ch'uan (747-834), as recorded in the *Blue Cliff Record*:

> Nan Ch'uan went to see Master . . . Pai Chang.
>
> Chang asked, "Have all the sages since antiquity had a truth that they haven't spoken for people?"
>
> Ch'uan said, "They have."
>
> Chang said, "What is the truth that hasn't been spoken for people?"
>
> Ch'uan said, "It's not mind, it's not Buddha, it's not anything."
>
> Chang said, "You said it."[184]

Pai Chang here tested his advanced friend with the fundamental hermeneutical question, probing to see if Nan Ch'uan still felt there was any dogmatic doctrine, even an esoteric one. Ch'uan bravely sallied forth by

[182] The *avyākṛtavastunī*, namely, that: 1) Buddha exists after death, 2) does not, 3) both does and does not, 4) neither does nor does not; 5)the world is finite, 6) infinite, 7) both finite and infinite, and 8) neither finite nor infinite; 9) the world has a beginning, 10) has not, 11) both has and has not, and 12) neither has nor has not; 13) the self is the same as the body, and 14) the self is different from the body.

[183] Skt. *sarvopalambhopaśamaḥ prapañcopaśamaḥ śivaḥ / na kiṃcitkasyacitkaścid-dharmo buddhena deśitaḥ //.*

[184] T. and J. C. Cleary, *The Blue Cliff Record* (Boulder: Shambhala, 1977), pp. 181ff.

standing up for what he took to be the tradition, thinking to get off easily since it was a "traditionless tradition" wherein the truth was nothing at all, yet somehow still there, and still possessed by the sages. Chang powerfully refutes him with the humorous reference to the fact that this was indeed not "unspoken truth" at all, since Ch'uan himself had just easily said it. Ch'uan realizes he has over-stepped, becomes insecure, and attempts to defer to Chang's authority.

> Ch'uan said, "I am just thus. What about you, teacher?"
> Chang said, "I am not a great man of knowledge either; how would I know whether it has been spoken or not?"
> Ch'uan said, "I don't understand."
> Chang said, "I've already spoken too much for you."

Whatever other depths or surfaces of meaning may be here, for our purpose one thing is abundantly clear. Pai Chang completely refuses to set himself up as authority for his disciple, and leaves him entirely on his own at the conclusion of the encounter. The commentator Yuan Wu interestingly relates it to the above idea of Nagarjuna, saying, "Old Shakyamuni appeared in the world and in forty-nine years never said a single word."

Tsong Khapa urges us to "listen with reverence" to the philosophy of enlightenment and yet we have discovered that the hermeneutical act of listening can only be performed by means of pure reason. The definitive teaching turns out ultimately to be sheer silence, an absolute negation of the ultimate expressibility of reality. And yet we must never mistake this silence of non-imposition of authoritarian dogma about the absolute for a portentous or referential silence that joins in the non-rational mysticism of the reificational, naively realistic use of language to refer mysteriously to essences and substances. It is a silence rather that by its pure negation of anything beyond us affirms our absoluteness and perfection, affirms our own reason's ability to understand for ourselves without being dominated by any outside authority. It is a silence of restraint on the part of the Buddhas, a refusal to put a barrier between ourselves and them, as if only they knew and we did not, and they had to tell us what It is. They go the crucial step beyond even telling us "That Thou Art!"[185] affirming that, if we are That Place in reality, just habitually fooling ourselves that we are not, we do not need to be told where we are. This is the ultimate encouragement for us to open our eyes to our actual complete adequacy. And it is for that inspiration that we should have reverence. And we can

[185] The *Mahāvākya*, or "Great Statement" of the Upanishads, the basis of the monistic nondualism of Shankara and other great Vedantic philosophers.

listen to the unimpeded eloquence that is ultimately never apart from that ultimate silence, really listen without greed for finding escape from ourselves, without perplexity from any assumption that it is beyond our capacity, and with joy in the knowledge that the listening is part of the transformative path. We will return to this more fully in the final section.

3. With the Critical Discrimination that realizes

Here we must locate the process of study and reflection upon the import of the *Essence* in precise psychological terms, in relation to the phenomenology of the path to enlightenment. For this, we may briefly outline the main points of Tsong Khapa's "Silver Book," as we may call it, bearing in mind the story recounted above.[186] *The Great Transcendent Insight* is the final one third of his *Great Stages of the Path to Enlightenment*, written under a silver sky full of the Sanskrit twenty emptinesses. It is an enormous and difficult work in its own right. Fortunately, it was summarized by Tsong Khapa himself, in his *Middle Stages of the Path to Enlightenment*,[187] written in 1417 in his very last years, upon special request for a master summary of the longer version. In what follows, we will condense still further his *Middle Transcendent Insight*, which will allow the student of the *Essence* to locate his contemplations in terms of the sophisticated psychology of the path of development toward enlightenment.

Tsong Khapa begins the section by discussing the relation of critical, analytic meditation to one-pointed quiescence meditation, to which the previous section of the book was devoted.

> We should not be satisfied with merely that Quiescence wherein the mind, thought-free, stays where purposefully focused on a single object, even where we also have clarity free of dullness and the especially beneficial joyous bliss. We must cultivate Transcendent Insight by generating the wisdom that is unmistakenly certain of the import of Thatness.[188]

Given our general sense of "meditation" and its goals, Tsong Khapa's statement challenges us as directly today as ever it did his contemporaries.

[186] That is, the "transcendent insight" section of the LRC.

[187] *Lam rim chung ngu*, TKBS, vol. pha. For a full translation of that section of that work, see Thurman, *Life and Teachings of Tsong Khapa*. Parts of the following section appeared in the *Tibet Journal*, 4 (Winter 1978) "Tsong Khapa on Analytic Meditation," pp. 3-16, and are included here by kind permission of the Library of Tibetan Works and Archives, Dharamsala.

[188] LRC, TKSB, pa, ff. 337b-338a.

Why indeed should we not be satisfied with the clarity and bliss of one-pointed samadhi? Tsong Khapa in answer quotes the *King of Samadhi Scripture*:

> Those mundane persons who cultivate samadhi
> Yet do not rid themselves of the notion of self
> Get very agitated when their afflictions return. . . .
> Yet if they discern precisely the selflessness of things
> And if they meditate on that exact discernment,
> That causes the attainment of Nirvana;
> No other cause whatever will bring peace.[189]

Current notions of "meditation," as *dhyāna*, samadhi, and so on, have been formed by popularized religious disciplines, such as Yoga, Vedantistic TM, the Americanized *Vipassana*, and pop Zen. The goals of these simplified disciplines must be considered somewhat escapist by Universal Vehicle standards. That is, whether they call it *nirvikalpasamādhi* (thoughtless trance), *nirguṇabrahman* (unqualified godhood), *anupadhiśeṣanirvāṇa* (remainderless nirvana), or *satori*, these disciplines seek permanent escape from the ills of existence in a transcendently altered, radically "other," state of blissful peace. Thus "meditation" for them is mainly contentless and one-pointed, since the ultimate contentlessness is their goal, the supreme anaesthetic their choice over present and future pains. The Universalists, including Unexcelled Yoga, rigorous nondualism, and real Zen, on the contrary, are critical of the notion of transcendence as a state, define "absolute" as "a-relationality," and thus consider that "entrance into the absolute" is a contradiction in terms. They affirm the terrible, wonderful insight of the nondualist *Transcendent Wisdom Scriptures*, that there is *nowhere to escape*. Nirvana becomes *apratiṣṭhita*, "unlocated," "stateless," and Nagarjuna even insists that Nirvana is no different from *samsara*. In this situation, it is natural that wisdom (*prajña*) should be more important than meditation (*dhyāna*), that a Buddha's perfect enlightenment should consist of perfect compassion (a perfect body), as well as perfect knowledge (a perfect mind), and that meditative soteriology (*śamatha*) should require indispensably the discipline of philosophical analytic insight (*vipaśyana*).

Tsong Khapa first refers to the definitions given in the *Elucidation of Intention*, that "He who practices quiescence and transcendent insight will be freed from the bondages of negative conditionings and of signs;"[190] and comments that:

[189] TKSB, pa. f. 338b.
[190] LRChung, pha, f. 132a.

> "Negative conditionings" here refers to instincts underlying mental processes, which instincts increasingly generate a distorted subjectivity. "Signs" refers to the continuous habitual adherence to mistaken objects which reinforce those instincts. The former are abandoned by transcendent insight, and the latter by peaceful quiescence.[191]

This psychological analysis shows clearly why both one-pointed quiescence meditation and discursive analytic insight meditation are necessary for genuinely transforming enlightenment. Quiescence concentration counters our habitual bondage of involvement with the infinite variety of perceptual and conceptual signs, and transcendent insight drills into the deeper layers of consciousness to expose, reform, and transform the subconscious instinctual patterns that anchor those habits. Tsong Khapa illustrates this with a famous metaphor from Kamalashila's *Stages of Meditation*,[192] where attainment of enlightenment is compared to discernment of the figures of deities painted on the walls of a dark temple. To see them clearly, one needs a light both very bright and also protected from any disturbing wind. Without the light of analytic insight, Reality will not be discerned no matter how long one may dwell in one-pointed, thought-free concentration. And without the windshield of calm quiescence, the flickering flame of even the accurate conceptual understanding of selflessness will never burn long or brightly enough to give the full picture of Reality. Thus, quiescence and insight are mutually indispensable.

Tsong Khapa gives elaborate instructions in the technique of concentrative quiescence. The practice is analyzed into nine states of mind arranged in order of development, and cultivated by bringing into play six mental forces and four conscious attitudes. The connection between these can best be represented in a diagram (Table B).[193]

Choosing an object, these nine states can be progressively cultivated, and one-pointed concentration and transic absorption in that object can be developed. The question then becomes how to choose the object. There is a sophisticated typology of altered states of consciousness, and if one chooses these higher states of immeasurable love, compassion, joy, equanimity, infinite space, infinite consciousness, nothingness, and the state beyond consciousness and unconsciousness,[194] in that order, one can

[191] TKSB, pha, f. 132a-b.

[192] *Bhāvanākrama*.

[193] See Hopkins, *Meditations on Emptiness*, p. 645, for a diagram similar in layout, but different in terminology.

[194] The realm of pure form is divided into the four main sectors of immeasurable love, compassion, joy, and equanimity, each of which is, respectively, subdivided into three, three, three, and eight realms. These are Brahma-heavens of superior bliss, though none of them represents a stage of liberation in and of itself. The Beatific Bodies (*Saṃbhogakāyā*)

TABLE B. The Technique of Concentrative Quiescence

Nine States	*Six Forces*	*Four Attitudes*
1. Focus	Learning	
		Forced control (1 and 2)
2. Steady focus	Reflection	
3. Repeated focus		
	Mindfulness (3, 4)	
4. Increased focus		
5. Discipline		Intermittent control (3, 4, 5, 6, 7)
	Alertness (5, 6)	
6. Calm		
7. Quiescence		
	Effort (7, 8)	
8. One-pointed concentration		Unbroken control
9. Equipoised trance	Expertise	Natural control

become totally absorbed into those form and formless realms, physical and mental heavenly states. But these realms are considered to be somewhat dangerous, as they are genuinely totalistic experiential realms, and yet even they are temporary, as imaginatively constructed as this desire realm or gross sense realm of differentiated objects. Therefore, it is considered essential to cultivate transcendent insight alternatively with the early stages of quiescence practice, in order to remain clearly aware of the relativity and conventionality even of heavenly states from the beginning, lest one become overwhelmed experientially, mistake them for absolutes, and become trapped by them into losing track of the liberative central way. We should note that the experiential realm of nothingness is included here, indicating that even without liberation from the reificatory habit pattern of the unexamined mind, one can experientially attain a direct experience of nothingness, which is clearly not the realization of emptiness. This is psychological evidence for the important Centrist insistence that emptiness is not nothingness, and must never be confused with it.

coexist with the highest Brahma forms in the highest form realm heaven, Akanishtha. "Beyond" it lie experientially the formless realms, as listed in the text. It is interesting to note that, even in Individual Vehicle sources, Buddhas always attain Buddhahood from the form realm, not from the formless realms, although they range into the latter at will, in the process of focusing their extreme concentrative stability. Phenomenologically, it is important to gain a good picture of these realms from Abhidharma sources in order to know clearly what Nirvana *is not*, according to the Buddhist psychology of altered states.

Turning to transcendent insight, first Tsong Khapa separates the analytic meditations into two basic types; the analytic investigation of the five aggregates, twelve experiential media, and eighteen experiential elements,[195] and the critical inquiry into the twofold selflessness. The former is the cultivation of wisdom of the Individual Vehicle Abhidharmic scientists, the latter that of the Idealist and Centrist philosopher-yogis. The aggregates, media, and elements are convenient schematizations of mental and physical phenomena that enable the investigator to come to a rigorous understanding of reality, especially by failing to discover therein any independent, self-sufficient, personal self, which liberates him from his instinctual reification of one. Although the process of this investigation is worked out with great thoroughness and sophistication, its level of subtlety is not very great according to the Universalists, since it pays very little attention to the objective selflessness of the aggregates, media, and elements themselves.

Far more subtle is the inquiry into the twofold selflessness, or emptiness of persons and objects. Tsong Khapa, in another work, divides that process into five stages, which connect with the Universalist typology of the five paths. These can be schematized as in Table C.[196]

From this scheme, which itself could be the subject of an entire work, we should take note of several things relevant to the *Essence*. The first stage is indispensable for anyone wishing to enter any of the paths. Therefore, philosophy is the first stage of practice of the transformative meditative path. Further, the second stage is still within the sphere of the advanced reaches of philosophical deliberation, and the third stage is in the range where philosophical penetration has become combined with

[195] These are the central Abhidharma schemata of the psychosomatic complex, used in critical insight meditation in the Individual Vehicle schools. The following diagram may be useful.

Eighteen Elements		
	Twelve Media	
sight	visibles	visual consciousness
hearing	sounds	audial consciousness
smell	scents	olfactory consciousness
taste	tastes	gustatory consciousness
touch	textures	tactile consciousness
mentality	ideal objects	mental consciousness

[196] Sources for this table are: TKSB, pa, f. 173b2; 'Jam dbyangs bZhed-pa, *Grub mtha chen mo*, cha, ff. 326ff(27); Hopkins, *Meditations on Emptiness*, Ch. VI; A. Berzin, "Lam Rim Man Ngag" (Ph.D. dissertation, Harvard University, 1972), pp. 550ff. See also diagram reproduced in *Tibet Journal*, 4 (Winter 1978), p. 16.

TABLE C. The Five Stages

1. Initial cultivation of experience of philosophical view in simulated transcendent insight 2. Simulated transcendent insight with simulated quiescence	Accumulation Path of store of intuitive wisdom
3. Real insight and real quiescence	Experiential Path, heat, peak, tolerance, triumph
4. Direct realization of Thatness	Insight and Meditation Paths, bodhisattva stages to eighth
5. Transcendent insight in the context of deity yoga in the Unexcelled Yoga Tantras	Bodhisattva stages eighth-tenth and perfect Buddhahood

single-minded concentration, moving toward the moment of triumph through the stages of intensity, peak, and tolerance of the Experiential Path (*prayogamarga*). This also shows that a systematic development of concentration is essential to reaching the conclusion philosophy aims for, the "complete clarity" wherein all the perplexities are resolved. The reason for the need for concentration is that the misknowledge that causes the naive realist's reification of the unsatisfactory world of the alienated life-cycle is instinctually embedded in the unconscious, not only contained in misleading conceptual, philosophical theories and world views. Therefore, the critique of erroneous views opens the intellect to the true nature of "truthless" reality, but this openness must be sustained and focused in order to penetrate deeper into the underlying structures of our perceptual and conceptual instinctual habit patterns. Alternatively, without a precise conceptual treatment of distorting views at the beginning, no amount of concentration will liberate us from instinctual misknowledge. Indeed, it will work the other way, and bring us into the heightened experience of distortion, the absolutist reaching experiential ratification of one form or another of an alien absolute, and the nihilist reaching experiential ratification of his view of nothingness. Neither can ever become aware of the power of his own reificatory instincts without the critical wisdom of philosophical investigation. And once they "experience" what they believed on faith or by cultural conditioning, they are usually stuck, at least for that lifetime. Therefore, the path of philosophy, as represented in the *Essence*, is an indispensable part of the path to enlightenment, not at all an intellectual sidetrack.

Tsong Khapa was himself faced by just the same sort of objection to the urgency of rigorous critical analysis and philosophical inquiry. His contemporaries objected that since the instinctual, unconscious self-habits are the root of the samsaric life-cycle, how does the philosophical inquiry that removes intellectual, conscious self-notions manage to eradicate them? Tsong Khapa answers that instinctual self-habits also hold things to exist as if real in themselves and not merely established on the strength of conventions. Thus, "although such mental habits do not hold their objects through analysis of the meaning of conventional expressions (as do intellectual mental habits), if the objects thus held were to exist in fact, they would have to be discoverable by the analytic cognition that analyzes the manner of existence of the referents of conventional expressions."[197] Thus, philosophical analysis exposes the pattern of objective existence unconsciously reified by instinctual self-habits and, having exposed it, refutes its applicability to reality. The meditative, sustained application of this criticism to the instinctual unconscious habits is thus the path of overcoming them. Therefore, Tsong Khapa says, one should not imagine that "texts negate only intellectual habits with their objects."

Although the *Essence* and other Centrist and Idealist philosophical works are written as general inquiries into philosophical issues, they presuppose the framework of the path of transcendent insight, in which the problems they investigate become especially relevant at certain junctures. Thus, Nagarjuna's *Wisdom* is said to have begun with its refutation of production because, of the ten equalities used as meditative themes during the sixth bodhisattva stage on the path of meditation (included in stage 4 in the scheme above), the equality of all things due to their lack of intrinsically real production is the easiest to begin with.[198] Of course, Nagarjuna is not writing only for bodhisattvas at such an advanced stage. But he pursues his philosophical investigation in the pattern of a simulated transcendent insight meditation to enable the student to begin to develop the wisdom he will need when ultimately he does reach such advanced stages. Thus, much of the discussion of the *Essence*, when brought out of the book into one's sustained reflection, can be fitted into the framework of transcendent insight. This becomes apparent when we outline this framework and give some examples.

[197] See the great *Essence*, Ch. V, Section 1.

[198] Chandrakirti makes this remark in the MA, ad. k. 5 (de la Vallée Poussin, *Madhyamakāvatāra par Chandrakīrti*, St. Petersburg: Biblioteca Buddhica, 1907, pp. 80-81), and Tsong Khapa mentions it in the *Essence*; see the great *Essence*, Ch. VII n. 3.

The philosophical analysis that frames transcendent insight may be divided into two movements: 1) the determination of personal selflessness, and 2) the determination of objective selflessness. Each of these in practice contributes to the cultivation of both types of wisdom: 1) the spacelike equanimous wisdom, and 2) the illusionlike aftermath wisdom. The first of these is cultivated by concentrated focus on the reasonings contained in the four keys: 1) ascertainment of the negatee, 2) ascertainment of logical concomitance, 3) ascertainment of impossibility of true unity, and 4) ascertainment of impossibility of true plurality. These latter two keys are replaceable by other reasoning patterns, such as Nagarjuna's "diamond smithereens" (six keys) or the royal reason of relativity (three keys), or the sevenfold analysis of the chariotlike self (nine keys).[199]

"Ascertainment of the negatee" (key number one), is most important in that the meditator will never know if he has succeeded in negating a false object if he does not know what the object would be like in the first place. Of paramount importance here is to keep clear that we are not looking for our empirical, everyday self, but rather for a fixed, unique, independent, intrinsically identifiable, substantially real self, which is still "our self." To assure ourselves that this is worth looking for, since we may nowadays be philosophically pragmatist enough to see the futility logically, we must examine our behavior toward persons and events and especially toward our own identity when it is threatened and so on, to see that we habitually assume in ourselves the presence of just such a fixed identity. Our preoccupation with "I"-"Me"-"My"-"Mine" arises

[199] The first two keys are invariably keys one and two following in the text. After those two are established, the negatee identified and the commitment to concomitance made, the "diamond smithereen" reasoning begins, following the pattern at the beginning of the *Wisdom*: "Things are not produced from self, from other, from both self and other, and from neither self nor other; because self-production would be pointless and endless, other-production would allow everything to produce everything at all times uncontrollably, production from both would entail the flaws of both previous possibilities, and production from neither would be causeless, hence a non-production." The royal reason of relativity also begins after the first two keys are in place, as follows: "Things are empty with respect to any intrinsically identifiable reality; because they are relative." And the sevenfold analysis uses the example of a chariot, beginning with the third key: " 'Chariot' and its parts ['self' and aggregates] are not the same, not different, 'chariot' is not in the parts, parts are not in the 'chariot,' 'chariot' does not possess the parts, is not the conglomerate of the parts, and is not the configuration of the parts; because sameness would obviate the need for the special designation 'chariot,' and difference would require that 'chariot' lack the function of the parts, and that it be perceived apart from them, and so on." The diamond smithereen reasoning is not analyzed at length in the *Essence*, but is examined in this section further. The reason of relativity is expounded in the great *Essence*, Chs. III and VII. The sevenfold analysis is briefly recounted in Chapter VII. See Hopkins, *Meditations on Emptiness*, Ch. V, pp. 491-522; Ch. VII, pp. 538-57; Ch. VIII, pp. 558-608, for an excellent and detailed presentation based on 'Jam dbyangs bZhed-pa's *Grub mtha chen mo*.

TABLE D. Orders of Self Posited by Schools

	Personal Self		*Objective Self*	
Schools	*gross*	*subtle*	*gross*	*subtle*
Analysts, Traditionists	permanent, unique, independent	self-sufficient	none explicit	none explicit
Idealists	permanent, unique, independent	self-sufficient	independent external objects as such	intrinsically real designative bases; subject-object dichotomy
Idealist Dogmaticists	permanent, unique, independent	self-sufficient	subject-object dichotomy	truth-status of objects
Traditionist Dogmaticists	permanent, unique, independent	self-sufficient	none	truth-status of objects
Dialecticists	self-sufficient	intrinsically real, objective, identifiable person	none	intrinsically real, objective, identifiable objects

from this unconscious assumption. Thus, the first key in a sense establishes the relevance of the inquiry, as well as its target.

The extensive analysis in the *Essence* of the notions of the various schools concerning the measure of the negatee can be brought under this heading in practice. Is the personal self an independent, self-sufficient, substantial self-notion, which when refuted leads to selflessness? Is this a gross or a subtle selflessness? What is the difference between intrinsic identifiability, intrinsic objectivity, intrinsic reality, and so on? It will serve the reader very well in keeping track of these discussions to have some schematization of the various orders of self as posited by the various schools at the gross and subtle levels (Table D).[200]

[200] This table is based on Hopkins, *Meditations on Emptiness*, p. 470, although I have adapted it to the terminology and context of the *Essence*. His monumental doctoral dissertation is based on the Dialecticist section of 'Jam-dbyangs bZhed-pa's *Grub mtha chen mo*, an important work by one of Tsong Khapa's successors in the direct lineage of the *Essence*, as well as in the same scholastic tradition. 'Jam-dbyangs bZhed-pa's work, in Hopkins' literal translation and exposition, is naturally, therefore, complementary to the *Essence*, and can be studied in connection with the *Essence* by those who wish to wrestle strenuously with the profundities and subtleties of central way philosophy. An initial difficulty for a scholar who works in English is that each translator has his own set of key

TABLE E. Types of Status (*siddhatvaṃ*)

I	*II*	*III*	*IV*
ultimate, absolute (*paramārtha-*) real (*tattva-*) authentic (*samyak-*)	truth- (*satya-*)	intrinsically identifiable (*svalakṣaṇa-*)	intrinsically real (*svabhāva-*) objective (*svarūpa-*)

It can be seen clearly that the progression among the Individualist and Universalist schools is in terms of subtlety, moving from the critical realism of the Analysts to the radical conventionalism of the Dialecticists. This scheme can be used for reference during study of the *Essence*, as Tsong Khapa pursues the distinctions between the various schools on these crucial points.

A further schematization concerning the identification of the negatee will be of great help to the student of the *Essence* in keeping track of the various qualifications used to describe the status of objects examined in critical insight investigations of the various schools. The diagram of the main types of absolute or ultimate status under consideration by "rationality analytic of ultimacy" is as in Table E, developed from P. J. Hopkins' brilliant layout in his dissertation.[201]

The Dialecticists do not discover any of these types of reality status in any object, ultimate or conventional, absolute or relative. The Dogmaticists negate all of them ultimately, but affirm types III and IV as necessary to conventionally valid things. The Idealists consider all ultimate and relative things as possessing all of these types of status, negating their presence in imaginatively constructed things, except for certain kinds of imagined things, such as space. These types of reality-status are often combined, as the subtletly deepens in the dialogues between and within the schools; for example, "intrinsically identifiable, intrinsically real, objective status" (*svalakṣaṇasvabhāvasvarūpasiddha*) may be predicated of something. But this need not be too confusing if the basic categories are kept in mind.

---

terms. But these can be linked through the glossaries each provides, and is not an insurmountable barrier to uncovering the texture of thought in either work.

[201] This table is based on Hopkins, *Meditations on Emptiness*, p. 483, and my use of it here is a salute to his ingenuity. It is the neatest way I can think of to present the different types of reality-status clearly and concisely. His whole section, Ch. V, pp. 478-86, on the "measure of the negatee" in Dialecticist critical insight philosophy and meditation, is extremely helpful in getting this first key clear.

The types of status in column I are derived ontologically in terms of transcendent experience; that in column II, also ontologically, with some weight on linguistic referentiality. Intrinsic identifiability (column III) is epistemological in derivation, with a strong awareness of the role of language in world-construction. The types in column IV are derived epistemologically, with a strong concern for the groundedness of valid perceptual experience. All of them are crucial for understanding the precise scope and subtlety of penetration of insight meditation, and the table should be referred to during the study of the *Essence*. Disagreement over the range of presence of these status-types actually defines the views of the different schools, which determines how an individual practitioner of any of them identifies the negatee, which itself determines the depth and completeness of the transcendent experience attainable.

The second key, the key of ascertainment of concomitance, is startling to us at first due to the popular idea of the opposition of meditation and logic. For the second key amounts essentially to a commitment to binary logic, to the law of the excluded middle, a commitment to respect the outcome of the inquiry by an a priori affirmation of its rigorous framework. If we now seek the "true self" as our own, we must find it as either truly the same as us (that is, our observable empirical aggregates of mind and body), or as truly different (that is, as a soul that is other, but still relates to our observable empirical aggregates). If we cannot find it in either mode, then we must accept that *it is not there*, not allowing ourselves the way out that "well, it must be there somehow in some impredicable fashion." In short, there is no third alternative, no illogical mode of being allowable for a logically absolute entity. This is, of course, a commitment we make to the structure of our language and conceptuality. This commitment made by Buddhist philosopher-yogis such as Nagarjuna, Chandrakirti, Padmasambhava, and Tsong Khapa should challenge once and for all our popular notions that meditation is somehow "irrational mysticism." It is just like the two-reality theory. Rather than a mystical theory arguing for the absoluteness of the absolute, it is a logical theory acknowledging the binary structure of our language, and hence the relativity even of the concept of the arelational absolute.

All of the investigations in the *Essence* concerned with the role of validating cognitions, perceptual and inferential, the relation of language to the inexpressible ultimate as well as to the objects of the ordinary relative world, and indeed the implications of the above for the hermeneutical scheme of interpretable and definitive, with its bearing on the relation between teaching and practice or realization, can be brought into individual reflection under the heading of this key. For the many theories that tend to rob language and reason of their transformative power are elaborated under the impetus of the instinctually governed self-habits or objectivity-habits, which resist exposure of the fallaciousness of their reified objects and generate an intuitive sense of the rightness of their own patterns of constructing and perceiving the world. This key therefore functions to block the hold over us of these uncritical intuitions and to prevent us from indulging the apparent counter-intuitiveness of the dictates of critical wisdom concerning emptiness and relativity, until, through continuous cultivation, our wisdom itself becomes our intuition in the direct experience of emptiness. The analogy of the drunk whose vision is distorted and sees two moons in the sky is very useful here, thanks to the ingenuity of the Eleventh Dalai Lama.[202] Before we have even begun the philosophical inquiry into the nature of reality, we are like a person so drunk he has no idea what planet he is on, who intuitively feels there are two moons there when he sees them. When we have the second key in place, we are like the drunk who thinks, "Ah, either there are two moons there, or this is my drunken hallucination. I'll ride my rocket over there and see. If I don't find two, then I'll know thereafter there is only one, even though I'll see the two until I sleep it off." And, when we have begun to develop the intuition of critical wisdom after some mastery of even simulated transcendent insight, we are like the drunk who sees the two moons, yet thinks automatically, "Ah, there's the moon!" without having to go through any further analytical inquiry. The further issue as to whether a Buddha can ever "get drunk" is more complicated than it seems, since, although all his instinctual habits of distorted perception are gone, Buddhist scholars would not wish to say that he is incapable of seeing the world as imagined by those who still suffer under misknowledge; else how could he interact with them through compassion and assist them in their own enlightenments? But this goes beyond the second key.

Once this key has been ascertained, we begin the actual search for the self as either truly the same as or truly different from the five aggregates (*skandha*): form, sensation, recognition, emotional creations, consciousnesses. To follow Tsong Khapa's presentation of the analysis:

Thus, if self and aggregates were a single entity with intrinsically real

[202] This comes from a verse of mKhas-grub rGya-mtsho, the Eleventh Dalai Lama, quoted in dKon-mchog 'Jigs-med dbAng-po's commentary on Rol-bai rDo-rje's *Song of Mother Emptiness*, translated by R. Thurman with Paul Nietupski, *Vajra Bodhi Sea*, Vol. VI, Series 13, Nos. 60-66, San Francisco, 1974. The full quotation is: "When the analysis of the authentic view is perfectly accomplished, the mere arisal of the appropriate objects in mental or sensory consciousness brings forth a cognition certain of those objects' emptiness, without requiring any further reason or proof. For example, a person whose senses are addled derives certainty of one moon from the actual appearance of a double moon in his sight—on the strength of his prior knowledge of the lack of two moons."

status, three [refuting] faults accrue. The first is that there would be no point in asserting a "self," since if the two were intrinsically really established as a single entity, they would never be at all differentiable; since the two being absolutely established as a single entity could necessarily never appear as different to a cognition that perceived them. The reason for this is that, while there is no contradiction for a false, superficial thing to appear differently from the way it really is, such a difference contradicts a thing's truth-status, since a truly established thing must really exist in just the way it appears to any [valid] cognition. Thus, we assert the intrinsically objective status of the self in order to establish an agent for the appropriation and discarding of the aggregates, and that is no longer plausible once the self and the aggregates become a single entity. As [Nagarjuna] argues in the *Wisdom*, "When you assert that there is no self except for habitual appropriation; [I answer] if the appropriation [function] itself were to be the self, then your self does not exist." The second fault is that the self would become a plurality. If the self and the aggregates were really the same, then just as one person has many aggregates, so he would come to have many selves. Or else just as the self would become many, so there would be the fault that the aggregates would become one; as [Chandrakirti] says in the *Introduction to the Central Way*, "If the aggregates were the self, as they are many, so the self would become many. . . . "

The third fault is that the self would become endowed with creation and destruction, as (Nagarjuna) says in the *Wisdom*: "If the aggregates were the self, then it would become endowed with creation and destruction," i.e., just as the aggregates are endowed with creation and destruction, so the self would become subject to creation and destruction, since the two are a single entity. If you think this merely is an acceptance of the momentary creation and destruction of self or person each instant, while admittedly there is no fault in accepting this merely conventionally, the opposition here asserts the intrinsic identifiability of the person, and so must assert intrinsically objective creation and destruction of that person, which assertion has three faults.

The first [Chandra] states in the *Introduction Commentary*: "What is intrinsically identifiably disparate by being intrinsically identifiably earlier and later cannot logically relate later to earlier, since the priority and posteriority are independently, self-sufficiently established, it is not suitable that they should depend on each other. . . . "

The second [fault accruing to assertion of intrinsically identifiable creation and destruction] is the fault of missing the effects of action committed, and it amounts to the impossibility of bringing the agent of action and experiencer of effect together on the basis of the mere "I." The third fault, that of experiencing an evolutionary effect without committing any action, is the absurd consequence of a single individual continuum having to experience all the effects of actions accumulated by all other individual continua. These two faults are [argued] on the key point that if the person is really objectively established, his prior and later moments may not logically constitute a single continuum. And [Nagarjuna concurs] in the *Wisdom*, "If man and god were [truly] other, then they would not properly constitute [successive states of] a single process."

Now, one wonders what are the faults in the self being intrinsically established as other than the aggregates. [Nagarjuna states] a fault in the *Wisdom*: "If [the self] is other than the aggregates, then it would not have the character of the aggregates." If the self were intrinsically other than the aggregates, then it would not have the created character of the aggregates, of production, duration, and destruction, just as a horse is established as different from an ox when it does not have the character of an ox. Here you might think, "Well, is not that [self as radically other] how it is?" But, [such a self] could not logically serve as the object which is the basis on which the instinctual [mental] habit designates the convention of "self," since [such a radically other self] is uncreated, just like a sky-flower or like Nirvana. Furthermore, if [the self] existed with a [radically] other nature than that of bodies such as "physical," etc., then it should be apprehensible thus [with that other nature], just as body and mind are apprehended differently. But since there is no perception of self in that way, it does not exist as a separate thing. [Nagarjuna concurs] in the *Wisdom*: "The self is not logically something other than appropriation; if there were something other without appropriation that could yet be perceived it would be logical, but there is no such object." And [Chandra concurs] in the *Introduction*: "Thus, there is no self other than the aggregates, because you cannot establish the perception of anything other than the aggregates."[203]

This example of reasoning in the third and fourth keys can be applied against any of the various types of gross and subtle notions of self given in the scheme above. There are also many other reasonings used by the different schools. In fact, all the reasonings in the *Essence*'s sections on each school that give their "chief reason to negate the negatee," can be brought into one's own reflections in the place of these third and fourth keys, whether there be but one key, or up to five. The same "key" pattern may be used in the context of the objective selflessness, as well. Indeed,

[203] LRChung, pha, ff. 178aff; see Thurman, *Life and Teachings of Tsong Khapa*, pp. 108-112.

in the *Essence*, the investigation of objective selflessness is much more emphasized, according to the Dialecticist distinctive specialty of holding that the instinctual, addictive level of misknowledge habituated to a sense of personal self is itself the objective self-habit, and therefore, even personal self-habits cannot be transcended without transcending objective self-habits ultimately. This leads them to another of their special positions, namely, that the Individual Vehicle Saints themselves do achieve the realization of objective selflessness, although it is only hinted at by the Buddha in the Individual Vehicle, never taught explicitly or extensively. In opposition to all the other Universal Vehicle schools, the Dialecticists consider that the advanced Individualist practitioner needs no more than the hints dropped by the Buddha to attain real sainthood. Otherwise, the Dialecticists feel, one repudiates too severely the attainment of the Individualist Saint, and, in effect, abandons the validity of the Individual Vehicle altogether, which is the cardinal sin of abandoning the efficacy of the Buddha's liberative technique.[204]

Having fully mastered these reasonings against the existence of the intrinsically identifiable self, that is, having sought it in the above ways and having not been able to find it, and having coupled that nonfinding with the commitment to the binary structure of logical possibility, a certitude of personal selflessness arises that is not just a mere assertion but a logically established inference. We proceed to apply the same analysis to the habitual property-notions (*atmīyagraha*) and easily cognize the absence of intrinsically identifiable property, just as the cognition of the nonexistence of the eye of a son of a barren woman follows closely upon the cognition of the nonexistence of the son of a barren woman. We continue to concentrate on the conclusive nonfinding through the four keys until omnidissolving analytic attention has penetrated all scannable subjective objects as well as objective objects, when there is an experience of the loss of even the conventional mere "I," the empirical ego as it were, which is no cause for alarm because there is no more any intrinsically real loss than there ever was any intrinsically real self. However, this experience itself, by no means the final goal, is called the spacelike equanimous knowledge of emptiness of personal self, and is an important stage in that it is the first nonconceptual taste of the nonsubstantiality of all habitual frames of reference. It is not by any means any sort of "leaping into the void" or even a very full cognition of emptiness (which, always remember, *equals* form/relativity, and so on, and does not underlie them), and is compared to feeling like water poured into water.

Now we arise from the spacelike equanimous wisdom of selflessness

[204] See the great *Essence*, Ch. V, Section 1B,b.

into the illusionlike aftermath wisdom, where all interdependent phenomena appear as transparent and dreamlike, yet where the causality-involvement of the conventional, designatory "I" is inescapable, and hence the commitment to compassionate cultivation of one's skill in liberative technique unshaken. Tsong Khapa has summarized this stage in his *Concise Stages of the Path* as follows:

> Cultivating both emptinesses, the spacelike equanimity and the illusionlike aftermath, it is praiseworthy to follow the transcendent way of the bodhisattvas with the integrated practice of wisdom and liberative technique.[205]

Tsong Khapa clarifies with arguments the meaning of the "aftermath illusory wisdom," and distinguishes between the subjective hallucinationlike experiences incidental to various kinds of mental concentration that so easily lend themselves to misinterpretation as ultimate goals and the precise philosophical awareness involved in this wisdom.

> Although not even an atom of such things as persons being born or death-migrating can be found to resist analysis when investigated by the reasoning analytic of ultimate reality, we must adhere to an understanding of the doctrine of the arisal of good and bad effects in regard to illusory things. Otherwise, by the force of gaining stability in mere one-pointedness of mind unfocused on anything at all, not cultivating a focus on an impeccable view of ultimate actuality, when we arise, apparent things such as mountains are no longer massively solid as before but arise indistinctly like fine smoke or like a rainbow. But this is not the arisal of illusoriness stated in the scriptures. It is a perception of [things'] emptiness of a certain coarse impenetrability, and not the perception of the voidness of intrinsic reality of even those apparent objects; because "absence of massiveness and solidity" is definitely not properly the import of "emptiness with respect to intrinsic reality." Otherwise, it would be impossible for truth-habits to function when rainbows, etc. were involved, and it would be impossible for cognition realizing truthlessness to arise where a solid object was concerned. . . . Then what is the unmistaken import of "illusory" here? For example, just as there is certitude of the falseness or illusoriness of [magic] horses and elephants based on the eye-consciousness' seeing the magic horses and elephants and the mental consciousness' certitude that the horses and elephants do not exist as they appear, so there is born a certitude of the false appearance or illusoriness of a person

[205] Verse from Tsong Khapa's *Lam rim bsdus don*. For translation of full text by A. Berzin, see Thurman et al., *Life and Teachings of Tsong Khapa*, pp. 59-66.

> based on both the undeniable appearance of that person in conventional cognition and the ascertainment by philosophical cognition of that person's emptiness with respect to objectively established intrinsic reality.[206]

The rigorous nonduality here is also noteworthy, in that there is no reification or romanticization of any state of dissolution, there is no artificial goal set for the philosopher-yogi, such as that he must "attain ego-loss," wipe out his naughty "I," and so forth. Rather he is encouraged to accept as incontrovertible the everyday conventional sense of "I," while attaining simultaneously the rational certitude of its intrinsic nonreality. Thus, the cultivation of these two simultaneous cognitions, after having attained through accurate analysis the spacelike trance wisdom, is the "aftermath dreamlike wisdom."

This understanding of personal selflessness, in terms of lack of individual, self-sufficient self, is still coarse in some respects, at least according to the Dialecticist Centrist school as upheld by Tsong Khapa. Having attained it, the usual practice is to take impersonal objects into consideration and engage in similar analyses, in order to realize objective selflessness. Things are divided into created phenomena and uncreated noumena. The "created" category is divided, in accord with Abhidharmic science, into physical (*rūpa*), mental (*citta*), and anomalous creations (*viprayuktasaṃskāra*), and the "uncreated" category is in turn divided into space, the two cessations, and emptiness itself. These seven items are then contemplated with analyses similar to that in the four keys above until it is realized that all are merely dependently designated.

Of all the analytic reasons, Tsong Khapa relies most heavily on the "royal reason," the reason of relativity, which serves as the supreme method of realizing subtle objective selflessness. He states:

> There are two main resistance points that obstruct the pure view: one is the reificatory view or absolutist view that has a fixed orientation toward truth-habits that hold to the truth-status in things. The other is the repudiative view or nihilistic view, which goes too far by not assessing the measure of the negatee and becomes unable to incorporate in its system the certitude about the cause and effect of relativity, losing all ground of recognition about anything such as "this is it" and "this isn't it." These two views are completely abandoned by the negation of intrinsic reality based on the reason that brings certitude that from such a causal condition such an effect occurs. For the ascertainment of the import of the thesis radically refutes absolutism, and the ascer-

[206] LRChung, pha, ff. 184ff.

tainment of the import of the reason radically refutes nihilism. . . . This reason of relativity has two forms—being "dependent production" and "dependent designation."[207]

Tsong Khapa praises this "royal reason" as the distinctive specialty of Nagarjuna and Aryadeva and their followers, as well as of the teaching of the Buddha.

Tsong Khapa then moves to an elaborate discussion of the two realities, ultimate and superficial, mentioning their actual identity and conceptual difference (*ngo bo gcig dang ldog pa tha dad*), their verbal meanings, their subcategories, and so forth. He particularly focuses on the false view (as held, for example, by rNgog-lo above) about the two realities which holds that the ultimate reality is not an object for any cognition, even a Buddha's. This objection reminds us of contemporary interpreters of the two realities who forget that they are categories of "knowables" (*jñeya*), facts, and by calling them "epistemological" rather than "ontological," end up saying "really there is only one reality." Tsong Khapa forcefully argues that while *ultimately* ultimate and superficial, Nirvana and samsara, are not different, *superficially* (conventionally, empirically) they are completely opposite. Just as conventional realities are objects for mundane cognitions, so ultimate realities are objects for transcendent cognitions, such as the holy wisdom of spacelike equanimity, the Buddha's inconceivable wisdom, and so on. Otherwise, the Body of Truth would be merely talk, the bodhisattvas' efforts would be in vain, the Buddhas would be unperfected, and so forth. Tsong Khapa thus reminds us that, although *ultimately* the "transcendent" is no more existent than the "mundane," *empirically* it is no less existent, and hence through cultivation of transcendent insight, we can come to direct awareness of it empirical factuality.

Tsong Khapa concludes this "Silver Book" by exhorting the student to master swiftly the ordinary Universal Vehicle path of—essentially—renunciation of the misknowledge-dominated life-cycle, love and compassion for all sentient beings, and transcendent wisdom concerning the true nature of reality. He urges him then to find a qualified guru and to plunge into the ocean of the Unexcelled Tantras. This emphasizes the point that, in the above scheme of "five stages of transcendent insight," stage one is indispensable.[208] Tsong Khapa is insistent that there is no alternative to the cultivation of the profound view of emptiness, that

[207] LRChung, pha, ff. 186bff.

[208] Thus, even the fifth stage of transcendent insight, that combined with the deity yoga of the Unexcelled Yoga Tantras, can be entered upon only after the first stage of critical, philosophical reflection has been mastered and a conceptual authentic view developed.

there is no better method than that of following the ways of the Champions, and that claims of the Tantrics that their "Great Perfection" and "Great Seal"[209] teachings are superior and render the Centrist way obsolete are fallacious, since neither go beyond emptiness; although both are based on the authentic view, their methodology of cultivating the "critical discrimination" he urges is less refined and effective. However, once the central way has been intellectually mastered through unerring simulated transcendent insight, stages two, three, and four can indeed be combined with the type of transcendent insight cultivated in Unexcelled Yoga Tantra deity yoga practice to accelerate greatly the progress through those stages. This is not the place to go into deity yoga, more than to say that the imagination, the mental function that constructs the world of misknowledge and hence that function which the Idealists and Dogmaticists make such efforts to correct, is harnessed to a positive end in Unexcelled Yoga.[210] At the same time that the falsely constructed dichotomous world is cut open by the diamond saw of wisdom, the constructive imagination itself is rechanneled into reconstruction of a higher-order conventional reality. The key point of the psychology underlying this remarkable process is that in Unexcelled Yoga transcendent insight, the objects appearing falsely in the superficial realm, that is appearing intrinsically objective when they are merely relativistically established, can be perceived conventionally simultaneously with critical wisdom's perception of their emptiness. In the other types of transcendent insight, conventional reality is perceived by misknowledge-governed perceptions, and only alternatively is ultimate reality experienced by intuitive insight. Critical wisdom penetrates apparent intrinsic objectivity, conventional objects themselves disappear temporarily under the pressure of ultimacy-analytic rational cognition leading into spacelike samadhi intuition, to redawn in aftermath illusory intuition, like the two moons of the drunk, or like the reflection of the moon in water. Subsequent progress proceeds by means of an oscillation between these two intuitions; hence it is relatively slow, as the wisdom side and the compassion side cannot be cultivated at the same time.

Therefore, the Unexcelled Yoga Tantra transcendent insight is more nondualistic and more effective in its procedure. Relativity and emptiness are simultaneously cognized, in what is called the indivisibility of appearance and emptiness (*snang stong dbyer med pa*). This is important

[209] Tib. *rDzogs chen*, central teaching in the Nyingma school, and *Phyag rgya chen po (Mahāmudrā)*, central in the Kagyupa school. For a more detailed discussion of the views involved in these teachings, see "Essence of Nectar" (my translation) in Thurman et al., *Life and Teachings of Tsong Khapa*, pp. 213ff.

[210] See Tsong-ka-pa, *Tantra in Tibet*, for a discussion of deity yoga.

even in the *Essence*, which without explicitly bringing up the context of the Vajra Vehicle works in this vein in the context of the "equivalence of emptiness and relativity." Through knowledge of relativity, absolutism is avoided; through knowledge of emptiness, nihilism is avoided. As Tsong Khapa says in his *Three Principles of the Path*: "While appearance eliminates absolutism, emptiness eliminates nihilism, and you know emptiness manifest as cause and effect. Then you will not be deprived by extremist views."[211] This is also how the "royal reason of relativity" presents the special transcendent insight of Unexcelled Yoga Tantra, through the cultivation of the wisdom penetrating the simultaneous mutual affirmation of emptiness and relativity.

In sum, the "intellectual discrimination that realizes" is not to be relegated merely to some preparatory plane of practice, and the study of the *Essence* can be confidently pursued as central to the supreme path.

4. The Thatness of the Teaching

"Thatness" unavoidably brings up the issue of ultimate truth. The Sanskrit *tattva* is literally "that" plus "ness," an abstract noun made from the demonstrative pronoun and the abstract suffix.[212] It can be translated as "truth," "reality," even "fact," depending on the context. I assign "Thatness" to its use in the direct sense of "absolute reality." It emphasizes the immanence of the absolute, its being right "there" as reliable truth before one. It is contrasted with "Suchness" (*tathatā*), which emphasizes the elusiveness and transcendentality of the absolute. It is "there," but not just as "that," as only "such," or "like that," always having something more to it than can be conceived or perceived. The "Thatness of the Teaching" is thus the compellingly liberative Truth of the Teaching of Enlightenment, the *Sad Dharma* of all Buddhas, its ground of absolute reality which it manifests in all its transcendentality, as immanent before the student.

But what is this "Thatness?" What sort of claim is made about it? Why should this teaching have more "Thatness" than anything else? How is it known? Can it be proved? Or only proclaimed? If it is totally immanent in everything, are we already enlightened, and so why should

[211] This verse from Tsong Khapa's seminal *Three Principles of the Path*, full translation available in Thurman et al., *Life and Teachings of Tsong Khapa*, and in G. Wangyal, *Door of Liberation* (New York: Lotsawa, 1978).

[212] *Tattva*, Tib. *de nyid* or *de kho na nyid*, can mean "truth," "reality," or "principle," though in Buddhological translations it is often rendered as "Thatness." It indicates the absolute as immanent, contrasted to *tathata* (Tib. *de bzhin nyid*), "Suchness," which indicates the absolute as ever elusive, or transcendental.

we worry about it? If it is totally transcendent, what can it have to do with our situation? If it is some mixture of the two, what is "absolute" about it? How can it affect our knowledge, expression, and action? These are the crucial questions for philosophy.

Many modern interpreters of central way thought have pondered these issues, and their verdicts may be summarized as falling into two camps. One camp has taken the transcendentalist option, considering "Thatness" to be the same as "Suchness" in referring "mystically" to an inexpressible Absolute, utterly beyond all human faculties, expressions, and reasons, merely pointed out as object of "mystic," that is, non-rational or trans-rational, contemplation. Reason must be discarded, they urge, and a courageous "leap of faith" is essential for communion or even union with this Absolute.[213] The other camp has taken the "immanentist" option, considering "Suchness" to be the same as "Thatness," both expressing critiques of all Absolutes, born of a sophisticated epistemology and analysis of logic and language. For them, the goal is to realize that there is no "Goal," to still the over-reaching aspirations of human reason, and to settle in the absolute relativity of the everyday, making the best of it from birth to death. Reason must be harnessed to its proper object, shorn of its pretensions, and the courage to live life must be drawn from other human resources, from culture, community, and faith affirmed by sheer will, disdaining the scaffolding of reason.[214]

The former hold the message of the central way to be that *samsara is Nirvana*. The latter hold it to be that *Nirvana is samsara*.

Either of these positions may be partially correct. Each has its own evidence, arguments, and advantages. But both share the view that, according to the central way, philosophy as such, as the rational, critical pursuit of ultimate understanding, is a failure. Its scope is ultimately limited by its final unreliability. It cannot take us to absolute truth. There is an ineluctable barrier in the nature of reality itself. If the absolute is finally an utter transcendence, we must leap blindly beyond on sheer courage born of the despair of reason. If the absolute is finally an utter non-existence, we must shut off reason and have the will to carry on, playfully perhaps making meaningful the meaningless as we go along.

Against these two interpretations—options widely favored even in India and Tibet as well[215]—Tsong Khapa has the audacity to argue that

[213] See T. Stcherbatski, *Conception of Buddhist Nirvana* (Delhi: Motilal Banarsidass 1980); T.R.V. Murti, *Central Philosophy of Buddhism* (London: Allen & Unwin, 1955). They represent the modern version of the Jo-nang position.

[214] See F. Streng, *Emptiness, A Study in Religious Meaning* (New York: Abingdon, 1967); M. Sprung, ed., *The Two Truths in Buddhism and Vedanta* (Dordrecht: Reidel, 1973). They represent the modern version of the position of Jayananda, or rNgog Lotsawa.

[215] See notes 213, 214 above.

the Absolute, the Ultimate Truth, Reality, can be proven, expressed, and experienced, and that human reason can thus serve as the solid ground for ethical, creative, and liberative action in the world. He affirms this interpretation as in accordance not only with Dignaga's perception of the Buddha as "personification of reason" (*pramāṇabhūta*),[216] and with Maitreyanatha's perception of him as "Real Connoisseur" (*arthajño*),[217] but also with Nagarjuna's salutation of him as "Supreme Philosopher" (*vādatāṃ varaṃ*). Nagarjuna would have to be considered cynical and insincere to praise Shakyamuni as the best of philosophers, of *Vādis*, those who stand for something and speak for something, if he merely meant either that the best philosopher only uses philosophy to show its inadequacy to Truth or that he merely abandons philosophy for linguistics, sociology, or theology.

But it is not enough to uphold Nagarjuna's good faith and sincerity. As Tsong Khapa's claim is that Thatness is susceptible of rational proof, we must examine his argument critically to see if it holds together. And before that, we must examine the evidence for the two previous interpretations, then establish against them that there is such a thing as "rational proof" for Centrist philosophers.

The first camp above, the monistic absolutists, base their interpretation on a number of passages of Nagarjuna's *Wisdom* (MMK), as well as on statements of Aryadeva in his *Experientialist Four Hundred* (CŚ) and comments by Chandrakirti and others. Since the *Wisdom* is fundamental to all Centrists, we will attend to those passages. In his verse of salutation at the beginning, Nagarjuna refers to "the quieting of fabrications, the supreme bliss," as the goal of the Buddha's teaching, which clearly affirms the soteric aim of Centrist thought. "Fabrication" (*prapañca*) refers to the imaginative construction, or reification, of realities that do not exist in themselves. By the critique of all metaphysical speculation, language is seen as inapplicable to reality, fabrications are stilled, and the supreme bliss of union with the real Absolute is attained. Nagarjuna further refers to "the peace of the quieting of views" (MMK, V, 8) and to "emptiness, the transcendence of all views" (MMK, XIII, 8), where "view" is a metaphysical view, all of which must be abandoned, and yet this is not just capitulation to the world but rather a transcendence into a real emptiness. "Liberation occurs by ending addiction and evolution, which come from thought, which comes from fabrications; and fabrications terminate in emptiness" (MMK, XVIII, 5). This absolute union may be

216 See above, n. 12.

217 Maitreya begins his *Ornament of the Universal Scriptures* with this unique epithet, otherwise unattested in the Buddhist literature, which usually prefers *Dharmajño* or *Sarvajño* for the Buddha. See our forthcoming translation of the MSA.

inexpressible and beyond reason, but it is still surely "there," and is the Highest Good; "where the range of mind ends, the expressible ends. [How like the early Wittgenstein's statements in the *Tractatus*!] Ultimate reality is unoriginated and undestroyed, just like Nirvana" (MMK, XVIII, 6). And this absolute reality is attained experientially, is personally experienced by a Buddha, who is its personification, in a sense; "Those who mentally fabricate the Buddha, who is beyond both fabrication and termination—they all are ruined by their fabrications and do not behold the Transcendent Lord (*Tathāgata*)" (MMK, XXII, 15). There really is a "beyond," inexpressible as it may be, and through ceasing to clutter it with fabrications, a "mystic" can transcend them and occupy that "beyond" as a Transcendent Lord, one who has "gone beyond to Suchness" (*tathatāgata*). From that position, a sage can ultimately only maintain a mystic silence, pointing beyond by saying nothing. "The quieting of all perceptions, the stilling of all fabrications, that is the Highest Bliss! The Buddha never taught any doctrine to anyone" (MMK, XXV, 24). And the path to attainment of the referent of this silence is only to be trodden by the mystic, after abandoning the metaphysical speculations of philosophy; "when misknowledge is terminated, mental creations will not evolve. And the termination of misknowledge is accomplished by intuitive wisdom and its contemplation" (MMK, XXVI, 11). These passages contain the main soteric message of the *Wisdom*, the absolutists maintain, and its other analyses of all attempts at philosophical formulation of the workings of causation, perception, meaning, and even transcendence and liberation are fundamentally antinomial in nature, meant to lead to the despair of reason needed to impel the mystic leap into union with the absolute.

The other camp, the existential relativists, adopt a more subtle position philosophically, and are slightly more difficult to distinguish from the Centrists themselves. They base their interpretation on a different set of passages from the *Wisdom*. They discount the apparent referentiality of the soteric passage above by saying that the "beyond" does not refer to an ontological beyond, a pure, undifferentiated "space" of liberation, but rather to a temporal "beyond," the space of living achieved after a fundamental epistemological insight into the workings of language and cognition. They see Nagarjuna as concerned with epistemology, not ontology, and ultimately with the semantic limitations of language itself.

In the opening salutation, they point to the antinomies cited by Nagarjuna: "no destruction, no creation, no cessation, no permanence, no coming and no going, no unity and no plurality." They understand the critical analyses of all forms of expression to explode the pictures created by language, showing their failure to correspond with factual processes in the world. Thus, "if the 'going' is in the 'being gone through,' then two goings are the consequence; that underlying the 'being gone through' and that which is the going" (MMK, II, 5). "Two goings being consequent, so are two goers, since a 'going' is impossible without a 'goer' " (MMK, II, 6). Thus, the inconsistencies inevitably attendant on the habitual assumption of the intrinsic meaningfulness of words collide with our habit, and induce an epistemological change, whereby we come to realize that our words, the fuel of our fabricative thoughts, are empty, that is, fundamentally meaningless. This position is unassailable philosophically, they claim, since "when one argues by means of emptiness and an opponent tries to answer, none of his statements serve as answers, since his proofs always remain to be proven" (MMK, IV, 8). Thus the basic message of the *Wisdom* is that language is antinomial, ultimately meaningless; logic is useless and at best indeterminate; and this position itself is not taken as logically necessary, but only out of despair of reason—indeed, all rational activity—as pointless. "If activity etc. are pointless, there is no good nor bad, no right nor wrong. If right and wrong do not exist, neither do the effects they bring about. If there is no effect, that obviates the path, leading to heaven or to liberation; and all activities consequently are pointless" (MMK, VIII, 5, 6).

The greatest temptation is to take this understanding of the pointlessness of reason as itself a rationally substantiated position, and Nagarjuna clearly warns against that; "one who adopts emptiness as a view is thereby pronounced incurable" (MMK, XIII, 8). The most important delusive reification to abandon is that of a real absolute, a real liberation beyond the world; "the Nirvana of created things is in no way whatsoever possible. Also the Nirvana of a being is in no way whatsoever possible" (MMK, XVI, 4). Liberation is the cure of such naive, spiritualistic dualisms as impel us to seek escape from life in ultimate liberation; "who does not reify Nirvana nor repudiate samsara, why should he worry about Nirvana and samsara?" (MMK, XVI, 10). We must accept that the "Transcendent" is a mirage, and reconcile ourselves to the fact that life, the chain of causes and effects of relativity, is all there is; "The Buddha taught the Dharma, which is the conservation of evolutionary energy (*karmaṇo 'vipraṇāśas*); since empty, it is not annihilated, since it is a life-cycle, it is not permanent" (MMK, XVII, 20). Not only is there no Absolute beyond the world, there is no being to have attained that Absolute, to be personally grounded therein; "there is nothing unappropriated, nor any appropriation at all, nor anything non-appropriative; however could there be any Transcendent Lord?" (MMK, XXII, 7). Indeed, the Transcendent Lord is this-worldly, is completely in the world; "the intrinsic reality of the Transcendent Lord is the intrinsic reality of this life. The Transcendent Lord has no intrinsic reality, and free of intrinsic reality is this life!" (MMK, XXII, 15). But this resignation, this abandonment of the illusion of the transcendental, crushing as it may seem, is in fact a liberation, for "just life and transmigration, appropriative and dependent, is taught to be Nirvana, when free of appropriation and dependence" (MMK, XXV, 9). The epistemological insight into conceptual delusion has liberated us from the illusion of bondage; our bondage is no longer bondage once we abandon hope for liberation, understanding it as chimerical! The single world of skeptical relativism is driven home to us; "The limit of samsara is the limit of Nirvana. Even the most subtle anything is not found between them" (MMK, XXV, 24).

Under this interpretation of the fundamental meaninglessness of words and the ultimate uselessness of philosophy, except for its discovery of this fact about itself as a spur to its abandonment, it is more than fair to ask why did Nagarjuna write the *Wisdom*? Why did the Buddha teach at all? Why do the Centrists say a single word? In fact, this question can also be put to the absolutists as well. But they both have a ready answer, based in the texts, and this answer is most crucial to our concerns about reason. In brief, they say that Nagarjuna's *Wisdom* is not a book, in the ordinary sense; it has no thesis or argument. It is there as a kind of "horror house" for philosophers; those caught up in the philosophical disease can enter there if they want, and in the various chambers they will encounter the sight and sound of the grotesqueness of their own philosophizing in the trick mirrors and special effects kindly arranged by Nagarjuna. This will so shatter their misplaced confidence in reasoning, they will abandon the enterprise, and leap into mystic contemplation, per the absolutists, or embrace the only world left with desperate existential courage, per the relativists. This ingenious construction of Nagarjuna follows the tradition of all Buddhas, who, themselves standing for nothing in particular in a philosophical sense, can and do say anything at all that fits the situation, in order to help others give up their delusions, their unswerving aim. As Nagarjuna himself says: "Buddhas mention 'self,' and also teach 'selflessness,' as well as teaching that there are no such things as self and selflessness" (MMK, XVIII, 6). "The Buddha's Doctrine is that all is Reality, unreality, both Reality and unreality, and neither Reality nor unreality" (MMK, XVIII, 8). So Centrists in their anti-philosophical tradition, be it mystic absolutism or skeptic relativism, should not espouse any particular position. " 'All is empty' should not be asserted, nor should 'all is not empty,' 'all is both [empty and non-empty],' nor 'all is neither [empty nor non-empty].' Each is maintained [only] in the context of conventional reality" (MMK, XXII, 11). As for the Buddha himself, he simply never taught any doctrine whatsoever to anyone at any time.

This completely noncommittal interpretation of Centrism is further buttressed by Nagarjuna's statement in the *Rebuttal of Objections*: "If I were to have any thesis whatsoever, I would be liable to that fault; but I am completely faultless, because I have no thesis" (VV, 29). Aryadeva agrees with this stance: "Whoever takes no position at all, either 'existence,' 'non-existence,' or 'both existence and non-existence,' cannot be refuted even if [one tries] for a long, long time" (CŚ, XVI, 25). And Chandrakirti concurs as well: "The fault you just advanced . . . applies to whoever has a definite position; but this consequence is not applicable to me, since this position does not exist for me" (MA, VI, 173). Tsong Khapa finally mentions some contemporary skeptic relativists in Tibet who are even more radical in their assertion of this "positionless position." He reports that they deny that anything is established by any sort of validating cognition, and they take this to be the reason for refuting holders of philosophical views only by means of dialectical consequences of the opponents' own assertions. They believe that ultimate truth cannot be proven, and that even the theory of ultimate and superficial realities is only for the opponent's benefit and not the Centrist system. When further pressed, they will even say, Tsong Khapa reports, that they never really made such statements as the above, but only appeared to in the eyes of others.[218] That is really the most remarkable evasion of all; I am not really writing this book, except insofar as you, dear readers, may think I am!

But Tsong Khapa insists that these would-be Dialecticist Centrists, or interpreters of the school, are in fact the chief antagonists (*pūrvapakṣin*) of the school! And indeed, I shall now, following Tsong Khapa, proceed to argue that the absolutist and relativist interpretations I have given extensively above along with their sources in the fundamental *Wisdom* are both quite distorted, badly misrepresent the philosophical contribution of the Centrists, and, most important, do not hold water.

Philosophically, their most important common view is that Nagarjuna's "emptiness" puts a stop to the workings of thought, indeed to all the workings of causation, communication, and cognition. Curiously, both absolutists and relativists esteem him for that, the former because this leads to the mystic leap that reaches their goal of the monistic absolute, the latter because this confirms their own existential embrace of the stark reality of their situation in the inevitable, unitary world. But Nagarjuna's own contemporaries who understood him in such a way,

[218] See the great *Essence*, Ch. V, Section 2c.

as annihilating the workability of the world and the viability of the path of transcendence, did not esteem him for that, as they considered it contrary to common sense as well as philosophical reason. They condemned him for it resoundingly. In the famous XXIVth chapter of the *Wisdom*, this antagonist states that if everything were empty, then it would be inevitably consequent that everything would be annihilated, all causation, all meaning, all reason, all virtue, all understanding. Nagarjuna's reply to them is the classic refutation of this misunderstanding. He completely reverses the burden of defense, as it were, pointing out that precisely the opposite is true. If everything were *not* empty, then it would be inevitably consequent that everything would be annihilated, all causation, all meaning, all reason, all virtue, and all understanding. In this, he straightforwardly affirms his *position*, his *thesis*, namely, that everything is indeed empty of intrinsic reality. And he clearly affirms his commitment to the workability of the world, including the possibility of the path to its transcendence. This is clearly a philosophical position, rationally expounded, grounded in the observed fact of relativity. Let us hear the steps of his reply (MMK, XXIV, 7-19).[219]

"Let us explain this. You do not know either the use, sense, or referent of 'emptiness,' and therefore you do yourself such damage." Is this an appeal to meaninglessness? He faults his opponent precisely for not knowing what he is talking about, for misapprehending the "meaning" of "emptiness." He affirms that it has a "use," a "sense," and that it refers to something, "something" meaning for him a possible object of experience, a "knowable" (*jñeya*). "The Buddhas' teaching of the Dharma relies on the two realities: the social, superficial reality, and the reality of Ultimate Import." There *are* such persons as "Buddhas," they *do* teach, and they do not teach only One Reality, or one unreality. They teach two realities; a relative one that is superficial—lying on the surface—and social—conventionally structured by culture, which shapes consciousness through language; and an Ultimate Absolute that is profound, transcendent, yet real, *knowable*, and hence of supreme import, being ultimately liberative and transformative. "Those who do not discern the difference between these two realities do not understand the profound, the principle of the Buddha-Doctrine." Any conflation of the two, misapprehension that samsara is *just* Nirvana, or that Nirvana is *just* samsara, misses the

[219] It is important to show how Nagarjuna himself defended his position against the antagonist who mistakes emptiness for nothingness, and considers Centrism philosophically incoherent. The fact that the modern absolutists and relativists feel that they are commending Nagarjuna for this ultimate incoherence, as thereby revealing philosophy's limitations, does not get them out of being subject to his rebuttal. For they still are conceding his ultimate failure to "make sense" *as a philosopher*, whether or not they may praise him as a "mystic" or as a skeptical epistemological psychologist.

profound principle, the Thatness of the Teaching of Enlightenment. "Without employing the conventional, the Ultimate is not taught. Without understanding the Ultimate Reality, Nirvana is not attained." The conventional is inevitable and indispensable for communication. The most important communication is teaching. The most important subject of teaching is Ultimate Reality, as it is most important to know it; for its knowledge results in the attainment of liberation, Nirvana, the highest bliss, which is the best thing that can happen to a sentient being. The relative world is there, but so is its transcendence, and the path of liberation is indeed proclaimed to be viable.

Misunderstanding of this is also dangerous, he cautions; "A wrongly viewed emptiness destroys the weak intelligence, like a clumsily held snake or an ill-worked spell. Thus the ascetic's mind was quite averse to teaching, knowing how hard it is for the dull-witted to fathom this principle." Snake-venom is valuable in medicine, and healing spells were common in India, though it takes skill to use them properly. The problem lies not in the medicine, but in the lack of skill of the practitioner. "This rebuttal you repeatedly level against emptiness is not the faulty consequence of our position; it does not logically apply to emptiness." He acknowledges his "position," and takes responsibility for its consequences. He assumes the force of logic, and upholds the compelling nature of rational argument. He insists that emptiness does not logically defeat logic, which implies that logical reasoning confirms emptiness as the factual nature of things. And emptiness is presented as the key to the viability of things. "Everything works properly which properly works with emptiness. And nothing works properly which does not work properly with emptiness." So emptiness is not a critique of logic, language, and validating cognition, but makes them all work properly by critiquing illogic, misuse of language, and delusive cognition. This is manifestly Nagarjuna's very explicit claim.

And then he turns the critique back on his opponent. "You are merely projecting the faults of your position (that is, non-emptiness) upon ours, like a man on horseback forgetting the horse beneath him." Non-emptiness, the habitual naive reification of intrinsic realities in things, is what makes their interaction and causal cohesion and understanding problematic, preventing their working properly. For, "if you regard things as existent by virtue of their intrinsic reality, you thereby regard them as bereft of causes and conditions. And thereby you are condemning effects, causes, agents, actions, activities, originations, cessations, and even fruitional goals." If everything were self-constituted from its own intrinsic reality, as naive realism habitually perceives and conceives, then each thing would be essentially isolated from everything else, unsusceptible to relationships, unchangeable, fixed just as it is in its pristine intrinsicality. The world would, in fact, cease to work, and the path of liberation would also become impossible. No one could become transformed from unliberated to liberated. No seed could absorb nourishment from soil and water and rupture itself into a sprout. The world would screech to a halt. Therefore, only the fact of each thing's emptiness of that falsely presumed intrinsic reality enables it to change, move, grow, and transform. Emptiness is thus not the ending of things, but their relatedness, their interactiveness, and also their provability and knowability. "Whatever is relativity, we proclaim that emptiness. It is dependent designation. It is also the central way. Nothing whatsoever is found which is not relativistically originated. Therefore, nothing whatsoever is found which is not empty. So if all things were *not* empty, there would be no origination and no destruction."

Tsong Khapa remarks that this famous set of fourteen verses should be used as a free-floating appendix to every other critique in the *Wisdom*.[220] It is not just a matter of answering once a single opponent. The Centrist philosopher himself, the student of the central way, continually experiences little misapprehensions of emptiness as a sort of termination of everything, repeatedly confusing it with nothingness, even though he clearly knows intellectually that it is something different from nothingness. This is because the instinctual habit of reifying intrinsic reality in persons and things is so deeply engrained in our thoughts and perceptions. We *feel* intrinsic reality is "there," in ourselves and in things, and each time analytic investigation finds it to be absent, we automatically reify that absence into a little real disappearance, as if something solid had vanished before us. Emptiness then feels as if it has cut off a piece of the world, prevented its working, and we should reflect on the sequence of the fourteen verses. This puts the problem back where it belongs, reverses the wonder, as it were, from "how can things relate?" to "how could they not relate?" From "how can things be empty?" to "how could they *not* be empty?"

Nagarjuna announces his pragmatic and straightforward philosophical approach in the very first substantive in his salutation, "relativity" (*pratītyasamutpāda*),[221] announcing what he observes to be the case before mentioning what can be realized (the "Supreme Bliss" emphasized by the absolutists) by understanding what is not the case (non-cessation, etc., the antinomies emphasized by the relativists). As for the usefulness of logic and language, his every critique presupposes a commitment to

[220] In RG, p. 36.

[221] Taking the eight qualifications, *anirodham* etc., as adjectival compounds qualifying *pratītyasamutpādam*.

rigorous thought, as misconception and illogic are only overcome by rigorous critical reason. The "intuitive wisdom" he recommends to terminate misknowledge is not uncultivated, naive intuition. Indeed, the unphilosophical ordinary person perceives intrinsic realities in things *intuitively*, that is, habitually, instinctually, so "non-rational," or "mystic," intuition would only confirm misknowledge. "Wisdom" (*prajña*) is the "critical investigation of facts" (*dharmapravicaya*), which only becomes "intuitive" when it has firmly reached its conclusion and transcended misleading thinking. Un-wise, naive intuition untempered by critical insight is precisely "mystic" and "non-rational," leading to experiential ratification of an alienated Absolute somewhere "out of the world," or to experiential ratification of an alienated bondage in "meaningless," that is, "mysterious," "thrown-ness" in a closed world of unalterable suffering. Wise intuition is the fruit of long philosophic cultivation of critical insight, developed in sustained contemplation of the profound nature of things, until reason transforms instinct and habit, and what one knows rationally to be the case is intuitively felt to be the case. This is a position that balances complexity and integrates both realities without collapsing them to one side or another, to the habitual simplicity of just this or just that. It is thus the position of the central way.

Therefore Nagarjuna does not say only that samsara is just Nirvana (the absolutist) or that Nirvana is just samsara (the relativist); he says, "There is no distinction at all of samsara from Nirvana. There is no distinction at all of Nirvana from samsara" (MMK, XXV, 19). The absolutist is correct: there is an overriding soteric aim. There is a Nirvana, a supreme bliss. But salvation is not "mystic," a "leap into the void" having discarded reason, and Nirvana is not a place outside the world; it is a situation that includes the world within its bliss. Samsara cannot be distinguished from it. It is in Nirvana that samsara is embraced completely. In the ultimate reality, there is no duality of any sort, and samsara and Nirvana are the same actuality. But the relativist is also correct. "Perfection" is always correlated with "imperfection"; there is no escape from inevitable relativity. Nirvana is not an intrinsically real intrinsic reality that mysteriously violates its nature and projects unilaterally absolute meaningfulness into the world. Nirvana cannot be distinguished from samsara. It is just here now, and the full experiential acceptance of that is liberation, which is not a going elsewhere. But truly being "here" is not an abandonment of the Absolute, a capitulation to the mysteriousness of meaninglessness, a relative meaninglessness. It is rather an Absolute being here, a triumphal commitment to sensible duality. For part of relativity is the ideal of the Absolute. It is also a misuse of language to proclaim "relativity" without allowing meaningfulness to its complementary concept, "Absolute." And so the noumenal is as much an object, a knowable, as the phenomenal. Indeed, it is the Supreme Knowable, known by transcendent wisdom, and that knowledge transforms all other knowledge without annihilating it. So nonduality is not a unity, a monistic absolutism, and it is not a chaotic plurality, a spiritually nihilistic relativism. It is wisdom's relativistic absolutism, Nirvana absorbing samsara in liberation, and compassion's absolutistic relativism, samsara preserving Nirvana as its liberating transcendence.

Returning to teaching, expression, and reason, the Buddhas "teach no doctrine," keep silent ultimately, as a critique of authoritarian dogmatism, not to mislead the philosophically naive into thinking that Truth can replace fact. They do not dogmatically repeat "emptiness," or "nonemptiness," "both," or "neither," in the specific contexts of the naive students' tendency to misapprehend emptiness as nothingness, the tendency to intensify the reification of habitually perceived intrinsic objectivity in things, the tendency to become attached to a dogmatic form of indeterminacy, or the tendency to mystic abandonment of reason in fixated alienation, respectively. And they can teach any of these four alternatives in therapeutic opposition to whichever fixation the student suffers. This is standard teaching procedure for any good teacher of philosophy, getting the student to see the other side of questions. But the very great difference between this and mere skeptical sophistry, is that a Buddha, or a Nagarjuna, does this in order to lead the student to his own philosophical "position," his "thesis" that all things mundane and transcendent are empty of intrinsic reality.

Therefore, as Tsong Khapa explains in the *Essence*, the claim of "no position," "no thesis," made by the great Centrists, is misunderstood if taken out of context as a blanket avowal of sophistry, a disdain of philosophic integrity, an arrogant refusal to abide by the conventions of sincere communication. On the contrary, it is simply a refutation of the ultimate status of any position, the intrinsic identifiability of any object, which is tantamount to an affirmation of the conventional validity of reasoning, and a pledge of commitment to the conventional validity and compellingness of reason in general. The Centrist acknowledges that anything disappears under analysis, but this for him does not invalidate all logic; it rather returns it to its proper sphere of operation, namely, the relative world with its absolute transcendence.

This point is so crucial to our proof, we should follow it in somewhat more detail. We must consider the specific contexts of the statements that "we have no position," to avoid overgeneralizing the central way as sophistry. The most extensive exposition of the issue is by Chandrakirti in his *Introduction Commentary* (ad. MA, VI, ks. 170-178). Chandrakirti first refutes the realist's picture of causation as the intrinsically identifiable production of intrinsically identifiable effect from an intrinsically identifiable cause. This he does with the usual Centrist method of analysis as to whether such a real cause produces its effect by contact with it or without contact with it. He pushes the realist thus to pinpoint the intrinsic referentiality of "cause," and so forth, down to the presumed intrinsically objective referents. Such ultimacy-seeking investigation, of course, fails to discover any absolute basis of the designations "cause," and so on, and the realist's picture of causation is exploded. Chandra then remarks that he does not have that problem, since for him all mundane things exist; illusory causes produce illusory effects, able to interact because they lack intrinsic objectivity. The realist then tries to evade the thrust of the critique by applying the same dialecticist consequence to Chandrakirti. He does not understand that Chandra is serious in his acceptance of "illusory," that is, merely relative, causation. He analyzes Chandra's analysis; "Does your critique refute the refutee by contact with it or without contact with it? If 'yes' (on either option), then the same fault rebounds on you. So your critique is self-contradictory, you overthrow your own thesis, and your refutation cannot refute anything." He goes even further, speaking to our main issue here directly: "If you now try to quibble further by reversing the same consequence back again on the statement I just made, then you are irrationally repudiating all things. Superior persons do not approve you, as you are just a sophistic skeptic refuting everything without taking a position of your own!" This is an exact formulation of the interpretations given above (absolutist and relativist). And it is in the teeth of this challenge precisely that Chandrakirti says that the consequence he applied to the realist's picture of causation cannot be rebounded back on him because he has no such position. He further states in the *Commentary* that this is the same context in which Nagarjuna made his similar statements (MMK, IV, 9; VV, 27), and Aryadeva made his (CS, XVI, 25).

The key here is in the "such." Surely, it cannot be thought that Chandrakirti is so foolish that he would admit to what he is accused of, that is, having no position at all, and consider that admission a rebuttal of the accusation! He acknowledges that such a "dualistic analysis" would apply to one who has a "definite position," so "such" can be taken to mean "definite." And he states that "definite" here means "intrinsically identifiable," or "intrinsically real." In short, his denial of a "definite position" is simply part of his unremitting critique of the realist's picture of things as intrinsically objective. Just as that picture does not hold up in strict correspondence to the process of causation, so it does not hold up in strict correspondence to processes of reason and cognition. He does not hold an intrinsically identifiable position because there is no such thing. It would be an ultimate position, and all presumed "ultimate things" disappear under critical analysis. The realist thinks he himself is holding an intrinsically identifiable position and that Chandrakirti should inevitably do the same. This is precisely the confused notion, the misuse of language, that Chandrakirti is trying to cure.

Chandra then encourages the realist that he also ascribes to the workability of things. Details on the solar disc can be seen in mirror image during eclipses; the mirror and the solar disc are neither in contact nor out of contact, yet the details emerge in the merely conventional reality. One can use a mirror image of one's face to preen oneself, and in the same way one can perfect one's face of wisdom by the reflection of reason; so "you should acknowledge that the probandum is understood, even if not established by [intrinsically identifiable] logical processes." And he finally makes explicit the difference between his commitment to logic and his critique of intrinsically identifiable logical processes that are as implausible as intrinsically identifiable "production," "going," "fire and fuel," and so on. "If the reason causing understanding of one's probandum were intrinsically really established, it would be a real thing to be understood, and the probandum would exist with intrinsic objectivity. Then the analytic investigation of 'with contact or . . . etc.' would apply, and it would not be found to exist. So [your rebuttal applies] only [to such a position] as you believe [us to hold]." Aware that his opponent misapprehends the way he holds his position, Chandrakirti feels compelled to answer, as did his central way ancestors in the same situation, that he has *no such position*.

And Nagarjuna and Aryadeva agree in saying that the realist's critique will never succeed in refuting a position that he is only imagining the Centrist to be asserting. The Centrist considers all logic a conventional, ultimately illusory, though relatively valid or invalid, process, and can never be rejected for holding an absolutistic thesis of emptiness, since he never proposes such a thesis. That does not mean that he does not acknowledge conventionally valid propositions (the only kind possible), conventionally propose emptiness, and argue for it logically and rationally. So he cannot properly be termed a skeptical sophist with no position of his own. In fact, Chandra goes on to say, the Centrist's position is so overwhelmingly sensible, so well grounded in empirical observation of the facts of the world, it is easy for him to prove his point, as there are many examples of illusory realities: mirror images, the moon in water, mirages, and so on. On the other hand, the advocate of intrinsic reality has an impossible task in finding an example to establish the pervasion of his syllogisms, since a phenomenal intrinsic reality can nowhere be discovered under analysis. And he laments, "O why does this world become delirious, caught in the net of harmful dogmas?"[222]

The problem is clearly the same as in the controversy between the Dogmaticists and the Dialecticists, though the latter is on a much more subtle level, as has been explained above.[223] The Dialecticist is concerned to treat critically the misconception of intrinsic identifiability, the philosophical correlate of the instinctual misperception of intrinsic objectivity in things. His most delicate treatment lies in the isolation of the Dogmaticist insistence on private reason supported by the habitually secure private object, and in its critical dissolution by revealing it to be tantamount to an ultimate reason and an ultimate object, both of which are absurd for any Centrist. The most powerful reason advocated by the Dialecticist is known as the "reason of relativity," namely, "all things are empty of intrinsic identifiability; because they are relativistically originated." Contemplation of the thesis cures absolutism, and contemplation of the reason cures nihilism. At the most advanced level of philosophical subtlety, this royal reason unpacks into four consequences.[224] The Dialecticist prefers a consequential mode of reasoning to the advancing of independent syllogisms; it is more effective in producing understanding in another's mind, for it fits more closely with that other's starting view and introduces doubtfulness into that view as prelude to any new suggestion. Too often the Dogmaticist independent syllogisms will be misunderstood by the opponent as tacitly confirming his own absolutism about the way thought works, defeating the Centrist's purpose at the outset. Therefore the imperative consequence is the preferred methodology of proof for a Dialecticist, although he can use a syllogism when he wishes, since, as we have shown, he does have his own position.

The first of the four consequences is, "if things stood on intrinsic identifiability, its repudiation would be their destruction, and emptiness would be the destructive cause. Such being irrational, things do not exist [identifiably]" (MA, VI, 34). First, let us recall that intrinsic identity is that irreducible anchor of reference in a thing to which its name fits. It is thus what must be discovered by analysis seeking the ultimate meaning

[222] Comparing this more detailed exposition of MA, VI, 170-178, with Tsong Khapa's handling of the "no position" question in the *Essence* (Ch. V, Section 2C) provides an excellent illustration of why the *Essence* is such a difficult work. Tsong Khapa only uses MA, VI, 173, and some passages from its commentary as the basis of his elucidation, which is indeed the key passage. Hence, he achieves the elliptic elegance of thought of the *Essence*. But scholars who are unfamiliar with the MA find it hard to comprehend without more explication. Thus, the *Essence* gives the essential keys, but most of us need an enormous background study to really appreciate it.

[223] See above, Introduction, VIII, 1.

[224] These four consequences are given in the great *Essence*, Ch. VII.

of designations, not content with their mere conventionality. It is the private object that the Dogmaticist needs to anchor his universe of facts, and the basis of his use of private reasons. It is, for the Centrists, an empirical fact that the philosopher yogi who deeply contemplates things in critical insight meditation does not discover any such thing at the core of things. He thus experiences the disappearance of objects of his penetrating inspection, entering what is called the "holy equipoised intuition" focused on emptiness. This experience empirically verifies the logical incompatibility between intrinsic identity and relativity. The consequence thus imperatively incumbent on the advocate of intrinsic identity is that the putative intrinsic identity that was once there has been destroyed by the equipoised intuition, as what was once there and is no longer must be considered destroyed. And emptiness, absolute, uncompounded, unchanging, and so forth, must be posited as the cause of that destruction. This consequence is based on empirical facts of cognition that are acknowledged by the Dogmaticist, who accepts the reality of such equipoise, and it refutes intrinsic identity as ontologically impossible.

The second consequence is that, if things had intrinsic identities, conventional things would withstand ultimacy-seeking analysis. Chandrakirti states it as "when one analyzes these things, they are not found to stand anywhere short of that with ultimate nature. Therefore, social, conventional reality should not be analyzed" (MA, VI, 35). This consequence is also based on the observation that things dissolve under ultimately penetrative analysis, which is common knowledge for Centrist philosophers. The smallest subatomic particle disappears when one attempts to pin it down ultimately. It becomes a mere probability, impossible to determine whether it is a wave or a particle. Tables and chairs and houses and human beings come apart, piece by piece, mental event by mental event, and nowhere is anything durable, analysis-resistant, to be discovered. This kind of "diamond-cutting analysis" is the precursor for the holy equipoise. So, the Dogmaticist scholar, or the Dogmaticist realist within the philosopher yogi himself, (such as the speaker of the other voice in Wittgenstein's later works), must abandon the insistence on intrinsic identity under the compulsion of this consequence, based on common experiences, and an important epistemological point is made: "social, conventional reality should not be analyzed," referring of course to ultimacy-seeking analysis.

The third exceptional consequence used by the Dialecticist to overcome the intrinsic identifiability habit is called "the consequence of the non-negation of ultimate production," Chandrakirti formulates it as "the very reasons proving the irrationality of self-production and other-production in the ultimate sense also prove their irrationality in the conventional reality; so whereby will your 'production' come to pass?" (MA, VI, 36). The Dogmaticist realist wishes to distinguish "intrinsic identity" from "intrinsic reality," refuting the latter in the Centrist tradition, but feeling helpless without the former in wishing to maintain some logical order in the conventional world. He argues for a "conventional intrinsic identity." Chandrakirti considers this a mistaken use of language, as "conventional" means precisely "relativistically, that is, non-ultimacy-analytically, designated," and therefore there can be nothing intrinsic, that is, non-relational, in conventional relativity. This consequence thus logically connects "intrinsic identity" and "intrinsic reality" and shows that the Dogmaticist habit has reimported a hidden ultimacy incongruously back into the relative world. This then becomes imperative for the Dogmaticist who will not waver on his philosophical commitment that reason dictates the impossibility of ultimate production. This consequence is based on the Dialecticist commitment to the viability and rigorous effectiveness of conventional reason, once freed from the insurmountable inconsistencies of the absolutist picture of rational processes.

The fourth imperative consequence is that of the "wrongness of the authoritative statement that things are empty with reference to intrinsic reality." Chandrakirti gives it in his *Introduction Commentary*, following the previous verse, by quoting the Buddha's statement in the *Kashyapa Chapter* of the *Jewel-Heap Scripture*. "Kashyapa, furthermore, the central way is the genuine insight into things; it does not make things empty by means of emptiness, but [realizes that] the very things themselves are emptiness" It is highly significant, contra the above-mentioned absolutist and relativist interpretations of Centrist thought, that the last of the four exceptional consequences should be based on the validity of scriptural authority, on the commitment to the reliability of definitive meaning statements. Of course, only statements of emptiness, of exclusion or absolute negation of intrinsic reality are accepted as definitive in meaning, as explained above. But still there is a commitment to the meaningfulness, reliability, and authority of at least those statements. This is the opposite of some general notion of the uselessness or meaninglessness of language. It is the affirmation of the supreme value of true expression. It is an imperative consequence for the Dogmaticist because he cannot deny the correctness of the definitive meaning statement, and if his insistence on intrinsic identifiability is inconsistent with it, he must abandon his insistence.

Here there may be a final objection to the critical philosophy of the central way, namely, that its definitive statement is purely negative, it does not present any positive reasoning, only negations, and so, in spite of all the high-flown talk of logic and reason, is it not just a systematic skepticism, replete with good old *epoché* and final *ataraxia*?

In response to objections such as this, Tsong Khapa concludes the *Essence* with a section that considers whether the negative thesis "all things lack intrinsic reality" contains any sort of valid probandum, a cognitive object susceptible of rational proof.[225] His discussion is extremely lucid, and we need not recapitulate it in its entirety here, but only make the major points that are necessary to convey the full picture of the relation between reason and enlightenment, between philosophy and transformative experience. First, "emptiness" is obviously a negation of intrinsic reality. Among the two types of negation (exclusion or absolute negation, which negates its negatee only, without implying anything else; and implicative, or choice, negation, which implies some other fact while negating its negatee), "emptiness" is an exclusion negation. It merely negates intrinsic reality. It does not imply the existence of intrinsic realitylessness. According to the traditional examples, "this man is not a Brahmin" is a choice negation, in that it implies that he is of different but similar caste. "A Brahmin should not drink beer" is an exclusion negation, since it does not imply what else he should drink, merely excluding his drinking of beer. Thus, "all things lack intrinsic reality" does not imply anything else about all things; it just excludes their possible possession of intrinsic reality.

Tsong Khapa's argument turns on three possible interpretations of the negation "emptiness": that it merely excludes its negatee, but does not prove anything, on the one extreme; that it proves the actual existence of intrinsic realitylessness, on the other extreme; and that its exclusion of its negatee *is* itself the proving of realitylessness, the central position here. He rejects the first possibility as weakening too much the logical viability of negation. If negation of the possible presence of a pot on the table fails to prove that there is no pot on the table, we would never be able to know anything about where not to look for it. He rejects the second possibility as putting too much weight on the function of negation. The negation of the pot's possible presence on the table does not even address the question of whether the pot's absence exists on the table. If we wanted to prove that, we should say "an absence of a pot exists on the table," and the proof of that assertion involves many more complex philosophical questions than merely establishing that the pot is not there. And the Centrists never argue in any text that "emptiness exists." They do not formulate their syllogisms as "intrinsic realitylessness exists in all things." They merely state that things lack intrinsic reality. And further,

[225] See the great *Essence*, Ch. VII.

to forestall such a naive reification of emptiness itself, they often state that emptiness itself is lacking in intrinsic reality, that emptiness itself is empty.

However, Tsong Khapa does argue that the negation of intrinsic reality *does prove intrinsic realitylessness* by negating its negatee. This does not make it an implicative, or choice, negation; the two operations, excluding the negatee and proving the negation, are simply logically equivalent. And here I will cite the key passage from the *Essence* below, as his own formulation is so perfectly clear.

> An example [of exclusion negation] is the expression "there is no smoke in the lake," which merely excludes the presence of smoke in the lake without indicating [the existence of] anything else. However, it does not [thereby] fail to show that the lake is free of smoke, nor does the corresponding cognition fail to ascertain the smokelessness of the lake. Likewise, the expression "there is no intrinsic reality in the sprout" merely rules out any intrinsic reality in the sprout, but why should that preclude the expression's expressing and the cognition's ascertaining the intrinsic realitylessness of the sprout? Therefore, the words express the absence of the smoke in the lake in their very exclusion [of it] and the cognition ascertains the absence of the smoke in its very exclusion [of it from the lake]; because the exclusion of the negatee and the determination of the negation are [mutually indispensable], the lack of either one entailing the lack of the other. In the same way, the scriptural references teaching intrinsic realitylessness express intrinsic realitylessness in their actual negation of intrinsic reality, the rational cognition negative of intrinsic reality cognizes intrinsic realitylessness in its actual negation of intrinsic reality, and the reason negative of intrinsic reality proves intrinsic realitylessness in its actual negation of intrinsic reality. These [facts] must be accepted, and one must not assert that the scriptural references have no subject, the cognition has no object, and the reason has no probandum.

This is the challenge of the central way philosophers. It is not a mystic absolutism that demands that the philosopher should throw away his reason as hopelessly inadequate to some ineffable Absolute, to spring from his despair into a Great Beyond. It is not a skeptical relativism that calls for the abandonment of metaphysics, that curbs reason's urge to know completely the nature of ultimate reality by proclaiming its unknowability and virtual non-existence, turning the philosopher's attention to the world of everyday, telling him "philosophy is obsolete, look at the troubles it has caused you, work on linguistics, sociology, theology, or poetry." It challenges the philosopher to push reason to its conclusive insights into the nature of reality, the meaning of life, the possibility of goodness and beauty. It claims that the true nature of reality can be proven compellingly, albeit the proof is not itself a substitute for the actuality of the Absolute. It claims thus that language can express what is most necessary to express, that reason can prove what is most necessary to prove, and that understanding—wisdom ultimately become intuitive—can realize what is most essential to realize. It opens wide the broad path of philosophy, the love of wisdom, and urges that all human beings must tread that path to realize their full humanity in enlightenment.

But what of "enlightenment"? What is involved in the proof of emptiness of intrinsic reality? What is the cognition of emptiness? How does wisdom take a non-objective object, the ultimate object, as its object? It is often said that it does not perceive by way of normal misknowledge-governed subject-object dichotomy. It perceives by way of non-perception, by pure negation. Then how is it transformative? Tsong Khapa provides a clue about the complex balance required on the central way of nondualism. Everything disappears in ultimacy-seeking experience; ultimate reality is by definition transcendent and undifferentiated. And yet the world is not destroyed. It is there on the surface, when not subjected to absolutist standards. In a sense it *is* the surface of the ultimate, which is ultimately one inconceivably multifaceted surface. Tsong Khapa sheds a unique ray of light on the epistemology of nondualism with a formulation in the *Essence* that I have not found elsewhere in the Centrist literature.[226] He states that there are three perceptual habits in experience: the perception of objective existence in things, the perception of objective non-existence of things, and the perception of things unqualified as regards objective status, the non-judgmental, oblique, or peripheral perception. The unenlightened person, who has not attained the authentic view of reality, experiences normally the first and third of these perceptions, usually mixed up together unconsciously. And then—and this remark is startling and provocative—the enlightened person with the authentic view *can experience all three* of them. This means that "enlightenment" is not a state of consciousness fixated on some "beyond." The second perceptual experience is achieved in transcendent experience, in the holy equipoise intuition, where subject and object merge like water poured into water, and everything disappears under emptiness-seeking critical analysis, supercharged in combination with one-pointed concentration. But emptiness itself has no intrinsic identity, no intrinsic reality. It *is* the intrinsic reality of all things, which is precisely their lack of intrinsic reality. So naturally it is senseless to claim that the

[226] See the great *Essence*, Ch. V, Section 2C.

lack of intrinsic reality has intrinsic reality. This is the meaning of the "emptiness of emptiness." Therefore the transcendent experience wherein the world is perceived concretely to disappear is epistemologically an experience of absolute nothingness. It is the second perceptual habit above, the perception of objective nonexistence, which, we must carefully note, is not a "perception of emptiness."

Of course, the strict precision of the Centrist psychology does not permit an expression like "experience of nothingness" to stand unchallenged. "If Nirvana were a nothing, how could it be non-appropriative? For no Nirvana-nothing is found without appropriation" (MMK, XXV, 8). That is, "nothingness" is also without intrinsic identity, it is only a concept for the absence of something. It is thus only meaningful within the realm of appropriation. Thus an "experience of nothingness" can only be an experience of being on the threshold of the loss of all "somethings." When the transcendent insight dissolves the subtle subjectivity, the apparent threshold, and the apparently objective nothingness looming beyond, there can be no further "experience." The next subjective experience event must be the threshold on emerging from such a trance, even if it be moments, hours, or days later; as is sometimes reported. So clearly enlightenment is not presented as a dwelling in the experience of obliteration. Wisdom's diamond drill penetrates the apparent nothingness as inexorably as it does the apparent somethingness.

This is not to say that the "habitual perception of objective nonexistence" that an enlightened person is capable of —which distinguishes him or her from the unenlightened—is anything less than the subjective experience of *death*, indeed is the epistemological description of the "great death" so often mentioned in the Zen literature. The proof of realitylessness is the logical iron rail that directs the cognition to full confrontation with the total dissolution of all subjectivity and objectivity into an experience of absolute nothingness. But it is also the catapult beyond this great cognitive "black hole" of absolute compression, since its critical wisdom energy dissolves the apparent objective existence of objective non-existence. Thus, emptiness dawns immediately as the magnificent panorama of relativity, through its absolute negation of the intrinsic reality of nothingness. The great death is the threshold of the dawn of enlightenment, in which the clear light of wisdom reveals the immense field of play of great compassion.

In fact, it would seem that the transcendent experience of a "real nothingness" is simply the final isolation of the private object, the distilling of its essence by squeezing it analytically out of the differentiated objects in which it is habitually invested, and the direct confrontation of it itself. When it too is realized to be non-existent objectively, the world is back, but this time a real world of relativity, understood as empty of intrinsic identity. Finally the philosopher *intuitively* knows that "nothing" refers to nothing! But from the addition of this experience to his repertoire, the master of the authentic view has achieved the central way of balance between being and nothing. Not bound any longer by the apparent "thereness" of intrinsically identifiable reality of things, he still can see it as others do. but he also understands things' elusiveness, their lack of intrinsic identity, their Suchness. The simultaneous awareness of these two realities of things, this cognitive "double exposure," grants him the freedom from attachment to apparently objective necessities, and the freedom to engage in relativities to bring about the happiness of living beings, including himself. Thus the true integration of samsara and Nirvana is not achieved by collapsing either one into the other. The central way is harmonious balance and intuitive wisdom is the non-dual integration of both in equilibrium.

As Tsong Khapa himself puts it, "Appearance dispels absolutist extremism and emptiness dispels nihilism; when emptiness dawns as cause and effect, you will not be deprived by any extremist views."[227] The balance of the central way can be further expressed as an ability to embrace simultaneously objective existence and objective non-existence of all things, in integrated compassion and wisdom. Ultimately this compassion becomes the "illusion-body" (*māyādeha*) of liberative great bliss, and this wisdom becomes the wisdom-mind of clear light brilliance (*prabhāsvara*). This kind of exquisite expression of the supreme integration (*yuganaddha*) is the language of the Unexcelled Yoga Tantras, and must be reserved for future works.[228]

Tsong Khapa himself does not unpack his epistemological formulation to this degree in this context. He simply makes one of his characteristically provocative "capping" remarks: knowing which habit patterns are operative in unenlightened and enlightened persons, "one will put a stop to the following false views: [the view] that rationality does not put a stop to all perception [controlled] by mental constructions such as 'this is it'; [the view] that all practices before the generation of the authentic view, such as cultivation of the will to enlightenment [of love and compassion], are but truth-habits or sign-habits [and therefore worthless

[227] *Lam gtso rnam gsum*: *snang bas yod mtha sel ba dang / stong pas med mtha sel shing stong pa nyid / rgyu dang 'bras bur 'char bai tshul shes na / mthar 'dzin lta bas phrog par mi 'gyur ro //.*

[228] See my forthcoming *Vajra Hero*, on the *Esoteric Communion* tradition. The "double exposure" image was invented by Professor T. Unno, and seems most apt for the balance of opposites of the central way.

pursuits]; and [the view] that after one may claim to have generated in mind the authentic view, there will be no intentionality in all one's acts."[229]

These three statements form the perfect frame for the conclusion of this introduction.

First, if it is a false view that reason cannot terminate misknowledge-governed habitual perceptions, the correct view is that reason, through its proof of emptiness by the reason of relativity, leads directly and inexorably, without any gap or leap, to the confrontation with the ultimate truth of truthlessness. Philosophy is thus vindicated as a complete path of liberation and transformation; the conclusively reasonable mind is esteemed as completely capable of transcending the unreasonable prejudiced mentality trapped in the vicious circle of inconclusive rationalization. One should therefore resist the temptation to discard critical reason and relapse into experiential confirmation of mundane intuition, habitually conditioned by prejudice, and hold out until critical wisdom experientially becomes the reliable and liberating intuition of reality.

Second, if it is a false view that the will to enlightenment, the spirit of enlightenment that is love and compassion, is not genuine before enlightenment and hence to be postponed until some presumed threshold is achieved, the correct view is that love is valid and essential at any point in the path. One cannot therefore excuse oneself from the responsibility of compassionate acts on the grounds that one had better wait until after enlightenment, and so remain self-involved in that ultimate self-interest of gaining individual enlightenment. One *is* enlightened when one acts enlightened, that is, for the sake of others, whatever one's cognitive state may be. Buddha is as Buddha does. It is all too often forgotten by students of the central way, with their rigorous philosophical attention to metaphysical and epistemological questions, that, as Nagarjuna says, "emptiness is essentially compassion" (*śūnyatākaruṇāgarbhaṃ*) (RA, k.398). Nagarjuna's fundamental central way work is called *Wisdom*, and so he confines himself therein to the pathways of critical reason. At no moment, however, is he, or should the student be, unaware that wisdom is but the doorway for the energy of compassion. The razor-sharp sword of critical wisdom cuts through the fetters of conceptual excuses that obstruct the open dynamic flow of compassion, full sensitivity to the sufferings of other beings who are the fabric of relativity, and overflowing love that radiates happiness to them, once all self-concern has melted in the bliss of self-fulfillment in the great emptiness of selflessness. Wisdom smashes the hard atoms of intrinsic identities; compassion is the all-powerful energy released to reshape relativity into the gentle jewelline forms of pure lands of bliss.

[229] See the great *Essence*, Ch. V, Section 2C.

Finally, if it is a false view that enlightenment prevents all intentionality, all will, and is either aloof anaesthesia or some inconceivable spontaneity, the correct view is that the Buddha-will is released infinitely in sensible activity directed to the benefit of all sentient beings. We need not insist that the Buddhas be silent, we need not feel abandoned by a detached Body of Truth, and we may expect to discover an appropriate variety of Bodies of Beatitude and Emanation throughout the universe working for the welfare of us and all beings. We may recognize the Great Death as the gateway to the Boundless Life. Pure reason thus does not destroy the world through its absolute negation of intrinsic reality, its proof of universal emptiness. It compels the confrontation with reality, and it impels beyond any "beyonds" into the total commitment to compassionate transformation of the relativity that dawns in that confrontation. Love, while not being merely reason, is the conclusive outflow of the perfection of reason. The white hot passion for pure reason attains its consummation in the supreme experience that becomes the supreme reason for compassion. Philosophy also does not just end. The love of wisdom goes beyond its original goal and becomes the wisdom to love. The central way thus unifies also the individual interest with the general interest, as relative concerns become the ultimate concern. And those relative concerns can be fulfilled because of the stability and liberative inexhaustibility of the ultimate concern. But I must reserve the ethical consequences of the central way for a further work. I only mention this aspect here to establish that the central way philosophers never accept the divorce of the ethical from the metaphysical, and work on wisdom only in the constant awareness that it *is* compassion. To repeat Nagarjuna's statement, the philosopher enters the "practice of enlightenment, profound, awesome, emptiness whose essence is compassion."[230]

To conclude with the golden silence that issues effortlessly in the golden speech of Tsong Khapa and the Centrist masters, it is not the portentous, referential silence of the mystic, nor the defeated, resigned silence of the relativist. It is the contented silence of having said all that is necessary, valuable, and helpful, and it is the loving silence that unconditionally affirms the complete integrity of each individual member of the audience. It is a silence that takes them all in, in their intrinsic perfection, their limitless potential, their fundamental well-being, and loves them unconditionally as they are. It does not feel the need to tell them even that they are perfect, that "they are That." It fits with the insight that they all really know deep down that they are indeed. And finally, it is a silence

[230] P. L. Vaidya, ed., *Madhyamakaśāstra* (Darbhanga, 1960), p. 310 (Ratnavali, IV, ks. 14-16).

that fearlessly wells forth in lucid speech, in liberative words, when that is intuitively felt to be a more effective way to bring out the best in people. But such speech does not "break" such silence. It is balanced with it. It is the integration of silence and speech that is the central way. And so now I will be silent, having hopefully built an appropriate forum, invited the audience with appropriate interests, prepared them with the key background and central questions, and introduced the speaker. Now I can step aside, as you are ready to listen to Tsong Khapa's Speech of Gold.

THE SHORT *ESSENCE OF TRUE ELOQUENCE* EULOGY OF BUDDHA SHAKYAMUNI FOR HIS TEACHING OF RELATIVITY

Reverence to the Guru, Manjughosha![1]

I praise that perfect Buddha,
The Supreme Philosopher,
Who taught us relativity;
Free of (real) cessation and creation,
Beyond nihilism and absolutism,
With no (real) coming and no (real) going,
Neither unity nor plurality,
The quieting of fabrications, bliss supreme![2]

I bow down to him whose insight and speech
Make him unexcelled as Sage and Teacher;
The Victor, who realized (ultimate truth),
Then taught us it as relativity!

Misknowledge itself is the very root
Of all the troubles in this fleeting world;
Who understood that and then reversed it,
Taught universal relativity.

Thereupon, how could it be possible
That the Geniuses[3] would not understand
This very path of relativity
As the vital essence of your teaching?

Such being the case, who could discover
Anything even still more wonderful
To sing your praises for, O Savior,[4]
Than your teaching of relativity?

[1] This poem was written on the morning of Tsong Khapa's final enlightenment, directly from the experience itself, as mentioned in the Introduction, VII. It gives the quintessence of his realization, closely resonant with the great *Essence*, Ch. III.

[2] Tsong Khapa here quotes the opening verses from Nagarjuna's *Wisdom*.

[3] Tib. *blo ldan*, that is, bodhisattvas of especially keen intelligence and courage.

[4] Tib. *mgon po*, usually translated "Protector," but stronger than that in this usage, as the protection is cosmic, from the miseries of the samsaric life-cycle itself.

"Whatever depends upon conditions
Is empty of intrinsic reality."
What excellent instruction could there be,
More amazing than this discovery?

Although the naive can seize upon it
As just confirming their extremist bonds,
The wise use that same (relativity)
To cut their way out of fabrication's trap.

This Teaching is not to be found elsewhere,
So you alone are entitled "Teacher";
A term of consolation for escapists,[5]
Like soothing a fox by calling him "lion!"

O wondrous Teacher! O wondrous refuge!
Wondrous philosopher! Wondrous Savior!
I pay full homage to that great Teacher
Who well expounded relativity!

O benefactor! To heal all beings,
You proclaimed (profound relativity),
The unrivaled reason to ascertain
Emptiness, the essence of the Teaching.

How can anyone who would understand
The profound law of relativity
As contradictory, or unestablished,
Ever fully understand your system?[6]

Your position is that, when one perceives
Voidness as the fact of relativity,
Voidness of reality does not preclude
The viability of activity.

Whereas when one perceives the opposite,
Action is impossible in voidness,
Voidness is lost during activity;
One falls into anxiety's abyss.

Thus, experience of relativity
Is most recommended in your Teaching,
And not that of absolute nothingness,
Nor that of intrinsically real existence.

[5] Tib. *mu stegs pa*, those who hope for salvation as escape from the world through observing religious rites and frequenting holy places.

[6] Here he refers to the "royal reason of relativity," which some critics find contradictory or inconclusive. See the great *Essence*, Ch. III.

The non-relative is like a sky-flower;
So there is nothing non-relational.
Things' existence with objective status
Precludes dependence on cause and condition.

Thus you proclaimed that just because no thing
Exists beyond relative occurrence,
So nothing can really exist beyond
Voidness of intrinsic reality.

If things had any self-reality,
Since such could never be reversed, you said,
Nirvana would become impossible,
Since fabrications could not be reversed.

Dauntless in the assemblies of the wise,
You clearly proclaimed in your lion's roar,
"Let there be freedom from identity!"
Who would ever presume to challenge this?

All systems are completely viable,
Since lack of intrinsic reality
And relativity do not conflict;
Never mind they complement each other.

"By the reason of relativity
There are no grounds to hold extremist views!"
For this excellent statement, you, Savior,
Are unexcelled among philosophers.

"All this objectively is emptiness!"
And "From this cause will occur this effect!"
These facts are mutually non-exclusive;
Certainties, they reinforce each other.

Than this, what could ever be more wondrous?
Than this, what could ever inspire more awe?
For this one principle, if you are praised,
It is real praise; and otherwise not so.

Those held in the slavery of confusions,
Helplessly resent you, (so free and clear),
Small wonder they find intolerable
The sound of "non-substantiality."

But those who assert "relativity,"
The precious treasury of your discourse,
When they resent the roar of emptiness;
Really, they never cease to amaze me!

They hold unexcelled relativity,
The gateway to identitylessness,
As a real identity just by name;
Ah, how cleverly they deceive themselves!

They should be led by whatever technique
To that good path ever pleasing to you,
That incomparable shore of haven,
Well-traveled by the highest holy beings.

Reality, unmade and non-related,
Relativity, made and relative;
How can these two facts be brought together
In one instance, without contradiction?

Therefore, the relatively occurrent,
Though ever free of self-reality,
Appears as if intrinsically real;
So you said all this is like illusion.

From this very fact one well understands
(The Centrists') statement that, the way you taught,
Those who would strive to challenge (your Teaching)
Rationally can find no fallacy.

Why? Because this your elucidation
Makes utterly remote the tendencies
To reify and repudiate things[7]
Empirical and hypothetical.

This very fact of relativity,
The reason one sees your speech is matchless,
Generates the certitude of the reason
Embodied in all your other teachings.

From real experience, you teach so well,
Those who train themselves as your disciples
Go far beyond every kind of trouble,
Having reversed the root of all evil.

[7] These two extremist habits are carefully analyzed in the great *Essence*, Ch. II.

But those who turn away from your Teaching,
Though they struggle wearily long and hard,
Continue just to invite more problems,
Sticking to habitual views of self.

O wonder! When the wise do understand
The difference between these two (trainings),
How can they fail to feel (most gratefully)
Reverence for you from their inmost hearts?

Not to cite the richness of your teachings,
To achieve mere general understanding
Of just the meaning of some small portion
Confers, even that, the highest pleasure.

Alas, my mind conquered by confusion,
Though I came from afar to seek refuge
In the profusion of your excellence,
I could not embody its smallest part.

Yet when I stand before the Lord of Death,
And the stream of life is not quite ended,
I will consider myself fortunate
To have even this slightest faith in you.[8]

Of teachers, the Teacher of relativity,
Of wisdoms, the wisdom of relativity;
These are like imperial victors in the world,
Making you world champion of wisdom, over all.

Whatever you taught is penetrated
By means of relativity itself,
And since that really becomes Nirvana,
No deed of yours does not deliver peace.

O Wonder! Whoever hears your Teaching,
Finds liberating peace in everything;
And so who could possibly not respect
Those who strive to uphold such a Teaching?

[8] These two verses, written *after* an experience of unexcelled enlightenment, are very thought-provoking. The first indicates that the holder of the authentic view is still sensitive to the vulnerability of the misknowledge-oriented person, the perceptual habit of objective existence. The second then relates to the achievement of the "great death," the perception of objective non-existence, and the transcendence of that transcendence via faith and compassion, will-to-enlightenment and will-of-enlightenment.

As it overcomes all oppositions,
Is free from internal contradictions,
And fulfills both main goals of human beings,
My delight ever grows for this system.

For its sake you gave again and again,
Throughout long incalculable aeions,
Sometimes your body, other times your life,
Your loved ones, and vast treasuries of wealth.

When I see such excellences as yours,
Seeing how your heart anchors the Teaching,
Just as a steel fish-hook hooks tight the fish;
How sad my fate, not to hear it from you!

The very energy of that sadness
Keeps my mind unwavering (from the Teaching),
As the attention of the anxious mother
Never wanders from the beloved child.

Even when I reflect upon your speech,
Thinking "That Teacher, radiantly haloed
With veils of light-rays, ablaze with glory
Of magnificent signs and holy marks,
Spoke in this way with his heavenly voice!"
Then the image of great Shakyamuni
Just flashing in my mind's eye, heals me well,
As the moon's rays heal the pangs of fever.

Though that good system is so marvelous,
Unskilled persons get totally confused
In every respect, as if they were
All entangled like a coconut's hairs.

Having understood this problem, I then
Schooled myself in (the writings of) skilled sages,
Studying with manifold exertions,
Seeking your intent again and again.

And I studied numerous treatises
Of the Buddhist and the non-Buddhist schools,
Yet unremittingly my intellect
Was still tormented in the trap of doubt.

So I went to the night-lily garden
Of the treatises of Nagarjuna,
Prophesied to elucidate rightly
The principle of your final vehicle,
Free of the extremes of being and nothing.

There I saw, by the kindness of the Guru,
All illumined by garlands of white light,
The true eloquence of the glorious Moon (Chandrakirti),
Whose expanding orb of taintless wisdom
Courses freely in the sky of Scripture,
Dispels the darkness of extremist hearts,
Eclipses constellations of false truths;
And then, my mind at last obtained relief![9]

Of all his deeds, his speech is the supreme;
And for this very reason, true sages
Should commemorate a perfect Buddha
For this (teaching of relativity).

I renounced the world on the example of that Teacher,
My study of the Victor's speech is not inferior,
I am a Buddhist monk, diligent in yoga-practice,
And such is my reverence for that most eminent Seer!

By my Guru's kindness I was thus fortunate to meet
The liberating Teaching of the unexcelled Teacher,
And I dedicate this virtue as a cause of all beings'
Being looked after by the holy spiritual teachers.

May the Teaching of that Benefactor, until world's end,
Be undisturbed by the winds of perverse prejudices,
And achieving faith in the Teacher by understanding
The natural way of the Teaching, may it be ever full!

May I uphold the wholesome system of Shakyamuni,
That illumines the principle of relativity,
Through all my lives, though I give up body and even life!
And may I never give it up, even for an instant!

[9] This beautiful metaphor, playing on the convention that the white *kumuda* lily blooms in moon-rays, as the red lotus blooms in the sunshine, is echoed again in the conclusion of the *Essence*. The white moon-lily is the special symbol of Nagarjuna. It is quite unearthly, when we think it through carefully.

May I spend all day and night in the consideration
Of liberative techniques to propagate this success
Which was achieved by that best Leader through countless trials,
By making strenuous efforts the essence (of his lives)!

As I make effort on this way with pure high resolve,
May the gods Brahma, Indra, and all the World-protectors,
Good Mahakala, and the other Dharma-guardians
Be my constant friends forever and never let me down![10]

[10] The colophon states, "This *Essence of True Eloquence*, a praise of the Unexcelled Teacher Lord Buddha, the unsolicited best friend of all peoples, from the perspective of his teaching of profound relativity, was composed by the learned monk, bLo-bzang Grags-pai dPal, at the royal mountain retreat of Tibet, the heavenly retreat of O-de-gung-gyal, otherwise known as Victory Monastery. The scribe was Nam-mkha dPal."

THE GREAT *ESSENCE OF TRUE ELOQUENCE,* DISTINGUISHING THE INTERPRETABLE AND THE DEFINITIVE MEANINGS OF ALL THE SCRIPTURES OF THE VICTOR

PROLOGUE

Reverence to the Guru, Manjughosha!

Shambhu, Meghavahana, Hiranyagarbha,
Anangapati, Damodara, and the other (gods),
All puffed up with self-infatuation,
They roar their lordship o'er the worlds;
And yet, before the vision of His Body,
They pale like fireflies in the sun!
Then down they bow their sparkling diadems
In reverence to the lotuses of His feet!
I pay homage to that Lord of Sages,
The God of all the gods![1]

I bow devoted to Maitreya and Manjughosha,
Vast oceans, treasuries of jewels of eloquence,
Rippling with mighty waves of enlightened deeds,
Hard to fathom in their depths of wisdom,
Hard to measure in their great expanse of love!

I bow my head to the feet of Nagarjuna and Asanga,
Who pioneered the ways for Champions of philosophy,[2]
With two interpretations of Sugata's sacred discourse,[3]
And made that superb Doctrine of that Victor,
Shine like sunlight throughout the triple world!

[1] Shambhu is Shiva; Meghavahana, Indra; Hiranyagarbha, Brahma; Anangapati, Kama; and Damodara, Vishnu. See Introduction, II, for speculation on the mention of these deities.

[2] Tib. *shing rta chen po gnyis* (Skt. *mahāratha*). Nagarjuna and Asanga are sometimes themselves called "Champions," literally "Great-Charioted," and sometimes they play the role of "Founders of the Champion's Way" (*shing rtai chen poi srol 'byed*). It seems safe to infer that the imagery became blurred in the Tibetan tradition, once the epithet was divorced from its origin in the very common Sanskrit epic epithet *mahārathaḥ*, which is an attributive compound (*bahuvrīhi*) meaning "he who has (or drives) a great chariot," that is, "Champion," or "Mighty Warrior." The use of the epic epithet for great philosophers brings into play military imagery in the sense of viewing the attainment of enlightenment as a battle with the psychic demons such as ignorance, as well as acknowledging the philosophical battle of controversies.

[3] Tib. *bder gshegs gsung rab tshul gnyis shing rtai srol.* The two trends (*dvinaya*) in the Universal Vehicle Scriptures are known as the "profound" (*gambhīra*) and the "magnificent" (*udāra*). The profound trend is emphasized in the teachings of emptiness or self-

Respectfully I bow to those Master Scholars,
Best heralds of the non-decline of Buddha's Teaching,
Who upheld the two systems of the Champions,
And opened the eyes of millions of geniuses—
To the ornaments of the Holy Land of India,
Aryadeva, brave Buddhapalita, Bhavaviveka, Chandrakirti,
Vasubandhu, Sthiramati, Dignaga, and Dharmakirti![4]

There have been many who did not realize That Place,[5]
Although they strived, were not lowly in accomplishments
From direct experience, and were learned in the Doctrine,
And even dedicated themselves to the path of philosophy.[6]

But I have seen It quite precisely,
By the grace of my Guru, Savior Manjughosha,
And I am going to explain it from great love.
You who aspire to Peerless Philosophy,[7]
Listen with reverence,
With the critical discrimination that realizes
The Thatness of the Teaching!

(The Lord said), in the *Questions of Rashtrapala Scripture*:[8]

The way is empty, peaceful, and uncreated.
Not knowing that, the living beings wander.
Moved by compassion, he introduces them
With hundreds of reasons and technical procedures.

---

lessness, or identitylessness, which are systematized by Nagarjuna in the Centrist philosophical method. The magnificient trend is emphasized in the teachings of compassion and love of the spirit of enlightenment (*maitrīkarunābodhicitta*), which are systematized by Aryasanga in the Experientalist philosophical method.

[4] See Introduction V, for lives of these philosophers.

[5] Tib. *gnas de*, meaning the place of ultimate reality, the realization of voidness-relativity, and so forth.

[6] Gun-thang 'Jam-dbyangs explains (in the *Legs-bShad sNying-poi Yang-snying*, p. 16) that "not lowly in accomplishments from direct experience" refers particularly to Dol-bupa (1292-1361), the founder of the Jo-nang. "Learned in the Doctrine" refers particularly to rNgog-lo-tsva-ba (1059-1109), Sakya Pandita (1182-1251), and Bu-ston Rinpoche (1290-1364). And "dedicated themselves to the path of philosophy" refers particularly to Phyapa Chos-seng, etc., those masters of the Sakya school who developed the teaching of logic, known as the "eight great lions of philosophy." See Introduction, VI. For information on the Jo-nang school, see D. S. Ruegg, "The Jo Nan Pas: A School of Buddhist Ontologists," *Journal of the American Oriental Society*, 83 (1963), 73-81.

[7] *smra ba zla med* = Buddhahood, no less.

[8] P. L. Vaidya, ed., *Mahāyānasūtrasaṃgraha*, (Darbhanga, 1961[Buddhist Sanskrit Texts, 17]) Vol. 1, p. 154, II, k.310: *sūnyaśca sānta anutpādanaya avijānād eva jagad udbhramati / teṣām upāyanayayuktiśatair avatārayasi api krpālutayā //*.

Having seen the extreme difficulty of realizing the actuality of things, without which there is no liberation from the world, the compassionate Teacher introduced living beings to that realization through the many doors of reasoning and technical procedures. Thus, the discriminating should exert themselves in the techniques for realizing Thatness. This depends on the discrimination between the interpretable meaning and the definitive meaning of the teachings of the Victor.

It is not possible to discriminate between these two on scriptural authority alone, on some statement such as "This is interpretable meaning, and this definitive meaning." Otherwise, the Champions' elaboration of explanations of the problem of discrimination between interpretable and definitive would have been pointless. Further, many different interpretations of interpretable and definitive have been declared in the scriptures themselves. Finally, since it cannot be established in general by referring to scriptural statements alone, as no such statement would be valid in every case, neither can it be established by a mere (scriptural) statement in any particular case.

The Champions of Philosophy, foretold to discern the interpretable and the definitive in the teachings, elucidated their inner meaning. Hence, we must seek that meaning by following their determinations (established) by reasonings that fault alternative interpretations of definitive meaning scriptures, proving their definiteness as uninterpretable meaning. Thus, ultimately, we must discriminate with impeccable reasoning.[9]

Should we accept theories violating reason, their teacher could not become the personification of validating cognition.[10] For, even the ultimate reality of things includes means of proof through logically established reasoning.[11]

[9] Skt. *yukti*, Tsong Khapa also gives four types of *rigs pa* (*yukti*), that is, reasonings; namely, "relational reasoning" (*ltos-pai-rigs-pa, āpekṣāyukti*), which investigates the superficial, the ultimate, and their respective bases, perceiving causal relationships; "functional reasoning" (*bya ba byed pai rigs pa, kṛtyānusthānayukti*), which investigates things and their functions, perceiving the tendencies of things to function certain ways; "logical reasonings" (*'thad pas sgrub pai rigs pa, upapattisiddhayukti*), which establishes its objectives without violating validating cognition, attending to whether a cognition is supported by the valid evidences of perception, inference, or scriptural dogma; and finally, "natural reasonings" (*chos nyid kyi rigs pa, dharmatāyukti*), which accepts either the commonsensical natures (wetness of water, and son), or the inconceivable natures, or the actual natures of things, without inquiring whether these natures are confirmed by other reasons. This categorization occurs in the context of an analysis of the sixfold investigation (*paryeṣṭi*) that is part of analytic meditation (*vipaśyanā*).

[10] Tib. *tshad mai skyes bu* (Skt. *pramāṇabhūta*). This famous epithet of the Buddha first occurs in Dignaga's *Pramāṇasamuccaya*. See Introduction, II.

[11] The type of reasoning mentioned here corresponds to type three in the fourfold classification given above in n. 9. It is necessary to receive this statement with the greatest care and precision. Tsong Khapa does not say that ultimate reality is *encompassable* by rationalization, thus violating a basic tenet of the Universal Vehicle, that is, ineffability and

Seeing the ramifications of this, the Lord (declared):

> O Bhikshus, just as a goldsmith gets his gold,
> First testing by melting, cutting, and rubbing,
> Sages accept my teachings after full examination
> And not just out of devotion (to me).[12]

inconceivability of the ultimate. He does insist, however, that reason is the approach to ultimate reality, as precursor of meditation and insight, and so on. Hence, our rational mind must not reject itself a priori, but must use itself to the full.

[12] This verse is known to the commentators as being from the *Vimalaprabhā* commentary on the *Kālacakra*, although it appears in the Pali Canon as well. The Sanskrit occurs as a quotation in the D. Shastri *Tattvasaṃgraha* (Varanasi: Bauddhabharati, 1968), k. 3587: *tapācchedācca nikaśāt suvarṇam iva pānditaib / parikṣyā bhikṣavo grāhyam mad vaco na tu gauravāt //.*

5. Nagarjuna.

6. Aryasanga.

7. Aryadeva.

8. Vasubandhu.

9. Dignaga.

10. Dharmakirti.

11. Tsong Khapa, founder of dGa-ldan school of Tibetan Buddhism, surrounded by episodes from his biography.

12. Icon of "refuge assembly," with Tsong Khapa in the center, Shakyamuni Buddha in his heart, surrounded by myriad gurus of profound (to his left), magnificent (to his right), and mystic practice (above him) lineages, as well as numerous emanations of Buddhas, bodhisattvas, ishtadevatas, dharmapalas, and lokapalas (on the tree before him).

Chapter I

STATEMENTS FROM THE *ELUCIDATION OF INTENTION SCRIPTURE*

1. INQUIRY TO RESOLVE CONTRADICTIONS

(Paramarthasamudgata) states, in the *Elucidation of Intention Scripture*:

> The Lord proclaims in many discourses the intrinsic identity[1] of the aggregates, their characteristics of production and destruction, their abandonment, and full understanding. As with the aggregates, so does he proclaim the twelve media, the dependent origination, and the four foods. Thus does he proclaim the intrinsic identity, the thorough knowledge, the abandonment, the realization, and the meditation of the four holy truths; the intrinsic identity, variety, plurality, abandonment and full understanding of the elements; and the intrinsic identities, resistances, remedies, initial productions, maintenances, preservations, developments, and increases of the thirty-seven accessories of enlightenment. On the other hand, the Lord also proclaims the intrinsic unreality, non-production, non-cessation, primordial peace, and natural total liberation of all things. I wonder about this and earnestly inquire of the Lord the actual meaning of his proclamation of the intrinsic unreality, non-production, non-cessation, primordial peace, and natural, total liberation of all things.[2]

[1] Tib. *rang gi mtshan nyid.* (Skt, *svalakṣaṇa.*) This is the key word of the entire treatise. Its meaning in this context of the ontological debate between the Idealists and the Centrists is not to be confused with its meaning in the Abhidharma—"defining characteristic"—or with its meaning in the Logical literature—"particular" or "ultimate particular." See below, Ch. V, n. 11. bLo-bzang Phun-tshogs, *Zin Bris*, f. 13aff., further qualifies the use of "intrinsic identity" here, by saying that here it is not merely a general sort of intrinsic identity, but is specifically "intrinsic identity as the basis of identificatory constructs" (*rang 'dzin rtog pai zhen gzhir rang gi mtshan nyid kyis grub pa*), since otherwise there would be no point of contradiction, as both Individualist Traditionists and Idealists accept an intrinsic identity which establishes a thing in its own right (*rang ngos nas grub pai rang mtshan du grub*).

[2] SN VII (Lamotte, *Explication*: Tib. p. 65, Fr. p. 192). Tsong Khapa abbreviates the quote, by abbreviating the enumerations of things covered. For information on the various categories, see the Glossary.

There is verbal contradiction between the statements in some scriptures that all things are devoid of intrinsic reality and those of others that proclaim the intrinsic identity, and so on, of the aggregates, and so on. Yet the scriptures should be free of contradictions. Hence (Paramarthasamudgata) inquires into the intended meaning of the declarations of intrinsic unreality, thereby also inquiring by implication into the intended meaning of the declarations of intrinsic identity, and so on.

Here, it is not correct to interpret "intrinsic identity" as the *Great Chinese Commentary*[3] does, as "distinctive characteristic." The scripture itself, in the section on the imagined nature,[4] clearly explains it to refer to "intrinsically identifiable status." Furthermore, (if it were "distinctive characteristic"), it would entail the logical fallacy that the explanation of the imagined nature as "identity-unreality" would be invalid, since there are distinctive characteristics even in things of imagined nature.[5]

Although other commentaries explain the "variety" and "plurality" of elements otherwise, we may take them to refer to the eighteen elements and the six elements, respectively, considering their subsequent occurrence in the scripture. "Preservation" means not forgetting.

2. ANSWER RESOLVING THE CONTRADICTION; THE INTERPRETATION OF UNREALITY INTENDED BY SUCH DECLARATIONS; BRIEF STATEMENT

In the *Elucidation of Intention*, (the Buddha) teaches intrinsic unreality intending the three unrealities:

> Paramarthasamudgata! I teach the intrinsic unreality of all things intending the following three types of such unreality: identity-unreality, production-unreality, and ultimate unreality.[6]

In the *Compendium*, (Asanga) states:

[3] *Āryagambhīrasaṃdhinirmocana ṭīkā*, by Wen Tshig (Chin., Yuan Tsho, 614-695 C.E.) (TG, C, vols. 39-41). This comment found at p. 39, f. 316b7: "*De la rang gi mtshan nyid ces bya ba ni bye brag gi mtshan nyid yin te / ji skad du gzugs ni thogs pa dang bcas pao zhes bya ba nas / rnam par shes pa ni rnam par rig pao / zhes bya bai bar du. . . .* ("Here, 'defining characteristic' is a 'particular characteristic.' For example, as [that of] 'form' is impenetrability . . . and as [that of] 'consciousness' is knowledge. . . .") Obviously Yuan Tsho takes *svalakṣaṇa* in its Abhidharmic meaning. See n. 1. above.

[4] Skt. *parikalpita-svabhāva*.

[5] That is, imaginatively constructed realities, or conceptually created things that have no reality according to this system, still have peculiar, or defining, characteristics within their conceptualized sphere. See above, n. 1.

[6] SN VII (Lamotte, *Explication*: Tib. p. 67, Fr. p. 193).

With what intention does the Lord declare the unreality of all things? He declares it wherever necessary to train (disciples), intending the three types of such unreality.[7]

Also, in the *Thirty*, (Vasubandhu) states:

The intrinsic unreality of all things is taught intending the three types of unreality of the three types of reality.[8]

Therefore, anyone who maintains that the statements of the intrinsic unreality of all things in scriptures such as the *Transcendent Wisdom* intend all superficial things and do not intend the absolute, contradicts the *Elucidation* and the treatises of Aryasanga and Vasubandhu, and also departs from the system of the Holy Father and Son.[9]

Detailed Explanation[10]

The inquiry into the intention of the statement of intrinsic unreality asks both the intention in declaring unreality and the actual mode of unreality, and the answer deals with both in order. To explain the first, (the Buddha) collected all the statements of unreality or identitylessness[11] with regard to all different categories of things, from form to omniscience, into three unrealities, intending that the explanation of their mode of unreality be easy to understand, since all superficial and ultimate things are contained within these three. However, though (the Buddha) needed to use such a technique, who is there in his right mind who would say that the ultimate was not included among the things declared to be unreal, when the

[7] *Yogacaryābhūmiviniścayasaṃgrahaṇī* by Āryāsanga, TG, C, zi, f. 17a2-3.

[8] Vasubandhu, *Triṃśikāvijñaptikārikāh*, k. 23. (Skt. S. Levi, *Vijñaptimātratā siddhi*, p. 14): *trividhasya svabhāvasya trividhāṃ niḥsvabhāvatāṃ / saṃdhāya sarvadharmānāṃ deśitā niḥsvabhāvatā //.*

[9] Tib. *'phags pa yab sras*, refers to Nagarjuna and Aryadeva, sometimes including (as sons) Buddhapalita, Chandrakirti, and so on.

In this paragraph, Tsong Khapa makes his opening critique of the Jo-nang school, the advocates of "other-voidness" (*gzhan stong*), who believed that the ultimate was an ultimately real void, devoid of everything else. Tsong Khapa returns to refute them frequently.

[10] Both P and K texts omit this heading *rgyas par bshad pa*, confusing it with the *gnyis pa ni* below (K. f. 6a2). Nevertheless, we have placed it here as logically necessary, as otherwise the *de gnyis rim pa bzhin ston pa las dang po 'chad pa ni* (K. f. 5b4) is left hanging, and the "Detailed Explanation" section would otherwise begin in the middle of the analysis of the two, intention and actual mode.

[11] Tib. *ngo bo nyid dam rang bzhin med*. Tsong Khapa here equates the two words as synonyms, and, indeed, both can serve as translations of *niḥsvabhāva*. The Tibetan words have different emphases, however, which serve to stress the ambiguity in the Skt. *svabhāva*. Where it is used in the ontological sense, meaning "own-being" or "intrinsic reality," the Tibetans prefer *ngo bo nyid*. Where it is used in the conventional sense, meaning simply "nature," they prefer *rang bzhin*, although when it is used as "self-nature," that is, stressing the *sva-* (*rang*) prefix, they equate it with *ngo bo nyid*.

Mother Scripture,[12] etc., declared that all things, such as the five aggregates, the twelve media, and the eighteen elements, are non-existent, identityless, unreal; and particularly mentions the intrinsic unreality of all the synonyms of the absolute, such as "emptiness," the "ultimate element," and "reality," etc.?[13]

To answer the second aspect of the question, that is, the mode of unreality—as one might wonder what are the three unrealities that contain all things, said to be intrinsically unreal, and what is their mode of unreality—let us explain the first. In the *Elucidation*, (the Buddha) declares:

> What is the identity-unreality of things? It is the imaginatively constructed nature. Why? It is a nature established by names and symbolisms, and is not substantiated by intrinsic identity. Therefore, it is called "identity-unreality."[14]

The first question and answer equates the imagined nature with identity-unreality. Giving reasons for that, he states the affirmative reason that it is established by names and conventions, and the negative reason that it is not established by means of any intrinsic identity. The following two unrealities should be understood by a similar breakdown into affirmative and negative reasons.[15]

The identity-reality which does not exist in the imagined is interpreted as establishment or existence by intrinsic identity. Here, the criterion for existence or non-existence with intrinsic identity (respectively) is whether (something) is established independent of, or dependent upon names and symbolic conventions. This system of interpretation, wherein (nominal) establishment is not concomitant with existence, is in radical disagreement with the (system) of the Dialecticist Centrists, wherein existents are established (precisely) on the strength of nominal conventions. Thus, the

[12] Tib. *yum gyi mdo* (Skt. Mātāsūtra refers to the *Prajñāpāramitāsūtras*, especially the *Satasāhasrikā*. The Tibetans retained the Universal Vehicle tradition of regarding the Transcendent Wisdom as a goddess, and hence her scripture, a conventional part of herself, is fittingly called *Jinamātā*, "Mother of all Victors." In the Tibetan philosophical tradition, certain major texts such as this are referred to by nicknames, which I have preserved in the translation.

[13] Tsong Khapa goes after the Jo-nang-pas again, using a somewhat stronger tone to highlight the preposterousness of their theory. See above, n. 9.

[14] SN VII (Lamotte, *Explication*: Tib. p. 67-68, Fr. p. 194). Here, Tib. *brda* (Skt. *saṃketaḥ*) is rendered "symbolic convention" or "symbolism" rather than merely "sign," following a comment by Tshe-brtan Lha-rams-pa, quoted in *Zin Bris* f. 15b, who cites Sthiramati as authority. Pandeya, *Madhyāntavibhāga*, p. 97; *samketah* (=) *saṃjñāsaṃjñisaṃbandhajñānaṃ*.

[15] That is, production-unreality is affirmed by conditional production, and is negatively established by refuting intrinsic production; ultimate unreality is affirmed as pure object, and is negatively established as ultimate unreality of the relative.

two systems disagree also on the meaning of existence and non-existence with intrinsic identity. Nevertheless, when we hold to the existence with intrinsic identity of this (system), we also hold to the establishment with intrinsic identity of the Dialecticists; and there are some cases wherein it is not so held according to the former, and yet it is so held according to the latter.[16]

In regard to the second unreality, in the *Elucidation*, (the Buddha) declares:

> What is the production-unreality of things? It is the relative nature of things. Why so? Production (of something) occurs by force of other conditions, and not by that thing's own nature. Therefore, it is called "production-unreality."[17]

Actual production, or real production, being nonexistent in the relative, is production (of a thing) by itself, mentioned in the phrase "not by that thing's own nature." It is equivalent to independent production. As (Asanga) states in the *Compendium*: "Because created things are dependently originated, they are produced by influence of conditions, and not from themselves. This is called 'production-unreality.'[18]

Thus, this system declares the unreality of such real production in the relative, yet does not declare its unreality to be due to non-establishment with intrinsic identity.

There are two interpretations of the third unreality, the first of which establishes ultimate-unreality in the relative. The *Elucidation* statement (is):

> What is the ultimate unreality of things? (It is) those dependently originated things which are unreal because of ultimate-unreality. Why

[16] Tsong Khapa hints at an important point. The Idealist believes that intrinsic identifiability (that is, intrinsic identity-status) is necessary for any sort of existence, hence "merely name" is negative of existence for him. The Dialecticist, on the other hand, admits no intrinsic identifiability, not finding any ultimate essence of anything that can resist analysis of referents of designations, hence for him "merely name" negates intrinsic identity, yet leaves undisturbed conventional existence; indeed, makes it possible. See Ch. V n. 21 and 33.

Thus, the Idealist holds intrinsic identifiability of relative and perfect as their objective, non-nominal existence. The Dialecticist sees that as the perception of intrinsic identifiability, and considers it an error, whereas the former considers it a necessity. Finally, although the Idealist does not not consider himself to hold the imagined as intrinsically identifiable, yet, as he thinks it can be found through analysis conventionally (although disappearing ultimately), he still holds to its intrinsic identifiability according to the Dialecticist. See *Zin Bris*, f. 18b, and *mTha dPyod*, ff. 33b-34a (. . . *sems tsam pas kun btags rtog pas btags tsam min par rang ngos nas mi grub par mi 'dod kyang kun btags rang ngos nas grub par 'dod pai phyir/*). SERA, f. 7b2ff.

[17] SN VII (Lamotte, *Explication*: Tib. p. 68, Fr. p. 194).

[18] MS X; TG, C, zi, f. 17a3-4; D, zi, f. 1666-7.

so? Paramarthasamudgata! I teach that, among things, the ultimate is the pure object and, since the relative nature is not the pure object, it is called "ultimate-unreality."[19]

The relative is called "ultimate-unreality" because it does not exist in the ultimate reality. For, if we objectify the ultimate and meditate on it, defilements will come to an end, but if we objectify the relative and meditate on it, we cannot purify ourselves of the defilements.

In that case, why not interpret the imagined also as ultimate unreality? Although this would be appropriate, insofar as the imagined is not the pure object either, still, only the relative is established as ultimate-unreality and not the imagined, because of the power of the relative when objectified to stop erroneous constructive thought.

Why? Although there is no such doubt with regard to the imagined, the following doubt is liable to arise (with regard to the relative): "If it is acknowledged that defilements are purified through meditation that objectifies the relative as being empty of the imagined, then, as we take the so-qualified relative as object, it becomes the 'pure object' and hence becomes the ultimate."[20]

Furthermore, the suspected fallacy (of relative amounting to the ultimate) has no bearing, just as there is no contradiction between the fact that the conviction of sound's impermanence abolishes the holding of sound as permanent and the fact that the contemplation of sound itself does not abolish the sense of permanence.[21] Also, although the relative is not established as the ultimate when the ultimate is taken to be the pure object, the question of its establishment as another sort of ultimate will be explained below.[22]

In regard to the second interpretation of the ultimate unreality, the *Elucidation* statement is:

> Furthermore, the perfect nature of things is called "ultimate-unreality." Why? Paramarthasamudgata! The objective selflessness of things is called their "unreality." It is the ultimate, manifest by the fact of the intrinsic unreality of all things. Therefore, it is called "ultimate-unreality."[23]

[19] SN VII (Lamotte, *Explication*: Tib. p. 68, Fr. p. 194).

[20] Thus, one reason for calling the relative "ultimate unreality" is to forestall this doubt about its possible equivalence with the ultimate perfect.

[21] The analogy here is between sound and the relative, and sound qualified by impermanence and the relative qualified by non-existence of the imagined. In both cases, the unqualified object, when contemplated, does not give the desired result in understanding.

[22] This refers to ultimacy as intrinsically identifiable status as mentioned in VS section of Ch. II (Explanation in the Compendium").

[23] SN VII (Lamotte, *Explication*: Tib. p. 68, Fr. p. 194).

The perfect, the objective selflessness of things, is the pure object, and hence also the ultimate. It is manifest in the unreality of the selves of things, and, because it is established by that fact alone, it is called "the intrinsic unreality of things," and hence the "ultimate-unreality."

(The Buddha) also declares, (elsewhere) in the *Elucidation*: "If the nature of the conditional and the nature of the ultimate were different, then the mere selflessness and the mere unreality of conditional (things) would not be the nature of the ultimate."[24]

Furthermore, in the section on the examples in (the *Elucidation*), (Buddha) states that (the ultimate) is established as (mere) selflessness, just as space is established as mere formlessness. Hence, it is extremely clear that the perfect, the objective selflessness, is established as the absolute negation of mental fabrication, which is just the negation of the objective self in the case of conditional (things). Therefore, the belief that this scripture's teaching of the import of reality is definitive in meaning is contradictory to the belief in the independent status, that is, reached without exclusion of a mentally objectified negatee, of an immutable perfect, which is not interpreted as an exclusive negative, a mere exclusion of negatee.[25]

This system calls the perfect the "ultimate-unreality of things," because it is the mere negation of the self-actuality of things, and does not believe it to be unreal because of a lack of intrinsically identifiable status of the actual negation itself.[26]

Exposition of Examples

In regard to the examples illustrating the three unrealities, the *Elucidation* statement is:

> The identity-unreality should be regarded as being like a sky-flower. Paramarthasamudgata! Production-unreality should be regarded as being like a magical creation, as should the first of the two ultimate-unreal-

[24] SN III (Lamotte, *Explication*: Tib. p. 45, Fr. p. 177). That is, the nature of the conditional is ultimate unreality. If the nature of the ultimate were different it would have to be wholly (or partially, at least) real. But the selflessness and unreality of conditionals is precisely the ultimate itself. Thus, if the ultimate itself had a real nature, it would entail an absurd hypostatization of a "real unreality."

[25] Presupposed in this passage is knowledge of the standard two types of negation: implicative, or choice, negation, which establishes another fact by implication when negating its explicit object, and absolute, or exclusive, negation, which only negates its negatee, implying absolutely nothing else. See Ch. VII. Of course, Tsong Khapa is again refuting the Jo-nang theory of the ultimate status of the ultimate. See above, n. 13.

[26] This stresses that the Idealists cannot conceive of either of the two truths without intrinsic identifiability. They accept ultimate unreality as the absolute negation of the subject-object dichotomy, which they equate with the subtle objective selflessness.

ities. Paramarthasamudgata! Just as space is manifest through the mere absence of form and is all-pervasive, so the other ultimate-unreality should be regarded as manifest through objective selflessness and as all-pervasive.[27]

The likening of the imagined to a flower of the sky illustrates the fact that it is merely an imaginative construction, and does not illustrate its non-existence among objects of knowledge. The way in which the relative is like illusion will be explained below, and the meaning of the simile for the perfect is self-evident.

Thus the mode of unreality intended by such statements is explained. If unreality is explained otherwise, that is as the non-establishment with intrinsic identity of all three natures, it is (a case of) insistence on the literal meaning of the scriptures declaring unreality. Thereby we adopt either nihilism or annihilism, since repudiation of all three natures brings us to the view of meaninglessness. Thus, in this system, if the relative were not established with intrinsic identity, it would be repudiated, since production and cessation would be impossible, and if the perfect were not established with intrinsic identity, it could not serve as the ground of things.

Here, we might suppose that, although the view of lack of intrinsically identifiable status might be allowed to represent repudiation of the latter two natures, how could it involve repudiation of the imagined?[28]

The reason is that the latter two natures would become non-existent if not established with intrinsic identity, hence the imagined also would become totally non-existent, deprived of its basis of designation and designative conventions (themselves partaking of the relative nature).

Furthermore, (the Buddha also declares) in the *Elucidation*:

They do not understand correctly the profound authenticity of my intentional instructions: "All these things are only unreal. All these things are only unproduced. All these things are only unceased, only primordially peaceful, only naturally liberated!" Although they admire that teaching, they are obsessed with its literal meaning only, and from that basis, they arrive at the view of nothingness and meaninglessness in all things. Having gotten these views of nothingness and meaninglessness, they repudiate all the natures in all things. They repudiate the imagined nature of things, as well as their relative and perfect natures. Why? Paramarthasamudgata! The imagined nature can be known when the relative and perfect natures exist. But those who see identitylessness

[27] SN VII (Lamotte, *Explication*: Tib. p. 69, Fr. p. 195).

[28] That is, as the imagined has already been denied intrinsically identifiable status, by its very name, identity-unreality.

in the relative and perfect natures repudiate the imagined nature also. Therefore, they are said to repudiate all three natures.[29]

This system holds that "literal insistence" means to accept as taught the statements from the scriptures that teach intrinsic unreality, such as "All things are ultimately devoid of reality, devoid of essential nature, and devoid of intrinsic identity."

"To see identitylessness in the relative and perfect natures" means to view them both as not established with intrinsic identity, and from "why" on, he teaches the reason this becomes repudiation of all three natures. If one takes literally the declaration of non-existence of production and cessation with intrinsic identity, then the relative is repudiated; and it can be seen (easily) how this becomes repudiation of the other two natures as well. For in this system, production and cessation, if they are not established with intrinsic identity, must therefore be non-existent.

The Intention of the Declaration of Productionlessness

If such is the mode of unreality, with what intention does he declare non-production, etc.? This is declared intending the first and last unreality. In regard to the first, the *Elucidation* statement is:

> I teach all things to be unproduced, unceased, primordially peaceful, and naturally liberated, intending the fact of identity-unreality. Why? Paramarthasamudgata! What does not exist with intrinsic identity is not produced. What is not produced does not cease. What is not produced and does not cease, that is originally peaceful. What is originally peaceful, that is naturally liberated. And, as for the naturally liberated, there is not the slightest thing to be done for its liberation.[30]

By setting forth lack of intrinsically identifiable status as the reason for the non-existence of production and cessation in the imagined, he teaches that for production and cessation to exist they must be established with intrinsic identity, and hence that production and cessation are established with intrinsic identity in the relative. Because freedom from production and cessation, being the uncreated, cannot possibly belong to the totally addictive realm,[31] he teaches "primordial peace" and "natural liberation," since it is (free from) addiction, here same as sorrow.

In regard to the final unreality, the *Elucidation* statement is:

[29] SN VII (Lamotte, *Explication*: Tib. p. 77, Fr. pp. 200-201).
[30] SN VII (Lamotte, *Explication*: Tib. p. 69, Fr. p. 195).
[31] Tib. *kun nas nyon mongs pai chos* (Skt. *sāṃkleśikadharma*). See Glossary.

> Again, I teach all things to be unproduced, unceased, primordially peaceful, and naturally liberated, intending the fact of ultimate unreality as manifest through objective selflessness. Why? This ultimate unreality manifest through objective selflessness subsists alone, eternally and permanently. It is the uncreated essence of things, free of all emotional addictions. And because it is free of all addictions, it is orginally peaceful and naturally liberated.[32]

The *Great Chinese Commentary* explains that "eternally" refers to the infinite past, and that "permanently" refers to the infinite future.[33]

Here, one might well wonder about the meaning of thus neglecting to take the middle unreality as the basis of non-production, etc., since all three (natures) have already been taken as the basis of unreality. Furthermore, what does (Asanga) mean by explaining non-production, etc., in terms of all three natures, in the *Abhidharma Synthesis*?

> Because of the identity-unreality of the imagined nature, the production-unreality of the relative, and the ultimate-unreality of the perfect, things are said to be unproduced, unceased, originally peaceful, and naturally liberated. With what intention? (The intention is that) without intrinsic reality, there is no production, without production, there is no cessation, and without cessation and production, there is original peace, and natural, total liberation.[34]

The *Great Chinese Commentary* explains that the scripture does not declare the relative as the intended basis of productionlessness, etc., in order to show that dependent origination is not without purpose.[35] And the *Abhidharma Synthesis* explanation (of non-production in the relative) is in terms of the non-existence of production from self and of production without cause. Since there are production and cessation established with intrinsic identity in the relative, the declaration of the non-existence of production and cessation does not intend the relative. And since most of the relative is included in the totally addicted, it is the intention of this scripture not to make it the basis of the latter two expressions.[36] Thus the *Synthesis* explanation intends that, as there is no intrinsic reality, interpreted as the types of reality excluded in each of the three natures,

32 SN VII (Lamotte, *Explication*, pt. 9: Tib. p. 70, Fr. p. 195).

33 SNT: TG, P, ti, f. 327b3.

34 AS III: TG, P, li, f. 124b3-6.

35 SNT: TG, P, ti, f. 330a5-7. Tsong Khapa's accurate paraphrase.

36 The "latter two expressions" are "primordial peace" and "natural liberation," conveying utter freedom from any sort of addiction.

so there is no production and no cessation, and so also there is primordial peace and natural liberation.[37]

3. DESCRIPTION OF THE THREE NATURES

Granted that the imagined nature is equivalent to identity-unreality, what is it in itself? The *Elucidation* statement is:

> The imaginatively constructed nature is the establishment by names and conventions of substantive natures such as "form-aggregate," etc., and qualitative natures, such as "production of the form-aggregate," or "cessation of the form-aggregate," or "the form-aggregate is abandoned and fully known," etc., in conditional processes, which are the ground of the imagined nature, and the object of constructive thought.[38]

The last three[39] expressions, from "conditional" to "thought," refer to the designative base of the imagined, and the rest (of the quotation) describes the process of imaginative construction. The processes of "substantive" (or ascriptive) designation, such as "this is the form-aggregate," and of "qualitative," or descriptive designation, such as "the form-aggregate is produced," will be explained in detail (below).[40]

Granted the relative is equivalent to production-unreality, what is it

[37] At this point, it becomes clear that the "wonderer" above who questions the intention of the statement of production-unreality, citing AS, etc., is none other than the Jo-nang theoretician, who needs every unreality to apply to the relative to support his claim that only the ultimate is real, that only the ultimate is ultimately existent. Of course, Tsong Khapa is here refuting him from the Idealist point of view, which is especially effective since the Jo-nang-pa stakes his case on his own peculiar interpretation of the "three-unreality" theory.

[38] SN VII (Lamotte, *Explication*: Tib. p. 81, Fr. p. 203). This definition, of great importance for our grasp of the philosophical thrust of the Idealist, can be more freely rendered: "The imagined reality" designates the world of conditional processes, which are its ground as object of conceptual constructions, when this world is verbally and conventionally structured into a world of natural entities, as [evinced in perceptions accompanying such] expressions as "This is the form-aggregate," and of natural qualities, as [evinced in perceptions accompanying such] expressions as "The form-aggregate is produced," "it is ceased," "it is abandoned," "it is fully understood," and so on. Thus, as long as our perceptions are habitually entangled in our conventional, verbalized descriptions of the world, that is, as long as we have not seen the unreality of the "structured, verbally, conceptually, and imaginatively constructed world," we do not perceive the "real" relative, the inexpressible processes that we are.

[39] Tib. *dang po* means, of course, "first." I have used "last" here as the three phrases, from "conditional" to "constructions," which are the first in the Tibetan order, are last in the English order.

[40] The processes of ascriptive designations, that is, designations that ascribe substance to phenomena, and descriptive designations, which describe the behavior of those ascribed entities, will be exemplified in the applications of the three natures to the various things at the end of this subsection.

in itself? The *Elucidation* statement is: "The relative nature consists of conditional processes, which are the ground of the imagined nature, and the object of imaginative construction."[41] The first phrase shows its own actuality, the second, that it is the designative base of the imagined, and the third, of what it is the object.[42]

Granted the perfect is ultimate unreality, what is it in itself? The *Elucidation* statement is:

> The perfect nature is that very same conditional process, the ground of the imagined nature and object of imaginative construction, as it intrinsically lacks precisely the reality (attributed to it) in the imagined nature, which is not established therein, which is the objective selflessness, the ultimate reality, and the pure object.[43]

Here, the perfect is described as the "objective selflessness," or "ultimate reality," which, when objectified and meditated upon, will purify defilements. What is "objective selflessness?" It is the fact of intrinsic unreality, also called "actuality." Of what is the reality non-existent? "Precisely the reality" indicates the above-mentioned imagined nature, the word "precisely" excluding anything else. Hence, this means that the perfect is not taken as the unreality of the other two natures, but precisely as the unreality of the imagined nature alone.

The first part of the quotation, from "conditional process" to "construction," indicates the relative as that which is empty, and "the imagined nature not established therein" makes it very clear that the perfect is the emptiness of the relative with respect to the imagined. Hence, the belief that this scripture's teachings are definitive in meaning is contradictory to the belief that the perfect is the emptiness of the last reality with respect to the first two realities.[44]

In regard to the mode of emptiness, the existence of something possibly existent elsewhere is not negated, as in the case of an area devoid of a pot, but the relative is empty of the establishment of the imagined, as in the case of a person's being empty of substantial existence. Thus, the scripture declares, "the imagined nature, which is not established therein. . . ."[45]

[41] SN VII (Lamotte, *Explication*: Tib. p. 81, Fr. p. 203).

[42] Here again, "first" and "third" are opposite in the translation, due to the inverted word-orders of the two languages.

[43] SN VII (Lamotte, *Explication*: Tib. p. 82, Fr. p. 204).

[44] The Jo-nang theory of "other-voidness" (*gzhan stong*) is even more clearly refuted here, for if, as they do, you take this scripture as definitive, you must accept as stated that the perfect is the relative devoid of the imagined only, and not the former devoid of the two latter. See above, n. 9.

[45] bLo-bzang Phun-tshogs, *Zin Bris* (f. 20a), here comments that mKhas-grub in *sTong Thun* (f. 69bff.), while granting Tsong Khapa's point that the Idealist view cannot be too

In regard to the "imagined" which is negated, the reason why this scripture does not mention any imagined other than that of ascriptive and descriptive designation, on both occasions of description of the imagined, will be explained below.[46]

Just as they are applied to the form-aggregate, the three natures are stated to apply to each of the other four aggregates, the twelve media, the twelve links of dependent origination, the four foods, the six elements and the eighteen elements. As for the holy truth of suffering, its designative base is the same as above, its imagined nature is established by names and symbolic conventions, ascriptively as "truth of suffering," and descriptively as "realization of the truth of suffering," its relative nature is as above, and its perfect nature is as above, with the statement that is is "unreality with respect to the (imagined) reality only." Likewise, (the three natures) apply to the other holy truths. Also, they are applied to the seven divisions of the accessories of enlightenment, the designative base as before, the imagined being ascriptive (designations), such as "perfect concentration," and descriptive (designations), such as "its resistance," "its remedy," etc., and their other two realities being stated as in the case of the truth of suffering. All of these are recited by Paramarthasamudgata to the Teacher to affirm his understanding of the explanation of the three unrealities that intends the method of presenting the three natures of each thing, from the form-aggregate to the components of the path, mentioned in the inquiry resolving contradictions above.

4. INQUIRY INTO THE MEANING THUS ESTABLISHED; EXPOSITION OF THE *ELUCIDATION OF INTENTION*

There are three types of scriptures: those that teach that things are existent by intrinsic identity; those that teach that things are not established by

easily twisted to fit theories such as that of the Jo-nang-pas, still feels that the Jo-nang tendency is present even in the Idealist view, due to their absolutism of believing the relative to have an ultimate truth-status.

[46] dPal-'byor Lhun-grub offers a useful summary of types of imagined realities (SERA, f. 13a3ff.). In general, there are two types of imagined realities, the totally non-existent (*mtshan nyid yongs chad*), and the categorical (*rnam grangs kyi . . .*). The first type is exemplified by personal and objective selves (that is, totally non-existent). The second type has two subtypes, the verbally established and that not established verbally. The first is exemplified by ascriptive and descriptive designation, equated to identity-unreality in SN. Examples of the second are space, and knowable objects in general. The SN is only concerned with the verbally established categorical type, since the issue is intrinsic identifiability; hence the totally non-existent and the non-verbal categorical are not involved. That is, the SN is soteriologically practical, since the mental habit of verbalizing mental construction, becoming either reification or repudiation, arises through not understanding the imagined reality of this type, and is abandoned by realizing this imagined reality's lack of intrinsically identifiable status. See also *mTha dPyod*, f. 50a1-3.

intrinsic identity; and those that show fine discrimination between establishment and non-establishment by intrinsic identity. Thus, there are two types according to whether or not they discriminate between existence and non-existence of intrinsic reality. The discriminating (scriptures) are definitive in meaning, as they cannot be interpreted otherwise, and the non-discriminating are interpretable in meaning, since they must be interpreted otherwise. Thus, by implication from the above explanations, we can understand that two types of scriptures are interpretable in meaning, and one type is definitive in meaning.

(Now), Paramarthasamudgata asks the Teacher, how this implicit result should be applied to determine the interpretable and the definitive among the three wheels (of Dharma)[47] in the context of their temporal sequentiality. The *Elucidation* statement is:

> First of all, the Lord, in the Deer Park at Rshipatana in Varanasi, for the sake of those involved in the disciple-vehicle, turned a wondrous, amazing wheel of Dharma, such as had never before been turned in the world by men or gods, by showing the aspects of the four holy truths. Nevertheless, even that wheel of Dharma turned by the Lord was surpassable, provisory, interpretable in meaning, and disputable.
>
> Then, the Lord, for the sake of those involved in the Universal Vehicle, turned a second wheel of Dharma, even more wondrous and amazing, by proclaiming emptiness, starting from the fact of the unreality, productionlessness, ceaselessness, primordial peace, and natural liberation of all things. Nevertheless, even this wheel of Dharma was surpassable, provisory, interpretable, and disputable.
>
> Then, the Lord, for the sake of those involved in all vehicles, turned the third wheel of Dharma, using the finest discrimination, starting from the fact of the unreality, productionlessness, ceaselessness, primordial peace, and natural liberation of all things. And this turning of the wheel of Dharma by the Lord is unsurpassed, not provisory, definitive in meaning, and leaves no grounds for dispute.[48]

Partial Explanation of Its Meaning; Verbal Meaning

Yuan Tsho explains:

> In regard to the turning of the first wheel, the first phrase indicates its location, the second, its disciples, and from "turned" to "truths" describes the wheel itself. "Aspects of the four holy truths" indicates the principal subject. "Wondrous" is praise. "Nevertheless" indicates

[47] The concept of the "Wheel of Dharma" is elucidated in what follows.
[48] SN VII (Lamotte, *Explication*: Tib. p. 85, Fr. p. 206).

it is not definitive. "Surpassable" indicates a specific teaching above it. "Provisory" indicates that it is a teaching valid for specific occasions. It is "interpretable," because it deals with existence and not with emptiness. "Disputable" indicates its rebuttal by other (teachings), and its serving as basis for the arguments between the sectarians of the Disciple Vehicle.[49]

That is, the scripture means: by "surpassable," that beyond it there is another definitive meaning; by "provisory," that if its meaning is taken literally as taught, it gives rise to criticism from others, such a meaning further indicated by the alternate translation, "with inherent opposition," given by the *Chinese Commentary*; by "interpretable," that the meaning must be otherwise interpreted; and by "disputable," that there are contrary arguments, since the Teacher did not explicate the meaning as "it is thus."

In regard to the second wheel, from "starting . . . " to "things" shows the principal subject. "For the sake . . . ," etc., shows the disciples for whom the wheel was turned. Some commentaries explain "by proclaiming emptiness" as meaning the teaching of objective selflessness, but the *Chinese Commentary* gives also an alternative reading, "by unmanifested aspects," the meaning of which is stated to be "hidden." This alternative translation is also correct, as the two latter wheels are shown to be similar in having realitylessness as their principal subject and different in their teaching procedures. The middle wheel does not discriminate between existence and non-existence of realities, hence "by unmanifest aspect," and the final wheel does so discriminate, hence "using the finest discrimination." Taking this (middle) wheel in comparison with the third wheel, the Tripitaka Master Yuan Tsho explains no more than "surpassable," and, although he cites the explanation of the Indian master, Paramartha, I do not quote it, since it does not seem apt. My interpretation is like the former (master's, that is, Yuan Tsho).[50]

[49] SNT: TG, P, thi, ff. 64b-65a.

[50] SNT: TG, P, thi, f. 70a. The Indian master "Genuine Truth" (*rgya gar gyi mkhan po yang dag bden pa*) is presumably Paramartha (Nanjio, Appendix II, 104-105), who did a translation of the first five chapters of SN (Nanjio, p. 156), and who worked in China from 548 to 569, a century before Yuan Tsho, although there is no record of a SN commentary by Paramartha either in the Tibetan or Chinese canons. However, Yuan Tsho quotes the opinions of this master at every step in his massive SNT (which, incidentally, appears to have been lost in the original Chinese, as Nanjio has no record of it), so it is from these quotations that Tsong Khapa is familiar with the ideas of this master. It is noteworthy that Tsong Khapa takes such pains to show his agreement with the Chinese master in most points of interpretation of the scripture. To understand his motive in quoting at such length from Yuan Tsho's commentary, we must remember the famous bSam-yas debate, from which the Chinese Buddhist scholars gained a bad reputation in Tibet. Tsong Khapa perhaps wishes to clear the name of Chinese Buddhist scholarship from this popular

Yuan Tsho explains:

> In regard to the third wheel, its principal subject is the same as that of the middle wheel. The disciples of the first two wheels were those of the Individual Vehicle and Universal Vehicle, respectively, and both were included in the final wheel, hence, "for the sake of those involved in all vehicles." "Finest discrimination" refers to the previously explained application of the three natures to each thing such as form, etc., and to the according differentiation of three modes of unreality. The "this" in "this turning . . . " refers to the just-mentioned wheel of fine discrimination, that is, the *Elucidation of Intention* and other scriptures of equally fine discrimination, and does not refer to (the other wheels), whose scriptures do not thus discriminate between the intrinsically real and unreal. "Unsurpassed," etc., indicates the greatness of this wheel, it being supremely wonderful, none other excelling it. "Not provisory" means that there is no later occasion when it is refuted. "Definitive in meaning" means that it shows accurately what exists and what does not, and hence it does not "leave any grounds for dispute."[51]

Yuan Tsho's explanation here agrees with mine, being just the reverse of my previous explanations of the (opposite terms) such as "surpassable," except in the case of (our explanations of "provisory") and "not provisory" (respectively).[52] (I understand this qualification as referring to the fact that) the discourses of the former two (wheels) give occasion to the criticism of their literal meanings, and the final wheel does not, because their literal meanings (respectively) do and do not require interpretation. (Finally), as to the question of "disputability," ("indisputable") means that there are no grounds for analytical dispute by experts as to whether or not the meaning of a scripture (of the wheel in question) is determined according to its teaching of (either) intrinsic reality (or) lack of intrinsic reality; it does not indicate that other sorts of disputes are impossible.

---

stigma, by showing how the Chinese scholar's interpretations were in many ways preferable to the Indian master's. This may seem far-fetched, but there is no other explanation for the length of the quotations from SNT, quite unmatched in the rest of our text, and not fully warranted by the difficulty of the subject, which is, after all, not nearly as problematic as the more philosophical sections.

[51] SNT: TG, P, thi, f. 79aff.

[52] The difference is very slight, Tsong Khapa not in actual disagreement with Yuan Tsho, and he mainly emphasizes the content of the teaching itself, as being literally accurate in the third wheel, and as requiring interpretation in the other two wheels. This highlights the Idealist theory of interpretable-definitive: namely, that whether or not a teaching is literally acceptable is the criterion to determine its interpretability-definitiveness.

The *Chinese Commentary* calls the first wheel "the wheel of Dharma of the four holy truths," the second, "the wheel of Dharma of identitylessness," and the third, "the wheel of Dharma of determination of the ultimate," or else, to accord with this very scripture, "the wheel of Dharma of fine discrimination."

According to the way in which this scripture formulates interpretable and definitive, there are two categories of teachings, discriminating and undiscriminating, and the grounds on which a scripture is classified (as one or the other) is whether it states invariably that things have intrinsically identifiable reality, whether it states that there is nowhere such a reality, or whether it discriminates explicitly between existence and nonexistence of such a reality (in particular things). According to the above explanation, this is made very clear in the "inquiry resolving contradictions" in the scripture, the answer given, the statement of the way of explanation of intrinsic unreality that intends the application of the three natures to each of all things, and the statement of the interpretable and definitive among the scriptures taught at different times.

Thus, the first wheel is shown to be interpretable in its statement of the existence of intrinsic identity in things, beginning with the four truths, and not merely in its being taught among the Buddha's earliest teachings. For example, there is no need to clear up any doubts about the (status) of such precepts as that first stated to the ascetics at Benares: "Make your lower robe circular!"

Similarly, the second wheel consists of the statements of intrinsic realitylessness. There is no need to demonstrate the interpretability of other scriptures of that time-period which are not concerned with realitylessness, as the doubt mentioned in the inquiry resolving contradictions does not arise from them.

The third wheel, while explained to be definitive in meaning, consists of statements of explicit discrimination as explained above, and not of every teaching given during that time-period. This is abundantly clear from the scripture itself. For example, the brief Discipline taught at the Parinirvana was declared at the very end (of the Buddha's life), yet is not classified as definitive in meaning by this scripture.

What does this scripture seek to establish by thus differentiating between interpretable and definitive? It seeks to teach disciples not to take literally teachings that do not specifically discriminate between things, but (categorically declare them all) either to be established by intrinsic identity, or not to be so established. For, although the imaginatively constructed is not established by intrinsic identity, the other two realities are indeed so established. Thus the scripture seeks to teach the disciples that emptiness, which is the relative devoid of the imagined, is the final ultimate and the goal of the path. Therefore, the first two wheels (of Dharma) are stated to be interpretable in meaning, and the final wheel to be definitive.

Some people believe, relying on this scripture, that, as all scriptures promulgated in the third time-period must be definitive in meaning, certain statements (about the "Buddha-essence") made to educate the heterodox who were fascinated by soul-theories, must be taken literally. Thus, they believe that the above-mentioned "fine discrimination" means the discrimination between the truth-status of the ultimate nature and the truthlessness of all things possessing that nature, which are not intrinsically real in the slightest, merely being postulated by the erroneous intellect.[53]

There are still others who imagine that, if discrimination between interpretable and definitive were determined by this scripture, the implication (advocated by those) above would follow. Hence, they refute this scripture, saying that its rule of interpretable-definitive is not to be taken literally. Both of these (types of scholars) appear to be arguing from a merely casual discrimination between interpretable and definitive, without examining in detail the inquiry resolving contradictions, the way the Teacher answers it, and the formulation of the interpretable-definitive (rule) that is based upon them.

[53] These are the Jo-nang-pas again, who base their belief in the definitiveness of the *Tathāgatagarbhasūtra* on their misinterpretation of the SN formulation, as they feel all scriptures of the later time period must be definitive. The "others" then mentioned make the same mistake but draw the opposite conclusion, and are presumably certain Centrist scholars of the Sakyapa school, who refute the Idealists for the wrong reasons.

Chapter II

EXPLANATIONS OF THE SCRIPTURES STATEMENTS

MASTER ASANGA'S CHIEF RELIANCE ON THE *ELUCIDATION OF INTENTION*

In the *Compendium*, Aryasanga commends the "ultimate" chapter of the *Elucidation*: "Know the ultimate, with its five characteristics, as described in the *Elucidation of Intention*!"[1] He commends the "nature" chapter as teaching the three natures: "View the nature of things as described in the *Elucidation of Intention*!"[2] He also quotes from the scripture the inquiry resolving contradictions, and commends the "realitylessness" chapter as teaching interpretable-definitive: "View the nature of the realitylessness of things as described in the *Elucidation of Intention*![3]

Also he cites the *Elucidation* statements about the eightfold group of consciousnesses and about final genealogical determinism.[4] In the "reality" chapter of the *Bodhisattva Stages*, in its commentaries, and in the *Universal Vehicle Compendium*, he determines, with a variety of explanations, the *Elucidation* statement (set forth in Chapter I above) that the relative being empty of the imaginatively constructed, which is ascriptive and descriptive designation, is the perfect. Finally, the explanations of the meaning of reality in the *Ornament of Universal Vehicle Scriptures* and the *Center and Extremes*, etc., and the essential points taught in their commentaries, are very much in agreement with the meaning of

[1] VS, TG, C, zi, f. 44b3; P, i, f. 47b5; D, zi, f. 44a2-4. Tsong Khapa gives the quote in elliptical form.

[2] VS, TG, C, zi, f. 55b5; P, i, f. 60a2; D, zi, f. 54b6-7.

[3] VS, TG, C, zi, f. 57b7; P, i, f. 60b2; D, zi, f. 56b7-57a1.

[4] Tib. *rnam shes tshogs brgyad pa* refers to the six sense-consciousness—eye, ear, nose, tongue, body, and mind-consciousnesses, plus the two consciousnesses peculiar to the Idealist system, namely, addicted mentality (*kliṣṭamanas*) and fundamental conscioiusness (*ālayavijñāna*).

Tib. *mthar thug rigs nges pa* refers to the Idealist theory that living beings belong to certain genealogies (*gotra*), such as discipline-lineage, solitary sage-lineage, bodhisattva-lineage, and that there are certain beings who can never attain liberation, being of a genealogy that is forever fixed in the samsara (*icchāntika*).

this scripture. Therefore, the determination of the meaning of this scripture appears to be fundamental to his system.

PROCEDURES TO DETERMINE REALITY ON THAT BASIS

1. GENERAL PROCEDURE TO ELIMINATE TWO EXTREMES

EXPLANATION IN THE *BODHISATTVA STAGES*; PATTERNS OF VIEWS WHICH REIFY AND REPUDIATE

(Asanga) states, in the *Bodhisattva Stages*: "How is (reality) discovered? It is discovered by the avoidance of the misapprehension which reifies what does not exist and the misapprehension which repudiates what does exist."[5] What are "reification" and "repudiation," as mentioned here? The *Bodhisattva Stages* gives their definitions:

> (Reification) is the habitual conviction arising from the reification of an intrinsic identity, (actually) inexistent, which is a reality posed by verbal designation of substances such as the formful and of things such as form.
>
> (Repudiation) is the repudiation of authentic actuality, saying "it does not exist at all, anywhere," although it exists ultimately with an inexpressible nature, and serves as support and basis of designative verbal signs.
>
> It should be recognized that these two ruinous activities are utterly destructive of our religious discipline![6]

The first two parts of this quotation describe the two (mental patterns), and from "it should be recognized" on, it shows how they ruin the profound Universal Vehicle teaching. From "actuality" to "signs" indicates the designative base of the imaginatively constructed. "Reality posed by verbal designation" is the "reality" verbally designated, and not the designative word itself, as the *Compendium* clearly explains.

Other passages in the *Bodhisattva Stages* are to be understood in the

[5] BBh (Skt. edited by N. Dutt, Patna: K. P. Jayaswal, 1966) p. 30, l. 6—*katham vidyate / asadbhūtasamāropasaṃgrahavivarjitaśca bhūtāpavādasaṃgrahavivarjitaśca vidyate /.*

[6] BBh, ed. Dutt, p. 30, l. 26; p. 31, l. 5—*yaśca rūpādīnāṃ dharmānāṃ rūpādikasya vastunaḥ prajñaptivādasvabhāvaṃ svalakṣaṇaṃ asadbhūtasamāropato 'bhiniviśate / yaścāpi prajñaptivādanimittādhiṣṭhānaṃ prajñāptivādanimittasanniśrayaṃ nirabhilāpyātmakatayā paramārthasadbhūtaṃ vastvapavādamāno nāśayati sarvena sarvaṃ nāstīti / . . . yair doṣair rūpādike vastuni asadbhūtasamāropād pranaṣṭo bhavati asmad dharmavinayād iti veditavyaḥ //.* The Tibetan closely corresponds with the Sanskrit, except it does not repeat the phrase *rūpādike vastuni asadbhūtasamāropād* in the last sentence, which phrase is indeed somewhat redundant.

same way; that "reification" is the conviction that the verbally designated reality has intrinsic identity, when in fact it does not exist by intrinsic identity; that the basis of designative verbal signs, that is, their support, is the designative base of the imagined; and that "repudiation" is the notion that this same (relative), which is ultimately existent in an inexpressible way, does not exist at all anywhere. Thus, "reification" is the notion that the imagined exists ultimately, "repudiation" is the notion that the other two natures do not exist ultimately. For, the first (reality) exists (only) superficially, and the other two do exist ultimately.

While, in order to parallel the explanation of "repudiation" as the view of the inexistence of the ultimately existent, "reification" should be explained as the view of existence of the ultimately inexistent, here it is not made verbally explicit that the notion of ultimate existence of the (imagined) is the notion of its intrinsically identifiable existence, said to be "reification." Nevertheless, since the meaning of the treatise is that where there is intrinsically identifiable existence, there also is ultimate existence, ("reification" here) is tantamount to the reification of an ultimate existence of the imaginatively constructed.

Although in the *Elucidation*, the relative is called "processes which are the ground of the imagined reality, and the basis of ascriptive and descriptive designation," and in this text, (Asanga) refers obviously to the relative by the statement (that repudiation is the notion of) "the non-existence of the ultimately existent basis of designative verbal signs," it is not wrong to explain it as both (the latter two realities), since, if the relative were ultimately inexistent, the perfect would also become ultimately inexistent.

In the *Bodhisattva Stages* (Asanga) declares: "Upon repudiation of the mere actuality of things such as form, etc., there is neither reality nor designation, and both together have no validity."[7] Therefore, repudiation of relative actuality does not take the form "it does not exist conventionally," nor the form "generally, it does not exist," but, as stated previously, takes the form "the ultimately existent is non-existent."

Procedures to Negate Both Extremisms

If such is the pattern of reification and repudiation, how are they to be abandoned? As will be explained below in detail, the extreme of reification is negated by showing that everything is ultimately empty with respect to ascriptive and descriptive designations. Immediately after the last quotation, (Asanga) negates repudiation thus:

[7] BBh, ed. Dutt, p. 31, l. 6—*rūpādīnāṃ dharmānāṃ vastumātram apavādato naiva tattvaṃ nāpi prajñaptiḥ tadubhayam etan na yujyate /.*

Thus, for example, if the aggregates, such as form, exist, it is possible to designate "person." If held as non-existent, there being no actuality, there is no designation "person." Likewise, if the simple actuality of things such as form exists, it is possible to ascribe words designative of things such as form to them. If they are held to be non-existent, with no actuality, there is no ascription by designative words. If the designative base is held to be non-existent, designation becomes non-existent, since it becomes unfounded.[8]

The antagonist whose position is negated as being "repudiation" is not likely to be found among the heterodox. And, among the orthodox of the Individual Vehicle, there is no theory that things such as form, which are the designative base of verbal and conventional expressions, are non-existent with respect to intrinsic identity. Therefore, as the *Compendium* explains, (the antagonist) is a Universal Vehicle philosopher, an advocate of realitylessness who maintains that things are not established by intrinsic identity. His position is definitely not that things such as the relative are generally inexistent, or conventionally inexistent, but is that they are not established in the ultimate. Therefore, the negation, "if the simple actuality does not exist," refutes the position that an ultimately existent, real actuality (of things) is inexistent, as explained above.

According to this (Idealistic) system, it is not necessary that the imagined be non-existent, if not established by intrinsic identity, or not existent ultimately. However, if the other two realities are not established by intrinsic identity, or in the ultimate, they do not exist at all. (This system) holds that the relative, which consists of mind and mental functions arising dependent on their own causes and conditions, has ultimate production through intrinsically identifiable production, and that otherwise, if it were no more than the mere designation "production," an intellectual supposition, then there would be no such thing as production in the actuality of mind and mental functions.

Therefore, (this system) is not satisfied with the answer that "there is no repudiation of relative process, since such process does exist superficially, according to the mere adherence to production and cessation by erroneous cognition."[9] It considers that one who adopts the position that "although relative causality is causality according to the error of the

[8] BBh, ed. Dutt, p. 31, 1.7—*tadyathā satsu rūpādiṣu skandheṣu pudgalaprajñaptir yujyate / nāsatsu nirvastukapudgalaprajñaptiḥ / evaṃ sati rūpādīnāṃ dharmānāṃ vastumātre sa rūpādidharmaprajñaptivādopacāro yujyate / nāsati / nirvastukaḥ prajñaptivādopacāro / tatra prajñapter vastu nāstīti niradhiṣṭhāṇa prajñaptirapi nāsti /.*

[9] The entire following paragraph exhibits the Idealist view of the Centrist's position, who, as an extreme nihilist in the former's opinion, is the chief antagonist.

truth-habit about causality, the relative itself is not (ultimately) established as causality, just as a rope is a snake according to the erroneous cognition supposing a snake in a rope, but is not generally experienced as having snake-status"—such a one cannot abandon repudiation, as he has no foundation on which to establish the effects of actions, that is, happiness and suffering from virtue and vice; and that if one admits any other sort of causality, it has to be causality established by intrinsic identity, thus equivalent to ultimately existent (causality). Hence, they explain that (such a position) becomes the chief form of nihilism, since there is no designation without a designative base, and since it is impossible for all things to be mere designations and still to have real functional efficiency. In the *Bodhisattva Stages*, (Asanga) declares:

> Thus, some people hear the exposition of the intended meaning of the scriptures that are hard to understand with their Universal Vehicle (spirit) and their profound emptiness, and do not understand correctly the meaning of the explanations. Their view (distorted) by mere mental constructions springing from the irrationality of incorrect analysis, they proclaim: "All this is mere designation. This is reality. Who sees it thus, truly sees!" According to them, as there is no simple actuality of a designative base, designation itself becomes entirely inexistent. How then could "mere designation" be a reality? Therefore, by that formula, they repudiate both reality and designation. And, since they repudiate both reality and designation, they should be known as the chief nihilists![10]

(Aryasanga) further declares, in the same text:

> So intending, (Buddha) said, "The view of person (as real) is harmless, but not the misapprehension of emptiness!" The former is merely ignorance with regard to an object, and does not repudiate all objects of knowledge, and hence, on that basis, one is not reborn in hell. One still believes other teachings, does not deviate from the basic precepts, and thus one does not come to ruin. The latter is just the opposite.[11]

[10] BBh, ed. Dutt, p. 31, 1. 10—*ato yā ekatyā durvijñeyān sūtrāntān mahāyānapratisaṃyuktān gambhīrān śūnyatāpratisaṃyuktān abhiprāyikārthanirūpitān śrutvā yathābhūtaṃ bhāṣitasyārthamavijñāya 'yoniśo vikalpyāyogavihitena tarkamātrakenaiva dṛṣṭayo bhavanti evamvādinaḥ / prajñaptimātram eva sarvam etacca tattvaṃ / yaścaiva paśyati sa samyakpaśyatīti / teṣāṃ prajñaptyadhiṣṭhānasya vastumātrasya abhāvāt saiva prajñaptiḥ sarvena sarvaṃ na bhavati / kutaḥ punaḥ prajñaptimātraṃ tattvaṃ bhaviṣyatīti / tadanena paryāyena taiḥ tattvam api prajñaptirapi tadubhayamapi apavāditaṃ bhavati / prajñaptitattvāpavāditācca pradhāno nāstiko veditavyaḥ /.*

[11] BBh, ed. Dutt, p. 31, l. 20—*idañca saṃdhāyoktaṃ bhagavatā / varam ihaikatyasya pudgaladṛṣṭir na tu eva ekatyasya durgṛhītaśūnyatā iti / tatkasya hetoḥ / pudgaladṛṣṭiko jantur jñeye kevalaṃ muhyenna tu sarvaṃ jñeyam apavādet / na tato nidānam āpāyeṣu upapadyeta / nāpi dharmārthikaṃ duḥkhavimokṣārthikañca paraṃ visaṃvādayet na vi-*

That being so, (Asanga quotes the scriptural formula): "When one thing does not exist in another, that other is empty of the one, but what remains (of that other) does exist. Such insight is the accurate penetration of emptiness."[12]

He then comments that the meaning of the first phrase refers to things such as form, etc., being empty of the entities verbally designated in them, and the "existent remainder" means the existence of the pure actuality which is the designative base, and of the simple designation itself. The "emptied out" is the imagined, the "empty" is the relative, and the emptiness of the latter with respect to the former is the perfect. The relevance of their existence and non-existence is as explained above.

Thus, abandoning the extreme of reification eliminates absolutism, and abandoning the extreme of repudiation eliminates nihilism, and hence non-duality is manifested. Such emptiness is explained to be the final ultimate. (Still) in the *Bodhisattva Stages*, (Asanga) states:

> The actuality implicit in the nature of the teaching that liberates from existence and non-existence with respect to the above things and nothingness, is non-duality. And non-duality is the central way, the avoidance of the two extremes, which is called "unexcelled."[13]

Explanation in the *Compendium*; The Antagonist's Opinion and Inquiry into Its Meaning

In the *Compendium*, (Asanga) states: "Some followers of the Universal Vehicle say, through their own misapprehension, that all things exist superficially, and nothing exists ultimately."[14]

The Centrists express the differentiation of existence and non-existence of things thus: "all things exist conventionally, though they are non-existent in the ultimate." (The *Compendium* continues):

> At that, we must say, "Sir! What is the ultimate? And what is the superficial?" Thus interrogated, if they answer, "The ultimate is the

pralambhayet / na ca śaithiliko bhavet shikṣāpadeṣu / . . . (reverse in other case). (Tsong Khapa abbreviates this quote without altering the meaning.)

[12] This formula is mentioned again below in the MAV section. Here Asanga quotes it in BBh without identifying the original source. It seems to be one of those ubiquitous formulae that arose originally from the Buddha's discourses, found in numerous texts. Vasubandhu gives a most precise form in his comment on MAV I, ad. 1.2; Skt. edited by R. C. Pandeya (Delhi, Motilal Banarsidass, 1971), p. 9, ls. 14-16; *evaṃ yad yatra nāsti tat tena śūnyam iti yathābhūtaṃ samanupaśyati yat punar atra 'vaśiṣṭham bhavati tat sad ihāstīti yathābhūtam prajānatītyaviparītaṃ śūnyatālakṣaṇam udbhāvitaṃ bhavati /.*

[13] BBh, ed. Dutt, p. 27, l. 4—*yat punaḥ pūrvakena ca bhāvena anena ca abhāvena ubhābhyāṃ bhāvābhāvābhyāṃ vinirmuktaṃ dharmalakṣaṇasaṃgrhītaṃ vastu / tad advayaṃ / yad advayaṃ tan madhyamapratipad antadvayavarjitaṃ / niruttaretyucyate /.*

[14] VS, TG, C, zi, f. 43a3-4; D, zi, f. 42b5.

realitylessness of all things. The superficial is the apprehension of realities in things without intrinsic reality. Why? Because those things which do not exist, are perceived as superficial, as designations, as mental formulations, and as conventions."[15]

Thus, the answer given to the question about the two realities is taken as the antagonist's position. In asking "what is the ultimate?" he asks for exemplification of ultimate truth, and does not ask for the locus of the non-existence that is ultimate non-existence, that is, what sort of inexistence is called "ultimate inexistence." Otherwise, the answer that "the realitylessness of all things is the ultimate" would be incorrect, because the Centrist does not posit any ultimate existence by virtue of any existence of the objective selflessness accepted as ultimate.[16] Likewise, in asking "what is the superficial?" he asks for that according to which the superficial is established as reality, as in the expression, "superficial reality," and does not ask what is the convention that is the locus of the existence which is conventional existence. Otherwise, the answer that "the apprehension of reality in realityless things is the superficial" would be incorrect; because the Centrist believes that such (false apprehension) is the truth-habit, and hence its supposed object does not exist even conventionally, and also because the "reality" negated in the expression "realitylessness" must be taken as reality which is truth.[17]

Refutation of the Antagonist's Opinion; Exhibition of Contradiction in His Theory

First of all, to refute the (antagonist's) description of the superficial, the *Compendium* statement is:

> At that, you must explain yourself; do you believe that the apprehension of reality occurs from a verbal and superficial cause? Or do you believe that it is merely verbal formulation and superficiality? If it

[15] VS Ch. 10, TG, C, zi, f. 43a5-7; D, zi, f. 42b6-7.

[16] That is, the ultimate is selflessness, and so on, but does not itself ultimately exist. This relates to the idea that the ultimate is the absolute negation of the negatee which is any sort of a self, substantiality, intrinsic identity, and so on, but this pure negation is not an *existence* of an absence. This very crucial point will be touched upon again and again. Noteworthy here is that, since this section is dealing with the Idealist view, this latter is being given credit for understanding of the Centrist position in its more precise subtlety, at least on this point.

[17] As usual, in Centrism, whatever concerns the conventional seems more puzzling than what concerns the ultimate. Tsong Khapa here hints at the fact that, in the Centrist system, there is nothing substantial in the superficial that might serve as ground or locus, that is, no intrinsic identity, no truth-status, and so on, and that superficial existence ultimately is only established by ultimate error, which is not to say that it has no coherence within its own framework, if left entirely out of the analysis carried on by rational cognition analytic of reality.

occurs from a verbal and superficial cause, then it cannot be said to be non-existent. If it is merely verbal formulation and superficiality, then it is impossible to call it "formulation" and "superficial," as (these terms) will have no basis.[18]

This means that the superficial, which is the notion of a reality where there is no reality in the ultimate, is an internal verbalization, which is either produced by a homogeneous previous cause, or else is a sheer designation by superficial verbalizing mental construction. In the first case, "it cannot be said to be inexistent, if causally produced" means "it cannot be said to be ultimately inexistent," because the context is the argument about ultimate existence and inexistence, and because the antagonist asserts ultimate non-existence, and not general non-existence. In the second case, it is impossible for it to be sheer imagined designation, because there is no designative base, and because if verbalization and superficiality were merely mentally constructed designations, then other things (that is, the ultimate) also would be just the same.[19]

As for the negation of the (antagonist's) description of the ultimate, the *Compendium* statement is:

> At that, you must explain yourself: Sir! Why is it that what is apprehended is non-existent? Thus questioned, if you answer: "Because it is a false thing," then you must say if that falseness exists or not. If it exists, then it is incorrect to say that the realitylessness of all things is itself the ultimate. And if it does not exist, then it is incorrect to say that what is apprehended is without reality because it is a false thing.[20]

This means that is is not correct to say that the intrinsically identifiable intrinsic identity apprehended in things does not exist, because that (statement) is faulted by the evidence of such apprehension. And if one objects that it is not faulted by the cognition that apprehends such, because that cognition is itself a false thing, it is not correct; because, if that falsity existed with intrinsic identity, realitylessness could not possibly be ultimate, and if it did not (so) exist, as it would also be an error, its apprehension would not exist. Although here also the analysis should be in terms of ultimate existence and non-existence, the above analysis (in terms of intrinsic identity) is employed as similar in meaning and as easier to understand.

Thus, here, without demonstrating the flaw in (the assertion of) ultimate non-existence and conventional existence of both imagined and

[18] VS, TG, C, zi, f. 43b3-4; D, zi, ff. 42b7-43a2.

[19] All meaningfulness would collapse, as the ultimate could be designated the "superficial," or anything could be designated as anything. Also, nothing could be anything, as designation would have no basis of application.

[20] VS, TG, C, zi, f. 43b5-6; D, zi, 43a2-4.

perfect, he indicates discrepancies through analysis of ultimate existence and non-existence of superficial consciousness and false consciousness, thereby negating (the assertion of) ultimate non-existence and superficial existence of the relative. The relative is the subject (qualified by) the perfect, and the means of designation and the designative base of the imagined, therefore, these experts chiefly debate the ultimate existence and non-existence of the relative.

Furthermore, in the *Compendium*, (Asanga) declares:

> The insistence on the imagined reality in the relative and the perfect should be recognized as the extreme of reification. The extreme of repudiation is the repudiation of intrinsic identity in asserting that the existent relative and perfect realities do not exist. The pattern of the import of reality should be realized by means of the procedure avoiding these two extremes.[21]

Thus, the assertion that there is no intrinsically identifiable status in the latter two realities, which do exist by intrinsic identity, repudiates intrinsic identity. Hence, this text agrees with the *Bodhisattva Stages* about the two extremes and the procedure to avoid them.

The imagined is non-existent in the ultimate, and not non-existent in the conventional. The *Compendium* statement is:

> Those suppositions established by names and internal formulations, are they or are they not the (imagined) reality? Conventionally, they should be stated to be that reality. Ultimately, they should be stated not to be that reality. The imagined reality, which is the object of consciousness based on names habitual in internal verbalization . . . is designatively existent, and is non-existent ultimately.[22]

Therefore, simply by the fact that such as the imagined (reality) of the two selves is inexistent among knowable objects, all of the imaginatively constructed is not inexistent.[23] Hence, its substantial existence and ultimate existence are negated, but its designative existence and conventional existence are affirmed.

Therefore, (we should explain the following) statement from a certain great commentary of the *Elucidation*:

> The imagined is non-existent in both realities; the dependent origination, which is the relative with its subject-object duality, is super-

[21] VS, TG, D, zi, f. 94b2-5.

[22] VS, TG, C, zi, f. 32a5-6; D, zi, f. 32a2-3, 7, this quote being picked out in pieces from a longer passage.

[23] For an outline of the different types of imagined realities, see above, Ch. I n. 46.

> ficially existent, and the perfect, which is also ultimate, exists in the mode of realitylessness, existing ultimately.[24]

This is not the intended meaning of that scripture. Furthermore, it shows a serious lack of discrimination to claim that this work was composed by Aryasanga, since it contradicts the explanation of the *Universal Vehicle Compendium* that internal and external subject and object are the imagined; it contradicts the *Bodhisattva Stages* and the *Compendium* by proving the non-existence of externals citing the *Elucidation*; it quotes the *Determination of Validating Cognition*, and so forth. Finally, the *Compendium* quotes most of the chapters of the *Elucidation*, except for the preface, and settles the difficult questions thoroughly, so it does not appear that this master need have composed an extra commentary.

Also, some recent authors have departed from this system by explaining the intention of Aryasanga and Vasubandhu as being the non-existence of the imagined, even conventionally, the conventional existence and the ultimate inexistence of the relative, and the ultimate existence of the perfect. Especially their belief that, since the meaning of conventional existence of the relative is that the erroneous intellect merely supposes the existence of production and cessation therein, production and cessation do not exist in things is the ultimate repudiation of things. Since thereby the other two realities are repudiated as well, this is the chief nihilism repudiating all three natures, as explained above in the *Bodhisattva Stages*, and should also be recognized as irreconcilably contradictory to the position that the *Elucidation* is definitive in meaning.[25]

Elimination of Contradiction in (Asanga's) Theory

Here, one may object, "if it is true, as the *Bodhisattva Stages* and the *Compendium* declare, that the relative is ultimately existent, how can it fail to contradict the (following statements)? The *Elucidation* statement is:

> If the reality, the ultimate, and the objective selflessness of things were each to be different in character, as, for example, the branches of the holy path are different in character from each other, then reality, the ultimate, and objective selflessness would each have a cause. Were they

[24] *Āryasaṃdhinirmocanasūtravyākhyāna*, TG, P, co. This commentary has been falsely attributed to Asanga, though, as Tsong Khapa argues, it is not really his work.

[25] Again, the Jo-nang-pas are the target of this refutation. Note that in tracing a similar position in the *Saṃdhinirmocanavyākhyāna*, and likewise refuting it, Tsong Khapa implies that the Jo-nang mistake had been made previously in India as well. bLo-bzang Phuntshogs, *Zin Bris* (f. 29b4), suggests that Bu-ston suspected that this commentary (above, n. 24) may have been written by one Nāgadhvaja (*Klui-rgyal-mtshan*).

to arise from causes, they would be created. Were they to be created, they could not be ultimate.[26]

"Thus, what is created is not ultimate. The *Center and Extremes* states that 'the ultimate is unique,' and its commentary states that 'the ultimate reality should be known as the sole perfect reality.'[27] Further, the *Scripture Ornament* states: 'The nature of the ultimate is that which purifies. It is not existent, not non-existent, not the same, and not other, not produced and not ceased, not decreased and not increased, nor even is it to be purified.'[28] Here, in the passage on the five characteristics of the ultimate, it is declared to be without production and cessation, etc., the commentary stating that 'it is not existent' with regard to the imagined and the relative, and 'not non-existent' with regard to the perfect. Finally, the *Compendium* also states: 'Should causality be said to exist superficially, or to exist ultimately? It should be said to exist superficially. . . . Should imagination be said to exist superficially, or to exist ultimately? It should be said to exist superficially.' "[29]

To explain how these statements do not contradict (the ultimate existence of the relative), there are two modes of establishment (of something) as superficially existent or as ultimately existent. First conventional existence is presented as existence established on the strength of conventional expressions, and ultimate existence is presented as existence by intrinsic identity not established on the strength of conventional expressions. This (first mode) is exemplified by many statements in scriptures, such as "that is on the strength of mundane conventions, and not in the ultimate." This (mode of establishment) is the basis of the arguments about ultimate and conventional existence and non-existence between the Centrists and the Realists, both heterodox and orthodox. And the *Bodhisattva Stages* and the *Compendium* make the above statements of the conventional existence and ultimate non-existence of the first reality, and of the ultimate existence and the conventional non-existence of the latter two realities, in terms of this (mode of establishment). Furthermore, the *Compendium* states:

[26] SN IV (Lamotte, *Explication*: Tib. p. 51-2, Fr. p. 181).

[27] MAV III, k. 10 (Pandeya ed., p. 95): *paramārthāntu ekataḥ* //. MAVBh: *paramārthasatyamekasmāt parinișpannādeva svabhāvād veditavyaṃ* /.

[28] MSA VI, k. 1 (Skt., Levi ed., p. 22)—*na sanna cāsanna tathā na cānyathā na jāyate na vyeti na cāvahīyate / na vardhate nāpi viśudhyate punarviśudhyate tat paramārthalakṣaṇaṃ* //. These five characteristics are different from the five characteristics mentioned in the SN and VS (above, n. 1), which are given in *Zin Bris* (f. 22a ff.): "The ultimate has five characteristics; those of inexpressibility, of non-duality, of really being beyond difference and sameness, and of being utter uniformity of experience." These five characteristics are discussed in the first four chapters of the SN at some length.

[29] VS, TG, C, zi, f. 295b7, 296a2; D, zhi, f. 288b7, 289a2.

The object of that consciousness that is based on names habitual in internal formulation does not exist either substantially or ultimately insofar as its existence would be by intrinsic identity of things such as form, etc., which have names such as "form," etc. Therefore, that which is imaginatively constructed from what is not existent as the reality of those things having names such as "form," etc., should be known as designatively existent. (However), the things that have names such as "form," being objects of that consciousness of nominal things which excludes habitual internal formulations, which (objects) exist by their inexpressible nature, should be understood as existent both substantially and ultimately.[30]

In regard to substantial existence and designative existence, the *Compendium* statement is:

It is proper that designated intrinsic identity, which does not require or depend on other things, should be known as substantially existent. And it is proper that designated intrinsic identity, which requires and depends on other things, should be known as designatively existent, and not substantially existent.[31]

Here, the latter is exemplified by the designation of "self" or "living being" depending upon the aggregates. In this system, there is no contradiction between the designative existence that cannot be apprehended out of relationship with other things and must be subject to dependence, and intrinsically identifiable status not established on strength of convention. Hence, although such as the instincts of the fundamental consciousness are declared to be designatively existent, this does not preclude their ultimate existence, (according to the first mode above). However, such ultimate existence would be precluded by the designative existence resulting (merely) from verbal and conceptual designation.

In regard to the second mode of establishment (of superficial and ultimate existences), the *Center and Extremes* states: "The ultimate is considered threefold: as object, attainment, and practice."[32]

In comment, (Vasubandhu) declares that the "object-ultimate is reality, because it is the object of the holy wisdom," where "holy" specifies the wisdom which is immaculate equipoise. As it is an object, it is called "ultimate-object," or "ultimate." It is reality, equivalent to selflessness,

[30] VS,TG, C, zi, ff. 32a6-32b1; D. zi, f. 32a2-5.

[31] VS,TG, quotation as yet unlocated.

[32] MAV III, ad. ks. 11av, 12 cd (Pandeya ed., pp. 95, 99): *arthaprāptiprapattyā hi paramārthastridhā mataḥ* / (comm.) *arthaparamārthastathatā paramasya jñānasya artha iti kṛtvā* // . . . (p. 99) (k.) *viśuddhigocaraṃ dvedhā ekasmādeva kīrtitaṃ* //. (comm.) *pariniṣpannādeva svabhāvāt* / *na hyanyasvabhāvo viśuddhijñānādvayagocaro bhavatīti* //.

and is also the ultimate which is the pure object. It is stated thus, since it is only the perfect, the other two realities being non-existent therein. The *Center and Extremes* further states: "the pure object is twofold, proclaimed to be one alone," and the commentary adds, "it is declared to be the perfect reality, the other two realities not being objects of both kinds of pure wisdom," the two wisdoms being the wisdoms that purify the two obscurations.[33]

Here, we might suspect that such wisdom would itself also become an object, since this system asserts that that wisdom is apperceptively self-conscious. There is no such fault (in the system), however, since, regarding whatever object, (the system) intends it to be an object for the realization of the meaning of ultimate reality.

Therefore, such an ultimate is uncreated. However, in this system, non-establishment in this sort of ultimate does not preclude establishment in an ultimate which is existent by intrinsic identity, not established on the strength of convention. The *Synthesis of the Essence of Intuition* states, intending the first mode of ultimate existence: "Liberated from subject and object, consciousness exists in the ultimate. It is celebrated in the scriptures of the experientialist yogi, who crosses the ocean of the mind."[34]

It is necessary to differentiate accurately these two sorts of ultimates, since many of the Centrist treatises argue against the Experientialists about the existence and non-existence of the relative, not in terms of convention, but in terms of ultimate existence and non-existence. And there are many occasions in the treatises of the Brother-Masters on which they depend on the second mode of establishment of the ultimate.[35]

About the mode of the superficial existence of the first two realities, the *Compendium* statement is: "Causal process and imaginative construction exist superficially by reason that they motivate the addictions and are the basis of designations."[36]

It is first stated herein, in agreement with the *Abhidharma Synthesis*, that that which motivates addictions when apprehended is established as superficially existent, which (statement) complements the *Elucidation* explanation of the ultimate as the pure object. Second, it states that the

[33] The two obscurations are "addictive" and "objective" (*kleśāvaraṇa* and *jñeyāvaraṇa*), and, according to this system, are purified by the concentrative wisdom of the four truths and by the aftermath wisdom of the five sciences, respectively.

[34] *Jñānasārasamuccaya* (attributed to Aryadeva?), TG, P, tsa k. 26.

[35] Occasions such as those brought out in the objection above, in answer to which the first mode of ultimate existence—namely, intrinsically identifiable existence—is used to avoid the accusation of internal contradiction of postulating a created ultimate, have been illustrated in answering the objection. The second mode, that of the ultimate as "pure object," is illustrated in the following quote, as in many other passages in the works of Asanga and Vasubandhu.

[36] VS,TG, C, zi, ff. 295b6-296a3. (Tsong Khapa's quote is a rather accurate paraphrase.)

reality designated by verbal and symbolic conventions, which becomes the basis of conventionally designative signs, is said to be existent conventionally. "Causal process" is explained to be that on which the words of formulations are based.

Again, in the *Principles of Elucidation* (Vasubandhu) states:

> The superficial reality and the ultimate reality were declared intending the objects that deceive common consciousness and the object of transcendent consciousness. Since verbalization is superficial, the reality known thereby is the superficial reality, that is, that to which verbalizations apply. For example, a ford crossed by foot is called a "foot-ford," and a ford crossed by boat is called a "boat-ford."[37]

The *Compendium* states that the holy wisdom, which is the equipoise of realization of ultimate reality, exists in the ultimate, intending the absence of the above two reasons for establishing its superficial existence. And it states the aftermath wisdom exists both superficially and ultimately, asserting its conventional existence from the point of view of its apprehension of conventional signs.

Superficial existence, as the cause of perceptions motivating addictions and as the signification-process that is designative base for conventional expressions, does not preclude ultimate existence which is establishment by intrinsic identity. As the *Principles of Elucidation* states, (some things) exist in both the first mode of the ultimate, and in the latter mode of the superficial:

> Concerning the argument of the Individual Vehicle sectarians regarding the statement of the *Scripture on Ultimate Emptiness* that action and retribution exist, but the agent is not apprehended, "if (such existence and non-existence) are in the ultimate, it cannot be said that all things are realityless, and if they are in the superficial, then the agent would exist, and it could not be said that it is not apprehended;" we answer that if it is known what are the superficial and the ultimate, existence in them both is known. What are they? The superficial consists of names, verbalizations, designations, and conventions, and the ultimate is the intrinsic identity of things. Thus, action and retribution exist both as names and as intrinsic identities, and hence they must be admitted as existent whatever one's belief.[38]

In regard to the belief in their existence in the ultimate, it is not precluded in this system, as it does not accept literally the declaration of the

[37] Vasubandhu's *Vyākhyāyukti* (VY), TG, P, si, f. 110a5-7.
[38] VY,TG, P, si, f. 127b7-128a3.

realitylessness of all things. The person, (or agent), exists superficially, but not substantially. Action and retribution exist superficially, and also substantially, but they do not exist in the second mode of ultimate establishment, as they are objects of common consciousness and not the objects of transcendent consciousness, because its object is the inexpressible general nature (of all things). Finally, the explanation of the *Principles of Elucidation* is very clear (on the point) that the above (Individualist) argument applies to the position of some other Universalists, that all things exist superficially, and not by intrinsic identity.[39]

The *Center and Extremes* divides the superficial reality, the vague reality, into three: "The vague (reality) consists of designations, cognitions, and intimations."[40] Thus, (of the) three, the designative superficial, the cognitive superficial, and the intimative superficial, it is necessary to know the latter, which is connected with the third reality (that is, the perfect), to explain the intention of the statements from other scriptures that suchness, etc., are superficially existent.[41]

Thus, if we differentiate precisely the modes of existence, substantial and designative, superficial and ultimate, of the lower and higher theories, as well as the various interpretations of them within one philosophical school, we are able to master fully the important theories and we may come to understand the many designatively and superficially existent (things), asserted (dogmatically) by the Realists, that the Centrist must prove to them are non-existent in the ultimate. Otherwise, the differentiation of the lower and higher philosophies is just for fun.

1. GENERAL PROCEDURE TO ELIMINATE TWO EXTREMES (CONTD); EXPLANATIONS IN OTHER TREATISES

Explanation in the *Ornament of Universal Vehicle Scriptures*

The *Scripture Ornament* explains that the declaration of realitylessness intends the non-existence of the reality supposed by the naive and of the three characteristics of created things: "Realitylessness is admitted, be-

[39] This whole paragraph is an intricate mixture of paraphrased quote and the author's exposition, so I have left out the quotation marks to avoid obscuring the argument. See VY text, following quote located above, n. 37.

[40] MAV III (Pandeya ed., p. 94) k. 10bc: *prajñaptipratipattitaḥ / tathodbhāvanāyaudaraṃ. . . .*

[41] dPal-'byor Lhun-grub exemplifies the three types of superficial as follows (SERA, f. 27a ff.): The imagined reality exemplifies the "designative superficial," relative cognitions exemplify the "cognitive superficial," and the perfect reality exemplifies the "intimative superficial," in that this latter provides a functional base for the intimative expression "perfect reality."

cause (things) do not exist as selves, or with intrinsic identities, do not endure in intrinsic objectivity, and do not exist as they are perceived."[42]

The *Synthesis* also explains that the *Hundred Thousand* declares realitylessness intending the realitylessness of these two as well as of the three unrealities. Things are realityless since they are not independent, but depend on conditions. This means that they are not born from their own selves, as the *Central Way Illumination* explains. Things are realityless since they do not exist by their intrinsic natures, and, once ceased, are not born again with the same natures. And they are realityless since they do not endure another second in any intrinsic objectivity, as their production and non-cessation is (merely) instantaneous. In short, things are explained as realityless in the three times: the future sprout not born by its own power, the past sprout not born again with the nature of the sprout, and the present sprout not remaining a second instant established as itself.[43]

Vasubandhu explains[44] that there is no reality because the realities otherwise insisted upon by the naive, such as the imagined reality, or purity, happiness, permanence, and self, do not exist. "Otherwise" means they persist in their convictions through (the misapprehension of) substantial difference of subject and object.

As there is no reality, there is no production; as no production, no cessation, etc.; each subsequent condition is established by reason of each preceding condition. The *Scripture Ornament* states: "Realitylessness is established since each (thing) is the basis of each subsequent one, and hence (are established) non-production, non-cessation, primordial peace, and natural liberation."[45] Further: "Tolerance of non-production of things is recommended, in the light of their beginning, sameness, otherness, intrinsic identity, self, transformation, addiction, and excellence."[46]

This explains the mode of non-production of things referred to in such statements as "tolerance of non-production of things is attained." "Beginning," as the commentary explains, refers to the non-existence of an original production in worldly life; "sameness" to the fact that a past thing previously produced is not reproduced in its own nature; "other-

[42] MSA XI, k. 50 (Skt. Levi ed., p. 50): *svayaṃ svenātmanā 'bhāvāt svabhāve cānavasthiteḥ / grāhavattadabhāvācca niḥsvabhāvatvam iṣyate //.*

[43] AS III, TG, P, li, f. 124b2-3. Tsong Khapa's argument gives an accurate paraphrase of the AS here.

[44] Tsong Khapa here refers in general to the *Abhidharmasamuccayavyākhyā* by Vasubandhu.

[45] MSA XI, k. 51 (Levi ed., p. 67): *niḥsvabhāvatayā siddhā uttarottaraniśrayaḥ / anutpādo 'nirodhaścādiśāntiḥ parinirvṛttiḥ //* (Levi's restoration).

[46] MSA X1, k. 52 (Levi ed., p. 68): *ādau tattve 'nyatve svalakṣaṇe svayamathānyathābhāve / saṃkleśe 'tha viśeṣe kṣāntiranutpattidharmoktā //.*

ness" to the non-existence of production at a future time of what did not exist previously. This means, as the *Central Way Illumination* explains, that nothing is produced without precedent, and no living being is produced for the first time in the cyclic world, because they are produced alike in type to what came to an end (previously). "Intrinsic identity" refers to the imagined, which is never produced. "Self-"production does not exist in the relative. Production that is "transformation" does not exist in the perfect. Non-production of "addiction" lies in attainment of the knowledge of (its) extermination. And the "excellence" of non-production lies in the Truth Body of the Buddha.

Such explanation of the interpretation of realitylessness and of the way of non-production constitutes the system that does not accept literally the exposition of all things as ultimately devoid of reality and that of created things as ultimately unproduced. It shares with the two Individual Vehicle schools the interpretation of the realitylessness (of happiness, purity, permanence, and self), which is insisted upon (as reality) by the naive, and of the realitylessness of the phenomena of past, present, and future. The present is excepted by the Analysts, who assert it to be the basis of the durative function after production, and of the destructive function after that.

(At this point), one may protest that, since the *Elucidation* declares the relative to be illusory, and the *Scripture Ornament* declares all created things to be illusory, they do not mean that (the relative) is truly established, (as has been maintained above). Nevertheless, the description (of something) as being "like illusion" does not invariably show it not to be truth. This rather depends on the method of use of similes such as "illusion." The *Scripture Ornament* shows the method of use of the simile, "illusion," in the statement: "Artificial imagination is said to be illusory, and the error of duality is said to be like an illusory creation."[47]

Vasubandhu explains that the meaning of the first phrase is that the application of the magical spell to the bases of the illusion such as sticks and clods, etc., is like the imaginative construction of the relative. And the meaning of the second phrase is that the appearance of the magical effects in the forms of horses and elephants, etc., is like the appearance of the relative as dichotomous subject and object.[48] Furthermore, the *Scripture Ornament* declares: "The ultimate is admitted, insofar as that (duality) does not exist therein. And where that (duality) is apprehended, there is the superficial reality."[49]

[47] MSA XI, k. 15 (Levi ed., p. 59): *yathā māyā tathābhūtaparikalpo nirucyate / yathā māyākṛtaṃ tadvat dvayabhrāntirnirucyate //.*

[48] Vasubandhu's *Mahāyānasūtrālaṃkāravṛtti*, ad. XI, k. 15.

[49] MSA XI, k. 16 (Levi ed., p. 59): *yathā tasmin na tadbhāvaḥ paramārthas tatheṣyate / yathā tasyopalabdhis tu tathā saṃvṛttisatyatā //.*

The commentary explains that the ultimate is the non-existence of subject-object-duality in the relative, just as the elephants, etc., do not exist in the illusions, and that such imagination of the artificial is apprehended as the superficial reality, just as the illusion is apprehended as actual horses and elephants. Thus, the *Scripture Ornament* does not declare "illusion" as a simile of the appearance of reality in internal and external created things, of which (reality) they are devoid (in fact), but explains the scriptures' declarations of "illusoriness" as illustrating the appearance of the six inner media as self and life, etc., when they do not (actually) exist as such, and of "dream-likeness" as illustrating the appearance of the six external media as the field of involvement of personal self, when (in fact) they do not exist as such.

The *Universal Vehicle Compendium*, in supplying the meanings for the similes of the relative, such as "illusion," employed in the *Mother Scripture*, explains "illusion" as the simile employed to dispel the doubt: "If there are no external things, how do we apprehend objects?" It explains "mirage" as the simile employed to dispel the doubt: "If there are no external things, how are mind and mental functions produced?" And it explains "dream," etc., as the similes employed to dispel the doubt: "If there are no external things, why do we act on the basis of attraction and repulsion?"[50]

Thus, even in regard to (such an obvious thing) as the method of employment of similes such as "illusion" for untrueness, we must distinguish without confusion the methods of employment of similes for the different types of untrueness in the Idealist and the Centrist theories.

Explanation in the *Discrimination of Center and Extremes*

In the *Center and Extremes* (Maitreya) states:

> Artificial imagination exists, (but) therein duality does not. Herein emptiness exists, and that (imagination) exists therein.
>
> It is not empty, and not non-empty; thus, everything is explained. Through existence, non-existence, and existence, such is the Central Way.[51]

The first verse teaches the nature of emptiness; and the second teaches the same thing understood as the Central Way. It teaches emptiness accurately, in order to show what is declared to be the unmistaken re-

[50] MS, Ch. II, TG, P, li, f. 21b5-7. (Lamotte, *La Somme du grand vehicle*, II, 122-23).

[51] MAV I, ks. 2, 3 (Skt., Pandeya ed., pp. 9, 13): *abhūtaparikalpo 'sti dvayaṃ tatra na vidyate / śūnyatā vidyate tvatra tasyām api sa vidyate // na śūnyaṃ nāpi ca 'śūnyaṃ tasmāt sarvaṃ vidhīyate / sattvādasattvāt sattvācca madhyamapratipacca sa //.*

alization of emptiness, the authentic knowledge of existence and non-existence, which is expressed as "when one thing does not exist in another, that other is devoid of the one, but what remains (of the other) does exist."[52] "In another" means the empty, which is (the process of) "artificial imagination," that is, the relative. The "one thing" that does "not exist" means the duality of substantially different subject and object, that is, the imagined. "Therein duality does not (exist)" teaches the emptiness of that relative with respect to this imagined. That being non-existent, what is that remaining existence? "Artificial imagination" and "herein emptiness exists" show both relative and perfect (as what remains). "And that exists therein" dispels yet another doubt.

Sthiramati clearly shows agreement with Vasubandhu's explanation of the meaning of "the empty" and of "that of which it is empty." The *Subcommentary* states:

> Some people think that all things are totally realityless, like the horns of a rabbit, and thus repudiate everything. "Artificial imagination exists" is declared to refute them, and "by intrinsic reality" should be added (to complete the sense).[53]

The expression "artificial imagination exists" is not complete in itself, the remainder to be added being this "by intrinsic reality." Thus, it is not that artificial imagination merely exists, it exists by its intrinsic reality, or exists established by intrinsic identity, such modes of existence being the same in the case of the perfect also.

In regard to the way in which the second phrase dispels doubt, the same (*Subcommentary*) declares:

> Is this not contrary to the scriptures, which declare that all things are empty? It is not contradictory. "Therein duality does not exist" means that artificial imagination is empty, because free of the nature of subject and object, and not that it is totally realityless. Hence, it does not contradict the scriptures.[54]

To rebut the argument that the intrinsically real status of the relative contradicts the statement that all things are empty of intrinsically real existence, he states that emptiness of intrinsic reality is stated intending

[52] Scriptural formula given above, Ch. II, n. 12.

[53] MAVT by Sthiramati (Pandeya ed., p. 9): *kecit virundhanti sarvadharmāḥ sarvathā niḥsvabhāvāḥ śāśaviṣānavadityataḥ sarvāpavādapratiṣedhārtham āha, abhūtaparikalpo 'stīti / svabhāvatā iti vākyaśeṣaḥ /.*

[54] MAVT (Pandeya ed., p. 9): *nanvevaṃ sūtravirodhaḥ - sarvadharmāḥ śūnyā iti śāstre vacanāt / nāsti virodhaḥ yasmāt - dvayaṃ tatra na vidyate / abhūtaparikalpo hi grāhyagrahakasvarūparahitaḥ śūnya ucyate na tu sarvathā niḥsvabhāvāḥ / ato na sūtravirodhaḥ //.*

that imagination, which appears as dichotomous internal subject and external object, is empty with respect to such (dichotomous) reality, and not that intrinsically identifiable reality is totally non-existent. This alone is the meaning of the treatises of the Brothers, and, as they also explain (the relative) as ultimately existent, there is definitely no explanation in their system of the relative as empty in itself.[55]

In regard to the way in which the third phrase dispels doubt, the *Subcommentary* states:

> If one protests that, since duality is totally non-existent like a rabbit's horns and artificial imagination ultimately exists by its intrinsic reality, then emptiness becomes non-existent; (we say) not so. "Emptiness exists therein" means that emptiness does not become non-existent, because the very non-existence of subject and object in artificial imagination is itself emptiness.[56]

It is obvious how doubt about the non-existence of emptiness might arise, since "artificial imagination exists and duality does not exist" indicates existence of the former and non-existence of the latter, (and thus the perfect is not mentioned).[57] The argument "artificial imagination ultimately exists by intrinsic reality" assumes (its opponent's) position to be that establishment by intrinsic identity is equivalent to ultimate existence, and the argument rebuts from just such a position, not saying "such is not our position."

This master also declared, in the *Thirty Commentary*:

> The chapter was composed in order to refute these two kinds of extremism: the notion (of some) that objects, like consciousness, (exist) substantially, and the notion of others that consciousness, like objects, exists superficially and does not exist ultimately.[58]

Therefore, the statement that the relative is not totally non-existent refutes the position that nothing at all exists ultimately, like the passages from the *Bodhisattva Stages* earlier, and does not refute a position that (the relative) does not exist among knowable objects.

The fourth phrase dispels doubt of wondering why it is not (universally)

[55] Further refutation of the Jo-nang theory, as in Ch. I.

[56] MAVT (Pandeya ed., pp. 9, 10): *yadyevaṃ dvayaṃ śāśaviṣānavat sarvathā nāsti / abhūtaparikalpaśca paramārthataḥ svabhāvato 'styevaṃ śūnyatā 'bhāvaprasaṅgaḥ / naitadevaṃ yasmāt - śūnyatā vidyate tvatra - iyameva hi śūnyatā yā grāhyagrahakarahitatā 'bhūtaparikalpasyeti na śūnyatāyā nāstitvaṃ bhavati /.*

[57] bLo-bzang Phun-tshogs (*Zin Bris*, f. 40a), explains that since only the relative (that is, construction) and the constructed (that is, duality) are mentioned, one might doubt that the perfect (that is, emptiness) really exists, as in the above quote from MAVT.

[58] *Triṃśikavṛtti* (by Sthiramati), TG, P, ri, f. 142a5-143b1 (Levi ed., *Vijñaptimātratāsiddhi*, p. 15).

realized, if emptiness of duality is always existent in artificial imagination, by showing the fact that, as the imagination mistaking dualistic appearance exists in that emptiness, it obscures (that realization).

The second verse is declared in order to refute those extremisms that are not the central way, which maintain one-sidedly that all things are empty, that they are non-empty, that they exist, or that they do not exist. All things are not empty with respect to imagination and emptiness, and they are not non-empty with respect to subject-object-duality, (all things being either) created imaginative construction or uncreated emptiness. According to Vasubandhu, this explanation should be taken in agreement with the teaching of the *Mother Scripture*, etc., that "all this is neither uniquely empty, nor uniquely non-empty," and it does not indicate the perfect by "not empty," nor the other two realities by "not non-empty." (The third phrase) should be understood according to the explanation of Vasubandhu and Sthiramati, "existence" meaning imagination, "non-existence" meaning duality, and "existence" meaning the mutual existence of both imagination and emptiness. Any explanation that opposes these (masters), such as that, as one of those two (imagination and emptiness) exists otherwise, the other is empty, should not be taken as explaining (correctly) the belief of these (masters). And Sthiramati explains that this import is the same as that declared in the *Kashyapa Chapter*, after explaining existence and non-existence as two extremes, that between them lies the central way of critical examination of things. Thus he explains this very system of the "pure information" (school) as the meaning of the central way; although other Centrists hold the latter school to be superior to the former, (in fact) this system makes the two equivalent.[59]

We have thus expressed the method of explanation in each section, according to Vasubandhu and Sthiramati. Dignaga also, in his *Concise Meaning of the Transcendent Wisdom*, explains the import of the *Eight Thousand* in agreement with the *Universal Vehicle Compendium*.[60] And Dharmakirti, in the *Treatise on Validating Cognition*, declares the reality of the relative to be the emptiness of substantially different subject and object: "Therein, if either were non-existent, both would be destroyed. Therefore, emptiness of duality is the reality of that (relative)."[61]

[59] The Idealists thus consider themselves to be the true Centrists, not members of a lower school, and Tsong Khapa subtly agrees, by using the word "other."

[60] Dignaga's *Prajñāpāramitāpiṇḍārtha*, ks. 27-29 (Skt. ed., Tucci, *Journal of Royal Asiatic Society, Calcutta*, 1947, pp. 56-59): *prajñāpāramitāyāṃ hi triṇi samaśritya deśanā / kalpitaṃ paratantraṃ ca parinispannam eva ca // nāstītyādipadaiḥ sarvaṃ kalpitaṃ vinivartate / māyopāmādidṛṣṭāntaiḥ paratantrasya deśanā // caturdha vyāvadānena parinispannakīrtanaṃ / prajñāpāramitāyāṃ hi nānyā buddhasya deśanā //.*

[61] *Pramāṇavārtika* (PV) II, k. 213 (Skt. edited by S. D. Shastri, Varanasi: Bauddha Bharati, 1968, p. 164): *tatra ekasyāpyabhāvena dvayamapyavahīyate / tasmāt tadeva tasyāpi tattvaṃ yā dvayaśūnyatā //.*

Further, he explains the meaning of the scriptures' declarations of the realitylessness of things in the same way:

> The inherence of difference in things is based on the difference of that (subject and object). That being itself an error, difference in things is also an error. No nature exists other than the aspects of subject and object. Therefore, because of emptiness of (that) nature, realitylessness is proclaimed.[62]

The differentiation of things in regard to their production, etc., is not effected by means of mere apperception, but by means of the same consciousness that perceives duality. Dualistic perception is a delusion. Since it is false, what it establishes also becomes false. There is no nature of anything other than subjects and objects, and the nature of such apparent duality is proclaimed to be realitylessness, since it does not exist as it appears. Furthermore, he declares in his *Treatise*: "All natures of such things as aggregates are specifically qualified as functional, and not real. Hence, they are (ultimately) free of natures."[63]

Statements of the form aggregates, etc., as natural things, and of formability, etc., as their natures, all are qualified by functionality. Although their basis exists substantially, they are not established in reality through their aspect of functionality. Hence he explains that this is intended by the declaration of emptiness with respect to nature, which (theory) he holds in common with the Individual Vehicle schools. Finally, the *Treatise on Validating Cognition* makes the same point earlier stated in the *Compendium*:

> If (one objects): "everything is without (functional) power (ultimately)," (we answer) "the power of the seed, etc., is visible in the sprout, etc." (And if one) maintains "that is superficial (only)," (we answer) "then how could (the sprout) ever come to be?"[64]

[62] PV II, ks. 214-15 (Shastri ed., pp. 164-65): *tadbhedāśrayini ceyaṃ bhāvānāṃ bhedasaṃsthitiḥ / tadupaplavabhāve ca teṣaṃ bhedo 'pyupaplavaḥ // na grāhyagrahakākārabāhyamasti ca lakṣaṇam / ato lakṣaṇaśūnyatvānniḥsvabhāvaḥ prakāśitaḥ //.*

[63] PV II, k. 216 (Shastri ed., p. 165): *vyāpāropādhikaṃ sarvam skandhādīnāṃ viśeṣataḥ / lakṣaṇaṃ sa ca tattvaṃ na tenāpyete vilakṣaṇaḥ //.*

[64] PV II, k. 4 (Shastri ed., p. 100): *aśaktaṃ sarvam iti ced bījāderañkurādiṣu / dṛṣṭa śaktiḥ mata sa cet saṃvṛtyaḥ 'stu yathā tathā //.*

This verse parallels the argument given above from the VS wherein the Centrist objects to the idea of any sort of compounded ultimacy, for him a contradiction in terms, and the Idealist objects to relegation of functional things to mere superficial status. bLo-bzang Phun-tshogs (*Zin Bris*, ff. 42b ff.) comments: "When [Dharmakirti] has explicitly stated, in terms common to both Traditionists and Idealists, that ultimate functional efficiency is an example of ultimate existence, an objector says: 'Wrong, because all cognitions have no power of functional efficiency ultimately.' He answers: 'They do, because we observe the power of seeds, etc., to produce sprouts, etc.' Objector: 'That doesn't follow, since that power is only admitted as superficial.' He answers: 'Well then, does the seed perform the function of producing the sprout from its own intrinsic condition (*rang gi sdod lugs kyi*

As for the details of the methods of explanation of these teachers, I do not discuss them, fearing prolixity.

2. SPECIFIC NEGATION OF THE EXTREME OF REIFICATION

Description of Reification—The Negatee

Repudiation, one of the two logical negatees of this system, is only philosophically postulated, and furthermore, as explained above is (mainly) in the system of the orthodox advocates of realitylessness. In reification, there are both conscious theoretical and unconscious instinctual varieties, the conscious reification being the (philosophical) systems of the Realists, both heterodox and orthodox. In regard to unconscious reification, as the reification of the personal self will be shown below, here we should explain the reification of the objective self, because although the objective self is a theoretical postulate, it is the object (that would have) to be proven (to secure) the objective self maintained unconsciously,[65] and also because the (objective self) is the chief logical negatee.

Although in many texts of this system, the objective self-habit is explained to be none other than the habitual notion of the substantial difference between subject and object, the *Elucidation* teaches the objective self-habit to be the habitual notion that ascriptive and descriptive designations are established by intrinsic identifiability in the relative. This is implied by its explanation of objective selflessness as identity-unreality, which is the non-establishment by intrinsic identifiability of the relative according to ascriptive and descriptive designation. Furthermore, the *Bodhisattva Stages*, the *Compendium of Determinations*, and the *Compendium of the Universal Vehicle* take pains to prove that emptiness devoid of the content of this habitual notion is the ultimate meaning of the central way, and is the perfect, which is objective selflessness. Therefore, if we do not know just what is this imaginatively constructed (reality) which is reified as the objective self in the relative, we will not know decisively the objective self-habit and the objective selflessness of this system.

The imagined (reality), in question when the objective self-habit is taken as the habitual notion that the imagined is established by intrinsic iden-

---

ngos nas)? Or not? If not, the seed intrinsically prevents production of the sprout, and production of effects would not occur even superficially. Thus, if effects are produced, they must be admitted to be produced ultimately, and to assert "superficial production" is to deny any sort of production whatsoever.' "

[65] That is, if the unconscious objective-self-perception habit were to be justified, it would have to secure the type of objective self that is philosophically postulated by the conscious, intellectual reification of objective self.

tifiability, is that reality verbally and conventionally designated in such things as the aggregates, ascriptively through statements such as "This is form!" and descriptively through such statements as "This is production of form!" Since the aggregates, etc., do exist just that much,[66] the notion that they exist there is not reification. Reification is the habitual notion that the aggregates exist by intrinsic identity as such and such (designated) entities.

Here, an objector might well demand reasons to prove the absence of a number of contradictions in this system (that he might perceive to be as follows): (first), if the negation of the intrinsically identifiable status of form, etc., as being the objective basis of names and signs, negates (only) their being the direct objective basis of expressions, then it is unnecessary to prove the relative to be devoid of that (imagined reality), since the Realists have already established the non-phenomenality of objective universals and verbal universals as actual contents and means of expressions.[67] Furthermore, (by the same reason), since the proof of (the relative's) emptiness with respect to that (sort of imagined reality) does not establish objective selflessness, (there being no objective selflessness in the Individualist schools), meditation on such (inferior) emptiness will not purify the objective obscurations, which contradicts the *Elucidation* explanation that the emptiness of the relative with respect to the establishment by intrinsic identifiability of the imagined (reality) is the perfect, objective selflessness, and the *Bodhisattva Stages* explanation that such emptiness is the object causing the purification of the objective obsurations. In the negation of form, etc. as being the conceptual objects of expressions, when the existence by intrinsic identity of the ground differentials of conceptual objects is negated, the relative will be negated as established by intrinsic identifiability, and even if (only) the intrinsic identifiability of the categorical differentials of conceptual objects is negated, it is (still) invalid (as an interpretation of this system) since the Traditionists have proved the non-phenomenality of universals as the object of inferential validating cognitions.[68]

[66] That is, as relative entities susceptible to designation.

[67] The thrust of this argument is that the Traditionists have already proven the non-phenomenality of universals, yet have not thereby arrived at understanding of objective selflessness, which this objector believes to be missing in the Individual Vehicle. See AK II, ad. k. 47 (LVP, Vol. II, 238 ff.).

[68] The objector here argues that Tsong Khapa is missing the central idea of the Idealists, that is, that lack of substantial subject-object dichotomy is the subtle emptiness, when he takes the imagined reality, that is, substantive and qualitative designation, as the negatee of the negation called "objective selflessness." The objector is confusing the Traditionist logicians' (that is, Dignaga, etc.) separation of perception and inference (with their respective objects) with the Idealists' separation of the imagined from the relative. "Differential" (*ldog pa [vyāvṛtti] – gzhan sel* [*apoha*]) is the Buddhist way of designating a universal, indicating that a conceptualized object (a "named object") is not a thing in itself containing the universal quality referred to by the name, but is only the opposite of everything else that

Furthermore, since the statement from the *Life Migration Scripture*: "Such and such a name expresses such and such a thing, but does not exist therein, and this is the ultimate nature of things,"[69] is established for the Individualist schools also, the ultimate, as emptiness (of the relative) with regard to the imagined, of the *Elucidation of Intention*, appears to amount to nothing more than this. Finally, it could not be correct to explain this pattern of emptiness as objective selflessness, the object used for purifying objective obscurations, since it does not indicate the pure consciousness that negates substantial difference between subject and object.

Let us now explain.

This pattern of emptiness is not already established by the Individual Vehicle schools, because the *Bodhisattva Stages* explains it to be the object of the wisdom purificative of objective obscurations and to be the unexcelled central way avoiding the two extremes, and because the *Universal Vehicle Compendium* declares that realization of this (pattern of emptiness) is realization of pure consciousness. Therefore, the Individualist schools do have philosophical assertions which amount to that reification which is the opposite of this (pattern of emptiness); that is, their habitual notion that form, etc., are established by intrinsic identity as ascriptively and descriptively verbally designated. In negating this reification, the *Bodhisattva Stages* refutes with scriptural reference, so the target of the refutation is also (a member of an) orthodox (school); and since the refutation would not apply to the advocates of realitylessness, nor to a particular type of Experientialist, (it must apply to) the Individual Vehicle

---

it is not. (For example, a "horse" is a "horse" because it is a non-non-horse, and not because the mysterious universal "horseness" resides in it.) "Ground differential" (*gzhi ldog*) is the actuality of a thing that may be taken as a conceptual object, that is, its non-conceptual basis, and "categorical differential" (*rang ldog*) is the thing as a conceptual object.

This objector is essentially confused between the Idealists' form, and so on, as mere *things susceptible to expression*, which constitute the relative and are thus intrinsically identifiable in their system, and the Traditionists' form, and so on, not as mere things, but as *functional bases of conventional expressions*, which are both intrinsically identifiable and distinctively characterized as such in their system.

The Idealist subtlety and precision of understanding of the process of verbalizing instinct, as relating to the three-reality theory and the presentation of the subtle objective selflessness, is, so to speak, "out of the league" of the Traditionists, who are formally content with distinguishing the objects of perception and those of inference, denying a certain type of reality-status to universals, objects of the latter, while unwittingly projecting a more subtle type of objective existence even to these universals.

[69] This scripture is not found in K, but the quote itself occurs in BBh (Dutt ed., p. 33) as an Individualist source used to refute the Traditionists: *yena yena hi namnā vai yo yo dharmo 'bhilāpyate / na sa saṃvidyate tatra dharmānāṃ sa hi dharmatā //*. A parallel verse occurs in Nagarjuna's *Bhāvasaṃkrānti* (TG, P, tsa) Ch. V., k. 3: *gang las gang byung ming de ni / gang las gang byung chos de rnams / de ni med par 'gro pa yin / chos de med pas chos nyid yin //*.

schools. And therefore, (it) refutes them with three references established for them, without quoting the *Elucidation*.[70]

(Having thus answered the objections in general, turning to the description of reification itself), to describe first of all unconscious reification, the *Compendium* statement is: "It should be recognized that naive people habitually insist on an intrinsic reality, which accords with names and expressions, in things subject to expression, because of five reasons."[71]

The first reason is then explained as the fact that (such naive people), when asked "what is the reality of that thing called 'form'?" they answer "its reality is form!" and not "its name is 'form'!" That means that when thus questioned, they give the name of a thing as its reality, and are unable to say "the reality of that thing called 'form' is merely its designation by the name 'form'." Therefore, when something is designated by the expression "form," if we examine the appearance of that thing which is the basis of designation, say by the expression "blue form," it appears to be established on the strength of its own objective condition; not merely verbally and conventionally posited.

The holding of that "blue" to be established as it appears is the reification which holds an intrinsically identifiable status (to underlie) the designation of something blue by the name "form." The above explanation has established that naive people have this (habit), and since the two realistic (Individualist) schools believe such a habit-pattern to have validity, where is the (Idealists') similarity to their system, in which, although the categorical differential of the verbally expressible is defined as mere conceptual designation, its ground differential serves as its intrinsic identity?[72] Thus we can understand particularly the process of

[70] See n. 68 above. The other two references are from the *Arthavargīya* (BBh, Dutt ed., p. 33) and the *Saṃthākātyāyanamārabhya . . . sūtra* (BBh, Dutt ed., p. 33).

[71] VS, TG, C, zi, f. 20b1; D. zi, ff. 21aff. bLo-bzang Phun-tshogs (*Zin Bris*, ff. 43b6-45a6) paraphrases the other four reasons from the VS: "2) When one investigates things with general and particular natures in order to find the referents of expressions such as 'this and this . . .' one reflects 'their reality is form' and not 'their reality is merely their verbal designations.' 3) When so investigating, one is displeased when one does not find that the reality of a thing is form [itself], and is not displeased when one does not find the reality of a thing to be mere verbal designation. 4) Because, although things are not established by intrinsic identity in their referential bases, one conceptually presumes them to be so. 5) Naive people are bound by the signs of expressions" (that is, their minds are irresistibly drawn to apparently real things by expression of their names).

[72] Tsong Khapa here answers the objection above (see n. 67), saying that it is wrong to think the Idealists' theory resembles the Realists' theories at all, in spite of the superficial resemblance between the Traditionist theory of the unreality of universals and the Idealist theory of the imagined, as ascriptive and descriptive designation, being nonexistent in the relative (since Realists accept the reality of externals, and the Idealists most certainly do not), and since the Traditionists are still much more naively realistic about the inherence of universals in their objective ground.

In the *Drang nges bzhi 'dril*, (f. 211 [106a] ff.), 'Jam-dbyangs bZhed-pa comments:

"Though the Traditionists accept the lack of intrinsic identifiability of such as blue being the conceptual base of a blue-perceiving conceptual cognition, they do posit the intrinsic identifiability [of such as blue] as conceptual base of that blue that serves as ground differential of the conceptual object of that [conceptual cognition], whereas the Idealist does not accept the intrinsic identifiability [of blue] as the conceptual base of that blue, not only as categorical differential but also as ground differential; because if a thing exists, Idealists accept the concomitant fact of such [as blue] being devoid of intrinsic identifiability as conceptual base of blue-perceiving conceptual cognition." Thus, by dividing the differential nature of a conceptual object into "categorical" and "ground," the Traditionist allows a subtle degree of objectification of conceptuality to creep into the object itself, whereas the Idealist more strictly acknowledges the ineffability of the perceptual, by holding both differentials of the conceptual object to be mental, part of the imaginatively constructed reality. Thus, their recognition of the relative's emptiness of the imagined qualifies as a form of objective selflessness, and the Traditionist's recognition of the non-phenomenality of universals does not.

But it is still difficult to understand this refined subtlety, unless we understand how these different views affect an actual case of perception. This is brilliantly unpacked by mKhas-grub, in his *sTong thun chen mo*, quoted in the *bZhi 'dril* following:

In this context of the Idealists, according to the mental orientation of an educated person, when blue appears in the visual consciousness seeing blue, there are not only the appearance of blue as blue and the appearance of blue as an external object, but also the appearance of the blue that serves as locus or basis of the designations of that blue as "blue," as "this blue of the nature of form," and as "this blue as produced." How is the presence of these appearances known? It is known; because when visual consciousness takes that very blue which appears in the mode of blue as an object of recognition and conceptually cognizes it, that visual consciousness automatically elicits the conceptual cognition which applies the designation "this is blue," and then that cognition or that visual consciousness automatically can elicit the impulse to answer the query, "what is the nature of that object called 'blue' " by "its nature is form" as it conceptually adheres in visual consciousness to the same appearance of blue appearing like blue. For that reason, when blue appears in visual consciousness as the blue that serves as the basis of the designation "blue," it is proven that that type of appearance which is the appearance of blue being the basis of the designation "blue" in the intrinsic objectivity of its phenomenal condition is present. And that is the meaning of the appearance of blue as intrinsically identifiably the blue that serves as the basis of the designation "blue." And similarly, it resembles the meaning of blue appearing intrinsically identifiable as the form, etc. which serve as bases of designations such as "this blue is form by nature," "this blue is the production of this," and so on. Yet, such appearances in visual consciousness are not appearances arising by the power of the objective condition of blue, nor are such appearances produced from the causality of such appearance of blue in visual consciousness leaving a seed of an instinct for homogeneity. It is just an appearance arising by the power of a beginningless instinct formed by the continuous habit of conceptual cognition of substantive and qualificative designations such as "this is blue," "this is form," "this is the production of form," and so on. And that instinct is called "articulative instinct" by the Idealists.

Since that appearance is simply arisen by the power of the instinct deposited by conceptual cognition's habit of applying designations, it is called "appearance simply posited by names and symbols," and "appearance posited by power of conceptual cognition." Now, just as form, etc. appear to sense-cognition as the bases of substantive and qualificative designations, the conventional existence of that form, etc. as the bases of substantive and qualificative designations is similar (in meaning) to the above-explained "appearance simply posited by names and conceptual cognition." And the appearance of form, etc. in sense cognition as intrinsically identifiably the bases of substantive and qualificative designations, and the intrinsic identifiability of form, etc. as they appear as the bases of designations, also are similar to the above mode of being designated by reification in regard to the imagined, as well as the process of reification in regard to other things. And similarly, when subject and object occur dualistically, the holding of them both to exist as they appear, substantially different, is the reification that is the objective self-habit. The answers to the remaining objections will be explained below.

The Procedure to Negate It; Actual Negation

The *Elucidation of Intention* does not give any reasons proving the relative to be devoid of the imagined. Hence, as this must be understood,

---

names and conceptual cognitions; yet they are not established as even conventionally existent according to their designations. Therefore, form, etc. being the conventional bases of substantive and qualificative designations constitute the (conventionally) existent imagined reality, and form, etc. being the intrinsically identifiable bases of substantive and qualificative designations constitute the (conventionally) non-existent imagined reality. When form etc. appear in sense cognition, the Traditionist asserts that there is appearance (of form etc.) as being the loci of usage of designations such as "this is form etc.," and that there is intrinsically identifiable status of those (form etc.) according to their appearance. Further, both Traditionist and Idealist do not accept that, when form appears in sense-cognition, it appears as the basis of the categorical differential of the designation "form." Moreover, they both do accept that, when form appears in sense-cognition, it has a way of appearing as the basis on which the name "this form" is applied, and that conceptual cognition adheres to that appearance of form in sense-cognition and uses the designation "this is form." But where they disagree is over whether such appearance has or does not have intrinsically identifiable status according to its appearance.

Thus the expression "basis of conceptual cognition" is applied to form, etc. appearing in sense-cognition in the following way; when form, etc. appear in sense-cognition as if established in the objective condition of the phenomena as the bases of the application of the names "this form" etc., when inferential conceptual cognition takes those appearances and designates them "this form," etc., and when those conceptual cognitions adhere to the (intrinsically identifiable) establishment of (form, etc.) as they thus appear in sense-cognitions and thereby repeatedly reinforce the articulative instincts existing in the mental continuum. And this is the meaning of the frequently used expression "form, etc. as the bases of conceptual cognition," which is not the same as just "form being the object of adherence of conceptual cognition." Therefore, this is a concise and easily understandable way to explain the reason for the difference between the Idealists' position on the lack of intrinsic identifiability of form, etc. as the bases of adherence of conceptual cognition, and the Traditionists' position on the lack of intrinsic identifiability of form, etc. as the objects of adherence of conceptual cognition.

To reformulate this in arguments: it is imperatively consequent that they are different; because the Idealist asserts that the lack of intrinsic identifiability of form, etc. as bases of conceptual cognitions' adherence does not encompass merely the categorical differentials of the bases of conceptual adherence, but encompasses what serve as the ground differentials of those bases, namely, the objects according to the mode of appearance wherein form, etc. appear in sense-cognitions arisen from constitutive instincts as the bases on which are applied designations such as "this is form," etc.; and the Traditionist system asserts that objects according to such appearance invariably have intrinsically identifiable status, since such sense-cognitions are not mistaken with respect to their perceptual objects. Therefore, there is an extremely great difference between them, since the Traditionist still accepts the validity of the conceptual habit-pattern that holds to the

the *Bodhisattva Stages* and the *Compendium* give three reasons each.[73] The *Universal Vehicle Compendium* also states:

> To answer the question, "What makes it clear that the reality of the relative is not as it appears in the imagined reality?" (We say) it is established because of the incompatibility between their natures, the incompatibility of multiplicity of nature, and the incompatibility of confused natures; because there is no cognition prior to names, because of multiplicity, and because of vagueness.[74]

To express simply the proof of the relative being empty of the imagined because of incompatibility between the natures of the two; if the fact of a round-bellied thing being the locus or basis of the expression "pot" were to be established by the intrinsic identifiability or reality of round-belliedness, it would not be established on strength of conventions, and hence, the conventionally subjective cognition, without requiring any convention, would arise thinking "pot" in regard to the round-bellied thing, before there was any designation of the name "pot."

(To express simply) the proof through the incompatibility between something being one and its having many natures; since, according to the antagonist's position, the giving of many names to one thing, as in calling Indra, "Shakra," "Shatakratu," "Gramaghataka," etc., must be on the strength of the thing itself, (the names being) existent in the thing as they appear to imaginative construction, that one thing would become many.

(Third, to express simply) the proof through the incompatibility of confusing the entities of distinct things; since, according to the antagonist, when two people are called by the same name, for example, "Upagupta," there is no difference in the way the cognition "Upagupta" arises (in regard to each of them), and since name and imagination apply to each of them on the strength of their objective reality, the two must become one entity.

Since the habitual notion that form, etc., are established ultimately,

---

intrinsic identifiability of form, etc. appearing in such a way in sense-cognitions, whereas the Idealist asserts that the upholding of the intrinsic identifiability of such appearances in sense-cognitions is (precisely) the objective self-habit.

Tsong Khapa assumes in his readers familiarity with a philosophical tradition in which the difference between "conceptual object" (*zhen yul*) and "conceptual basis" (*zhen gzhi*) is clear to just this degree of epistemological subtlety and precision.

[73] dPal-'byor Lhun-grub (SERA f. 38a6) remarks that the BBh gives the reasons of multiplicity, natural contradiction, and confusion, and the VS gives the same three reasons as the MS.

[74] MS II, TG, P, li, ff. 20b7-21a1. (Lamotte, *La Somme*, pp. 118-19).

or by intrinsic identity, as the bases of conceptual adherence, is similar to the habitual notion that (form, etc.) are established by intrinsic identity as the grounds of verbal designations,[75] the illiterate person, who does not know the names of things, still has (the unconscious habit of) reification which is the negatee; and the reasons to negate it are similar also.

The *Bodhisattva Stages* negates (reification by reasoning that), while a thing exists before the name is attached to it, that thing (according to the Realists) should be a non-entity before it is designated by its name, and otherwise, if it were to exist before the designation, the cognition "form" would arise, even prior to the name. Although the Individualists (attempt to evade this refutation) by saying that, although there would be such faults as nominal cognition arising prior to conventional information if the direct object of conventional designation were objectively intrinsically identifiable, no such faults accrue if form, etc., are established by intrinsic identity as the ground of conventional designation and as the basis of conceptual adherence, still (the refutation is) similar (in application to them).

Thus, although form, etc., being the bases of conceptual adherence cannot be negated (conventionally) in spite of their being the verbally and conventionally established imagined (reality), because they are (conventionally) established by validating cognition, the same (conceptual basis status) being established through the intrinsic identity of those things (can be negated), since an imagined reality set up by words alone cannot possibly be a knowable object. Hence, among things established verbally and conventionally, there are those established by validating cognition and those not so established.[76]

Nevertheless, this system asserts that as soon as something is merely established nominally and conventionally, it cannot participate in causality. The two Realist schools do not know how to establish the existence of those things such as form, etc., once their establishment by intrinsic identity as the bases of conceptual adherence and as the grounds of symbolic designation is negated. Intrinsic identity (*svalakṣaṇa*) here is not that ultimate particular (*svalakṣaṇa*) common to the logicians.[77]

[75] The two types of intrinsic identifiability here are Tib. *rtog pai zhen gzhir rang mtstan gyis grub pa* and *ming du btags pai gnas su rang mtshan gyis grub pa.*

[76] dPal-'byor Lhun-grub (SERA f. 38b3 ff.) remarks that this means that the fact of nominal and conventional establishment is neither concomitant with establishment by validating cognition (*tshad mas grub pa*) nor concomitant with non-establishment by validating cognition; because form as basis of conceptual adherence is established by validating cognition, while being the verbally constructed, yet form as basis of conceptual adherence *established by intrinsic identity* is impossible among knowable objects (and thus not established by validating cognition), yet is another type of verbally constructed reality.

[77] dPal-'byor Lhun-grub (SERA f. 40b4 ff.) explains that the "intrinsic identity" (*svalakṣaṇa*) involved in the status question is not the ultimate particular (*svalakṣaṇa*) of the

It is not contradictory for consciousness, as the basis of conceptual adherence, to be the imagined reality that is not established ultimately, and for (the same) consciousness to be ultimately established (in its relative nature), just as, for example, a pot's absence, being an absolute negation, is not prevented from sharing a common ground with the location (from which it is absent) by (the supposed) contradictoriness of an absolute negation and a phenomenon.

Therefore, although the statement, "Such and such a name," etc., is from a scripture canonical in the Individualist schools, it is not that there is no difference between the way they explain it (and the way this system does). For example, the expression "root-consciousness" that is used in the Mahasamghika school is explained by this system as the fundamental consciousness.

Since the above-explained habitual notion of existence by intrinsic identity, or in the ultimate, of ascriptive and descriptive designation is the chief type of objective obscuration, the determination of the nonexistence of its object is correctly equivalent to the object purificative of objective obscurations.

Finally, how are these reasonings applied to arrive at "pure information?" When we negate the ultimate establishment of things, from form to omniscience, as being the grounds of designation by verbal expressions and the bases of conceptual adherence, we reach the pure information free of subject-object-duality, with the realization that there is nothing unmistaken about the habitual notions of the imagination that perceive the substances and qualities of expressible things by depending on expressive names, expressible referents, and the connection between name and referent, since all such conceptualizations are devoid of their apparent objectivities. The *Compendium of the Universal Vehicle* states:

> Thus, such a bodhisattva who strives to reach pure information truly understands that those names made of letters, the content of mental formulations that appear as letters and meanings, are no more than mere mental constructs. He truly understands that meanings based on letters are no more than mere mental formulations. He truly understands that names are no more than mere designations of substances and qualities. Therefore, apprehending the fact that all are merely mental formulations, and not apprehending any objective identifiability in nominal things, with their ascriptive and descriptive designations, he enters pure information itself, with regard to mental constructions

---

logicians, which is equivalent with functional efficiency (*arthakriyaśakti*), because in the theories relating to the three realities, including those of Dharmakirti himself, the perfect is intrinsically identifiable and yet has no functional efficiency.

of apparent words and meanings, by means of the four thorough investigations, and the four authentic realizations.[78]

Here, one might object that although this is a negation of subject and object based on the constructions of mental consciousness, there is no philosophical negation of subject and object depending on the non-conceptual consciousness controlled by instincts, so how can it be valid as entrance into pure information?

This is not a fault, because the rational negation of blue existing by intrinsic identity as the basis of conceptual adherence which holds the object dichotomously apart proves that the perception of blue, in which "blue" appears as a basis of adherence, is mistaken in its apparent object, since that appears to have intrinsic identifiability. And that proof proves that that object "blue" does not exist as a substance different from the consciousness in which it appears.

Here again, one might protest that, when the ultimate status of consciousness as the basis of conceptual adherence is rationally negated, apperceptive self-consciousness, in which that consciousness appears, is established to be mistaken in its apparent object, because (consciousness) appears therein to have intrinsic identifiability. And once that is established, the philosophy of the Experientialist is demolished, since consciousness is without intrinsically identifiable status according to actual experience.

This is not a fault, because consciousness does not appear in apperception as a basis of conceptual adherence, although "blue" does appear as the basis of the conceptual adherence insistent on the externality of the blue in the perception of "blue." (The appearance of something) being an object of adherence cannot arise in apperception, etc., where dualism declines, which does not exclude its appearance in the dualistic perception of blue. The reason that when a basis of conceptual adherence appears, it must appear dualistically, is that whenever such a general notion arises in thought, it definitely arises with a dualistic appearance. Nevertheless, it is not the same in the case of this (apperceptive) consciousness, because, although it also arises generally in thought, it arises in the form of pure experience. And one cannot say, "It is the same since there definitely must be dualistic appearance in constructive thought!" because dualistic appearance in constructive thought is not equivalent to the arisal of a (specific) object with a dualistic appearance. Otherwise, it would be necessary to admit the impossibility of the occurrence of the decline of dualistic appearance in constructive thought. And that is not

[78] MS III, P, li, f. 28a1-5. (Lamotte, *La Somme*, p. 162).

correct, since then it would become impossible for dualistic appearance to decline (in any experience).

It is not to be imagined that blue does not appear to non-conceptual (consciousness) as the basis of conceptual adherence, since it is only so established on the strength of mental construction (itself); because (in that case) (sticks and clods) would not appear to non-conceptual consciousness as illusory horse and elephant, since they are only so established on the strength of mental construction.

Therefore, the *Elucidation of Intention* statement that emptiness (of the relative) with respect to the imagined, which consists of ascriptive and descriptive designation, is the perfect does not fail to negate substantial dichotomy between subject and object as well. (Furthermore), that scripture clearly states the negation of (the reality of) external things, in the section on serenity meditation. And it does not indicate the imagined reality in general, in which there are many things, such as all universal characteristics, space, etc., because these are not relevant in the context of establishing the emptiness (of the relative), with respect to such (a specific type of) imagined reality, as the perfect. Because, although those many things have an existence that cannot be established by names and symbols (alone), they have no intrinsic identifiability, because they are merely conceptually constructed.[79]

As for the negation of subject and object depending on external things, the *Compendium of Universal Vehicle* gives the reasoning (associated with the similes of) dream and reflection, etc.; the *Twenty* gives the reasoning negating the indivisibility of atoms; Dharmakirti gives the reasoning negating homogeneity in the production of the characteristics of subject and object; and Dignaga gives the reasoning negating the objective status of molecules and atoms.[80]

[79] See Ch. I n. 46.

[80] dPal-'byor Lhun-grub paraphrases (SERA ff. 44b7 ff.) MS: "Although the relative appears as external object, it does not so exist; because, although a dream horse appears, it does not exist as a real horse, and because, although the reflection of an image appears in a mirror, it [the image] does not exist there"; and *Viṃśatikā* (ks. 11-14): "There are no external objects, because they are not atomic, nor are they gross. The first is proved by the fact that there is no indivisible atom, because when a central nucleus stands surrounded by atoms in ten directions, they cannot relate [if indivisible] with or without connection of sides, or with or without interstices. The first is proved by the fact that, if they were connected on all sides, they would occupy the same spot, and the molecule itself would be an atom, and if they were connected on one side, they would become divisible. The second is proved by the fact that if atoms were connected with interstices a pot would not hold water, and by the fact that the nucleus would have to have directional facets to face eastern and western atoms, hence would be divisible"; and PV: "Blue is not an external object, because it is not perceived by blue-perception, because it does not impart form similar to itself; because if it did, it would have to be beautiful or ugly in itself, as it is perceived as beautiful or ugly" (PV II, k. 341). For Dignaga's argument in *Ālaṃbanaparīkṣa*, see Stcherbatski, *Buddhist Logic* I, pp. 518-21.

In regard to the *Compendium of the Universal Vehicle* statements that all the *Mother Scripture* declarations of non-existence negate the imagined reality, if we do not understand the *Elucidation*'s procedure to negate the imagined, we will interpret them as (referring to) only the imagined reality which is substantial difference between subject and object, and we will be forced into many positions that are altogether incorrect even in the Experientialist system, for it would be extremely difficult on such an interpretation to explain the statements of the total incomprehensibility of such things as permanence and impermanence, etc.

It might even become necessary to maintain that the statements of "total incomprehensibility" refer to the (time of) the equanimity (of holy wisdom), and the statements of "comprehensibility" through specific discrimination refer to the time of the aftermath-discernment(-wisdom); but saying this would be catastrophic!

The *Bodhisattva Stages*, the *Universal Vehicle Compendium*, and the *Abhidharma Synthesis* mention the four thorough investigations and the four authentic realizations[81] as the determination of the view of pure information, and the antidote of the objective obscurations, which are those mental constructions that also serve as foundation for the addictions. And in order to understand them, it appears necessary to understand exactly the negatee, reification, and the reasoning negating the (reality of the) imagined, as stated in the *Elucidation of Intention*. Also, as it seems especially necessary to know the way of entrance into pure information through negation of subject-object substantial difference by the reasonings (above), I have merely opened the door of analysis for the

[81] Skt. *saṃyakparyeṣṭi* and *-parijñāna*. *Zin Bris* (f. 47a1 ff.) outlines the four thorough investigations, those of name- (*nāmaparyeṣṭi*), referent- (*arthaparyeṣṭi*), substantive-designation- (*svabhāvaprajñaptiparyeṣṭi*), and descriptive-designation-investigations (*viśeṣa-prajñapti-paryeṣṭi*. 1) "The analytic understanding by authentic reasoning that the verbal names, involved in mental formulations of verbal thoughts in which verbal names and their referents appear dualistically, are mere imaginative constructions, as they are not established in fact as they appear to be, within their expressed referents objectively present." 2) "The correct understanding that the referents derived from the words which are mental formulations not intrinsically identifiably established as the bases of the predicative words are no more than mere imaginative construction." 3) "The correct understanding that the referents of ascriptive designations such as 'form' which depend upon names such as 'form,' referents such as the formful, and the name-referent-connection, are no more than mere imaginative constructions." 4) "The correct analytic understanding that the descriptively designated referents such as 'form is produced,' which depend upon verbal expressions such as 'form production,' their expressed referents, and the word-referent-connection, are no more than mere imaginative constructions as they are not intrinsically identifiable."

The four authentic realizations are generally represented as the results of the above four investigations. In other words, when the investigations penetrate into their respective areas, they eventually yield the realization of emptiness, which in this system is the emptiness of lack of substantial subject-object duality.

intelligent, having observed they have not yet begun to investigate (this question).

Elimination of Protest

Here, some might protest: "(We might allow that) the *Elucidation of Intention* states that the addictions are produced by habitual adherence to the imagined reality in the relative, evolutionary action is accumulated thereby, and thus one wanders in cyclic life; and when the identity-unreality of the imagined in the relative is seen, the sequence is reversed. (Further, perhaps), all three—disciple, solitary sage, and bodhisattva—attain liberation by this same path and practice, their path of purification and their purity being the same, stated to be 'without a second,' with no other pattern of emptiness of the relative with respect to the imagined than that explained above. But then, is the meaning of this scripture taken to be that the Individualists realize objective selflessness? Or is it not? If it is so taken, then the above explanations of the distinctiveness (of the Universal Vehicle) are contradicted. And if it is not so taken, how is the meaning of the scripture to be explained?"

(Let us explain); the *Bodhisattva Stages* declares that ascriptive and descriptive constructions, as well as materialistic constructions,[82] create the ground of phenomenal fabrications, which are (themselves) the objects of those imaginative constructions. On that basis, the futile views arise, and thereby the other addictions are produced and we travel around cyclic life. And, when we know that the objects held by the constructions do not exist, by means of the four thorough investigations and the four authentic realizations, this process is reversed.

Thus, (Asanga) believes that the objective self-habit, which holds ascriptive and descriptive designation to be intrinsically identifiable in things, acts as the root of the futile views, just as those Centrists who believe that the Individualists have no realization of objective selflessness hold that the objective self-habit acts as basis for personal egoism.[83] However, since, although the termination of objective self-habits eliminates per-

[82] Tib. *ngo bo nyid du rtog pa, khyad par du rtog pa*, and *ril por 'dzin pai rtog pa* = Skt. *svabhāvavikalpa*, *viśeṣa-vikalpa*, and *piṇḍagrahavikalpa*. BBh (Dutt. ed., p. 34) classifies thought-constructions into eight types: substantive (ascriptive) (*svabhāvavikalpa*), qualificative (descriptive) (*viśeṣavikalpa*), materialistic (*piṇḍagraha-*), egoistic (*aham iti-*), possessive- (*mama iti-*), pleasure- (*priya-*), displeasure- (*apriya-*), and neutral (*tadubhay-aviparīta-*) thought constructions (*vikalpa.*). Among these, materialistic construction is defined as taking such things as forests, armies, and so on, as real whole entities by lumping the particulars together by means of their universal conventional designations.

[83] This refers to Bhavaviveka and the Dogmaticists, since the Dialecticists make a specialty of their system the defense of the realization, authentic yet crude, of objective selflessness on the part of the Individual Vehicle saints.

sonal self-habits, the non-termination of objective self-habits does not (necessitate) the non-elimination of personal self-habits; the non-elimination of the ultimate basis of the life-cycle does not preclude liberation from the life-cycle. Therefore, although we may take "this same path" as the path of realization of the emptiness of the relative with respect to the imagined reality, we need not take it as the path of objective selflessness, because the *Abhidharma Synthesis* declares the relative devoid of the imagined in terms of personal selflessness also. Furthermore, the sameness of the path of purification and of purity itself is declared because of the fact that there is no difference between the Universal Vehicle and the Individual Vehicle with regard to the purification of addictions through the realization of personal selflessness and with regard to the liberation which is the mere elimination of addictions.

By implication from the *Elucidation of Intention* explanation of the meaning of the Universal Vehicle Scriptures as being that the establishment of the aggregates, etc., is the relative, the reification of objective self is the imagined, and the emptiness of that (former) with respect to that (latter) is the perfect, which is objective selflessness, we can understand the meaning of the Individual Vehicle Scriptures as being just that arrangement of the three realities which establishes the emptiness of the relative, consisting of the aggregates, with respect to the imagined, which is the personal self, as the perfect, which is personal selflessness. Therefore, the disciple for whom the first wheel was proclaimed was receptive to the realization of identity-realitylessness in terms of personal selflessness, and not in terms of objective selflessness, as the *Elucidation of Intention* explains by implication. And that is the meaning of the statement that the wheel of Dharma of fine discrimination was for the sake of disciples engaged in all vehicles.

(Again, some might protest that) if, taking the relative as the "empty" on all occasions of emptiness with respect to the imagined, which is (either) ascriptive and descriptive designation (or) substantial subject-object-difference, we must take the emptiness with respect to the two ways of (imagined) existence above as the perfect, then how is this reconciled with the statement of Vasubandhu from the *Supercommentary*, in which, taking the perfect as the empty, it is declared to be empty with respect to the other two realities? (As follows:) " 'Eye' means the ultimate eye. 'With respect to the eye' means the 'imagined eye' and the 'constructed eye.' 'Empty' is defined as 'free.' The same should be applied to such expressions as 'the ear empty with respect to the ear.' "[84]

[84] *Āryaśatasāhasrikāpañcaviṃśatisāhasrikāṣṭādaśasāhasrikāprajñāpāramitābṛhaṭṭīkā* (P. pha), thought by the objector to be the work of Vasubandhu, but attributed by Tsong Khapa and other Tibetan scholars to Damshtrasena. See Ruegg, *Théorie*, pp. 325-27. "Constructed" expresses Tib. *rnam brtags* (Skt. *vikalpita*), which intends the relative specifically in its role as basis of the imagined (*parikalpita*).

(Let us explain:) the basis upon which objective self-habits hold to (their notion of) objective self must be that which is taken as "the empty" when determining the perfect, which is objective selflessness, in any Experientialist or Centrist system. For example, when we wish to eliminate the suffering of terror when we perceive a snake in a rope, taking the rope as the empty, we must show it to be empty with respect to the snake, and it would be inappropriate to take the emptiness of the rope with respect to the snake as the empty, and to declare that that (emptiness) is empty with respect to the existence of (both) the rope and the snake as different things!

In regard to objective self-habits, such notions as the existence of indivisible atoms, of objects which are their aggregates, of instantaneous consciousness, temporally indivisible, and of consciousness which is a continuum of such (temporally indivisible consciousness), etc., are the conscious designations made only by those whose minds are affected by philosophy, and exist only for those philosophers, and not for other living beings. Therefore, the demonstration of an emptiness which is the non-existence of only those (notions) does not injure in the slightest the unconscious self-habits inherent from beginningless time. Hence, it is necessary to demonstrate that the basis upon which unconscious self-habits hold a self is empty with respect to the self supposedly held, and we must understand the negations of philosophical designations to be (no more than) factors of the negation of that (unconsciously presupposed self).

Through such considerations, since unconscious living beings perceive a self in just this relative reality, which consists of internal and external things such as names and forms, the objects of sight and hearing, we must determine emptiness by taking that same thing as the empty. Since the error (of living beings) is not in holding the existence of the other two realities as different things in the perfect, how can the formula "the perfect is emptiness with respect to the discrete existence of the other two realities" be the determination of selflessness?

Furthermore, to hold to the existence of an objective self is not (the same as) to hold to the existence of some other thing, such as to hold to the existence of a fire on the pass. Since the external objects and the internal subject of our own mind appear to be disparate, and we hold them to be established (in fact) as they appear, the remedy of that (habit) is the demonstration that the appearance of subject and object is not established as a substantial subject-object-dichotomy, and is not (simply) the demonstration that subject and object do not exist there as different things.

Therefore, the *Discrimination between Center and Extremes Com-*

mentary declares that (this pattern of emptiness) is not like a temple being empty of monks, but is like a rope being empty with respect to a snake, which statement also applies to the pattern of emptiness with respect to objective self.[85] Therefore, if we contemplate emptiness in a pattern such as that wherein the emptiness of the relative, which is the basis upon which self is held, with respect to the imagined, which is the self as held, is the perfect, and do not allow (ourselves to fall into the trap described in) the popular saying, "Throwing the effigy out the west gate, when the demons are causing trouble at the east gate";[86] (then, that meditation) will act as an antidote to self-habits. But if we contemplate emptiness in any pattern different from that system, self-habits will not be disturbed at all.

As for the explanation of the *Supercommentary*, the "imagined eye" means the expressive verbal universals and expressible objective universals that appear in constructive thought. The "constructed eye" means the apparent eye whose nature is to hold those (verbal universals, etc., to exist) in the objective visual media; and the "ultimate eye" is taken to be the perfect which is known by equanimous, individually introspective intuition, free of subject-object dichotomous appearance, and which is inexpressible, free of expressive and expressible verbal and objective universals. Therefore, since that ultimate nature of eye, according to the wisdom of the holy equanimity, is free of (both) dualisms of apparent words and referents and of subject and object, that object of equanimity is said to be empty with respect to the other two realities, since the former dualism (word-referent) is the imagined, and the latter (subject-object) is the relative (as imagined).

The same text continues:

> The imagined eye is that thing called "eye" which perceives things in the form of expressions and referents. The constructed eye is dichotomous appearance of visual forms which retain the nature of subject and object. And the ultimate eye is the perfect reality which is individual introspection free of all appearances, which is inexpressible, free of expression and referent. . . .

Thus, since, when you meditate on attention toward the ultimate,

[85] MAVB (Pandeya ed., p. 12): *yadi śāśaviṣānakalpanena dvayaṃ kathaṃ tenābhūtaparikalpasya śūnyatāsaṃbhavaḥ? anyena hyanyasya śūnyatā dṛṣṭā, yathā bhikṣubhirvihārasya / naitad evaṃ / yathārajjurmāyā va svātmanyavidyamānena sarpākārena puruṣādina vā prabhāsate / tatra kasyacid grāhanivartanārthaṃ sarpapuruṣādibhiśca śūnyatā ityucyate /.*

[86] This proverb arises from popular exorcistic rites, wherein a scapegoat made of barley flour and ritually set up to receive all the negative force to be exorcised is subsequently flung out of the house in which the rite is performed—obviously it has to be flung in the direction from which the disturbance is coming.

things constituted by creation do not appear, you should understand that they do not ultimately exist, but exist (only) superficially![87]

Hence, (the statement of the perfect as empty of the other two realities) is explained as the non-existence of dualistic appearance according to the holy equanimity. Therefore, this is not the way to determine the perfect, objective selflessness, which is the basic view (of the system).

The *Supercommentary* explains "ultimate existence" simply as existence according to the holy equanimity. Nevertheless, how could that be the ultimate existence involved in the argument about ultimate existence and non-existence, since what is admitted by equanimity in the intuitive understanding of reality is only that admitted to exist as object of its own particular subjectivity? The fact that this (*Supercommentary*) definitely does not admit ultimate existence capable of withstanding analysis by reasoning analytic of reality is known from the expression of total negation specifically aimed at such an admission in the section on emptiness-emptiness, ultimate-emptiness, and uncreated-emptiness, but I do not cite these, fearing prolixity.[88]

Finally, since the *Mother Scripture* itself, executing the analysis of the three realities of each thing from form to omniscience, explains the emptiness of the relative, the empty, with respect to the imagined, the negatee, as the perfect, the ultimate, the "ultimate (eye)" must be explained as the relative eye empty of the imagined eye. Therefore, it does not seem appropriate to explain the meaning of the scripture as the emptiness of the latter with respect to the two former, (even) in the context of the (holy) equanimity.

(Indeed,) this (*Supercommentary*) is not the work of Vasubandhu; because it negates the (ability of) both the relative and the perfect to withstand analysis by reasoning analytic of reality,[89] because it refers to the *Transcendent Wisdom Eighteen Thousand Commentary*'s comment on the eight attitudes of the great personages of the Individual Vehicle,[90]

[87] *Bṛhaṭṭīkā*, TG, P, pha; quotation unlocated.

[88] Tsong Khapa mentions this point without elaboration only to lend more weight to his overall refutation of Jo-nang-pas, which we have already observed above in numerous passages, since these latter claim the *Bṛhaṭṭīkā* as an authoritative source for their theory of the ultimacy of the ultimate. See Ruegg, *Théorie*, p. 326 n. 1.

[89] That is, if it were Vasubandhu's work, it would have him espousing the Centrist position on this point, and contradicting the Idealist adherence to the relative and the perfect as intrinsically identifiable.

[90] Tib. *Nyi Khri Rnam 'Grel* (lit. *Commentary on Twenty Thousand*) is given in Skt. as the *Aṣṭādaśasāhasrikāprajñāpāramitāvṛtti* (lit. . . . *Eighteen Thousand*) listed as the work of Bhadantavimuktasena, who was a disciple of Vasubandhu. Thus, if the *Bṛhaṭṭīkā* were Vasubandhu's work, he would be quoting his own disciple, which is highly unlikely, especially since the latter probably wrote his commentary after Vasubandhu had done most of his writing. bLo-bzang Phun-tshogs (*Zin Bris*, f. 53b2) lists the "eight attitudes of the Great Individualist" as: reduced desire, contentment, industriousness, solitariness, equi-

and because it is in complete disagreement with the explanation of the *Principles of Elucidation*, in which Vasubandhu demonstrates that the meaning intended in the *Mother Scripture* must be understood according to the *Elucidation of Intention*. Rather, it was written by Damshtrasena, as was well known to the scholars of the old school.

3. THUS, THE PROCEDURE TO DISTINGUISH INTERPRETABLE AND DEFINITIVE

Such being the Brother-Masters' method to explain the reality of things, (to turn to the rule of interpretable-definitive,) the *Twenty* states the intention of the first wheel's explanation of subject and object in terms of the (existence of) external things: "Consciousness and appearance, each arising from its own seeds;—the Muni declared there are two kinds of media, that (of consciousness) and that (of appearance)."[91]

Again, the same text declares the need (for the first wheel): "(The Teacher) declared the existence of the media such as the visible, etc., for the sake of the people disciplined thereby; (he declared it) on the strength of this intention, as (on another occasion he declared the existence of) a magically created being."[92]

The teaching of the origination of consciousness, such as vision of visibles, etc., from internal and external media was for the sake of (producing) the realization of the non-existence of the perceiver, etc., apart from those media. The refutation of the literalness (of this teaching) consists of the reasonings refuting external things. Since the imagined, which is ascriptive and descriptive designation of things, is included in the objective element and the objective medium,[93] the statement that (all media and elements) are established by intrinsic identity, without differentiating those two (that is, objective element and medium), is interpretable in meaning.

The *Abhidharma Synthesis* explains that the *Extensive (Transcendent Wisdom)* declares the realitylessness of all things intending the three unrealities. The *Universal Vehicle Compendium* explains the second wheel

---

poise, mindfulness, wisdom-cultivation, and displeasure with mundane distractions, and states that these are mentioned in the context of the third "spiritual conception" (*cittotpāda*), out of the twenty-two conceptions of the spirit of enlightenment that form the subject matter of that commentary.

[91] *Viṃśatikā*, k. 9 (Levi, ed., p. 11): *yataḥ svabījād vijñaptir yadābhāsa pravartate / dvividhāyatanatvena te tasya munir ābravīt //.*

[92] *Viṃśatikā*, k. 8 (Levi, ed., p. 10): *rūpādyāyatanāstitvaṃ tadvineyajanaṃ prati / abhiprāyavaśād uktam upapāduka-sattvavat //.*

[93] The *dharmadhātu*, eighteenth of eighteen *dhātus*, and the *dharmāyatana*, twelfth of twelve *āyatanas*; that is, the element and the medium, respectively, of mental objects.

to be interpretable in meaning, thereby indicating the *Mother Scripture* and similar scriptures, wherein all declarations of non-existence indicate the imagined, all metaphors such as illusion, etc., indicate the relative, and the four purifications indicate the perfect. The *Principles of Elucidation* refutes the literal acceptance of the explanations of realitylessness in the *Mother Scripture*, believing it to be included in the second wheel, as otherwise the *Elucidation of Intention* interpretation of realitylessness would not be definitive in meaning.

The way in which this (second wheel of Dharma) is explained as interpretable is quite different from the way in which the declarations of subject and object in the first wheel are considered interpretable. For, the existence of the media of eye and of visibles is declared intending the seed and the appearance, of which each arises from the development of its own seed, called "the instinct which evolves into visual consciousness;" which intentional meaning would not be suitable as the expressed meaning of the Individual Vehicle Scriptures. On the other hand, the three modes of unreality, which are the intended meaning of the declaration of realitylessness (in the middle wheel), are explained as the (express) meaning of the *Mother Scripture*. Furthermore, the existence of the external media is explained as the meaning of Individual Vehicle Scriptures, whereas the belief in the ultimate, total non-entity (of things), without differentiating the modes of unreality, is not explained as the meaning of the *Mother Scripture*.[94]

Therefore, (this system) does not explain that the *Mother Scripture* is interpretable in meaning because it intends the ultimate realitylessness of all things without differentiation. Rather, it explains that such (as the *Mother Scripture*'s position) is interpretable in meaning from the point of view of its need for further explanation, since it is not fit to be literally accepted, hence is not definitive just as it stands.

Their method of further explanation is to explain the ultimate realitylessness of imagined things as their non-establishment by intrinsic identity, the ultimate realitylessness of relative things as their non-establishment in that ultimate which is the pure object, and the ultimate realitylessness of perfect things, which are themselves the ultimate, as their non-existence as the objective self.

Therefore, they do not believe that the disciples for whom the *Mother Scripture* was declared are those who admit its literal meaning, but rather they believe them to be those who realize the meaning of that scripture

[94] Tsong Khapa thus points out a sense in which the Idealist is using a double standard; saying the first type of statement is plainly wrong, "interpretable" meaning "subsequently contradicted," and that the second is just not literally explicit, "interpretable" then meaning "to be further explicated."

according to the explanation of the *Elucidation of Intention*. Hence, the intentions of the last two wheels are the same.

The *Elucidation of Intention* clearly explains that, having, in spite of one's admiration, refuted the literal acceptability of the meaning of the *Extensive Transcendent Wisdom*, (one discovers) another meaning beyond the literal, which other meaning is definitive. Thus, it calls the *Mother Scripture* "interpretable in meaning," since it does not clearly explicate that (other) meaning, and cannot be literally accepted. The refutation of literalness consists of the above statement that literal acceptance leads to the repudiation that holds all three realities not to be established by intrinsic identifiability.

The *Principles of Elucidation* shows the internal contradiction in the literal statements of realitylessness, etc.:

> The *Transcendent Wisdom* teaches repeatedly such things as the realitylessness of all things, as well as teachings such as (are included in the passage) from "the bodhisattva wishes to enter the state of flawlessness . . . " up to "specifically repents all sins . . . ," If the expressions such as realitylessness, etc., had only literal meaning, they would contradict all these other precepts. Since there would be nothing at all to undertake, it would be impossible to accept that from such a cause, such comes to be. Or else, in regard to a certain precept, one would feel "what is there to undertake?" Therefore, such expressions are not to be taken literally. How then? (They are to be taken as) having a deeper intention.[95]

His rule of contradiction is mainly that, if there were no reality, the relative would become impossible, insofar as precepts, such as "if you wish to attain this and this, learn the *Mother Scripture*," and the desire to attain, and causality, such as that involved in the maxim, "from charity, great wealth accrues," all would become impossible.

Further, even those who accept the *Mother Scripture* as definitive in meaning accept the repeated statements of ethical choice and causality, etc., in conventional terms and not in ultimate terms. Thus, while they do not believe in any general absolute non-reality or conventional non-existence, they apply (qualifications such as "ultimately," "conventionally,") in general, although the scripture does not employ such qualifications in each case. Thus, this means that even (these followers of the *Mother Scripture* acknowledge) that causality, etc., become impossible if "ultimate non-existence" (of everything) is literally accepted. And the

[95] VY, TG, P, si, ff. 116b7-118a2.

Bodhisattva Stages and the *Compendium* also negate (acceptance of) the ultimate non-establishment of everything, explaining it as repudiation.

Since the differentiation of interpretable and definitive meanings of scriptural statements concerned mainly with the ultimate hinges on the existence and non-existence of logical refutation of literalness, we can answer this argument of (the Idealists) if we know well how to negate ultimate existence, and also how to establish with validating cognition causality and bondage-liberation, etc., in things (whose absolute existence has been) thus refuted. Otherwise, if we maintain that "if production were to be established by validating cognition, it would become ultimate production; but, as production is only according to the claim of production by erroneous cognition, all things (such as production of sprouts, etc.) are superficially valid," then, since we cannot rebut their refutations, it would be preferable for us to depend on the interpretations of the Experientialists.[96]

Although there are many approaches to the method of explaining (scriptures) as interpretable in meaning, intelligent persons should understand that the Experientialist method of explaining the second wheel as interpretable in meaning is precisely as above.

The *Elucidation of Intention* declaration of the three types of wheels (of Dharma) is not in terms of the assemblies in attendance, nor in terms of the periods of the teacher's life, but is established according to the contents (of the scripture); and they are (understood) in terms of their determination of the meaning of selflessness.

First, one wheel in Varanasi declared personal selflessness and the real existence of most things, such as the aggregates, without negating their truth-status, except in very few cases. Then, one wheel refuted the truth-status of all things such as the aggregates without any discrimination. Finally, there was one wheel of particular discrimination through the method by which the first reality is not established by intrinsic identity, and the latter two realities are established by intrinsic identity. And other scriptures that teach subjects different from these are not involved in this analysis of interpretable and definitive meanings.

The *Transcendent Wisdom Instruction* explains:

> Only those scriptures whose meaning is literal are definitive in meaning. No other meaning is contained in such meaning, and its meaning is definitely just that; hence it is "definitive meaning." How is that mean-

[96] Tsong Khapa here chides the Dogmaticists, whose position closely resembles the argument he illustratively mentions, saying that the way they try to answer the Idealists is not successful, and they would do better to adopt the Idealist view than present a distorted Centrist view. Certain pseudo-Dialecticists might also be included.

ing determined? By that scripture itself, by another scripture, or by both (itself and others).[97]

Examples of the first type (that determine their own definitiveness) are the *Mission to Lanka* and the *Elucidation of Intention*, etc., considering the fact that they clearly differentiate the existence and non-existence of realities (of different things), according to this belief. An example of the second type is the *Eight Thousand*, etc., considering the fact that they do not differentiate existence and non-existence of reality as does the *Elucidation of Intention*. And an example of the third type is the *Eighteen Thousand*, considering the fact that in its *Questions of Maitreya* chapter, it contains an explanation of interpretable meaning and an elimination of the error of insistence on literalness, and the fact that the *Elucidation of Intention* also explains its interpretable meaning. This (distinction between the second and third types) is made essentially because the *Questions of Maitreya* chapter is absent from the middle-length *Transcendent Wisdom*. Thus, (Ratnakarashanti) believes that the arrangement of the three realities in the *Questions of Maitreya* is the same in meaning as that of the *Elucidation of Intention*.

Such would be valid, were they in fact the same, but, since Vasubandhu proved the *Mother Scripture* declarations of realitylessness, etc., to be interpretable in meaning, by means of the *Elucidation of Intention*, etc., the Brothers do not intend that their demonstration of the inherent contradictions of the *Mother Scripture* should be disproved by the *Questions of Maitreya*. These two are quite similar and hard to distinguish, but were they to be the same, (Ratnakarashanti) would become an Idealist, since he could not possibly explain the intended meaning of the *Mother Scripture* as the ultimate realitylessness and conventional existence of all things. This subject, upon analysis, is quite far-reaching in its implications, hence I will explain it below in the Centrist section.[98]

[97] *Prajñāpāramitopadeśa* by Ratnakarashanti (according to TG attribution), although there are some who claim this is Vasubandhu's work; quotation unlocated.

[98] See Ch. VI.

Chapter III

THE ESSENTIAL CENTRIST MESSAGE

1. STATEMENTS FROM *THE TEACHING OF AKSHAYAMATI SCRIPTURE*

The Savior Nagarjuna and his (spiritual) son (Aryadeva) did not differentiate interpretable and definitive by means of a direct reference from a source in a scripture differentiating the two. Nevertheless, (the matter) is explained by implication from the way in which they explain the meaning of the scriptures. Furthermore, the *Lucid Exposition*, the *Wisdom Lamp Commentary*, and the *Central Way Illumination*[1] take the *Teaching of Akshayamati* as authority when they set forth the interpretation of interpretable and definitive. Therefore, that scripture should be taken as authoritative here. The *Teaching of Akshayamati* statement is:

> Which scriptures are definitive in meaning? Which are interpretable? Those teaching superficial realities are interpretable in meaning. Those teaching ultimate realities are definitive in meaning. Those teaching various words and letters are interpretable. Those teaching the profound, the difficult to see, and the difficult to understand, are definitive. Those scriptures that teach as if there were an owner in the ownerless, using various expressions such as "self," "living being," "life," "soul," "creature," "person," "humanity," "mankind," "agent," "experiencer," etc., are interpretable. Those scriptures that teach the doors of liberation, the emptiness of things, signlessness, wishlessness, inactivity, non-production, creationlessness, non-occurrence, beinglessness, lifelessness, personlessness, and ownerlessness, etc., are definitive in meaning. Rely on the latter, not the former.[2]

[1] By Chandrakirti, Bhavaviveka, and Kamalashila, respectively.

[2] *Akṣayamatinirdeśasūtra* (AMN) TG, P, ga (Skt. PPMMV p. 14, ls. 5-9): *katame sūtrāntā neyārthāḥ katame nītārthāḥ / ye sūtrāntā mārgāvatārāya nirdiṣṭāimā ucyante neyārthāḥ / yeṣu sūtrāntesu ātmāsattvajīvapoṣapuruṣapudgalamanujamanuṣyakārakavedaka nānāśabdairākhyāyante yeṣu cāsvāmikaṃ sāsvāmikatvena nirdiṣṭāṃ te neyārthāḥ / ye sūtrāntāḥ phalāvatārāya nirdiṣṭā ima ucyante nītārthāḥ / yāvad ye sūtrāntāḥ śūnyatānimittāpraṇihitānabhisaṃskārājātānutpādā bhāvanirātmāniḥsattvanirjīvaniḥpudgalāsvāmikavimokṣamukha-nirdiṣṭāḥ te ucyante nītārthāḥ /.*

The Sanskrit is more abbreviated than the Tibetan, as might be expected from manuscripts much later than that from which the Tibetan translation was made. Also, this version equates "interpretable" with "cause," and "definitive" with "effect."

The first two phrases align interpretable and definitive with the two realities in distinguishing them from the point of view of subject-matter. The next two phrases do not depart from this arrangement, since "teaching the superficial" is teaching various meanings employing various expressions, and "teaching the ultimate" is teaching the meaning that is difficult to understand, which is the universality of the cessation of mental fabrications. The last two phrases describe the methods of teaching involved in teaching the superficial and the ultimate. To teach as if self and living beings exist is to teach the superficial, which does not apply to merely that, but also to all teachings of the existence of functional things which require an agent. To teach the emptiness and non-production of things is to teach their realitylessness, and to teach the non-existence of living beings, etc., is to teach personal realitylessness; and such a method of teaching teaches the ultimate. From the fact that both (persons and things) are mentioned (as non-existent here), it follows that both are shown to be existent in the former (superficial) teaching (although only persons are referred to there explicitly). The teaching of the ultimate is not a matter of taking some other permanent thing as a ground and expounding it as non-production, etc., but is rather an indication of the truthlessness of such grounds as persons and things such as aggregates etc., since the ultimate reality is the mere exclusion of their truth-status.

The *Lucid Exposition* explains that the (following) differentiation of interpretable and definitive in the *King of Samadhi Scripture* agrees with the above: "The specialty of the scriptures of definitive meaning is known according to the teaching of emptiness by the Sugata. And all teachings which mention 'person,' 'living being,' and 'creatures' are known to be interpretable in meaning."[3]

To be sure, scriptures of interpretable meaning do "lead" disciples, but that is not the meaning of the "to-be-led" (*neya*) (portion of the term *neyārtha* [interpretable meaning]). Rather the meaning of the "to-be-led" is the process of interpretation, in which it is necessary to "lead" the (obvious) meaning of the scripture around to a different meaning.

There are two types of needs for interpretation. The first (arises when a statement is obviously figurative, and) requires interpretation: for example, the statement "having killed father and mother . . . " wherein "father" must be interpreted as "evolutionary entanglement" and "mother" must be interpreted as "craving." The second (arises when a statement lends itself to misinterpretation through a confusion of realities), as, for example, when (someone misinterprets) the statement "from bad and

[3] SRS, Skt. PPMMV 1s. 11-12: *nītārthasūtrāntaviśeṣa jānāti yathopadiṣṭā sugatena śūnyatā / yasmin punaḥ pudgalasattvapuruṣa neyārthato jānāti sarvadharmān //*. (Ed. corrects from Tib. *-puruṣo* for *puruṣa*, and *neyārthatāṃ* for *neyārthato*) (p. 14).

good actions arise the effects of suffering and happiness," by saying that its reality is just what is said, and there is no other reality of those (actions and effects). (It then becomes necessary) to explain that the (ultimate) reality of those two things (can only be understood) by interpreting the statement's obvious meaning otherwise.[4]

Therefore, the *Central Way Illumination* declares: "How do we define definitive meaning? It is that which is explained logically and in terms of the ultimate, since it cannot be interpreted by others in any other way."[5]

If interpretable and definitive were to be equated with inexplicit and explicit meanings, "logically" would be enough, but "in terms of the ultimate" is stated, since the former is not enough. Therefore, according to the (second) method explained above for alternative interpretation of the meaning of a statement, such a statement as "sprout is produced from seed," is interpretable in meaning, since, although there are rational means of validation of its explicit meaning, it is not in terms of the ultimate.

Therefore, since the statement of the non-existence of true production of things is logical and its explicit meaning cannot be interpreted otherwise, as if it were not the reality of those things, scriptures with such (statements) are definitive in meaning, because they cannot be otherwise interpreted according to either of the (above) two processes of interpretation.

(In sum), the scriptures themselves are taken as that characterized as interpretable or definitive, being established as such according to whether or not their meaning needs to be otherwise interpreted. In this case, interpretable and definitive correspond to superficial and ultimate, which (correspondence) is illustrated in the *Facts of the Stages* declarations of the four reliances; reliance on the teaching and not the teacher, reliance on the meaning and not the words, reliance on the definitive meaning and not the interpretable meaning, and reliance on the holy wisdom and not on (ordinary) consciousness.[6]

The *Ornament of Wisdom-Illumination Scripture* declares that "definitive meaning is the ultimate."[7] Since the *Teaching of Akshayamati* statements of non-production, etc., teach the ultimate, only non-production, etc., are the ultimate, and only indications of that are to be

[4] That is, although this statement is acceptable conventionally, when it is taken as ultimate reality, as if it were made in ultimate terms, it has no truth-status ultimately, and hence must be interpreted otherwise to understand ultimate reality, or emptiness.

[5] *Madhyamakāloka* (MAlok), TG,D, f. 149v4-5.

[6] These four reliances are not peculiar to Asanga's *Bhūmivastu*, but can be found with variations in the AMN, the BBh, and the MSA. See *Gun Thang*, p. 45 ff.

[7] *Jñānālokālaṃkārasūtra*, KG, P, ga. (Also called *Sarvabuddhaviṣayāvatāra-*.)

accepted as definitive in meaning. It is not to be supposed that, since on particular occasions the negatees are without qualification, non-production, etc., are not literally intended, hence not definitive. For, when such qualification as, for example in the *Hundred Thousand*, "It is in terms of popular conventions, and not in terms of the ultimate," is applied to the production of things on one occasion, it is to be understood as applied by implication on other occasions also, and hence even those statements which do not explicitly mention (such qualification) are literally acceptable.

2. EXPLANATION OF THEIR MEANING; SAVIOR NAGARJUNA'S EXPLANATION

The Equivalence of Relativity and Realitylessness

The scriptures declare both the existence and the non-existence of production and cessation, etc., some of them explaining the statements of non-production, etc., as definitive in meaning, and some of them explaining them as interpretable in meaning. If there were any logical refutation of the literal validity of the explanations of the non-existence of production, etc., in the ultimate or by intrinsic identity, then it would be correct to explain the objective self, which is that negated in "selflessness," as merely the imagined reality which is the intrinsic identifiability of things posited by ascriptive and descriptive designation, and which is substantial subject-object dichotomy, and to explain the ultimate reality as the absence of those (selves). However, there is no such refutation, because the existence of reality established in the ultimate, or by intrinsic identity, would utterly preclude the dependence of effects on causes and conditions.

Therefore, in the face of the fact of the non-existence of establishment by intrinsic identity because of dependence on conditions, if we insist that, without intrinsic identifiability, bondage-liberation, action-abstention, and cause-effect, etc., would become non-existent, then that insistence is to take the ultimate proof of emptiness of intrinsically identifiable reality as the ultimate refutation of emptiness! This explanation is the system of the Champions founded by the Savior Nagarjuna, which teaches the reasoning proving that the meaning of the *Mother Scripture* and those scriptures that agree with it cannot be otherwise interpreted but is definitive in itself; and teaches the reasoning refuting the literal validity of those scriptures that disagree with it.

As for the *Elucidation of Intention* statement that those who see no intrinsically identifiable status (in things) hold the view that repudiates all three natures, it does not refer to everyone who sees in that way, but only to those disciples who lack superior intelligence. Therefore, the Teacher declared such according to the mental capacities of the disciples, and not as his own belief. For, since the disciple of superior intelligence realizes emptiness with respect to intrinsic identity from the necessity of establishment of causality itself, such a vision (of absence of intrinsic identity) becomes a method to negate views that repudiate reality. (However), for the (less than superior) disciple, the *Mother Scripture* becomes interpretable, and the *Elucidation of Intention* definitive in meaning, just as (Aryadeva) states in the *Four Hundred* that it is better to teach "self" than to teach "selflessness" to the disciple who is not properly receptive to the teaching of selflessness.[8]

The *Wisdom* mentions the argument that (attempts to) refute the literalness of the *Mother Scripture*, etc., by arguing that all arrangements of life and liberation would be invalid, since production and destruction of things would be impossible if they were empty of intrinsically identifiable reality, (as follows:) "If everything is empty, there will be no production and no destruction, and the consequence of the non-existence of the four holy truths will be inevitable for you!"[9] To this (Nagarjuna) answers: "If everything is *not* empty, there will be no production and no destruction, and the consequence of the non-existence of the four holy truths will be inevitable for you!"[10] (emphasis added).

He states that the import of emptiness of intrinsic reality is equivalent to the import of relativity, since in the case of non-emptiness of intrinsic reality, relativity, which is production and destruction, would be impossible, and all arrangements would be invalid; whereas all these are very much appropriate in the case of emptiness of intrinsic reality.

Through logical determination of this very rule in the Centrist treatises, the Master (Nagarjuna) explains that there is not the slightest logical refutation of the literalness of the scriptures that declare the truthlessness of production, etc., and since there is no other way to explain them as interpretable, they are very much established as definitive in meaning. Intending this, the *Lucid Exposition* declares: "The Master composed this Centrist treatise in order to show the difference between scriptures of interpretable meaning and those of definitive meaning."[11] Thus (Chan-

[8] CŚ VIII, k. 5.

[9] MMK (called *Wisdom* according to Tib. *rtsa shes* 'nickname') XXIV, k. 1 (Inada, p. 144): *yadi śūnyamidaṃ sarvamudayo nāsti na vyayaḥ / catūrṇāmāryasatyānāmabhāvaste prasajyate //*.

[10] MMK XXIV, k. 20 (Inada, p. 148: *yadyaśūnyamidaṃ sarvamudayo nāsti na vyayaḥ / catūrṇāmāryasatyānāmabhāvaste prasajyate //*.

[11] PPMMV I, p. 13, 1.9: *evedaṃ madhyamakaśāstraṃ pranītamācāryeṇa neyanītārthasūtrāntavibhāgopadarśanārthaṃ /*.

drakirti) answers the objection that statements of the existence of the eight (properties), from cessation to diversity, and the statement of their non-existence (in the description of relativity), are mutually contradictory. He then continues:

> Not knowing the intention of such teachings, one feels doubt; "Herein, which is the teaching whose meaning is true? Which is the teaching with ulterior intention?" Some of lesser intelligence understand interpretable meaning as if it were definitive. Hence, the Master composed this treatise, in order to clear away both doubts and confusions through references and reasoning.[12]

The *Scripture Synthesis* answers the question about the profound by quoting the scriptures that teach the profound such as the *Hundred Thousand*, the *Diamond Cutter*, and the *Seven Hundred*, etc. Further, the *Canon of Reason* makes certain the impossibility of interpreting the meaning of these (scriptures) otherwise than taught. Therefore, (the Master) believed these to be definitive in meaning, and statements differing from them to be intentional.

The *Disclosure of the Spirit of Enlightenment* declares that the statements that negate external things and establish reality in mind alone are not literally intended: "the Muni declared—'All these things are only mind!'—in order to eliminate the fears (of emptiness) of the naive. (Nevertheless,) that is not the reality (of things)."[13] (Finally,) the *Jewel Garland* declares:

> Just as the grammarians make one read the grammar, the Buddha teaches the Dharma according to the tolerance of the disciple. To some he teaches the Dharma to refrain from sins, to some to accomplish virtue, to some as dependence on dualism, and to some as freedom from dualism; (finally) to some he teaches the profound, terrifying practice of enlightment, whose essence is emptiness and compassion.[14]

The first sentence states that the Teacher teaches the Dharma in accord with the intelligence of the disciple. The next two phrases refer to the

[12] PPMMV I, p. 13, 1s. 22-24: *yasyaivaṃ deśanābhiprāyānabhijñātayā saṃdehaḥ syāt —kā hyatra deśanā tattvārthā kā nu khalu ābhiprāyikīti yaścāpi maṇdabuddhitayā neyārthāṃ deśanāṃ nītārthāmavagacchati tayorubhayor api vineyajanayoḥ ācāryo yuktyāgamābhyāṃ saṃśayamithyājñānāpākaraṇārthaṃ śāstramidamārabdhavān //.*

[13] *Bodhicittavivaraṇa*, Nagarjuna, TG, P, tsa, k. 13.

[14] RA IV, k. 94-96 (edited by P. L. Vaidya, Darbhanga, 1960, *yathāiva vaiyākaraṇo mātṛkāmapi pāṭhayet / buddho 'vadattathā dharmaṃ vineyānāṃ yathākṣamaṃ // keṣāṃcidavadaddharmaṃ pāpebhyo vinivṛttaye / keṣāṃcitpuṇyasiddhyarthaṃ keṣāṃcid dvayaniśritaṃ // dvayāniśritamekeṣāṃ gambhīraṃ bhīrubhīṣanaṃ / śūnyatākaruṇāgarbhamekeṣāṃ bodhisādhanaṃ //.*

teachings concerned with ascendant status[15] (in the world). The next phrase refers to the teaching of the non-existence of personal self and of the existence of both subject and object for those in the class of the two disciple schools. The next phrase refers to the teaching of the existence of the emptiness of duality, that is, the non-existence of the subject-object dualism, for certain disciples in the Universal Vehicle class. The rest of the passage refers to the teaching of the awesome Dharma of (integrated) realitylessness and great compassion for the disciples of extreme intelligence who are oriented toward the Universal Vehicle.

Therefore, as long as we are not capable of the establishment of all arrangements such as bondage-liberation, etc., upon the doctrine of truthlessness, we must differentiate some things that are untrue from some things that are true. For it is necessary to lead (such disciples) gradually, by teaching partial aspects of selflessness, and it is not proper to present universal emptiness when (it would be misinterpreted to mean that) there is no basis upon which to establish causality. Therefore, (the Buddha) declared the procedure of refuting reality in persons and almost not refuting it in the aggregates, and the procedure of refuting substantial subject-object difference and not refuting the reality of the emptiness of duality (itself).[16]

However, when we are able to realize the very import of relativity as the import of realitylessness, there is no point in making any such differentiation, because we are quite capable of the admission of the validity of all arrangements upon that very basis which is the negation of intrinsic reality. Nevertheless, even for those in the Supreme Vehicle class who are in little danger of nihilistic views about causality, etc., there are a great many who, although somewhat roughly negating truth, the negatee, fail to negate it precisely. For, in the face of precise negation, so many lose sight of the functional basis of all systems verified by validating cognitions. Hence, the *Elucidation of Intention* differentiation of interpretable and definitive still appears to be an extremely skillful technique for guiding a great many disciples to the Universal Vehicle.

Finally, as that scripture is explained to be teaching according to its disciples, we can understand the teachings that agree with it, as the same. Thus, we can understand how Asanga, the author of the treatises elucidating its intention, explains also according to the inclinations of his disciples, and does not accept the meaning he explains as his own personal interpretation.[17]

[15] Skt. *abhyudaya*. Opposite of *niḥśreyasa*.

[16] That is, the procedures of the Individual Vehicle and the Idealists, respectively.

[17] Tsong Khapa refers especially to Aryasanga, whom he believes to have elaborated the whole Idealist system in adaptation to the needs of the period and people, while himself having attained the true understanding of the central way, as revealed in his commentary on the RGV in particular.

Celebration of That Fact as the Essential Import of All Scriptures

The Master praised the Lord in many treatises from the point of view of his declaration of relativity, having seen this very declaration of the equivalence in meaning of emptiness by intrinsic reality and relativity to be of the highest excellence, distinguishing our Teacher from other teachers. (The Lord's declaration was:) "By the very reason that origination depends on causes and conditions, things have no intrinsically identifiable reality."

(The Master salutes the Buddha as follows,) from the *Wisdom*:

> I praise that perfect Buddha, the Supreme Philosopher, who taught us relativity, free of cessation and creation, without annihilation and permanence, with no coming and going, not a unity nor a plurality, (which is the) quiescence of mental fabrications and the supreme bliss![18]

Also from the *Philosophical Sixty*: "I salute Shakyamuni, the herald of relativity, by which law, creations and cessations are abandoned!"[19] And from the *Rebuttal of Objections*: "I salute that incomparable, perfect Buddha, who made the declaration of the equivalence of meaning of emptiness, relativity, and the central way!"[20] And from the *Inconceivable Praise*: "I salute the Incomparable One, whose wisdom was matchless and inconceivable, and who declared the realitylessness of interdependently originated things!"[21]

The first (of these quotations) declares that relativity is free of cessation, etc., eight (attributes). The second declares that it is free of them by reason of being relativity. The third declares that "relativity," the "central way," and "emptiness of intrinsic reality" are synonymous. And the fourth teaches that cessation, etc., are free of intrinsically identifiable existence for that very reason.

All the Discourses of the Teacher proceed from the two realities, the ultimate and the superficial. Since we will not understand the reality of the teaching if we do not know the differentiation of these two, we also will not understand the procedure to explain the Discourses from the point of view of the two realities. For, all teachings of various subjects that are dependently designated and dependently occurrent, are in terms

[18] MMK I, salutatory verses. Inada, p. 38: *anirodhamanutpādamanucchedamaśāśvatam / anekārthamanānārthamanāgamamanirgamam // yaḥ pratītyasamutpādaṃ prapañcopaśamaṃ śivam / deśayāmāsa saṃbuddhastaṃ vande vadatāṃ varam //.*

[19] YS., k. 1.

[20] VV, k. 72 (edited by P. L. Vaidya, Darbhanga: Buddhist Sanskrit Texts, 1960, p. 295: *yaḥ śūnyatāṃ pratītyasamut pādaṃ madhyamāṃ pratipadaṃ ca / ekārthāṃ nijagāda praṇamāmi tam apratimasaṃbuddham //.*

[21] *Acintyastavana*, k. 1.

of the superficial reality, and the ultimate is no more than just that emptiness which is the lack of intrinsic identifiability by that reason (of relativity).

The *Emptiness Seventy* statement is:

> The peerless transcendent Lord taught this relativity of things because of the fact of their emptiness of reality. The ultimate meaning is no more than that, but the Lord Buddha correctly designates all varieties of things, relying on conventional expressions.[22]

Its commentary explains that the ultimate "is no more than that emptiness of reality of all dependently originated things." Thus, since (the Master) accepts the ultimate reality in this way, and establishes it as merely the exclusion of the self, the negatee, in relativity, the ground of negation, the systems of both the Champions agree, except for some differences on the qualification of the negatee, and it is incorrect to establish the ultimate reality in any other way. Furthermore, as for the belief in the truth-status of that (ultimate reality) itself, the *Wisdom* states: "Who entertain the view of emptiness are declared to be incurable!"[23] that is, that it is an incurable view, and the *Transcendental Praise* states it to be ridiculous: "Since you taught the nectar of emptiness in order to eliminate all mental fabrications, whosoever becomes attached to that (in itself), you find utterly ridiculous!"[24]

Since the existence of relativity as nature-possessor and ultimate reality as nature, that is, as support and supported, is (presented) according to conventional cognition and not according to the rational cognition of immaculate equanimity, according to this latter there is of course no contradiction, such as that of existence of a nature without any nature-possessor, (since all duality is eliminated in the pure-object-ultimate). And in regard to existence in the (other kind of) ultimate, that involved in the analysis of the reality of things existent by intrinsic identity, since an isolated nature cannot remain without a nature-possessor, the former (Idealist) system maintains that if the relative reality were empty of intrinsic identifiability, the perfect would also become unestablished by intrinsic identity. Moreover, this (Centrist) system declares, "Since the created is not established, how can the uncreated be established?" Thus, both systems agree repeatedly with the scriptural statement, "If form itself were not apprehended, how could the reality of form possibly be apprehended?"[25]

[22] ŚS, k. 65-66.

[23] MMK XIII, k. 8 (c.d) (Inada, p. 93): (*śūnyatā sarvadṛṣṭīnāṃ proktā niḥsaranaṃ jinaiḥ/*) *yeṣāṃ tu śūnyatādṛṣṭistānasādhyāṇ babhāṣire //.*

[24] *Lokātītastava*, k. 1.

[25] Of course, the two systems draw quite different conclusions from this fact, the Idealists

(Finally), the statements in the *Philosophical Sixty* that "liberation is the only truth," that is, that it alone is true, and that created things are false and prove to deceive, must be understood by interpreting the meaning of "false" and "untrue" as "deceptive," and the meaning of "true" as "non-deceptive." Hence the "truth" in question here is not that truth which is established by intrinsic identity, which is in question during the analysis of establishment and non-establishment in reality. These created things are said to be "false," or "deceptive," as they deceive the naive-minded by appearing to be established by intrinsic identity, when in fact they are not so established, as for example, (someone) is said to be deceiving if he pretends to be helpful, when he is not really helpful at all. Similarly, liberation, the ultimate reality, is said to be "true," or "non-deceptive," because it is not deceptive by appearing (to be established by intrinsic identity), as in the former case (of the superficial), to the person who directly beholds it.[26]

The heterodox schools, who do not believe in the relativity which is the dependent origination of persons and things, but believe in the truth (-status) of both, fall into the abyss of the absolutistic and nihilistic views. And those orthodox schools who, in spite of their admission of the relativity of both (persons and things) believe in their establishment in reality or by intrinsic identity, also come under the influence of absolutistic and nihilistic views.

Therefore, (Nagarjuna) believes that this very rule of the admission that persons and things which are dependently originated are devoid of intrinsic reality, like the reflection of the moon in water, is the best door to the abandonment of absolutistic and nihilistic views for those who desire to be free of them. As the *Philosophical Sixty* declares:

> Those who insistently reify an independent self or world—alas!—they are deprived by views (such as those of things' being) permanent or impermanent. And those who believe that dependent things are still established in reality—how could they fail to be affected by the fallacies such as permanence etc.? But those who believe that dependent things are neither real nor invalid, but are like the reflection of the moon in water—they are not deprived by views![27]

---

maintaining that both relative and perfect must therefore be established by intrinsic identity, and the Centrists maintaining that therefore both ultimate and superficial are not established by intrinsic identity. Here, Tsong Khapa wishes to emphasize the fact that both agree that, at least, one alone cannot be ultimate, as regards the ultimate which is establishment by intrinsic identity. Hence, the Jo-nang theory that the ultimate alone is established by intrinsic identity, or in truth, etc., is denied any support from the authority of either system.

[26] This is another blow to the Jo-nang belief.

[27] YṢ, k. 44-46.

Absolutism is eliminated by the fact of the non-establishment in reality (of persons and things), and nihilism is eliminated by the fact of the functional capacity of each thing, as it is not invalidated by losing that capacity (just because it is not established in ultimate reality). Therefore, while admitting the emptiness of the intrinsic reality of these internal and external things, to maintain that such emptiness is annihilation of the superficial contradicts the systems of both the Champions, who emphatically maintained that relativity is free of both permanence and annihilation. Nevertheless, there are many self-styled Centrists who still believe that, or else hold the similar belief that superficial things are empty even of their own entities, both beliefs being misunderstandings of the meaning of the expression "self-empty." They further claim that "there is no method that demonstrates to us that these internal and external things of relativity are free of absolutism and nihilism!"[28]

It is not surprising that the heterodox, who advocate the permanence of things, should not admit relativity, believing things to be established in truth, since that is the prescription of their own teachers. However, the belief in the truth-status (of things), while asserting relativity, which is the origination (of things) dependent on causes and conditions, is utterly absurd. Thus, the *Philosophical Sixty* declares:

> For the believers in "Being," who live by upholding a supreme thing, to stay on such a path is not surprising in the least. But, for those who believe in universal impermanence, relying on the path of the Buddha, to continue to uphold the supremacy of intrinsically real things with arguments—that really is astonishing![29]

Thus he declares the absurdity of those who believe that production and cessation, etc., as defined cannot be reconciled with non-existence in truth, or with (non-existence) by intrinsic identity.

Since this freedom of relativity from permanence and annihilation is so extremely difficult to understand, the Teacher himself thought that if he taught the profound teaching as he understood it, others would not understand it, hence he should stay for some time without teaching.[30] As it is stated in the *Wisdom*: "Thus, knowing the profundity of this

[28] This position is similar to the Jo-nang in sacrificing the relative for a notion of a solitary absolute, but differs slightly in emphasis, tending toward nihilism, whereas the Jo-nang tends toward absolutism. The two positions in the text are called *rang stong* and *chad stong* respectively, and the Jo-nang position, *gzhan stong*.

[29] YṢ, k. 41-42.

[30] Compare PPMMV, p. 217, 1s. 13-16: *adhigato mayā dharmo gambhīro gambhīrāvabhāso 'tarko 'tarkāvacarah sūkṣmaḥ paṇḍitavijñavedanīyaḥ / sacettamahaṃ pareṣāmārocayeyaṃ pare ca me na vibhāvayeyuḥ sa mama vighātaḥ syāt cetaso 'nudayaḥ syāt / yannvahamekākyaraṇye pravivikte dṛṣṭadharmasukhavihāramanuprāpto vihareyaṃ //.*

teaching to be so difficult to understand for those of lesser intelligence, the Muni's heart was very much averse to the teaching of the Dharma!"[31]

However, it seems that (Nagarjuna), the first great Champion, did not (believe) this (realization) in itself to be that difficult, as he explains that the difficulty of understanding is for those with less than superior intelligence, for whom a misunderstanding of this rule may be disastrous (and not for those with the superior intelligence). Thus, he goes on to encourage (us) by saying that we should strive to understand the meaning of reality, avoiding neglect of either both word and meaning or else just meaning of this system, and avoiding the nihilism which finds no place to establish causality, etc.; as in the *Jewel Garland* (as follows:)

> Thus, by such misunderstanding, one is ruined. But by true understanding, one attains immediate happiness and ultimate enlightenment. Therefore, abandoning repudiation and the nihilistic view, make the supreme effort for authentic knowledge to accomplish all goals![32]

The Master's many other statements of logical reasonings in his explanations of the profound meaning of the scriptures should be recognized as factors contributing to the realization of this (rule of emptiness-relativity), and thus we should train ourselves in the meaning of the central way. Finally, since I have already explained this pattern of reasoning frequently elsewhere, and since I intend to compose a commentary on the *Wisdom*, I will not go any further here.[33]

[31] MMK XXIV, k.12 (Inada, p. 146): *ataśca pratyudāvṛttaṃ cittaṃ deśayituṃ muneḥ / dharmaṃ matvāsya dharmasya maṇḍairduravagāhatāṃ //.*

[32] RA II, 1s. 22-23 (Vaidya ed., p. 302): *durjñātena tathānena vināśamadhigacchati / samyagjñātenātra sukhaṃ bodhiṃ cāpnotyanuttaraṃ // tasmādatra pratikṣepaṃ dṛṣtiṃ tyaktvā ca nāstikīṃ / samyagjñānaparaṃ yatnaṃ kuru sarvārthasiddhaye //.*

[33] Tsong Khapa refers here to the LTC portion of LRC, composed several years earlier, and to the RG, which he composed immediately after completing the work here translated.

Chapter IV

EXPLANATIONS OF THE FOLLOWERS OF SAVIOR NAGARJUNA

The chief follower of the Master was Aryadeva, who explained the system of the Master extensively in the *Experientialist Four Hundred.* The great Centrists, such as Buddhapalita, Bhavaviveka, Chandrakirti, and Shanṭarakshita, accepted his authority as equal to the Master's. Hence, the ancients called the treatises of these two masters "The Paradigm Treatises." Here, we will formulate the ways in which (those great Centrists) explained the ultimate intention of the "Holy Father and Son." There were many other brilliant sages, such as Aryashura and Nagabodhi, but their treatises on the central way are not available in translation (into Tibetan). Thus, we will explain the distinctive systems of those masters whose treatises are available.

THE DOGMATICIST CENTRIST EXPLANATIONS OF THE HOLY TREATISES

I. MASTER BHAVAVIVEKA'S EXPLANATION

1. ULTIMATE PRESENCE AND ABSENCE OF REALITY IN PERSONS AND THINGS

The *Wisdom* is the principal Centrist treatise by the Master. It has eight major commentaries: the *No Fear from Anywhere*, and those by Devasharma, Gunamati, Gunashri, Sthiramati, Buddhapalita, Bhavaviveka, and Chandrakirti.[1] Avalokitavrata explains that Bhavaviveka follows Devasharma's *White Exaltation.*[2] As for the *No Fear from Anywhere*, in comment on the twenty-seventh chapter, it cites evidence from the *Four Hundred*: "As the revered Aryadeva declares: Very rarely does it happen

[1] Of these eight commentaries, we have in Tibetan the texts of only four—the first and the last three—as did Tsong Khapa; and of those four, only Chandrakirti's PPMMV remains in Sanskrit. Nanjio lists a partial version of Sthiramati's commentary: Nanjio, 1316.

[2] Avalokitavrata—*Prajñāpradīpaṭīka* (PrPrT), Ch. XXVII.

that there are teacher, listener, and that worth hearing. Hence, in short, cyclic life is neither limited nor limitless!"[3] This means that the *No Fear from Anywhere* is not an autocommentary, as is also recognized from the fact that not even the smallest fragment of its commentary is cited in the commentaries of Buddhapalita, Bhavaviveka, or Chandrakirti.

As for Bhavaviveka's elucidation of the intention of the Holy Ones, his explanation of the ultimate two selflessnesses becomes clear when his determination of the three realities is understood.

According to the *Wisdom Lamp*:

> Now if it is suggested that the reality of the imagined, which consists of verbal and mental expressions such as "form," does not exist at all, such (a suggestion amounts to) a repudiation of the facts, since it repudiates verbal and mental expressions themselves;[4]

(this master) believes in the existence of the identity-reality in the relative; since he explains that if the imagined, suggested to be without identity-reality, is understood as ascriptively and descriptively designative words and mental constructions, both of which are classified among the aggregates, then repudiation (of the facts) ensues, (which repudiation proposes) the non-existence of identity-reality in the relative. Furthermore, since the *Elucidation of Intention* explains identity-realitylessness as non-establishment by intrinsic identity, and since these (Dogmaticists) also determine the meaning of that scripture, it is clear that (Bhavaviveka) believes the relative to have an intrinsically identifiable reality.[5]

In the *Wisdom Lamp*, (he formulates) his opponent's position: "The imagined reality is identity-unreality since it is not included in any of the five (categories); that is, name, causal process, mental construction, real knowledge, or reality."[6]

(This is) the position of the *Compendium* that the imagined is not included in the five (categories), among which "name" is defined as an anomalous creation and "causal process" is defined as the imagined's designative base. (The imagined) cannot be any of the first four, as it is

[3] Aryadeva, *Catuḥśataka*, Ch. VII, k. 5. *Akutobhaya*, TG, C, tsa, f. 98a4-5 (work attributed to Nagarjuna; authorship disputed, later chapters overlap with BMMV).

[4] *Prajñāpradīpamūlamadhyamakavṛtti* (PrPr), Ch. XXV, TG, C, tsa, f. 243b6.

[5] That is, since identity-unreality equals lack of intrinsically identifiable status, then identity-reality equals intrinsic identity; hence Bhavya's belief in the existence of intrinsic identity in the relative is confirmed.

The Idealists also posit identity-reality, or intrinsic identifiability, in the relative, rejecting it in the imagined only. Yet Bhavya faults them for an excessively strong rejection of the imagined, as intrinsic identity, as they do not qualify it with the phrase "in the ultimate sense." This shows his own sense of the necessity for a conventional intrinsic identity in the relative.

[6] PrPr, Ch. XXV, TG, C, tsha, f. 243b5 (not quoted literally).

not a thing, nor can it be reality, since it is merely conceptual designation.[7] In regard to the *Center and Extremes'* equation of "name" with the imagined, Sthiramati explains that "name" there stands for its referents, and not the actual name itself.[8] Further, in all such expositions, the "causal process" equated with the relative includes only causes which are created things, although the *Compendium* states that among causes there are also uncreated things.[9] Thus, (acknowledging) that (for the Idealist) the imagined is identity-unreality by reason of its non-inclusion in the five (categories), nevertheless, (for Bhavaviveka) such non-inclusion is not the meaning of identity-unreality.[10]

It seems to be difficult to distinguish between (the positions of Bhavya and the Dialecticists) with regard to conventional existence, due to the fact that the treatises of this master are full of expressions such as "non-establishment by intrinsic reality," "non-production by intrinsic reality," and "substantial non-establishment," etc., and the Dialecticist treatises often mention "reality," "intrinsic reality," and "intrinsic identity" with reference to conventional existence. Therefore, his explanation above of the meaning of the existence and non-existence of the identity-reality mentioned in the *Elucidation of Intention* is the clearest source (for the demonstration) of this master's belief in the conventional intrinsic identifiability of things.

Therefore, he believes it possible to realize both selflessnesses true to definitions, even without realizing the lack of intrinsically identifiable reality in persons and things. As for the negatee he posits as negated by the two selflessnesses, it is not merely intrinsically identifiable status, as will be explained below.

Furthermore, in the *Wisdom Lamp*, he shows the fault of inappropriateness of example in the argument that the imagined reality, being a referent designated by names and mental constructions of any common person, and not (itself) a means of designation, is without identity-reality, just as a snake designated in a rope (has no identity-reality).

> If you venture "the objects mentally constructed by someone with both (name and concept) are non-existent, just like the cognized snake in a rope," (then I reply that) the imagined is not non-existent, since, al-

[7] VS, here not literally quoted. TG, C., zi, f. 23b7; D., zi, f. 22b2.

[8] MAVT ad. III, 13 (Pandeya ed., p. 131): *namnaḥ parikalpitena saṃgrahaḥ / evamadhikarasaṃgrahaḥ parikalpitena namno na svabhāvasaṃgraha iti yad uktaṃ niḥsvabhāvasiddhatvāt parikalpitaḥ svabhāvo nimittādipañcavastubhir na saṃgṛhīta iti tanna virudhyate, tatra svabhāvasaṃgrahasya vivakṣitatvāt /.*

[9] The uncreated can be a cause for the Idealist in its capacity as a base for names, etc.

[10] That is, since he believes it means ultimate lack of intrinsic identity. See *Zin Bris* II, ff. 10-11.

though (in that case) the similarity (between rope and snake) fools the cognition and the imagined object does not exist there (in the rope), conventionally speaking the (snake) is not non-existent in (some other) coiled snake (that is, altogether).[11]

This means that it is not correct to use the non-existence of the referent of the designation "There is a snake (in a rope)" as an example of the non-existence (in things such as form) of identity-reality of the referent of the ascriptive and descriptive designations "This!" and "This is . . . " For an opponent could reply that, just as the object of the cognition "snake" exists conventionally speaking in a coiled snake—granted it does not exist in a rope—the object of the cognition "form" exists, conventionally speaking, in form, granted that the object of the cognition "feeling" does not exist in form.

Here, since "exists" and "does not exist" mean "has . . . " and "has not identity-reality," he is saying that the objects of ascriptive and descriptive designations upon form, etc., are not without identity-reality, conventionally speaking. He states that it would be contrary to common sense if there were no snake in a coiled snake, "as if there were no object of the cognition 'This is a snake!' in a coiled snake, conventionally speaking." (However,) he allows that an advocate of the central way may negate things in the ultimate sense, meaning that if the object of the cognition (in the form of) "This is a snake" of a coiled snake were proved without identity-reality in the ultimate sense, such would (accord with) the Centrist system. Therefore, he continues in the *Wisdom Lamp*, if one wishes to show the identity-unreality of the imaginatively constructed, which is ascriptive and descriptive designation, one must admit the reasoning of the Centrists.[12]

This reasoning is given in the *Wisdom*: "Where the realm of mind stops, there is nothing to verbalize. Reality has no production and no cessation, just like Nirvana."[13]

[11] PrPr, XXV, TG, C, tsha, f. 243b7; P., tsha, ff. 303b7-304al; Tsong Khapa here paraphrases. This is the clearest evidence for Bhavya's assertion of conventional intrinsic identity. In this example, the Idealist intends that rope = relative, snake = imagined, lack of snake in rope = identity-unreality. And Bhavya changes the example to indicate that rope = relative in the ultimate sense; snake = the conventional relative; snake lacking in the rope = ultimate intrinsic identitylessness (identity-unreality); snake existing in snake = conventional intrinsic identity (imagined existent in the relative).

[12] PrPr, XXV, TG, C, tsha, f. 224a1: *kun brtags pa med pa ma yin te / de la rnam pa 'cha bas blos gros grub pas kun brtags pai don med kyang tha snyad du sbrul 'khyil pa la sbrul med do zhe na ni / grags pas gnod par 'gyur ro / ci ste don dam pas dngos po sel bar byed na ni / dbu mai tshul gyis rjes su zhugs ba yin te / don dam pas sbrul rdzas su yod pa ma yin pai phyir dang / ngo bo nyid las skyes med pai phyir /*. See also TJ, C. dza, f. 214b ff.

[13] MMK XVIII, k.7: *nivṛttamabhidhātavyaṃ nivṛtte cittagocare / anutpannāniruddhā hi nirvāṇamiva dharmatā //*.

This is not to say that the Centrist reasoning is necessary in order to negate the ultimate establishment in any round-bellied thing of the entity posited there by the verbal designation "pot." For, as he states in the *Blaze of Argument*, both Experientialists and Centrists agree in explaining that whatever is posited by verbal signs does not actually inhere in the reality of things, since such (non-verbal) persons as the deaf and the dumb can still recognize things such as pots, and such animals as cows can recognize their own and others' calves by means of smell and color; and so on.[14]

Therefore, the conceptual objects of designations such as "this is form!" and "this is production of form!" are (only) the referents of the designations. Conventionally speaking, they do exist by intrinsic identity; hence do not have identity-unreality. So, by negating (their) ultimate existence, he explains the meaning of the scripture as the non-existence of identity-reality in the ultimate sense. Thus, the object intended as the "imagined" in the statement "there is no identity-reality in the imagined" is none other than the imagined in the ultimate, and the statement that it is posited by names and conventions merely means that it is verbal and conceptual designation. Thus, he does not consider the relative to have been declared to be without identity-reality; for, if the relative were not established by intrinsic identity as actual process of ascriptive and descriptive designation, it would be pointless even for the Experientialist system to explain the imagined as identity-unreality.[15] Therefore, he maintains that the meaning of the scripture is that the perfect is the ultimate emptiness with respect to the substance and production of form, and is not as the Experientialists explain it (that is, the perfect as the relative devoid of the imagined). Likewise, this master believes that the lack of self-production, mentioned in the declaration of production-unreality of the relative as lack of intrinsic production, is synonymous with the lack of essential production and lack of identifiable production mentioned in other scriptures, and he interprets all of them as meaning non-production in the ultimate. That being so, and real production being production established by intrinsic identity, (it is clear that) he believes in production established by intrinsic identity, conventionally speaking, since he always employs the qualification "ultimately" when he negates such (establishment) in things. In the case of the Experientialists, however, while they accept the *Elucidation of Intention*'s "self-production" and other scriptures' "intrinsically real production" as similar in meaning, they interpret both as lack of independent production, and thus believe

[14] TJ, TG, C. dza, f. 215a1 ff.

[15] Since the relative itself is the basis of the imaginatively constructed, it cannot be identity-realitylessness.

that such non-production need not imply ultimate non-production. (Finally), since (Bhavaviveka) believes that the relative would have to be established as it appears if it were to be established in truth, which would invalidate the scriptural statements of illusoriness, he explains the *Elucidation of Intention* as (teaching the relative's) emptiness of intrinsic reality.[16]

2. CONVENTIONAL EXISTENCE AND NON-EXISTENCE OF THINGS EXTERNAL

Let us explain this (master's) position as to whether superficial phenomena are objective (external things) or subjective (products of consciousness). Although the Holy Father and Son did not explicitly pronounce upon the existence or non-existence of external things on the conventional level, this master believes that external things exist conventionally, that the sense-consciousnesses perceive things in determinate form and not as indeterminate,[17] and that both (external things and internal consciousnesses) are sequential as causes and effects.

Thus, (he maintains that) the *Ten Stages* statement that "the three realms are simply mind" is intended to refute any creator of the world other than the mind, such as heterodox schools assert, and is not intended to refute (the existence of) external things. Further, since he believes that even this statement of the *Mission to Lanka*—"The externally apparent does not exist, and a variety appears in the mind, similar to bodies, belongings, and places; (but) I say it is simply mind!"—does not refute external things, one should reflect on whether he believes the refutation of external things can never be the meaning of any scripture.[18]

In the *Wisdom Lamp*,[19] he explains the first statement (above) as meaning that external things do not exist by intrinsic reality, and that the "production of the variety in the mind, similar to things such as body, belongings, and places" means the fact that (the mind arises) having aspects (imparted by and) similar to those things. He explains "simply mind" as above.

(He further maintains that) it is not so that atoms do not appear as objective conditions of sense-cognitions when they aggregate (with other

[16] That is, Bhavya makes a difference between "reality-status," "truth-status," and "ultimate-status," which he negates, and "intrinsically identifiable status," without which he cannot understand the relative.

[17] That is, he does not subscribe conventionally to the strict definition of perception (*pratyakṣa*) by the Traditionist Idealist logicians, as essentially indeterminate (*rnam med*).

[18] Bhavya expresses these points in TJ, TG, C, dza, f. 207b4 ff.

[19] PrPr XXV, TG, C, tsha, f. 247ab ff.

atoms) as form and sound, etc. (He maintains that) armies and forests, etc., are aggregations based on different types (of atoms) and hence are not substantially existent; whereas molecules of homogeneous atoms, dependent upon one basis, form (objects such as) pots, etc., hence are substantially existent.[20] He even maintains that cognitions perceiving two moons, etc., would not arise without an external objective support, since (such perceptions) must arise based upon apprehension of one moon. (He argues that) if there were no external (objects), scriptural declarations that sense-cognitions occur from objective conditions would be repudiated, since their occurrence from objective conditions would be impossible either conventionally or ultimately.

Therefore, he does not accept (the theory of) the fundamental consciousness, for if he did, there would be no point in admitting external objects, since the occurrence of consciousnesses perceiving objects would be derived from the development of the instinctual propensities of that (fundamental consciousness), without any external objects. Thus, since he does not admit that (fundamental consciousness), he does not posit any addicted mentality, as he states in the *Heart of the Central Way*, "the term 'consciousness' definitely indicates the self."[21]

Further, he does not believe in apperceptive self-consciousness, stating in the above text: "How could any mind itself be perceived apart from the perception of objects?"[22] For he refutes even in conventional terms the following arrangements, which are clearly the rule if apperception is admitted: that consciousness arises as a dual perception in the aspects both of external objects and of itself, appearing as actual experience of the aspect of subjectivity not apparent externally; that apperceptive self-consciousness is experience subsequent to a prior objective perception; and that the two (consciousness and apperception) are (related as) objective condition and subject (respectively). His system seems to agree with master Jñanagarbha's interpretation of the central way, insofar as he also does not refute intrinsically identifiable status (in things) conventionally, and he (also maintains) the existence of external things.[23]

[20] PrPr XXV, TG, C, tsha, f. 248a1 ff. Conventionally, of course.

[21] MH, TG, C, dza, f. 21b3, reading / *rnam par shes pai ming gis ni* // *de la bdag tu btags par 'gyur* / for / *rnam shes zhes byai rnam grangs kyis* // *bdag ni nges par bstan pa yin* /.

[22] MH, TG, C, dza, f. 20b5; text reads / *yul du snang bar ma gtogs par* / *sems kyi bdag nyid gzhan ci yod* / instead of Tsong Khapa's / *yul du snang las gzhan gyur pai* // *sems nyid ji 'dra ba zhig snang* /, which variance indicates either that Tsong Khapa's text was differently worded, or, more remarkably, that he was quoting from memory, getting the sense right but altering the wording.

[23] This master's major work is the *Analysis of the Two Realities*.

3. THE MAIN REASON FOR NEGATION OF ULTIMATE EXISTENCE

What is the main reason for negation of existence in the ultimate, according to this master? Except for occasional negations by means of a negative reason, he (usually) refutes (ultimate existence) by means of (the technique of) "perception of an inconsistent fact."[24] (In) other (cases), considering ease of examples that conform to reason and probandum, he sets forth arguments such as the following: "The eye does not see form in the ultimate, because it is a sense-faculty, like the auditory sense-faculty;" or "the earth-element is not the ultimate reality of solidity, because it is an element, like water."[25] Thus, he emphasizes (the technique known as) "confutation through similarity of reason,"[26] which is often used in the treatises of the Holy Father and Son. His intention is that if solidity and sight of form were established as ultimate entities, then differences of solidity and non-solidity in things similar (by virtue of being) elements and of sight and lack of sight of form by things similar (by virtue of being) sense-faculties would be impossible, since reasons cannot be found to support such differences. Thus, if (something) exists in the ultimate, it should exist on the strength of its own objective condition, and not just be set up on the strength of cognition according with its appearance. Hence it should be independently existent, requiring nothing else. Therefore, there would be no valid evidence supporting the discernment of such differences (in different things). For example, if smoke were to occur independent of any cause, the absurdities that it could occur from anything or that it could not occur from fire would become obligatory.

Thus if identifiable existence (of anything) were possible in the ultimate, it would have to stand exclusive and isolated in its own essence, as something apart from the actualities of cause, condition, and aggregation. Hence, such things as elements and their composites, aggregates of eight kinds of atoms, and mind and mental functions, without mutual dependence, would not exist at all. Thus all things which arise from combinations of causes and conditions and which cannot exist apart from them must be stated to be ultimately and substantially inexistent. He prefers to demonstrate the faults (of ultimate existence) by showing that

[24] Tib. *'gal zla dmigs pa nyid kyis 'gog pa*. Skt. *viruddhopalabdhi*. This is equivalent to saying that Bhavya employs a positive syllogism exposing an idea contradictory to that of his opponent, rather than a negative consequence, reducing the opponent's position ad absurdum. The former is the characteristic Dogmaticist methodology.

[25] See PPMMV I for Chandrapada's refutation of this practice and MH, I, 26 and following comment in TJ.

[26] Tib. *rgyu mtshan mtshungs pai mgo snyoms*. See below, n. 28.

nothing may exist apart from aggregation and that an ultimate existent would have to exist independently, rather than negating (ultimate existence) as other masters prefer,[27] through the analysis of unity and multiplicity of parts and wholes.

Our intelligence will expand tremendously in reasoning (power) when we thoroughly understand the key reasonings employed by the great followers of the Holy Ones. Hence, we should learn thoroughly this system's reasoning that if something were to exist in the ultimate, the confutation of similarity of reason arises.[28]

II. EXPLANATION OF SHANTARAKSHITA AND KAMALASHILA

1. ULTIMATE PRESENCE AND ABSENCE OF REALITY IN PERSONS AND THINGS

Since Shantarakshita shares the position (expressed in Kamalashila's) explanation in the *Central Way Illumination*[29] of the meaning of the *Elucidation of Intention* statements of identity-unreality and production-unreality, which accords with Bhavaviveka's (interpretation), he also believes in a conventional reality established (in things) by intrinsic identity. This can be understood also from their acceptance in common (with Dignaga, etc.) of the reasonings employed to establish causality in the *Seven Logical Treatises*.[30]

2. CONVENTIONAL EXISTENCE AND NON-EXISTENCE OF EXTERNAL THINGS

Do external objects exist or not, conventionally? The *Wisdom Lamp* states:

[27] See Ch. II, re Dharmakirti, etc., and below, re Shantirakshita, etc.

[28] *mTha dPyod* illustrates this reasoning, which he calls "consequence that confutes through similarity of reason," as follows: "sound-hearing-ear-sense must see form; because form-seeing-eye-sense sees form ultimately." Bhavya, of course, uses the method obversely in the form of a positive syllogism rather than a consequence.

[29] MAlok, TG, C, sa, ff. 148a1 ff.

[30] That is, Shantarakshita accepts Dharmakirti's idea that functional efficiency (*artha-kriya*) is the criterion of reality. Thus, to be real in any sense, even conventionally, a thing must have some intrinsic identity to have any functional efficiency. This demonstrates his position that things on the conventional level must have identifiable status. The *Seven Logical Treatises* are enumerated in the Introduction, n. 56.

Although some people first accept (the theory of) pure information, and later wish to abandon it completely, it would be better (to avoid it from the first, as it is better) to stay far away from mud, rather than getting soiled and having to wash yourself off. Therefore, it is correct to realize the selflessness and non-production of consciousness just as one realizes the realitylessness of external things.[31]

The *Wisdom Lamp Commentary*[32] here explains that this refers to the system of certain Experientialists, who first, when still involved with superficial reality, negate external things and accept pure consciousness, and later, when they wish to realize ultimate reality, accept that even pure consciousness must be abandoned. That is, it is better to teach realitylessness from the beginning rather than first presenting one with the reality of (pure) consciousness and later refuting such reality. This view that the realitylessness of consciousness should be realized just as is the unreality of external things clearly negates the idea of certain Centrists that a disciple must necessarily be taught in such stages. Accordingly, although the *Wisdom Lamp*'s refutation of the position, "those two should not be contemplated simultaneously but by stages," that "it is not necessary to be stingy about simultaneous meditation (of both) from the beginning" is explained by the *Commentary* (to refute) the belief of "certain Experientialists," (I) consider (that belief) to resemble (Shantarakshita's).[33] Therefore, although such a system (as that mentioned by Bhavaviveka) does occur occasionally (in works prior to Shantarakshita), still, master Jñanasena's belief that master Shantarakshita, with the composition of his major treatise, founded that Centrist theory that poses the conventional non-existence of external things, is correct.[34]

To quote the *Autocommentary* of the *Central Way Ornament*:

Those who wish to answer all false criticisms based on the premise of the fact of causality should investigate the nature of those superficial things—"Do they have only the nature of mind and mental phenomena, or do they have the nature of external things?"—Concerning the latter thesis, some (do not accept it,) saying—"The treatises declare 'mind-only' to refute (the reality) of agent and experiencer (and do not mean it literally)"—while others (do accept it,) considering "What is involved in causality is exclusively consciousness alone, and whatever is objectively established, that resides in consciousness."[35]

[31] PrPr, XXV, TG, C. tsha, f. 248b5-7. Tsong Khapa's version is rather different in style, although the meaning is not altered.

[32] PrPrT, TG, C, wa, zha, za, by Avalokitavrata, Ch. XXV, TG, C, za, ff. 303a2-304a1.

[33] PrPrT, TG, C, za, f. 303b4-7.

[34] Jñanasena (alias Jñanagarbha), author of *Two Realities*.

[35] *Madhyamakālaṃkāravṛtti* (MAlamV), TG, C, sa, f. 78b5-7, quoting MH, see above, n. 19.

Here, Shantarakshita quotes from the *Heart of the Central Way*, and sets forth the belief in external things we have described above. He records his own belief under "while others . . . considering. . . ."

In regard to the authority of which scriptures he relies upon, he makes that clear in the same *Autocommentary*: "Such an interpretation is in agreement with all the statements occuring in the *Dense Array* and in the *Elucidation of Intention*, etc. We also consider the *Mission to Lanka* statement appropriate—'External form is non-existent—one's own mind appears as external things.' "[36]

Thus, depending on the method of "mind-only," one can understand with little difficulty the realitylessness of personal self, personal possessions, and the subject-object dichotomy. Subsequently, those of no small intellectual might, with intense efforts, may analyze that mind with respect to its (possible) natures of unity or multiplicity and, thereby seeing no essence (of the mind) in the ultimate (sense), may understand the central way that abandons all extremes. According to the *Ornament of the Central Way*: "The unreality of external things is to be realized depending on the (principle of) mind-only. Thus depending, utter selflessness is to be realized in that (mind) as well."[37]

He further quotes the *Mission to Lanka*: "I explain non-production as the reversal from cause and condition, the negation of (external) causes as well, and the establishment of the mind alone. Things have no external existence, nor can the mind be apprehended—in order to abandon all views, (I teach) the nature of non-production."[38]

The *Central Way Ornament Elucidation* comments that the first of these verses teaches the non-production of the Idealist system, and the second teaches the non-production of the Centrist system.[39] The Universal Vehicle is attained through the doors of these two methods, that of pure information through the emptiness of external things in the conventional, and that (of the central way) through the intrinsic unreality of all things in the ultimate. The *Central Way Ornament* continues: "Holding the reins of reasoning, while mounted on the chariot of the two methods, through the realization of their meanings, Universal Vehicle status will be attained."[40]

Now, as he must explain this system of the conventional non-existence

[36] MAlamV, TG, C, sa, f. 79a3-4.

[37] MAlamV, TG, C, sa, f. 79a5. Actually, the sentence preceding this quote is almost an exact quote from Shantarakshita, ibid., f. 79a4-5; hence, the "*Dbu ma rgyan las*" is probably misplaced in our edition.

[38] MAlamV, TG, C, za, f. 79b4-5.

[39] *Madhyamakālaṃkāra pañjikā* (MAlamP), TG, C, sa, f. 128b5.

[40] *Madhyamakālamkāra* (MAlam), TG, C, sa, f. 79b6.

of external things as being the inner intention of Savior Nagarjuna, which treatise of the Master teaches this, in his opinion?

The *Central Way Ornament* quotes the following verses in order to prove the non-existence of external things:

> Herein is no production at all
> Nor is there any cessation.
> Production and cessation both
> Are exclusively mind-only.
>
> Things referred to as "primary elements," etc.,
> Are really comprised in consciousness;
> And by that knowledge, one gains freedom.
> Are they not, then, false presumptions?[41]

The latter of these two verses occurs in the *Philosophical Sixty*. The first verse teaches mind-only, while the second answers the question about the mention of primary elements and their material combinations by stating that it is the consciousness itself that appears as such things, and thus they are included in consciousness. Whether it concerns consciousness or external things, the proposition that (either one) exists in the ultimate sense is a false presumption since they are not apparent to the wisdom of reality.

Now the *Central Way Ornament Elucidation* explains that the first verse is quoted from the *Mission to Lanka*. However, Ratnakarashanti takes both verses to be Nagarjuna's, and thus he believes Centrism and Idealism to be the same, since the Master taught mind-only also.[42] It is evident that he was misled by Shantarakshita's quoting of the verses in one continuum; but there are other instances of verses by different authors being quoted in continuum.

This system admits the reality of determinants (of cognition) such as blue and yellow, and interprets Dharmakirti's position as being the same—thus (Shantarakshita) is a Centrist who (is like the Idealist who) believes determinate cognition[43] to be conventionally true. He postulates apper-

[41] MAlam, f. 79b5-6. The first verse is actually from the *Mission to Lanka*, as Tsong Khapa and Kamalashila (in the *Elucidation*) point out. Only the second verse is Nagarjuna's, being YṢ, k. 35. Tsong Khapa is very polite to Shantarakshita in the following paragraphs, but it is evident from the way in which the verses are quoted in the *Ornament* that the latter master mistook the first verse for Nagarjuna's (introducing it as " '*dir yang gsungs pa*," not "*mdo las gsungs pa*," an unidentified "stated" always assumed in this text to be the original master's). Further, Shantarakshita misses that the YṢ verse contains a formulated opinion (first phrase) and its rebuttal. Hence, it goes against his argument, rather than supports it.

[42] Ratnakarashanti's *Prajñāpāramitopadeśa* is a work in which the attempt to harmonize Centrism and Idealism is made.

[43] *Sākārajñāna*.

ception on the conventional level, and although he does not clearly state whether or not he admits fundamental consciousness, it is obvious he tends not to admit it.[44] (Incidentally,) the Pandit Sahajavajra states that the interpretation of Lva-ba-pa puts him in the category of Centrists who (are like the Experientialists who) believe cognitive determinants to be conventionally false, since for him determinants such as blue and yellow do not even have conventional reality.[45]

3. EXPLANATION OF THE MEANING OF THE *ELUCIDATION OF INTENTION*

Well then, does this system interpret the meaning of the *Elucidation of Intention* according to the explanation of the Experientialists? Or otherwise how does it interpret it?

In the *Central Way Illumination* (Kamalashila) explains that the *Elucidation of Intention* teaching that the ulterior intention of (the statement of realitylessness is) the three unrealities is a verification of the definitive meaning status of the *Mother Scripture*, etc.:

> On that account, the Lord's teachings of non-production, etc. were declared only in terms of the ultimate. Hence, by teaching the ulterior intention (of the teachings) to be the three unrealities, (the *Elucidation*) establishes their authority as the sole definitive meaning, as (those teachings) show the central way free of both extremes.[46]

Furthermore (he continues), that teaching (of the *Elucidation*) is declared for the sake of dispelling the mental habits of reification and repudiation that prevent access to the ultimate—repudiation of the superficial reality (of things), and reification of the existence of things that are (supposedly) permanent, etc., yet that do not exist conventionally, and of the (ultimate) existence of form, etc. as they appear. Repudiation is avoided by refutation of the literalness of statements of non-production by demonstration that such statements are made in terms of the ultimate,

[44] dPal-'byor Lhun-grub (SERA, f. 28a2) comments that it is obvious that Shantarakshita does not need *ālaya*, because he posits *manovijñāna* as the designative base of "person," whereas those who admit *ālaya* invariably posit it as designative base for "person."

[45] The truth/falsity of determinants (*rnam pa*) is originally an Idealist problem, hinging on whether one posits that the sense consciousness seeing blue, etc., is mistaken cognition or not. Shantarakshita feels that Dharmakirti thought such cognition to be non-mistaken. Dharmottara, etc., hold the opposite view. And Mahasiddha Lva-ba-pa feels such cognition is definitely mistaken, hence that such cognitive determinants are essentially false. See *Zin Bris*, f. 16b.

[46] MAlok, TG, C, sa, f. 150a2-3.

and further by establishment of the need for accepting the existence of production and cessation conventionally.[47]

Experts accept the equation of the relative with the production-unreality, due to the fact that things are produced dependent on conditions and not from their own selves alone, with the pronouncement that "the dependently occurrent is emptiness with respect to self-existence." Similarly, the *Questions of Anavatapta* states that what is produced from conditions is not produced with intrinsic identity—"What is produced by conditions is not produced—there is no intrinsic reality of production in it."[48] Therefore, since it is produced from causes and conditions, it is not necessary that the relative exist in truth, for otherwise even false things such as illusions would be true phenomena. And that is why the *Elucidation of Intention* declares the relative to be "like illusion," intending that there is no distinction between illusion and truthlessness. Therefore, things such as impermanence when held to be ultimately existent are imagined realities, which are stated to be identity-unreality, since they are not established as they are represented. This (above line of reasoning) avoids reification.

It is not contradictory to explain identity-unreality as the ultimate non-establishment of the relative, since (naive realism) adheres to the reality of the imagined in the relative itself, and hence it is necessary to demonstrate the absence of such an imagined identity-reality in the relative.[49]

In regard to the fact that the *Elucidation of Intention* explains the identity-unreality as being due to the lack of intrinsic identifiability of the imagined (only), and does not mention identity-unreality as the lack of intrinsic identifiability of the other two realities, this master considers that it signifies that the very same lack of ultimate status of the other two realities is being explained as the identity-unreality which is the lack of intrinsic identifiability of the imagined. And (for him) it is extremely clear that reification is avoided by (taking) ultimate lack of intrinsic identifiability as the meaning of identity-unreality, whereas repudiation is abandoned by the fact that conventionally there is an identity-reality which is intrinsic identifiability. Therefore, while this master and the Experientialists agree (in asserting) that causality is repudiated if the relative is lacking in intrinsic identifiability, this master differs in his

[47] Note how this resembles Asanga's refutation of literalness of statements, and yet how Kamalashila still maintains a Centrist stance, by validating a non-literal scripture on the ultimate level, thus reconciling SN and AMN.

[48] Tsong Khapa follows the text (MAlok, TG, L, sa, f. 150a) with a paraphrase. Skt. from PPMMV, p. 105: *yaḥ pratyayairjāyati sa hyajāto notāsya utpādu svabhāvato'sti / yaḥ pratyayādhina sa śūnya ukto yaḥ śūnyatāṃ jānati so'pramattaḥ //.*

[49] That is, since relatives are not as they appear, they are not established ultimately. *Zin Bris*, f. 18a.

qualification that the lack of intrinsic identifiability is "in the ultimate," whereas the Experientialists argue that if something has intrinsically identifiable status, it must exist ultimately. As for the meaning of the *Elucidation of Intention* statement that the relative is empty with respect to the imagined, since those phenomena of the relative are lacking in intrinsic identifiability as the real referents of ascriptive and descriptive designations of form, etc., as "such and such," this master maintains his belief in (the imagined as) the conceptual object, just as Bhavaviveka (does) as explained above.[50] Furthermore, in the *Central Way Illumination* (Kamalashila) interprets the statements of non-production, etc., as intending the ultimate realitylessness which is objective selflessness. To answer the argument that the statements of some scriptures that all things are realityless and unproduced, etc., are interpretable in meaning (since) the *Elucidation of Intention*, etc., reveal the ulterior intention of the scriptures' meaning, he states:

> therefore, the exposition of intention (of a statement) does not preclude (that statement's) definitiveness of meaning; because the very fact (that their intention is exposed) establishes the statements of non-production, etc., as definitive in meaning, eliminates any contradiction with experience, etc., and gets rid of any assumptions of literalness. To quote the *Holy Elucidation of the Intention* itself. . . .[51]

"Therefore" is explained as meaning that all things are exclusively without reality, due to the realitylessness stated by the *Elucidation of Intention* as ultimate realitylessness, being both ultimate and manifested by the realitylessness of things. And this (above quote further) explains that the *Elucidation of Intention* exposition of the ulterior intention of the statements of realitylessness, etc., establishes their definitiveness of meaning by refuting their literal acceptability. This system equates literal acceptance (of "non-production," etc.) with the notion of utter non-existence of production and cessation etc., saying that the Centrist admits non-production in the ultimate sense, but accepts production, etc., in the conventional sense, and hence should not insist upon the literalness of statements of productionlessness, etc. It thus equates admission of the ultimate non-existence (of production etc.) with the non-acceptance of the literal meaning (of such statements).[52]

[50] That is both masters retain conventional intrinsic identifiability in the relative, refuting such only in the ultimate sense, and thus assert the conventional relative reality of imagined phenomena as conceptual objects. See pp. 266, 268.

[51] MAlok, TG, C, sa, f. 151b4-5.

[52] That is, statements without the qualification "ultimate," which, if taken literally, would be understood as repudiating conventional production, and so forth.

We might now object that, if such is the case, it contradicts the *Elucidation of Intention* explanation of the second wheel of Dharma, which teaches "realitylessness" and "non-production" as interpretable in meaning, since (according to this position) the *Elucidation of Intention* establishes those (teachings) to be definitive in meaning.

Although (Kamalashila) does (not) explicate the rebuttal of this contradiction in the *Central Way Illumination*,[53] his intention is that, granted that there would be a contradiction if one and the same scripture were both stated to be interpretable in meaning and also established as definitive in meaning by showing its intention, not (only) one scripture is involved, but (many) scriptures that are similar only insofar as they belong to the middle wheel of Dharma. That is to say, teachings such as "there is no form," in a scripture such as the *Transcendent Wisdom Heart*, where the qualifications "in the ultimate" and "in truth" are not explicitly applied, are not fit to be accepted literally as taught, and thus are interpretable, requiring further interpretation by supplying the qualifications "in the ultimate," etc., since "eye" and "ear," etc. are only non-existent ultimately and are not non-existent conventionally. However, this analysis also means that the scriptures such as the *Transcendent Wisdom Hundred Thousand*, which apply such qualifications as "in the ultimate sense" to their negatees, are established as literally definitive in meaning; thus, the statement that the second wheel is interpretable in meaning does not apply to all (the scriptures) of the second wheel.

Now, the *Elucidation of Intention* refutes the (type of) literal acceptance of statements of productionlessness, ceaselessness, and realitylessness which holds "That is just so!" but does not refute (the type of) literal acceptance which accepts *ultimate* realitylessness, etc. Fitting these two facts together, (Kamalashila) asserts that, although the acceptance of the non-existence of substance, production, and cessation with intrinsically identifiable status would be (erroneous) literal acceptance, this scripture's teaching of identity-unreality due to non-existence of intrinsically identifiable status refutes the ultimate existence (of that intrinsically identifiable status, and thus is definitive in meaning). He (is compelled to) explain it in that way by his crucial belief in the validity of intrinsic identifiability in the conventional sense.

In sum, he believes that the *Elucidation of Intention* establishes scriptures such as the *Mother Hundred Thousand* as definitive in meaning, because the *Elucidation of Intention* teaches that "of the two kinds of scriptures taught in the second wheel of Dharma to those devoted to the

[53] *Zin Bris*, f. 18b, remarks that most later commentators consider this passage to be a strong criticism of Kamalashila.

Universal Vehicle, those that apply the qualifications such as "ultimately" and those that do not, one should not take the statements of the latter literally, but should understand according to the former kind that production and cessation, etc., exist conventionally and do not exist ultimately."[54] By these reasonings, we can completely understand his method of explaining the interpretability of the first (wheel of Dharma).

If the meaning of this scripture is not the formulation of the three reality theory of the Experientialist, does (Kamalashila) believe that no scripture has such a meaning?

In the *Central Way Illumination*, he states that when the *Elucidation of Intention*, the *Mission to Lanka*, and the *Dense Array* fail to refute intrinsic reality of the mind on certain occasions when external objects are negated and mind-only is established, they are teaching in accordance with the inclinations of those who must be led gradually, being unable to realize all at once the realitylessness of all things.[55]

Thus, he interprets the meanings of these scriptures by differentiating the above teachings from those teachings given to disciples who are capable of realizing the realitylessness of all things all at once. And, although master Shantarakshita does not explicitly settle the question of the three realities in the same manner, (from) at least those of his works that have been translated (into Tibetan), (it appears that) the intentions of both masters are the same.

The *Central Way Illumination* teaches in detail the style of path founded by Bhavaviveka, in which the meaning of the *Elucidation of Intention* statement of the three realities is interpreted according to the Centrist, not the Experientialist, system. Knowing the subtleties of both methods of scriptural interpretation, one will understand the various techniques of reasoning and scriptural interpretation of the Great Champions.

4. INTERPRETATION OF THE MAIN REASON REFUTING ULTIMATE EXISTENCE

A. Identification of the Logical Negatee

If one accepts only the conventional reality of intrinsically identifiable status, then of what sort is the negatee, which is not merely that (status), but is said to be "true," "real," and "ultimate" status?

It is extremely important to identify the negatee, as otherwise there would be no clear awareness of either the mental habit holding to truth-

[54] SN VII, paraphrased by Tsong Khapa.
[55] MAlok, argument first formulated, TG, C, sa, f. 156b5. Refuted up to 157a2.

status, etc. (in things) or of the general (character) of the negatee thus held. Then our sense that such (truth-) status (in things) is impossible would be merely a dogmatic aversion, and no matter how often we assert "this is the fault inherent in such status and this is the proof of its non-existence," we will reach no solid understanding of the import (of these assertions).

Commenting on the statement that "earth," etc., are not ultimately the realities of the elements, (Bhavaviveka) says in the *Blaze of Arguments*:

> "Ultimate object" (*paramārtha*) is called "object" (*artha*) because it is a knowable (object), which is to say it is something to be examined and understood. "Ultimate" (*parama*) has the meaning of "supreme." Thus the (parallel [*karmadhāraya*]) compound "ultimate-object" (*paramārtha*) is formed, as it is both an "object" and an "ultimate." Otherwise, (analyzing the compound as a genitive *tatpuruṣa*) it is called "object of the ultimate" as it is the object of the ultimate, non-conceptual intuition. Further, (as an attributive compound, [*bahuvrīhi*]) (it means) "that (object) conforming with the ultimate," as that "ultimate meaning" exists for the wisdom that conforms to the realization of the ultimate.[56]

Of the three (meanings) mentioned, the latter is significant here (in our concern to understand "ultimate status"). Bhavaviveka continues:

> There are two kinds of ultimates. One is non-operational, transcendent, immaculate, and unfabricated, and the other is operationally involved and endowed with fabrication, known as "pure mundane intuition conforming to the stores of merit and wisdom." Thus, there is no fault, with regard to this (latter kind of ultimate), as employed to qualify our thesis.[57]

Here, (we) must accept (as a type of ultimate) the rational cognition analytic of the ultimate, not (reserving ultimacy for) only the holy aftermath rational cognition.[58] Therefore, when the basis of the analysis of

[56] TJ III, k.26, TG, C, dza, f. 59a6-59b. Orally reconstructed by Dr. V. V. Gokhale (Poona, 1971): *paramārthaḥ ityatra artha iti jñeyabhūtatvāt / sa arthaḥ parīkṣyaḥ gamyaścaityarthaḥ / parama iti śreṣṭhaḥ ityasya paryāyaḥ / paramārthaḥ iti samāsaḥ / arthaśca asan paramaśca iti paramārthaḥ / apica paramasya artho 'san 'vitarkajñānasya paramārtha bhūto iti paramārthaḥ / apica paramārthānurūpaḥ paramārthāvabodhānurūpaprajñāyāṃ tat paramārthabhāvāt /.*

[57] TJ, TG, C, dza, f. 60b3; *Zin Bris*, f. 20ab.

[58] That is, the wisdoms usually aligned with the two types of ultimate would be the holy-equipoise-wisdom, and the holy-aftermath-wisdom. But Tsong Khapa includes rational cognition analytic of the ultimate with the latter.

existence and non-existence by the Centrists and other (philosophers) is said to be "non-existent ultimately," what is meant is that that basis (objects, etc.) does not exist in the face of reason analytic of the ultimate, and that such (rational cognition) does not establish them (as ultimately existent). This (above) is the clearest explanation (of this point) in the treatises of this master (Bhavaviveka); and (the type of ultimacy involved) is not identified so clearly in the writings on the two realities of master Jñanagarbha, nor in the *Central Way Ornament* and its *Autocommentary*.

In the *Central Way Illumination*, the three wisdoms are termed "ultimate," since their object is the ultimate reality:

> All cognitions arising from hearing, reflecting, and meditating upon (the meaning of) reality are termed "ultimate" because they have the object which is undeceiving, and because the aim of these (cognitions) is ultimate. They may further be distinguished as either direct or (inferentially) indirect, and by these (mundane) things are known to be exclusively unproduced (ultimately). Therefore, the expression "(things are) ultimately unproduced" means that they are not established (as ultimately existent) by these authentic cognitions.[59]

(Things are) said to be unproduced on the strength of the consideration of these (cognitions), since they are not established as produced according to (these) authentic cognitions. The two selflessnesses are "ultimate" as they are corroborated by (correct) reasoning, and are "objects" as they are the objectives of those aspiring to realization and the abandonment of obscurations and are the aims of infallible ultimate intuition—hence they are taught as having the nature of the "ultimate object." Accordingly, if "reality" is taken to refer to rational cognition, it, and not conventional cognition, negates intrinsic reality. And, if "reality" is taken to refer to actual ultimate reality, it is not found to exist by rational cognition analytic of ultimate reality. This is explained in the *Subcommentary* of the *Ornament*.[60]

This indicates that things such as production, etc., are not established as the actuality of things, for if such production of things was to exist in actuality it would have to be established by cognition of the true and the ultimate, and it is in fact not so established—and that very fact is also termed "ultimate non-production."

How would production have to be established to be established in actuality? For example, when one sees in hallucination a stick or a clod

[59] MAlok, TG, C, sa, f. 228a2-4; D. f. 229b1-3.

[60] MAlamP, TG, C, sa, f. 84ab ff.; D. f. 86b5-87a. Thus "ultimate existence" does not itself ultimately exist in a dualistic manner.

as an illusory horse or an illusory elephant, although such things appear to such (distorted) cognition, one cannot say that that stick does not appear to be such (as a horse). Likewise, when a sprout appears to be produced from a seed, although such is no more than an appearance to (visual) cognition, it cannot be said that that sprout does not arise from that seed (at all). But then, one might suppose in that case, is that not "ultimate production," since objectively the sprout is produced from the seed?

This does not fault (Kamalashila's position), for, although there is an appearance of horse or elephant, as far as the source of the mistake (that is, stick or clod) is concerned, such an appearance is on the strength of the cognition of hallucinating vision, and is not produced from its own natural conditions; otherwise, it would appear even without any hallucination. Likewise, in the case of the seed's production of the sprout, it is not produced on the strength of its own objective existence and is only presented on the strength of its appearance to conventional cognition. Therefore, the perception of the production of the sprout on the strength of its own inherent condition, not merely as presented on the strength of appearance to its (corresponding) subjective cognition, would be the perception of ultimate production. And thereby can be known (what is meant by) "existence of ultimate or true production"; and thereby can be understood the (problem of) existence and non-existence of ultimate, real, and true production of all other things.

The *Central Way Illumination* states that "all living beings perceive such a real, inherent self in things as is indicated (by their conditioning), and all things thus falsified by their mental habits are said to exist only superficially."[61]

The superficial cognition that mistakenly perceives (things') reality where there is ultimately unreality and which arises from beginningless instincts, pretends to all living beings as if there were a true existence of things; and thus what exists according to their habitual thoughts is said to be "superficially existent." Since ultimate existence is taken as the reverse of that (type of existence presented by falsifying cognition), it is explained in contrast to it. And, (on this point), the systems of all the Dogmaticist Centrists are similar.

(In regard to criteria of validity within the superficial,) although conventionally existent (things) cannot be established (merely) on the strength of appearance in non-analytical cognitions such as the two unconscious self-habits, they can be established conventionally on the strength of their appearance in conventional cognitions that are not faulted by other validating cognitions. Thus, in the system of this master, although there is

[61] MAlok, TG, C, sa, f. 227a3-4.

such a thing as a conventional reality established on the strength of appearance to such (unfaulted, conventional) cognition, it must be qualified as "not (merely) established on strength of appearance to purely subjective cognition." Although he does indeed admit the ultimate reality of those emptinesses which are the emptinesses of those (conventional) objects with respect to the (hypothetical) objects of truth-habits, those (emptinesses themselves) are not established on the strength of (objective) realities which (themselves) are not established on the strength of their own appearance to their corresponding subjectivities. This is how to understand the meaning of "emptiness of emptiness" (in this system).

The above-mentioned "truth-habit" is the unconscious truth-habit of this system, which does exist for living beings unacquainted with signs, although not by way of connection of name and referent. Therefore, although one can (refute its intellectual objects by) arguing that if the object of the truth-habit were to exist, then it could withstand analysis by reasoning analytic of the ultimate, indivisible things would exist, and (so would) intrinsic reality with the three qualities,[62] etc., the (philosophical) holding of such (untenable positions) is not the (only) function of the truth-habit, since their refutation (by itself) does not establish the actual (experience) of truthlessness.

Due to the fact that imprecise identification of the object of the truth-habit of this (master) entails the granting of truth-status to every object of rational cognition, certain scholars of former times adopted such a belief (in truth-status). Others asserted the utter absence of any object of rational cognition. And still others asserted the existence and non-existence of the objects (of rational cognition) by distinguishing between the (differentials) of "reason" and "inference."[63]

In conclusion having identified this unconscious objective self-habit, one understands all reasonings negating objective self as either its actual negation or as a factor of it. One should understand the thrust of this (practical) teaching as (inculcative of) repeated analysis of whatever is internalized in the pattern of one's own mental processes, through learning, teaching, and thinking (upon this matter). Indeed, ultimately, such an attitude is required on all other occasions of the expositions of selflessness by any of the Buddhist (philosophical) schools.

[62] bLo-bzang Phun-tshogs (*Zin Bris*, f. 23a) explains that the "three qualities of an intrinsic reality are: 1) intrinsic non-creation by causes and conditions; 2) unrelatedness to any other thing; and 3) unchangeability into any other condition.

[63] Tib. *ldog pa*. Skt. *vyāvrtti*. Literally, "exclusion," being the Buddhist equivalent of a "universal." This last position represents a Logician-Centrist syncretism where inference has no ultimate object, but "reason" extended to include "intuition" does.

B. Reasoning Negating the Negatee

What is the chief reasoning used to negate the above negatee?

With some exceptions, the reason used to negate the negatee of this system is the reason (called) "non-perception of the related fact."[64] Nevertheless, the *Central Way Ornament*, relying on the *Mission to Lanka* and the *Meeting of Father and Son*, expounds its proofs by means of the reasoning known as "absence of (true) unity and multiplicity," and the *Central Way Illumination* employs (the reasonings known as) "the diamond-smithereens," "negation of production from existent (causes) or non-existent (causes)," "negation of production through four alternatives," and "absence of unity and multiplicity." It finally employs the "reason of relativity" which is a reason (defined as) "perception of the inconsistent fact."[65]

The conclusive scope of the demonstration of the internal contradiction in an opponent's (position affirming ultimate existence) is as follows: the absolute status of anything is refuted by showing first of all, in the face of no matter what assertion of Buddhist or non-Buddhist school, the impossibility of an indivisible, a thing without a multiplicity of parts such as periods of time, parts of physical objects, or aspects of cognitive objects. Then one demonstrates that, whereas conventional objects may exist as unitary things while established as composed of many parts, as far as absolute status is concerned, there are inevitable inconsistencies. If part and whole are ultimately different, there can be no connection between them, and if part and whole are absolutely the same, then the whole becomes a multiplicity. (Shantarakshita and Kamalashila) expound (such arguments), being thoroughly conversant with reasonings such as that of Aryadeva, "There is no finger apart from the joints, etc."[66]

To exemplify (their fuller line of reasoning) as in the *Central Way*

[64] Tib. *'brel zla ma dmigs pa.* In regard to a "non-perception of related fact" (negative) reason, dPal-'byor Lhun-grub has some clarifying comments: (in paraphrase) "non-perception" negative reasons are twofold—1) those arising from non-perception of an imperceptible, and 2) those arising from non-perception of a perceptible. Each of these is again twofold: 1a, 2a) non-perception of related fact reasons, and 1b, 2b) non-perception through perception of contradictory fact reasons. Among types 1a and 2a, there are four subtypes: i) cause–non-perception, ii) concomitance–non-perception, iii) identity-non-perception, and iv) effect–non-perception. For further exemplification he refers us to *Drop of Logic* (NB); see Stcherbatski, *Buddhist Logic II.*

[65] Tib. *'gal zla dmigs pa.* This refers to types 1b and 2b in the schema in note above. These are known as the five great reasons. The first two are included in type "cause–non-perception." The third is included in type "effect–non-perception." The fourth is included in type "concomitance–non-perception." But the fifth is labeled "(non-perception) through perception of contradictory fact," since ultimate existence and relativity are mutually exclusive. See *mTha dPyod* f. 222b ff.

[66] CŚ: *tshigs las sor mo gzhan med de. . . .*

Illumination, "to refute (ultimate) production of one thing from another, (first) the (cause) is restricted to being either permanent or impermanent, and then production from a permanent thing is refuted. Then, (production from) an impermanent thing is restricted to being either simultaneous or sequential, and production from a simultaneous (cause) is refuted. Then, a sequential (cause) is restricted to being either destroyed or undestroyed (in its production of effect), and production from a destroyed (cause) is refuted. Then production from a formerly undestroyed cause is restricted to being either obstructed or unobstructed, and production from an obstructed (cause) is refuted. The refutation thus far is rather simple. Then production from an unobstructed (cause) is restricted to being either wholly unobstructed or partially unobstructed; then, in the former case, there must be a confusion of two things occuring at different times, and an atom and (its aggregative effects such as) a molecule must be confused as single object,[67] (the causal atoms) being wholly unobstructed; or else in the latter case, as (the supposed indivisible cause, being 'partially' unobstructed) would have parts, it would be a superficial (production, no longer absolute)."[68]

Further, the conclusive scope of the demonstration of inconsistencies (in the advocacy of ultimate production) lies in the refutation through the analysis of sameness and difference in wholes and parts. Thus, there are many doors of reasoning demonstrating the faults of such (assertions) as (ultimate) production from something else.

The ultimate refutation accomplished by master Jñanagarbha in his *Analysis of the Two Realities*, where his actual reasoning negating truth-status is the refutation of (ultimate) production through four alternatives, is quite similar to those (above-mentioned) of Shantạrakshita and Kamalashila.[69]

(Finally), all of these (reasonings) are the great paths of philosophical analysis of the followers of Savior Nagarjuna, and thus should be learned by those who wish to expand their intelligence in reasoning. And if one understands the reasonings of these (masters) of the Dogmaticist school, one will easily understand the reasonings in the other (schools), so there has been no digression.

[67] The atom being undestroyed and unobstructed, it would be perceived simultaneously with its aggregative effect.

[68] Malok, TG, C, sa, ff. 166a ff.

[69] *Satyadvaya* (SDV) TG, C, sa. Jñanagarbha is classed in Tibetan tradition as a Traditionist-Dogmaticist-Centrist, along with Bhavaviveka, as they accept the reality of external objects, and do not admit the existence of separate apperceptive consciousness (*svasaṃvitti*). Shantarakshita, Kamalashila, Aryavimuktasena, Haribhadra, and so on, are classified as Experientialist-Dogmaticist-Centrists, as they deny external objects, and admit apperceptive consciousness.

Chapter V

DIALECTICIST ELUCIDATION OF THE HOLY INTENTION

THE QUESTION OF INTRINSIC REALITY IN PERSONS AND THINGS

1. THE DISTINCTIVE SPECIALTY OF THEIR NEGATION OF INTRINSIC REALITY IN PERSONS AND THINGS

A. The Distinctiveness of Their Negation of Intrinsically Identifiable Intrinsic Reality

Bhavaviveka found many faults with Buddhapalita's explanation of the *Wisdom*, but he did not criticize him out of disagreement over the two selflessnesses.

Avalokitavrata explains:

> The great teachers of the central way, the Holy Father and Son, Bhavaviveka, and Buddhapalita, all show the method of the *Transcendent Wisdom* by explaining that inner and outer relativity exists conventionally, functionally efficient as mere illusion, and does not exist ultimately, being without substantiality.[1]

(In effect, he considers that) both masters (Buddhapalita and Bhavaviveka) explain the patterns of ultimate reality and of illusory, conventional existence in the same way. Furthermore, Jñanagarbha, Shantarakshita, and Kamalashila do not propose any difference between the selflessnesses of their systems and those of the system of Buddhapalita and Chandrakirti. Chandrakirti (on the other hand), while accepting that Buddhapalita, through correct interpretation of the intention of the holy (masters), presents the ultimate and the conventional without differing from his own system, still insists that his (and Buddhapalita's) system is distinct from the systems of the other Centrists. Thus, in the *Introduction to the Central Way Commentary* (he states):

[1] PrPrT, ad. MMK XXIV, k. 14.

Let the experts please be certain that what we expound here in the course of our rebuttal of any other system accords with the doctrine of emptiness, and that such is not the case with other treatises, just as (they are certain that) this doctrine known as "emptiness" is not taught flawlessly in any treatise other than the *Wisdom*. And thus, the proposition advanced by some, that "the Centrists conventionally accept the very same things for which the Traditionists posit ultimacy," should be recognized as merely an expression of utter ignorance of the actual meaning of the *Central Way Treatise*.[2]

He then goes on to quote and dismiss a similar statement about the Analyst system (and the Centrist system), and he finally concludes "Thus, since it is inappropriate that (this) transcendental doctrine should resemble (in any way) a mundane doctrine, experts may be certain that this system is distinctive (from all others)."[3]

He argues for the distinctiveness of his own system from that of other Centrists and attributes their belief that the Realists' absolute is the Centrists' conventional to their ignorance of the actuality of the central way. His reason is that in his own system nothing is admitted to be established by intrinsic identity, even conventionally, and those (Realists) establish (everything, ultimate and superficial) on that basis only. Since if either of the two realities is confused the other will be confused, it is incorrect that the transcendental teaching which does not confuse the two realities should resemble a mundane teaching which does confuse them both. Thus, this system of the holy masters has nothing in common with the Realists' theories, not only with regard to the ultimate but even with regard to the superficial.

Now when (Jñanagarbha, in) the *Autocommentary* of the *Analysis of the Two Realities*, quotes the verse: "What is absolute for one is superficial for another; just as (the same woman) is regarded as mother by one and wife by another";[4] and the *Subcommentary*[5] identifies the verse as being Nagarjuna's, it is (obvious) from (the above passage of) the

[2] MABh XI: (Poussin, ed., *Madhyamakāvatāra de Candrakirti*, p. 406, ll. 9-14. dPal-'byor Lhun-grub comments here that this proposition is advanced by certain Dogmaticists in criticism of the Dialecticists, but actually the criticisms fall back upon themselves, since the intrinsic reality taken as ultimate by the Traditionists is accepted as superficial only by the Dogmaticists and not by the Dialecticists, who deny intrinsic reality even superficially. mKhas-grub clarifies this (*sTong Thun*, 74a2), quoting Jñanagarbha, who made the comment: "One's absolute is another's conventional—just as the mother of one is the wife of another," and then emphasizing Chandrakirti's negation of this via the negation of any conventional intrinsic reality, or intrinsic identity. See below, n. 4.

[3] MABh XI, Poussin ed., p. 407, lines 1-3.

[4] *Satyadvayavibhāgavṛtti*, TG, C, sa, f. 3b3 ff., f. 10a3-4.

[5] *Satyadvayavibhāgapañjikā*, TG, C, sa, f. 15b1 ff., f. 37b4 (attributed in C. to Shantarakshita).

Introduction Commentary that such is not the case. As for the allegation that Shantarakshita wrote the (above) *Subcommentary*, while it may be a case of (another author with) the same name or a case of borrowing the name, it is not (the Shantarakshita who is) author of the *Central Way Ornament*, etc. For (not only does Kamalashila) refute, in his *Compendium of Principles Elucidation*,[6] this author's explanation of the purpose of composing a treatise (which he would not do if it was his own master's explanation), (but also) this author approves the literal meaning of the statement of (Jñanagarbha in) the *Autocommentary* to the effect that the theory of the non-existence of the apparent subject-object(-duality) is contradicted by perception and refuted by common sense, (which is precisely opposed to the position of Shantarakshita).

Furthermore, it is incorrect to object that "if the difference between the negatees of the two Centrist schools were no more than that (presence and absence of intrinsically identifiable production conventionally), why does Chandrakirti not make a specific refutation of that (insistence of the Dogmaticist on conventional, intrinsically identifiable production)?"[7] (For, in fact, Chandrakirti does just that) in the *Introduction Commentary*, (first formulating the Dogmaticist argument as follows):

> It is fine to negate production from self and other since there is no ultimate production, but it is undoubtedly the nature of the objects of perception and inference such as form and sensation, etc., to be produced from something else (conventionally). If you do not admit that, why mention two realities, as there would only be one reality left? Thus, production from something other does indeed exist.[8]

The objection is that, although in the negation of intrinsically real causality it is proper to negate other-production in the ultimate, "real" or "intrinsically identifiable" other-production must be admitted conventionally, or else the superficial reality would be annihilated. To rebut

[6] Tib. *tshad mai de kho nyid bsdus pai 'grel pa.* TA,C,ze, f. 133a7 ff. This corresponds to the TSP, and Tsong Khapa here refers to the fact that the way the author of the *Satyadvayapañjikā* explains the purpose of writing a treatise is very similar to the arguments made in the long antagonist's erroneous position (*pūrvapakṣa*) given in TSP, p. 2, 1. 17; p. 3, 1. 12. The basic disagreement is that the author of the *Satyadvayapañjikā* writes that the purpose (*prayojana*) is expressed by the author to overcome the prejudice of the reader that the "treatise is unnecessary, like counting the teeth of a crow," whereas Kamalashila feels that a student with such a crude misapprehension would not be the intended reader of such a book, so one would not compose a statement of purpose merely to overcome such a prejudice. See *Zin Bris* II, f. 25a.

[7] This objection is raised by kLong-chen Rab-'byams-pa, who disallows this distinction between the negatees of the Dogmaticists and the Dialecticists, according to dPal-'byor Lhun-grub.

[8] MABh VI, ad. k. 34: Poussin ed. p. 119, ll. 10-15.

this (Chandrakirti) methodically proves the non-existence of identifiable production in both realities.[9] And this is established to (counter) the (Dogmaticist) Centrist theory that intrinsically identifiable production exists conventionally, though not ultimately, and is not (directed) at (any theory of) the Realists.

B. Description of the Negatee and Proof of its Non-existence

a. Habitual Modes of Intellectual and Unconscious Reifications, and Proof of Their (Object's) Non-existence

What sort of (mental) habit holds (things) to be intrinsically identifiable?

To describe first of all the pattern (of this mental habit) of the philosophers; they investigate the meaning of the conventional expression "person" in such uses as "this person performed this action and experienced this result," by such (analysis) as "is the 'person' the very same thing as 'his' own aggregates? Or is 'he' something different from them?" When they discover whichever possibility, either sameness or difference (to be the case), it gives them a basis for establishing that "person," and they are then able to establish his accumulation of evolutionary action and so forth. If they do not find (any such basis), they are unable to establish (either "person" or his "actions," etc.). Hence they cannot rest content with the mere use of the expression "person." Thus, such establishment of "person" through analytic investigation into the referent of the conventional expression "person" is the establishment of person as having intrinsically identifiable status. And all the Buddhist philosophers, from Analysts to Dogmaticists, hold (their various types of "persons") in this kind (of pattern).[10]

Similarly, (this pattern of establishment of intrinsically identifiable status) holds with regard to all things, either created, such as forms and sensations, etc., or uncreated, inclusive of the Traditionist (concept of) space established as that absolute negation which is the mere absence of concrete impenetrability. (That is,) in establishing the existence of anything believed to be verified by validating cognition, (these philosophers) cannot do so if no (intrinsically objective) referent is discovered upon the investigation into the status of the object which is indicated by the

[9] See below.

[10] dPal-'byor Lhun-grub comments on the objects held in this pattern by the different schools: the Mahagirika (*sa-sgrog-ri-pa*) admits the "person" as all five aggregates; the Agamika as only consciousness (*vijñāna*); the Vatsiputriya as an inexpressible non-excluded middle; the Traditionists as *manovijñāna* and its *anubhava*; the Idealists, Vasubandhu, etc., as *ālayavijñāna*; Dignaga, etc., as *manovijñāna* and *svasaṃvitti*; Dogmaticists, Bhavya, etc., as *manovijñānasaṃtāna* (like *ālaya*).

expression of a particular name, and thus do establish existence (of something) when the opposite (that is, ultimate discovery of objective referent) holds true. Finally, the intrinsic identity (*svalakṣaṇa*) involved in (this sort of) intrinsically identifiable status is altogether quite different from the "ultimate particular" (*svalakṣaṇa*) explained precisely as "functional capacity" in the logicians' treatises, and from the "defining characteristic" (*svalakṣaṇa*) explained as that which characterizes (something as) different from everything else, such as heat in the case of fire, in the *Abhidharma Scripture*, etc.[11]

It is the method of Chandrapada not to accept even conventionally the presentation of such a sort of existence, his own method of presenting the conventional (being exemplified) in the *Lucid Exposition*:

> Moreover, this example is incorrect because the expressions "pestle" and "Rahu" do exist among mundane conventions, established without analysis, and do apply to their referents, body and head (respectively), just as the designations "person," etc., (exist conventionally and apply non-analytically to conventional entities, although ultimately there is no such thing as a referent of "person").[12]

This statement answers (the argument) that one can use the conventional expression "hardness is the intrinsic identity of earth," although there is no earth that is not hard, since designation and referent are conceptually appropriate, just as people employ the conventional expressions "body of a pestle" and "head of Rahu," although there is nothing more (to a pestle) than a body, and nothing more (to Rahu) than a head.

The (gist of) the answer is that it is correct, according to conventions

[11] For "ultimate particular," see Stcherbatski, *Buddhist Logic I*; and for defining characteristic, see de la Vallée Poussin, *L'Abhidarmakośa*, I, that is, *svalakṣaṇadharaṇād iti dharmaḥ* etc. This and the preceding paragraph form a key passage for the understanding of the meaning of "intrinsic identity" (*svalakṣaṇa*), as used throughout Tsong Khapa's investigation, and is indeed the passage which provides the basis of my translation.

[12] PPMMV, I, Tib. p. 53; Vaidya ed., pp. 22-23: *api ca pudgalaprajñaptivat śarīropādānasya śilaputrakasya upādātuḥ laukikavyavahārāṇgabhūtasya viśeṣaṇasya avicāraprasiddhasya sadbhāvāt / śiropādānasya ca rāhorupādātuḥ sadbhāvād, ayuktam etan nidarśanam //.*

T. Stcherbatski translates this passage in his *Nirvana* (p. 151), but his interpretation differs from Tsong Khapa's. He comments in a note that "a *cheda* is needed after *prajñaptivat*," which he supplies, and then takes the "like the designation person" phrase to be a separate argument by the "Buddhist Logician" whom he considers to be Chandrakirti's opponent here, rather than Bhavaviveka. This seeming difference may not prove too serious if we consider that Bhavaviveka is actually the "Logician" among Centrists. The serious drawback Tsong Khapa would find in the great Russian's interpretation is the way in which the latter forces on the text his preconceived notion that the "Prasangika (Dialecticist) rejects all logic, monistically." For Tsong Khapa here is precisely showing how Chandra is presenting the validity of Dialecticist "pragmatic" logic, while refuting the illogicality of Bhavya. We follow the Tibetan translation of *śilaputraka* as "pestle" (*mchi gu*), rather than "statue," as Stcherbatski has it.

of social communication, for a speaker to dispel the doubt of a listener with the expressions "pestle" and "Rahu," since the latter has formed the notions of "body" and "head" from hearing the corresponding words and is wondering, "whose body?" and "whose head?" Thus, the speaker wishes to eliminate the possibility of reference to any body other than that of the pestle, or to any head other than that of Rahu. However, this example does not correspond to the case of the expression "hardness is the intrinsic identity of earth," there being no earth which is not hard, and hence no need to dispel any such doubt.[13]

(Chandrapada) then goes on to give another reason for the inappropriateness of the example, explaining that the example of the two expressions is inapplicable to (a case of essential) non-difference (expressed verbally by different terms), since (in fact) the things "body" and "head" and the qualifications "pestle('s)" and "Rahu('s)" prove to be different in terms of mundane convention. (Of course, Chandrakirti is quite aware that) when one investigates the referents of (these) expressions, they are not found to be different things, since Rahu's head alone is called "Rahu," and since the referents of "pestle" and "body," when sought out, are not to be found apart. (Now) it is when (this point) is brought out as an argument (in favor of the applicability of the example that Chandrakirti is impelled to) state (most) succinctly (his position on the presentation of the conventional). Immediately following the above quotation (in the *Lucid Exposition*, (he states):

> If you propose that the example is indeed applicable since (pestle and Rahu) are proved to be nothing different from body and head, since only those (latter) can be apprehended, I say that is not so; for, in the usage of social conventions, such a sort of analysis is not employed (as that seeking essential identity, etc.), and further, the things of the world are (only) existent (insofar) as unexamined critically.[14]

Thus, the argument that, although just such an entity and identity exist for the listener, when the meaning of that conventional expression is examined, they are not established (even conventionally) as entity and

[13] The crux of the critique of Bhavya's attempted use of this analogy lies in the concept of "intrinsic identity," which Chandra finds out of place in the conventional reality. He could not object to the expression "hardness of earth," which would indeed be parallel to "head of Rahu," etc. But Bhavya's statement contains that extra part, that is, hardness = intrinsic identity, which is properly a philosophical statement, that is, belongs to the domain of rational cognition investigating the ultimate, and therefore cannot be established conventionally, where things can only be established without analysis, through the conventional acceptance of correlative terms. All of Chandra's arguments below eventually boil down to this main point, and confusion can be avoided by bearing this in mind.

[14] PPMMV, Tib. p. 53; Vaidya ed., p. 23: *śarīraśirovyatiriktasya arthāntarasya 'siddhas tanmātrasya upālambhāt siddham eva nidarśanam iti cet / naitadevaṃ / laukikavyavahāre itthaṃ vicārāpravṛtter avicārataśca laukikapadārthānāṃ astitvāt /.*

identity, since no "pestle" and "Rahu" are found apart from the body and the head—(that argument evinces) the method of presenting the (conventional) existence of things of other philosophers explained above.[15] And Chandrakirti answers them, saying that "existence" is a social convention, and, as it cannot be presented through such analysis, it is presented non-analytically.

The manner of this non-analytic presentation (is demonstrated) immediately after the preceding passage: "Although analytically, there is no self apart from forms, etc., from the social superficial point of view such (self) has its existence dependent on the aggregates. Thus, as 'Rahu' and 'pestle' are similar in this respect, your example is not established."[16]

"There is no self" means that there is no analytically discoverable ground on which to establish "Devadatta," since, when examining the expressions "Devadatta's body" and "Devadatta's mind" to find the basis of reference of "Devadatta" and the mode of existence of his body and mind, no Devadatta is discovered, either as merely his body and mind or as something apart from them. This means that "Devadatta" is not established by intrinsic identity and not that he does not exist at all, as he does exist superficially depending on his aggregates. This, he indicates, is the way to understand both examples.

As for the manner of establishing things (in general), he continues:

> Likewise, analytically it is obvious that there is no identified (referent) in such things as "earth" apart from such (identities) as "hardness," and there is no unsupported identity apart from the identified (referent)—thus, it is just superficial, and therefore the masters (Nagarjuna and Aryadeva) presented existence in terms of merely mutually dependent status.[17]

[15] That is, those who must analytically discover an identifiable objective entity or referent underlying a verbal identity or designation.

[16] PPMMV I; Vaidya ed., Skt. p. 23; *yathaiva hi rūpādivyatirekena vicāryamāṇa ātmā na saṃbhavati, api ca lokasaṃvrtya skandhānyupādāya asyāstitvaṃ, evaṃ rāhuśilaputrakayor apīti nāsti nidarśanasiddhiḥ* /. Following PPMMV quotes run continously from this passage.

This passage is quite straightforward if we bear in mind that the example "head of Rahu" etc. does not parallel the "intrinsic identity of earth," since that is not existent as a mundane conventional concept, but is quite parallel to any concept that is conventionally useful. This makes the ellipsis in *evaṃ rāhuśilaputrakayor api* quite unconfusing, and we avoid a mistake such as Stcherbatski's who takes it: "but your example does not mean that the same applies to the statue and to Rahu" (*Nirvana*, p. 152). Whereas, precisely because the same *does* apply to the examples, they do not parallel the essentially analytic expression "hardness is the intrinsic identity of earth."

[17] PPMMV, *evaṃ pṛthivyādīnāṃ yadyapi kāṭhiṇyādivyatiriktaṃ vicāryamāṇaṃ lakṣyaṃ nāsti / lakṣyavyatirekena ca lakṣaṇaṃ nirāśrayaṃ tathāpi saṃvṛttireveti parasparāpekṣayā tayoḥ siddhyā siddhiṃ vyavasthāpayaṃ babhūvur ācāryāḥ* /.

By "thus, it is just superficial," Chandrakirti means that, as mentioned above (n. 13),

That is to say, in presenting "earth" and "hardness" as referent and identity, it cannot be done by establishing them as the discovered object of the above-mentioned analytic quest of the designative bases of the conventional terms used for identified referent and identity, as such things can only be presented as existent in terms of their mutual relationship. He then continues to explain with (further) reasons the necessity to accept his method of presenting persons and things as the only sure one:

> This is necessarily to be accepted in precisely that way only; otherwise, the superficial would not be the superficial, and would either lack validity entirely or would become (ultimate) reality. (Further), not only such things as "pestles" become impossible when submitted to the logical analyses that will be demonstrated here, but even (the aggregates) such as "forms," "sensations," etc., have no existence. Thus (according to your understanding of the superficial) you would have to assent to their utter non-existence even superficially, just like the "pestle," etc. As such is not the case, this (mistaken procedure of presenting the superficial analytically) is out of the question.[18]

Having thus declared himself, Chandrakirti concludes by stating that one must consult the *Central Way Introduction* to learn the correct method of presenting the dependently designative (superficial reality).[19] This shows that when conventional existence is presented as something discovered analytically, it is so presented by logical processes that inquire into (questions of) ultimate status, and thus such a thing does not exist superficially, but exists ultimately. By so showing (it is clear that he equates) "intrinsically identifiable status" with "ultimate status."

Here one may object, "why should this be a distinctive feature of your (Dialecticist system), as the Dogmaticist Centrists also do not attribute conventional existence to things discovered by philosophical analysis? Do they not also refute the presentation of superficial things as things discovered by rational analysis, as for example in the *Two Realities*: 'Since it exists as it appears, analysis is not applicable: things are faulted by becoming other (than they appear to be) when subjected to analysis'?"[20]

"hardness of earth" is all right just as a superficial expression, like "head of Rahu," "Devadatta's body-mind," and so on, and where Bhavya has gone wrong is in adding the analytic, non-conventional concept of "intrinsic identity."

[18] PPMMV, *avaśyaṃ caitad evam abhyupeyaṃ / anyathā hi saṃvṛttir upapattyā na viyujyate, tad eva tattvam eva syāt, na saṃvṛttiḥ / na ca upapattyā vicāryamāṇānāṃ śilaputrakādīnām eva asaṃbhavaḥ / kim tarhi vakṣyamānaya yuktyā rūpavedanādīnām api nāsti saṃbhava iti teṣām api saṃvrtyā śilaputrakādivat nāstitvam astheyam syāt / na caited evam iti asad etat /.*

[19] See MA VI, k. 32 ff.

[20] SDV, TG, C, sa, k. 21, f. 2b4. (C has a variant *mang* for *snang*, but *Zin Bris* supports

This objection arises from a lack of discernment regarding the analytic methods of the two types of Centrists, by means of which they inquire into the question of ultimate status (in things). The Dialecticist accepts simply the above sort of analysis as analysis of (something's possession or lack of) ultimate status, as witnessed by the above quotations and their frequent explanations that existents are merely nominal, symbolic, and conventional. "Mere nominality" means, as aforementioned, the undiscoverability of anything through investigation into the meaning of conventional expressions, and does not mean that names exist and things do not, or that there is nothing which is not a name. (Finally,) although they do not accept everything proposed by the verbally ascriptive conventional intellect as conventionally existent, neither do they accept any conventionally existent things somehow not posited by conventionally ascriptive intellect.

The Dogmaticist Centrists (on the other hand) believe that forms and sensations, etc., cannot be presented (as conventionally existent) on the strength of conventionally ascriptive intellect, but can be so established on the strength of their appearance in undistorted sense cognition, etc. Therefore, there is a great difference (between the two systems) in regard to the type of cognition involved in the question of (something's) establishment "on the strength of cognition." Thus, they believe that the simple analysis of things, not as established on strength of such (undistorted, etc.) cognition, but as existent or non-existent on the strength of their intrinsically objective condition, serves as the analysis of the question of their ultimate status, and they do not accept the above (Dialecticist) analytical method alone (as resolving the question of ultimate status). Therefore (it is evident that) they accept intrinsically identifiable status (as) conventionally (existent). And consequently (the two systems) also differ as to what is excluded by the word "merely" in the scriptural statements such as "merely nominal" and "merely designative."[21]

We might suppose here, as the mundane person engages in a great deal of analysis—"Is it happening or not?" or "Is it produced or not?"—that it must be improper to reply to such inquiries, "It happens!" or "It is produced!"[22] However, this type of inquiry and the above analytic method

Tsong Khapa's reading, as does SDVV, f. 10a7). This objection would be the school of kLong-chen-pa again.

[21] That is, the Dialecticist believes that "merely" excludes the possibility of discovery of anything intrinsically established through the analysis of the meaning of any sort of expression, either conventionally or ultimately, and the Dogmaticist believes that the "merely" excludes ultimate status of relative things, not excluding conventional intrinsically identifiable status.

[22] That is, since the philosophical analysis described above does not discover any coming or going or production when seeking the meaning of the corresponding expressions, and we might be thinking that philosophical analysis and ordinary inquiry were essentially the same processes.

are utterly different. The mundane person is not inquiring into coming and going through analysis into the meaning of the use of the conventional expressions "comer," "goer," "coming," and "going" out of dissatisfaction with (the fact that they are) merely conventional usages. He is rather making an unreflective[23] inquiry into the unreflective usage of the expressions "coming" and "going." Therefore, how can there be any contradiction between accepting such investigations (as proper to common parlance and the acceptance of the undiscoverability of the meaning of conventional expressions through philosophical analysis)?

Such holding to intrinsically identifiable real existence arrived at through analysis of the meaning of conventional expressions is not the habit-pattern of unconscious self-habits.[24] Yet it is that (unconscious self-habit) which binds living beings in the life-cycle, and thus it is that very (habit-pattern) which philosophical reasoning must principally refute. What is the habit-pattern (of unconscious self-habits)?

(Unconscious self-habits) hold to the existence of things internal and external as if they existed in their own right, not merely established on the strength of convention. When such (self-habits) hold persons such as "Yajña" in that way, they are (called) "personal self-habits," and when they hold things such as "eye" and "ear" in that way, they are called "objective self-habits." By this fact, the two selves also can be understood (as not intrinsically different but different with reference to the objects involved).[25]

Although this mental habit does not hold (objects in this way) after analysis of the meaning of expressions, if the objects thus held (as objectively real) were to exist in fact, they would have to be discoverable by the analytic cognition that analyzes the manner of existence of the referents of conventional expressions. Therefore, since there is no contradiction between the fact that non-analytic, unconscious self-habits with their objects are the principal rational negatees and the fact that the treatises contain only analytic negations (on the theoretical plane), one (should) not adhere to the notion that "the texts merely negate intellectual mental habits with their objects."[26]

Although persons whose intelligence is unformed by theories and living

[23] Tib. *rang dga ba*.

[24] From the beginning of this section, the theoretical or intellectual self-habit has been under discussion, and now Tsong Khapa turns to the description of the instinctual or unconscious self-habits, although the two sections are not separated.

[25] This most important definition fails to dawn in full import if we are not clear what is meant by "hold" (*'dzin pa*, *graha*) here. It is not the holding of an intellectual stance or opinion, but is rather the actual mode of perception.

[26] Although delivered with a light touch, this point has the greatest importance in understanding the role of philosophical study in Buddhism.

beings bereft of symbolic awareness would not be able to verbalize "existence of objects (in their own right) not established on strength of conventionally verbalizing intellect," still the meaning (as present in their perceptions) exists for them. If this were not the case, then even the meaning of the holding of (the two types of) self would cease to exist (for these beings), (if it is argued that such mental habits could not exist in beings who could not verbalize them).[27]

Although the Experientialists and the Dogmaticists assert that the two selves, which, as negated in persons and things, underlie the two selflessnesses—along with the ways they are conceptualized—are quite different objects, this system distinguishes selflessnesses with respect to their bases of reference, but does not assert a difference in "selves" that are actually non-existent.[28]

In the *Central Way Introduction*, in the following: "This selflessness was proclaimed to be of two types, on account of the division between persons and things, in order to liberate living beings . . . "[29] (Chandrakirti) states the distinction (as made) according to the distinction between persons and things and does not state it as made from the point of view of (any sort of) two selves. Furthermore, in the *Four Hundred Commentary*, he explains: "As for 'self,' it is a reality or substance of things that does not relate to anything else. As it does not exist, there is selflessness. That again is understood as twofold because of the distinction between persons and things; namely, personal selflessness and objective selflessness."[30] Here, an "unrelated reality" is an independent reality, which would be existence with the mode of being of an objective entity, not merely as a nominal designation.

Here one might suppose that if (we maintain that) all Buddhist schools from Analysts to Dogmaticists believe things admittedly established by

[27] This argument anticipates a common objection against the validity of philosophical inquiry in the Buddhist enterprise, namely, that theoretical analysis cannot affect unconscious mental patterns which exist even in beings who have no access to theoretical concerns. Tsong Khapa in effect retorts that then beings ignorant of philosophy would be enlightened—not knowing the word "egoism," they would not be egoistic through self-habits.

[28] dPal-'byor Lhun-grub comments (SERA II, f. 14b4) that both Experientialists and Dogmaticists define "subtle personal selflessness" as realization of voidness of a substantial, self-sufficient person. Experientialists define "subtle objective selflessness" as realization of non-existence of external objects coupled with the non-existence by intrinsic identity of things as referents of their names. Dogmaticists define "subtle objective selflessness" as realization of things' non-existence in their own right. Dialecticists, however, define both types as realization of persons' and things' lack of intrinsic identity. See schema of various selflessnesses in the Introduction, Table D.

[29] MA VI, k. 179ab, Poussin ed., p. 301: *bdag med 'di ni 'gro ba rnam dgrol phyir / chos dang gang zag dbye bas rnam gnyis gsungs /.*

[30] CŚT, TG, C, ya, 29a6 ff. XII, ad. k. 13. (Bhattacarya ed. [Calcutta: Visvabharati Books, 1931], p. 151): *tatrātmā nāma yo 'parāyattasvarūpaḥ svabhāvaḥ / (tadabhāve nairātmyaṃ/) tacca dharmapudgalabhedāddvaitaṃ pratipadyate / dharmanairātmyaṃ pudgalanairātmyaṃ ceti /.*

validating cognition to have intrinsically identifiable status,[31] then we contradict (our) previous explanation of the Experientialists' rejection of intrinsic identity and postulation of verbal and conventional status in regard to the admitted existence of the imagined (nature of reality), as constituted by ascriptive and descriptive designation.[32] (However,) we are not liable to this fault, for, granted that they do state that what can be established by ascriptive and descriptive designation is "not established by its intrinsic identity," they do not admit (such non-establishment as equivalent to) the quest and non-discovery of a designative base to which (something's) name is assigned.[33] Therefore they do hold to intrinsically identifiable status as explained in this (Dialecticist system). Although their treatises explain the ascriptively and descriptively designated as "merely verbal," they interpret "mere verbal designation" as (meaning) that there is no real object as apparent to the perception of the dualistic cognition of disparate subject and object. This differs from the (meaning of) "mere verbal designation" in this system.

b. Meaning of Statement of Twofold Selflessness, Even in the Individual Vehicle

The Experientialists and the Dogmaticists believe that the Individual Vehicle Canon does not teach objective selflessness, but teaches only personal selflessness, which (latter) therefore needs no further explanation in the Universal Vehicle, having been determined in the Individual Vehicle. However, the system of the two masters[34] rejects both of these ideas.

First, in regard to the way in which the Individual Vehicle Canon teaches objective selflessness, Buddhapalita states:

> As examples of the selflessness of created things, the Lord used "illusion," "echo," "reflection," "hallucination," "dream," "ball of foam," "bubble," and "plantain trunk." He also stated things to have no actuality, no reliable reality, but to be mental fabrications and false. When he stated "all things are selfless," he meant they were without reality, the word "self" meaning "intrinsic reality."[35]

He explains that since the Individual Vehicle Canon contains the use of the metaphors "foam," "bubble," "reed," "hallucination," and "il-

[31] As explained at the beginning of this section.

[32] Above, Chapter II.

[33] Indeed, the Experientialists could not admit this, or they would violate their own understanding of the three natures, wherein the relative (*paratantra*) is precisely the designative base of the imagined, and could not be discovered. See Ch. I n. 16.

[34] Tib. *slob dpon gnyis*, that is, in this case, Buddhapalita and Chandrakirti.

[35] BMMV VII, TG, C, tsa, f. 193b6-8.

lusion," for the five aggregates, respectively, and also the statements "all these are false," and "all things are selfless," it does teach the unreality of all things, "self" meaning "intrinsic reality."

(Chandrakirti) states, in the *Introduction Commentary*, that the Individual Vehicle teaches objective selflessness, and he cites quotations from Individual Vehicle Scriptures such as "form is like a ball of foam."[36] He explains, in the *Philosophical Sixty Commentary*, that (Nagarjuna) does not give the reasonings to reject nihilism, as these are explicit in the Individual Vehicle, but does give the reasonings to reject absolutism, because, although (the Individual Vehicle contains) statements such as "there is only one holy truth, and that is Nirvana, whose nature is non-deceptive," these statements are not frequent, uninterrupted, and set forth in a continuous exposition.[37]

In this context, Bhavaviveka rejects (Buddhapalita's interpretation), saying that "these examples demonstrate that the apparent personal self does not exist, and hence teach personal selflessness, not objective selflessness. The meaning of the word 'self' is not the 'intrinsic reality of things,' but is the 'self of a person.' If the Individual Vehicle taught objective selflessness, the Universal Vehicle would be pointless."[38]

(In response, Chandrakirti in the *Introduction Commentary*) supports (Buddhapalita), giving evidence from the *Jewel Garland*, and declaring that "(Buddha) teaches not only objective selflessness in the Universal Vehicle, but also the stages, the transcendences, the vows, and the two stores, etc., and therefore (the Universal Vehicle) is not pointless."[39]

Chandrakirti further proves that such is the position of the Master (Nagarjuna), quoting the *Wisdom*:

> The Lord knew things and their non-existence,
> Hence, in the *Advice to Katyayana*,
> He accomplished the negation
> Of both existence and non-existence.[40]
>
> The Lord declared as "falsehood"
> Everything that is deceptive.
> All created things are deceptive,
> Therefore, they are false.[41]

[36] MABh, Poussin ed., p. 19, ls. 17-23, l. 15.

[37] YṢV, TG, C, ya, f. 4b3, Tsong Khapa's paraphrase of: *de bas na pha rol dag la gsal bai phyir de yang rigs pa mi bshad do // yod pa bzlog pa ni dge slong dag 'di lta ste / mi slu bai chos can mya ngan las 'das pa 'di ni bden pai mchog gcig puo /.*

[38] PrPr, TG, C, tsha, f. 113a6-b4. (Ch. VII)

[39] MABh VI, Poussin ed., p. 20.

[40] MMK, 15. 7: *kātyāyanāvavāde cāstīti nāstīti cobhayaṃ / pratiṣiddhaṃ bhagavatā bhāvābhāvavibhāvinā //.*

[41] MMK, 13.1: *tanmṛṣā moṣadharma yad bhagavānityabhāṣata / sarve ca moṣadharmāṇaḥ saṃskārās tena te mṛṣā //.*

He also quotes the *Philosophical Sixty*:

> When the Victors declare
> That Nirvana is the sole truth,
> What intelligent person would then presume
> That other things were not rejected?[42]

Thus as (Chandrakirti) proves definitively from the *Wisdom* that the meaning of "falsehood" is "unreality which is emptiness with respect to intrinsic reality," and faults any other interpretation, it must definitely be accepted that the thought of the holy (masters) is that even the Individual Vehicle Canon expounds objective selflessness. Nevertheless, this does not (seek to) establish that there are no statements in the Individual Vehicle Canon to the effect that "there is a reality in things which is established by intrinsic identity," as such statements do occur there frequently.

In regard to personal selflessness (generally), according to all Individual Vehicle and Universal Vehicle philosophers, it is postulated as merely the non-existence of a substantial, self-sufficient person, distinct in nature from the aggregates. As for the pattern (of belief in such a person), the self that is the basis of the notion "I" is held to resemble the master of the aggregates and the aggregates are held to resemble its servants, since the "I" is held to control them, and they to belong to it, as expressed in such notions as "my forms" and "my sensations."[43]

Thus, when (such a self) appears self-sufficient and distinct in nature from the aggregates, like master and slaves, and it is assumed to exist in reality, then that is the habitual adherence to its substantial existence. When that (type of self) is negated, the person (is admitted by these philosophers) as a "mere designation" upon the aggregates, the (word) "mere" ruling out the existence of the self as something other than the aggregates.

In regard to the method of designation, Bhavaviveka in the *Blaze of Argument* states that "thus, conventionally we designate consciousness with the word 'self' because (thereby) the conglomerate of body and faculties is designated according to the scriptural statement, 'Conscious-

[42] YṢ, k. 36: TG, C, tsa, f. 20b5.

[43] There is a great variety of opinion about the exact relation of the conventional "I" and the aggregates. The Tibetan Dialecticists differ among themselves, although 'Jam-dbyangs Bzhed-pa's famous dicta, that "the 'I' and the aggregates are intermixed like water poured into water"; and "the 'I' and the aggregates are the same entity, but conceptually different (*ngo bo gcig dang ldog pa tha dad*)" are well accepted. More controversial is the proposition that the "I" is a component of the fourth, the "creation" (*saṃskāra*) aggregate. While this would hold insofar as "I" is a syllable and a word, hence a member of *vyañjana-*, *nāma-*, and *pada- kāyā-saṃskāras*, the conventional "I" as ego may not be part of any aggregate, or it could not designate them with proper binarity. But this is an extremely subtle question.

ness is the self, because it takes rebirth.' " Thus, he cites the scriptural statement that the aggregates are designated as a "living being," just as an assembly of pieces is designated a "chariot." He continues to make his case, with statements from certain scriptures in which the mind is called the "self," such as "If the mind is controlled, happiness will be attained," and "When the self is controlled, heaven will be obtained," and with reasonings such as "the self appropriates the aggregates, and consciousness takes rebirth; therefore consciousness is established as the self."[44]

This master does not assert any fundamental consciousness, hence (for him) the consciousness that appropriates the body is the mental consciousness, and other (philosophers) who do not admit a fundamental consciousness are in agreement. Those who assert a fundamental consciousness assert its actual continuum as the person. As for the scriptural references that these (philosophers use to support) their assertions about the personal self, they are too numerous to mention.

According to Chandrakirti's system, although (these philosophers) do negate the substantial existence of such a (self-sufficient) person, they do not (thereby) negate the intrinsically identifiable status of the person, and thus do not (accept it) as merely a conventional designation. Hence, since their holding to its (intrinsically identifiable) existence is tantamount to adhering to the person as true, it is (still) the personal self-habit, just as (holding things as true) is the objective self-habit.

Above all, he explains that the direct realization and subsequent meditation upon the non-existence of that self-sufficient, substantial self, which is (also) the very object the heterodox hold as the real, internal agent, a "soul" construed as different from the aggregates, do not reduce in the slightest the habitual reality-notion (explained) above in regard to forms, etc. Thus (such meditations do) not apply to the elimination of addictions such as desire which arise from the notion of the reality of the aggregates.

Thus, he states, in the *Central Way Introduction*:

> When you understand selflessness through your yoga (method,)
> You do not realize the (ultimate) reality of forms, etc.
> Greed, therefore, initiated on perception of form,
> Will (still) arise, since you have not realized the (ultimate) nature of those (objects).[45]

and in the *Philosophical Sixty Commentary*:

[44] TJ, III, TG, C, dza, f. 80b2-3.
[45] MA VI, v. 131, Poussin ed., p. 253.

> It is completely impossible to eliminate addictions for those who, although they want to do so, still perceive an intrinsic reality in forms, etc. To show this, (Nagarjuna) declared: "What could stop the great poison of addictions in those whose minds have the place? Even when they are in (an indifferent) state, they will be seized by the snake of addictions."[46]

Here, "place" means the object which gives rise to truth-habits, (namely), a (supposed) intrinsically identifiable status (in things).

As for (the previous) method of others to present the person as designatively existent, it is not (corroborated by) the meaning of this statement in the Individual Vehicle Canon: "Just as 'chariot' designates the assembly of its parts, so superficially 'living beings' designates the aggregates"; because (if they did accept this meaning, they would know that) just as the "chariot" ascribed to the parts cannot properly be a part, so the "person" designated as ascribed to the aggregates cannot properly be an aggregate.[47]

It might be supposed, nevertheless, that since "chariot" is ascribed to the assemblage of the parts, the chariot thus being precisely the assemblage itself, it is (the same) also with the aggregates (and the "person"). (However,) the very fact that something is an ascriptive designation necessarily rules it out as being (itself) the referent designated, just as (events) caused by the elements are designated as "blue" and "eye," etc. (yet those elements and events are not merely the words "blue" and "eye," etc.). And, as such (designations) as "pot" are similar (in this respect) to the "self," there need be no uncertainty in regard to them (either).

(Chandrakirti) states this point in the *Introduction*: "The scripture states that it is ascribed to the aggregates; therefore, the 'self' is not the mere conglomerate of the parts."[48]

Again, it might be supposed, from the scriptural statement, "When the ascetics and priests think 'the self,' they are looking only at these five aggregates," that these (five aggregates) are the self, as they are mentioned there as the object of the view of self. However, (such statements) do not teach the aggregates as being the object of the view of self by way of positive proof, but rather the word "only" refutes the existence of any

[46] YṢV, ad. k. 52.

[47] This quote is used by Bhavaviveka in the passage quoted above, (see n. 44), to corroborate his contention that the "self" is conventionally accepted as consciousness. Tsong Khapa here refutes his use of this quotation in such a way, as the fact that "self" designates the aggregates means that it cannot be, even conventionally, one of the aggregates, such as consciousness (that is, *vijñāna skandha*).

[48] MA VI, k. 135, Poussin ed., p. 258.

object of the view of self other than the aggregates. This is confirmed in other scriptures, where statements such as "form is not the self" refute the possibility of each one of the aggregates being the self. As (Chandrakirti) expresses it in the *Introduction*:

> If the aggregates are admitted as self because of statements
> By the Teacher—"The aggregates are the self!"
> (It is a mistake).
> He (merely) negates the self as other than the aggregates,
> As proven by other scriptural statements—
> "Form is not self," etc.[49]

This statement also gives insight into the verbal meaning of the expression "futile view."[50]

These (reasonings above) acknowledge the conventional existence of the objective object (the mere "I") of unconscious "I"-habits, which have two kinds of objects, objective and aspective. The aspective object is the intrinsically identifiable status of the self, as held in the thought "That self exists by its intrinsic reality," and does not in fact exist, even conventionally. (Similarly,) the (objective) object of unconscious futile views, which are (forms of) possessiveness, is (the designation) "mine." And the aspective (object) is held to be the intrinsically identifiable status of "mine."[51]

Here the objection may be raised that if the aggregates are not properly the object of unconscious self-habits, the scriptural negations (such as) "forms etc. are not the self" are inappropriate, because those (aggregates mentioned) are not properly the object or basis of the unconscious futile views which hold (those aggregates) as the self.

This criticism does not apply, since both the mental habits holding self and aggregates as the same and the mental habits holding self and aggregates as different are intellectual mental habits and not unconscious (mental habits). Yet still, if there were (an object) as supposed by the unconscious futile views, it would not exist in any other way than as either the same or different (from the aggregates), and therefore negating (those possibilities) through such analysis would still be appropriate.

The foregoing has demonstrated that scriptural authority supports (this

[49] MA VI, k. 132, Poussin ed., pp. 254-55.

[50] "Futile views" or "views toward a destructible assembly (lit. after Tib. *'jig tshogs la lta ba*)," therefore mean views that regard the aggregates as intrinsically existent, and hence are "futile," as the aggregates are constantly fluctuating, only superficially existent phenomena.

[51] Tib. *dmigs pai yul* (*ālaṃbanaviṣaya*) and *rnam pai yul (ākāraviṣaya*). SERA identifies the latter with *zhen yul* (*abhiniveśya*); from this clue we can conclude that the former indicates the object as presented unconsciously in perception, and the latter concerns the automatic influence of conceptual orientation.

position) and does not fault it. (To give proof by) reasoning, it is not reasonable for the consciousness or any other aggregate to be the self, since the aggregates are appropriated by the self, and the self is the appropriator of the aggregates; otherwise, agent and action would become the same.

This very (argument) is the intention of the holy (masters), as witnessed by the statements from the *Wisdom*: "if firewood were the fire, then agent and action would be the same";[52] and "by (the example of) wood and fire, all processes of the self and appropriation, together with (notions) such as 'pots' and 'wool,' are completely explained."[53]

Furthermore, (Nagarjuna) states, in the *Wisdom*: "Appropriation should be understood as similar. . . ."[54] Just as action and agent exist in designative dependence on each other and have no intrinsically real status, so should the appropriated and the appropriator be represented.

(For example,) one can easily employ the expression "Yajña sees" based on (his) eye's seeing of forms, and one can easily employ the expression "his eye sees forms" based on Yajña's looking at forms, and yet this will not be contradicted by the facts that (in the first case) the eye that sees the forms is not Yajña, and (in the second case) that the Yajña who looks at forms is not an eye. Likewise, while it is admitted that one can use conventional expressions such as either "I was sick and am cured" or even "my eye was sick and is cured" when one's eye is sick and is cured, nevertheless, social conventions do not establish the actual eye itself as both the self and the property of the self. By this example, one should understand the remainder of the experiential media,[55] internal and external, in relation to the self; that is, depending on one of them the other is represented as "hearer" (of sound), etc.

Now the heterodox (scholars), perceiving that it is inappropriate to posit such things as eye, etc., as the person, posit a "person" who is a seer, etc., and is substantially different from those (things such as eye). And other orthodox Buddhist scholars, perceiving the flaws in (the postulate of) substantial difference, posit consciousness or some other function of the aggregates as the person. (But) those who understand the teachings of the Victor as being unmistaken are liberated by the realization that there is no reality (in things) other than that which is merely designated conventionally. This is declared in the *Introduction Com-*

[52] MMK X, 1 (ab): *yadīndhanaṃ sa ced agnir ekatvaṃ kartṛkarmaṇoḥ* /.

[53] MMK X, 15: *agnīndhanābhyāṃ vyākhyāta ātmopādanayoḥ kramaḥ / sarvo niravaśeṣeṇa sārdhaṃ ghaṭapaṭādibhiḥ* //.

[54] *MMK VIII, 13: evaṃ vidyād upādānam . . . vibhāvayet* //. Tsong Khapa's explanation follows PPMMY, Vaidya ed., p. 80, 1s. 3-9, closely.

[55] Tib. *skye mched*. Skt. *āyatana*; the other ten being sound, ear, etc.

mentary.[56] (A caution here is that) one must know how to represent properly the accumulation of evolutionary action and the experience of effects in the light of the fact of the mere designativeness (of things).

Therefore, since (Chandrakirti), according to his determination in the *Introduction* and its *Commentary* of the intended meaning of scriptural statements such as "just as 'chariot' designates, etc.," understands personal selflessness as the lack of intrinsic reality (of person), tantamount to the undiscoverability of the referent of the conventional expression "person," having sought it in seven ways, his explanation is utterly distinctive from others. And the substance of the intention of the *Buddhapalita Commentary* is the same.

2. ON THAT BASIS, THE DISTINCTIVENESS OF THEIR METHOD TO ELUCIDATE THE HOLY INTENTION

A. Distinctiveness in (Interpretation of) Realization of Selflessness, the Gross and Subtle Self-habits, etc.

The unexcelled distinction of Buddhapalita and Chandrakirti's elucidations of the intention of the Holy Father and Son, setting them apart from other elucidations, is their representation of the two realities, wherein all the structures of the life-cycle and of Nirvana are perfectly viable. (Thus, they) establish the existence (of things) on the strength of convention, (those things) having no reality not established on the strength of convention. (And this reconciles the facts that) investigation of the referents of conventional expressions for "persons" and "things" discovers nothing at all either the same or different, etc., and yet conventional expressions such as "Yajña" and "eye" are definitely to be employed.

(The fact that) "conventional existence" and "conventional production," etc. mean (that the existent is) established as such on the strength of convention (is corroborated in the following) statements, first from the *Dharma Digest*:

> Worthy son! Being in the world consists of habitual adherence to (the notions of) production and cessation, and thus the Tathagata, with his great compassion, in order to avoid generating terror in people, declares that "(things) are produced and ceased" on the strength of conventions. However, worthy son, here, nothing at all is produced . . . [57]

[56] MABh VI, Poussin ed., p. 254 ff.
[57] *Āryadharmasaṃgītimahāyānasūtra*, quoted MABh, Poussin ed., p. 258.

and from the *Emptiness Seventy*:

> The Buddhas declare (that things) "are," "are produced," "are destroyed," "exist," "do not exist," "are inferior," "mediocre," or "superior," on the strength of social conventions, and not on the strength of reality.[58]

Furthermore, the *Mother Scripture*, etc., state that "(things) exist as mundane conventions."[59] Therefore, the Centrist must represent (existence) as conventional. However, although mundane convention does employ formulations such as "the sprout is produced from the seed," they are employed only without investigation into the referent of the conventional expressions through analysis as to whether it is produced from itself or from something else, etc. (This is) because the holy masters explained (conventional expressions) in just that way. It is also because the ascription of "person" to something substantially different from the aggregates and so on is definitely inappropriate as the meaning of non-analytic mundane conventional expressions, this system's presentation of that meaning being apparent from the above explanation of (its) interpretation of "person." For, in the world, the self and its possessions are represented as master and slaves.

It being thus necessary to understand in accordance with this explanation that such is the rule of the ultimate existence and non-existence of persons and things, and that (hence) also such is the (rule of) twofold selflessness, there is no way to arrive at the realization of personal selflessness while still asserting philosophically the existence of an objective self. (This is supported in) the *Introduction Commentary* where it is said that without destroying the mental habit of an objective self, personal selflessness is not realized.[60]

This is the superior position of the holy masters. In the *Philosophical Sixty*, in saying: "There is no liberation through 'existence,' nor will 'non-existence' take one beyond this world—the Great Ones are delivered by thorough knowledge of both reality and unreality,"[61] (Nagarjuna) states that there is no liberation as long as both absolutism, which holds things as having intrinsically identifiable existence, and nihilism, which sees cause and effect as impossible, are not destroyed, and that there is liberation when the actuality of reality and unreality is known, free from the two extremes. "Liberation" here is not properly interpreted as mean-

[58] *Śūnyatāsaptatī* (ŚS) k.1.

[59] *The Transcendent Wisdom Hundred Thousand* contains such formulations in many passages.

[60] MABh, I, Poussin ed., p. 19 ff.

[61] YṢ, k. 5.

ing (liberation) from objective obscurations, as (Chandrakirti's commentary) specifies (it to be liberation) from this cyclic existence (that is, from addictive obscurations).

Similarly, (Nagarjuna) saying in the *Jewel Garland*: "thus, it is delusory to hold this miragelike world to 'exist' or 'not to exist'; and the deluded are not liberated. The absolutist goes to heaven, the nihilist to bad migrations. But one who does not rely on duality, knowing reality accurately, does become free,"[62] declares that the avoidance of the two extremes of being and nothingness is necessary for liberation from cyclic life.

Thus, when teaching objective selflessness as the negation of subject-object substantial dichotomy, the Universal Vehicle teaches a gross and a subtle (form of that) objective selflessness, the (first) failing to negate intrinsic reality in the (remaining) cognition devoid of duality, and (the latter) negating intrinsic reality in that (cognition) as well. And just as we take only the latter as definitive in meaning, so, with the Disciple Canon's teaching of both a gross and a subtle personal selflessness, we should accept the subtle selflessness as definitive in meaning, since the reasons are the same in all respects.[63]

This being the case, the (Dialecticist) method of equating the self-habits with the two obscurations[64] is also different. Whereas the other Centrists understand objective self-habits as objective obscurations, this system takes them to be addictive (obscurations). Thus Buddhapalita[65] (explained) how (Nagarjuna) wrote the *Wisdom*, having seen the danger for living beings in the variety of sufferings, to teach them the true reality of things in order to liberate them. He further explained how, although "reality" means "lack of intrinsic reality," the eye of intelligence (of living beings) is obscured by the darkness of delusion, and they think there is an intrinsic reality in things, whereby their attraction and aversion (for these things) arises. (Finally, he explained) how the illumination through the knowledge of relativity clears up the darkness of delusion, the intrinsic unreality of things is seen, and attraction and aversion do not arise, thus

[62] RA, I, 56-57: *marīcipratimaṃlokamevamastīti gṛhṇataḥ / nāstīti cāpi moho 'yam sati mohe na mucyate // nāstiko durgatiṃ yāti sugatiṃ yāti cāstikaḥ / yathābhūtaparijñānān-mokṣhamadvayaniśritaḥ //.*

[63] That is, just as the Dogmaticists consider the Idealist understanding of the statements of lack of subject-object dichotomy as not requiring negation of intrinsic reality of pure consciousness itself to be only a crude understanding of objective selflessness, with the subtle one going one step further and realizing the negation of that reality in consciousness as well, they should acknowledge the same possibility in the Individual Vehicle of coming to a more subtle understanding of the deeper aspect of personal selflessness, although it is not emphasized in the teachings.

[64] Tib. *sgrib gnyis* (*kleśāvaraṇa* and *jñeyāvaraṇa*).

[65] BMMV, I, TG, C, tsa, f. 155b2-156a1 (paraphrased by Tsong Khapa).

deprived of any ground. To corroborate (his statement) he cites (Aryadeva's) *Four Hundred*: "The seed of existence is consciousness, and objects are its sphere of activity. When the objects are seen to be selfless, the seed of existence is stopped."[66]

Thus, "delusion," grouped with desire and hatred (as one of the three major addictions), is explained as consisting of truth-habits about things and as the seed of existence, and it is further stated that its abandonment requires the realization of selflessness, which itself is the realization of the intrinsic unreality of things. Therefore, (Buddhapalita) believes the actual holding to the truth of personal and objective things to be addictive misknowledge.

(Chandrakirti also) clearly explains the holding of things as truth to be addictive misknowledge, the first of the twelve links (of dependent origination), in his *Four Hundred Commentary*: "Consciousness, attached to things under the influence of addictive misknowledge which causes excessive reification of intrinsic reality in things, is the seed of the cyclic process. And, when it entirely ceases, it is established that the life-cycle ceases";[67] and in his *Introduction Commentary*:

> Misknowledge, whose nature is the obscuration of the understanding of the real nature (of things) and the reification (of reality) in things without intrinsic reality, is utterly false. . . . Thus, the superficial truth is established under the influence of the addictive misknowledge included among the (twelve) factors of existence.[68]

Both personal and objective self-habits are present in this unconscious misknowledge, and hence the personal self-habit also is addictive misknowledge. For this reason, there is no contradiction involved in the fact that sometimes misknowledge, and sometimes unconscious futile views, are said to be the root of cyclic existence. Now the objective of such unconscious self-habits is the basis of the "I"-habit, hence the mental habit holding other persons to have intrinsically identifiable status is not (among) the futile views, although it is a personal self-habit.

This interpretation is the superior position of the Holy Father and Son, as (Nagarjuna), saying in the *Emptiness Seventy*: "The Teacher proclaimed that misknowledge is the consideration that things arisen from causes and conditions are real, and from that the twelve factors arise,"[69] declares further that terminating misknowledge with the realization of

[66] CŚ, XIV, k. 25 (Bhattacarya ed., p. 230) (restored as follows): *bījaṃ bhavasya vijñānaṃ viṣayāstasya gocaraḥ / dṛṣte viṣaya-nairātmye bhavabījaṃ nirudhyate //.*

[67] CŚT, XIV, ad. k. 25 (Bhattacarya ed., p. 230).

[68] MABh, VI, ad. k. 28, p. 107 ls. 5-8; 17-19.

[69] ŚS, k. 61.

things' emptiness of intrinsic reality terminates all twelve factors (of dependent origination).

(Aryadeva also) states that the realization of relativity is necessary for the termination of the misknowledge included in the three poisons, as in the *Four Hundred*: "Delusion gets into everything, just as the physical sense (pervades) in the body; hence by conquering delusion, all addictions are also conquered. When relativity is realized (in things), delusion does not arise; hence all our efforts herein are only to explain that message."[70] The meaning of "relativity" is repeatedly stated in this system to be "emptiness of intrinsic reality."

Therefore, all the reasonings of the central way are factors of the eradication of the habit-pattern of misknowledge, the root of the life-cycle. Hence, having identified how our own unconscious misknowledge maintains its hold, we should strive to terminate it, and should not amuse ourselves with expertise in mere hair-splitting with other philosophers!

One might well wonder, if indeed unconscious personal self-habits and unconscious objective self-habits are without difference in habit-pattern, what about all those explanations of the Dogmaticists?

The notion of the existence of a self-sufficient, substantial person, distinct in nature from the aggregates, holds the person to be substantially different from such things as feet and hands, etc., and hence is not present in those whose minds are uninfluenced by theories. (Chandrakirti) states this in the *Central Way Introduction*: "When an ordinary man plants a mere seed, he says, 'I made this son!' or 'I have planted a tree!'; hence there is no production from other (things) even in social conventions."[71]

And Buddhapalita also states: "(The ordinary person) when he plants a seed of a tree and it grows, points to the tree and employs the expression 'I planted this tree!' "

Hence he does not hold the (seed and the tree) to be substantially different. If the contrary were true, that is, if it were conventionally ordinary to think of substantially different things producing each other), the absurd consequence would be that when a (juniper) tree grows, one could employ the expression "I planted a myrobalan tree!"[72]

If we apply this reasoning, we must say (with Chandrakirti in the *Introduction*): "When an ordinary person hurts his hand, he says and thinks 'I am hurt!'; hence there is no substantial difference between the two in (the conventions of) the world."[73]

Such things as these are not only expressed by ordinary people, but

[70] CŚ, VI, ks. 10-11 (TG, C, tsha, f. 7b2-3).
[71] MA, VI, k. 32, p. 114.
[72] BMMV, I, TG, C, tsa, f. 157b2-3(Ch. I).
[73] The location of this quotation has not been found.

are also accepted necessarily in such a manner. If we could not establish that the tree is planted and the person is hurt because of (the apparently objective) fact that the planted seed is not a tree and the hurt hand is not a person, then such (expressions and considerations) would be impossible, and the whole (conventional) order would be demolished. The essence of these (above) reasonings dictates that we interpret as intellectual the objective self-habits explained as unconscious by the Dogmaticist philosophers.[74]

Such being the case, one wonders what to do with objective obscurations. There is no clearer identification (of objective obscurations) in the indisputable treatises of the Father and Son or in the whole Dialecticist literature than (the following) identification (of Chandrakirti's) in the *Introduction Commentary*:

> The instinct for misknowledge is the hindrance to complete comprehension of knowable things. It also exists as the instinct for desire, etc., and is the cause of corresponding functions of body and speech. Further, that instinctual propensity for misknowledge, desire, etc., is only eliminated in (attainment of) Buddhahood or omniscience, and not in any other (persons or stages).[75]

"Such functions of body and speech" belong to the saints, who exhibit the unfortunate propensities of body and speech called "jumping monkeylike" and "contemptuous toward others," which propensities have been eliminated by the Teacher, yet are not eliminated by them.[76] "Also" points out that the instinct for desire, etc., is also a hindrance to the full comprehension of knowables. Hence, the instincts of all addictions constitute the objective obscurations, and all factors of the error of dualism, their effect, are included within those (objective obscurations).

(Chandrakirti defines) "instinct" itself as "that which defiles, infects, and goes along with the mental process, its synonyms being 'lower limit of addictions,' 'habituation,' and 'root.' "[77]

Although there is no other way to abandon these objective obscurations than the above-explained path of realizing the ultimate reality, the dif-

[74] That is, objective self-habits as truth-habits specially defined as holding things to have objective status intrinsically, not just presented as apparent in undistorted sense-cognition.

[75] MABh, XI, ad. k. 31, Poussin ed., p. 393, l. 17-394, l. 3.

[76] Tib. misprint *rmangs mo* for *dmans mo*. Chandrakirti mentions these two types of instinctive propensities that still afflict Arhats and not Buddhas: the physical propensity to walk in an ungainly manner, jumping along, as if one had been a monkey in a previous life, and the verbal propensity to speak to others in a condescending and contemptuous way, as if one had been a brahmin priest accustomed to speaking to low-caste women. MABh, Poussin ed., p. 393: . . . *sngon spreur gyur pa mchongs shing mchongs shing 'gro ba dang sngon bram zer gyur pai dmangs mor brjod pai kun tu spyod pa*. . . .

[77] MABh, Poussin ed., p. 393, ls. 7-10.

ference of the abandonments in the Individual Vehicle and in the Universal Vehicle arises from the (various) degrees of completeness of the factors of the method and from the duration of the time of familiarity (with the method).

The above indications enable us to understand the differences as to interpretability and definitiveness between the various methods of liberation from the various obscurations, through the realization of the selflessnesses in the various forms of the two self-habits. And the key points (are found in) the many different scriptural statements that identify the two self-habits and (explain) the gross and subtle forms of the two selflessnesses.

Since the interpretation, condition, and actuality of the instincts are difficult questions when one does not accept any fundamental consciousness, I should explain them here; but I will not undertake this since the matter cannot be settled briefly, and I hesitate to digress to much.[78]

In sum, these distinctive specialties (of the Dialecticist system), different from other philosophical systems, have arisen regarding the questions about whether or not (the two selflessnesses) are understood by the (various practitioners of) the Universal Vehicle and the Individual Vehicle, about the two self-habits, and about the two obscurations, for the reason that the interpretations of the truth-habits regarding persons and things are different, and hence the selflessnesses of both (persons and things) are also different.[79]

B. Distinctive Specialty of Allowing the External Objective without Allowing Apperceptive Consciousness and Fundamental Consciousness

Since such is the way of representation of persons and things, it is not possible to make distinctions such as "conventionally, 'persons' such as 'stream-winners' exist, but 'persons' such as 'hell-denizens' do not," because they are similar insofar as they are equally non-existent ultimately and equally existent conventionally. Likewise, among things (categorized as) aggregates, elements, and media, it is not possible to make a distinction such as that "corporeal things do not exist, but mind and mental functions do," because they are equally existent or equally non-existent in terms of (either of the) two realities.

All the postulates of those other Centrists who claim equal existence of the external objective and the internal subjective,[80] and of certain

[78] See MA, VI, ks. 38-40 and commentary.

[79] See Introduction, VIII, 3, and notes 193, 196, 200, 201.

[80] That is, Traditionist-Dogmaticist, Bhavaviveka, etc.

Centrists[81] and Idealists who claim that the subjective exists and not the objective, amount to no more than the claim that, for something to exist, it must have intrinsically identifiable status, and that, if something has no such intrinsic identity, it cannot exist. This (Dialecticist) system also accepts the impossibility of the intrinsically identifiable status of the external objective (world), but disagrees over the question of a (consequent) necessity for the (utter) non-existence of the external objective. Therefore, if one understands in general how to represent the existence of anything whatsoever, in spite of its lack of intrinsic identifiability, one is well able to understand the reasonings for the impossibility of differentiating the existence and non-existence (in terms of the same reality) of the objective and the subjective. (Conversely,) without that (general understanding), one cannot understand (those reasonings).

Therefore, (Chandrakirti) states in the *Four Hundred Commentary* that reasonings such as "there is no objective (realm), because neither gross nor subtle (forms) of matter exist, because the negation of indivisible atoms also negates gross (substances) which are their aggregates," can negate the indivisibility of objective (things), but cannot negate the very existence of objective (things), since (such a conclusion) is faulted both by scriptural authority and by common sense.[82]

In regard to (interpretation of scriptural references germane to the status of the external objective), according to Bhavaviveka, the meaning of the *Ten Stages* statement that "the three realms are merely mind" is not that the word "merely" negates those (external objects), but clearly that it negates any sort of world-creator other than the mind, (and Chandrakirti agrees with this interpretation). (However), Chandra does not accept Bhavaviveka's explanation that the (*Mission to Lanka*) statements such as "the externally apparent does not exist" do not negate external objects. (Chandra) rather explains that, although the scripture does teach that (negation of the external), it is interpretable in meaning. Thus, he refutes (the Experientialist use of these references) by saying, in the case of the *Ten Stages*, not that the scripture is interpretable in meaning, but that (negation of the external) is not the scripture's meaning; and by

[81] That is, Experientialist-Dogmaticist, Shantarakshita, etc.

[82] CŚT, TG, C, ya, 28b ff., IX, ad. ks. 6, 12-19. Tsong Khapa especially refers to the passage after k. 19 (Bhattacarya ed., pp. 55-56, Skt. restored): *tasmāllaukikā bhāvā lokottaraparidarśanavicārāpraviṣṭā loke yathā bhavanti tathābhyupagantavyāḥ* / *yathā vijñānaṃ laukikaṃ tathā paramāṇur apīti nyāyāvatāre 'pi paramāṇuḥ nirākartuṃ* (B. *prakāśayituṃ*) *na śakyate* / *tasya nyāyasya* (B. *bhūnasya*) *lokāgamavirodhena viruddhatvāt* / .
I presume Bhattacarya's *bhūnasya* is a misprint for *bhūtasya*, which would follow from his mistranslation of Tib. *gsal ba* by *prakāśayitum*, where *gsal ba* is clearly used in its sense of to "clear away," "get rid of," that is, refute, not in its sense of "to illuminate." Once that misunderstanding is cleared up, we can return to the Tib. *dei rigs pa la*, reconstructing the obvious *tasya nyāyasya*.

saying, in the case of this *Mission to Lanka* reference, not that (negation of the external) is not the scripture's meaning, but that the reference is interpretable in meaning.[83] (Chandra's) intention is that one should accept as taught both the *Mother Scripture*'s instruction that the five aggregates are all indiscriminately empty with respect to intrinsic reality and the Abhidharmic explanations that all five equally have their particular and universal natures; because the objective and the subjective are similar in that the analysis of the mode of existence of the referents of verbal designations (of such things) discovers no (substantial referents), and yet as both are posited as superficially existent on strength of verbal conventions, there is no difference (between the objective and the subjective superficially either). Therefore, such discriminations (between the objective and the subjective) in regard to their existence and non-existence contravene the conventions of common parlance as well as the representations of the ultimate, and hence are wrong about both realities. As (Aryadeva) says, in the *Four Hundred*:

> (In regard to subject and object) to say
> "The one exists, yet the other does not!"
> Is not proper ultimately, nor conventionally.
> Thus, one cannot even use the expression.[84]

Thus, this is also the intention of the Holy (Nargarjuna).

As for the meaning of such statements as: "Such (things) as the so-called (four) elements are really comprised in consciousness,"[85] (it is that) forms, minds, mental functions, and anomalous creations are designated as elements, etc., according to their representation in the consciousness that perceives them; because if they were not so represented, they could not be represented as separately existent. Thus, those things such as elements are included in the category of consciousness, being merely its representations. And therefore, such an (authoritative) reference is not a negation of external objects, its meaning being as (above and as) elucidated in its own commentary. Thus, when the creative purity of consciousness is directly known as unproduced with respect to its intrinsic reality, then also the variety of objects it represents (will be known) as free (of intrinsic reality) and (their apparent objectivity will) decline, just as a (mirror-)image terminates when the (original) form terminates.[86]

83 Tsong Khapa refers to Bhavaviveka's refutation of the Idealist system in Ch. V. of the TJ, and to Chandrakirti's refutation of the Experientialist interpretation of the *Ten Stages* and *Mission to Lanka* references in MA VI, ks. 84-97, Poussin ed., pp. 239-53.

84 CŚ, XVI, k. 24 (Bhattacarya ed., p. 295): *ekaṃ sadasadekaṃ ca naidaṃ tattvaṃ na laukikam / tenedaṃ sadidamasad vaktum eva na śakyate //.*

85 VṢ, k. 47 (C. tsa, f. 21b4).

86 Tsong Khapa here paraphrases YṢV (TG, C, ya, 21a5-6): *gang gi tshe rnal 'byor pas yod pa med pa yin pai don sgro 'dogs pai rnam par shes pai tshangs pa de brdzun pa bslu bai chos can du mthong zhing rang bzhin gyis skye ba med par mthong ba dei tshe nges*

Nor does the non-acceptance of the fundamental consciousness fault (this position). For, the fundamental consciousness is (only) asserted to (serve) as a basis of effects of evolutionary actions, (especially) the development of evolutionary effects of actions arising after a long time, since actions are terminated in their own second moment, and there is (supposedly) no effect arising from a terminated thing. And hence, when one can present phenomena even without intrinsic identifiability, a (posited) fundamental consciousness is no longer necessary, since a terminated thing is perfectly admissible as a phenomenon. As (Chandra states) in the *Introduction*:

> Since things are not really ceased intrinsically,
> This is possible without a fundamental;
> Understand how evolutionary effects can arise sometimes
> Even long after evolutionary actions have ceased![87]

Not only is it easy to abandon absolutistic and nihilistic views in regard to both realities when one knows how to represent a realityless causality by rejecting intrinsic identifiability even superficially, but also the coherence of the evolutionary effects of actions is viable even without admitting any fundamental consciousness. As Chandra states in the *Introduction Commentary*:

> Therefore, not only does intrinsic realitylessness (enable one) to abandon utterly absolutism and nihilism with regard to both realities, but also the coherence of the effects of actions, even when the actions are long terminated, is viable without imagining any such things as the continuity, retentiveness, and possession of a fundamental consciousness.[88]

"Therefore" refers to his previous explanation of how one intrinsically realityless thing produces other intrinsically realityless things.[89] Although it is necessary, upon denying fundamental consciousness, to rebut other criticisms such as the charge of the incompatibility of the final mind in death with the initial mind in (the subsequent) birth, Chandra does not

---

par de shes te / ji ltar gnas pai sems rang gi ngo bos skye ba med par shes pas des bskyed pa 'byung ba chen po la sogs pa ma lus pa dag kyang gzugs 'gags na gzugs brnyan 'gags pa bzhin du 'bral bar 'gyur na. . . .

[87] MA, VI, k. 39.

[88] MABh, VI, ad. k. 39. Chandrakirti here refers to three Abhidharmic concepts: 1) *vijñānasaṃtāna* 2) *avipranāśa*, and 3) *prāpti*, the latter two of which are included as *viprayukta* (anomalous) functions that connect the force of action to an agent; the former, like an IOU, connects a debt to a debtor, the latter ties action to agent as if by a rope. See *Zin Bris*, f. 36b5.

[89] Chandra has explained this in MA, VI, k. 37cd-38ab, and following: *ji ltar der ni gzugs brnyan sogs stong las // shes pa de yi rnam par skye 'gyur ltar // de bzhin dngos po thams cad stong na yang // stong nyid dag las rab tu skye bar 'gyur /.*

explain them, thinking that knowing this (above) rule enables one to know the others. And I will not digress to explain them here, fearing prolixity.[90]

(Finally), the key point in not positing the fundamental consciousness is the acceptance of external objects, for if one does assert (the existence of external objects) one must agree with the statement of the *Center and Extremes*:

> (One may say) "Consciousness arises, seeing
> Things, beings, selves, and ideas,
> (But) those objects do not exist (in fact)";
> (And) if they don't exist, neither does it![91]

(Chandrakirti) explains the method of proving that a terminated thing is a phenomenon in his *Lucid Exposition* and in his *Philosophical Sixty Commentary*, and I intend to explain it in my super-commentary on the *Wisdom*.[92] (Finally), the representation of the three times (past, present,

[90] Tsong Khapa clearly explains the details of presenting the coherence of action without any postulate of fundamental consciousness in his *Dbu-ma-dgongs-pa-rab-gsal* (GRS), pp. 230 ff. The gist of the explanation is that the Dialecticist does not need the devices of the other schools because he does not see the termination of the act to be intrinsically real, and, therefore, a terminated thing for him can be efficient, hence the finished action can give its fruit in the future (a logical analogue of Lao Tzu's famous dictum that the emptiness of the bowl gives it its function, not its surface!).

[91] MAV, I, k. 4 Pandeya ed., p. 14): *arthasattvātmavijñapti pratibhāsaṃ prajāyate / vijñānaṃ* (,) *nāsti ca 'sya 'rthas* (,) *tadabhāvāt tadapyasat* //. Stcherbatski (*Discrimination between Middle and Extremes*, Calcutta: Biblioteca Buddhira Reprint, 1971, p. 60) translates: "the mind itself appears to us as a projection of things [inanimate], as well as living bodies, [as the ideas of a Self and his sensations]. Their objects do not exist however, and without them unreal are also these [ideas]." His Aga block print differs somewhat from our text and the C text, but the essential meaning does not vary. It is interesting that in this case, Tsong Khapa uses an Idealist text to show how even they recognize the contingency of consciousness on its objects, albeit unwitting of the implications for their fundamental consciousness theory.

[92] Tsong Khapa refers to PPMMV, VII, and the commentary in RG, VII. bLo-bzang Phun-tshogs (*Zin Bris*, ff. 37b1-38b2) gives the following comment worth quoting in full: "As for the way scripture and reasoning establish the destroyed as phenomenal (*zhig pa dngos por sgrub pa*) Chandra states [PPMMV, VII, Vaidya ed., p. 72, l. 23]: 'According to the advocate of instantaneity who asserts the causelessness of termination, how can instantaneous things be established, there being no termination, like sky-flowers, it being causeless? And how can he establish creations free of termination? Thus his whole position is incoherent!' To rephrase this proof: for those who assert that termination, a thing's non-duration for a second instant, ensues from the cause of the thing['s production itself], with no other cause, and that the terminated thing hence is causeless and non-phenomenal; it is consequent that things are not instantaneous, there being no cause of their termination/non-duration, and there being no cause of the terminated thing. . . ." But as Chandra goes on to say, the Dialecticist accepts that the terminated is phenomenal (*bhava*), with respect to its own function (*svarūpāpekṣaya*), but not because of any intrinsic reality of ceasing phenomena such as forms, etc. "The scriptural proof of the phenomenality of the terminated: in the *Ten Stages* it is stated, 'even death has a dual function, one terminating creations, one causing the non-interruption of misknowledge,' thus it has causal efficacy. Thus 'a dead being as a terminated thing is produced by a cause and produces its effect;

and future), through the key point of admitting a terminated thing as a phenomenon, is a major distinctive specialty (of this system).[93]

(Chandrakirti) states the position of the protagonist who asserts apperception and the refutation (of that position) in the *Introduction Commentary* (along the following lines): "Memory is impossible without prior experience, hence memory is produced from experience. There is memory of the prior object—'Such was seen'—and of the prior subject—'I saw.' Hence, there is experience of such (subjective prior states) as the cognition of blue. Further, if that (cognition) was experienced by some different cognition, that (second cognition) would have to be experienced by still another, which would entail (the fault) of infinite regress. Or, if the prior cognition were to be experienced by a later cognition, that later cognition would not encompass other objects such as form. Hence, a (cognition) must experience itself, as it is certain that there are only the two (possibilities of simultaneity or successiveness) in experience. Therefore, subsequent memory establishes that the prior experience of a past object includes an apperceptive consciousness."[94]

---

hence is phenomenal.' YṢ also states that (k. 21): 'termination is perceived as the quiescence from the actual termination of the cause.' This indicates phenomenality of the terminated, causally produced, as the extinguished flame is caused by exhaustion of oil in the wick."

Tsong Khapa (RG, VII, pp. 187-91) follows a similar pattern of explanation of this point, elaborating the arguments in more detail, and adding the example of the Abhidharmic inclusion of the characteristics birth, duration, and termination, in the category of anomalous functions (*viprayuktasaṃskāra*), all of which obviously must be considered as phenomena. These arguments are extremely subtle, the gist of them boiling down as usual to the fact that the Dialecticist claim of phenomenality is made only in conventional terms, as are all their claims. And in the non-analytic conventional it is simpler and more coherent to admit the phenomenality of the terminated, as obviously it performs a function, as in the adduced cases. The Realist, who sees claims as having to pertain to some of objective, absolutistic workings of causality, avoids allowing the terminated any sort of causal function, reserving such function instead to what he calls "incompleteness of cause," so as not to be pushed into the position of hypostatizing an absence. This is crucial for him, since the ultimate absences, cessation, and so forth, are for him by definition non-phenomenal.

[93] Tsong Khapa further elaborates this point in RG, XIX, p. 343, where he frankly admits the Dialecticist's conventional claim of the phenomenality of the three times to be similar to the non-Buddhist Vaisheshikas, with the difference that the latter make their claim absolutistically, and go the extreme of positing a past, present, and future in the past and in the future, subdividing into three each of the three categories. For the Dialecticist the past is always past, the first instant of the terminated sprout being the termination of the sprout, the next being the termination of the first instant of the terminated sprout, and so on. *Zin Bris*, f. 38b1 explains: "the future sprout is accepted as phenomenal, having a cause in the non-completion of the termination of the previously existent condition. Thus, whereas past and future are asserted by the lower Buddhist schools as being absolute negations [of presentness], this system accepts both as phenomenal and hence as implicative negations, not absolute negations." Thus, by the key of recognizing the convenience of allowing the reality of three times in the non-analytic conventional, the mystery of why actions may result in delayed effects is cleared up [still, as ever, on the conventional level!] without resorting to an abstruse psychology such as that involved in the theory of the fundamental consciousness and its inherent seed-potentialities.

[94] Tsong Khapa here paraphrases the exposition of the MA, VI, ad. k. 73 ff., Poussin ed., p. 167 (LVP, p. 350): Chandrakirti identifies the antagonist here as any Experientialist

(Chandra answers:) "If this proof is made in terms of substantially existent (mental states, etc.), then, as there is no such (substantially existent) memory, your (reason is) as (difficult) to prove as your probandum. Or, if (the proof) is in conventional terms, as that (apperception) is not established for your antagonist as the cause of memory (even conventionally), your proof of the existence of apperceptive consciousness by the existence of memory is like proving the existence of water-crystal and fire-crystal by the existence of water and fire."[95]

As this antagonist's (syllogism) is (an inference) reasoning from an effect, (Chandra) takes it in terms of its holding apperception as the probandum. That being done, an example is not found, since even if (this

---

who asserts the Traditionist opinion (*mdo sde pai phyogs khas blangs nas . . .*), and the *Zin Bris*, f. 38b1 ff. mentions the locus classicus of this argument as being in PV (II, k. 485a, Shastri ed., p. 239), Skt. *smrter apyātmavit siddha*, etc., and also mentions that Traditionists, Experientialists, and Idealist-Dogmaticists will advance this argument.

Some clarification is needed regarding the two reasons given by the antagonist here, that is, that of infinite regress and that of restriction of consciousness to itself, for the impossibility of a cognition to be cognized by another cognition. The MA reads: "That [blue-cognition] is not properly experienced by another cognition. Why? Because the [fault of] infinite regress would be consequent if it were experienced by another cognition. If you assert that a cognition discerning blue is discerned by immediately subsequent consciousness, you must also accept another experiencer of that consciousness of the cognition of blue, and as that again must have still another, you are stuck with the fault of infinite regress. Further, there would be the fault of consciousness' non-discernment of any other objects [than prior consciousness], as all consciousness-continua would have other consciousnesses as their objects, and living beings have only a single stream of consciousness."

This passage is muddled by Poussin (LVP, p. 350), who thinks *jñāna* and *vijñāna* (Tib. *shes pa* and *rnam par shes pa*) should be distinguished as *idée* and *connaissance*, respectively, as well as failing in his edition to catch three mistakes: *shes pas* for *shes pai* (168, l. 2), *yongs su gcod* and *yongs su mi gcod* (l. 5), and *yul yin pa* for *yul can yin pa* (l. 6), which render his edition and translation totally opposite to the sense, as attested by TG, C, a, f. 269a3-4; Tsong Khapa's GRS, p. 285; and 'Jam-bzhed's *mTha dPyod*, ff. 402 ff.

Tsong Khapa comments in his GRS, p. 285: "As for the consequence of infinite regress, if blue-discerning-cognition is itself discerned by another subsequent cognition, then does that [subsequent] cognition [itself] require another cognition to assess it? Or not? If not, then the former cognition does not need [the subsequent]. If it requires it, then still another is required, and the fault of infinite regress ensues, and that fault entails the fault that the original blue cognition is not even established as an experience. Second, as for the consequence that [consciousness] could not discern any other object, if the prior cognition was discerned by a later [cognition], that [latter] could not discern any other objects, such as forms, sounds, etc., as it could not transfer [its attention], as the whole stream of consciousness would have other prior cognitions as its object. The concomitance of that [proposition] is not uncertain, as each later cognition would discern a prior cognition, being produced with its apprehension of the prior, and would not apply itself to a distant external [object], transferring itself from the proximate internal objective sector."

[95] As Chandra phrases it himself in the original (MA, Poussin ed., p. 169, ls. 17-20): "There is no [need for] the existence of a magical water-crystal [to be inferred from] merely seeing some water, nor for [inferring] the existence of a magical fire-crystal from merely seeing some fire, since water and fire may occur without them, from rain or from rubbing two firesticks together, and so on. In just the same way, we will here show how memory occurs without any apperceptive consciousness."

antagonist) were to propose, "there is an experiencer of blue-cognition, because of the existence of a subsequent memory; just as (in the case of) blue (which is perceived and subsequently remembered)," although there is a mere conformity to the reason and probandum in the example, invariable concomitance between them cannot be established. Hence, the example is not mentioned explicitly, like the fact that apperceptive consciousness is the probandum. And, although (such a syllogism) might prove the (existence of) mere experience, as that would be (proving the) already proven, it is not (formally) proposed, like that (fact that apperception is the probandum).[96]

According to (Chandrakirti's) system, the non-existence of apperceptive consciousness does not preclude the production of memory, as he shows in the *Introduction*:

> As I have no (intrinsically) other memory
> From that (cognition) experiencing objects,
> I will remember "I saw (it)!"—
> This is the system of social conventions.[97]

This verse does not refute the above-explained reason for holding that the production of memory is excluded by the absence of apperceptive consciousness. It (merely) refutes the notion of apperceptive consciousness above, which depends (logically) on a special sort of (intrinsically other) memory (for whose production it is necessary). The notion is that, since when one remembers a prior seeing of blue as "I saw it before," one is remembering that former seeing as seen by oneself, that (special) sort of memory would be precluded if the former blue-cognition did not experience itself, and thus that former (cognition) was self-consciously apperceptive.

(However), (Chandrakirti) proves that the notion "I saw it before" occurs not by the influence of apperceptive consciousness, but by the influence of the application of both the prior experience of the blue object and the later memory-cognition to one (and the same) object. And further,

[96] bLo-bzang Phun-tshogs (*Zin Bris*, f. 39a3) illustrates what would have been a formal syllogism to express the view of the Traditionist-Idealist (labeled as a case of causal reasoning, *kāryānumāna*, see *Stcherbatski, Buddhist Logic* II, p. 70): "Consider blue-cognition; it has apperceptive consciousness as a means of experiencing itself; because it is remembered at a later time." However, this is not formally set forth by them, to avoid the embarrassment of inability to find a homogeneous example, apperceptive consciousness being a unique case. For, indeed, the color blue itself is not apperceptively conscious just because it is remembered! The question is, however, somewhat left up in the air, citing an objector who says that the PV commentators and PV, II, k. 485, do indeed employ some formal syllogisms. bLo-bzang Phun-tshogs then dubs this an extremely difficult point and recommends our close examination of the problem.

[97] MA, VI, k. 75, p. 171.

in order to prove that, he argues that since the (same) object which is first experienced and discerned by the prior cognition of blue is remembered by the later blue-cognition, it is not not experienced and not not discerned. As he states: "according to me it is because experience and memory are not intrinsically identifiably other." If merely that reason (of identifiable otherness) were (enough to establish apperception), then Maitreya's experience would be remembered by Upagupta. Therefore, if those two (memory and experience) were established as substantially different, as the opponent would have it, the natural (conventional) mind would hold notions of (their) substantial otherness, it would not hold that what was perceived by the former blue-cognition is perceived (also) by the later memory, it would be impossible for experience and memory to have the same object, and it would be impossible for the memory "I saw it before" to occur. But according to us, those two are not substantially different and the natural mind has no such notions, and hence (we can) show that it is not impossible for memory to hold "I discerned it" about an object discerned by a previous cognition. Furthermore, (memory) accedes to an object by force of the attraction of a prior experience, being without any independent motivation to discern any object, as is not the case with any other (hypothetical independent cognition, such as the second instant of blue-cognition, etc.)

Thus, this non-acceptance of apperceptive consciousness, even conventionally, is the ultimate in the negation of intrinsic identifiability, even conventionally. Although he does not state explicitly whether or not (this negation is accomplished) by restricting experience to self-experience or other-experience, he means to pose no such alternative, just as, in not accepting the lamp's self-illumination while accepting its luminosity, he does not restrict it to the alternative of illumination by itself or by other means.

One might object that in the case of the lamp there is no fault of non-substantiation by validating cognition even if it does not illuminate itself; and yet consciousness is different from the lamp, since it becomes non-substantiated by validating cognition if it is not taken as self-consciously apperceptive. (Then we reply): "How would you answer the argument that if a lamp does not illuminate with respect to itself and does not illuminate with respect to any other, it is not established thus as luminous, nor as anything else, and hence is not established by validating cognition?" If you consider that, although it is not luminous with respect to itself or to any other, it illuminates pots, etc., hence is established as luminous, well then, (we suggest) it is just the same in the case of consciousness! If you further object that, since the actual cognition of objects itself depends on apperceptive consciousness, without apperception the object-cognition is not substantiated, we repeat that it is still just like the case of the lamp. And if you still imagine that in that case you will take your stand on the fact that lamps illuminate themselves by themselves, (we must insist that) this is wrong, as then it would be impossible for darkness to obscure them, and also darkness itself would obscure itself. And if you accept that, then darkness would be invisible. In short, since consciousness is designated through its dependence on objects, it is without intrinsically identifiable status, and objects themselves are just the same. By this reason, not only are these two (subject and object) conventionally mutually dependent, but the further point is that due to the mere interdependent designativeness (of things), apperceptive consciousness is inadmissible.

This can also be understood from the reason refuting apperceptive consciousness given (by Nagarjuna) in his *Rebuttal of Objections*:

> If (you think) validating cognition is self-substantiated, then your validating cognition is substantiated without requiring any objects, since the self-established depends on no other.[98]

But you object that the "I" in the memory "I saw blue before" is the person, and since that is excluded from blue-cognition, how can memory of it be memory of blue-cognition?

Although eye-consciousness perceiving blue and person seeing blue are mutually exclusive, there is no contradiction in saying "I saw blue" depending on that cognition's perception of blue. So, how can that memory of "person," "I saw blue before," based on the memory of blue-cognition's seeing blue, exclude the memory of blue-perceiving-cognition?

C. Distinctive Specialty of Non-acceptance of Dogmaticist Logical Privacy[99]

a. Origin of The Negation of Private Dogmaticism and Other Methods to Explain Its Import

The scriptures definitely contain the meaning that if one interprets them in one way, one must accept private dogmaticism, and if one interprets them in another way, it is inappropriate to do so.

[98] VV, 41, Vaidya ed., p. 288; *yadi ca svataḥ pramāṇasiddhir anapekṣya te prameyāni / bhavati pramāṇasiddhir na parāpekṣa hi siddhir iti //.*

[99] Tib. *rang rgyud*, Skt. *svatantra*. This term is applied to a type of argument based on the same type of logical mark or reason first by Chandra in PPMMV, I, where he roundly rejects Bhavaviveka's use of it. Hence the name "Svatantrika-Madhyamika" for Bhavaviveka and his followers. The precise philosophical translation of this term is extremely difficult in English, the literal "independent" accomplishing little. It is only made possible

Nevertheless, nowhere in all the translated treatises of the orthodox schools is it made explicit that inquiry into the question of private dogmaticism and public dialecticism[100] (reveals that) private arguments are invalid and dialectical arguments valid, except in the treatises of Chandrakirti and his followers.

---

by the work of L. Wittgenstein, who in the *Philosophical Investigations* refutes for the first time in Western philosophy the concept of a "private language," and a concept of a "private object," which ordinary people and philosophers have assumed and theorized, respectively, to be the basis of language and experiential reality. Chandrakirti, with his proto-Wittgensteinian theories of: 1) conventionality as the non-analytical, and 2) the task of philosophical analysis as being the unravelling of false views or conceptual knots by means of removing the unconscious absolutism prevalent in our habitual use of language and in our unconsciously language-governed perceptions and so on, means just this "private mark," "private view," and so on, by his use of *svatantra*. I have used this term here, sometimes paired with the term "dogmaticist," which describes the type of argument that results from the sense of the arguer that he is moving from a privately established objective basis. This contrasts with the Skt. *paraprasiddha*, Tib. *gzhan grags*, or "public," "dialectical," type of argument, that operates in full cognizance of the conventionality of language, and more deeply therefore, of the conventionality of views. To justify this correlation, which will startle the knowledgeable reader for various reasons, one must consider the definition of the terms in Sanskrit and Tibetan. Tsong Khapa himself equates *rang rgyud* to *rang dbang*, which in numerous contexts means simply "independent" (lit. "self-powered"). This accords at first glance with the Sanskrit *svatantra*, translated into Tibetan both by *rang rgyud* and *rang dbang*. And thus Stcherbatski, for example, in his *Central Conception of Buddhist Nirvana*, translates the expression *svatantrānumāna* as "independent argument." There is, however, one factor left unexplained by this equation of Tsong Khapa and Stcherbatski. Namely, if they are identical, why did the pandits and lotsawas who translated the Centrist texts employ the expression *rang rgyud* at all, when their practice was to adhere rigidly to single translations of Sanskrit terms, to preserve coherence with the originals and to preserve ambiguities? Skt. *tantra* can mean "system," "method," "tradition," "continuum," and "control," and yet the *dbang* translation only evinces the latter sense. It seems therefore that the Tibetan-Indian translation teams were aware of this ambiguity and wished clearly to specify the senses of "system" and "continuum" by using *rgyud* in every case in this context. In Tibetan psychological language, *rang rgyud* is very common and means clearly "one's own personal mental process," or "private stream of consciousness." Thus they wish to say something more than merely "independent," rather "independent in system," "acting as if manifesting an independent, personal, private process." Thus, I have chosen "private," correlated with "dogmaticist" (*Oxford English Dictionary, Compact Edition*, Oxford University Press, 1971, p. 583: "dogmatic = proceeding upon *a priori* principles accepted as true"), in certain contexts. This gives the combinations "private syllogism" (*svatantrānumāna, rang rgyud rjes dpag*), "private reason" (*rang rgyud rtags*), and in general, when Tsong Khapa uses the shorthand for the whole method simply *rang rgyud*, simply "the private," or "the dogmaticist" (approach). See n. 100 below.

100 dPal-'byor Lhun-grub (SERA, f. 42b) and bLo-bzang Phun-tshogs (*Zin Bris*, f. 41a) agree that Tsong Khapa means that if you read the scriptures as indicating the intrinsic identifiability of things, then the private reason and the dogmaticist reasoning process is appropriate; and if not, not. Note that in this context the private, dogmaticist reasoning is contrasted with the consequentialist, dialectical reasoning process (that is, *svatantra* vs. *prasanga*), which merely takes off from the antagonist's position leading its consequences out into a reductio ad absurdum. Thus, the "privately oriented" philosopher attempts to lay down formal, dogmatically grounded arguments proving his privately established opinions. The "publically oriented" dialectical philosopher, on the other hand, merely seeks to free his opponent from his self-contradictory stance through a dialectical application of

This becomes explicit in (Chandrakirti's) pioneering of the system of the Champions when, in the *Lucid Exposition*,[101] in the context of showing the inapplicability of Bhavaviveka's criticism of Buddhapalita's elucidation of the (opening) stanza (of the *Wisdom*), "not from self, not from other . . . ," he set forth many proofs that Buddhapalita did not maintain any private dogmaticism, and that (further) it would be irrational for (any) Centrist to be privately dogmatic, (setting forth also) many refutations of the contrary opinion. And it is explicit also when, in the *Four Hundred Commentary*,[102] in the context of refuting the assertions of Master Dharmapala, he briefly outlined the procedure to refute private dogmaticism.

As far as Bhavaviveka was concerned, he did not think there was any disagreement between himself and Buddhapalita about whether or not to accept private dogmaticism. He seemed (simply) to assume that (Buddhapalita's) system did not live up to (an assumed tacit) acceptance of private dogmaticism. This is the key to (Bhavaviveka's) failure to assert any distinction between himself and Buddhapalita in regard to the negatees (used) in their negations of intrinsic reality in persons and things.[103] Avalokitavrata, a follower of Bhavaviveka, was familiar with the *Lucid Exposition*, hence one might expect him to explain, in his commentary on (Bhavaviveka's) refutation of Buddhapalita in the *Wisdom Lamp*, whether or not he found Chandrakirti's criticism of Bhavaviveka to be applicable.[104] Likewise, one might expect Shantarakshita, Kamalashila, and their followers to set forth a rebuttal of Chandrakirti's refutation of private dogmaticism.[105] (However, the fact is) none of them did so.

---

consequences, aware that his own positions are conventionally based and determined, and hence flexible in his approach. In Wittgenstein's sense, the "dialectical" philosopher is a kind of therapist, seeking to cure the sicknesses of absolutism and nihilism. See Introduction for fuller discussion, "Peerless Philosophy" section.

101 PPMMV, I, *Vaidya* ed., pp. 5 ff.

102 CŚT, XVI, ad. k. 21-22 Bhattacarya ed., pp. 289-90). dPal-'byor Lhun-grub (SERA, f. 53b) outlines Chandra's argument here as follows: "There is no genuine private reason; because there is no valid cognition privately established; that is, not posited on strength of three-aspected convention; because logical reasons merely exist as postulated by the convention of the three aspects."

103 That is, Bhavaviveka does not even consider the possibility that anyone might argue non-dogmatically, that is, without a basis in a private reason, because he assumes there to be a certain degree of objective validity, or intrinsic identifiability in empirical things. Herein lies the very heart of his controversy with the Dialecticists.

104 PrPrT, I. Apparently, on internal evidence, such as other references to Chandra in this massive commentary, Tsong Khapa considers Avalokitavrata to be later than Chandrakirti. Thus, his silence during this crucial debate is most curious, as a rebuttal of Chandra's powerful attack on Bhavaviveka is called for there more than anywhere else.

105 It is sure that Shantarakshita or Kamalashila should also have answered Chandrakirti's charges against the Dogmaticist method, elements of which they incorporated in their own Centrist works, MAlam and MAlok. Thus the later Dogmaticists for some reason did not take Chandra seriously enough, or felt unable to respond. A close reading of these two little known works would give us a better idea.

In general, the two (Dialecticist) masters took as the ultimate in profound and subtle reasonings both those reasonings proving the perfect viability of all systems such as causality in the absence of the intrinsic reality that is negated as intrinsic identifiability even conventionally, and also (those reasonings) negating that negatee (of intrinsic identifiability) by the very reason of relativity, asserted clearly to be the relativity of (all things), transcendental and non-transcendental. Moreover, among these (ultimately subtle and profound reasonings), (they) took this negation of dogmaticist privacy as the most subtle (of all).

In this regard, a certain pandit argues that the private logical reason would be appropriate if there were substantiation by validating cognition of both reason and the invariable concomitance proving the probandum; but it is not appropriate, such not being the case. (For) it is wrong to assert that a logical reason can be authoritatively substantiated for both protagonist and antagonist, since the protagonist does not know what is established by validating cognition for the antagonist, as he cannot the details of the other's thoughts by either perception or inference; nor does he know what is established by validating cognition for himself, as it is always possible his judgment is in error.[106]

(But we respond that) this (approach) is utterly wrong, for if such were the case, it would also be inappropriate to refute (an antagonist with a public syllogism), even if one (based one's argument upon) the assertions of the opponent (and not upon one's own private assertion). For, one could not know the antagonist's position, not knowing his thoughts, and one's own refutation through advancing (the antagonist's) fallacies could be wrong, as it would always be possible that one's judgment about those fallacies could be mistaken.

(This same pandit) argues that the reason that the invariable concomitance (of reason with probandum) is not established by validating cognition is that perception, although it can cognize the concomitance of the presence of fire with the presence of smoke in a kitchen, does not cognize the concomitance of the presence of fire with the presence of smoke in all times and places; and further, inference does not cognize the concomitance of the probandum-property with a reason present at all times and places. Thus, (he concludes) concomitance is established by mere conventional assertion, and not by any validating cognition.

This (argument) also is entirely wrong, because it negates (the valid cognizability of concomitance) by distorting the import of the exposition of the method for establishing concomitance given in the logical texts.

[106] bLo-bzang Phun-tshogs (*Zin Bris*, f. 41a3) identifies this certain pandit as Jayananda, who was a commentator on the MA. Ba-so's *Mchan-'grel* on LTC (30) concurs kha. 234a), remarking further that the Tibetan Khu-lo-tsva-ba was Jayananda's disciple.

For the import of the (logical) treatises is certainly not that the proof of the concomitance of presence of fire with presence of smoke, based on (the example of a kitchen), is a proof of the concomitance of presence of fire of a kitchen with presence of smoke of a kitchen. Otherwise, the reason of presence of smoke in an occasionally smoky kitchen would prove the presence of fire of that kitchen (always). This is because, if the reason of presence of occasional smoke proved the invariable concomitance of the presence of fire, then concomitance would be proved between whatever is taken as reason and whatever is taken as (probandum-) property[107] (just by taking two things in that relationship). And it is also because the mode of proof of that would be as mentioned above (as denied to be the import of the treatises). Thus, if the kitchen is the base for certification of the invariable concomitance of fire-presence with smoke-presence, and the invariable concomitance is the thing to be certified there, you (Pandit), if (concomitance is) as you think, just show us an additional exemplary case as a basis for certification of concomitance![108]

Similarly, how could the proof, based on the (example) pot, of the concomitance which proves the impermanence of sound by the reason of (its) production be no more than a proof of the concomitance of the pot's impermanence with the pot's production? Thus, do not wrongly construe (the nature of concomitance), since the method to certify the reliability for all times and places of precisely the establishment of concomitance of fire-presence and impermanence with mere smoke(-presence) and (mere) production (respectively), unspecified as to time and place, is the mention (as examples) of the "smoke(-presence)" of this time and place and of the "production" of this time and place. Therefore, having followed this reasoning, still to insist that the precise reversal of the argument rebuts (my refutation of your position) is like a drowning man's clutching at a bunch of straw![109]

Now, (such a pandit) might say that the face-value or habitual perception of things[110] is established without analysis by commonsensical

[107] This discussion presupposes Dignaga's alignments of perception (*pratyakṣa*) with particulars (*svalakṣaṇa*) and ultimate reality (*paramārtha*) and of inference (*anumāna*) with universals (*sāmānya*) and superficial reality (*saṃvṛti*), without invalidating either reality.

[108] That is, since the pandit has misunderstood the function of the example (*dṛṣṭānta*) in establishing the concomitance of the provable property (*sādhyadharma*) with the logical reason (*hetu*), and thus attempts to render his syllogism overly particularized, he will be unable to adduce any further example to establish the concomitance; the concomitance has become for him a particular, rather than a general, relationship between two particulars.

[109] To rephrase the last passage of this argument, Tsong Khapa means that, since it is precisely the particularity of the instantiating example that enables the proof of the universality of the concomitance between reason and probandum, it is a desperate maneuver to insist that that very particularity of the example actually precludes the universality of the concomitance.

[110] Tib. *dngos po stobs shugs sam 'dzin stangs*.

validating cognition, having refuted any validating cognition unerring about its objects, giving the fact that the opponent's system and not his own asserts the ability (of things) to withstand rational analysis as the reason that the negated fallacy does not rebound upon himself. Nevertheless, he does not seem to (be able) to discern the difference between the analysis as to conventional status and the analysis as to actual status (of things), or the difference between the two types of Centrists' (respective) analyses of actual status (of things). Finally, although he constantly declares that "there is no intrinsic identity, even conventionally," still, since he seems not to know how to represent such (systems) as causality in the (condition of) the mere nominal designation (of things), as the referents of conventional designations cannot be discovered when (analytically) sought, according to the above explanation,[111] his assertions are no more than (empty) talk.

Again, some other (scholars) assert that the import of lack of the private reason and private thesis is that the truthlessness which is the simple exclusion of truth is not something that can be proved, and that the false views (of antagonists) are negated by consequences based on the antagonist's assertions or the ultimate implications of those assertions, there being absolutely nothing established by validating cognition.[112]

Still others say that all schemes of ultimate and superficial (realities) are presented only for the view of others, and not as one's own system. And they even say that "even that statement itself was not made by me, but only appears (to be so made) in the view of others![113] (But) such talk never happened among the refuters of private dogmaticism of ancient times, and is merely the chatter of latter-day (philosophers).

The majority of these above persons, while asserting the special negatee of this system, negate the validated cognizability of relativity, and thus are the chief target of our critique. However, I already explained and refuted their (theories) in my *Stages of the Path of Enlightenment*, and so I will not enlarge upon them here.[114]

[111] Tsong Khapa especially refers to the discussion of the sheer non-analytic conventionality of the superficial reality expounded in the section discussing the "head of Rahu, etc." argument.

[112] bLo-bzang Phun-tshogs (*Zin Bris*, f. 41a3) identifies this other scholar as the same Jayananda who wrote a subcommentary on the MA; but Ba-so Chos-rje, in his LTC *Mchan-'grel* (30) f. 473), identifies the "other" as Khu Lo-tsva-ba, Jayananda's disciple.

[113] bLo-bzang Phun-tshogs (*Zin Bris*, f. 42b3) identifies the final two "certain persons" as, respectively, rMa-bya Byang-chub brTson-'grus, one of the eight major disciples of Phya-pa Chos-seng, known as the "Eight Great Lions of Reasoning," and Khu-lo mDo-sde-'bar, a disciple of Byang-chub brTson-'grus. Byang-chub brTson-'grus is said to have expounded his nihilistic theory in his *'Thad pai Rgyan*, which text I have been unable to locate. Khu-lo translated the VV.

[114] *LRC Mchan*, f. 391b. Tsong Khapa begins a section refuting the main critiques of the Dialecticist's special method of equating emptiness with relativity, sorting them into

b. Existence of Reason Proving Probandum but Non-existence of Private Reason

i. How There Is Proof of Probandum by Reason

Our own interpretation (is as follows): if you assert the intrinsically identifiable status mentioned in the *Elucidation of Intention*, you definitely must employ private (syllogisms), like the orthodox Realists and Bhavaviveka, etc. If you do not admit even conventionally any intrinsically identifiable thing, there is no doubt that you must not employ private

---

four groups: those who unsuccessfully attempt to refute the Dialecticists by analysis of the implications of a thing's withstanding or not withstanding rational analysis; those who attempt to do so by analysis of whether or not a thing is established by validating cognition; those who attempt to do so by analysis of implications of whether or not there is production from four extremes; and those who take the negation of all four alternatives of a phenomenon's existence, non-existence, both, or neither as refuting the Dialecticist's special emptiness-relativity equation. bLo-bzang Phun-tshogs (*Zin Bris*, f. 42b3) states that the refutations of the above nihilists are executed in the context of the arguments given under the fourth heading.

LRC Mchan, f. 411a1: "To demonstrate the inaccuracy of [using] the refutation of all four alternatives of existence, non-existence, [both and neither] of phenomena as a rebuttal [of the Dialecticist arrangement of the two realities]: 'In the Centrist treatises, all the four alternatives . . . etc., . . . of phenomena or of intrinsic reality are negated. There are no things not included therein, and hence reasoning negates everything [mundane as well as transcendental].' This is the idea. [We answer:] This, as above explained, negates, out of two kinds of "phenomena," intrinsically established phenomena as having whatever sort of existence asserted in either reality. However, it does not negate the causally efficient phenomena in the conventional reality. Further, in regard to the non-phenomenal or non-created things, it also negates any sort of asserted intrinsically established non-phenomenal things. Likewise, it negates the simultaneous existence and non-existence of such a sort of [intrinsically real] phenomenon, and negates an intrinsically established neither existent nor non-existent thing. And so should the mode of negation of all four alternatives be understood. And if someone insists that there is no such qualification [of the four theses] but, having refuted both existence and non-existence of a thing, one then negates that it is both, and then negates that it is not both, and then insists that there is no problem from the direct contradiction in assertions, [all I can say is] I don't argue with madmen." (Note: Here Tsong Khapa is saying that the misinterpretation of the tetralemma arising from failing to understand that "intrinsically real" must be supplied before each thesis naturally presents the Centrist as a madman, and the self-styled Centrist who attempts to adopt such a position should indeed be treated as such!)

"Furthermore, when one negates self or intrinsic reality as objectively established in the aggregates, the wisdom that considers there to be no intrinsic reality or self arises. If one even negates the intrinsic realitylessness that is the object of that wisdom then the Centrist view is destroyed, because one has destroyed the object of the wisdom that realizes the intrinsic realitylessness of things. Here, one should ask the one who asserts the refutation of both existence and non-existence of intrinsic reality—'How is it that you accomplish the refutation of the intrinsic realitylessness that is the object of the wisdom that ascertains that the aggregates have no intrinsic reality?' If he replies that, 'according to the *Wisdom* statement "If there were the slightest non-empty thing, then there could be a slightest empty thing. But if there is no slightest non-empty thing, how can emptiness come to exist?" as there is nothing non-empty, then the emptiness that is intrinsic realitylessness does not exist;' [then we can rejoin] that 'empty' and 'non-empty' here are to be taken, as in all

dogmaticism. Thus, the negation of the subtle negatee likewise comes down to this. This is not (a question of) not asserting private dogmaticist (syllogisms) in the belief that if there is no intrinsically identifiable thing even conventionally, then the establishment of the probandum of our own position, the means of proof proving that, validating cognitions, and their objects are all prohibited. In the *Introduction Commentary*,

---

parts of the treatise, as 'empty' and 'non-empty' with respect to intrinsic reality. Thus, 'non-empty with respect to intrinsic reality' means 'established with respect to intrinsic reality.' Thus it is utterly ridiculous to insist that 'because there is not the slightest thing that is established by intrinsic reality, the emptiness which is the absence of intrinsic reality does not exist.' Further, the ascertainment that there is no objectively established intrinsic reality in such things as sprouts considers 'there is no intrinsic reality in the sprout,' and does not consider either 'there is' or 'there is not that intrinsic realitylessness [as a thing itself].' This is very easy to understand [as it would be parallel to] considering a closing of the eyes as a [physical] looking within one's own face!

"Thus, although it is logical to negate rationally the existence of emptiness to get rid of the notion of the 'existence of intrinsic realitylessness,' as it is improper to hold to the existence of the non-existence of intrinsic reality, one must acknowledge that one is refuting the object of a cognition that maintains the existence of the non-existence of intrinsic reality, and is not refuting the object of the wisdom that realizes intrinsic realitylessness in the sprout. When we negate the objectively established intrinsic reality of the sprout, we become certain that there is no intrinsic reality, and even when another cognition might consider 'that very intrinsic realitylessness exists,' we do not rationally negate its object,but we [rationally] negate the assertion that that emptiness itself is objectively established!

"Well, one wonders how the thought that that intrinsic realitylessness intrinsically really exists arises. When one apprehends the intrinsic realitylessness of the sprout, the thought arises that although the intrinsic reality of the sprout is not established, the intrinsic realitylessness of the sprout is intrinsically really existent. For example, in the absence of a pot, no thought arises of the truth of the existence of the pot, but the thought arises of the truth of the absence of the pot. Such being the case, if [the original opponent] had said that, since there is not the slightest thing not empty by intrinsic reality, even the emptiness which is the intrinsic realitylessness of the sprout does not exist as objectively established, then that would have accorded with the genuine reasoning [of Nagarjuna]. Even [Chandra], in the CŚT, states that [passage] to be the negation of the intrinsically objective establishment of emptiness: 'If "emptiness" had any sort of objective status, then things would be endowed with intrinsic reality; hence there is no such [status in emptiness]. To explain this, it is stated [by Aryadeva]: "If there were anything non-empty, then emptiness would be produced from something; thus, since there is no such [non-empty] thing, [emptiness] becomes a medicine." ' If such were not the case, negating the existence of emptiness as intrinsic realitylessness would entail the non-existence of intrinsic realitylessness, and would entail the existence of objectively established intrinsic reality, and it would be impossible to negate all forms of intrinsic reality."

(Tsong Khapa here goes on to cite the Experientialist argument about a realityless word negating reality of things, and so on, and then the *Wisdom* on the incurability of holding emptiness as a view, and so on. He concludes by equating the holders of this type of nihilism, who think that the Centrist must refute conventional causality, more specificially, must refute, even conventionally, the object of wisdom realizing emptiness, with the view of the Hva shang Mahayana of the bSam-yas debate, who held that good thought was as bad as bad thought, and so forth. This passage continues up to *LRC Mchan* 414b4.)

This extensive refutation of the misinterpretation of Centrism as nihilism is useful to clear away all doubts about the philosophical sincerity of the Centrists, such as have arisen among the majority of previous Western interpreters of the central way. So I have quoted it at length.

when (Chandra) negates both positions through the analysis—"The cause produces the effect through contact or without contact?"—as proof that the fault lodges with the opponent, (he states): "Accordingly, this examination applies to (the view that) the produced and the producer (are) intrinsically identifiable. . . ." Thus he states that the fault (arising) from the alternative analysis accrues to the belief in intrinsically identifiable cause and effect, and that there is no such fault in the position (that cause and effect) are without intrinsic reality, just like illusion.[115]

Then, when the opponent uses his own arguments to rebut him, he answers:

> The fault you just advanced—"Does the refutation refute the refutand through contact or without contact?"—applies to whoever has a definite position, but this consequence is not applicable to me since this position does not exist for me.[116]

As the reason for the dissimilarity of the two, he states in the verse that he has no position of his own, and in the commentary, he adds: "Because refutation and the refutand do not have intrinsically real status."

Thus, he explains "positionlessness"[117] as meaning the lack of intrinsically real or intrinsically identifiable assertions, which has the same meaning as the reason explained for dissimilarity (of positions) in the passage on causality.

In this context (Chandra) goes on to quote (the *Transcendent Wisdom Scripture*):

> When Shariputra questioned Subhuti with the analysis, "Do produced things obtain an unproduced attainment, or a produced attainment?" he answered, "Neither is acceptable." And then to the question, "Then is there no attainment or realization?" he answered, "Though those two do exist, (their existence) is not in the manner of a duality."[118]

He then quotes further: "Those two and the (stage of) stream-winner, etc. are (existent) as mundane conventions; in the absolute, there is no attainment and no realization." (And continues to comment):

[115] MABh, VI, ad. k. 170, Poussin ed., pp. 292-296. See Introduction, VIII, 4.

[116] MA, VI, k. 173, Poussin ed., p. 294.

[117] Tib. *phyogs med pa*; Skt. *apakṣatva*. It is important to connect this clarification of the Dialecticist "positionlessness," or "thesislessness," with the famous PPMMV, I passage where Chandra asserts he need not have any thesis, the famous VV statement to that effect, and the famous statement of Aryadeva, a major source of the false conclusion that has been drawn by the many mentioned above that the Centrists are not philosophers, that they stand outside the philosophy game, that they are nihilistic with respect to logic, etc. See n. 125 below.

[118] MABh, VI, ad. k. 173.

Here, because of the logical consequence of duality, he negates the getting of attainments as either produced or unproduced things. Since duality is inapplicable in (the condition of) unreality, he accepts the reaching of attainments as non-analytic mundane conventions; likewise, although refutation and refutee do not exist either through contact or without contact (in the ultimate), one should know that refutation refutes the refutee conventionally.

Further: "Refutation devoid of intrinsic reality refutes the refutee, and a reason, even without (intrinsic) validation, being devoid of intrinsic reality, proves the probandum."[119]

Thus, he declares that all proof and refutation should be taken according to the dialogue between the two Elders. "Attainment" means that to be acquired. As for the (suggestion that), when questioned through analysis as to what attainment is acquired, if neither is admitted, then (perhaps) there is no obtainment of result (at all), that is to hold that, when analysis discovers no (result), it negates any (possibility). "(Though those two) do exist" refers to (things merely) not found by rational cognition, and not (totally) negated—hence, they are said to exist. The statement that "it is not in the manner of a duality" means that neither of the two analysands, "produced" or "unproduced," are discovered. The rest of the quotation elucidates the import that "ultimate non-existence" is the analytic non-discovery (of anything) in the manner of duality, and "existence" is conventional existence. Although this is perfectly clear, since the words "analytic" and "non-analytic" are difficult, one must know all the above-explained four methods of analysis.[120] "Duality is inapplicable in (ultimate) unreality" means that if one admits intrinsically identifiable existence, or existence that is not merely established by force of convention, dichotomous analysis is applicable, but if (one admits) unreality or intrinsic realitylessness, such analysis is not applicable.[121]

[119] MABh, ad. k. 173, Poussin ed., p. 296.

[120] Tib. *sngar bshad pai dpyod lugs bzhi po*. It is difficult to tell exactly which four methods of analysis Tsong Khapa intends here, and the commentaries do not explicate. After much thought, I suggest the following four: 1) analytic rational cognition seeking reality analyzing all assertions about the ultimate through binary analysis as in the above quote from the *Transcendent Wisdom*; 2) Experientialist analysis of imagined realities to discover their lack of intrinsic identity; 3) Dogmaticist analysis of things to see whether or not they exist on the strength of their own objective condition, as presented to undefective sense cognition; and 4) Dialecticist analysis of conventional expressions, out of dissatisfaction with their mere conventionality, to seek real referents. A further type of analysis is, of course, the unreflective common-sense analysis of the usage of ordinary expressions on the conventional level. The appreciation of these various types of analysis is essential to understand the precise meaning of the "non-analytical conventional reality."

[121] It is not applicable because such an admission entails the assertion of the non-analytic nature of conventionality. Hence, no conventionally intended and understood statement need be submitted to such analysis.

Thus, in the *Lucid Exposition*, he states that validating cognitions and their objects are presented in mutual dependence, once intrinsically real status is denied them.[122] And (Nagarjuna), in his own commentary on *Rebuttal of Objections*, states with examples that one can prove a probandum even without intrinsic reality.[123]

In general, with the rule (from the *Wisdom*): "To whatever emptiness is appropriate,"[124] (Nagarjuna) states repeatedly that for the position of emptiness with respect to intrinsically identifiable reality, all systems of the samsaric life-cycle and of Nirvana are valid. Thus, if we hold as invalid the function of logical reasons proving probanda and the function of validating cognitions apprehending their objects, it merely demonstrates the feebleness of our intelligence.

As for the meaning of the *Rebuttal of Objections* statement, "if I had any position, then there would arise that fault for me," it is the same as (the above lines of Chandra), ". . . applies to whoever has a (definite position) . . . "; and likewise the following statement, "(but) since I have no position, there only is no fault for me," has the same meaning as (the above), "since this position does not exist for me this consequence is not applicable." Therefore, the import of "thesislessness" and "positionlessness" (should be understood) according to the explanation of the *Introduction Commentary*.[125]

(Further, Aryadeva) states in the *Four Hundred*:

> Whoever takes no position at all,
> Either "existence," "non-existence," or "both existence and non-existence,"
> Cannot be (successfully) refuted
> Even if (one tries) for a very long time.[126]

This is not an authoritative source for (the Centrist's) non-assertion of proof of probanda even in the non-analytic conventional. For, although (Aryadeva) states that he cannot be faulted because he has no position, (Chandra) explains, in the *Introduction Commentary*, "because of the fact of the inappropriateness of these dualistic (analytic) theories in regard to the designatively existent, (an opponent's) refutation and rebuttals will

122 This in rebuttal of the charge of nihilism.

123 VV, ad. k. 27.

124 MMK, XXIV, k. 17ab: *śūnyatā yasya yujyate tasya sarvaṃ ca yujyate /.*

125 VV, k. 29 (cited PPMMV p. 6, 1. 2): *yadi kācana pratijñā syān me tata eva me bhavet doṣaḥ / nāsti ca mama pratijñā tasmān naivāsti me doṣaḥ //.* See above, n. 116. This is a clear example of Tsong Khapa's critical scholarship. It also confirms the view that the PPMMV cannot be properly understood, at least as reflecting the system of Chandra, with no critical comparison with his explanations of the same points in his other works, particularly MABh, CŚT, and YṢV.

126 CŚ, XVI, k. 25 (cited PPMMV p. 5, l. 25): *sadasatsadasacceti yasya pakṣo na vidyate / upālambhaś cireṇāpi tasya vaktuṃ na śakyate //.* See above, nn. 116, 125.

never succeed in faulting the Centrist in any way."[127] (That is), since refutation through (dualistic) analysis such as "is the attainment produced or unproduced?" is inapplicable to the non-analytically posited designatively existent, established by force of conventions, criticism through dualistic analysis will never succeed in refuting (the Centrist).[128] Therefore, when (Chandra) in the *Lucid Exposition* uses these (above) references as evidence for the statement "because he does not assert any other position,"[129] given as the reason for the improperness of a Centrist's use of private dogmaticism, (he is only giving) evidence for the (fact that) the Centrist does not assert ultimate status or does not properly assert the intrinsic identifiability (of anything). And the statement "if there is no such (assertion) and if such (another type of assertion) is improper" negates private dogmaticist (reasons), and does not negate a mere reason's proof of its probandum. "Dualistic theory" is stated to have three patterns: the theory that the negatee is a truth, and that the negation negating it is (also) a truth; the theory that (the negatee) has intrinsic identifiability and (its negation) total non-existence; and the above-explained dualistic theory (about production and non-production, etc.).[130]

ii. Rule of Non-Assertion of Private Reason

Here, one might imagine that, if intrinsically identifiable position, reason, and example are never possible, then not only private dogmaticism, but also all functions are invalidated. Nevertheless, this system establishes the validity of all functions, such as proof of probanda, (precisely) by negating that (intrinsic identifiability). Thus, what might be the reason for the impropriety of the admission of the functional effectiveness of (conventional) private reasons and probanda (in particular)?

(Chandrakirti) explains this in the *Lucid Exposition* in three (parts): (giving) the reasoning negating the private (approach), the way in which the opponent tacitly accepts that reasoning, and the reason why his own approach is not likewise subject to the same criticism.[131]

[127] MABh, VI, ad. k. 175, Poussin ed., p. 297. Immediately after this statement in MABh, Chandra quotes CŚ, XVI. 25, as given above n. 126.

[128] At least in regard to the Centrist's establishment of the conventional reality.

[129] PPMMV, I, Vaidya ed., p. 5, l. 24 (Stcherbatski's *Nirvana*, p. 95): *na ca mādhyamikasya sataḥ svatantrānumānaṃ kartuṃ yuktaṃ, pakṣāntarabhyupagamābhāvāt* /.

[130] The first type of theory is that of an absolutist logician, such as a Naiyayika; the second, that of a nihilistic logician, such as a Charvaka; and the third, that of a Buddhist logician, who still has the same problems, but in a more subtle form.

[131] This begins PPMMV, Vaidya ed., p. 8, l. 13. The second thrust of the argument as pointed out by Tsong Khapa begins on p. 10, 1. 6. The final point is covered, p. 11, ll. 13-22. This is interesting initially, as it shows the relevance of these passages of PPMMV, which have been considered by some scholars as unnecessary, since they thought Chandra

(First), (Chandra) criticizes Bhavaviveka's syllogism, "Internal media are certainly not self-produced absolutely, because they exist, just as consciousness itself exists,"[132] (in the following manner):

> Your use of the thesis-qualification "absolutely" is unnecessary from your own standpoint, since you do not accept production from self even superficially. (If you maintain that) it relates to (the standpoint of) others, it would be better to refute (your) heterodox (opponents) without any such qualification, since they muddle the two realities and should be refuted in terms of both.[133] (Further), since it is inappropriate to refute the claim of self-production in mundane conventional terms, it is inappropriate to employ such qualifications in that (context); for the mundane person assents to the mere arisal of an effect from a cause without any analytic inquiry into whether it is produced from self or from other.[134] Again, if it is the case that (you) wish to refute even the superficial production of the eye, etc., which your opponent believes to be absolute, this then entails with respect to yourself either the thesis-fault of subjectlessness, or the reason-fault of groundlessness, since you yourself do not accept eye, etc., as absolutely (existent).[135] If you object that my critique is inapplicable since, although absolute eye, etc., are not established, superficial eye, etc., exist, (I must ask you) then what is qualified by "absolutely"? If you venture that it qualifies the negation of production since you are negating ultimate production of superficial things such as eye, etc., (I must insist) that this is wrong, because you

---

had gone far enough when he said that the "Centrists have no thesis, etc." Thus, he has been seen as polemically rubbing Bhavaviveka's nose in the dirt, as it were. But our evaluation of the passage must be changed if we acknowledge that: a) Chandra does indeed accept the function of logic and philosophy, and so on, and b) it is particularly Bhavaviveka's *kind* of logic that he refutes. Then these passages follow from Chandra's general refutation as the exemplification of the unworkability of the private argument in a particular case.

132 Bhavaviveka employs this syllogism in his discussion of non-production in PrPr, I, as also in TJ, Samkhya chapter. The Skt. is quoted by Chandra in PPMMV, I; Vaidya ed., p. 8, l. 15: *na paramārthataḥ adhyātmikāni āyatanāni svata utpannāni, vidyamānatvāt caitanyavad iti /.*

133 Tsong Khapa follows PPMMV, Vaidya ed., p. 8 ff. in paraphrase of the main points: *kim arthaṃ punar atra paramārthata iti viśeṣaṇam upādīyate? lokasaṃvṛtyābhyupagatasya utpādasya apratiṣidhyamānatvāt / pratiṣedhe ca abhyupetabādhāprasangāditi cet naitad yuktam / saṃvṛtyāpi svata utpattyanabhyupagamāt / . . . paramatāpekṣaṃ viśeṣaṇam iti cet tadayuktam / saṃvṛtyāpi tadīyavyavasthānābhyupagamāt / satyadvayāviparītadarśana-paribhraṣṭā eva hi tīrthikā yāvad ubhayathāpi niṣidhyante tāvad guṇa eva saṃbhāvyata iti /.*

134 PPMMV: *na cāpi lokaḥ svata utpattiṃ pratipannaḥ, yatas tadapekṣayāpi viśeṣaṇa-sāphalyaṃ syāt / loko hi svataḥ parata ityevamādikaṃ vicāram anavatārya karaṇātkāryam utpādyate ityetāvanmātraṃ pratipannaḥ /.*

135 PPMMV: *yadi saṃvṛtyā utpattipratiṣedhanirācikīrṣuṇā viśeṣaṇam etad upādīyate, tada svato 'siddhādhāro pakṣadoṣaḥ, āśrayāsiddhau va hetudoṣaḥ syāt / paramārthataḥ svataś cakṣhurādyāyatanānām anabhyupagamāt /.*

did not state (it in) that (way), and because, even if you had stated it thus, it would entail the fallacy of subjectlessness with respect to the other party.[136]

To rebut this critique, (Bhavaviveka) argues that, when the Buddhist proves the impermanence of sound in (arguing with) the Vaisheshika, (the subject and probandum) are considered in general, and not as specifically qualified; because, if it was considered (as qualified specifically), there would be no means of establishing the probandum. For if the subject was considered to be "sound as a transformation of elements," it would be unestablished for the Vaisheshika, and if it was considered to be "sound as a property of ether," it would be unestablished for the Buddhist. Thus, just as (in that case) mere sound in general, with qualifications disregarded, is considered to be the subject, so (in this case) the mere eye, etc., are considered as subject, disregarding all qualifications such as "absolute" and "superficial," and there is no fault of the non-establishment of subject.[137]

In answer, (Chandra) refutes (Bhavya) by demonstrating the arguments such as (that based on) the mutually exclusive difference between the erroneous and the non-erroneous (objects and cognitions), in the light of Bhavya's own claim that the intrinsic actualities of subjects such as "eye" are not discovered by mere erroneous (cognitions). The gist of these (arguments is as follows). It is inappropriate to posit "mere eye, etc.," disregarding qualifications in light of the two realities, as subjects of the syllogisms proving the absence of production from self of eye, etc.; because the validating cognition that encounters that subject is a cognition that is unmistaken about the intrinsic reality of eye, etc. (according to your own system); and because, as unmistaken cognition does not mistake intrinsic reality, the object it encounters cannot be an erroneous object that falsely appears to have intrinsic identifiability when it actually does not. In regard to the way in which the first reason is admitted (by Bhavya), in a philosophical system that claims that whatever exists, exists by virtue

[136] PPMMV: *saṃvṛtyā cakṣurādisadbhāvād adoṣa iti cet, paramārthata ityetattarhi kasya viśeṣaṇam? sāṃvṛtānāṃ cakṣurādīnāṃ paramārthata utpattipratiṣedhād utpattipratiṣedhaviśeṣaṇe paramārthagrahaṇamiti cet, evaṃ tarhi evameva vaktavyaṃ syāt; saṃvṛtānāṃ cakṣurādīnāṃ paramārthato nāstyutpattiriti, na caivam ucyate / ucyamāne 'pi parair vastusatām eva cakṣurādīnām abhyupagamāt, prajñaptisatām anabhyupagamāt parato 'siddhādhāro pakṣadoṣaḥ syād iti na yuktam etat /.*

[137] PPMMV: *atha syāt-yathā anityaḥ śabda iti dharmidharmasāmānyam eva gṛhyate na viśeṣaḥ; viśeṣagrahaṇe hi sati anumānānumeyavyavahārābhāvaḥ syāt / tathā hiyadi catur mahābhautikaḥ śabdo gṛhyate sa parasyāsiddaḥ / athākāśaguṇo gṛhyate sa bauddhasya svato 'siddhaḥ / (tathā vaiśeṣikasya śabdanityatāṃ pratijānānasya yadi kāryaḥ śabdo gṛhyate sa parato 'siddhaḥ / atha vyaṇgyaḥ sa svato 'siddhaḥ) . . . tasmād yathātra dharmadharmisāmānyamātram eva gṛhyate evam ihāpi dharmimātram utsṛṣṭaviśeṣaṇaṃ grahīṣyata iti cet /.*

of its own objectivity, (a cognition) that errs in its perception of intrinsic identifiability cannot be represented as (validly) discovering its proper object. Any sort of validating cognition, either non-conceptual or conceptual (that is, perception or inference), must be unmistaken about the intrinsic identity of its validly cognized object, whether perceptual or conceptual. Thus, a validating cognition must derive its validity from an object which, not being merely a conventional, nominal designation, has intrinsic objectivity or intrinsic reality as its own actual condition; and this is just what (Bhavya's) own system claims. (Finally), the second reason is established by the fact that an object's being discovered by such a type of validating cognition precludes its being an erroneous object. Likewise, an object's being discovered by erroneous cognition precludes its being a non-erroneous object. Therefore, (Bhavya) has not been able to avoid the fault of (his syllogism's) having an unestablished subject (as Chandra previously pointed out).[138]

(Here) some might object that, "just as, in regard to the validating cognition perceiving sound, there is no need to establish it to be qualified as either permanent or impermanent, having first restricted it to such an

[138] In this extremely difficult and subtle passage, bearing importantly on the fundamental difference between the Dogmaticist and Dialecticist outlooks, Tsong Khapa departs from his close paraphrase, and reformulates Chandra's argument in a more formal mode. Thus, after giving the pertinent portions of the Sanskrit, I give a literal translation of it.

PPMMV: yasmād yadaivotpādapratiṣedho 'tra sādhyadharmo 'bhipretaḥ, tadaiva dharmiṇastadādhārasya viparyāsamātrāsāditātmabhāvasya pracyutiḥ svayamevānenāṇgīkṛtā / bhinnau hi viparyāsāviparyāsau / tadyadā viparyāsena asatsattvena gṛhyate, taimīrikeṇaiva keśādi, tadā kutaḥ sadbhūtapadārthaleṣasyāpyupalabdhiḥ // yadā ca aviparyāsād abhūtaṃ nādhyāropitaṃ vitaimīrikeṇaiva keśādi, tadā kuto 'sadbhūtapadārthaleṣasyāpi upalabdhiḥ, yena tadānīṃ saṃvṛtiḥ syāt? ata evoktam ācāryapādaiḥ / yadi kiṃcidupalabheyaṃ pravartayeyaṃ nivartayeyaṃ vā / pratyakṣādibhir arthais tadabhāvān me anupālambhaḥ // iti // yataścaivaṃ bhinnau vipayāsāviparyāsau, ato viduṣām aviparītāvasthāyāṃ viparītasyāsaṃbhavāt kutaḥ sāṃvṛtaṃ cakṣuḥ yasya dharmitvaṃ syāt? iti na vyāvartate 'siddhādhāro pakṣadoṣaḥ, āśrayāsiddho vā hetudoṣaḥ / ityaparihāra evāyaṃ //.

"[That is not so;] because, when as here the negation of production is accepted as probandum, [Bhavaviveka] himself postulates that it would be a grievous error for its basis, the subject [of the syllogism], to have an intrinsic nature established merely by erroneous [cognition]. The erroneous and the non-erroneous are different. And when through error the non-existent is considered existent, like fine hairs seen by the ophthalmic, then where will there be perception of that touching the category of the real? And when, through non-erroneous [cognition], there is no imposition of the unreal, like real hair seen by the visually acute, then where will there be a perception of that touching the category of the unreal, whereby such would become a superficial thing? Therefore the Master said [VV, k. 30]: 'If anything were to be perceived as objects by perception, etc., it would be confirmable or refutable; but because there are no such things, I cannot be gainsaid.' Thus, since erroneous and non-erroneous are different, and for the wise the erroneous cannot intrude upon the non-erroneous reality, then how can a superficial eye be the basic subject of his [syllogism]? Thus, [Bhavaviveka] has not eliminated the faults . . . etc."

In sum, Chandra argues from the fact that the Dogmaticist believes in the objective reality of objects having intrinsic identifiability, and hence cannot by his own lights leave the subject of the syllogism as a mere unqualified generality. See *Zin Bris*, ff. 43b ff.

alternative, in order for it to serve as a means of establishing the subject sound, so it is not necessary to establish cognition as qualified as either erroneous or non-erroneous, having first restricted it to such an alternative, in order to show it to be the validating cognition that is the means of establishing the subject. In the same way, even though the validating cognition perceiving sound, having restricted sound to being either permanent or impermanent, finds no permanent sound nor any impermanent sound, that does not preclude its perceiving (mere) sound. Likewise, even though the validating cognitions perceiving eye, etc., do not find eye, etc., as either true objects or false objects, having restricted them to being either true or false, that does not preclude their perceiving (mere) eye, etc. Therefore, those arguments that it is inappropriate to hold mere eye, etc. as subjects (of Bhavya's syllogism) are invalid."[139]

Since such doubts as these would never even arise for Bhavaviveka and his followers or for the Realist sages, Chandrakirti does not explicitly dispel them. Nevertheless, since they do arise for my contemporaries who do not understand this dispute, I will explain. When one examines whether an object is established by validating cognition or not, to pronounce it "established by validating cognition," it is necessary to cognize the indicated object as established as it appears to a non-conceptual validating cognition, or as established as it is ascertained or constructed by a conceptual validating cognition. And that means that it is a genuine object, since it is presented as established as it appears to us or is ascertained by us, and since (our) cognition is presented as non-erroneous in its perceptual object or in its ascertained or conceptual object. Thus, there is no question of (an artificial separation between the object and its cognitive status, as if) the object alone were restricted to an alternative (of being true or false, etc.) and its cognitive status were not so restricted to that alternative. And therefore, since a genuine object is presented as that discovered by a cognition unmistaken with regard to its intrinsic identity, how can the truth or falsity of an object be a question of alternative analysis of the object and not of (the object) as presented to cognition? (Of course) these (methods of verifying objects) are the methods of establishing (objects) by validating cognition used by the disputants who claim that existents exist by their intrinsic objectivity (such as the Dogmaticists), and not our (Dialecticist) method (of establishment of objects by validating cognition).

Thus, the Dogmaticist position is that, although genuine objects such as eye(-medium) are perceived by non-erroneous cognitions, they need

[139] These "contemporaries who do not understand the dispute" are not identified in any of the commentaries I have so far obtained, though it is clear they are among the majority still influenced by the legacy of Shantarakshita.

not be established as qualified as either conventionally or ultimately objective, (that is) with their status in light of the two realities (determined), and that, although it is proper to analyze the ultimate existence or non-existence (of an object) when it is considered as that qualified (by ultimacy or superficiality), how can criticisms expressed through examination of (an object's) qualification by (one or the other of) the two realities be applicable when (the object) is merely considered as a general subject (of a syllogism)? But Chandra considers that objects so (posited by Dogmaticists) become objectively existent, which is just the same in meaning as "ultimately existent," thus cannot possibly be "merely subjects," since (fundamentally) considered so qualified (as ultimately existent, etc.). And he thus refutes (the contention that) (eye, etc.) are merely considered as unqualified general subjects (of the syllogism).[140]

If the essence of these (arguments) is understood, one can know the reasons why the Dogmaticists explain that "the analysis of the superficial reality divides it into true and false (objects), because although both can appear (to ordinary cognitions), (the former) are able to perform functions, and the (latter are) not able to perform functions,"[141] and yet they do not divide the subjective (cognitions) into true and false. (And one can also know the reasons) why the Dialecticists represent both subjects and objects as true or false according to the mundane (usage) itself, and yet do not so present them in their own system (all in the superficial being false).

Finally, if (the Dogmaticists venture that) the subject (of the syllogism) is presented as established (merely) by erroneous cognition, in which things do not have the intrinsic identifiability they appear to have to both conceptual and non-conceptual cognitions, then the probandum (of the syllogism), namely, intrinsic realitylessness, would already have been established; and how could it be acceptable for an opponent for whom this remains to be proven? Therefore, (even in this case, Bhavaviveka) would still have the fault of unestablished subject (according to his own lights).[142]

[140] This passage succinctly summarizes the main pivot of this dispute, which is the Dogmaticist notion of the objective reality of empirical objects, which notion belies their deeper feeling of reliance upon their normal perceptions. It is this feeling that Chandra takes such pains to expose and open to question, for he considers it to be the subtle form of realism that prevents the Dogmaticists from fully realizing the central way. bLo-bzang Phun-tshogs records that this is one of the extremely subtle points that surfaces in the discussion around the negation of the private reason. It is noteworthy in relation to Wittgenstein, since here in the Dogmaticist case also, the notions of the private reason, inference, and syllogism, and so on, are based on the considering of the objects of perceptions "private objects," that is, objects that can be pointed to by the non-erroneous perceiver, that have intrinsic findability or intrinsic identifiability, that they really, indubitably "see."

[141] MAlam, k. 4.

[142] This final point puts yet another obstacle in the way of the Dogmaticist with his

(Here, the puzzled contemporaries[143] further object that) if objects discovered by mistaken cognition and non-erroneous knowable objects were contradictories, then also the object discovered by inferential rational cognition and the ultimate reality would also be contradictories; because it is inadmissible that (ultimate truth) could be discovered "merely," by erroneous cognition and hence must be discovered by cognition unmistaken with regard to the intrinsic reality (of its objects). And further, all superficial (objects) would become (ultimate realities), because they are encountered by the Victor's phenomenologically omniscient intuition; and yet the word "merely" excludes their discovery by an unmistaken cognition.

The first criticism does not apply, because, although inferential rational cognition is a mistaken cognition insofar as it is mistaken in regard to (the mode of existence of) its apparent object, it is not the case that everything it discovers is the result of mistaken cognition. For example, our (correct) perception of the sound of a conch, which is both sound and (intrinsically) false, does not preclude our failing to perceive a false sound.[144] (In regard to the second criticism,) a suspicion (such as the objector's) might well arise when considering the context, but the express intention of the speaker is to refute that (superficial objects) are discovered by analytic cognition that analyzes the modes of existence (of those objects), thus he says "merely," and he does not refute (the possibility) that such objects can be encountered by non-erroneous cognitions; because as (Chandrakirti) says in the *Lucid Exposition*, "We say 'what's the use of such application of fine analysis to mundane conventions?' as the superficial is found to have its self-existence merely by erroneous cognition."[145] Although this mode of explanation (of Chandra's) does

---

insistence on the "private, valid object," and so on, trying to put forth a merely general, unqualified object as subject.

143 This objection seems to follow from the previous objections, and so must have been current among Shantarakshita's followers in Tibet, among Nyingmapas, Sakyapas, Kagyupas, and even some Kadampas.

144 Tsong Khapa refers to the subtle point about inference and conceptual thought in general that, while it is mistaken ontologically in the sense that its habitual construction of the mode of existence of the objects and terms that appear to it is false, yet it can analytically arrive at the fact of its erroneousness, and can conceptually cognize the true mode of existence, and thus know it, while yet not overcoming its perceptual habits. This subtlety may be expressed by saying that ultimate reality, although conceded not to be expressible in words in the sense of not being encompassable by words, is nevertheless approachable by words, and indeed, only so approachable. One points out the moon, and another can look in the right direction to see it. If no one would point, having decided that it was senseless since one cannot put one's finger right on it, then another would not know in which direction to look for it.

145 PPMMV, VII, ad. k. 32, although it is not sure that this is the exact passage Tsong Khapa intends. In fact, Chandra repeats this statement often in PPMMV.

not correspond with his explanations elsewhere concerning the admission (by Bhavaviveka) that the ultimate status of the basic subject (of the syllogism) is lost, there is no discrepancy with his theory on the refutation of private dogmaticism.

These (above explanations aim to) refute the import (of Bhavya's methodology); now, we should refute his example.

When the Buddhist proves the impermanence of sound to the Vaisheshika, both systems do not verify (sound) with any validating cognition that finds sound (either) as a property of ether (or) as an elemental transformation. Nevertheless, they can point to "this thing" which is the mere sound that is the goal of validating cognitions. However, the case is different when the advocate of emptiness of intrinsic reality proves to the advocate of non-emptiness of intrinsic reality that eye, etc. are not produced from themselves. For not only can they not discover any objective existence or any objective non-existence, but also they cannot point out to each other, "such a thing as 'this' we both encounter as the actual thing to use as subject of argument."[146] Thus, the contention of the Dogmaticists such as Bhavaviveka, that although there is no pointing out of any general (object) disregarding that kind of qualification (such as "encounterably objectively existent" or not), one can apprehend a general subject disregarding such qualifications as "ultimately" or "truly established or not," cannot be maintained; because if something exists objectively, it is a thing that exists truly. Thus, as this (disagreement) occurred on account of the key point of the disagreement about the measure of the negatee, also in the case of the proof of the impermanence of sound, the two systems can show that "sound is established" even though not according to their respective systems' qualifications, as long as that does not involve any validating cognition, as might be expressed by "(we) both (accept) a validating cognition encountering sound that serves as a validating cognition for this kind of manifestation of sound." (Now) this (analysis) is in terms of the protagonist's assertion of objective

[146] This passage parallels PPMMV, I, Vaidya ed., p. 10 l. 1: *nidarśanasyāpi nāsti sāmyaṃ, tatra hi śabdasāmānyam anityatāsamanyaṃ ca avivakṣitaviśeṣaṃ dvayor api saṃvidyate / na tu evaṃ cakṣuḥ sāmānyaṃ śūnyatāśūnyatāvādibhyāṃ saṃvṛtyā angīkṛtaṃ nāpi paramārthataḥ / iti. . . .*

It is difficult to follow why the two cases are different if we assume that it is just "the eye-medium" that is pointed to, as in the example it is just a sound pointed to. We have to bear in mind that for the Dogmaticist, there is no "mere eye-medium," but an "objectively existent mere eye-medium," as the Dogmaticists will not allow of any "mere" thing, even conventional or superficial existent. Indeed, the Dialecticist does not see such an object, so there is nothing agreed upon to be pointed out to both. Here again we see the notion of the "private object" as understood by the Dogmaticist interfering with the interactions of the conventional level, as understood by the Dialecticist to operate only in the "public" realm, where the category of "objective existence" does not apply.

existence, but even if the Dialecticist were to play the role of protagonist, he could not show any method of establishing (a subject generally) by a validating cognition encountering the subject, disregarding qualification as to objective existence or non-existence, to such an antagonist (who asserts objective existence).

By means of these reasonings, you should also understand the method of (proving Bhavya's fault of) non-establishment of the reason.[147]

(Chandrakirti) appropriately criticizes (Bhavya) by specific analysis as to whether the subject is discovered by true or false cognition, since Bhavaviveka himself criticizes (the Analysts) as to the meaning of their reason in the syllogism "the internal media are productive causal conditions, because the Victor said so," by analysis in the light of the two realities, saying "if you say that it is in a superficial sense, it is unsatisfactory to you yourself, and if you say it is in an ultimate sense, it is unsatisfactory to me."[148] And the reason for this is the key point that the two realities are set up as those discovered (respectively) by cognitions that truly see knowable objects and by cognitions that superficially or falsely see knowable objects. As (Chandra) states in the *Introduction*:

> Through true and false perceptions of all things,
> They are held as having two realities;
> The object of true perception is Thatness,
> That of false perception said to be superficial reality.[149]

Here, when one only uses the twofold analysis relating to the two realities in regard to the reason, one must ask, "what is the sense of the reason?" However, when one makes a threefold analysis (of the reason) including the (possibility of) a mere (general) (reason) unqualified by either of the two (realities), one must ask "What do you set forth as a reason?[150]

[147] See below, where Bhavaviveka cannot verify with his own brand of valid cognition any ground of applicability of reason in an argument of the Analysts.

[148] PPMMV I, Vaideya ed., p. 10, l. 6 (ref. to TJ IV, where Bhavaviveka uses this mode of analysis against the Individualists): *ittham caitadevaṃ yat svayam api anena ayaṃ yathokto artho 'bhyupagataḥ tarkikena / santi eva ādhyātmikāyatanotpādakā hetvādayaḥ, tathā tathāgatena nirdeśāt / . . . asya paropakṣiptasya sādhanasya idaṃ duṣanam abhihitam anena - ko hi bhavatām abhipreto atra hetvarthaḥ? saṃvṛtyā tathā tathāgatena nirdeśāt, uta paramārthata iti? saṃvṛtyā cet svato hetor asiddhārthatā, paramārthaś cet . . . asiddhārthatā viruddhārthatā vā hetor iti. . . .*

[149] MA VI, k. 23, Poussin ed., p. 102.

[150] That is, as the third possibility is based on the disputants' basic sense of what can be pointed to without any qualification, their presuppositions about the "objective world," or "evident non-analytic conventionality" are brought into play and question. Thus, it is open to question in this case whether there is any object at all that can be pointed to as reason or logical subject. This recalls Wittgenstein's passionate remark to the advocate of the private object: "in what sense have you *got* what you are talking about and saying that only you have got it? Do you possess it? *You do not even see it!*" (*Philosophical Investigations*, paragraph 398)

(Chandrakirti) states as the reason why the above criticisms do not similarly apply to his own methodology, his non-acceptance of private dogmaticism: "Syllogisms proving probanda in our own system are sufficient if established for the antagonist, since their only purpose is to refute his false imaginations."[151] (He goes on to explain) that it is sufficient if either party (to a dispute) accepts (a subject, reason, etc.), giving the example of a mundane dispute, and that even Dignaga, who asserts that in (formal) proof and refutation, it is necessary that both establish (subject and reason, etc.), should in fact accept the former method, since (even he does admit that) refutation through scripture and personal inference are only established for oneself.[152]

The meaning of "private dogmaticism" is (illustrated) in certain contexts in the *Wisdom Lamp* where (Bhavya) generates syllogisms for establishing his probanda, having certified the status of his reason and his subjects both (in proof and refutation) with validating cognition, that is, privately, from the objective condition of the referents, without deriving (his position) from the assertions of his antagonist. These (passages) are marked by expressions such as "it is stated in 'independent' (*rang dbang du*) terms," or "in terms of refutation" where (the Tibetan) "independent" (*rang dbang*) is synonymous with (the Tibetan) "private" (*rang rgyud*).[153]

(In conclusion), (the Dialecticist) accepts both reasons and probanda without accepting private reasons and probanda, since the probanda are not yet established by antagonists who assert that existents are intrinsically, objectively existent, and since he cannot certify that "such and such is the method for establishing by a validating cognition an object which is not qualified, as above, as either objectively existent or as ob-

[151] PPMMV I, Vaidya ed., p. 11, l. 6 (*Nirvana*, p. 117): *na vayaṃ svatantrānumānaṃ prayuñjmahe parapratijñāniṣedhaphalatvādasmadanumānānām* . . . Tsong Khapa is not quoting directly here.

[152] Tsong Khapa here parallels PPMMV I, Vaidya ed., p. 11, ll. 13-20 (*Nirvana*, p. 119, with ref. to *Buddhist Logic II*, p. 172).

[153] See above, n. 99. Note that Tsong Khapa can only point to the common usage by Bhavaviveka of Sanskrit *svatantra* which Tibetan translators of PrPr have rendered by *rang dbang*, not by *rang rgyud*; so he has to show the virtual synonymity of the two terms in Tibetan. This indicates that, just as in the modern "logical privacy" controversy, it is *not* the subtle substantivist or Dogmaticist who considers "autonomous" objectivities, signs, reasons, cognitions, and actions based on them to be logically "private". He just sees them there before him, and assumes others also do so. It is thus the Dialecticist, who sees no such autonomies in anything, who must *force* him to recognize the absurd "logical privacy" of his autonomous, intrinsically identifiable world, thought, and activities. Thus, the terminology of privacy and publicness (*rang rgyud* and *gzhan grags*) could naturally only be developed by the Dialecticist and imposed on the unwilling Dogmaticist, in hopes of freeing him from the trap of his subtle substantivism, of course.

jectively inexistent. And when (a Dialecticist) sets forth a public syllogism proving the realitylessness of the objective status of a sprout, employing the reason of relativity and the example of a mirror-image, he does not call (his syllogism) "public" and "not established for both (parties)" because he himself does not assert the concomitance between the sprout and relativity or between relativity and intrinsic realitylessness, but because, as above, (his reason, etc.) will not be established independently by validating cognition for his antagonist. Thus (a "public syllogism") means that (it employs reasons, subjects, etc., which are) not established for both (parties) by validating cognition in such a (private) manner.[154]

Although the sprout and its relativity are established by natural, conventional, validating cognitions in the mental processes of both protagonist and antagonist, that (type of validating cognition) is confused for the antagonist with (a presumed) validating cognition encountering intrinsic objective existence, and the two are not distinct for him until his (authentic) view is generated. Hence the protagonist is unable to show him (anything established by merely conventional validating cognition) until such time (as his confusion is gone), even though the protagonist himself distinguishes (the two types of validating cognition). Although Dialecticists among themselves may demonstrate methods of establishment (of subjects, etc.) by validating cognitions without deriving them from each other's assertions, (they employ) validating cognitions presented in verbal, conventional terms, and not presented in terms of the intrinsic objectivity of the phenomena (involved). Hence, (the employment of) private dogmaticism is inappropriate (for them also).

In regard to (phenomena) such as a sprout, there are three perceptual habits: one holding it to be objectively existent; one holding it to be objectively inexistent; and one holding it without qualifying it in either way. If the distinction is clearly understood that all three of these habit-patterns exist in the mental process of one in whom the authentic view is generated, but that only the first and the last are present in the mental process of one in whom no authentic view has been generated, then one will put a stop to the following false views: (the view) that rationality

[154] This definition of *paraprasiddhānumāna* indicates that it is not the same in Dialecticist usage as in the Logicians' usage, where it is considered a fault of a thesis, as only established for one party in a debate. On the contrary, for the Dialecticist it is established for both parties, on a common-sense level (although the absolutist, or "privatist," is philosophically unaware of that fact), and is established for neither party by any independent validating cognition, although the absolutist again does think that some things are so established and some things are not. Thus, our translation "public inference" and "public syllogism" fit very well here, stressing the utter conventionality of the basis of establishment of subject, reason, concomitance, and so forth. See above, n. 99.

does not put a stop to all perception (controlled) by the mental constructions (such as) "this is it"; (the view) that all practices before the generation of the authentic view, such as cultivation of the will to enlightenment, are but truth-habits, or sign-habits; and (the view) that after one lays claim to having generated in mind the authentic view, there will be no intentionality in all one's acts.[155]

Therefore, it is not enough, when proving a probandum with a public reason, for the antagonist only to accept it. The subject, probandum,[156] and the reason, etc. must be established by (conventional) validating cognition recognized from one's own point of view, and even the antagonist must definitely or somewhat accept it. Otherwise, if (the antagonist) is mistaken about the conceptual object, he will be unable to generate the view that realizes ultimate reality. And this very fact of the indispensability of conventional validating cognition as the cause of encountering the supreme reality is the import of (Nagarjuna's famous) statement: "Without relying on conventions, the supreme reality will not be understood."[157]

(Finally), one might suppose that, according to this (critique by Chandrakirti), the Dogmaticists such as Bhavaviveka—since they (by implication) assert what amounts to ultimate or true status (of phenomena)—should not be classified as Centrists. (However), we cannot say "I accept that as a pot," when we ascertain its roundness yet are not sure that it is a pot, since it is yet to be established by validating cognition. And we cannot say that the Vaisheshika is not a philosopher who asserts a whole substantially different (from its parts), even though (in our view) he proves by validating cognition what amounts to be the non-existence of the whole "pot" substantially different from its parts. Just so, those (Dogmaticist) sages are Centrists, since they clearly assert truthlessness, refuting with numerous rational methods the true existence of phenom-

[155] That is, a) aware that generation of correct view entails perception of non-existence of objective reality in things, one trusts that reasoning leading to this authentic view does not fail to put a stop to verbalized constructions such as "this is it!" (accompanied by the mysterious inner pointing out that Wittgenstein talked about); b) aware that since the third type, non-qualified perception, does exist for one who has not yet generated the authentic view, mental cultivations such as will-to-enlightenment, and so on, can be practiced without bringing truth-habits, and so on, into play; and c) aware that the realizer of authentic view can still function mentally in all three ways, so one does not expect and await a hypothetical "enlightened state," where one's mind is a blank, where one cannot plan one's compassionate activities, where things must be "spontaneous," and so on, and so forth.

This little epistemological disgression on the experience of enlightenment and its relationship to ordinary experience is of profound significance and worthy of repeated contemplation. See Introduction, VIII.

[156] Reading *chos can gnyis* as an abbreviation for *chos dang chos can gnyis*.

[157] MMK XXIV, k. 10: *vyavahāramanāśrityā paramārtho na deśyate / paramārthamanāgamya nirvāṇaṃ nādhigamyate //*.

Chapter VI

AVOIDANCE OF CONTRADICTION BETWEEN THE (DIALECTICIST) SYSTEM AND THE SCRIPTURES

AVOIDANCE OF CONTRADICTION WITH THE *ELUCIDATION OF INTENTION*

Now one may wonder, if the interpretations of the other masters are as explained above, how does this master interpret the differentiation between reality and realitylessness with reference to the three natures and the method of presenting interpretable and definitive meanings of the *Elucidation of Intention*?

On this subject, there is no clear explanation in the original treatises of Nagarjuna and Aryadeva, nor did Buddhapalita explicate the details of this (question). However, (Chandrakirti), in the *Introduction Commentary*, explains four theories (of the Idealists) to be interpretable in meaning: (namely), the theories that the first two natures (respectively) do not and do exist with intrinsic identifiability; that there is a fundamental consciousness; that there are no external objects; and that there is final genealogical determinism. His own words are as follows, (first quoting an Idealist):

> "This scriptural reference makes it clear that even other scriptures of that same type are interpretable in meaning."
>
> Which are the "scriptures of that same type?" (They are) such as the *Elucidation of Intention*, teaching the three natures, imagined, relative, and perfect, with the imagined utterly non-existent and the relative utterly existent; and (teaching that) "the grasping consciousness is deep and subtle, all seeds streaming (therein) like flowing water; thus I do not show it to the naive, thinking it inappropriate, lest they construe it as a self." And such as these are explained to be interpretable by the scripture: "Just as a doctor prescribes medicines for the sickness of invalids, so the Buddha teaches even 'mind-only' to some living beings."[1]

[1] MA, VI, k. 95cd, Poussin ed., p. 195; MABh, VI, Poussin ed., pp. 195-56. The SN

Thinking that the last (of the four doctrines) could be understood as interpretable from the proof of (the doctrine of) the unique vehicle executed (by Nagarjuna) in the *Scripture Synthesis*[2] (Chandra) in the *Introduction Commentary* proves by reason and reference the interpretability of the first three (doctrines), this quote showing the (proof of) their interpretability through scriptural reference. There are two kinds of "mind-only" references, those that negate external things and those that do not. With reference to the type of scripture that makes such statements as "the externally apparent does not exist,"[3] (Chandra states) that the *Mission to Lanka* clearly shows their interpretability. For, the statements of "mind-only" are not in terms of the Teacher's own system but in terms of the inclination of the disciples, just as the doctor does not give medicine to particular patients out of his own whim, but in accord with the particular pattern of the patient's sickness.

(Chandra) continues, saying, "likewise the mention of Buddha-essence in the Buddha's discourses . . . " and concludes his quotations by saying, "thus, such kinds of scriptures, all of which are accepted as definitive in meaning by the Idealists, are clearly shown to be interpretable in meaning by this (very) scriptural reference."[4] This passage is explained (by Jayananda) in his *Subcommentary* as showing the interpretability of the statements of "mind-only," by using the statements of the interpretability of the "Buddha-essence" as examples, and he also explains "this scriptural reference" as referring to the *Ten Stages* refutation of the world-creator in the context of the realization of relativity.[5] (But) this is incorrect, since (Chandra) in his own commentary uses the interpretability of "mind-only" statements as the example, and then proves the interpretability of all scriptures taken as definitive by the Experientialists by reason of the statement of the interpretability of the Buddha-essence (doctrine). Thus, "by this scriptural reference," in this context referring to one of two (preceding quotes), refers to the *Mission to Lanka* indication of the interpretability of the Buddha-essence (doctrine) and of the (fact that)

---

quote, "The grasping consciousness . . . " is the concluding verse of SN, V. Lamotte (*Explication*, p. 58) restores this verse as: *ādānavijñāna gambhīrasūkṣmo, ogho yathā vartati sarvabījo / bālāna eṣo mayi na prakāśi, mā haiva ātmā parikalpayeyuḥ //*. The scriptural quote, "Just as a doctor . . . " is from the LAS, Vaidya ed., p. 54 (Skt. *āturi āturi bhaiṣajyaṃ yadvad bhiṣak prayacchati / cittamātraṃ tathā buddhaḥ sattvānāṃ deśayanti vai //*, also quoted *Subhāṣitasaṃgraha*, f. 25, LVP, p. 250).

bLo-bzang Phun-tshogs (*Zin Bris* II, f. 49b4 ff.) mentions a fifth Idealist doctrine also shown to be interpretable by this reference, namely, the doctrine of the permanent phenomenal existence of the Buddha-essence (Tib. *snying po rtag dngos yod par*), discussed by mKhas-grub at length in *sTong Thun*.

[2] Tsong Khapa follows the tradition that accepts Nagarjuna's authorship of the *Sūtrasamuccaya*. Therein, the *ekayāna* proof runs from TG, C, ki, f. 190 ff.

[3] *phyi rol snang ba yod min te / . . .* common phrase in Idealist scriptures.

[4] MABh, VI, Poussin ed., p. 196, l. 12 to p. 198, l. 15, here expounded in paraphrase.

[5] Jayananda's MAT a subcommentary on MA often criticized by Tsong Khapa.

realitylessness is to be understood as the inner (gist) of all the scriptures.[6] And, as for the *Ten Stages* refutation of any other creator (than the mind), this is stated as evidence for the fact that the "only" in the expression "mind-only" does not exclude external things, and not as evidence showing that the negation of external things is interpretable in meaning. "Such kinds of scriptures" refers to those that give teachings such as those in the *Elucidation of Intention* above, and does not show that the Idealists assert the definitiveness of scriptures that show the Buddha-essence (doctrine) to be interpretable! There is no question about both these points. Our own view is that (Chandra's) quotation of the statement of the interpretability of the Buddha-essence (doctrine) is the (scriptural) proof that the *Elucidation of Intention* doctrine of the fundamental consciousness is not to be taken literally.

In this regard, it is first necessary to understand that the teaching of the (Buddha-) essence is not literally intended, as the *Mission to Lanka* states:

> Those scriptures that teach according to the inclinations of living beings are erroneous in meaning, not giving the message of Thatness. A teaching which is like a mirage, deceiving thirsty beasts by having no water, may generate devotion in the naive-minded, but is not the message that establishes the wisdom of the Holy Ones. Therefore, you should follow the (intended) meaning, and should not be attached to the expression.[7]

Further, in the *Mission to Lanka*, Mahamati questions:

> The Lord promulgates the Buddha-essence in the discourses, saying it is naturally radiant, primordially pure, endowed with the thirty-two marks, and existing within the bodies of all living beings. You say it is like a precious gem, wrapped in a filthy rag, being permanent, stable, and eternal, but wrapped by the defilement of the aggregates, elements, and sense-media. How is this Buddha-essence-theory different from the soul-theory of the heterodox? For the heterodox also espouse a soul as permanent, inactive, qualityless, all-pervading, and indestructible.[8]

[6] Refers to MABh passage given in n. 4 above.

[7] LAS, Vaidya ed., p. 33 (passage preceding that quoted MABh, Poussin ed., pp. 196-97 (LVP pp. 251-52)): . . . *sūtrāntaḥ sarvasattvāśayadeśanārthavyabhicāriṇī, na sa tattvavyavasthānakathā / tadyathā mahāmate mṛgatṛṣṇikā mṛgollāpinī udakabhāvābhiniveśenābhiniveśyate, tasyāṃ codakaṃ nāsti, evameva mahāmate sarvasūtrāntadeśanā dharmā bālānāṃ svavikalpasaṃtoṣanaṃ, na tu sa tattvāryajñānavyavasthānakathā / tasmāttarhi mahāmate arthānusāriṇā bhavitavyaṃ na deśanābhilāpābhiniveṣṭena //.*

[8] (LAS Vaidya ed., following the above, quoted MABh, etc.): . . . *tathāgatagarbhaḥ punarbhagavatā sūtrāntapaṭhe 'nuvarṇitaḥ / sa ca kila tvayā prakṛtiprabhāsva-*

In answer, the Lord said that the Buddhas teach the Buddha-essence (intending) the objective selflessness, the non-apparent object, with its synonyms such as "emptiness," "signlessness," and "wishlessness," in order to avoid the fear of selflessness on the part of the naive and to educate the heterodox who are attracted to soul-theories, and thus it is not the same as the heterodox soul-theories. Present and future bodhisattvas should not become attached to it as a self. Thinking that those beings whose thoughts have been dominated by soul-theories will more quickly come to enlightenment if their thoughts dwell in the sphere of the three doors of liberation, the (Buddhas) teach the Buddha-essence to that end. Thus one should understand the Buddha-essence as corresponding to selflessness, in order to eliminate heterodox views. I quote (and paraphrase) here no further, fearing prolixity.[9]

Thus, (Chandra) proves the non-similarity between the theory of the Buddha-essence and the theory of the existence of self by the reason that (the Buddha's) statement intimates as its intended basis the emptiness which is objective selflessness, out of the need to eliminate the (disciples') fear of selflessness and gradually to lead those attached to soul-theories toward selflessness. Such being the case, the soul-theorists are intending just what they are teaching, whereas the Teacher's intended meaning, which he considers when teaching, and his literal meaning are utterly different. When the soul-theorists teach the permanent, and so on, self, they are at all times certainly and firmly committed to their own literal meaning, whereas the Teacher sometimes teaches as if his literal meaning were true, but then later (indicates that he did so) in order to lead (the disciples' minds) around to the intimated meaning he was intending. Thus, (Chandra shows we) must see through the (apparent) similarity, saying "the two are not the same." This clearly shows that if we literally accept the teaching of Buddha-essence as previously expounded, we would be the same as the theorists of soul-existence; and that very fact is the refutation of the explicit (teaching of the Buddha-essence). Thus, what intelligent person would dispute whether or not such statements (of Buddha-essence) in other scriptures are established as interpretable in mean-

---

raviśuddhyādiviśuddha eva varṇyate dvatriṃṣallakṣaṇadharaḥ sarvasattvadehāntargataḥ mahārghamūlyaratnaṃ malinavastraparivesṭitam iva skandhadhātvāyatanavastraparivesṭito (rāgadveśamohaparibhūtaḥ parikalpamalamalino) nityo dhruvaḥ śāśvataścānuvarṇitaḥ / tat katham ayaṃ bhagavān tīrthakārātmavādatulyas tathāgatagarbhavādo na bhavati / tīrthakārāpi bhagavān nityo 'kartā nirguṇo vibhur avyaya ityātmāvādopadeśaṃ kurvanti //.

[9] *(LAS Vaidya ed., following above): bhagavān āha / na hi mahāmate tīrthakārātmavādatulyo mama tathāgatagarbhavādopadeśaḥ / kim tu . . . śūnyatābhūtakoṭinirvāṇānutpādānimittāpraṇihitādyānāṃ padārthānāṃ tathāgatagarbhopadeśaṃ kṛtvā . . . bālānāṃ nairātmyasaṃtrāsapadavivarjanārthaṃ . . . deśayanti / na . . . bodhisattvair ātmābhiniveśaḥ kartavyaḥ /*, etc.

ing, when this scripture has shown the intimated basis, the need, and the refutation of literalness? It is very clear about the inappropriateness of literal acceptance, using the example of a mirage, and saying, "one should follow the (intimated) meaning, and should not be attached to the (literal) expression." If, in spite of this, one does not accept the elucidation of (Chandrakirti), but accepts the interpretability of this teaching from rational refutation of its literalness, that being the personal precept of the Indian sages, and yet still does not admit that the above scripture demonstrates the fact (of the Buddha-essence's interpretability), then one merely exhibits one's own true nature!

Further, in the *Scripture Synthesis*, (Nagarjuna) introduces all the above-quoted scriptural passages with the remark, "the Tathagata, by teaching a variety of doors to the (Great) Vehicle in terms of (the inclinations of) the disciples, teaches this very profound ultimate reality." "This profound ultimate reality" refers directly to the just previously quoted references from the *Transcendent Wisdom*, etc., teaching the emptiness which is objective selflessness.[10] And "in terms of the disciples" means that such explanations are influenced by the inclinations of the disciples, which has the same meaning as (Chandra's) statement above that "this is the teaching to generate devotion in the naive, and is not the teaching of ultimate reality."

As for the way in which literal acceptance (of the Buddha-essence theory) is the same as the advocacy of the existence of self, (this literal acceptance may be formulated as the assertion that) the Buddha-essence exists as literally taught, the Buddha not having taught the Buddha-essence thinking of the intimated meaning of emptiness, non-production, or selflessness, etc., which is the mere exclusion of the fabrications of objective self or of identifiably existent production, but (having meant it) literally as he taught it. And the (Buddha-essence's) permanence is not merely that indestructibility which is the mere exclusion of the negatee, destruction, but is a permanence which arises as an established entity, like (the colors) yellow or blue, not needing to be represented as the exclusion of negatee. Such being the case, as there is no difference (between this position and) the type of permanence (maintained) by the non-Buddhist advocates of the permanent self, (this position) amounts to an assertion of a permanent phenomenon. The refutation of this (theory) is (accomplished by) the elucidations in the higher and lower orthodox schools of the reasonings refuting the permanence advocated by the heterodox (philosophers), since those (Buddhist scholars) do not accept any such (permanent) thing.

Once one asserts the determination of a permanent thing that is not

[10] *Sūtrasamuccaya*, TG, C, ki, f. 207a2-3.

merely a negation excluding destruction, one is not suitably receptive to any sort of explanation of the two selflessnesses, taught to be the selfless reality which is the mere exclusion of the fabrications, the two "selves." As these scriptures have stated above, (the Buddhas) declare (the Buddha-essence, etc.) for the sake of those who are attached to self-theories, in order to eliminate their fear of selflessness.

Therefore, there are two modes (of teachings) with interpretable meaning. There are those interpretable meaning teachings for the sake of gradually leading to reality those Buddhists who are suitably receptive to explanations of the ordinary personal selflessness and the gross objective[11] selflessness; and showing the refutation of their literal meaning is extremely difficult. (Second,) there are those interpretable meaning teachings taught in order to educate those of the heterodox type who, as explained above, are not ready for the full explanation of even the ordinary personal selflessness, as they either openly advocate the heterodox self or else have a great habitual affinity for such views from their former lives; and it is easy to show the refutation of their literal meaning.

If thus the doctrine of the existence of a (Buddha-) essence which is permanent, etc., is interpretable in meaning, how does one establish the interpretability of (the doctrine of) fundamental consciousness?

The two expressions, "Buddha-essence" and "fundamental consciousness" are repeatedly declared to be synonymous; thus, from the *Dense Array Scripture*:

> The various realms are the fundamental consciousness, and so also are the Buddha-essences. The Tathagatas indicate that very nature by means of the expression "fundamental consciousness." Although the "essence" is renowned as the "fundamental," the feeble-minded are unaware of it.[12]

Likewise, the *Mission to Lanka* mentions that "the Buddha-essence, renowned as the 'fundamental consciousness,' is endowed with the seven (auxiliary) consciousnesses."[13] Thus, they are the same, being verbally

[11] Ordinary, or gross, personal selflessness is defined by all Buddhist schools other than Dialecticist as the non-existence of a permanent, unique, and independent person. The subtle selflessness of person is defined by these schools as the non-existence of a self-sufficient person. The Dialecticists define the two as non-existence of a self-sufficient person, and non-existence of an intrinsically identifiable person, respectively. As to gross selflessness of things, the Idealists define it as the non-existence of independent objects as such, and the Experientialist-Dogmaticists as the non-existence of subject-object difference. Since the Dialecticists themselves do not consider any objective selflessness other than the subtle lack of intrinsic identifiability of things to be genuine, Tsong Khapa may here be using "gross" (*rags pa*) in a less technical sense, referring to the kind of intimation of objective selflessness contained in the similes for the aggregates used even in the Individual Vehicle to indicate their general insubstantiality. See Introduction, VIII, 3, Table D.

[12] *Ghanavyūhasūtra* (Tib. *Rgyan-stug-po-bkod pa*).

[13] LAS, Vaidya ed.; *tathāgatagarbhaḥ ālayavijñānakīrtitaḥ saptavijñāninaḥ* /.

synonymous considering their intended meaning, in spite of the fact that they are not shown to be literally (and conceptually) equivalent, the one being permanent, the other impermanent, since the fundamental consciousness is taught intending the very same thing intended by teaching of the essence. Such being the case, the demonstration of the former's interpretability establishes the latter as interpretable in meaning.[14] Such is the view of Chandra, as he states in the *Introduction Commentary* that "it must be acknowledged that it is precisely emptiness that (the Buddha) indicated by the expression 'fundamental consciousness,' in order to introduce the intrinsic reality of all phenomena."[15]

Thus, although that intended is the same thing (when speaking of "essence" and "fundamental"), the disciples are different. The disciple for whom the "fundamental consciousness" is declared is suitably receptive to the teaching of the ordinary personal selflessness and of the objective selflessness which is (defined as) emptiness of subject-object-duality. (We know this) because such (a disciple) is unable to understand the intrinsic realitylessness of all persons and things; because the fundamental consciousness is presented out of the necessity of teaching emptiness with respect to external objects, as (Chandra) says in the *Introduction*:

> "Fundamental consciousness exists!" "Person exists!" "These aggregates alone exist!"—These teachings are for the sake of those who do not understand Thatness, the most profound of things.[16]

(Finally), the source that shows the interpretability of the differentiation of the first two (of the three) natures with regard to not existing and existing (respectively) with intrinsic identifiability is the *Mission to Lanka* passage quoted in the *Introduction Commentary* immediately after the scriptural citations that show the interpretability of the above doctrines; namely, the statement, "Mahamati, this inner understanding of the scriptures of all Buddhas has the nature of emptiness, productionlessness, non-duality, and intrinsic realitylessness. . . . " Thus, (the Buddha here)

[14] This distinction Tsong Khapa makes between the synonymity of the two expressions (*ming gi rnam grangs yin pa*), considering they both intend the same referent, and their literal-conceptual (*sgras zin gyi don*) difference (*gnyis mi gcig pa*) is somewhat obscure. He apparently means, as inferred from Chandra's view, which he subsequently expounds, that both are used by the Buddha intending emptiness, but their conceptual difference, being respectively permanent and impermanent, is part of the interpretable, conventional, pedagogical device.

[15] MABh, VI, ad. k. 41, Poussin ed., p. 131 (LVP, p. 321).

[16] MA, VI, k. 43, Poussin ed., p. 132 (LVP, p. 322): Poussin cites a Skt. version from *Subhāṣitasaṃgraha*: *evaṃ hi gambhīratarāṇ padārthān na vetti yastaṃ prati deśaneyam / astyālayaḥ pudgala eva cāsti, skandhā ime va khalu dhātavaśca //*. The Tibetan version was translated from a Skt. version that read *kevalam* for *dhātavaś*.

declares that any sort of scripture whatsoever should be understood as having this very meaning (of non-duality, etc.).[17]

Well then, how does this system present the interpretability and definitiveness of the three wheels (of Dharma)?

(Even) in the first wheel, the statements of intrinsic realitylessness of persons and things are definitive in meaning. (However, the explanation of) personal (selflessness) through negation of merely substantial self-sufficiency (of a supposed self) different in nature from the aggregates, rather than through negation of the intrinsic identifiability (of that supposed self) is interpretable in meaning. That intended by such (explanations) is the mere conventional existence (of self). As for the necessity (for such an interpretable teaching,) it is in order to avoid the arisal of nihilism (in such a disciple) from the teaching of the emptiness of persons and things with regard to intrinsic identifiability, to cultivate their mental processes by teaching the gross selflessness, and (finally) to introduce them to the subtle selflessness. And the refutation of the literal acceptability (of these teachings) consists in the reasonings negating intrinsically identifiable status (of things).

Next, in the second wheel, the statements that persons and things are empty with respect to ultimate or intrinsically identifiable existence while yet existing according to mundane conventionality are the ultimate in definitive meaning. They were taught to those Universalists able to understand the equivalency of relativity empty of intrinsic identifiability with emptiness with respect to intrinsic reality, since (causal processes) such as bondage and liberation are definitely non-viable (if presumed to) have intrinsically identifiable status, and it is indispensably necessary to accept the relativity of such (causal processes as) bondage and liberation. In the abbreviated teachings of such (second wheel scriptures) as the *Heart of Transcendent Wisdom*, such as "those five aggregates should be precisely viewed as empty of any intrinsic reality,"[18] the negatee is not explicitly qualified with the expression "in the ultimate," yet is implicitly so qualified, as such (qualification) must be understood from the context of the elucidations of (all) statements of emptiness with respect to intrinsic identifiability. Or, even if such were not the case, such (qualification) must be understood as implicit (in the abbreviated versions), since once the qualification "in the ultimate" is applied in such (extensive) versions as the *Mother Scripture*, it must be understood (as implicit) in

[17] MABh VI, ad. k. 95, Poussin ed., p. 198 (LVP, p. 252). LAS quote found Vaidya ed., p. 33: *etaddhi Mahāmate śūnyatānutpādādvayaniḥsvabhāvalakṣaṇaṃ sarvabuddhānāṃ sarvasūtrāntagatam /.*

[18] *Prajñāpāramitāhṛdaya; phung po lnga po de dag kyang rang bzhin gyis stong par rnam par yang dag par rjes su bltao.*

all scriptures of the same class. For example, when a contemporary author composes a treatise, and expresses himself consistently on a certain subject, we must understand (as implicit) (his consistent expression) in those contexts where he does not so express himself (for brevity's sake, etc.).

Finally, (in the third wheel), the statements of the lack of intrinsic identifiability of the first nature and of the intrinsically identifiable existence of the latter two natures (are interpretable in meaning). (They are) taught for those (disciples) of the Universal Vehicle class who would find no ground to establish cause-effect and bondage-liberation in the intrinsic realitylessness that is emptiness with respect to intrinsically identifiable status, in order to forestall their falling into the great nihilism from (misinterpreting) the teaching of the middle wheel and in order to introduce them to the subtle objective selflessness by cultivating their mental processes by means of the teaching of the gross objective selflessness. (These statements were made) intending the Idealist differentiation between the first nature and the latter two natures, as (respectively) being established verbally and conventionally and being identifiably established on the conventional level. The refutations of the literal acceptability (of this third wheel teaching) consists of the formulations of the Centrist treatises (to the effect that), although there is no rational refutation of the ultimate non-establishment of persons and things, all presentations such as causality are impossible if (things) are ultimately or intrinsically identifiably existent.[19]

Such is (Chandra's) method of presenting the interpretability and definitiveness (of the three wheels of Dharma), which, although in disagreement with the formulation of the *Elucidation of Intention*, is consistent with the *King of Samadhis* and the *Teaching of Aksayamati*.

We must not confuse the (above teachings about the) turning of the wheel of Dharma three times with the meaning of the (following) passage from the *Questions of King Dharanishvara*:

> Just as the jeweler perfects a gem by stages with the threefold cleansing and the threefold rubbing, so the Victor, knowing the scope of the impure living beings, makes those infatuated with the world tired at heart and causes them to engage in the religious discipline by means

[19] This last paragraph was resorted in translation into roughly the same order of presentation as the first two paragraphs: that is, 1) such and such a main theme is interpretable; 2) why; 3) intending what; 4) for what reason; 5) refutable by what reasonings—for clarity of comparison. Tsong Khapa, apparently tired of repeating himself in the same fashion, wove all the items together in his final paragraph into two rather convoluted sentences, quite intelligible in the abbreviated Tibetan. They are perfectly accurate, but, presented all at once as it were, might confuse the English reader not so accustomed to handling these doctrines.

of the doctrine of renunciation, such as "impermanence," "misery," "selflessness," and "ugliness." He causes them to realize the deep process of the Tathagata doctrine, by means of the teaching of emptiness, signlessness, and wishlessness. Next, he installs those living beings in the Buddha-realm by means of the teaching of irreversibility and the teaching of the purification of the three spheres (of acts, that is, agent, action, and patient). And those living beings, having become equalized in their various genealogies and faculties, realize deeply the ultimate nature of the Tathagata, and are dubbed "the unexcelled worthies for offerings."[20]

Thus, this (passage teaches) how a single person is led first into the Individual Vehicle. Then, being introduced into the Buddha-realm, the Universal Vehicle, finally he reaches the stage of attaining Buddhahood. (On the other hand,) the three wheels of Dharma are turned for the sake of Individual Vehicle and Universal Vehicle disciples of different characters. (This is also evident from the fact that) the *Scripture Synthesis* quotes this scriptural passage as a proof of the fact that there is ultimately one vehicle,[21] since even the Individualists enter (eventually) the Universal Vehicle and attain Buddhahood. Thus, as both the first two stages (mentioned in the passage) lead (the disciple) in the Individual Vehicle, the selflessness of that first stage is like the selflessness included in the four (aspects of the first holy truth, that is,) impermanence, etc., said in the *Four Hundred* to be a means of cultivating a (disciple's) character before teaching him the view of emptiness. Such (selflessness) is the absence of the self that is (presumed to be) independent among its possessions. (In the passage above), "irreversibility" means that once one enters that (vehicle) it is not necessary to go on any different vehicle.[22]

Here one might object that if the meaning of the scriptures is (both) as the Idealists elucidate it and (also) as the Centrists elucidate it differently, then it becomes a matter of internal contradictions for the speaker (of the scriptural discourses), and the meaning of the scriptures is (entirely) refuted.

Well now, is it the import of the Disciples' Canon that there is no permission for taking life, (even) depending on (certain) circumstances? Or is it not? If it is not, then there would be no difference between the Individual Vehicle and Universal Vehicle Canons with regard to whether taking life is prohibited or allowed. If it is, then, as the import of the

[20] *Dhāraṇīśvararājaparipṛcchasūtra* is unavailable in Skt., and is not quoted in surviving compendia, though quoted in *Sūtrasamuccaya*, itself only extant in Tibetan.

[21] Quote from *Sūtrasamuccaya* occurs in *ekayāna* section, TG, C, ki, f. 190 ff.

[22] This CŚ quote is not a direct quote from the text, although the gist of the statement is contained in CŚ, I.

Universal Vehicle Canon is indeed that, given certain (dire) necessities, taking of life is permitted, there is an internal contradiction for the speaker (of the canons). If I say that, what answer do you have? If you venture that while as far as the Individual Vehicle disciple is concerned there is never permission for taking life, there is no contradiction, since the speaker's intention is that (only) given certain special (cases of) Universal Vehicle (disciples) is there such permission, (then you have answered your own question). Where then is the contradiction in there being (statements about) intrinsic identifiability, considering the intellects of certain Universal Vehicle class disciples who are not (yet) receptive to the full explanation of the profound, and in there being (statements that there is) no intrinsically identifiable status in anything, considering those disciples who are receptive (and able) to understand the full import of the profound?

We cannot apply (this sort of intentional analysis) to statements such as "Having killed father and mother . . . ," where although the literal meaning is not the meaning of the expression, since that is determined by the speaker's desire, namely (that one should eliminate) existence and craving, since the speaker here wants this sort of disciple to understand the actual meaning as explicitly expressed (albeit symbolically). Therefore, our position is that the non-definitiveness (of a teaching) is proven by showing a (logical) refutation of its literal meaning, the explicit meaning having necessarily been expressed, since no subject of the expression is shown other than the literal one, and there must be some subject of expression (in any even interpretable teaching). Therefore, there are two kinds of cases, one where (a teaching) is both the expressed meaning of the scriptural passage as well as the intention of the speaker, and another where it is necessarily established as the meaning of the scriptural passage, even when it is not the intention of the speaker.[23]

THE DISAGREEMENT BETWEEN THE (*ELUCIDATION OF INTENTION*) AND THE *QUESTIONS OF MAITREYA* (CHAPTER OF THE *TRANSCENDENT WISDOM EIGHTEEN THOUSAND*)

(Here, it is commonly objected that) if the *Elucidation of Intention* presentation of the three natures is as explained in the Idealist system, do

[23] The gist seems to be that: 1) there is no internal contradiction in a passage that is intentionally to be interpreted differently by differnt disciples; 2) this is not just a case of literalness or non-literalness, there being different types of expressions and different intentions in different cases; 3) and of the two cases, the former are normally definitive and the latter interpretable.

we likewise accept the *Questions of Maitreya* chapter? Or do we not? If we do, then, as in the case of the *Elucidation of Intention*, it is not correct to accept the *Mother Scripture* literally. If we do not, then (how do we account for the fact that) the following passage—"Maitreya, consider that imagined form as insubstantial. Consider that constructed form as substantial, not because of its independence, but because of the substantiality of construction. Consider that ultimate form as neither substantial nor insubstantial, but as derived from the ultimate"[24]—agrees with the *Elucidation of Intention* by mentioning the substantiality of the relative and by proving the mere nominality of things from form to Buddhahood with the three reasonings (given above)[25] such as "because there would be no cognition prior to the name," etc.?

To explain: Maitreya, wishing to learn how the bodhisattva practices the transcendent wisdom, asked how he should learn (to understand) things from forms to Buddhahood, and was answered that he should learn them as being "mere names."[26] (Maitreya) then asked (further) about how to learn that forms, etc., were "mere names," since, as names such as "form" are apprehended along with the things that serve as their referents, "forms," etc. are not properly "mere names." If there is no referent, a name is not suitably a "mere name"; since, if the objective referent exists, the word "mere" excludes nothing, and if it does not

[24] This *Questions of Maitreya* chapter of the *Transcendent Wisdom Scriptures* is found only in the 18,000 and 25,000 line versions, as chapters 83 and 72 of the respective texts. E. Conze and S. Iida have edited a Sanskrit version of the chapter, which closely corresponds to the version found in the 18,000 line version, and loosely corresponds to that of the 25,000/version (it is included in *Melanges d'Indianisme à la Memoire de Louis Renou*, Paris: Editions E. de Boccard, 1968, pp. 229-242). E. Conze has translated this edited Sanskrit text and included it as Chapter 83 of his *Large Sutra on Perfect Wisdom* (Berkeley and Los Angeles: University of California Press, 1975, pp. 644-652), itself based on the 25,000 line version. Tsong Khapa's own analysis of the main issues of the chapter follows the Tibetan version in the 18,000 line version, KG, P, ga, ff. 317b-334b, and the direct quotes he gives here and below can be traced easily to Conze and Iida's Sanskrit version. His analytical paraphrases are very elaborate and involve references to a number of other texts, and are hard to attach to the rather more terse text of the Scripture, though they clearly adhere to its sense. The Sanskrit of this quote is as follows (Conze & Iida, p. 238): *yan Maitreya parikalpitaṃ rūpam idam adravyaṃ draṣṭavyaṃ. yad vikalpitaṃ rūpam idaṃ vikalpitaṃ rūpaṃ sadravyatām upādāya sadravyaṃ draṣṭavyaṃ, na tu svatantravṛttitaḥ. yad dharmatā-rūpan tan naivādravyaṃ na sadravyaṃ paramārthaprabhāvitaṃ draṣṭavyam.* Conze's own English version of this is found in his *Large Sutra*, pp. 648-649. bLo-bzang Phun-tshogs (Zin Bris II, f. 56b) elucidates the scripture's definitions as follows: "Here the imagined is the negatee, the imagined; the constructed is the relative, said to be substantial as existent by force of designative discrimination, not as independent; the perfect is not non-substantial, existing as the reality of the negation of the negatee, and not substantial, not existing as an imagined reality."

[25] See Ch. II, "Actual Negation" (of reification).

[26] Skt. in Conze & Iida, "Maitreya's Questions," p. 234; English in Conze, Large Sutra, p. 644.

exist, neither does the name, since it is without referential basis.[27] (The Buddha) then answers that (names) from "form" to "Buddhahood" are coincidentally designated upon their referents, that is, that nominal designation is coincidental. Since "coincidental" here has the meaning of "artificial," it refutes the intrinsic reality (of the referents or the names).[28]

If, as the Idealist would have it, this passage does not negate the truth-status of forms, etc., but (merely) negates the truth-status of "forms, etc." as nominally designated entities, then the intention of the above statement that (all things) from form to Buddha are mere names should be demonstrable (as meaning that) entities designated by such as "this form, etc." are mere nominal designations (which is not so stated in the passage). In the subsequent passage, where (Maitreya) asks if forms, etc., are non-existent with respect to any nature, and the (Buddha) says he does not say that, (Maitreya) again asks "then how is it?" and (the Buddha) replies that "they exist by mundane terms and conventions, but not in the ultimate."[29] Thus (if the Idealist interpretation were correct), then this statement that (all things) from form to Buddha are equally non-existent in the ultimate, and equally existent in the conventional would be wrong. Therefore, it is mistaken to urge that this chapter elucidates the interpretability of the *Mother Scripture* by showing the intention of the (scripture's) earlier statements that all things are ultimately non-existent and conventionally existent.

Therefore, the import (of the chapter) is that, since nominally designated things are artificial, that is, established as existent in conventional terms, there is no referent to which names are attached which (itself) is not established as merely conventionally existent. And since that is not to say that in general there is no phenomenal basis for using names, the statement of the existence of that (conventional referent) and the statement that (all things) are mere nominal designations are not contradictory.

Thus, (Maitreya) asks how it is correct that "form" should be coincidentally nominally designated, since the consideration "this form" does not arise by virtue of seeing a manifestation of form without (knowing)

[27] Tsong Khapa paraphrases here. English, Conze, *Large Sutra*, p. 645; Sanskrit, Conze & Iida, "Maitreya's Questions," p. 234.

[28] Tsong Khapa continues the paraphrase; Conze, *Large Sutra*, p. 645; Conze & Iida, "Maitreya's Questions," p. 234. The key phrase of the Buddha's here is: *āgantukam etan nāmadheyaṃ prakṣiptaṃ saṃskāranimitte vastuni, yad idaṃ rūpam iti.*

[29] Conze, *Large Sutra*, p. 646; Conze & Iida, "Maitreya's Questions," p. 236: *Maitreya āha: kiṃ punar Bhagavān sarvaśaḥ svalakṣaṇena rūpaṃ nāsti eva rūpam . . . na santi eva yāvad buddhadharmāḥ? Bhagavān āha: na-ahaṃ . . . vadāmi. Maitreya āha: kathaṃ Bhagavān rūpam asti . . . yāvad buddhadharmāḥ santi? Bhagavān āha: loka-saṃketavyavahārato Maitreya rūpam asti na tu paramārthato . . .* (abbreviations in edition).

the name "form," but arises by virtue of the name. (The Buddha) answers that it is correct for the thought "form" to arise since form is established on strength of convention, existing in that mode even before a name has been attached to it. (He) then asks Maitreya himself if a cognition that thinks "form" with regard to a phenomenon arises without depending on the name ("form"). (Maitreya) answers that such does not happen, and (the Buddha) states that for that very reason "forms, etc." are coincidental nominal designations.[30] This (passage) indicates that that reason is the proof that forms, etc., are established on strength of conventions, and is not proof of the opposite, as (he) implies that if form had intrinsically identifiable status, the thought "form" would have to arise without requiring any designation of the name ("form"); just as a sprout would grow without requiring any seed if it were established by its intrinsic identity. (Further), the statement of the coincidentality of designations of forms, etc., by the (further) reasons of a single thing having many names and many things being designable by one name,[31] means that it is mistaken (to think) that nominal conventions are used on strength of intrinsic identifiability and are not just established coincidentally on strength of conventions.

When one uses these (three) reasons to prove something, it is not at all required that they be used in the way they are used in the *Universal Vehicle Compendium*. For (Nagarjuna), in his *Subtle Weaving*, uses the latter two (of the three) reasons to negate the ultimate status (of phenomena): "Furthermore, ultimate status is not established because (realistic cognition) is not possible; because of the obvious fault of the confusion of multiple aspects of expressions and their referents, and because of the indeterminacy (of expressions with respect to their referents)."[32]

(Returning to the scripture), (Maitreya) asks if, when one apprehends phenomena from "form" to "Buddha," it is not so that one only perceives that reality of forms, etc., which consists of nominal and conventional designations. (The Buddha queries in turn then) that since there are phenomena which serve as referential bases of nominal designations, is it not the case that forms, etc., have intrinsically real status? (Maitreya) responds that, as for the reality of forms, etc., the referents of conventional designations such as "forms, etc.," it is no more than mere mental

[30] From this point, Tsong Khapa's paraphrase returns again to the beginning of the chapter (position in English and Sanskrit texts given above, n. 26), interpolating in his analysis the type of issue raised in the treatment of the process of verbal designation customary for the Idealists, as in Ch. II of the *Essence*.

[31] These two reasons are always used together with the reason called "no cognition prior to name" given in Ch. II of the Essence under "Actual Negation."

[32] *Vaidalyaprakarana*, P, C, tsa, f. 106a1 (paraphrased by Tsong Khapa here).

construction. (Finally the Buddha,) at that "mere construction" statement, responds: "Well then, what were you thinking when you questioned as before?"[33] This passage indicates that there is no contradiction between the statement that phenomena which are referential bases of names exist, although not as intrinsically identifiable entities, and the statement that such are mere nominal designations.

Thus (Maitreya) suggests that, if forms, etc., are merely names and conventions, would not the reality of forms, etc., then be apprehended, meaning thereby that it would be contradictory to say both the above "it is mere designation" as well as "its reality is not apprehended"; which means that it is not contradictory for the reality of form etc., to exist, since even one who advocates "mere designation" must accept (the relationship of) designation and referent. In answer, (the Buddha counters, asking that) if (those things are) mere nominal designations, do they have production and destruction, addictive defilement and purification? (Maitreya) then answers that they do not, and (Buddha finally) declares, "Well then, is the question 'If things are mere designations, wouldn't they have their own reality?' appropriate?"[34]

Then, as explained above, they engage in the exchange beginning "Well, are forms, etc., totally non-existent with respect to any nature?" indicating that the negations of reality, production, destruction, addictive defilement, and purification are in terms of the ultimate and that forms, etc., exist conventionally.[35] Thus, since even mere designations (only exist) in terms of convention, how can the mode of exposition (of this chapter) possibly agree with that of the *Elucidation of Intention*? Even the Brother-Masters (Asanga and Vasubandhu) did not consider that this chapter revealed the interpretability of (the rest of) the *Mother Scripture*, but that this chapter is the same (as the rest of the *Mother Scripture*) since it teaches the ultimate non-existence and conventional existence of all things; and hence, according to the explanation of the *Elucidation of Intention*, it is not fit to be literally accepted.[36]

(To understand how) this is not contradicted by the fact that (this scripture) states the relative (nature) to exist substantially, one must first know the scripture's mode of representing the three realities. To explain, the scripture identifies the imagined nature (as follows):

[33] Conze, *Large Sutra*, p. 646; Conze & Iida, "Maitreya's Questions," p. 236.
[34] Ibid.
[35] Here Tsong Khapa's paraphrase again reaches the passage given above, n. 29.
[36] Since Tsong Khapa uses the expression "thought" (Tib. *snyam du dgongs so*), we may safely assume that there is no particular passage in the brothers' writings elucidating this point. Tsong Khapa rather infers from the fact that the brothers did *not* use the *Maitreya Chapter* to support their Idealist philosophy that they made no claim that this chapter expounds the three natures in the same way as does the SN.

Maitreya, this imaginative construction of a form-reality founded on the name, concept, designation, and convention "form" (ascribed) to the phenomena of the conditional process (is the imagined reality, including all things) from imagined "form" to imagined "Buddha-qualities."[37]

Here, "founded on " means "apprehending in form the referent of the nominal designation." "Imaginative construction of a form-reality" indicates that the imagined is the reality which is imaginatively constructed, not (mere) imagination (itself).

The scripture goes on to identify the discriminatively constructed reality (as follows):

The discriminatively constructed (relative) reality is the articulation of those phenomena of conditional processes, utilizing mental processes inherent in the nature of mere construction; (it is) the names, concepts, designations, and conventions from "form," "sensation," "conception," "creation," and "consciousness" up to "Buddha-qualities." (It includes all things) from "discriminated form" up to "discriminated Buddha-qualities."[38]

Here, "those phenomena" refers to the subjects of expressions, and the mode of expressing them by utilizing discriminative construction (is described by the passage from) "forms," etc. By explaining the thus expressed "names, etc." as the "discriminatively constructed (relative) reality," (we can) understand that the previously indicated subjects and mental constructions are also the discriminated (relative reality), and thus (we understand that it includes) both (the function of) discriminative construction and the ground of discriminative construction.

The scripture then defines the ultimate reality (as follows):

(The ultimate reality is) the truth-limit, Thatness, the objective selflessness and the sole realitylessness, permanent and eternal, of constructed form with respect to imagined form, (including all things) from ultimate form to ultimate Buddha-qualities.[39]

[37] Conze, *Large Sutra*, p. 648; Conze & Iida, "Maitreya's Questions," p. 238: *yā Maitreya tasmin saṃskāranimitte vastuni rūpam iti nāma-saṃjñā-saṃketa-prajñaptivyavahāran niśritya rūpa-svabhāvatayā parikalpanā, idaṃ parikalpitaṃ rūpam . . . yāvat ime parikalpitā buddhadharmāḥ.* (Tib. omits *saṃketa.*)

[38] Ibid. *yā punas tasya saṃskāranimittasya vastuno vikalpamātra-dharmatāyāṃ avasthānatā vikalpa-pratītya-abhilapanatā tatra-idaṃ nāmasaṃjñāsaṃketaprajñaptivyavahāro rūpam iti . . . yāvad buddhadharmā iti. idaṃ vikalpitaṃ rūpam . . . ime vikalpitā buddhadharmāḥ.* (editors' abbreviations).

[39] Ibid. *(dharmadhātur) yat tena parikalpitarūpeṇa tasya vikalpitarūpasya nityaṃ nityakālaṃ dhruvaṃ dhruvakālaṃ niḥsvabhāvatā dharmanairātmyan tathatā bhūtakoṭir idaṃ dharmatā-rūpam . . . ime yāvad buddhadharmā.*

Here, "ultimate form" is the realitylessness of constructed form, objective selflessness, etc. And since that principle is selflessness and realitylessness of constructed form with respect to imagined form, the negated "self" or reality is the imagined reality. "Permanent," etc., indicates emptiness, which is ascertained at all times.

This method (is the same as) the Centrist presentation of the three natures, given by (Chandra) in the *Introduction Commentary*, where (Chandra explains) that, just as a snake is a (mere) imaginative construct in a rope, not (really) existing there, yet is not (a mere) construct but is established in an actual snake, so intrinsic reality is a (mere) imaginative construct in the created relativity of the relative nature, since (Nagarjuna has defined) intrinsic reality as non-artificial and non-relational, yet such (intrinsic reality) is actual in the sphere of Buddhas, not being merely imaginatively constructed; as one is called a "Buddha" who realizes the solitary intrinsic reality, free of all contact with created things. Thus, this way of presenting the three realities elucidates the inner gist of the scriptures. And thus the meaning of the *Mother Scripture* should be understood as (Chandra explains) in the *Introduction Commentary*.[40]

Here, the "constructed" (reality) is taken as the relative reality of all relative things from form to omniscience; and it is emphasized as the chief (reality). And that reality explained as the imagined, (consisting of) reality-imaginations from form to omniscience, is (itself) taken as the ground, or intrinsic reality, whose existence in the relative is (merely) imagined. Nevertheless, it is perfectly established as the object of a Buddha's ultimate gnosis. Furthermore, the ultimate reality of the relative is its emptiness with respect to the imagined, which is the relative existing ultimately, and that very reality exists as the object of the Buddha's ultimate knowledge. Thus, a single reality is presented as both imagined and also perfectly established when related to different grounds. Therefore, although there is no ultimate or superficial thing which is established as an intrinsic reality endowed with intrinsic identifiability, still the ultimate reality without the superficial reality is established as that which is represented as intrinsic reality of the absolute. Thus the question of existence and non-existence of intrinsic reality must be subtly understood.[41]

As for the statement (that a Buddha) understands clearly "the solitary

[40] MABh, VI, ad. k. 97, p. 201 (paraphrased) (LVP, p. 255). Poussin badly garbles this passage, taking the "being of the snake" as "the rope," and later reading *ma rig par* for *ma reg par*, etc.

[41] That is, the Centrists *conventionally* reaffirm even the imagined reality, *ultimately* refuting both relative and imagined, this being a way of reducing the three realities to two realities, conventional and ultimate.

intrinsic reality free of contact with created things," it negates the (dualism of) "identified" and "identity" (inherent in) the object of the direct realization of the ultimate reality; and I have already explained the non-contradictoriness of this point.[42]

The (subsequent) exhortation of the *Introduction Commentary* to think over whether the duality of subject and object is (merely) imaginatively constructed in the relative, since apart from the relative there are no subjects and objects, means that it is incorrect (to maintain) that the subject-object-duality alone is the imagined, since, there being no distinction between existence and non-existence of subjective and objective, they both constitute the relative and thus serve as the designative base of the imagined.[43]

Therefore, the "substantiality" mentioned in the *Questions of Maitreya* statement of "substantial existence and non-existence" is not the "substantial" of the pair "designative-substantial" employed in other treatises (of the Idealists), nor is it the "substantial" equated by the Centrists with intrinsically identifiable status; but signifies mere existence. Thus, "substantial non-existence of the imagined" intends the impossibility of (the imagined) existing as the reality of the relative, and does not (impugn) the existence of the imagined as object of names and signs, etc. And, as for the "substantial existence of the constructed (reality)," the scripture itself states it to be substantially established through the "substantial" existence of discriminative constructs (themselves), and not through some independently arisen phenomenon. Since "independent status" is just that which is explained in the treatises of the Father and Son Masters as intrinsically identifiable status, this (statement of "substantiality") is not the same as the statements of other (interpretable) scriptures that the relative is endowed with intrinsic identifiability.

"Substantial" existence established by the substantiality of discriminative constructs is the kind of existence sustained by the existence of discriminative construction, which means that it is not an intrinsically identifiable existence. Since among things established by discriminative construction there are both those that do exist conventionally and those that do not, this (kind of mentally established existence) may not be likened to the discriminative construction of a snake in a rope. (Finally), as to the statement that the absolute reality is neither substantially existent nor non-existent, it intends the above non-existence acording to the imagined and the existence as the intrinsic reality of the negation of that (imagined).

[42] See explanation of "identified"-"identity" relationship on p. 261, in terms of "nature" and "nature-possessor" (*dharmadharmin*).

[43] See above, n. 40.

Interpreted in this way, this chapter determines with question and answer the points liable to misinterpretation from the statements in the scripture's other chapters about the mere nominal designativeness of all things. It thoroughly differentiates the distinctions of existence and non-existence of the three realities, and thus should be recognized as establishing the authority of the previous expositions.

This *Questions of Maitreya* chapter seems to be a major source of error for those scholars who are liable to suspect that within the *Transcendent Wisdom Scripture*, the path which is the sole avenue of all the Victors of the three times, within that very scripture is (a chapter) which is determined to be interpretable in meaning like the *Elucidation of Intention*. And since the great Centrists do not seem to have elucidated the meaning of this very (chapter) in great detail, I have submitted the question to a detailed examination.[44]

[44] See Ch. II nn. 96, 97, showing how Ratnakarashanti makes this mistake about the *Questions of Maitreya* chapter.

Chapter VII

THE CHIEF REASON FOR NEGATION OF ULTIMATE STATUS

1. DESCRIPTION OF THE CHIEF REASON

Which does this system take to be the chief reason negating the ultimate status of things?

(Chandrakirti) states, in the *Introduction Commentary*: "(Nagarjuna) did not execute the analyses in the *Treatise* out of a love for debate, but taught the facts in order to liberate (living beings)."[1] All analytical reasonings in the *Wisdom* have as their sole aim the attainment of liberation by living beings. Living beings are chained in cyclic life by their habitual adherence to personal and objective selves. And since the chief cause of bondage is this habitual adherence to the two selves, in the person, object for the arisal of the thought "I," and in the things that (constitute) his process (of existence), those two are the chief bases of rational negation of habitual selfhood. Therefore, (all) reasonings are categorized as negating the two selves.

In the passage in the *Introduction Commentary* where the reasonings determining reality in the *Introduction* are categorized as determining the two selflessnesses,[2] (Chandra) states that the reasonings refuting four-extreme-production are demonstrations of objective selflessness. (He also) states that the Master (Nagarjuna), in beginning (the *Wisdom*) with "not from self, not from other . . . etc.," demonstrated with reasoning only the equality of the non-production of all things, from among the ten equalities stated in the *Ten Stages*[3] (to be contemplated) in entering the sixth stage, thinking that the other (nine) equalities were easier to dem-

[1] MA, VI, v. 118, Poussin ed., p. 231 (LVP, p. 280).

[2] MA, VI, ad. k. 179, Poussin ed., pp. 301 ff.

[3] MA, VI, ad. k. 5, Poussin ed., pp. 80-81. DBS (ed. Bagchi, p. 31): . . . *bodhisattvaḥ . . . ṣaṣṭīṃ bodhisattvabhūmimavatārati / sa daśābhirdharmasamatābhiravatārati / katamābhir daśābhiḥ? yaduta sarvadharmānimittasamatayā ca sarvadharmālakṣaṇasamatayā ca sarvadharmānutpādasamatayā ca sarvadharmājāta(sama)tayā ca sarvadharmaviktasamatayā ca sarvadharmādiviśuddhisamatayā ca sarvadharmaniśprapañcasamatayā ca sarvadharmānāvyūhānirvyūhasamatayā ca sarvadharmamāyāsvapnapratibhāsapratiśrutkodakacandrapratibimbanirmāṇasamatayā ca sarvadharmabhāvābhāvādvayasamatayā ca / . . .*

onstrate. Therefore, the chief reasoning proving the selflessness of things is the reasoning negating four-extreme-production.

Furthermore, this reasoning proving (selflessness) boils down to the cutter of the whole trap of false views, the royal reason of relativity itself. For, the very fact of the inter-relative occurrence of inner things such as mental creations and outer things such as sprouts, dependent on causes and conditions such as misknowledge and seeds, (corroborates) the negations "their production is empty with reference to any intrinsically identifiable intrinsic reality" and "they are not produced from self, other, both, or neither." As (Chandra) states in the *Introduction*:

> Things will never be produced from self, other, or both, or from a creator, or causelessly (randomly); thus, they are produced relatively. Thus, since things occur relatively these constructs cannot (withstand) analysis, and hence this reason of relativity cuts open the whole network of bad views.[4]

As for the chief reasoning negating personal self, (Chandra) states in the *Introduction*:

> While that (self) will never be established, either ultimately or conventionally, via seven modes, still, through social conventions without analysis, it is designated depending on its components.[5]

[4] MA, VI, ks. 114-15, Poussin ed., pp. 226-7; (LVP pp. 276-78). Poussin translates *rtog pa . . . brtag par mi nus* as "one cannot conceive such conceptions," rather than "such constructs cannot withstand analysis." Noteworthy from the comment on this passage is the locution for the *pratītyasamutpādayukti* that confirms our translation of "reason of relativity," namely, *rten cing 'brel par 'byung ba rkyen nyid 'di pa tsam gyi rigs pa*, which Poussin rightly reconstructs *pratītyasamutpāda-idaṃpratyayamātratā-yukti*. Then even more strongly, Chandra says, "by interpreting the meaning of dependent origination as merely such contingent conditionality, we cannot admit any intrinsic reality in anything at all" (*'di ltar rkyen nyid 'di pa tsam zhig rten cing 'brel par 'byung bai don du rnam par 'jog pas ni dngos po 'ga la yang rang bzhin khas (mi) blangs te*). Thus, we find strong support for translating *pratītyasamutpāda* as "relativity" (*idaṃpratyayatā*) in the context of Centrist logic.

[5] MA, VI, k. 158, Poussin ed., p. 277 (LVP, p. 320). The seven modes of reasoning are summed up in MA VI, ks. 151-55. This formal reasoning is succinctly given by Hopkins (*Meditations on Emptiness*, p. 560) "Except for only being imputed to the aggregates which are its basis of imputation, there is no self-subsistent self. For the aggregates . . . are not the person; the person is not an entity other than the aggregates . . . ; the person is not the support of the aggregates . . . ; the person ultimately does not depend on the aggregates . . . ; the person does not ultimately possess the aggregates . . . ; . . . is not the shape of the aggregates . . . ; . . . is not the composite of the aggregates. . . . For example, if a chariot is sought analytically, there is no independent chariot to be found." (This follows Ngag-dbang dPal-ldan's *Grub mtha chen moi mchan 'grel* (Sarnath, 1964, ff. dbu 129aff.). Hopkins then gives the reasoning in detail on following pages. In essence, the seven reasonings are based on the rejection of both sameness and difference as obtaining between the self and the aggregates, or between a chariot and its parts. The later five are basically further possible positions taken in the attempt to evade the first two negations.

Although no chariot is found when sought in seven ways, as identical with its components, different from them, possessing them, mutually dependent in two ways (with them), the mere composite (of them), or as the structure of their composite, it still is presented as designatively existent, designated depending on its components. In the same way, the person is presented. (He also) states that very (reasoning) to be the method for the easy finding of the view of the profound, and hence those reasonings should be acknowledged as the chief reasonings negating personal self.

(Chandra) also states in the *Introduction*:

> "How could it exist, if not in these seven ways?" The yogi finds no existence of this (self), and thereby easily penetrates reality as well—so here its status should thus be acknowledged.[6]

Since this (example of the chariot) is easier to understand at first than the non-discovery of the person when seeking in seven ways, as well as its designative status dependent on its aggregates, such is the sequence in practice. And this (reasoning) also boils down to the reason of relativity, since the import of the selflessness of the person is the non-discovery of any person in those seven ways because of the fact of its (mere) designation depending on the aggregates. Such being the case, the very negation of self-production, etc., four (extremes) and of intrinsic sameness or difference, etc., in seven (ways), by the reasons of relative production and dependent designation should be upheld as the principally significant of reasonings.

2. THE PROCESS OF REFUTING INTRINSIC IDENTIFIABILITY THEREBY

Well then, since this negation of intrinsically identifiable status (of anything) even in the superficial by those reasons of relativity appears to be the distinctive specialty of this system in elucidating the intention of the Holy Ones, how do they execute such an exceptional negation?

As this is extremely crucial, let us explain it. This (exceptional negation) is executed in the *Central Way Introduction* by three reasonings given in the basic verses and one given in the commentary.

The first of these (is called) "the consequence that the holy equipoise would destroy phenomena," (and it runs as follows): if things had an

[6] MA, VI, k. 160, Poussin ed., p. 279 (LVP, p. 321).

intrinsically identifiable reality, when the yogi realized directly the unreality of all things, his intuitive knowledge would annihilate things such as forms and sensations, since they should be apprehended (if they were real), yet they are not. A thing that formerly exists and later does not is called "destroyed," and (in this case) the cause of its destruction would be taken to be that intuitive knowledge. Since it is irrational for that (wisdom) to be a cause of destruction, intrinsically identifiable production is inadmissible at all times. (Chandra states) in the *Introduction*: "If things stood on intrinsic identifiability, its repudiation would be their destruction and emptiness would be the destructive cause. Such being irrational, things do not exist (identifiably)."[7]

Here one (Dogmaticist) might object that mere intrinsically identifiable existence does not entail that intuitive wisdom apprehend things, and, although ultimate existence does entail such apprehension, he does not assert such (existence of things), since intrinsically identifiable status is only conventional.

Although this is a direct rebuttal, it cannot evade (Chandra's consequence), as we will explain in the context of the next reasoning.

(The second of the four exceptional reasonings is called) the "consequence that conventional reality could withstand analysis," (and it runs as follows): if things were intrinsically identifiable, then if, for example, one were to analyze the objective referent of the conventional designation "production"—"Is this 'produced' sprout really the same as the seed? Or really different?"—it is necessary that the analytic (cognition) find (those things). Otherwise, they would become established merely on the strength of conventions since there would be no intrinsically identifiable objective referents.

However, when one analyzes (things) by investigating them in such a way, one does not find any such thing as production apart from that the nature of which is ultimate reality, where there is no production and no cessation.[8] Therefore, superficial things (should) not be asserted to be objects discovered by such analysis. (Chandra formulates this consequence) in the *Introduction* (as follows):

[7] MA, VI, k. 34, Poussin ed., p. 117 (LVP, p. 311). Poussin remarks that Chandra is here attacking the Idealists, which is not incorrect. However, as Tsong Khapa points out, insofar as Chandra here attacks the upholders of intrinsic identity (*svalakṣaṇa*), both Dogmaticists and Idealists are involved. Tsong Khapa explains this reasoning in somewhat more detail in GRS, p. 211 ff., adding nothing major; in fact, that later exposition seems to refer back to the way he worked it out in our text.

[8] This rather odd locution derives from Chandra's own in the succeeding quote, and is a rather indirect way of saying that through analysis one finds only the ultimate nature of things, which is to say one finds their ultimate unfindability.

When one analyzes these (mundane) things, they are not found to stand anywhere short of that with ultimate nature. Therefore, social conventional reality should not be analyzed.[9]

Here, as explained above, a certain (Dogmaticist) claims (that this consequence does him) no damage, the essence of his disagreement being his drawing a line between reasoning analytic of ultimacy and non-ultimacy and the method of analysis merely (seeking referents of designations) explained above, since, although (conventional reality) does withstand analysis by the (latter) type of analysis, he never claimed that it withstands analysis by reasoning analytic of the ultimacy or non-ultimacy (of things). This rebuttal is the fundamental one, and is essentially

[9] MA, VI, k. 35, Poussin ed., p. 120 (LVP, p. 313). Poussin is puzzled here (n. 2): "Faut-il avouer que je n'entends pas tres bien ma traduction?" although his translation is verbally accurate in the main except for his substitution of "il ne faut pas . . . " for "on ne doit pas . . . " (*mi bya*), and his Skt. reconstruction seems good—*tasmāddhi te bhāva vicāryamāṇas tattvātmavato bhavad arvāk / sthānaṃ na labhante tasmāllokasya vyavāhārasatye vicāro na kartavyaḥ //*, (an interesting example of how meaning is more than words!). I believe the locution "things whose nature is ultimate reality," which he renders "ce qui possede realite et 'soi,' " taking *tattvātma* as a *dvandva* compound rather than a genitive *tatpuruṣa*, to be his mistake.

Tsong Khapa's discussion of this second reasoning is worth quoting in some detail, from GRS, pp. 214 ff.: "Here one objects that 'ultimate non-production naturally depends on negation of self- and other-production, but the actualities of the objects of the two validating cognitions such as form and feelings are definitely to be produced from other things. If that is not admitted, then why talk of two realities? You will have only one in fact. Thus, there is production from other things.' This is the argument, apparently the assertion of ultimate non-production and conventional other-production, of a certain Dogmaticist. His contention that there will be only one reality if you do not accept superficially intrinsically real other-production means that if intrinsically identifiable production does not exist superficially, there is no genuine superficial [reality], which, being impossible, leaves only ultimate reality. In answer, [Chandra] says, 'granted this is true, for ultimately there are not two realities, as in scripture "Bhikshus, thus ultimate reality is unique, it is Nirvana whose nature is non-deception; all creations are deceptive in nature." This means that the meaning of the "reality" we admit is "non-deception," and we grant that this non-deceptive reality is unique.' 'In the ultimate sense' means 'according to vision of ultimate reality,' [and herein] there are not the two realities, superficial and ultimate, but only exclusively the ultimate reality, as was proclaimed. . . . In short, if things had intrinsic identifiability, creations would not be established as deceptive, and hence, as there would be no superficial reality, there would not be two realities; whereas on the premise of lack of intrinsic identifiability [can be based] both ultimate and superficial realities. . . . " Tsong Khapa then distinguishes between "reality" as meaning "non- deceptive," in answer to an objection, also clearing up a problem of a *Philosophical Sixty Commentary* statement that "Nirvana is a reality superficially," explaining that it means that Nirvana is established as being ultimate reality according to superficial cognition, not that it is a conventional reality. He then goes on to run over the actual verse and cite from MMK and CŚ to the effect that superficial reality is necessary to realizc ultimate reality, and so on. He closes with a relevant discussion of "analytic/non-analytic" as used here: "Here "analytic/non-analytic is analytic/non-analytic of the ultimate reality, and as it is crucial to understand what sort of analysis serves as ultimacy-analysis, it should be sketched. In the Dialecticist system, ultimacy-analysis consists in not being satisfied with conventional usage but seeking the referent of such designations as 'the sprout is produced' [thinking 'is it produced from self or other

the same (in thrust) as the previous rebuttal (given to the first consequence).

As for the reason why they cannot evade the damage of those (consequences), it is—as repeatedly explained above, and as given in Chandra's statements in this context and in many others that superficial existence is (equivalent to) social conventional existence—the very statement that whatever persons and things are established by social conventions are only established without the slightest analysis as to the mode of existence of the referents of the conventions; and thus that which, on the contrary, is analytically established to exist is ultimately existent. Therefore, if (something) is intrinsically identifiably existent, it must of necessity withstand analysis by rational cognition and must of necessity be apprehended by the intuitive wisdom that directly encounters the ultimate.

(Again the Dogmaticist) objects that ultimate existence of something is its existence on the strength of its own actual condition, not merely established on the strength of its appearance in non-defective cognitions such as sense-cognitions, and hence social conventional existence is not that established on the strength of verbal conventions, but is existence on the strength of appearance in non-defective cognition, while still not being existence established on the strength of a thing's own objective condition.

(We answer that) if such were the case, it would contradict the (scriptural) statement that all things are mere names, signs, and designations, and the statement that "(things) exist by social conventions and usages, and not in the ultimate sense." (For,) if there were some object found by analysis of the mode of existence of the referents of conventional designations, what would the word "merely" (in the former statement) exclude? And how could it be correct to say (in the latter statement) "it exists by social conventions," etc.? (And here finally,) while being completely out of touch with the way in which a common person accepts the referents of conventional designations, if one nevertheless says "(such

. . .']. Thus, this [type of analysis] should be understood as quite different from analysis using social conventions such as 'Where does it come from? Where does it go? Where is it, inside or outside?' and so on. [On the other hand], the Dogmaticists do not interpret merely such as ultimate-analysis, but rather understand it as the above-explained inquiry as to whether [a thing] is established as existent on the strength of its appearance to non-defective condition or on the strength of its objective condition. . . . These two different delineations of ultimacy-analysis arise from the essential difference of their different identification of the negatee [of selflessness]. If this is not grasped, and [analysis] is understood as like the case of having erred in thinking Devadatta had come when he had not, for example, and then considering all unanalyzed things as false and all analyzed things as not false—this is the system neither of Logicians nor Centrists; since for both there are many things established by validating cognition that are non-analytic in status."

and such) exists as a social convention," this is no more than (empty) talk, since one does not (in fact) accept the meaning.

The sevenfold analysis, (which proves) the impossibility of establishing as person any object found by analysis seeking the referent of the convention "person," and the reasonings such as the negation of production from other even conventionally, (which prove) the impossibility of establishing as production, etc., any objects found by analysis seeking the referents of conventions for things such as "production"—these should be understood from the detailed examinations (I have given them) elsewhere.[10]

Thus, there is no difference between the conventions for persons and things, such as "I saw" and "the sprout grows," and the conventions (of philosophy) such as "my substantial self saw" and "the sprout grows from a substantially different seed," in the sense that investigation of the mode of existence of the referents of (both-types of) conventions finds nothing (ultimately). Nevertheless, there is an extremely great difference (between them) with regard to whether or not their existence corresponding to their designations is faulted by other (conventional) validating cognitions; the former pair (of conventional objects) being conventionally existent, the latter pair not being existent even conventionally. And further, this (point) depends on the thorough discrimination of the difference between (a thing's) being faulted by rational cognition and its being unable to withstand analysis, as well as the extremely great difference between rational cognition's not finding the existence (of something) and its seeing the non-existence (of something). But I have already explained these extensively elsewhere.[11]

Here, someone, who has not accomplished the analysis of fine discrimination between the above (apparently similar types of conventions) yet negates ultimate status by a few likely reasons and maintains the existence of superficial things by means of a few erroneous cognitions, might think that (those conventions) can be established merely by their existence according to erroneous cognition, since their referents merely exist according to error. This (kind of attitude) ends up (as the position that) if (the propositions that) "happiness and suffering arise from the creator and from nature, etc." and "happiness and suffering arise from good and evil actions" are right, they are both equally right, and if wrong, are both equally wrong; since analytic cognition will not find (the referent of) even the latter when analyzing it as above, and even the former exists

[10] Although both of these topics are covered extensively in GRS, Tsong Khapa here would be referring to the treatment given in LTC, since that was the only major Centrist work he wrote prior to our text.

[11] This again refers to LTC, f. 391b ff. (see Ch. V n. 113), and to RG, I, p. 18ff.

according to erroneous (cognition). Therefore, (such a person holds that Chandra's statements) in the *Introduction*: "This (self) is irrational even as the ground of the 'I'-process, nor do we assent even to its superficial existence";[12] and also, "What the fundamentalists, disturbed by sleep of ignorance, imagine respectively (as real) each in their own (theory), and what (people) imagine in illusions and mirages—these are just what do not exist, even conventionally";[13] (that is, to the effect that) the imaginative constructions of the special theories of our own and others' schools and the objects such as horses and elephants apprehended in illusions or water apprehended in mirages are non-existent even superficially; both become incorrect. For, (unless they exist superficially) not even erroneous cognitions could apprehend them; since they do exist according to erroneous cognitions, they should become conventionally existent; and otherwise the rational negations such as "production from self or other is not established even conventionally" would become incapable of refuting anything at all.[14]

Here, (the above holder of the confused attitude about the status of conventions) cannot claim immunity (from the unacceptable consequences of his position) by asserting that he establishes superficial existence, not as those errors which belong to unreflective living beings from beginningless time, but merely as existence according to the error derived from the beginningless continuum of failure to analyze (the nature of reality). For, if such were the case (that is, that superficial existence is constituted by the specific error of lack of analysis), then even the conceptual objects of notions of permanence that hold prior and posterior as identical, (as well as the objects) of unconscious self-habits that adhere to the intrinsic identifiability of persons and things, would become conventionally existent.[15]

Therefore, granting that (something's) conventional existence precludes its discovery by rational cognition investigating its mode of ex-

[12] MA, VI, k. 122cd, Poussin ed., p. 240 (LVP, p. 288).

[13] MA, VI, k. 26, Poussin ed., p. 105 (LVP, p. 302). Poussin's suggestion in notes to translate *bdag nyid ji bzhin* as "each in his own way" would seem better to serve the sense here, as none of the commentaries take the *bdag nyid* here as *ātma*. For *Tīrthika*, literally "forder" (to salvation), "fundamentalist" I find conveys its sense, as "heterodox" corresponds to *phyi rol pa*.

[14] This very subtle passage may be confusing if we forget that Tsong Khapa is here drawing out the absurd conclusions of the position that the superficial, conventional reality is merely established according to erroneous cognition, which position makes its holder unable to distinguish between the genuinely superficially real, and the totally unreal.

[15] Tsong Khapa further exposes the conventional nihilist described in note 14 above. This person is definitely not the Dogmaticist, but is rather one of the pseudo-Dialecticists among Tsong Khapa's contemporaries. It seems to be a general tendency, as it can certainly be observed among students of the central way today, when dealing with the extreme subtleties of the Dialecticist method of establishing conventional realities.

istence, still it is definitely necessary that it not be refuted by validating rational cognition, and it is also necessary that it not be faulted by any other conventional validating cognition, because it is necessary that (a thing's) conventional existence be established by validating cognition.

Here, if one objects that such (a position) contradicts (the doctrine that) conventionally existent things are merely established on the strength of verbal conventions, (we respond that) this does not fault (our position). The word "merely" in the expression "superficially existent things such as persons are merely established on the strength of verbal conventions" excludes (the possibility that) the person is not established on the strength of verbal conventions, and does not exclude (the possibility that) the person is also established by validating cognition; nor does it give any indication that everything established on the strength of verbal conventions is (in fact) superficially existent.

If you wonder what sort of non-conventional status of (things) is excluded (by the above expression, we can explain that) if the referent designated by the convention "person" were to have intrinsically identifiable status, this would entail its having an existence by virtue of its own intrinsic reality and would not allow it to have existence (merely) by virtue of the subjective convention ("person"). (Thus,) this is the kind of (non-conventional status, that is, intrinsically identifiable status) that is ruled out (by "merely"). Although such a kind (of non-conventional status) is negated by rational cognition, the (conventional) existence of the referents of conventional expressions such as "Yajña sees" is (nonetheless) established,[16] since, if a conventional expression had no referent (at all), it would be faulted (even) by conventional validating cognition. And, in the context of a verbal convention and its referent, when a referent is found not to exist by its own intrinsic reality, its existence on the strength of convention is automatically established. Therefore, if one analyzes the mode of existence of the ultimate reality, it finally ends up as just the same. And so we assert that its existence is also established on the strength of convention, although we do not assert that the ultimate reality is established by conventional validating cognition. Furthermore, we say that the ultimate reality exists according to conventional cognition because of the fact that the notion of the existence of the ultimate is absent from the habit-pattern of rational cognition, which is not the same

[16] Our K text has a negative *mi* before "established," but the P text (nga, f. 181b8) does not, and the Dalai Lama also edited it out. Actually, this difficult passage becomes clear if we break the sentence after *tha snyad kyi don*, treat the phrase *med na tha snyad pai tshad mas gnod pas* as a conditional clause providing the reason for the final *yod par ni 'grub la*. It thus becomes an instance of rational cognition's disproof of the objective status of a referent being de facto proof of its conventional status, rather than a total annihilation of the referent.

as saying that (ultimate reality) is established by that (conventional validating cognition).

Buddhapalita also explains that the Victor spoke of production, etc., on the strength of conventions and that "production," etc., were established as mere expressions. Whereas the Dogmaticists assert that the non-defective cognition that establishes conventional existence is non-erroneous with regard to the intrinsically identifiable thing that is its perceptual or conceptual object, in this (Dialecticist system) there are a great many things that can be established as objective by (cognitions) erroneous about their apparent objects. Hence there is a great difference in (the determination of what is) defective and non-defective in the non-defective cognitions of these two (systems).[17]

Although (Chandra) calls this sort of existence on strength of convention "designative existence," it is definitely not the sort of designative existence where something is designated in the absence of any phenomenon. Thus, all (things) such as Buddhas and living beings as defined, and bondage and liberation as defined, are viable in this (interpretation of conventional existence), and are not at all viable in any other system. (Finally), in the face of the elucidation of this very fact by the two masters (Buddhapalita and Chandrakirti) as the ultimate intention of the Holy Father and Son, if one can see no ground for establishing (all empirical) systems with (all their) attributes, it is the result of the predominance of the ingrained habit of associating all normal causalities, etc., with intrinsically identifiable status. And since it (means that) still the import of relativity has not yet dawned as the import of emptiness by intrinsic reality, you should realize that you are standing at the point of greatest resistance to this system.[18]

(The third of the four exceptional reasonings is called) "the consequence of the non-negation of ultimate production," (and it runs as follows): if things' intrinsically identifiable status is not negated by the negation through analysis of whether production is from self or other,

[17] That is to say, "defective" cognition for the Dogmaticist is cognition that suffers from organic malfunction, that is, vision distorted by hallucinations, and so forth, whereas for the Dialecticist all conventional cognitions are defective in that they perceive things as apparently objective while the things are actually only designatively objective, but nevertheless these intrinsically defective cognitions may successfully establish the conventional, designative existence of objects. The difference here again turns on the Dogmaticist assertion of intrinsic identifiability of the conventional, which is anathema to the Dialecticist.

[18] Tsong Khapa here highlights how Bhavya's classic insistence on conventional intrinsic identifiability as indispensably necessary for the viability of the empirical world is the arch-antithesis of the Dialecticist system, whether leading to the subtle Dogmaticist form of absolutism, absolutizing the conventional, or to the subtle form of nihilism practiced by certain pseudo-Dialecticists of repudiating the conventional coherence of systems of causality, and so forth.

then negation of ultimate status also will not be accomplished through such analysis. Since that is irrational, intrinsically identifiable status can also be negated conventionally. By the essential point that intrinsic identifiability necessarily entails ultimacy, the reasonings negating ultimate production also negate conventional intrinsic identifiability. Therefore, intrinsically identifiable production does not exist in either of the two realities, as (Chandra) states in the *Introduction*:

> The very reasons (proving) the irrationality of self- and other-production in the ultimate sense also (prove) their irrationality in the conventional reality—so whereby will your production come to pass?[19]

(The fourth of the four exceptional reasonings is called the consequence of) "the wrongness of the (scriptural) statement that things are empty by intrinsic reality." (Chandra) in comment on the first (exceptional) reasoning in the *Introduction*[20] cites the *Kashyapa Chapter* to prove emptiness with respect to intrinsic identifiability:

> Kashyapa, furthermore, the central way is the genuine insight into things; it does not make things empty by means of emptiness, but (realizes that) the very things themselves are emptiness . . . likewise it does not make things signless, wishless, performanceless, non-produced, and non-occurrent by means of signlessness . . . and non-occurrence, (but realizes that) the very things themselves are signlessness . . . the very things themselves are non-occurrence. . . .[21]

(Chandra) also explains that this scriptural reference teaches the incorrectness of the (interpretation of) emptiness by the Idealist system. (Thus,) if things had an intrinsically identifiable reality, they would not be empty in their own nature, and "the very things themselves are emp-

[19] MA, VI, k. 36, Poussin ed., p. 122 (LVP, p. 315). In GRS, p. 218ff., Tsong Khapa makes a few further points about this verse: "the type of production that is refuted conventionally as well as ultimately is qualified as 'substantialistic' (*rdzas kyi bdag nyid kyi*), which can be equated to 'intrinsically identifiable,' since mere production would not be so refuted, as conventional production is not susceptible to analysis of the ultimatistic sort. Further, the belief that rationality analytic of ultimacy might not negate conventional intrinsically identifiable production would inevitably entail that ultimate production itself would not be negated, since intrinsically identifiable status is equivalent to truth-status and ultimate status."

[20] MA, VI, ad. k. 34 (above Ch. VII, n. 7).

[21] *Kashyapa Chapter* of the *Ratnakūṭa* Scriptures. This passage is also cited by Poussin in LVP, p. 312, n. 1: *yathoktaṃ bhagavatāryaratnakūṭasūtre / yan na śūnyatayā dharmān śūnyān karoti, api tu dharmā eva śūnyāḥ / yan nānimittena dharmān animittān karoti, api tu dharmā evānimittāḥ / yan nāpraṇihitena dharmān apraṇihitān karoti, api tu dharmā evāpraṇihitā / yaivaṃ pratyāvekṣā, iyam ucyate kaśyapa madhyamapratipad dharmānāṃ bhūtapratyāvekṣā. . . .* The quote goes on with the same pattern applied to *anabhisaṃskāra*, *ajāta*, *anutpanna*.

tiness" would be wrong. And if existence by a thing's own intrinsic reality were not refuted, then it would be necessary to demonstrate emptiness through an emptiness with respect to something else, which contradicts "it does not makes things empty because of emptiness." In short, (intrinsic identifiability of things) would mean that there is no self-emptiness which is emptiness by a thing's own nature. Therefore, if one does not assent to the emptiness of things with respect to the intrinsic reality which is intrinsic identifiability, though one may call it "self-emptiness," it does not get beyond "other-emptiness," and (Chandra means that) the Idealist doctrine that the relative is free of substantial subject-object-dichotomy does not negate (intrinsic identifiability) by taking the import of the relative to be intrinsic realitylessness.

Although (the various positions on the subtle objective selflessness) are similar insofar as they are modes of emptiness where the negation-ground does not exist as actuality of the negatee, and where that ground is empty with respect to the negatee, (only) the emptiness (of things) with respect to intrinsic identifiability means (their) emptiness in (their) own right, all other modes of emptiness not being emptiness (of things) in themselves. The reason is that, with the former type of emptiness, as long as there is no loss of concentration on the previously attained establishment by validating cognition, it is impossible for reifications to occur which, under the influence of theories, hold that ground as truly existent or existent in a way tantamount to that. Whereas, even when the latter (Idealist and Dogmaticist systems) do not lose the establishment by validating cognition of their objectives, this does not prevent reifications (holding) theoretically to (existence in) truth or (in something with) the meaning of truth.[22]

[22] Tsong Khapa considers this final passage important enough to repeat it word for word in his GRS, p. 214, but it is somewhat difficult to understand. It relates to the general question of "self-emptiness" and "other-emptiness." First, let us translate the context in which Tsong Khapa uses the sentence in GRS (p. 213ff.): "This [*Ratnakūṭa*] scriptural passage refutes the Idealist statement that the relative is empty because of its lack of substantial subject-object difference, and not with respect to intrinsic identifiability. . . . Yet, though such is the intended meaning of the expression 'things are empty in their own objectivities,' it is definitely wrong to assert that ' "self-emptiness" is a pot's emptiness of pot, since a pot's non-emptiness of pot by emptiness of truth is "other-emptiness" '; since, as a pot's emptiness of pot entails a pot's absence in a pot, and if a thing is absent from itself it is absent from whatever else, the pot would be totally nonexistent. . . . Such an emptiness as that is taken to be genuine by some, while others assent to this nihilistic emptiness, but both of these are outside of the relativity free of absolutism and nihilism so often proven by the Victor and his Sons. Especially, the nihilistic emptiness position that asserts that all superficially real things must each be determined to be empty with respect to itself is utterly wrong; all the four schools recognize this as nihilism and do not generate it in their own streams of consciousness. Therefore, . . . [then our same sentence follows]."

3. CONSIDERATION OF WHETHER THERE IS A PROBANDUM IN THE NEGATION "INTRINSIC REALITYLESSNESS"

Here, one may wonder, does the reason merely negate intrinsic reality in persons and things, when one asserts that (it is) "not established"? Or does the reason (actually) prove intrinsic realitylessness?

In this regard, since it is first of all necessary to understand the definitions of the two kinds of negation, let us explain them. When a negation is verbally expressed, it either excludes its negatee explicitly in words or else may be understood as functioning effectively to negate its negatee when it dawns in the cognition (through its implications). An example of the first mode is "selflessness," and of the second is "ultimate reality," which, although its excluding of negatee is not verbally explicit, functions effectively to exclude mental fabrications when its import dawns (in the mind). Thus (negation) is what is understood when a negatee is directly excluded.[23]

Now the first of the two (kinds of either implicit or explicit negation) is choice negation, which commits itself to something else when it directly excludes its negatee. As (Bhavaviveka) states in the *Blaze of Argument*, "choice negation negates the reality of something and thereby establishes the reality of something else similar to it. For example, the negation 'this (man) is not a brahmin' establishes that (the man) is of a lower class than the brahmin class, yet is similar to a brahmin by virtue of his learning, ascetic achievements, and so forth." Exclusion negation, (the second kind), does not imply anything else when it directly excludes its negatee. As (Bhavaviveka) explains in the *Blaze of Argument*, "Exclusion negation does no more than negate just the reality of something, not establishing anything other but similar. For example, the expression 'A

Further, bLo-bzang Phun-tshogs asserts (*Zin Bris*, *Dbu ma*, f. 66b4) that "the meaning of 'self-emptiness' is that a thing is not established as existing according to its own apparent objectivity."

In short, as long as this type of emptiness is present in awareness that has already verified it by means of validating cognitions, such awareness can never assent to theoretical presumptions about anything's objective-reality-status or anything like it, since anything that appears to the mind as objectively real is instantly cognized as being empty of the status corresponding to the appearance. A traditional example is that of a man who sees a double moon through visual distortion and simultaneously affirms his well-known cognition that there is only one, so seeing the double appearance, he says, "Ah, there's the moon!"

On the other hand, cognitions of other types of emptiness cannot have this effect, since they assent on some level to the validity of the mode of appearance of objects, thinking them to be indeed intrinsically identifiable, having intrinsic identities, conventionally true, and so on, or some other equivalent.

[23] These two modes of negation, verbally explicit and merely implicit, must be understood apart from the usual distinction between exclusion negation and choice negation (absolute negation and implicative negation), which are described immediately following.

brahmin should not drink beer!' only negates just that, and does not indicate that he does or does not drink any other kind of drink."[24] In these passages, (Bhavaviveka) uses "establishes" and "does not establish" interchangeably with "implies" and "does not imply," or else (exclusion negation would be presented as) not even negating its negatee.

Here, the difference between these two (types) is not that they negate using the words "is not" and "exists not," respectively; because both Chandra and Bhavya explain "it is not from self" as an exclusion negation, and one must understand "Boundless Life" (*Amitāyuh*) as a choice negation. Thus, for negation (to take place), it is not sufficient to exclude a negatee with regard to something by negating all other things (in general) as being it, but it is necessary that (the negation) take effect with the mode of exclusion (of the negatee) by one's verbal expression or with the mode of direct exclusion of the negatee in one's conceptual cognition.[25]

(In this regard) there are some who maintain that, while such expressions as "selflessness" are exclusion negations (in general), they are no longer such when put together with an object, as in "selflessness in persons," etc., and others assert that there is no exclusion negation together with an object, since then it implies something else as well. These are quite wrong, because although the particulars of the two types of negation are set forth in other treatises just as explained above, such expressions as "brahmins should not drink beer!" retain the character of exclusion negation even though they are conjoined with an object, and because (in such as that same expression) the object such as "brahmin" is the basis for judging whether or not something else is implied by the exclusion of the negatee, and is not (itself) the other thing implied.

There are four modes of implying something else (in a negation), implicitly, explicitly, both together, and by context, as (Avalokitavrata) cites in the *Wisdom Lamp Commentary*: "Choice negation (implies) other things showing them implicitly, explicitly establishing them, through both modes, and not by its own expression; the other (type of negation) is different."[26] Here, an example of implicit (choice negation) is "Yajña is fat and does not eat by day." An example of explicit establishment of something else is "it exists without being produced from itself," since

[24] TJ, III, ad. MH, III, k. 26. In calling these "choice negation" (*paryudāsapratiṣedha*) and "exclusion negation" (*prasājyapratiṣedha*) I am following B. K. Matilal, *Epistemology, Logic, and Grammar in Indian Philosophical Analysis* (The Hague: Moutorn, 1971), p. 165, with the corresponding qualifications.

[25] This sentence seems to rule out the mere exclusivity of ordinary reference, à la *apoha* theory, as a proper negation, reserving that term technically for a specific verbal and mental operation.

[26] PrPrT, TG, C, wa, f. 63b4-5.

exclusion of the negatee and establishment of another fact are contained in the same expression. An example of (choice negation through) both modes, where explicit and implicit implications are both in the expression, is "fat Yajna does not waste away without eating by day." And an example of (choice negation) not indicated in the expression (itself) is the statement "this is not a brahmin" made in the context where one knows for certain that a person is either a brahmin or a warrior but not which of the two. If any of these four modes of implication is found, (a negation is) a choice negation, and any other (negation) which does not imply any other thing is an exclusion negation.

Now, certain former (scholars) asserted that the Centrists use reasons and syllogisms for negating intrinsic reality, but not for proving intrinsic realitylessness.[27] This is incorrect, because genuine reasons without probanda and inferential validating cognitions without objects are impossible.

(Still) others maintain that the Dogmaticists have reasons and syllogisms for proving selflessness, but Dialecticists do not, since (Chandrakirti) explained, in the *Lucid Exposition*, that "we do not prove that this does not exist, but do refute the absolutistic constructions of others. Likewise, we do not prove the existence of this (conventional reality), but refute the nihilistic constructions of others, since we assert the establishment of the central way by clearing away the two extremisms."[28] (They also maintain) that consequences merely function to negate the premises of others,[29] and that, as in the *Introduction*, "the wise exclaim that the fruit of philosophical analysis is the elimination of imaginative constructions";[30] and that therefore (the Dialecticists) merely refute the systems of others and do not prove the non-existence of intrinsic reality.[31]

Explanation of only that necessary for mere exclusion of the negatee is not one of the Dialecticist distinctive specialties, because even (Bhavaviveka) explains, in the *Blaze of Argument*, that "(this) does no more than merely negate, as earth, etc., are not actually elements ultimately, and does not prove that they are actually anything else or that they are

[27] bLo-bzang Phun-tshogs (*Zin Bris*, *Dbu ma*, f. 69a4) indicates these to be Tibetans, but refrains from identifying them.

[28] PPMMV, XX, ad. k. 3 (Tib.: TG, C, a, f. 127b5 ff.), Vaidya ed., p. 169, l. 19 ff.): *na vayam asyāsattvaṃ pratipādayāmaḥ, kiṃ tarhi paraparikalpitaṃ sattvam asya nirākurmaḥ / evaṃ na vayam asya sattvaṃ pratipādayāmaḥ, kiṃ tarhi paraparikalpitam asattvam asya apakūrmaḥ / antadvayaparihāreṇa madhyamāyāḥ pratipādayitum iṣṭatvād /.*

[29] This is not a direct quote, although it closely corresponds to the phrase in PPMMV, I (TG, C, a, f. 8a2; Vaideya ed., p. 8, 1.1): *parapratijñāpratiṣedhamātraphalatvāt prasaṇgopādānasya . . . /*

[30] MA, VI, k. 117cd, Poussin ed., p. 230.

[31] These scholars, whose assertions are somewhat more sophisticated, as they allow that at least Dogmaticists use proofs, and so on, are not identified in the commentaries.

actually non-existent."[32] Therefore, the word "merely" in the statements that negation of intrinsic identifiability merely excludes the negatee and merely gets rid of false constructions indicates that (these statements) are exclusion negations, refuting the possibility of their being choice negations by ruling out their implying anything else, not merely negating their negatees within their logical scope; because, as explained above (exclusion negation) merely excludes its negatee without establishing anything else.[33]

An example (of exclusion negation) is the expression "there is no smoke in the lake," which merely excludes the presence of smoke in the lake without indicating (the existence of) anything else. However, it does not (thereby) fail to show that the lake is free of smoke, nor does the corresponding cognition fail to ascertain the smokelessness of the lake. Likewise, the expression "there is no intrinsic reality in the sprout" merely rules out any intrinsic reality in the sprout, but why should that preclude the expression's expressing and the cognition's ascertaining the intrinsic realitylessness of the sprout? Therefore, the words express the absence of the smoke in the lake in their very exclusion (of it) and the cognition ascertains the absence of the smoke in its very exclusion (of it from the lake); because the exclusion of the negatee and the determination of the negation are (mutually indispensable), the lack of either one entailing the lack of the other. In the same way, the scriptural references teaching intrinsic realitylessness express intrinsic realitylessness in their actual negation of intrinsic reality; the rational cognition negative of intrinsic reality cognizes intrinsic realitylessness in its actual negation of intrinsic reality, and the reason negative of intrinsic reality proves intrinsic realitylessness in its actual negation of intrinsic reality. These (facts) must be accepted, and one must not assert that the scriptural references have no subject, the cognition has no object, and the reason has no probandum.

Therefore, it does not seem to be correct to assert, with regard either to the Centrist, or even to the Logician, that reason merely negates intrinsic reality and does not prove intrinsic realitylessness. When it is said that the statement "earth is not ultimately the actuality of the element" merely accomplishes the negation of its being the actuality of the element ultimately, it means that that exclusion negation proves that probandum, and the statement "it does not prove that it is actually non-existent" does not mean that (the statement) does not prove that it does not exist as an element ultimately, but means that it does not prove there to be any reality of non-existence other than a pure negation. Therefore, granted

[32] TJ, I, edited by S. Iida, *Introduction to Svātantrika-Mādhyamika* (Ann Arbor: Xerox University Microfilms, 1968), p. 103 (Tib.); p. 104 (Eng.).

[33] See above definitions.

that it is valid to inquire whether something else is established other than mere exclusion of a negatee, how can it be cogent to inquire, having assented to the exclusion of a negatee, whether reason, word, and cognition have taken the negation as their object?

Here one might object that if the reason that rules out intrinsically real existence also proves intrinsic realitylessness, how is this reconciled with the Holy (Nagarjuna's) statement? "This negates existence itself, and does not embrace non-existence itself; just like saying 'it is not black' is not to say 'it is white.' "[34]

This means that just as, for example, to say "this is not black" when you want to show the mere absence of black, is a mere negation of black and is not an indication of something else such as "this is white," so when you assert that such as sprouts are ultimately intrinsically realityless, you are proving merely the negation of their ultimate, intrinsically real existence; and are not proving the existence of any truthlessness apart from that. (Bhavaviveka) in the *Wisdom Lamp* and (Avalokitavrata) in the commentary explain (this verse of Nagarjuna's) as meaning that the proof (of realitylessness) is not a choice negation, but is an exclusion negation, as (Avalokitavrata) states that "this can be understood from the example, since he does not say that 'it is not black' fails to show that the thing is not black, but that it does not show that it is white." (Incidentally,) Avalokitavrata states that "this reference comes from the *Investigation of the World.*"

The way in which confusion arises here may be expressed as follows: "that ultimate non-production of the sprout must be proven to be the case by rational cognition; hence, when the sprout is proven to be without ultimate production, the existence of ultimate non-production becomes the probandum, since the inference proves that fact." I am going to explain how rational cognition does not prove the existence of intrinsic realitylessness in my commentary on the *Wisdom.*[35]

If we realize that the probandum is the exclusion negation (itself), what we prove is the mere exclusion of ultimate production, and we understand that we do not prove anything else such as the existence of ultimate non-production.

[34] This verse, quoted here by Tsong Khapa as "by the Arya" (*'phags pas*), and in RG, p. 49, as "from the *Lokaparīkṣa*" (*'Jig rten brtag pa*), cannot be found in any of the works of Nagarjuna. It is quoted also by Bhavya in the PrPr, but without identification. My present conclusion is that the verse comes from a work of Nagarjuna's known to Bhavya and through him to Tsong Khapa, but not translated into Tibetan and now lost in India.

[35] Tsong Khapa addresses this question at length in his RG, I, pp. 44 ff., where this is one of the extreme views he takes pains to refute, the other being that the refutation of intrinsic reality is not itself a logical conclusion. Thus, the difficulty others have in accepting probanda in "realitylessness" is from the notion of probandum as a positive fact.

In regard to (Chandra's) statement in the *Lucid Exposition*, "we refute what others imagine exists, and do not prove any non-existence,"[36] an example of a notion to refute is (that of) utter non-existence, and it is refuted as follows: "Ultimate productionlessness is not to be held as truly existent;" and an example of not proving any absolute existence is (simply) not to prove the existence of ultimate production. Therefore, one can negate both the truth-status of the sprout and the truth-status of the truthlessness, since it is not the case that the exclusion of one determines the other, but one cannot negate both the truth-status of the sprout and the truthlessness of the sprout, since necessarily the exclusion of the one is the determination of the other. (Nagarjuna) clearly states in the *Rebuttal of Objections*: "If it were the case that the realityless (words) themselves were to eliminate some realitylessness, when intrinsic realitylessness was done away with, intrinsic reality would actually be established.[37]

Thus, if realityless words were to negate the intrinsic realitylessness of things, then things would become in fact intrinsically really existent. Similarly, ultimate existence and ultimate non-existence cannot both be negated. However, ultimate existence and ultimate existence of non-existence can both be negated.

In this regard, the (Buddhist) Realists cannot negate truth-status in both (negation and negatee), since they assert that if the negatee is untrue its negation is true, and if the negation is untrue its negatee is true. (On the other hand), the Centrists, having solidly established with scripture and reason the definitive meaning, the inconceivable, profound central path of abandonment of both those extremes (of absolutism and nihilism), succeed in spreading out in all directions the essence of the Doctrine of the Victor!

Now, the following question may be (fairly) put: "Since there seems to be a multitude of approaches by which the two Great Champions of Philosophy proceeded to differentiate between the interpretable meaning and the definitive meaning of the scriptures and by which the lordly sages specifically elucidated the intimate intention (of those Champions), which master of elucidation of the intimate intentions of those two (Champions) do you (Dialecticists) follow? You must (at last) proclaim which interpretation of definitive meaning you profess to be the conclusive ultimate."

I revere from the depths of my heart
All the excellent elucidations of these,

[36] PPMMV, see above Ch. VII n. 28.

[37] VV, k. 25 (Vaidya ed., p. 284): *naiḥsvabhāvyanaṃ cen naiḥsvabhāvyena varaṇaṃ yadi hi / naiḥsvabhāvyānivṛttau svabhāvyaṃ hi prasiddhaṃ syāt //.*

The Ornaments of the Sages of this world.
Yet when one's eye of intellect is opened wide,
As a night-lily garden bursts in blooms,
By the white light shining from Chandra's moon,
And Buddhapalita's appointed path is seen[38]—
Who is there who would not hold supreme
The most excellent system of Nagarjuna?

Such is my answer!

This way (I have explained above) should be understood to be the path of the determination of the ultimate reality (revealed) in all the scriptures, esoteric as well as exoteric, since there is a grave mistake (in thinking) that, while the systems of the two (philosophical) Champions for determining the ultimate reality by distinguishing the interpretable and the definitive among scriptures are evidently prevalent in the context of the Transcendence Vehicle, the great Siddhas and the Pandits who elucidated the scriptures of the Tantric Vehicle had a third alternative (system) for determining ultimate reality.

And it is for this reason that I saw that seeking reality without relying on the way of the Champions with their two systems is like a blind man's running guideless through a wilderness and that the previous accounts of ultimate reality by the mere dogmatists, who stand on a few scriptural phrases distinguishing interpretable and definitive, do not investigate thoroughly the treatises, and do not, in particular, understand the subtle points of (the Champions') reasonings; their accounts are essentially mere verbiage. I then became dissatisfied with having only a rough idea of many of the (deeper) points of meaning, and so made a comprehensive inquiry into the precise and general keys of those reasonings which the Champions have given us as eyes for looking upon the scriptures. Having done so, I composed this account of the *Essence of Eloquence* for the sake of those of subtle philosophical discernment who, unleashing mighty waves of efforts to determine the magnificence, the profundity, and that more profound than the profundity of the scriptures, have taken to heart the practical attainment of what they know, and earnestly desire that the Doctrine of the Victor may long be with us![39]

[38] Tsong Khapa here refers to his experience of unexcelled enlightenment at Ol Kha, when, the morning after his prophetic dream, he was rereading Buddhapalita's commentary on the Eighteenth Chapter of the *Wisdom*, and everything finally became clear to him. See Introduction, VII.

[39] Note that here, at the end of what is unquestionably one of the most intellectually sophisticated texts in the Centrist literature, Tsong Khapa asserts his own view of his proper readers as being those who take philosophy to heart, as it were, putting it into practice in the quest of self-transformation and transcendent attainment.

He embodies the essence of the Teaching,
The profound intention of the Victor,
Revealed by the Scripture of the Profound;

With vast learning in the many treatises
Of the two methodologies supreme
Of Buddha's philosophical traditions;

His precise discernment of their import
Contemplates aright the path of reason
Compelling to the hearts of subtle intellects;

Reknowned as melodious Manjughosha,
The garland of his fame spreads all around;
Ah, the foot of that Universal Lord!

Reverent, I adored it on the lotus of my heart,
My faith unwavering and powerfully intense,
And that most sweet reason of philosophers,
Who sees the real Thatness of the Holy Discourse,
Authored this book on the miraculous message.[40]

What other treatise thus elucidates
The import of that Discourse of the Buddha,
That great treasury of true eloquence,
So fitting the Champions' practical systems
Elaborated by the deep Nagarjuna
And the irresistible Asanga,
The two prize bulls of all philosophers?

Already expert in all the sciences
Of Bodhisattvas, veterans of heroes' deeds,
I still inquired ever more penetratingly
Into every further exact realization
Of those Places, so difficult to measure,
Of the profound and the magnificent;
And my heart became buoyantly delighted
With the splendid banquet of totally pure
Samadhis, brilliant wisdoms, and active ethics.

One minute one swells with joy of faith in the Victors,
The next, one remembers the kindness of the Champions;
Time again, reverence for the wise spiritual teacher,

[40] Here Tsong Khapa refers to his mentor, Manjushri, offering us a glimpse of his personal fusion of philosophy and revelation. See Introduction, VII.

Heartfelt compassion for the suffering living beings,
The wish for the long endurance of the Precious Teaching—
These feelings increase as if in mutual competition.
These times, when one feels the magic of the path
Of that Philosophy which bestows the discovery
Of That Place, so long desired, so hard to realize—
"Kyea-mah! How wonderful!"[41]
Though all alone, the shout of joy bursts forth!

The Moon of philosophers shines on such a one,[42]
Honoring him with garlands of brilliant praise;
"Contemplator of the highest wisdom!"
"Leader of those pure in ethical achievement!"
"Discoverer of the definitive meaning!"
"Principal heir of the Victorious Buddha!"[43]
The intelligent who wish to win such Buddha-honors,
Should immerse themselves in this clear exposition,
And purify the eyes of their intellects
With the path of philosophical reason.

By whatever merit I may have gained
Through this effort in the pioneering
Champions' Ways of the two great systems,
May the Victor's Holy Dharma be long upheld,
Just as it was by Nagarjuna and Asanga!

As the wise Heroes of Enlightenment,
Samantabhadra and Manjughosha,
Work constantly to delight the Victors,
So also may all my activities
Be ocean waves of wisdom's goodness!

[41] Tib. *kye-ma* is unfamiliar to us as an exclamation of glee or exaltation; we must use our imagination to locate it somewhere between "yippee!" and "alleluia!"

[42] At first I thought this "moon of philosophers" (Tib. *smra bai zla ba*) refers to Chandrakirti (Skt. *candra* means "moon"). But why should Chandrakirti especially be the one to laud the philosophical yogi who reaches "This Place?" To be sure, the "Secret Biography" has Manjushri tell Tsong Khapa that Chandrakirti is the unerringly reliable of the profound philosophers to elucidate Nagarjuna's central way. Another possibility is the goddess Prajñaparamita herself, who is transcendent wisdom, and also emptiness, the Mother of all Buddhas, as it would ultimately be she who would most fittingly garland the enlightened one with praise and honor for winning the profound insight into selflessness. Or it could be her in her guise as Mahamudra, the "Great Seal" or "Supreme Consort," who embraces the adept of transcendent wisdom when his or her realization opens as universal compassion, according to the exquisite symbolism of the Vajrayana.

[43] The implication of these epithets is that the perfection of wisdom, the fulfillment of the philosophical path, is simultaneously the consummation of ethics and meditation as well.

Colophon

This *Essence of True Eloquence*, which clarifies the distinctions between the interpretable meaning and the definitive meaning of the scriptures, by differentiating the two systems of the Champions of Philosophy, the system of "Mind-Only" of the Great Saint Asanga, and the system of realitylessness of the Savior Nagarjuna, was composed (in 1407) by the illustrious Easterner Tsong Khapa bLo-bzang Grags-pa, a Bhikshu of the Shakya Order, a scholar, and a philosopher. The scribe was the Shramanera sDom-brtson bSod-nams bLo-gros.

OM! All is well!

GLOSSARY OF TECHNICAL TERMS

Asterisk indicates Sanskrit reconstruction not attested.

English	*Sanskrit*	*Tibetan*
absolute (ultimate)	*paramārtha*	*don dam pa*
Absolute Body (Body of Truth)	*dharmakāya*	*chos sku*
absolute negation (exclusion negation)	*prasajyapratiṣedha*	*med dgag*
absolutism	*bhāvavāda, bhāvagraha, bhāvāntagraha*	*yod par smra ba, yod par 'dzin pa, yod mtha 'dzin pa*
absolutist extreme	*bhāvānta*	*yod mtha*
absolutistic extremism	*bhāvāntagraha*	*yod mtha 'dzin pa*
absolutistic imagination	*bhāvatvaparikalpana*	*yod pa nyid du yongs su brtags pa*
absorption	*samāhita*	*mnyam par gzhag pa*
accessories of enlightenment	*bodhipakṣikadharma*	*byang chub kyi phyogs chos*
accumulation path	*saṃbhāramārga*	*tshogs lam*
action (evolutionary)	*karma*	*las*
actuality (reality, Thatness)	*tattva*	*de nyid, de kho na nyid*
addiction (affect)	*kleśa*	*nyon mongs*
addictive mentality	*kliṣṭamana*	*nyon yid*
addictive misknowledge	*kliṣṭāvidya*	*nyon mongs can gyi ma rig pa*
addictive obscuration	*kleśāvaraṇa*	*nyon sgrib*
affect (addiction)	*kleśa*	*nyon mongs*
aftermath intuition	*pṛṣṭhalabdhajñāna*	*rjes thob ye shes*
aggregate	*skandha*	*phung po*
Analyst	*vaibhāṣika*	*bye brag smra ba*
analytic insight	*vipaśyana*	*lhag mthong*
analytic meditation	*savicārabhāvana*	*dpyad sgom*
analytic rational cognition	**savicārayuktijñāna*	*dpyod pai rigs shes*
annihilism	*ucchedadṛṣṭi*	*chad lta*
anomalous creation	*viprayuktasaṃskāra*	*ldan min 'du byed*
antagonist (opponent)		*phyir rgol*
apperception	*svasaṃvitti, svasaṃvedana*	*rang rig*
apperceptive self-consciousness	*svasaṃvedana*	*rang rig*

English	*Sanskrit*	*Tibetan*
approximate (gross, crude)	*audārika*	*rags pa*
arrangement (system, presentation)	*vyavasthāna*	*rnam gzhag*
articulation	*abhilāpana*	*mngon par brjod pa*
ascendance, ascendant status	*abhyudaya*	*mngon mtho*
ascriptive (substantive) designation	*svabhāvavikalpana*	*ngo bor brtags pa*
aspect	*ākāra*	*rnam pa*
aspective object	*ākāraviṣaya*	*rnam pai yul*
authentic realization	*parijñāna*	*yongs su shes pa*
authentic view	*samyakdṛṣṭi*	*yang dag lta ba*
basis (ground)	*ādhāra*	*gzhi*
basis of conceptual adherence	**kalpanābhiniveśya-ādhāra*	*rtog pai zhen gzhi*
basis of designation	*prajñapya*	*gdags gzhi*
basis (ground) of emptiness (emptied, the empty)	*yena śūnyatā, śūnyatādhāra*	*stongs gzhi*
basis of reference		*'jug gzhi*
categorical differential	**svavyavṛtti*	*rang ldog*
cause	*hetu*	*rgyu*
causal process	*nimitta, hetunimitta*	*rgyu mtshan*
Central Way	*Madhyamaka*	*dbU ma, dbu mai lam*
Centrism	*Mādhyamika (dṛṣṭi)*	*dbU mai lta ba*
Centrist	*Mādhyamika*	*dbu ma pa*
champion	*mahāratha*	*shing rta chen po*
champions' way	*mahārathanaya*	*shing rtai srol*
champions' way pioneer	**mahārathanayakara*	*shing rtai srol phye ba*
choice (implicative) negation	*paryudāsapratiṣedha*	*ma yin dgag*
class (gene, lineage)	*gotra*	*rigs*
cognition	*jñāna, buddhi*	*shes pa, blo*
conventional —	*vyāvahārika —*	*tha snyad pai —*
conventional validating	**vyāvahārikapramāṇa —*	*tha snyad pai tshad mai*
holy aftermath —	**āryapṛṣṭhalabdhayukti —*	*phags pai rjes thob kyi rigs shes*
rational —	**yuktijñāna*	*rigs shes*
sense —	*indriyajñāna*	*dbang shes*
ultimacy-analytic rational —	**paramārthavicārayukti—*	*don dam dpyod pai rigs—*
cognitive (objective) obscuration	*jñēyāvaraṇa*	*shes byai sgrib pa*
cognitive status		*blos grub pa*
coincidental	*āgantuka*	*glo bur ba*
common individual	*pṛthagjana*	*so so skye bo*

English	*Sanskrit*	*Tibetan*
conception (of the spirit of enlightenment)	*(bodhicitta-)utpāda*	*(byang chub kyi sems) skyes pa*
conceptual object	*abhiniveśya*	*zhen yul*
concomitance	*vyapti*	*khyab pa*
confutation through similar reasons		*rgyu mtshan mtshungs pai mgo snyoms*
conscious futile view	*parikalpita-satkāyadṛṣṭi*	*kun btags kyi 'jig lta*
misknowledge	*— avidyā*	*kun btags kyi ma rig pa*
self-habit	*— ātmagraha*	*kun btags kyi bdag 'dzin*
truth habit	*— satyagraha*	*kun btags kyi-bden 'dzin*
consciousness	*vijñāna*	*rnam par shes pa*
consequence	*prasaṇga*	*thal ba*
constructed (reality)	*vikalpitasvabhāva*	*rnam par brtags pai ngo bo nyid*
imaginatively constructed (reality)	*parikalpita*	*kun btags kyi ngo bo nyid,* yongs su brtags pai ngo bo nyid
constructive thought	*kalpana*	*rtog pa*
convention (verbal and symbolic)	*(nāmasaṃketa) vyavahāra*	*(ming dang brdai) tha snyad*
conventional cognition	*vyāvahārikajñāna*	*tha snyad pai shes pa*
conventional existence	*vyāvahārikasat*	*tha snyad du yod pa*
conventional status	*vyavahārasiddha*	*tha snyad du grub pa*
conventional truth	*vyāvahārikasatya*	*tha snyad bden pa*
— validating cognition	*vrāvahārikapramāṇa*	*tha snyad pai tshad ma*
conventionally ascriptive intellect		*tha snyad 'dogs pai blo*
conviction	*abhiniveśa*	*zhen pa*
creation	*saṃskāra*	*'du byed*
cyclic life (life-cycle)	*saṃsāra*	*'khor ba*
dedication	*pariṇāmana*	*yongs su bsngo ba*
defining characteristic	*svalakṣaṇa (Abhidharma)*	*rang gi mtshan nyid*
definitive meaning	*nītārtha*	*nges don*
dependent designation	*upādāyaprajñāpti*	*brten nas gdags pa*
dependent origination (relativity)	*pratītyasamutpāda*	*rten cing 'brel bar 'byung ba*
descriptive (qualitative) designation	*viśeṣavikalpana*	*khyad par du brtags pa*
designation	*prajñapti, vikalpa*	*gdags pa, brtags pa*
designative base (referential base)	*prajñapya, prajñapyārtha*	*gdags gzhi, gdags don*
designative edxistence	*prajñaptisat*	*gdags su yod pa*
determinate (cognition)	*sākāra (jñāna)*	*rnam ldan (gyi shes pa)*
determination	*viniścaya, nirṇaya, paricchinna*	*gtan la 'bab pa, rnam par nges pa, yongs su gcod pa*
determine, ascertain	*niścaya*	*nges pa*

English	*Sanskrit*	*Tibetan*
dialectical consequence	*prasaṅga*	*thal ba*
dialectical (public) reason	*paraprasiddhahetu*	*gshan grags kyi rtags*
diamond smithereen		*rdo rje gzegs ma*
differential	*vyāvrtti*	*ldog pa*
categorical —		*rang ldog*
ground —		*gzhi ldog*
direct objective basis of expressions		*brjod byed kyi dngos yul*
discerned	*parichinna*	*yongs su bcad pa*
discernment		*rnam dpyod*
discipline	*vinaya*	*'dul ba*
Discourse (Scripture)	*sūtra*	*mdo*
discriminated (constructed) reality	*vikalpitasvabhāva*	*rnam brtags kyi ngo bo nyid*
distinctive characteristic	*svalakṣaṇa (Abhidharma)*	*rang gi mtshan nyid*
distinctive specialty	*asādharaṇaviśeṣa*	*thun mong min pai khyad chos*
dogmaticism (privacy)	*svātantryā*	*rang rgyud*
Dogmaticist	*Svātantrika*	*rang rgyud pa*
Dogmaticist Centrist	*Svātantrikamādhyamika*	*dbu ma rang rgyud pa*
dogmaticist (private) inference/syllogism	*svatantrānumana (svārthaparārtha)*	*rang rgyud rjes dpag (rang don dang gzhan don)*
dogmaticist (private) reason	*svatantrahetu*	*rang rgyud kyi rtags*
dogmaticist (private) thesis	*svatantrapratijña*	*rang rgyud kyi dam bca*
dogmatist (sophist)	*tarkika*	*rtog ge pa*
dualism (dualistic theory)	*dvayavāda*	*gnyis su smra ba*
education	*śikṣa*	*bslab pa*
egocentric person	*arvāgdarśana*	*mtshur mthong*
egoism, "I"-habit	*ahaṃkāra*	*ngar 'dzin*
element	*dhātu*	*khams*
eloquence	*subhāṣita, pratibhāna*	*legs bshad, spobs pa*
eloquent elucidation	*subhāṣita*	*legs bshad*
Emanation Body	*nirmānakāya*	*sprul sku*
emptied out	*yad śūnyata*	*gang gis stong pa*
emptiness	*śūnyata*	*stong pa nyid*
— of personal self	*pudgala —*	*gang zag gi —*
— of objective self	*dharmātma —*	*chos bdag gi —*
— of relative with respect to imagined	**parikalpitaśūnyaparatantra*	*kun brtags kyis stong pai gzhan dbang*
— of subject-object substantial dichotomy	**grahyagrahakadravyabhedatvena —*	*gzung 'dzin rdzas tha dad kyis—*
other-emptiness	*paraśūnyata*	*gzhan stong*
self-emptiness	*svaśūnyata*	*rang stong*

English	*Sanskrit*	*Tibetan*
empty, the (basis of emptiness)	*śūnyatādhāra*	*gang stong pai gzhi*
enlightenment	*bodhi, buddhatvam*	*byang chub, sangs rgyas nyid*
equanimity	*upekṣa*	*btang snyoms*
establishment (status)	*siddha, siddhi*	*grub pa*
ethic (morality)	*śīla*	*tshul khrims*
evolution, evolutionary action	*karma*	*las*
evolutionary development	*karmavipāka*	*las kyi rnam par smin pa*
exclusion	*vichinna*	*rnam bcad*
exclusion (differential)	*vyāvrtti*	*ldog pa*
exclusion negation (absolute negation)	*prasajyapratiṣedha*	*med dgag*
existence	*sat*	*yod pa*
existent	*bhāva*	*dngos po*
experience	*anubhava*	*myong ba*
experiential medium (medium)	*āyatana*	*skye mched*
Experientialist	*yogācāra*	*rnal 'byor spyod pa*
expressible (subject)	*abhidheya*	*brjod bya*
expressive verbal universal	**abhidhānaśabdasāmānya*	*brjod byed sgra spyi*
external objective	*bāhyārtha*	*phyi don*
externally objective status	*bāhyārthasiddha*	*phyi don du grub pa*
extreme	*anta*	*mtha*
extremism	*antagraha*	*mthar 'dzin*
absolutistic —	*bhāvāntagraha*	*yod mthar 'dzin pa*
annihilistic —	*ucchedāntagraha*	*chad mthar 'dzin pa*
eternalistic —	*śāśvatāntagraha*	*rtag mthar 'dzin pa*
nihilistic —	*abhāvāntagraha*	*med mthar 'dzin pa*
extremist habit	*antagraha*	*mthar 'dzin*
extremist view	*antagrahadṛṣṭi*	*mthar 'dzin gyi lta ba*
fabrication	*prapañca*	*spros pa*
fact (reality, truth)	*satya*	*bden pa*
face value		*stobs zhugs*
final genealogical determinism	*gotraniyata*	*rigs nges pa*
form	*rūpa*	*gzugs*
form aggregate	*rūpaskandha*	*gzugs kyi phung po*
formable	*rūpya*	*gzugs su rung ba*
formability	*rūpyatā*	*gzugs su rung ba nyid*
formless	*ārūpya*	*gzugs med*
functional capacity	*arthakriya*	*don byed nus pa*
fundamental consciousness	*ālayavijñāna*	*kun gzhi rnam shes*
futile view	*satkāyadṛṣṭi*	*'jig lta*
instinctual —	*sahaja —*	*— lhan skyes*
unconscious —		

English	*Sanskrit*	*Tibetan*
gene (spiritual gene)	*gotra*	*rigs*
genealogical determinism	*atyantagotraniyata*	*mthar thug rigs nges pa*
generality (universal)	*sāmānya*	*spyi*
objective —	*arthasāmānya*	*don spyi*
verbal —	*śabdasāmānya*	*sgra spyi*
Great Community School	*mahāsaṃghika*	*dge 'dun chen po pa*
gross (self-habit, etc.) (approximate)	*audārika (ātmagrahādi)*	*(bdag 'dzin sogs) rags pa*
ground (base)	*āśraya, ādhāra*	*gzhi, gnas*
ground differential	**āśrayavyāvrtti*	*gzhi ldog*
ground of symbolic designation		*brda 'dogs pai gnas*
habit (notion)	*graha*	*'dzin pa*
habit-pattern (posture)	*muṣṭi*	*'dzin stangs*
habitual adherence	*abhiniveśana*	*mngon par zhen pa*
habitual notion	*muṣṭi*	*'dzin stangs*
heterodox (non-Buddhist)	*bahirdhā*	*phyi rol pa*
holy	*ārya*	*'phags pa*
Idealist	*vjñānavāda*	*sems tsam pa*
identifiability (intrinsic)	*svalakṣaṇasiddha*	*rang mtshan gyis grub pa*
identification	*lakṣa*	*mtshon pa*
identified	*lakṣya*	*mtshan gzhi*
identity (intrinsic)	*lakṣaṇa*	*rang gi mtshan nyid*
identity-unreality	*lakṣaṇaniḥsvabhāvatā*	*mtshan nyid ngo bo nyid med pa*
identitylessness	*alakṣaṇatva, niḥsvabhāva*	*rang mtshan med pa, rang bzhin med pa*
imagination	*parikalpana*	*yongs su brtags pa*
imaginatively constructed reality	*parikalpitasvabhāva*	*kun brtags kyi ngo bo nyid*
imagined nature	*parikalpitalakṣaṇa*	*kun brtags kyi mtshan nyid*
immanent reality (Thatness)	*tattva*	*de kho na nyid, de nyid*
implication	*abhisaṃdhi*	*dgongs pa*
implicative (choice) negation	*paryudāsapratiṣedha*	*ma yin dgag*
implicit meaning	*ayathāruṭa*	*sgra ji bzhin ma yin pa*
indeterminate (cognition)	*anākāra (jñāna)*	*rnam med (kyi shes pa)*
Individual Vehicle	*hīnayāna*	*theg dman*
Individualist	*hīnayānika*	*theg dman pa*
inference	*anumāna*	*rjes dpag*
personal — (internal)	*svārtha—*	*rang don—*
public — (syllogism)	*parārtha—*	*gzhan don—*

English	Sanskrit	Tibetan
inferential rational cognition	*ānumānikayuktijñāna	rjes dpag rigs shes
inferential validating cognition	*ānumānikapramāṇa	rjes dpag tshad ma
instinct	vāsana, anuśaya	bag chags, bag la nyal ba
instinctual (natural, unconscious)	sahaja	lhan skyes
intellectual futile view	parikalpitasatkāyadṛṣṭi	'jig lta kun brtags
intellectual misknowledge	parikalpita-avidyā	kun brtags kyi ma rig pa
intellectual self-habit	parikalpita-ātmagraha	bdag 'dzin kun brtags
intellectual reification	parikalpita-samāropa,	sgro 'dogs kun brtags
intellectual truth-habit	parikalpita-satyagraha	bden 'dzin kun brtags
intellectual supposition		blos rloms pa
intelligence (information) only	vijñaptimātra	rnam par rig pa tsam
intention	abhiprāya, abhisaṃdhi	dgongs pa
intention-ground		dgongs gzhi
intention-meaning		dgongs don
intentional	ābhiprāyiki	dgongs pa can
intentionality		zhe rtsis
internal verbalization	manojalpa	yid kyis brjod pa
interpretable meaning	neyārtha	drang don
intimation (intention)	abhisaṃdhi	dgongs pa
intrinsic —	sva—	rang —
— identity	svalakṣaṇa	rang gi mtshan nyid
— identifiability	svalakṣaṇasiddha	rang mtshan gyis grub pa
— objectivity	svarūpasiddha	rang gi ngo bos grub pa
— reality	svabhāva, svarūpa	rang bzhin, rang gi ngo bo nyid
— realitylessness (unreality)	niḥsvabhāva, niḥsvarūpa	rang bzhin med pa, rang gi ngo bo nyid med pa
— reality-status	svabhāvasiddha, svarūpasiddha	rang bzhin gyis grub pa, rang gi ngo bo nyid kyis grub pa
intrinsically —		
— identifiable status	svalakṣaṇasiddha	rang mtshan gyis grub pa
— identifiable intrinsic reality	*svalaṣaṇasiddhasvabhāvasat	rang mtshan grub pai rang bzhin yod pa
— identifiable intrinsic identity	*svalakṣaṇasiddhasvalakṣaṇa	rang mtshan grub pai rang mtshan
— identifiable intrinsic reality status	*svalakṣaṇasiddhasvabhāvasiddha	rang mtshan grub pai rang bzhin gyis grub pa
— identifiable intrinsic objectivity	*svalakṣaṇasiddhasvarūpasiddha	rang mtshan grub pai rang gi ngo bo nyid kyis grub pa
intuition (intuitive		

English	*Sanskrit*	*Tibetan*
wisdom)	*jñāna*	*ye shes*
holy aftermath —	*āryapṛṣṭhalabdha —*	*'phags pai rjes thob —*
holy equanimity —	*āryasamāhita —*	*'phags pai mnyam bzhag —*
invariable concomitance	*vyapti*	*khyab pa*
irrational	*na yuktitaḥ*	*rigs pa ma yin pa*
liberation (Nirvana)	*mokṣa, vimokṣa, nirvāṇa*	*thar pa, rnam par thar pa, mya ngan las 'das pa*
life (life-cycle)	*saṃsāra*	*'khor ba*
literal insistence	*yathārutābhiniveśa*	*sgra ji bzhin du zhen pa*
literal meaning	*yathārutārtha*	*sgra ji bzhin pai don*
logical scope	*yuktigocara*	*rigs pai yul*
Logician	*naiyāyika, prāmāṇika*	*rigs par smra ba, tshad ma pa*
Lord	*bhagavān*	*bcom ldan 'das*
magnificent	*udāra*	*rgya che ba*
materialistic construction	*piṇḍagrahakalpana*	*ril 'dzin brtags pa*
materialistic view	*piṇḍagrahadṛṣṭi*	*ril 'dzin lta ba*
meaning (object, referent, import)	*artha*	*don*
meaninglessness	*alakṣaṇata*	*mtshan nyid med pa*
medium	*āyatana*	*skye mched*
mental habit	*graha*	*bzung ba, 'dzin pa*
middle way (central way)	*madhyamapratipat*	*dbu mai lam*
migration	*gati*	*'gro ba*
misknowledge	*avidya*	*ma rig pa*
mutual dependence	*parasparāpekṣa*	*phan tshun ltos pa*
mutually dependent status	*parasparāpekṣasiddha*	*phan tshun ltos grub*
mutually dependent designative status	*parasparāpekṣaprajñāptisiddha*	*phan tshun ltos pai gdags grub*
naive	*bāla*	*byis pa*
name	*nāma*	*ming*
natural (innate, unconscious, instinctual	*sahaja, nija*	*lhan skyes*
natural conventional validating cognition	**sahajavyāvahārikapramāṇa*	*lhan skyes tha snyad pai tshad ma*
nature	*dharma, lakṣaṇa, svabhāva*	*chos, mtshan nyid, rang bzhin*
nature-possessor	*dharmin*	*chos can*
negate (refute)	*pratiṣedha, niṣedha*	*dgag pa, bkag pa*
negatee	*pratiṣedhavya, niṣedhya*	*dgag bya*
negation (refutation) (absolute/implicative)	*pratiṣedha*	*dgag pa*
negation-ground		*dgag gzhi*
nihilism	*abhāvavāda (graha)*	*med par smra ba ('dzin pa)*

English	*Sanskrit*	*Tibetan*
nihilist	*abhāvavādin*	*med pa pa*
nihilistic extreme	*abhāvānta*	*med mtha*
nihilistic extremism	*abhāvāntagraha*	*med mthar 'dzin pa*
Nirvana	*nirvāṇa*	*mya ngan las 'das pa*
nominal convention	**nāmavyavahāra*	*ming gi tha snyad*
nominal designation		*ming gis 'dogs pa*
non-analytic —	*avicāra*	*dpyod med*
— conventional validating cognition	*—vyāvahārika-pramāṇa	*— tha snyad pai tshad ma*
— natural self-habit	*— sahajātmagraha	*— bdag 'dzin lhan skyes*
— presentation	*— vyavasthāna	*— rnam gzhag*
non-perception of related fact reason		*'brel zla ma dmigs pai rtags*
noumenally omniscient intuition	*yathāvadjñāna*	*ji lta ba mkhyen pai ye shes*
noumenon (transcendent)	*dharmatā, paramārtha, lokottara*	*chos nyid, don dam, 'jig rten las 'das pa*
object of names and signs	**nāmasaṃketaviṣaya*	*ming dang brdai yul*
objective (external) objectivity	*bāhyārtha, bāhyārthasiddha*	*phyi don, phyi don du grub pa*
objective condition	*ālaṃbanapratyaya*	*dmigs rkyen*
objective object	*ālaṃbanaviṣaya*	*dmigs pai yul*
objective obscuration	*jñēyāvaraṇa*	*shes sgrib*
objective reality	*svarūpatva, svabhāvatva*	*rang gi ngo bo nyid*
objective-reality-status	*svarūpasiddha*	*rang gi ngo bo nyid kyi grub pa*
objective referent		*gdags don*
objective self	*dharmātma*	*chos kyi bdag*
— habit	*dharmātmagraha*	*chos kyi bdag 'dzin*
objective selflessness	*dharmanairātmya*	*chos kyi bdag med*
objective status	*svarūpasiddha*	*rang gi ngo bos grub pa*
objective universal	*arthasāmānya*	*don spyi*
obscuration	*āvaraṇa*	*sgrib pa*
orthodox (Buddhist)	*ādhyātmika*	*nang pa, rang sde*
other-emptiness	*paraśūnyata*	*gzhan stong*
particular, ultimate	*svalakṣaṇa (prāmanīka)*	*rang gi mtshan nyid (tshad ma pai)*
path of philosophy	*nyāyamārga, yuktimārga*	*rigs pai lam*
perception aggregate	*saṃjñāskandha*	*'du shes kyi phung po*
perception of inconsistent fact reason		*'gal zla dmigs pai rtags*
perceptual habit	*muṣṭi, graha*	*'dzin stangs, 'dzin pa*
perceptual object	**ābhāsaviṣaya*	*snang yul*
perfect —	*pariniṣpanna —*	*yons su grub pa —*
— identity	*— lakṣaṇa*	*— mtshan nyid*

English	*Sanskrit*	*Tibetan*
— nature	*— lakṣaṇa*	*— mtshan nyid*
— reality	*— svabhāva*	*— ngo bo nyid*
person	*pudgala*	*gang zag*
personal self (gross, subtle)	*pudgalātma*	*gang zag gi bdag*
personal self-habit (conscious, unconscious)	*pudgalātmagraha*	*gang zag gi bdag 'dzin*
personal selflessness (gross, subtle)	*pudgalanairātmya*	*gang zag gi bdag med*
phenomenon	*bhava, dharma*	*dngos po, chos*
phenomenally omniscient intuition	*yāvatjñāna*	*ji snyed mkhyen pai ye shes*
philosophy (reason, theory)	*vāda (nyāya, siddhānta)*	*smra ba (rigs pa, grub mtha)*
position (thesis)	*pakṣa (pratijña)*	*phyogs (dam bca)*
possession	*prāpti*	*thob pa*
possessiveness	*ātmīyagraha*	*bdag gir (nga yir) 'dzin pa*
precise (subtle)	*sūkṣma*	*phra mo*
present, to (represent)	*vyavasthāp-*	*rnam par gzhag pa*
presentation (representation, arrangement)	*vyavasthāna*	*rnam par gzhag pa*
presentation of the non-analytic conventional		*ma dpyad pai tha snyad du 'jog pa*
privacy, logical	*svātantrya*	*rang rgyud*
private (dogmaticist) reason	*svatantrahetu*	*rang rgyud kyi rtags*
private (dogmatic) syllogism	*svatantrānumāna*	*rang rgyud rjes dpag*
private (dogmatic) thesis	*svatantrapratijñā*	*rang rgyud kyi dam bca*
probandum	*sādhya*	*sgrub bya*
— property	*sādhyadharma*	*sgrub byai chos*
production unreality	**utpādanaiḥsvābhavya*	*skye ba ngo bo nyid med pa*
profound	*gambhīra*	*zab mo*
property	*ātmīya*	*bdag gi ba, nga yi ba*
protagonist		*sngar rgol*
public (dialectical) reason	*paraprasiddhahetu*	*gzhan grags kyi rtags*
public (dialectical) syllogism	*paraprasiddhānumāna*	*gzhan grags kyi rjes dpag*
pure information (intelligence)	*vijñaptimātra*	*rnam par rig pa tsam*
quality (property)	*dharma*	*chos*
qualitative (descriptive) designation	*viśeṣavikalpa*	*khyad par du brtags pa*

English	*Sanskrit*	*Tibetan*
rational cognition	**yuktijñāna*	*rigs shes*
conventional —	*vyāvahārika —*	*tha snyad pai —*
holy aftermath —	*āryapṛṣṭhalabdha —*	*'phags pai rjes thob —*
holy equanimity —	*āryasamāhita —*	*'phags pai mnyam gzhag gi —*
validating —	*prāmāṇika —*	*tshad mai —*
ultimacy analytic —	*paramārthavicāra —*	*don dam dpyod pai —*
rationality (reason, philosophy	*yukti, nyāya*	*rigs pa*
real (intrinsically) production	*svabhāvotpāda*	*rang bzhin gyis skyes pa*
real status	*svabhāvasiddha*	*rang bzhin gyis grub pa*
Realist	*bhāvavādin*	*dngos por smra ba*
reality	*tattva, svabhāva, svarūpa, satya*	*de nyid, de kho na nyid, bden pa, rang bzhin, rang gi ngo no nyid*
absolute (ultimate) —	*paramārthasatya*	*don dam bden pa*
constructed (imagined) —	*parikalpitasvabhāva*	*kun brtags kyi ngo bo nyid*
conventional —	*vyāvahārikasatya*	*tha snyad bden pa*
imagined —	*parikalpitasvabhāva*	*kun brtags mtshan nyid*
immanent — (thatness)	*tattva*	*de nyid, de kho na nyid*
intrinsic —	*svabhāva*	*rang bzhin, rang gi ngo bo nyid*
perfect —	*pariniṣpannasvabhāva*	*yongs grub kyi mtshan nyid*
relative —	*paratantrasvabhāva*	*gzhan dbang gi mtshan nyid*
transcendent — (suchness)	*tathata*	*de bzhin nyid*
ultimate (absolute)	*paramārthasatya*	*don dam bden pa*
reality-status	*satyasiddha, svabhāvasiddha*	*bden grub, rang bzhin grub*
realitylessness	*asatyatā, naiḥsvabhāvya*	*bden med, rang bzhin med, ngo bo nyid med pa*
reason (rational cognition)	*hetu, yukti, nyāya*	*rtags, rigs pa (rigs shes)*
reasoning	*yukti*	*rigs pa*
functional —	*kṛtyakaraṇa—*	*bya ba byed pai —*
logical —	*upapattisādhana —*	*'thad pas sgrub pai —*
natural —	*dharmatā —*	*chos nyid kyi —*
relational —	*āpekṣā —*	*ltos pai —*
referent	*artha, vastu*	*don, gzhi*
referent of designation	*prajñapyārtha*	*gdags don*
referential base		*gdags gzhi*
refute (negate)	*pratiṣedha*	*dgag pa*
refutation	*pratiṣedha, nirākaraṇa*	*bkag pa, sun 'byin pa*
reification	*samāropa, adhyāropa*	*sgro 'dogs pa*
relative (nature,		

English	*Sanskrit*	*Tibetan*
reality)	*paratantra*	*gzhan dbang*
relativistic origination	*pratītyasamutpāda*	*rten cing 'brel bar 'byung ba*
relativity	*pratītyasamutpāda, idaṃpratyayatā,*	*rten cing 'brel bar 'byung ba*
reliance	*pratiṣaraṇa*	*rton pa*
remedy	*pratipakṣa*	*gnyen po*
representation	*vyavasthāna*	*rnam par gzhag pa*
repudiation	*apavāda*	*skur ba 'debs pa*
resistance	*vipakṣa*	*mi mthun phyogs*
retention	*dhāraṇī*	*gzungs*
retentiveness (infallibility)		*chud mi za ba*
samsara (life-cycle)	*saṃsāra*	*'khor ba*
science	*vidyāsthāna*	*rig gnas*
Scripture (Discourse)	*sūtra*	*mdo*
self	*ātma*	*bdag*
objective —	*dharma —*	*chos kyi —*
personal —	*pudgala —*	*gang zag gi —*
self-consciousness (apperceptive)	*svasaṃvitti*	*rang rig*
self-emptiness	**svasūnyata*	*rang stong*
self-habit	*ātmagraha*	*bdag 'dzin*
self-production	*ātmotpāda*	*bdag las skyes pa*
selflessness	*anātmatā, nairātmya*	*bdag med pa*
sensation aggregate	*vedanāskandha*	*'tshor bai phung po*
sense faculty	*indriya*	*dbang po*
sense medium	*āyatana*	*skye mched*
serenity (quiescence, exuberance)	*śamatha, praśrabdhi*	*zhi gnas, sin sbyangs*
sign	*nimitta, saṃketa*	*mtshan ma, rgyu mtshan, brda*
sign-habit	**nimittagraha*	*mtshan mar 'dzin pa*
signification process	**nimittabhūta*	*mtshan mar 'gyur pa*
signlessness	*animitta*	*mtshan ma med pa*
social convention	*lokavyavahāra*	*'jig rten gyi tha snyad*
spheres, three (of an act)	*trimaṇḍala*	*'khor gsum*
spirit of enlightenment	*bodhicitta*	*byang chub kyi sems*
spiritual gene, genus	*gotra*	*rigs*
status	*siddha*	*grub pa*
subjective	*ādhyātmika*	*nang gi*
subjectivity	**grahakākāra*	*'dzin rnam*
subjectlessness	**asiddhadharmin*	*chos can ma grub pa*
substance	*dravya*, (*āśraya* with *dharma* as "quality")	*rdzas* (*gzhi* with *chos*)
substantial existence	*dravyasat*	*rdzas su yod pa*
substantial status	*dravyasiddha*	*rdzas su grub pa*

English	Sanskrit	Tibetan
substantial subject-object-dichotomy	*grāhyagrahakadravya-bheda	gzung 'dzin rdzas tha dad
substantive (ascriptive) designation	svabhāvaprajñapti	ngo bor brtags pa
subtle (precise)	sūkṣma	phra mo
suchness (transcendent)	tathatā	de bzhin nyid
superficial reality	saṃvṛttisatya	kun rdzob bden pa
cognitive —		shes pai —
designative —		btags pai —
intimative —		brjod pai —
supposition		mngon par rtog pa
symbol (convention)	saṃketa	brda
system	naya, vyavasthāna	lugs, rnam gzhag
systematizer (pioneer)		srol phye ba
technique (liberative)	upāya	thabs
thatness (immanent)	tattvam	de nyid, de kho na nyid
theoretical (conscious, intellectual) self-habit, etc.	parikalpitātmagrahādi	kun brtags bdag 'dzin sogs
theory (philosophy)	siddhānta	grub mtha
thesis	pratijñā	dam bca
thing	dharma	chos
thorough investigation	paryeṣṭi	yongs su 'tshol ba
tolerance	kṣānti	bzod pa
Traditionalist	sautrāntika	mdo sde pa
transcendence	pāramitā, niḥśreyasa	pha rol tu phyin pa, nges legs
transcendence vehicle	pāramitāyāna	phar phyin theg pa
transcendent reality	tathatā	de bzhin nyid
transcendent wisdom	prajñāpāramitā	shes rab kyi pha rol tu phyin pa
transcendental (opposite of mundane, social)	lokottara	'jig rten las 'das pa
true existence	*satyasat	bden par yod pa
true production	*satyotpāda	bden par skye pa
Truth Body	dharmakāya	chos sku
truth-habit	satyagraha	bden par 'dzin pa
truth-status	satyasiddha	bden par grub pa
truthlessness	asatyasiddha	bden par med pa, bden par ma grub pa
ultimacy-analytic rational cognition		mthar thug dpyod pai rigs shes
ultimate (reality) (absolute)	paramārtha (satya)	don dam (bden pa)
ultimate particular	svalakṣaṇa (prāmāṇika)	rang gi mtshan nyid (tshad ma pa)
ultimate production	paramārthotpāda	don dam du skyes pa

English	Sanskrit	Tibetan
ultimate status	*paramārthasiddha*	*don dam du grub pa*
unanalyzed existence		*ma brtags par yod pa*
unanalyzed social convention		*ma dpyad (brtags) pai 'jig rten gyi tha snyad*
unconscious (instinctual)	*sahaja —*	*— lhan skyes*
— futile view	*— satkāyadṛṣṭi*	*'jig lta lhan skyes*
— misknowledge	*— avidyā*	*ma rig pa lhan skyes*
— self-habit	*— ātmagraha*	*bdag 'dzin lhan skyes*
uncreated	*asaṃskrta*	*'dus ma byas*
unique vehicle	*ekayāna*	*theg pa gcig pa*
universal (generality)	*sāmānya*	*spyi*
objective —	*artha —*	*don —*
verbal —	*śabda —*	*sgra —*
Universal Vehicle	*mahāyāna*	*theg pa chen po*
Universalist	*mahāyānika*	*theg pa chen po pa*
unreality	*niḥsvabhāvatā*	*ngo bo nyid med pa*
identity —	*lakṣaṇa —*	*mtshan nyid —*
production —	*utpāda —*	*skye ba —*
ultimate —	*paramārtha —*	*don dam —*
unreflective (inquiry, usage)		*rang dga ba (i brtag pa, 'jug pa)*
vague reality	*audārikatattva*	*rags pai de kho na nyid*
validating cognition	*pramāṇa*	*tshad ma*
conceptual — (inferential)	*anumāna —*	*rjes dpag —*
conventional —	*vyāvahārika —*	*tha snyad pai —*
perceptual —	*pratyakṣa —*	*mngon sum —*
verbal designation	*nāmaprajñapti*	*ming gis gdags pa*
verbal formulation	*nāmābhidhāna*	*ming gis brjod pa*
verbal generality (universal)	*śabdasāmānya*	*sgra spyi*
Victor	*jina*	*rgyal ba*
view	*dṛṣṭi*	*lta ba*
will to enlightenment (spirit of)	*bodhicitta*	*byang chub kyi sems*
wisdom	*prajña*	*shes rab*
withstand analysis, ability to		*dpyad bzod pa*

LIST OF ABBREVIATIONS

All Tibetan works are referred to by their number in bibliography; the Sanskrit title may be given, however, if the original was Sanskrit, with the Tibetan translation surviving and used by Tsong Khapa. The English short title may also be given to correspond to the Tibetan short title used by Tsong Khapa.

AA *Abhisamayālaṃkāra, Ornament of Realizations* (90)

Conze, E. *Abhisamayālaṃkāra*. Rome: Serie Orientale Roma, 1954. Translation, referring to text of *8,000 Line Prajñāpāramitā Sūtra*.

Obermiller, E. *Analysis of the Abhisamayālaṃkāra*. London, 1933. Analysis of the text, according to the Tibetan tradition of exegesis.

AK *Abhidharmakośa, Treasury of Abhidharma* (115)

La Vallee Poussin, L. de. *L'Abhidharmakośa de Vasubandhu*. 6 vols. Paris and Louvain: Institut Belges des Hautes Études Chinoises, 1923-1931. French translation of text and autocommentary.

Law, N. N., and Dutt, N. *Abhidharmakośavyākhyā of Yaśomitra*. Calcutta, 1949-1957. Sanskrit edition, Chapters I-IV.

Wogihara, U. *Abhidharmakośavyākhyā of Yaśomitra*. Tokyo, 1932-1936. Sanskrit edition, Chapters V-VIII.

AMN *Akṣayamatinirdeśa, Teaching of Akshayamati* (36)

AS *Abhidharmasamuccaya, Abhidharma Synthesis* (58)

Pradhan, P. *Abhidharmasamuccaya* Santiniketan, 1950. Reconstruction of Sanskrit.

Rahula, W. *Le Compendium de la Super-Doctrine*. Paris, 1971. French translation.

BA *Blue Annals, Deb ter sngon po* (34)

Roerich, G. N. *The Blue Annals*. 2 vols. Calcutta, 1949, 1953. Translation of 'Gos Lo-tsva-ba (1392-1481).

BL T. Stcherbatski. *Buddhist Logic*. 2 vols. New York: Dover, 1962. Elucidation of Dharmakirti's system of logic, based on translation of NB (75), given in second volume.

BBh *Bodhisattvabhūmi, Bodhisattva Stages* (59)

Dutt, N. *Bodhisattvabhūmi*. Patna: K. P. Jayaswal Institute, 1966. Edition of the Sanskrit text from which quotes are given in notes.

Willis, J. *On Knowing Reality*. New York: Columbia University Press, 1979. Translation and study of Chapter IV.

BMMV *Buddhapalita-mūla-madhyamaka-vṛtti, Buddhapalita Commentary* (67)

C Chone Tanjur (*bsTan-'gyur*)

Stonybrook, N.Y.: Institute for Advanced Studies of World Religions, 1976. Microfiche publication.

ca. circa

Ch. Chapter

CŚ *Catuḥśataka*, *Yogācāracatuḥśataka*, *Four Hundred*, *Experientialist Four Hundred* (57)

Bhattacarya, V. *The Catuḥśataka of Āryadeva*. Calcutta: Visvabharati Books, 1931. Edition/reconstruction of Sanskrit text, embedded in commentary by Chandrakirti, Chs. VIII-XVI.

Vaidya, P. L., *Le Catuḥśataka d'Āryadeva*. Paris, 1923. French translation of verses without commentary.

CŚT *Catuḥśatatīkā, Four Hundred Commentary* (68)

Sanskrit text of Chs. VIII-XVI available in Bhattacarya's edition, above (CS).

D Derge Tanjur

Yamaguchi, Z., Takasaki, J., Ejima, Y. *sDe dge Tibetan Tripitaka bstan hgyur*: dbU ma Section (14 vols.); Sems tsam Section (16 vols.). Tokyo: Tokyo University Press, 1977-1982. Critical edition and reprint.

DBS *Daśabhūmika Sūtra, Ten Stages Scripture* (39)

Rahder, J. *Daśabhūmikasūtra*. Louvain, 1926. Sanskrit edition.

ed. editor; edition

f. folio (Tibetan books)

ff. following; folios (Tibetan books)

Fr. French

GRS *dbU ma dGongs pa Rab gSal* (14)

Tsong Khapa's commentary on Chandrakirti's *Introduction to the Central Way*.

GTSB *rGyal Tsab gSung 'Bum* (17)

rGyal Tsab's collected works.

Gun Thang Gun Thang bsTan pai sGron Me's commentary on the great Essence (24)

K Kalimpong text of the great *Essence* (2)

Hand edited according to notes of H. H. Fourteenth Dalai Lama.

k. (ks.) *kārikā*(s)

(Sanskrit verses).

KG Kanjur (*bKa 'Gyur*)

The Tibetan Tripitaka; Peking Edition. Tokyo and Kyoto: Tibetan Tripitaka Research Institute, 1956.

KGSB mKhas Grub gSung 'Bum (18)

mKhas Grub's collected works.

l. line

ls. lines

LAS *Lañkāvatārasūtra*, *Mission to Lanka Scripture* (44)

Suzuki, D. T. *Lañkāvatāra Sūtra*. 2 vols. London: Routledge, Kegan Paul, 1956. Sanskrit edition and English translation.

Vaidya, P. L. *Lañkāvatārasūtra*. Darbhanga: Mithila Institute, 1959.

LRC *Lam Rim Chen mo, Great Stages of the Path* (6)

Tsong Khapa's master synthesis of the Bodhisattva path teachings.

LRChung *Lam Rim Chung ba* (7)

Tsong Khapa's short *Stages of the Path.*

LRMchan *Lam Rim mChan 'Grel* (30)

Ba so's notes on LTC section of LRC.

LTC Final third of LRC

Sometimes referred to as a separate work on Madhyamika thought. Translated in Wayman, A. *Calming the Mind and Discerning the Real.* New York: Columbia University Press, 1978.

LVP La Vallee Poussin, L. de. *Madhyamakāvatāra de Candrakīrti.* Paris: Museon, 1907-1911. Partial French translation of MA.

MA *Madhyamakāvatāra, Introduction to the Central Way* (69)

La Vallee Poussin, L. de. *Madhyamakāvatāra de Candrakīrti.* St. Petersburg, 1926. Critical edition of Tibetan text printed in book form in Biblioteca Buddhica series.

MABh *Madhyamakāvatārabhāṣya, Introduction Commentary* (70)

La Vallee Poussin includes this text in his edition of MA, above.

MAlam *Madhyamakālaṃkāra, Central Way Ornament* (110)

MAlamV *Madhyamakālaṃkāra-vṛtti, Central Way Ornament Commentary* (111)

MAlamP *Madhyamakālaṃkāra-pañjikā, Central Way Ornament Elucidation* (87)

MAlok *Madhyamakāloka, Central Way Illumination* (88)

MAT *Madhyamakāvatāra-ṭīkā, Introduction to the Central Way Subcommentary* (83)

MAV *Madhyāntavibhāga, Discrimination between Center and Extremes* (92)

Pandeya, R. C., *Madhyāntavibhāgaśāstra.* Delhi, 1971. Edition of the Sanskrit, usefully printed together with MAVT and MAVBh.

Stcherbatsky, T. *Discrimination between Middle and Extremes.* Calcutta, 1971 Reprint of Biblioteca Buddhica XXX. Partial translation of first chapters, along with commentaries.

MAVBh *Madhyāntavibhāgabhāṣya, Center and Extremes Commentary* (116)

Also printed in Pandeya edition, above MAV.

MAVT *Madhyāntavibhāgaṭīkā, Center and Extremes Subcommentary* (113)

Also printed in Pandeya edition, above MAV.

MH *Mādhyamikahṛdaya, Heart of the Central Way* (64)

Sanskrit verses of this text, rediscovered by V. V. Gokhale, being edited by J. Takasaki, forthcoming from Tokyo University Press.

MMK *Prajñā-nāma-mūlamadhyamakakārikā, Wisdom, Fundamental Central Way Verses* (100)

There are many editions, translations, and studies of this seminal work, both traditional and modern, usually based on the version embedded in Chandrakirti's *Prasannapadā.* The Sanskrit version I have used for references in notes is: Vaidya, P. L. *Prasannapadāmūlamadhyamakavṛtti.* Buddhist Sanskrit Texts, vol. 10. Darbhanga, 1960.

Verses also edited in Inada, K. *The Mūlamadhyamakakārikās of Nāgārjuna.* Tokyo: Hokuseido, 1970.

MS *Mahāyānasaṃgraha, Compendium of the Universal Vehicle* (61)

Lamotte, E. *La Somme du Grand Vehicule*. 2 vols. Louvain: Museon, 1938-1939. Contains an edition of the Tibetan and Chinese texts, as well as a French translation.

MSA *Mahāyānasūtrālaṃkāra, Ornament of the Scriptures of the Universal Vehicle* (93)

Levi, S. *Mahāyāna-Sūtrālaṃkāra*. 2 vols. Paris, 1907. Provides a Sanskrit edition of the text with its autocommentary and a French translation.

Thurman, R.A.F. *Ornament of the Scriptures of the Universal Vehicle*, American Institute of Buddhist Studies, forthcoming. Provides an English translation based on consultation of Sanskrit, Chinese, and Tibetan texts and commentaries, edited by the author from the work of a team of translators.

n. note

Nanjio Nanjio, B. *A Catalogue of the Buddhist Tripitaka (Chinese)*. Oxford, 1883.

NB *Nyāyabindu, A Drop of Logic* (75)

Stcherbatski, T. *Buddhist Logic*. Vol. II. New York: Dover, 1972. Provides an annotated English translation of the complete text with commentary.

NTC *rNam Thar Chen-mo, Great Biography* (of Tsong Khapa) (31)

P Peking edition of Tibetan Tripitaka

Tibetan Tripitaka Research Institute. *The Tibetan Tripitaka; Peking Edition*. Tokyo and Kyoto: Suzuki Research Foundation, 1956.

p., pp. page(s)

PI Wittgenstein, L. *Philosophical Investigations*. New York: Macmillan, 1953.

PPMMV *Prasannapadāmūlamadhyamakavṛtti, Lucid Exposition* (71)

Vaidya, P. L. *Prasannapadāmūlamadhyamakavṛtti*. Gives Sanskrit edition I have used for references (see MMK).

PPP *Prajñāpāramitāpiṇḍārtha, Concise Meaning of Transcendent Wisdom* (81)

PrPr *Prajñāpradīpa, Wisdom Lamp* (65)

PrPrT *Prajñāpradīpaṭīkā, Wisdom Lamp Commentary* (63)

PS *Pramāṇasamuccaya, Synthesis of Validating Cognitions* (82)

Hattori, M. *Dignaga on Perception*. Cambridge: Harvard University Press, 1971. Harvard Oriental Series. Provides a reconstruction of the Sanskrit and an English translation of the chapter on perception.

PV *Pramāṇavārttika, Treatise on Validating Cognition* (76)

Nagatomi, M. *The Pramāṇavārttika of Dharmakīrti*. Cambridge: Harvard University Press, forthcoming. Harvard Oriental Series. Provides an English translation of the text.

PVi *Pramāṇaviniścaya, Determination of Validating Cognitions* (77)

RA *Ratnāvalī, Jewel Garland* (101)

Vaidya, P. L. *Prasannapadāmūlamadhyamakavṛtti*. Darbhanga, 1960. Includes a Sanskrit edition of the text.

Nagarjuna. *Precious Garland*. London: Allen & Unwin, 1975. Provides an English translation by P. J. Hopkins.

RG *Rigs pai rGya mtsho, Ocean of Reason* (9)

Tsong Khapa's supercommentary on Nagarjuna's *Wisdom*.

RGV *Ratnagotravibhāga-mahāyānottaratantraśāstra, Analysis of the Jewel Matrix, Jewel Matrix, Supreme Tantra* (94)

Johnston, E. H. *Ratnagotravibhāga-mahāyānottaratantraśāstra*. Patna, 1950. Provides an edition of the Sanskrit.

Obermiller, E. *Sublime Science of the Great Vehicle to Salvation*. Acta Orientalia, Vol. IX. 1931. Complete English translation.

Takasaki, J. *A Study on the Ratnagotravibhāga*. Rome, 1966. Complete English translation.

SDV *Satyadvayavibhaṅga, Analysis of the Two Realities* (84)

SDVV *Satyadvayavibhaṅgavṛtti, Two Realities Autocommentary* (85)

SERA dPal-'byor Lhun-grub's commentary on *Essence of True Eloquence* (22)

Used as textbook for hermeneutical studies at Sera Monastery (formerly Lhasa, now Karnataka, India).

Skt. Sanskrit

SN *Saṃdhinirmocanasūtra, Elucidation of the Intention Scripture* (53)

Lamotte, E. *Éxplication des Mystères*. Louvain and Paris, 1935. Provides an edition of the Tibetan text and a French translation.

SNT *Saṃdhinirmocanaṭīkā, Great Chinese Commentary* (on the *Elucidation of the Intention*) (121)

SRS *Samādhirājasūtra, King of Samadhis Scripture* (52)

ŚS *Śūnyatāsaptatī, Emptiness Seventy* (102)

Komito, D. "Nāgārjuna's Śūnyatāsaptatī." Ph.D. dissertation, University of Indiana, 1980. Provides a complete English translation.

SS *Sūtrasamuccaya, Scripture Synthesis* (104)

Joshi, L. M. *Sūtrasamuccaya of Nāgārjuna*. Patiala: Journal of Religious Studies, 1979. Provides an English translation.

TG Tanjur (*bsTan 'gyur*)

Institute for Advanced Studies of World Religions. *Chone Tanjur*. Stonybrook, N.Y., 1976, microfiche edition.

Tibetan Tripitaka Research Institute has published the Peking edition (see P above).

Yamaguchi, Z. et al. *sDe dge Tibetan Tripitaka bstan hgyur*. Tokyo: Tokyo University Press, 1977. Provides a critical edition of the sDe rge edition of the Tanjur, so far having completed *dbU ma*, *Sems tsam*, and *Tshad ma* sections.

mTha dPyod 'Jam-dbYangs bZhed-pa's critical commentary on the *Essence of True Eloquence* (25)

Textbook for Gomang College of Drepung Monastery, formerly Lhasa, now Karnataka.

Tib. Tibetan

TJ *Tarkajvāla, Blaze of Arguments* (66)

TKSB *Tsong Khapa gSung 'Bum, Tsong Khapa's Collected Works* (1-19)

TLP Wittgenstein, L. *Tractatus Logico-Philosophicus*. New York: Humanities Press, 1961.

Toh. Yensho Kanakura, ed. *A Catalogue of the Tohoku University Collection of Tibetan Works on Buddhism*. Sendai: Tohoku University, 1953.

sTong Thun mKhas-grub's critical work on hermeneutical philosophy written to analyze further certain problems raised by Tsong Khapa in the great *Essence* (18)

trans. translator; translation

Trimś. *Triṃśikākārikā, Thirty Verses* (118)

Levi, S., ed. *Vijñaptimātratāsiddhi*. Paris, 1925.

TS *Tattvasaṃgraha, Compendium of Principles* (112)

Jha, G. *Tattvasaṃgraha with Pañjikā*. 2 vols. Baroda: Gaekwad, 1937. Provides an English translation.

Shastri, S. D. *Tattvasaṇgraha of Ācārya Shāntarakshita, with the Commentary Pañjikā of Shrī Kamalashīla*. 2 vols. Varanasi: Bauddha Bharati 1, 1968. Provides a critical edition of the Sanskrit text.

TSP *Tattvasamgrahapañjikā, Compendium of Principles Elucidation* (89)

Kamalashila's commentary on TS; Sanskrit edition and English translation given under TS above.

v., vs. verse(s)

Vimś. *Vimśatikā, Twenty Verses* (119)

Levi, S. *Vijñaptimātratāsiddhi*. Paris, 1925. Sanskrit edition.

VP *Vaidālyaprakaraṇā, Subtle Weaving* (105)

VS *Viniścayasaṃgrahaṇī, Compendium of Determinations, Compendium* (62)

VV *Vigrahavyāvartaṇī, Rebuttal of Objections* (106)

Sanskrit ed. included in Vaidya, P. L. *Prasannapadāmūlamadhyamakavṛtti*. Darbhanga, 1960.

Bhattacarya, K. *The Dialectical Method of Nagarjuna*. Delhi: Motilal Banarsidass, 1978. English translation.

VY *Vyākhyāyukti, Principles of Elucidation* (120)

YBh *Yogācārabhūmi* (also *Bhūmivastu*), *Experientialist Stages* (also, in Tibetan parlance, *Facts of the Stages*) (60)

Partial Sanskrit edition: Bhattacarya, V. *Yogācārabhūmi*. Calcutta, 1957.

YṢ *Yuktiṣaṣṭikā, Philosophical Sixty* (108)

Loizzo, J. *The Philosophical Sixty with Chandrakirti's Commentary*. Amherst: American Institute of Buddhist Studies, 1978. Provides English translation from Tibetan (no Sanskrit text available).

YṢV *Yuktiṣaṣṭikāvṛtti, Philosophical Sixty Commentary* (72)

English translation, see YṢ above.

Zin Bris bLo-bzang Phun-tshogs' textual commentary on the great *Essence*, used in Sera Monastery, Karnataka (23)

BIBLIOGRAPHY OF PRINCIPAL SOURCES

Tibetan Works

From the *rJe yab sras gsung 'bum*, (Collected Works of Tsong Khapa, rGyal Tshab, and mKhas Grub) (TKSB, GTSB, KGSB), bKra-shis Lhun-po edition, printed in Delhi by Ngawang Gelek Demo, 1980; (also Lhasa edition available in microfiche, Institute for Advanced Studies of World Religions, Stonybrook, N. Y., 1976); Peking edition, Suzuki Research Foundation, Tokyo, 1956.

WORKS OF TSONG KHAPA (TKSB)

1. *gSan yig* (lineage lists), ka, 27ff.
2. *sTon pa bla na med pa la zab mo rten cing 'brel bar 'byung ba gsung pai sgo nas bstod pa legs par bshad pai snying po (Short Essence of Eloquence)*, kha, *Thor bu*, ff. 15a4-18b4.
3. *Rang gi rtogs pa brjod pa mdo tsam du bshad pa (Destiny Fulfilled*), kha, *Thor bu*, ff. 62a4-65b2.
4. *Byang chub lam gyi rim pai nyams len gyi rnam gzhag mdor bsdus (Short Stages of the Path*), kha, *Thor bu*, ff. 65b2-68b1.
5. *Lam gyi gtso bo rnam pa gsum (Three Principal Paths), kha, Thor bu*, ff. 230b4-231b5).
6. *Byang chub lam gyi rim pa chen mo (Great Stages of Path)*(LRC), pa, 481ff.
7. *Byang chub lam gyi rim pa chung ba (Medium Stages of Path*) (LRChung), pha, 201ff.
8. *gSung rab kyi drang ba dang nges pai don rnam par phye ba gsal bar byed pa legs par bshad pai snying po (The Essence of Eloquence*), pha, 91ff; also P, pha, ff. 260-350; also Kalimpong text, Kalsang Legshay, 1968, critically edited by H. H. Dalai Lama in working sessions, Dharamsala, 1971.
9. *dbU ma rtsa bai tshig leur byas pai rnam bshad rigs pai rgya mtsho (Ocean of Reason*, RG), ba, 281ff. Also printed edition, Varanasi: Jilaykhang, 1973, 486pp.
10. *dKa gnad brgyad kyi zin bris*, ba, 16ff.
11. *Rigs pa drug cu pai zin bris,* ba, 12ff.
12. *dbU ma lta bai khrid yig*, ba, 21ff.
13. *dbU ma rgyan gyi brjed byang*, ba, 16ff.
14. *dbU ma 'jug pai rnam bshad dgongs pa rab gsal (Illumination of the Inten-*

tion)(GRS), ma, 267ff. Also printed edition, Varanasi: Jilaykhang, 1973, 487pp.

15. *sPyod 'jug shes rab leui tikkai zin bris*, ma, 31ff.
16. *Legs bshad gser gyi 'phreng ba (Golden Rosary)*, tsa, 405ff, and tsha, 268ff.

rGyal tshab Dar-ma Rin-chen (GTSB)

17. *Shes rab kyi pha rol tu phyin pai man ngag gi bstan bcos mngon par rtogs pai rgyan gyi 'grel pa don gsal bai rnam bshad snying poi rgyan*, kha, 316ff.

mKhas grub dGe-legs dPal-bzang-po (KGSB)

18. *Zab mo stong pa nyid kyi de kho na nyid rab tu gsal bar byed pai bstan bcos bskal bzang mig 'byed (sTong Thun Chen mo)*, ka, 260ff.
19. *Ngo mtshar rmad du byung bai rnam thar dad pai 'jug ngogs* (*Haven of Faith*), TKSB, ka, 71ff.

'Jam-dbyangs Chos-rje bKra-shis dPal-Idan

20. *gSang bai rnam thar rin po chei snye ma*, TKSB, ka, 16ff.
21. *gSang bai rnam thar gsol 'debs*, TKSB, ka, 4ff. *Commentaries on the Essence and Related Works.*
22. dPal-'byor Lhun-grub. *Legs bshad snying poi dka 'grel bstan pai sgron me* (SERA). Buxaduar: Sera Monastery, 1968.
23. bLo-bzang Phun-tshogs. *Drang nges rnam 'byed kyi zin bris zab don gsal bai sgron me (Zin Bris)*. Mysore: Sera Byes Monastery, n.d.
24. Gun-thang bsTan-pai sGron-me. *Drang nges rnam 'byed kyi dka 'grel rtsom 'phro legs bshad snying poi yang snying*. Saranath: Pleasure of Elegant Sayings Press, 1968.
25. 'Jam-dbyangs bZhed-pa. *Drang ba dang nges pai don rnam par 'byed pai mtha spyod 'khrul bral lung rigs bai dur yadkar poi gan mdzod bskal bzang re ba kun skong (Mtha spyod)*. Mysore: Gomang Monastery, 1979.
26. Don-grub rGyal-mtshan (pupil of dKon-mchog bsTan-pai sGron-me). *Legs bshad snying poi rgya cher bshad pa drang nges bzhi 'dril* (from Gomang Monastery Library). New Delhi: Chophel Legdan, 1975.
27. 'Jam-dbyangs bZhed-pai rDo-rje. *Grub mthai rnam gzhag rang gzhan grub mtha kun dang zab don mchog tu gsal ba kun bzang zhing gi nyi ma lung rigs rgya mtsho skye dgui re ba kun skong (Grub mtha chen mo)*. Mussoorie: Dalama, 1962.
28. 'Jam-dbyangs bZhed-pai rDo-rje. *dbU ma 'jug pai mtha dpyod lung rigs gter mdzod zab don kun gsal skal bzang 'jug ngogs (db Uma mTha dpyod)*. Buxaduar: Gomang Monastery, 1967.
29. lCang-kya Rol-pai rDo-rje. *lTa mgur a mai ngos 'dzin*. Saranath: Elegant Sayings Press, 1968.
30. Ba-so Chos-kyi rGyal-mtshan, et al. *Lam rim mchan bzhi sbrags ma (also called MChan: 'Gral)*. New Delhi: Chophel Legdan, 1972. (LRMchan)

Historical Works

31. rGyal-dbang Chos-rje. *'Jam mgon chos kyi rgyal po Tsong Khapa chen poi rnam thar thub bstan mdzes pai rgyan gcig ngo mtshar nor bui 'phreng ba (rNam Thar Chenmo)*. Saranath: Elegant Sayings Press, 1968.
32. Bu-ston Rin-po-che. *rGya gar chos 'byung*, see Obermiller, *Buston's History of Buddhism.*
33. Taranatha. *rGya gar chos 'byung*, see Chattopadhyaya and Chimpa, *Tavanatha's History of Buddhism in India.*
34. 'Gos Lo tsva ba. *Deb ter sngon po* (BA), see Roerich.
35. Khetsun Sangpo. *Biographical Dictionary of Tibet and Tibetan Buddhism.* 12 volumes. Dharamsala: Library of Tibetan Works and Archives, 1972-1981.

Scriptures

36. *Akṣayamatinirdeśasūtra, Blo gros mi zad pai bstan pai mdo. Teaching of Akshayamati* (AMN). P, No. 842, Vol. 34; Sanskrit portions quoted obtained from PPMMV.
37. *Anavataptanāgarājaparipṛcchasūtra. Klui rgyal po ma dros pai zhus pai mdo. Questions of Anavatapta.* P, No, 823, Vol. 33.
38. *Buddhāvataṃsakanāmamahāvaipūlyasūtra. Sangs rgyas phal po che zhes bya ba shin tu rgyas pa chen poi mdo. Garland Scripture.* P, No. 761, Vols. 25-26.
39. *Daśabhūmikasūtra. Mdo sde sa bcu pa. Ten Stages Scripture* (DBS) (Part of the *Garland*). P, No. 761, Vol. 25.
40. *Dharmasaṃgītisūtra. Chos yang dag par sdud pai mdo. Dharma Digeṣt Scripture.* P, No. 904, Vol. 36.
41. *Ghanavyūhasūtra. Stug por bkod pai mdo. Dense Array Scripture.* P, No. 778, Vol. 29; Toh. 110.
42. *Jñānālokālaṃkārasūtra. Ye shes snang bai rgyan gyi mdo. Ornament of Wisdom Illumination Scripture.* P, No. 768, Vol. 6; Toh. 100.
43. *Kaśyapaparivarta. Od srung gi leu. Kashyapa Chapter* (Section of Ratnakuta). P, No. 760, Vol. 24; Toh. 87.
44. *Lankāvatārasūtra. Lan kar gshegs pai mdo. Mission to Lanka.* P, No. 775, Vol. 29; Toh. 107.
45. *Paramārthaśūnyatāsūtra. Individual Vehicle Scripture.* Unidentified.
46. *Pitāputrasamāgamasūtra. Yab sras mjal bai mdo. Meeting of Father and Son Scripture* (Part of *Ratnakūṭa*). P. 760, Vol. 23; Toh. 45.
47. *Prajñāpāramitāhṛdayasūtra. Shes rab snying poi mdo. Heart of Transcendent Wisdom Scripture.* P, No. 160, Vol. 6; Toh. 21.
48. *Prajñāpāramitāsaptaśatikasūtra. Shes rab kyi pha rol tu phyin pa bdun brgya pai mdo. Transcendent Wisdom Seven Hundred.* P, No. 737, Vol. 21; Toh. 19.
49. *Prajñāpāramitāṣṭasāhasrikāsūtra. Brgyad stong pa. Transcendent Wisdom Eighteen Thousand.* P, No. 734, Vol. 21; Toh. 12.

50. *Prajñāpāramitāṣṭādaśasāhasrikāsūtra. Khri brgyad stong pa. Transcendent Wisdom Eighteen Thousand.* P, No. 732, Vols. 19-20; Toh. 10.
51. *Prajñāpāramitāśatasāhasrikāsūtra. 'Bum. Transcendent Wisdom Hundred Thousand, Extensive Transcendent Wisdom, Mother Scripture.* P. No. 730, Vols. 12-18; Toh. 8.
52. *Samādhirājasūtra. Ting nge 'dzin gyi rgyal poi mdo. King of Samadhis Scripture.* P. No. 795, Vols. 31-32; Toh. 127.
53. *Saṃdhinirmocanasūtra. dGongs pa nges par 'grel pai mdo. Elucidation of the Intention Scripture, Intention Elucidation, Elucidation.* P, No. 774, Vol. 29; Toh. 106.
54. *Saddharmapuṇḍarīkāsūtra. Dam chos pad mai dkar poi mdo. Lotus Scripture.* P, No. 781, Vol. 30.
55. *Vajracchedikasūtra. rDo rje gcod pa. Diamond Cutter Scripture.* Toh. 16.

Scientific Treatises (Śāstra)

ARYADEVA

56. *Jñānasārasamuccaya. Ye shes snying poi kun las btus pa. Synthesis of Essence of Intuition.* TG, Vol. tsha.
57. *Yogācāracatuḥśataka. rNal 'byor spyod pai bzhi brgya pa. Experientialist Four Hundred, Four Hundred* (CŚ). TG, tsha; P, No. 5246, Vol. 95; Toh. 3846.

ASANGA

58. *Abhidharmasamuccaya. mNgon pa kun las btus pa. Abhidharma Synthesis, Synthesis* (AS). Toh. 4049.
59. *Bodhisattvabhūmi. Byang chub sems dpai sa. The Stages of the Bodhisattva, Bodhisattva Stages* (BBh). P, No. 5538, Vol. 110.
60. *Bhūmivastu. Sai dngos gzhi. Facts of the Stages.* Toh. 4035-37. Includes *Bāhubhūmika, Śrāvakabhūmi, Bodhisattvabhūmi*; this title used by Tibetan scholars when quoting from parts other than BBh.
61. *Mahāyānasaṃgraha. Theg chen bsdus pa. Compendium of the Universal Vehicle* (MS). P, No. 5549, Vol. 112; Toh. 4048.
62. *Nirṇayasaṃgrahaṇī* (more often called *Viniścayasaṃgrahaṇī*). *rNam nges (rnam par gtan la dbab pai) bsdus pa. Compendium of Determinations, Compendium* (VS). Toh. 4038.

AVALOKITAVRATA

63. *Prajñāpradīpaṭīka. Shes rab sgron mei rgya cher 'grel pa. Wisdom Lamp Commentary* (PrPrT). P, No. 5259, Vols, 96-97; Toh. 3859.

Bhavaviveka, Bhavya

64. *Mādhyamikahṛdaya. dbU mai snying po. Heart of the Central Way* (MH). P, No. 5255, Vol. 96; Toh. 3855.
65. *Prajñāpradīpamūlamadhyamakavṛtti. dbUma rtsa bai 'grel pa shes rab sgron me. Wisdom Lamp, Lamp of Wisdom* (PrPr). P, No. 5253, Vol. 95; Toh. 3853.
66. *Mādhyamikahṛdayavṛttitarkajvāla. rTog ge 'bar ba. Blaze of Arguments* (TJ). P, No. 5256, Vol. 96; Toh. 3856.

Buddhapalita

67. *Buddhapalitamūlamadhyamakavṛtti. dbU ma rtsa bai 'grel pa bud dha pa li ta. Buddhapalita Commentary* (BMMV). P, No. 5242, Vol. 95; Toh. 3842.

Chandrakirti, Chandrapada, Chandra

68. *Catuḥśatakaṭīka. bZhi brga pai rgya cher 'grel pa. Four Hundred Commentary* (CŚT). P, No. 5266, Vol. 98.
69. *Madhyamakāvatāra. dbU ma la 'jug pa. Introduction, Introduction to the Central Way, Central Way Introduction* (MA). P, No. 5261, Vol. 98; Toh. 3861.
70. *Madhyamakāvatārabhāṣya. dbU ma la 'jug pai bshad pa. Introduction Commentary* (MABh). P, No. 5263, Vol. 98; Toh. 3862.
71. *Mūlamadhyamakavṛttiprasannapadā. dbU ma rtsa bai 'grel pa tshig gsal. Lucid Exposition* (PPMMV). P, No. 5260, Vol, 98; Toh. 3860.
72. *Yuktiṣaṣṭikavṛtti. Rigs pa drug cu pai 'grel pa. Philosophical Sixty Commentary* (YṢV). P, No. 5265, Vol. 98; Toh. 3864. See Loizzo & Thurman.

Damshtrasena

73. *Śatasāhasrikāpañcaviṃṣatisāhasrikāṣṭādaśasāhasrikāprajñāpāramitābṛhaṭṭīka. Yum gsum gnod 'joms. Transcendent Wisdom Supercommentary* (falsely attributed to Vasubandhu). P, Vol. pha.

Dharmakirti

74. *Hetubindu. gTan tshigs kyi thigs pa. Drop of Reason.* P, No. 5712, Vol. 130; Toh. 4213.
75. *Nyāyabindu. Rigs pai thigs pa. Drop of Logic* (NB). P, No. 5711, Vol. 130; Toh. 4212.
76. *Pramāṇavārttika. Tshad ma rnam 'grel. Treatise on Validating Cognition* (PV). P, No. 5709, Vol 130; Toh. 4210.
77. *Pramāṇaviniścaya. Tshad ma rnam par nges pa. Determination of Validating Cognitions* (PVi). P, No. 5710, Vol. 130; Toh. 4211.

78. *Saṃbandhaparīkṣa. 'Brel pa brtag pa. Critique of Relations.* P, No. 5713, Vol. 130; Toh. 4214.
79. *Saṃtānāntarasiddhi. rGyud gzhan grub pa. Proof of Other Minds.* P, No. 5716, Vol. 130; Toh. 4219.
80. *Vādānyāya. rTsod pai rigs pa. Logic of Debate.* P, No. 5715, Vol. 130; Toh. 4218.

DIGNAGA

81. *Prajñāpāramitāpiṇḍārtha. Sher phyin bsdus don. Concise Meaning of Transcendent Wisdom.* Toh. 3809.
82. *Pramāṇasamuccaya. Tshad ma kun las btus pa. Synthesis of Validating Cognitions* (PS). P, No. 5700, Vol. 130; Toh. 4203.

JAYANANDA

83. *Madhyamakāvatāraṭīka. dbU ma la 'jug pai 'grel bshad. Introduction to the Central Way Subcommentary* (MAT). P, No. 5271, Vol. 99.

Jñanagarbha

84. *Satyadvavavibhaṅga. bDen gnyis rnam 'byed. Analysis of the Two Realities* (SDV). Toh. 3881.
85. *Satyadvayavibhaṅgavṛtti. bDen gnyis rang 'grel. Two Realities Autocommentary* (SDVV). Toh. 3882.

KAMALASHILA

86. *Bhāvanākrama. sGom pai rim pa. Meditation Stages.* P, No. 5310-12, Vol. 102; Toh. 3915-17.
87. *Madhyamakālaṃkārapañjikā. dbU ma rgyan gyi dka 'grel. Central Way Ornament Elucidation* (MAlamP). P, Vol. sa.
88. *Madhyamakāloka. dbU ma snang ba. Central Way Illumination* (MAlok). P, No. 5287, Vol. 101; Toh. 3887.
89. *Tattvasaṃgrahapañjikā. De kho na nyid bsdus pai dka 'grel. Compendium of Principles Elucidation* (TSP). P, No. 5765, Vol. 138.

MAITREYANATHA

90. *Abhisamayālaṃkāra. mNgon rtogs rgyan. Ornament of Realizations* (AA). P, No. 5184, Vol 88; Toh. 3786.
91. *Dharmadharmatāvibhaṅga. Chos dang chos nyid rnam par 'byed pa. Discrimination between Phenomenon and Noumenon* (DDV). P, No. 5523, Vol. 108; Toh. 4022.
92. *Madhyāntavibhāga. dbUs mtha rnam 'byed. Discrimination between Center*

and Extremes, Center and Extremes (MAV). P, No. 5522, Vol. 108; Toh. 4021.

93. *Mahāyānasūtrālaṃkāra. mDo sde rgyan. Ornament of the Scriptures of the Universal Vehicle, Scripture Ornament* (MSA). P., No. 5521, Vol. 108; Toh. 4020.

94. *Ratnagotravibhāgamahāyānottaratantraśāstra. rGyud bla ma. Analysis of the Jewel Matrix, Jewel Matrix, Supreme Tantra* (RGV). P, No. 5525, Vol. 108; Toh. 4024.

NAGADHVAJA

95. *Saṃdhinirmocanavyākhyāna. mDo sde dgongs 'grel gyi rnam bshad. Elucidation of Intention Commentary* (often falsely attributed to Asanga). P, Vol. co.

NAGARJUNA

96. *Akutobhaya. Ga las 'jigs med. No Fear from Anywhere* (falsely attributed, author unknown). Toh. 3829.

97. *Bhāvasaṃkrānti. Srid pa 'pho ba. Life-transmigration.* P, No. 5240, Vol. 95.

98. *Bodhicittavivaraṇa. Byang chub sems 'grel. Disclosure of the Spirit of Enlightenment.* Toh. 1800-1801.

99. *Lokātītastava. 'Jig rten las 'das par bstod pa. Transcendental Praise.* P, No. 2012, Vol. 46; Toh. 1120.

100. *Prajñā-nāma-mūlamadhyamakakārikā. dbU ma rtsa ba shes rab. Wisdom, Fundamental Central Way Verses* (MMK, PMMK). P, No. 5224, Vol. 95; Toh. 3824.

101. *Rājaparikathāratnāvalī. Rin chen 'phreng ba. Jewel Garland* (RA). P, No. 5658, Vol. 129; Toh. 4158. See Nagarjuna, Tucci, Vaidya.

102. *Śūnyatāsaptatī. sTong nyid bdun cu pa. Emptiness Seventy* (ŚS). Toh. 3827. See Komito.

103. *Śūnyatāsaptatīvṛtti. sTong nyid bdun cu pai 'grel pa. Emptiness Seventy Commentary* (ŚSV). P, No. 5231, Vol. 95; Toh. 3831.

104. *Sūtrasamuccaya. mDo kun las btus pa. Scripture Synthesis* (SS). P, No. 5330, Vol. 102; Toh. 3934. See Joshi.

105. *Vaidālyaprakaraṇā. Zhib mo rnam 'thag. Subtle Weaving* (VP). P, No. 5230, Vol. 95.

106. *Vigrahavyāvartanī. rTsod pa bzlog pa. Rebuttal of Objections* (VV). P, No. 5228, Vol. 95.

107. *Vigrahavyāvartanīvṛtti. rTsod pa bzlog pai 'grel pa. Rebuttal of Objections Commentary* (VVV). P, No. 5232, Vol. 95.

108. *Yuktiṣaṣṭikā. Rigs pa drug cu pa. Philosophical Sixty* (YṢ). P, No. 5225, Vol. 95; Toh. 3825.

RATNAKARASHANTI, SHANTIPA

109. *Prajñāpāramītopadeśa. Sher phyin man ngag. Transcendent Wisdom Instruction* (PPU). P, TG, Vol. 114.

SHANTARAKSHITA, SHANTIRAKSHITA

110. *Madhyamakālaṃkāra. dbU mai rgyan. Central Way Ornament* (MAlam). P, No. 5284, Vol. 101; Toh. 3884.
111. *Madhyamakālaṃkāravṛtti. dbU mai rgyan gyi rang 'grel. Central Way Ornament Commentary* (MAlamV). P, No. 5285, Vol, 101; Toh. 3885.
112. *Tattvasaṃgraha. De kho na nyid bsdus pa. Compendium of Principles* (TS). P, TG, Vol. 113.

STHIRAMATI

113. *Madhyāntavibhāgaṭīka. dbUs mthai 'grel pa. Center and Extremes Subcommentary* (MAVT). P, TG, Vol. 48; Toh. 4032.
114. *Triṃṣikāvṛtti. Sum cu pai 'grel bshad. Thirty Commentary* (TV). P, TG, Vol. 58.

VASUBANDHU

115. *Abhidharmakośa. Chos mngon pai mdzod. Treasury of Abhidharma* (AK). P, No. 5590, Vol. 115; Toh. 4089.
116. *Madhyāntavibhāgabhāṣhya*. Toh. 4027.
117. *Mahāyānasūtrālaṃkāravyākhyā. mDo sde rgyan gyi rnam bshad. Universal Vehicle Scripture Ornament Commentary* (MSAV). P, TG, Vol. 44; Toh. 4026.
118. *Triṃṣikākārikā. Sum cu pai tshig leur byas pa. Thirty* (Tr). P, TG. Vol. 58; Toh. 4055.
119. *Viṃṣatikā. Nyi shu pa. Twenty* (Vi). P, TG, Vol. 58; Toh. 4056.
120. *Vyākhyāyukti. rNam bshad rigs pa. Principles of Elucidation* (VY). P, Vol. 58; Toh. 4061.

VIMUKTASENA

121. *Aṣṭādaśasāhasrikāprajñapāramitāvṛtti. Sher phyin khri brgyad stong pai rnam 'grel. Transcendent Wisdom Eighteen Thousand Commentary*. See the great *Essence*, Ch. II n. 88.

YUAN TSO (WEN TSHIG)

122. *Aryagambhīrasaṃdhinirmocanasūtraṭīka. rGya nag gi 'grel chen. Great Chinese Commentary* (SNT). P, TG. Vols. 39-41.

Editions and Translations

Batchelor, S. *Shāntideva: A Guide to the Bodhisattva's Way of Life*. Dharamsala: Library of Tibetan Works and Archives, 1979.
Berzin, A. "Lam Rim Man Ngag: Oral Tradition of the Great Stages of the Path Teachings." Ph.D. dissertation, Harvard University, 1972.
Bhattacarya, V. *The Catuḥśataka of Āryadeva*. Calcutta: Visvabharati Books, 1931.
Bhattacharya, K. *The Dialectical Method of Nāgārjuna (Vigrahavyāvartanī)*. Delhi: Motilal Banarsidass, 1978.
Chang, G. C. C. *The Buddhist Teaching of Totality: The Philosophy of Hwa Yen Buddhism*. University Park: Pennsylvania State University Press, 1971.
———. *The 100,000 Songs of Milarepa*. Boulder: Shambhala, 1977.
Chattopadhyaya, A. *Atiśa and Tibet*. Calcutta: R. D. Press, 1967.
———, and Chimpa, L. *Tārānātha's History of Buddhism in India*. Simla: Indian Institute of Advanced Study, 1970.
Cleary, J. C. and Cleary, T. *The Blue Cliff Record*. Boulder: Shambhala, 1977.
Conze, E. *Abhisamayālaṃkāra*. Rome: Serie Orientale Roma, 1954.
———. *Large Sutra on Perfect Wisdom*. Berkeley and Los Angeles: University of California Press, 1975.
———. *The Perfection of Wisdom in 8,000 Lines and Its Verse Summary*. San Francisco: Four Seasons, 1973.
Dalai Lama, H. H. *The Buddhism of Tibet and the Key to the Middle Way*. London: Allen & Unwin, 1974.
de Jong, F. *Cinq chapitres de la Prasannapadā*. Paris: Geuthner, 1949.
Dhargyay, G. N. *Tibetan Tradition of Mental Development*. Dharamsala: Tibetan Library, 1978.
Dutt, N. *Bodhisattvabhūmi*. Patna: K. P. Jayaswal, 1966.
Eckel, D. M. "Bhāvaviveka: A Buddhist Critique of Nihilism." Ph.D. dissertation, Harvard University, 1980.
Fa Tsun. *Leau Yi Bu Leau Yi Fen Bye* (Chinese translation of *Essence of True Eloquence*). Microfilm copy made available to me by Dr. R. S. Y. Chi, Indiana University, Bloomington.
Gokhale, V. "Fragments from the Abhidharmasamuccaya of Asanga." *Journal of the Royal Asiatic Society, Bombay*, 23 (1947), 13-38.
Hattori, M. *Dignāga on Perfection*. Cambridge: Harvard University Press, 1971. Harvard Oriental Series.
Hopkins, P. J.; Kensur Lekden; and Tsong-ka-pa. *Compassion in Tibetan Buddhism*. Valois, N. Y.: Snow Lion, 1981.
Hopkins, P. J. *Meditations on Emptiness*. Ann Arbor: Xerox University Microfilms, 1972.
Hsuan Tsang. *Vijñaptimātratāsiddhi: La Siddhi de Hsuan Tsang*. Translated by Louis de la Vallee Poussin. 3 vols. Paris: Geuthner, 1928-1948.
Hurvitz, L. *Chih I*. Brussels: Institut Belges des Hautes Études Chinoises, 1962.
Iida, S. *An Introduction to Svātantrika-Mādhyamika*. Ann Arbor: Xerox University Microfilms, 1968.

Inada, K. *The Mulamadhyamakakārikās of Nāgārjuna*. Tokyo: Hokuseido, 1970.

Ingalls, D.H.H. *Materials for the Study of Nāvya-Nyāya Logic*. Cambridge: Harvard University Press, 1951. Harvard Oriental Series.

Jamspal, V. L., with Samten Chopel and P. Della Santina. *Nagarjuna's Letter to King Gautamīputra*. Delhi: Motilal Banarsidass, 1978.

Jha, G. *Tattvasaṃgraha with Pañjikā*. 2 vols. Baroda: Gaekwad, 1937.

Johnston, E. H. *Ratnagotravibhāga-Mahāyānottaratantraśāstra*. Patna: Jayaswal Institute, 1950.

Kaschewsky, R. *Das Leben des Lamaistischen Heiligen Tsongkhapa Blo-Bzaṅ-Grags-pa (1357-1419)*. Wiesbaden: Otto Harrassowitz, 1971.

Kato, B. *The Threefold Lotus Sutra*. Tokyo: Weatherhill, 1975.

Komito, D. "Nāgārjuna's Śūnyatāsaptatī." Ph.D. dissertation, University of Indiana, 1980.

Lamotte, E. *Éxplication des Mystères*. Louvain and Paris: Maisonneuve, 1935.

———. *L'Enseignement de Vimalakīrti*. Louvain: Muséon, 1962.

———. *La Somme du Grand Véhicûle*. 2 vols. Louvain: Muséon, 1938-1939.

———. *Traité de la grande vertu de la sagesse*. Louvain: Muséon, 1949-1967.

La Vallee Poussin, L. de. *L'Abhidharmakośa de Vasubandhu*. 6 vols. Paris and Louvain: Institut Belges des Hautes Études Chinoises, 1923-1931.

———. *Madhyamakāvatāra par Candrakīrti*. St. Petersburg: Academie Impériale des Sciences, 1907. Edition of Tibetan, Bibliotheca Buddhica IX.

———. *Madhyamakāvatāra de Candrakīrti*. Paris: Museon, 1907-1911. Partial translation: VIII, pp. 249-317; XI, pp. 217-358; XV, pp. 236-328.

———.*Mūlamadhyamakakārikās de Nāgārjuna avec le Prasannapadā commentaire de Candrakīrti*. St. Petersburg: Academie Impériale des Sciences, 1903-1913.

Levi, S. *Mahāyāna-Sūtrālaṃkāra*. Paris, 1907. Sanskrit and French.

Lhalungpa, L. *Life of Milarepa*. New York: Dutton, 1977.

Loizzo, J., with R. Thurman. "The Philosophical Sixty with Candrakirti's Commentary." Amherst: American Institute of Buddhist Studies, 1978. Manuscript.

Maxwell, N. *Great Compassion: The Chief Cause of Bodhisattvas*. Ann Arbor: Xerox University Microfilms, 1975.

Mullin, G. *Lives of The Six Ornaments*. Mundgod: Drepung Monastery Press, 1979-1980.

Nagao, G. *A Study of Tibetan Buddhism*. Tokyo: Iwanami Shoten, 1954.

Nagarjuna. *Precious Garland*. Translated by P. J. Hopkins. London: Allen & Unwin, 1975.

Nagatomi, M. *The Pramāṇavārttika of Dharmakīrti*. Cambridge: Harvard University Press, forthcoming.

Obermiller, E. *Analysis of the Abhisamayālaṃkāra*. London: Luzac, 1933.

———. *Buston's History of Buddhism in India and the Jewelry of Scripture*. Tokyo: Suzuki Research Foundation, 1975.

———. *Doctrine of Prajñāpāramitā as Exposed in the Abhisamayālaṃkāra of Maitreya*. Heidelberg: *Acta Orientalia*, 1932.

Pandeya, R. C. *Madhyāntavibhāgashāstra*. Delhi: Motilal Banarsidas, 1971.
Pasadika, B. "Nagarjuna's Sutrasamuccaya." *Journal of Religious Studies* (Patiala, Punjabi University) 7:1 (1979), 19-44.
Pradhan, P. *Abhidharmasamuccaya*. Santiniketan: Visvabharati Press, 1950.
Rahder, J. *Daśabhūmikasūtra*. Louvain: Institut Belges des Hautes Études Chinoises, 1926.
Rahula, W. *Le Compendium de la super-doctrine*. Paris: École Française d'Éxtrême Orient, 1971.
Roerich, N. *The Blue Annals*. Delhi: Motilal Banarsidass, 1976.
Ruegg, D. S. *Life of Bu Ston Rin Po Che*. Rome: Istituto Italiano per il Media ed Estremo Oriente, 1966. Serie Orientale Roma, XXXIV.
———. *Traité du Tathāgatagarbha de Bu Ston Rin Chen Grub*. Paris: Ecole Française d' Extrēme:Orient, 1973.
Schayer, S. *Ausgewahlte Kapitel aus der Prasannapadā*. Krakow: Polska Akademja Umiejetności, Prace Komisji Orjentalistycznej, 1931.
Shastri, D. *Abhidharmakośabhāṣya*. Varanasi: Bauddha Bharati, 1973.
———. *Pramāṇavārttikā*. Varanasi: Bauddha Bharati, 1968.
———. *Tattvasaṃgraha*. Varanasi: Bauddha Bharati, 1968.
Shastri, N. S. "Madhyamakāvatāra VI." *Journal of Oriental Research* (Madras): IV (1930); V(1931); VI(1932). Sanskrit restoration.
Sprung, M. *Lucid Exposition of the Middle Way*. Boulder: Prajna, 1979.
Stcherbatski, T. *Buddhist Logic, Vol. II*. New York: Dover, 1972.
———. *The Conception of Buddhist Nirvana*. Leningrad: USSR Academy of Sciences, 1927.
———. *Discrimination between Middle and Extremes*. Calcutta: R.D. Press, 1971. Reprint Biblioteca Buddhica XXX.
Streng, F. *Emptiness, A Study in Religious Meaning*. New York: Abingdon, 1967.
Suzuki, D. T. *Lañkāvatārasūtra*. London: Routledge and Kegan Paul, 1956.
Takasaki, J. *A Study on the Ratnagotravibhāga*. Rome: Istituto Italiano per il Medio ed Estremo Oriente, 1966. Serie Orientale Roma, XXXIII.
Tat, W. *Ch'eng Wei-Shih Lun: Doctrine of Mere-Consciousness*. Hong Kong: Dai Nippon, 1973.
Thurman, R.A.F. *Holy Teaching of Vimalakirti*. University Park: Pennsylvania State University Press, 1977.
———, ed. *Life and Teachings of Tsong Khapa*. Dharamsala: Library of Tibetan Works and Archives, 1981.
———, ed. *Ornament of the Scriptures of the Universal Vehicle*. Amherst: American Institute of Buddhist Studies, 1980.
Tsong-ka-pa. *Tantra in Tibet*. Translated by P. J. Hopkins. London: Allen & Unwin, 1978.
Tucci, G. *Bhavanākrama I and III*. Rome: Istituto Italiano per il Medio ed Estremo Oriente, 1958, 1971. Serie Orientale Roma, IX.
Vaidya, P. L. *Études sur Āryadeva et son Catuḥśataka*. Paris: Geuthner, 1923.
———, ed. *Lalitavistara*. Darbhanga: Mithila Institute, 1958. Buddhist Sanskrit Texts, 1.

Vadya, P. L., ed. *Lañkāvatārasūtra*. Darbhanga: Mithila Institute, 1961. Buddhist Sanskrit Texts, 4.
———, ed. *Prajñāpāramitāpiṇḍārtha*. Darbhanga: Mithila Institute, 1960. Buddhist Sanskrit Texts, 4.
———, ed. *Madhyamakaśāstra*. Darbhanga: Mithila Institute, 1960. Buddhist Sanskrit Texts, 10.
———, ed. *Rāṣṭrapālaparipṛccha*. Darbhanga: Mithila Institute, 1961. Buddhist Sanskrit Texts, 17.
———, ed. *Ratnāvalī*. Darbhanga: Mithila Institute, 1961. Buddhist Sanskrit Texts, 10.
———, ed. *Samādhirājasūtra*. Darbhanga: Mithila Institute, 1961. Buddhist Sanskrit Texts, 2.
———, ed. *Vigrahavyāvartanī*. Darbhanga: Mithila Institute, 1960. Buddhist Sanskrit Texts, 10.
Wangyal, G. *Door of Liberation*. New York: Lotsawa, 1978.
Wayman, A. *Calming the Mind and Discerning the Real*. New York: Columbia University Press, 1978.
———. *Yoga of the Guhyasamājatantra*. Delhi: Motilal Banarsidass, 1980.
———, and Lessing, F. *Mkhas-grub-rje's Fundamentals of the Buddhist Tantras*. The Hague: Mouton, 1968.
Willis, J. *On Knowing Reality*. New York: Columbia University Press, 1979.

Miscellaneous Works

Berger, P., with B. Berger and T. Luckmann. *The Homeless Mind: Modernization of Consciousness*. New York: Doubleday, 1974.
Berger, P., with T. Luckmann. *The Social Construction of Reality*. New York: Doubleday, 1967.
Demiéville, P. *Le Concile de Lhasa*. Paris: Hautes Études, 1952.
Govinda, L. A. *Creative Meditation and Multi-Dimensional Consciousness*. Wheaton: Theosophical Press, 1978.
———. *Foundations of Tibetan Mysticism*. New York: Dutton, 1960.
———. *Philosophy and Psychology of the Abhidhamma*. New York: Weiser, 1974.
Gudmunsen, C. *Wittgenstein and Buddhism*. London: Allen & Unwin, 1979.
Joshi, L. M. *God's Alternative: Buddhism and Theism*. London: Allen & Unwin, forthcoming.
———. *Studies in the Buddhistic Culture of India*. Delhi: Motilal Banarsidass, 1980.
Kajiyama, Y. *Bhāvaviveka and the Prāsaṅgika School*. Navanalanda Mahavihara Research Publication, I, Rajgir, Nalanda Press, 1957.
Kosambi, D. D. *Introduction to the Study of Indian History*. Bombay, 1957.
Matilal, B. K. *Epistemology, Logic, and Grammar in Indian Philosophical Analysis*. (The Hague: Mouton, 1971).
Murti, T.R.V. *The Central Philosophy of Buddhism*. London: Allen & Unwin, 1955.

Raju, P. T. *Idealistic Thought of India*. London: Allen & Unwin, 1953.
———. *Philosophical Traditions of India*. London: Allen & Unwin, 1971.
Rhys-Davids, T. W. *Buddhist India*. Delhi: Motilal Banarsidass, 1974.
Robinson, R. H. *Early Madhyamika in India and China*. Madison: University of Wisconsin Press, 1967.
Ruegg, D. S. *La Théorie du tathāgatagarbha et du gotra*. Paris: Ecole Française de Extrĕme-Orient, 1969.
Saunders, J. T., and Henze, D. F. *The Private Language Problem: A Philosophical Dialogue*. New York, 1976.
Shastri, D. N. *Critique of Indian Realism*. Agra: Agra University Press, 1964.
Snellgrove, D. L. with H. Richardson. *A Cultural History of Tibet*. London: Weidenfeld, 1968.
Sprung, M., ed. *The Two Truths in Buddhism and Vedanta*. Dordrecht: Reidel, 1973.
Stcherbatski, T. *Buddhist Logic Vol. I*. New York: Dover, 1962.
———. *Central Conception of Buddhism and the Meaning of the Word "Dharma."* Delhi: Motilal Banarsidass, 1979.
Takakusu, J. *Essentials of Buddhist Philosophy*. Delhi: Motilal Banarsidass, 1975.
Tambiah, S. J. *World Conqueror and World Renouncer*. Cambridge: Cambridge University Press, 1976.
Thapar, R. *A History of India 1*. London: Penguin, 1966.
Toynbee, A. *Mankind and Mother Earth*. London: Oxford University Press, 1976.
Tucci, G. *Tibetan Painted Scrolls*. Rome, 1949.
Vidyabhushana S. C. *History of Indian Logic*. Delhi: Motilal Banarsidass, 1971.
———. *Outline of Indian Philosophy*. Delhi: Motilal Banarsidass, 1971.
Warder, A. K. *Indian Buddhism*. Delhi: Motilal Banarsidass, 1970.
Warnock, M. *Imagination*. Berkeley and Los Angeles: University of California Press, 1978.
Weber, M. *The Religion of India*. New York: Macmillan, Free Press, 1958.
Wittgenstein, L. *The Blue and Brown Books*. New York: Harper and Row, 1958.
———. *On Certainty*. Oxford: Blackwell, 1969.
———. *Philosophical Grammar*. Oxford: Blackwell, 1974.
———. *Philosophical Investigations*. Translated by G. Anscombe New York; Macmillan, 1953.
———. *Remarks on Colour*. Berkeley and Los Angeles, University of California Press, 1977.
———. *Remarks on the Foundations of Mathematics*. Cambridge: MIT Press, 1967.
———. *Tractatus Logico-Philosophicus*. New York: Humanities Press, 1961.
———. *Zettel*. Berkeley and Los Angeles: University of California Press, 1970.

Reference Works

Chone Tanjur. Stonybrook, N. Y.: Institute for Advanced Studies of World Religions, 1976. Microfilm.

Das, S. C. *Tibetan-English Dictionary*, Alipore, 1960.
Edwards, P. ed. *Encyclopedia of Philosophy*. 4 vols. New York: Macmillan, 1967.
Hirano, T. *Index to the Bodhicaryāvatāra Pañjikā, Chapter IX*. Tokyo, 1966.
Nagao, G. M. *Index to the Mahāyāna-sūtra-alaṃkāra*. Tokyo, Iwanami Shoten, 1958-1961.
Nanjio. *A Catalogue of the Buddhist Tripitaka. (Chinese)*. Oxford: Clarendon Press, 1883.
Potter, K. *Encyclopedia of Indian Philosophies, Vol. I*. Delhi: Motilal Banarsidass, 1970. Bibliography.
Sakaki, R., ed. *Mahāvyutpatti*. Tokyo: Suzuki Research Foundation, 1962.
Sonam Angdu, ed. *Tibeto-Sanskrit Lexicographical Materials*. Leh: Basgo Tongspon, 1973.
Tibetan Tripitaka Research Institute. *The Tibetan Tripitaka; Peking Edition*. Tokyo and Kyoto, 1956. ("P" numbers refer to this edition with its romanized catalog)
Ui, Hakuju. *A Complete Catalogue of the Tibetan Buddhist Canons*. Sendai: Tohoku University Press, 1934 ("Toh." numbers 1-4569).
Yensho Kanakura, ed. *A Catalogue of the Tohoku University Collection of Tibetan Works on Buddhism*. Sendai: Tohoku University Press, 1953. ("Toh." numbers refer to this catalog, 5001-7083)
Zuiho Yamaguchi, Jikido Takasaki, and Yasunori Ejima. *sDe dge Tibetan Tripitaka bstan hgyur, dbU ma* section. 14 vols. Tokyo: Tokyo University Press, 1977.

INDEX

abandonment, 191, 283, 312
Abhidharma, 24, 25, 42; definition, 115
Abhidharma Sciences, 34
Abhidharma Scripture, 292
Abhidharma Synthesis, *see* AS
absolute, 55, 57, 92, 329; absolute-, 60; as Supreme Knowable, 160; nature, 117; negation, 56, 125, 127, 129, 165, 197, 239, 376; nothingness, 169, 178; production, 97; reality, 362; status, 139, 286
absolutely, as thesis qualification, 106
absolutism, 56, 58, 60, 62, 92, 111, 163, 177, 263, 300, 307, 315, 375n, 381
absolutist, 62, 165, 308, 342n; mysticism, 98; -nihilist, 135
absolutistic: constructions, 378; relativism of wisdom, 160; views, 262, 315
absurd consequence (*prasaṅga*), 95
accessories of enlightenment, 191, 203
accumulation path, 135
Action Tantras, 70
action-abstention, 256
actuality, 283
Adbhutavyuha (Tsong Khapa's Buddhaland), 83
addicted mentality, 271
addiction, 199, 221, 242, 243, 303, 309-10
addictive: defilement, 359; misknowledge, 309; obscurations, 221n, 308, 312
Advaitavedanta, 51
Advice to Katyayana, 300
aftermath: discernment, 242; illusory wisdom, 145
agent, 253, 305
aggregates, 85, 134, 140-41, 191, 192, 194, 203, 251, 300-304, 312, 314, 352, 366
aggregations, 271
allowing the external objective, 312-21
alternative reality (other-emptiness), 61
Amdo, birthplace of Umapa, 80
Amitabha, 34
AMN, *see Teaching of Akshayamati Scripture*
analysis: four methods, 330; in Wittgenstein, 96-97; mundane unreflective, 102; of part-whole, 273, 287; of person, 94; of self, 97; of unity/multiplicity, 273; referent-seeking, 102, 368; ultimacy-seeking, 164
Analysis of Jewel Matrix Supreme Tantra (RGV), 12, 56
Analysis of Two Realities (SDV), 271n, 287, 295
Analysis of Two Realities Subcommentary (SDVV), 289n-290
Analysts (Vaibhashika), 24, 42, 51, 93, 107, 138-39, 289, 291, 298, 340
analytic: cognition, 297, 338; concept, 295n; insight, 131; investigation into the referent of person, 291; methods of Centrists, 296; non-discovery, 330; rational cognition, 330n; reasonings, 364; status, 369
Anangapati (Kama), 187
annihilism, 198
anomalous creations, 146, 314
apparent: objectivity of name in named, 234; reality, 79
appearance: in non-defective cognition, 369; -side, 79; -emptiness, 148
apperception, 230, 240, 271, 277, 317, 318
apperceptive self-conciousness, 240, 271, 312, 317-20
argument, dialectical, 321; private (dogmaticist), 321
artificial imagination, 226-29

Aryadeva, 20, 52, 80, 84, 147, 161-62, 188, 253, 257, 265, 286, 294, 309, 310, 314, 328n, 329n, 331, 345; myth of, 36-38
Aryasanga, 27. *See also* Asanga
Aryashura, 265
Aryavimuktasena, 287n
AS (*Abhidharma Synthesis*), 44, 200, 221-22, 224, 242, 244, 248
Asanga, 12, 20-21, 26, 34, 42, 43, 51, 54, 72, 83, 117, 187, 192, 195, 200, 209-18, 243, 278n, 359, 383; legend, 28-32; personal view, 259n
ascriptive and descriptive designation, 239, 248, 256, 268, 279, 299; constructions, 243; designation, 203, 303
aspective object (of "I"-habits), 304
ASV (*Synthesis Commentary*), 224
Atisha, 52, 54, 71, 75, 88
atom, 270-72; -molecule-analysis, 287
authentic: cognition, 283; realizations (four), 240, 242n, 243; status, 139; view, 68, 80, 85, 168, 170, 171, 342-43
Avalokitavrata, 265, 288, 323, 377, 380
Avalokiteshvara, 34, 41

Ba-so Chos-rje, 326n
bare datum, as logically private object, 107
baseless superficial (critiqued by Idealist), 215-16
bases of conceptual adherence, 238-40
bases of reference, 298
basis of designation, relative nature, 198
BBh, see *Bodhisattva Stages*
Beatific Body (*Sambhogakaya*), 18, 87, 172
between-state, 77
Bhadantavimuktasena, 247n
Bhagavan Vajrabhairava, 82
Bhavaviveka, 39-40, 51-52, 55, 84, 93, 107, 188, 243n, 253n, 265-73, 281-83, 287n, 288, 293-95n, 300-303n, 312n, 313, 314n, 320n, 323, 327, 333-39, 341, 343, 373n, 376-78, 380; conventional identity, 104; subtle substantivism, 100; private object, 107
binary logic, commitment to, 140
bKra-shis Seng-ge, Kadampa scholar, 72
Blaze of Argument (TJ), 39, 52, 269, 272n, 282, 301, 376, 378
bLo-bzang Grags-pa, siddha, 66
bLo-bzang Phun-tshogs, 230n, 285n, 319n, 332n, 326n, 337n, 346n, 356n, 376n
Blue Cliff Record, 128
Blue and Brown Books, 99
BMMV (*Buddhapalita Commentary*), 84, 299, 306, 310
Bo-dong Phyogs-rgyal (Jo-nang-pa), 69
Bodhisattva, 3, 32, 83, 113, 136, 239, 243, 348, 383; ethic, 54; path, 75; practices, 356
Bodhisattva Stages (BBh), 75, 209-14, 218-19, 228, 231-33, 236, 238, 242-43, 251
Body of Beatitude (*Saṁbhogakāya*), 18
Body of Emanation (*Nirmāṇakāya*), 18
Body of Truth (*Dharmakāya*), 18, 147
bondage, 253, 256, 259, 352, 364; twofold (of conditionings and signs), 131
Boundless Life (Amitayus), 172
Brahma, 8-14, 184
Brahma Sūtras, 34
Brahamin-Buddhist debate, 91
Brahminical culture, 31
Brom-ston-pa, Kadampa founder, 69
Brother-Masters (Asanga-Vasubandhu), 221, 228, 248
bSod-nams Grags-pa, Sakya teacher, 73
Bu-ston, 50, 59, 68, 79, 218n
Buddha, 3, 20, 114-15, 156, 183, 197, 258, 260, 345, 348, 357-59, 361; as superior philosopher, 177; is, as Buddha does, 171; -essence, 61, 208, 346-50; his intention, 71; his liberative technique, 144; his philosophical traditions, 383; his silence (as not anti-rational), 154; -honors, 384; -nature, 55; -qualities, 360; -realm, 354; -will, 172
Buddhaguhya, 75
Buddhahood, 12, 64, 85, 135, 311, 354, 356
Buddhapalita, 39, 51, 54, 84, 188, 265, 266, 288, 299, 300, 306, 308, 309, 310, 323, 345, 373, 382
Buddhapalita Commentary, *see* BMMV
Buddhist, 334, 339, 350; education, 68; Holy Land, 84; Buddhist hermeneutics,

111-30; monk (Tsong Khapa), 183; critical philosophers, 92; philosophy, 8, 33-37; practitioners, 7
Bya-bral, hermitage, 83

Canon of Reason, 258
categorical differential, 232, 234
categories of teaching, two, 207
causal process, 221, 266
causality, 219, 250, 253, 256
ceaselessness, 204
celebration of relativity/emptiness-equivalence, 260-64
Center and Extremes (MAV), 209, 214, 219-21, 223, 226-28, 267, 316
central path, 54; of abandonment of extremes, 381
central way, 4, 10, 21, 26, 53, 133, 172, 173, 229, 260-64, 265, 275, 277, 288, 310, 328n, 374, 378; avoiding two extremisms, 217; defined (MAV), 226-27; Idealists', 214; of critical examination, 229; philosophers, 7, 167; position, 159; quietistic error about, 68; relativism/absolutism balance, 159; view, 79, 268
Central Way Illumination (MAlok), 224, 225, 233, 253, 255, 272, 277, 279-81, 284, 286-87, 323n
Central Way Introduction Subcommentary (MAT), 346
Central Way Ornament, *see* MAlam
Central Way Ornament Autocommentary (MAlamV), 274, 275, 283
Central Way Ornament Elucidation (MAlamP), 275, 276, 283
Central Way Treatise, *see* PM
Centrism (Madhyamaka), 6, 57, 127-28, 276, 328n
Centrist, 24, 40, 54, 59, 136, 279, 281, 288, 307, 323, 327n, 331, 332, 343, 344, 361, 379; exonerated of charge of nihilism, 161; literature, 382n; message, 253-64; philosophers, 329n; position of emptiness/relativity, 156; psychology, 169; reasoning, 269; schools, 290; set up by Asanga as antagonist, 215-18; stance, 278n; system, 245, 261, 268, 275; treatises, 257, 353; view, 251n; viewpoint (Asanga's), 30; way, 148
Centrists, 151, 164, 166, 219, 221, 229, 243, 263, 269, 274, 277, 283, 289, 308, 312, 313, 326, 354, 362, 363, 368n, 378, 381; as critical relativists, 93
cessation, of mental fabrications, 254
cessations, the two noumena, 146
champions, 21, 49, 148, 189, 261, 263-64, 382-83; of philosophy, 187, 385; system of, 323; two ways of, 384
Ch'an, 28, 37, 52, 121
Chandra (Chandrakirti), 22, 51, 54-55, 57, 84, 93, 107, 119, 126-27, 140, 151, 164-65, 188, 253n, 258, 265-66, 288, 290-314n, 316-19, 321-23, 328n, 329, 331-38, 340-51, 353, 361, 364-69, 371-84n; critique of substantivism, 100-102; error-free teacher, 81; moon of elucidation, 183; myth, 40-41; on positionlessness, 155, 160; privacy-refutation, 59, 106-10, 340-80
Chang, G.C.C., 121n
chariot: of two methods, 275; simile, 303, 366
Charvaka, 15-17, 332n
Chih I, 119-22
choice negation, 166, 376, 378, 379, 380; four types, 377. *See also* implicative negation
Chos-kyi dPal-ba, 70
clear light brilliance of ultimate wisdom, 170
Clearys, T. and J. C., 128n
cognitive: double exposure, 170; status, 336; superficial relative reality, 223
cognizability of absolute, 167
coincidentality (nominal designation), 357-58
common sense, 290, 313; analysis, 330n; validating cognition, 326
compassion, 11-12, 26, 57, 131, 171, 183; emptiness' essence, 258; universal, 60
Compendium (VS), 192-93n, 209-10, 212, 214-15, 217-22, 230-31, 236n, 251, 266-67
Compendium of Principles (TS), 53, 70, 75
Compendium of Principles Elucidation (TSB), 290

complete clarity, 102, 135
concept of space, Traditionist, 291
conceptual: aggregate, 7; basis, 234n; cognition, 377; nature, 117; object, 269, 343, 371, 373; thought, 338n, validating cognition, 336
Concise Stages of the Path (LRChung), 145
concomitance, 325, 342; ascertainment of, 140
conditional process, 201, 360
confutation via similarity of reason, 272-73
conscious attitudes, four, 132-33
consciousness, 276, 309; as self, 302; as referent, 271; alone, 274; aggregate, 305
consecrations, four, 82
consequence: dialectical, 329; four exceptional, 366-67, 373-74; of relativity, 163, 326
constructed eye, 244-46
constructed form, 356, 361
constructed reality, 361. *See also* imaginatively constructed nature
construction, discriminative, 360
constructions: ascriptive and descriptive, 243; imaginative, 243; materialistic, 243
contemplative trance, 73
continuity of fundamental, 302, 315
convention, 194, 332, 358; three-aspected, 323n
conventional, 92, 157; cognition, 146, 261, 283, 284; designation, 302, 326; existence, 215, 267, 288, 295, 304, 306, 359, 372, 373; existence of externals, 270-71; existence of self, 352; expressions, 261, 291, 305-306; external objective, 270; information, 238; intrinsic identifiability, 267, 278, 373n, 374; intrinsic identity, 106, 165, 266n, 268n, 273, 289; intrinsically identifiable production, 269; intrinsically indentifiable status, 271, 367; level, 339; objects, 286; other-production, 368n; production, 306; reality, 79, 118, 148, 164, 281, 285, 367, 374; reason, 165; sense of "I,"144, 146, 301n; status, 299; status of externals, 273-77; terms, 295; usage, 297; validating cognition, 80, 370, 372, 373; Dialecticist presentation of, 100-102, 292
conventionalism, Dialecticist, 100-102
conventionality, 94, 99-100, 108, 164, 215n, 322n, 330n; of theses, 154
conventionally: ascriptive intellect, 296; existent, 371; mutually dependent, 320; objective, 337; verbalizing intellect, 298
conventions, 99, 215, 343, 357, 360, 370; of social communication, 293; of common parlance, 314
Conze, E., 356n, 357
created phenomena, threefold, 146
creationlessness, 253
creator, 347, 370
critical: discrimination, 89, 130, 148; insight meditation, 164; philosophy, 93, 165; wisdom, 3, 89, 96, 135, 141, 171
CŚ (*Experientialist Four Hundred, Four Hundred*), 34, 38, 151, 155, 161, 257, 265-66, 286, 309, 314, 331, 354
CŚT (*Four Hundred Commentary*), 298, 309, 313, 323, 328n
cyclic life, 243, 266, 309, 364

Dalai Lama XI, 141n; XIV, 87, 372
Damodara (Vishnu), 187
Damshtrasena, 244n, 248
danger of emptiness misunderstood, 157
dbU-ma-dgongs-pa-rab-gsal (GRS), 316n
death, 72, 77, 316n
deathless enlightenment, 72
Deer Park at Rshipatana, 204
defective/non-defective sense-cognition, 373
definitive, 253, 255, 256, 280, 382; in meaning, 204, 249, 250, 251, 258, 279, 308; meaning, 111, 189, 251, 256, 277, 381, 384, 385; meaning for Individualists, 116; meaning statements, 165; scriptures, three types of, 119
definitive/interpretable, rule of, 116-26
definitiveness, 119, 207, 312, 347, 352, 353
deity yoga, 135, 148
delusion, 309-10
Dense Array, 275, 281, 350
dependent designation, 147, 158, 366
dependent origination, 191, 203, 262,

309. *See also* relativity
dependent production (form of relativity-reason), 147
dependently designative superficial, 295
designated identity, two types (dependent, designative), 220
designation, 212, 215; ascriptive and descriptive, 244
designative: base, 201, 212, 295, 299, 362; conventions (relative nature), 198; dependence, 305; existence, 373; existence as identifiable (Idealist), 220; existence as mere verbal designation, 220; status, 366; superficial imaginary reality, 223n; words and constructions, imagined, 266
designative-substantial, 362
designatively existent superficial (imaginary), 220
Destiny Fulfilled, 66-77
destroyed as phenomenal, 316n
determinants of cognition, 276
determinate-form-perception, 270
determination: of definitiveness, three ways of, 252; of the negation, 379
determining reality, 210-52
Devadatta, 294
Devasharma, 40, 265
dGa-gdong, retreat, 79
Dharma Digest, 306n
Dharma, three wheels of, 32
Dharmakirti, 12, 51, 58, 67, 74, 188, 229-30, 241, 273n, 276, 277n
Dharmapala, 39, 47, 323
Dharmottara, 277n
Dialecticism (*Prāsaṅgika*), 321
Dialecticist, 79, 108, 164, 165, 296, 313, 316n, 317n, 324, 329n, 337, 339n, 340, 341, 342, 350n, 368n; Centrist, 39, 51, 53, 55-56; Centrism, 103; Centrists, 105; Centrist hermeneutic, 123, 125, 127; consequences, 95; elucidation of the holy intention, 288-385; literature, 311; method, 308; outlook, 335n; school, 88, 146; system, 295, 299, 312, 345, 373; view, 85
Dialecticists, 80, 91, 138, 163, 195n, 289, 290, 327n, 336, 378, 381
Diamond Cutter, 258
diamond smithereens, reasoning of, 137
differentials, 232, 234n, 285
Dignaga, 12, 13, 44-47, 51, 58, 67, 73-74, 188-89n, 229, 273, 325n, 341; molecule/atom-objectivity-negation, 241; vision of Buddha, 151
direct objective basis of expressions, 232
Disciple-Canon, 308, 354
Disciple-Vehicle, 204
Discipline (Vinaya), 85, 86, 207
Disclosure of the Spirit of Enlightenment, 258
Discrimination between Phenomena and Noumena, 29
discriminative construction, 360
distinctive characteristic, 192
distinctive feature, 295
distinctive specialties, Dialecticist, 144, 288, 312
Doctrine of the Victor, 49, 187, 381, 382
Dogmaticism, 328
Dogmaticist, 105, 108, 165, 290, 323n, 367-69; Centrism, 40, 52; Centrists, 51, 55, 105, 295, 296; Centrist explanations, 265-87; Centrist hermeneutic, 125; Centrist theory, 291; Centrist systems, 284; methodology, 272; outlook, 335n; philosophers, 311; privacy (*rang rgyud*), term choice, 91, 93, 104-105; realist, 165; reasoning process, 322n; school, 88, 287; system, 375; -Dialecticist controversy, 88
Dogmaticists, 53, 79-80, 91, 148, 163, 164, 243n, 251n, 266, 289, 291, 298-99, 308n, 310, 336-37, 339, 343, 373, 378
dogmatism, 9
dogmatist, 90, 382
Dol-bu-pa, 50, 59-62
Don-grub Rin-chen, 66, 70-72
Donner, N., 121n
doors: of liberation, three, 253; of reasoning, 287
dPal-'byor Lhun-grub, 203n, 223n, 238n, 241n, 277n, 286n, 289n, 298n, 322n
dreamlikeness, 226
dualism, 13, 25, 311, 362
dualistic, analysis, 332; appearance, 229, 240; cognition, 299; consciousness, 126, 255; perception, 230; theory, three patterns, 332

duality, 226-27, 261, 308, 329, 330
Dzing-ji temple, Maitreya temple, 84

education, Buddhist, 68
educations, three spiritual, 115
egocentric (*arvāgdarśana*), 67; predicament, 17, 90; viewpoint, 90
egocentrism, 18
egocentrist, 95; absolutism, 92; approach in philosophy, 90; dogmatism, 17; misknowledge, 108; outlook, 95
egoism, personal, 243, 298
eight: attitudes of great Individualist, 247n; attributes of relativity, 258-60; kinds of atoms, 272
eightfold group of consciousness, 209
elements, 134, 191, 194, 312; six and eighteen, 192-203
eliminate contradiction of "ultimate relative," 218-23
elimination of protest (to SN's imagined), 243-48
eloquence, 18, 130, 187
Elucidation Commentary (*Saṃdhinirmocanavyākhyāna*), 218n
Elucidation of Intention, 27, 32, 113, 117-19, 125-26, 131, 191-209, 211, 217-19, 225, 248. *See also* SN
Emanation Body (*Nirmānakāya*), 18, 172
emptied out (imagined, *gang gis stong pa*), 214
emptiness, 3, 10-11, 50, 114, 124, 148, 151, 160, 165, 178, 204, 205, 226-28, 232, 243, 246, 253-54, 260-64, 298n, 328n, 331, 348-49, 351-52, 354, 361, 367, 374, 375, 384n; as a view, 153; as cause, 164; as knowable, 156; as relatedness, 158; as thought-exterminator, 155; by intrinsic reality, 301, 373; dawning as cause and effect, 170; doctrine of, 289; intrinsic-reality-negation, 166; not nothingness, 133; noumenon, 146; of duality, 229, 259; of emptiness, 57, 167, 169, 247, 285; of external things in conventional, 275; of intrinsic reality, 257, 263, 310, 339; of objects of truth-habits, 285; of personal self, 144; of relative with respect to imagined, 241; of subject-object duality, 351; of substantially different subject-object, 229; pattern of, 214; three interpretations of, 166; with respect to identifiable status, 353; with respect to nature, 230; with respect to self-existence, 278
emptiness: -essence (as compassion), 258; -existence, 166; -identitylessness, 169; -knowledge (avoiding nihilism), 149; -perception, 169; -side (*stong phyogs*), 79; -unreality, 194
emptiness/: causality-compatibility, 145; compasssion-indivisible, 171-72; relativity experience, 169; relativity equivalence, 149; relativity rule, 141, 264
emptinesses, twenty, 5
empty: defined as "free," 244; of intrinsic reality, 245; (*stong gzhi*) relative, 188, 214, 245
enlightened person, 168, 170
enlightenment, 7, 12-13, 21, 112, 141, 157, 168, 172, 343n, 348, 382n; claim of, 49, 50, 64-65; consummation of reason, 127; ultimate; 264; utterance of, 114
entity and identity, 293
entrance into pure information, 240, 242
epistemology, 58, 74; of enlightenment, 343n; of nondualism, 168
equalities, ten, 136, 364
equality of non-production, 364
equanimity, 242
erroneous cognition, 338, 371
Escapists, 178. *See also* Fundamentalists
Esoteric Communion (Guhyasamāja), 27, 59, 70, 76, 79-80, 82-83, 87
Essence, 13, 50, 85, 136, 160, 351; core, 123; final section, 166; inspiration, 78; key passage, 167; key to sacred tradition, 111; study as the path, 149
essence notions ("objects," "simples"), 93
established: by intrinsic identity, 299; by validating cognition, 238, 372; on strength of convention, 306
ethical, achievement, 384; choice, 250; choice (*blang dor*), 66; consequences of central way, 172; transformation of Tibet, 52
ethics, 383; Transcendent-Wisdom-, 67; -enlightenment, 171
evident non-analytic conventionality, 340n

evolution (karma), 151; and cessation (samsara/Nirvana), 73
evolutionary action, 243, 291, 306, 315
example, 272, 319, 332; of mirror-image, 34-42; of unrealities, 197-99
exclusion: negation, 165, 376, 377, 379, 380; of a negatee, 377-78, 380; of truth-status, 254
exclusive negative, 197
existential relativists, 152
experiential, media, 305; path, 135
Experientialist, 26, 52, 221, 233, 251, 269, 274, 277-79, 281, 298, 299, 313, 317n, 328n, 346; analysis, 330n; philosophy, 240; system, 242, 245; yogi, 221
Experientialist Four Hundred, see CŚ
Experientialist-Dogmaticist, 313n, 350n
Experientialist-Dogmaticist-Centrist, 287n
Explanatory Tantras, 76
expressibility of absolute, 167
Extensive Transcendent Wisdom, 248, 250
external object, 271, 276, 281, 316, 345-46
external objective, 273-77, 312
extremes of absolutism and nihilism, 381
extremism, 228-29
extremist: bonds, 178; hearts, 183; views, 149, 179
eye of intellect, 308, 382
eye-consciousness, 320
eye-medium, 339n

Fa Tsang, 121, 127
fabrication (*prapañca*), 151-52, 177, 376
face-value, 325
Facts of the Stages, 255n
faculties, 354
faith, 112, 181, 183
fallacy of subjectlessness, 333
falsehood, meaning of, 301
Father Tongue, liberative word, 65
fear of selflessness, 350
final genealogical determinism, 209, 345
final mind in death, 315
fine discrimination, wheel of Dharma, 244
Finely Woven, VP, 26
finest discrimination, 204-205
first wheel of Dharma, 206, 248, 352
five aggregates, 300
Five Books of Maitreya, 29, 34, 66
five categories (name, cause, construction, wisdom, reality), 266
five paths, 134-35
Five Stages, 27, 41, 76
five stages of transcendent insight, 134-35
foods, four, 191, 203
form, 290, 314; aggregate, 201, 203
formless states, four, 132
Four Hundred, see CŚ
Four Hundred Commentary, see CŚT
Four Philosophies (*siddhānta*), 35
four: alternatives, 327n; aspects of first holy truth, 354; consequences unpacked from royal reason, 163, 366-67; elements, 314; holy truths, 204, 257; investigations (thorough), 242n; keys, 137; major deeds of Tsong Khapa, 85; methods of analysis, 330n; modes of implication, in negation, 377; realizations, authentic, 242n; reasonings contra identity, 366; reasons for reification, 234n; reliances, 255; theories of Idealists (interpretable), 345; truths, 207; ways (in Tantric hermeneutics), 76
four-extreme-production, 364
fourth reliance, 126-30
freedom, 18; from identity, 179; from permanence and annihilation, 263; from true plurality, 143; from true unity, self/aggregate, 141-43
fun, philosophical, 223
functional capacity (efficiency), 238n, 263
functionality, 230
fundamental consciousness, 220, 271, 277, 302, 312, 315, 316, 317n, 345, 347, 350, 351
Fundamentalists, 371. *See also* Escapists
futile view, 243, 304, 309

Gampopa, 69
Ganden Monastery, 87
Garland Scripture, 24, 43, 83, 120, 121
Gautama, Shakyamuni Buddha, 112
genealogies, 354
general subject disregarding qualification, 107, 339
genius, 72, 177
genuine insight, 374

given private object, 95
God beyond gods (*Devātideva*), 8, 18, 187
going, critique of, 153
Golden Light Scripture, 23
Golden Rosary, 58, 63, 68, 73, 74
great: adepts, eighty-four, 41; compassion, 60, 114, 306; death, 169, 172
Great Champions of philosophy, 33, 281, 381
Great Chinese Commentary, 192, 200, 204-207
Great Elders, 34
Great Final Nirvana, 119, 120
Great Perfection, 148
Great Prayer Festival, 86
Great Seal (Mahamudra), 62, 148, 384n
Great Stages of the Path, 71, 75, 88, 130
Great Transcendent Insight, LTC, 130, 264n
Great Vehicle, *see* Universal Vehicle, 349
gross, objective selflessness, 350; personal selflessness, 308; selflessness, 138, 350n, 352-53; substances, 313
ground differential, 232, 234
ground, analytically discoverable, 294; of conventional designation, 238; of designations, 239; of symbolic designation, 238
groundlessness, 107, 127, 333
GRS, 367n, 368n, 370n, 374n, 375n
Gudmunsen, C., 25
Gun-thang 'Jam-dbyangs, 188n
Gunamati, 265
Gunashri, 265
guru, 80, 177

habit-pattern, 170, 297; of rational cognition, 372
habitual: perception, 325; reality-notions, 302; views of self, 181
habitual adherence, 243; to self-notions, 364; to naive reification, 157
Haribhadra, 287n
Heap of Jewels Scripture, 43
Heart of Transcendent Wisdom, 352
Heart of the Central Way (MH), 39, 271, 272n, 275
hell, 213, 312
herald of relativity, 260
hermeneutical: act, 129; enterprise, 113; questions, 88; schemes, scripture-based, chart, 122; strategies, 116-26
hermeneutics, science of interpretation, 112
Heruka Tantra, 47
heterodox, 208, 263, 302, 333, 348, 350; scholars, 305; schools, 262
Hevajra Tantra, 69, 76
Hiranyagarbha, Brahma, 187
history, 68, 70
holy: aftermath rational cognition, 282; equanimity, 247; equipoise, 366; equipoised intuition, 164; intention, 288, 306; truth of suffering, three natures of, 203; truth, four aspects of first, 354; truths, four, 191; wisdom, 255; wisdom, equipoise-, 220
Holy Father and Son, 22, 78, 80, 193, 265, 270, 272, 288, 306, 309, 373
Holy Land of India, Aryavarta, 33
Hopkins, P. J., 104n, 132n-38n, 365n
Hoshang Mahayana, 53, 328n
Hundred Thousand Transcendent Wisdom, 224, 256, 258
Hurvitz, L., 119n
hyperbolic imagining, Wittgenstein's, 95
hypothetical things, 180

"I": -habit, 309; -habit, unconscious, 304; notion, 301; -process, 371
icon of refuge field, 20
Idealism, 276
Idealist, 51-52, 136, 138, 148, 195, 251, 267, 308n, 313, 345-47, 350n, 353-54, 357, 362, 367n, 375; hermeneutic, 119; school, 88; scriptures, 27; similes, 226; system, 118, 261, 314n, 355, 374; system's non-production, 275; theory of genealogies, 209n; three natures, diagram, 118
Idealist-Dogmaticists, 51-52, 138, 317n
Idealists': negatee, 139; things susceptible to expression, 232n; view of identity, 197n
identifiable: existence, 272; objective identity, 294; production, 291; reality, 228; status, intrinsically, 192, 199
identification: of object of truth-habit, 285; of the negatee, 281, 368n

identified, 362; /identity, 294
identity, 362; and entity, 293; and identified (referent), 294-95; -teaching scriptures, 204. *See also* intrinsic identity
identity-reality, 194, 266-68
identity-unreality, 126, 192, 199, 200, 243, 244, 273, 278, 280; Centrist interpretation, 268; defined, 194; repudiation, 266; ultimate identitylessness, 268n; ultimate imagined, 269
identitylessness, 180, 193, 198, 204
ignorance, *see* misknowledge
Iida, S., 356n, 379n
illusion, 180, 225-26, 278
illusionlike aftermath wisdom, 145
illusory horses and elephants, 283-84
imagination, 148, 219, 226-28
imaginative construction, 198, 201, 237, 360, 371, 378
imaginatively constructed nature, 117-18, 194
imagined (nature), 192, 200-201, 217, 225, 243-46, 248, 278, 299, 345, 356, 359-60, 362
imagined reality, 238, 256, 278; as four misapprehensions, 224; as negatee, 247; described, 231-32; included among five categories, 267; typology of, 203n
imagined-identitylessness, 278; -non-production, 199
Immaculate Light, 70
immeasurables, four, 132
impermanence, 325, 334, 336, 339, 354
implicative negation, 166, 376. *See also* choice negation
import of relativity, 257, 259
inactivity, 253
incomprehensibility, total, 242
Inconceivable Praise, 260
independence, 138
independent: existence, 358; reality, 298; self, 262; status, 362; terms, 341; world, 262
Indian philosophy, 30-35
Individual Vehicle, 19-20, 42, 44, 85, 112, 117, 212, 238, 243-44, 299-301, 308n, 312, 350n, 354, 355; Canon, 303; disciples, 206; Saints, 144; Scriptures, 249; schools, 230, 233; sectarians, 222
Individualist, disciples, 120; eight attitudes of great, 247n; individual self-habit, 105; insight, 134; schools, 139, 233, 239; Scientists, 51
indivisible thing, impossibility of, 97, 285-86
Indra (Meghavahana), 8-14, 184, 187
inexpressibility of ultimate, 338n
inference, 113, 290, 324, 325n, 335, 338n; reasoning from an effect, 318
inferential, rational cognition, 338; validating cognition, 378
infinite regress, fault of, 317
initial mind at birth, 315
inquiry into contradictions (in SN), 191-92
insight path, 135
instantiating example, 325n
instinct, 132, 284, 312; articulative, 234n; defined, 311; for homogeneity, 234n; for misknowledge, 311; of all addictions, 311; of fundamental, 220
instinctual: misknowledge, 135, 144; propensities, 271, 311; self-habits, 136
insubstantiality, 350n, 356
integration: of samsara and Nirvana, 170; wisdom and compassion, 170
intellect, conventional, 296
intellectual, genius, 64; mental habits, 297; objective self-habits, 311; reification, 291; self-habit, 80, 136; wisdom, 126
intended meaning, 192, 348
intention, 305, 314, 355; holy, 288; inner, 276; of the Holy Ones, 266, 366; ulterior, 277, 279
intentional, analysis, 355; in meaning, 258
intentionality, 171-72, 343
interdependent designativeness, 320
internal: contradictions, 354-55; formulation, habitual, 220; media, 248, 333, 340; subjective, 312; verbalization, 217
interpretability, 281, 312, 346, 349, 350, 351, 352, 353, 357, 359; Idealist idea of, 119; modes of, 249; of middle wheel, 207
interpretable meaning, 111, 189, 204, 248-51, 253, 255, 257, 259, 279-80, 345-48, 363, 381-82, 385; as subsequently contradicted or explicated,

interpretable meaning (*cont.*)
249n; etymology of, 254; Individualist idea of, 116; two modes of teaching, 350; types of, 124
interpretable-definitive, 140; Centrist idea of, 123; Idealist idea of, 248-52; rule of, 207, 208
intimate intention, 381
intimated basis (meaning), 348-49
intimative superficial (perfect reality), 223
intrinsic identifiability, 107, 125, 138, 140, 160-61, 163, 195, 234, 237, 240, 241, 256, 292, 313, 315, 324, 332, 334-35, 337, 345, 351-52, 355, 361, 367, 371, 374-75, 379; habit, 94, 164; habit, key definition of, 291; of relative and perfect, 197
intrinsic identity, 165, 191n, 192, 194, 195, 198, 210, 212, 224, 227, 234, 238, 248, 251, 256, 262, 263, 267, 269, 289, 293-94, 301, 313, 326, 335-36, 367n; anchor of reference, 163; defining passage, 91, 93-94; first wheel teaching of, 207; non-conventionality, 101; refutation of, 104; substantial, independent, 220; varieties of, 292
intrinsic objective existence, 342
intrinsic objectivity, 92, 108, 138, 163, 224, 335, 342; dissolved, 148; reification of, 160
intrinsic reality, 108, 138, 165, 167, 206, 227, 267, 283, 300, 303, 304, 314, 328n, 334, 338, 357, 361, 372, 375-76, 379; intrinsically identifiable, 228; negation, 308; self, 299; three qualities of, 285; uncaused, unchanging, unrelated, 285n
intrinsic realitylessness, 167, 207, 315, 327n, 337, 342, 351-53, 375, 376, 379, 381
intrinsic referentiality, 161
intrinsic unreality, 191-92, 196, 202, 275, 308
intrinsically identifiable, 329; entities, 359; existence, 211, 260, 307, 353; intrinsic identity, 216; intrinsic reality, 288, 365; objective referent, 367; other-production, 290; person, 350n; production, 367, 374; property, 144; real existence, 297; reality, 260, 331, 367; reality of relative, 266; self, 144, status, 94, 139, 232, 257, 279, 291, 295, 296, 299, 302-303, 313, 320, 327, 358, 362, 366, 372-73; thing, 328, 373
intrinsically identifiably: existent, 369; other, 320
intrinsically objective: condition, 296; referent, 291; status, 139
intrinsically real: causality, 290; status, 139, 329; things, 263
Introduction, *see* MA
Introduction Commentary, *see* MABh
intuition: aftermath illusory, 148; infallible ultimate, 283; mundane, 171; nonconceptual, 282; of nothingness, 170; spacelike samadhi-, 148
intuitive: knowledge, 367; wisdom, 152, 159, 367, 369
invariable concomitance, 319, 324
investigation of referents of conventions, 306
Investigation of the World, 380
Invincible Lord (Ajita), Maitreya, 75
Ishvarasena, 47

Jam-dbyangs bZhed-pa, 134n, 137-38n, 301n
Jayananda, 56, 324n, 326n, 346; inconclusive critique of privacy, 105-106
Jewel Garland (RA), 171-72, 258, 264, 308
Jewel Heap Scripture, 24, 165
Jewel Matrix (RGV), *Supreme Tantra*, 29, 30, 54
jeweler simile, 354
Jñanagarbha, 271, 274n, 283, 287-90
Jo-khang, Lhasa cathedral, 86
Jo-nang-pa (school), 58-61, 193n, 202n, 208n, 218n, 263n
Joshi, L. M., 35n

Kadampa, 54, 66
Kama, Anangapati, 15
Kamalashila, 51-52, 132, 253n, 273, 277-81, 286, 287, 288, 290, 323; analysis, 97-98; hermeneutic, 125; interpretation, 273-87; position, 284
Kant, 55
Kaschewsky, R., 65
Kashyapa Chapter, 165, 229, 374

keys of selflessness meditation, four, 137
Khu-lo mDo-sde-'bar, 326n
Khu-lo-tsva-ba, 326n
Khyung-po Lhas-pa, 70, 79
King of Samadhi Scripture (SRS), 131, 254, 353
kLong-chen Rab-'byams-pa, 62, 290n, 296n
knowable fact (jñeya), 147
Krishna, 16

la Vallee Poussin, L. de, 289n, 365n, 367n, 368n, 371n
LAS, *see Mission to Lanka*
lack: of intrinsic identifiability, 261, 350n, 353; of self-production-ultimate, 269
Lalitavistara, 114
Lamotte, E., 191n, 346n
Lamp of Concentrated Practice, 38, 76
Lamp of the Path (of Enlightenment), 56, 75
Land of Snows, 63
leap: into mystic union, 154; of faith, 150; theory, critique, 55
Lho-brag mKhan-chen Nam-mkha rGyal-mtshan, 84
liberation, 17, 18, 151, 243, 307, 312, 364; as addiction-elimination, 244; city of, 66; of intelligence by analysis, 98; the only truth, 262
liberative, Dharma, 71; technique, 114, 184; Truth, 149
life, 168, 253; and liberation, 257; lacking reality, 154
Life Migration Scripture, 233
life-cycle, 117, 244, 297, 306, 331
lifelessness, 253
lily-garden of Nagarjuna's treatises, 183
lion's roar, "freedom from identity," 179
literal: acceptability refuted, 250; expression, 349; insistence on negations, nihilistic, 199; meaning, 348
logic, 12, 57-58, 67, 74, 113
logical, concomitance, 137; negatee, 85, 281; privacy, 320n, 341n; reason, 323n, 324, 331; refutation of literalness, 251
logically private language, 91
Logician, 238, 332n, 342n, 368n, 379; -Centrist syncretism, 285n
Long-chen-pa, *see* kLong-chen Rab-'byams-pa
Lord, 191-92, 260, 348; as personification of reason, 73; of Death (Yama), 181; of Sages, 187
Lotus Scripture, 112, 120
love, 19, 26, 63, 147, 171; of wisdom, 89
LRCMchan, 327-28n
LTC, 370n
Luminous Lamp (Chandrakirti's), 41
Lva-ba-pa, 277

MA (*Introduction*), 41, 54, 57, 77, 142-43, 155, 163-64, 295, 298, 302-304, 306, 310, 315, 317n, 319, 329, 340, 351, 364-68, 371, 374, 378. *See also Introduction*
MABh (*Introduction Commentary*), 160-62, 165, 288-90, 300, 306-11, 315, 317, 328, 330-31, 345-46, 351, 361-64, 366
Madhyamaka, *see* Centrism
magic creation simile, 197, 248
magnificence, 74, 382
magnificent, 188n, 383; deeds, 20, 32; deeds lineage, 52
Mahakala,, 36, 184
Mahamati, 351
Mahamudra, *see* Great Seal
Mahasamghika school, 239
main reason refuting ultimate existence, 281-87
Maitreya, 18-21, 34, 84, 187, 356-59
MAlam (*Central Way Ornament*), 52, 275-76, 283, 286, 290, 323n
MAlamP, *see Central Way Ornament Elucidation*
MAlamV, *see Central Way Ornament Autocommentary*
MAlok, *see Central Way Illumination*
Manjughosha, 3, 63, 65, 81-82, 187. *See also* Manjushri
Manjushri, 5, 41, 45-46, 58, 71, 73, 88, 127, 384n; angelic preceptor, 63; Holy Lord, 80; icon, myth, 34; in heart lotus, 89; incarnate as Sakya Pandit, 58; incarnate in Tsong Khapa, 84; inspirer 111; sword vision, 83; visionary presence, 77-82
Mara, 16

Master (Nagarjuna), 260, 265
Master Scholars, 33-36, 188
master-slave simile, 307
materialist, 16-17
materialistic constructions, 243
Matilal, B. K., 377n
Matrcheta, 36-38, 115
MAV, *see Center and Extremes*
MAVB, 219-20, 245-46
MAVT, 227-28
Māyajālatantra, 29
meaninglessness, 153, 198
measure of the negatee, 146, 339
media, 134, 194, 312; twleve, 191, 203; two kinds, 248
meditation, 130-31, 135, 191
meditative wisdom, 126
Meeting of Father and Son Scripture, 286
Meghavahana, *see* Indra
memory, 317-20; -cognition, 319
mental, consciousness, 302; constructions, 343; constructs, 239; fabrications, 254; forces, six, 132-33; formulations, 215, 239; functions, 272, 314; habit of the philosophers, 291; phenomena, 24, 274
mere, absence of concrete impenetrability, 291; construction, 360; designation, 301, 359, 366, 369; designativeness, 306; experience, 319; illusion, 288; mental construction, 358-59; names, 356, 369; nominality, 194-95, 296, 356; signs, 369; verbal designation, 299
merely designative, two meanings of, 296
methods of conversion, four, 120
MH, *see Heart of the Central Way*
Middle Stages of the Path, 130, 146-47
Middle Transcendent Insight, 130
middle wheel of Dharma, 206
Milarepa, 53, 69
Mimamsa, 14-17, 45
mind, 24, 274; and mental functions, 272
mind-only, 274-76, 281, 345; references, two kinds, 346; system, 385
Ming Emperor Yung Lo, 86
mirage simile, 308
misapprehension of emptiness, 213
misknowledge, 4, 92, 96, 124, 141, 159, 177, 309, 365, 371; addictive, 309; unconscious, 309
misknowledge-governed habitual perceptions, 171
Mission to Lanka (LAS), 27, 113, 119, 252, 270, 275-76, 281, 286, 313, 314, 327-28n, 346-47, 350-51
mKhas-grub rJe, 74, 202n, 234n, 346n
MMk, *see Wisdom*
mode of emptiness (relative of imagined), 202
monastic Order, 85
Mongols, 58
monism, Vedantic, 60
monistic absolutism, 160
moon of philosophers (Chandrakirti), 384
moon-in-water simile, 262
Mother Hundred Thousand, 280
Mother Scripture, 118, 194n, 229, 242, 247, 249-50, 252, 256-57, 277, 307, 314, 352, 356-57, 359, 361
Mother of All Buddhas, 384n
MS (*Universal Vehicle Compendium*), 195n, 209, 218, 226, 229, 231, 233-34, 236-37, 239-42, 248-49, 358
MSA (*Scripture Ornament, Universal Vehicle Scripture Ornament*), 29, 34, 75, 209, 219, 223-26
MSAV (*Scripture Ornament Commentary*), 225
mundane: analysis, 296; conventionality, 352; conventions, 292, 329, 338; intuition (prejudiced), 171; terms, 357; conventional terms, 333
Muni, 248, 264
Murti, T.R.V., 57, 150n
mysticism, 129, 140; as egocentrist tendency, 92; of Tantras, 68

Nagabodhi, 265
Nagadhvaja, 218n
Nagarjuna, 10, 12, 20-21, 24-25, 34, 36, 41, 52, 55, 72, 75, 80, 83, 84, 125, 128-29, 136, 140, 142, 147, 151, 153, 155, 159, 160, 161, 162, 172, 183, 187, 253, 257, 262, 264, 276, 289, 294, 300, 303, 305, 307-309, 314, 320, 328n, 331, 343, 345-46, 349, 361, 364, 380-83; explanation of, 256-64; legend of, 22-25, 30-31; refutes charge of nihilism, 156; relativity as peace, 103; Tantric, 76
naive, fear of emptiness of the, 258
naive intuition (as misknowledge), 159
naive realism, 25, 79, 118, 278

Naiyayika, 13-14, 17, 332n
name: as anomalous creation, 266; and form, 245
Nan Ch'uan, 128-29
natural: liberation, 191, 204; mind, 320; conventional validating cognition, 342
nature, 370; of reality, 168; /nature-possessor, 261, 362n
nectar of emptiness, 261
negatee, 137, 143, 267, 282, 286-87, 290, 326, 332, 352, 375, 381; described, 231-35, 291; logical, 281; measure of, 146; rational, 80, 297; refutand, 329; reification as, 242; self as, 261
negation, 165, 286-87, 332, 381; absolute, 56, 125; of conventional other-production, 370; of dogmaticist privacy, 324; of external objects, 314; of external things, 241, 347; of extremisms, 211-47; of four alternatives, 287, 327n; of indivisible atoms, 313; of intrinsically identifiable status, 104, 366; of intrinsic identifiability, 320; of subject and object, 240; of subject-object dichotomy, 241-42; of the external, 313-14; of truth-status, 124; of ultimate status, 374; rational, 364; two kinds of, 166, 376
negation-ground, 375
night-lily garden, 382
nihilism, 113, 118, 177, 198, 213, 263, 300, 307, 315, 328n, 335-53, 375n, 381; as absolutism, 95; charge denied by Wittgenstein, 98-99; cured by reason, 163; ethical, 53; no causality, 264; skeptical, 68
nihilist, 308, 371n
nihilistic: constructions, 378; emptiness (*chad stong*), 263n, 375n; relativism, 160; skepticism, avoided, 98; view, 79, 259, 262, 264, 315
Nirvana, 24, 179, 181, 268, 300, 306, 331, 368n; as highest bliss, 157; not absolutely existent, 153; the sole truth, 301; Tsong Khapa's, 87
Nirvana/samsara-relation, 150, 156, 159
No Fear from Anywhere, 265-66
no findable "this" (in Dialecticist context), 109
no position position, *see* positionlessness
nominal: cognition, 238; consciousness (habitual inner verbal), 220; designation, 335, 357-59, 363; status (of imagined), 194
non-acceptance of dogmaticist logical privacy, 320-44
non-analytic: cognitions, 284; conventional, 317n, 330n, 331; mundane conventions, 330; presentation, 294; status, 100
non-assertion of private reason, 332-41
non-conceptual: consciousness, 241; validating cognition, 336; wisdom, 126
non-defective cognition, 369, 373
nondualism, 168
nondualistic insight, 148
nonduality, 23, 73, 146, 160, 214, 351
non-egocentrist, philosophical, 90-91, 95-96
non-emptiness, 157, 160, 339
non-objective object, 168
non-perception-of-related-fact reason, 286
non-perception-perception, 168
non-phenomenality of universals, 232
non-production, 191, 199-200, 204, 253, 254, 256, 275, 280, 349, 351
non-qualified perception, 343n
non-substantiality, 179
non-substantiation by validating cognition, 320
nothingness: realm of, 133; -emptiness, 169; -experience, 169
noumenon, uncreated, 24
Nya-dpon dPal, 72
Nyaya, 45

O-de-gung-rgyal (Ol-kha retreat), 84, 184n
object-ultimate, reality, 220
objective, 313-14, 362; basis of names and signs, 232; condition, 270-71, 369; condition of referents, 341; element, 248; entity, 298; existence, 339-40; identifiabilty in nominal things, 239; medium, 248; non-existence, 340; object (of "I"-habits), 304; obscurations, 221n, 232-33, 239, 242, 308, 311-12; reality, 125, 337n; referent, 356; self, 138, 231, 245-46, 256, 307; self-habit, 144, 243, 245, 297, 302, 308-309; self-habit-varieties, 231-32, 245; status,

objective status (*cont.*)
328n, 342; universals, 232, 246; world, 340n
objective selflessness, 137, 143, 146, 196-98, 200, 202, 205, 215, 218, 232-33, 243-45, 247, 279, 298-301, 308, 348, 349, 351, 360, 364; as identity-unreality, 231; gross, 350
objective-: existence-perception, 168; non-existence-perception, 168; reality-status, 376n; self-reification, 231, 244; status-unqualified-perception, 168
objectively existent phenomenon, 337, 342
objectivity, 335; -habits, 141
Ocean of Reason (RG), 11, 88, 264n, 316n, 317n, 370n
omniscience, 9, 311, 361; noumenal and phenomenal, 49
ordinary personal selflessness, 350-51
Ornament of Essence of Exposition, 73
Ornament of Realizations (AA), 29, 54, 68
Ornament of Scriptures of Universal Vehicle, see MSA
Ornament of Wisdom-Illumination Scripture, 255n
orthodox, 212; Buddhist scholars, 305; schools, 262, 321
other-emptiness (other-voidness), 61, 193n, 202n, 245, 375
other-production, 290, 368n, 374
ownerlessness, 253

Padma Sambhava, 53, 140
Pai Chang, 128-29
Paradigm Treatises, 265
paramārtha, meaning analyzed, 282
Paramartha, 205n
Paramarthasamudgate, 191-92, 196-98, 203-204
part/whole-analysis, 97, 273
particular, 325n; discrimination, wheel of, 251; nature, 314
path: of enlightenment, 136; of philosophical reason, 384; of philosophy, 136, 188; of purification, 243; of reason, 74, 383; of the Buddha, 263; to enlightenment (phenomenology of), 130-49
pattern of emptiness, 233, 246
peace, 114, 181
peaceful, 132-33, 188
Peerless Philosophy, 89-111, 188
perception, 290, 324-25n, 335, 343; of inconsistent fact reasoning, 272, 286n; of related fact reasoning, 286n
perceptual: absolutism, 109; habits, three, 168, 342; objects, 373
perfect (nature, reality), 117-18, 126, 196-97, 200, 244-47, 269, 345; defined, 202; pure object, 221
perfect enlightenment, 64
performancelessness, 374
permanence, 138, 349
permanent: phenomenality of Buddha-essence, 346n; phenomenon, 349; self, 348-49
person, 223, 253, 291, 301, 303
personal: egoism, 243; inference, 341; possessions, 275; self, 138, 259, 275, 300, 302, 364-65; self-habit, 144, 244, 297, 309; selflessness, 118, 137, 146, 244, 251, 298-301, 306-307, 350n, 352; self-reification, 231
personification: of reason, 73, 151; of validating cognition, 189
personlessness, 253
Pha-tshab, 56
Phag-mo-gru, 79
Phenomenal-Noumenal Discrimination, 29
phenomenality, of the terminated, 316n; of three times, 317n
phenomenologically omniscient intuition, 338
philosopher, 56, 90, 164, 167, 179, 291, 302, 343, 385
philosophical: analysis, 92, 295-96n; cognition, 109, 146; reasoning, 297; view, 135
Philosophical Investigations (PI), 92-94, 96, 98-100, 102-103, 110, 322n, 340
Philosophical Sixty, see YS
philosophies (lower and higher), 223
philosophy, 50-52, 64, 89, 96, 103, 150, 172, 381-82n, 384; as path of liberation, 103, 171; love of wisdom, 21; Sutra (vs. Tantra), 80
Phya-pa Chos-seng, 50, 56-57
PI, *see Philosophical Investigations*

place, as object of truth-habits, 303
PM, *see Wisdom*
positionlessness, 61, 80, 154, 160, 329-31
possession (of fundamental), 315
possessiveness, 304
Poussin, *see* la Vallee, Poussin, L. de
PPMMV (*Lucid Exposition*), 22, 41, 54, 57, 93, 106-109, 253, 254, 257-58, 272n, 278n, 292, 294-95, 316, 323, 329n, 331-32, 338, 341, 378, 381
PPP, 229
practical Dharma as the three spiritual educations, 115
Practice Tantras, 70
Praise for Relativity, 85. *See also Short Essence*
Prajnaparamita, goddess, 3, 384n
Prāsaṅgikamādhyamika, Dialecticist Centrist, 39
Precious Garland (RA), 34, 171-72, 264
presentation of conventional, 292-99
presuppositions of philosophers, 56
primordial peace, 191, 204
principle of relativity, 183
principles of conversion, four, 120-21
Principles of Elucidation, see VY
privacy, 40, 103-11; defined and justified, 320n
private, 321n, 341; list of combinations, 105; dogmaticism, 320n, 323, 326, 332, 339, 341-42, 344; dogmaticist syllogism, 328; domain, 91; experiential data, 90; language, 90-91, 94, 108, 322n; mark, 322n; object, 91, 94, 104, 107-108, 164, 169, 337n, 339n, 340n; probanda, 341; reason, 163-64, 322n, 326, 327, 341; syllogism, 322n; thesis, 326; valid object, 338n; view, 322n
probandum, 272, 318, 319, 324, 328, 330, 341, 343, 378, 380; of negation, 166, 376; of syllogism, 337; -property, 324-25
production: from four extremes, 327n; from self, 333; from self and other, 290; intrinsically identifiable, 290; -unreality, 192, 195, 200, 278
productionlessness, *see* non-production
profound, 68, 188n, 355, 381-83; and magnificent scriptures, 75; emptiness, 213; insight into selflessness, 384n; intention, 383; philosophy, 51; reality, 118; teaching, 263; ultimate reality, 349; view, 20, 50, 79, 147; terrific, enlightenment-in-practice, 258
proof: and refutation, 341; of emptiness by relativity-reason, 167, 171; of identity-unreality by reasons of confusion, incompatibility, and multiplicity, 237; of universal emptiness, 172
property-notions, habitual, 144
provable property, 325n
proving intrinsic realitylessness, 378; selflessness, 378
PrPr (*Lamp of Wisdom*), 266-68, 270, 273-74, 323, 341, 380
PrPrT (*Lamp of Wisdom Commentary*), 253, 265n, 274, 377, 380
pseudo-Dialecticists, 251n, 371n
psychology, 317n; of the path, 130-49
public, reason, 105; dialecticism, 321; inference, 342n; syllogism, 324, 341-43
pure: consciousness, 233, 308n; information, 229, 239, 242, 274, 275
Pure Land Scriptures, 121
pure lands of bliss, 32, 171; negation, 379; objects, 196, 197, 202, 221, 232; reason, 172; object-ultimate, 196, 261
purification of the three spheres, 354
PV, *see Treatise on Validating Cognition*
PVi, 218

qualificative designations, 234n, 244
Questions of Anavatapta, 278
Questions of King Dharanishvara, 353-54
Questions of Maitreya Chapter, 252, 355-63
Questions of Rashtrapala Scripture, 114, 188
quiescence, 130; /insight-integration, 132

RA, *see Precious Garland*
rational: analysis, 327n; cognition, 283, 285, 330, 370, 371-72, 379, 380; cognition ultimacy-analytic, 148, 282; cognition of immaculate equanimity, 261; cognition, holy-aftermath-, 282; negatee, 80, 297; negation, 240, 364, 371
rationality, 113, 170, 342
Ratnakarashanti, 252n, 276

real: nothingness, 169; production, objective, 284; self, 284; status, 139, 281
Real Connoisseur, Buddha as, 151
realism, naive, 25
Realists, 219, 223, 232, 238, 289, 291, 327; sages of the, 336; systems of the, 231
reality, 168, 180, 218, 267, 308, 345; constructed, 361; discriminatively constructed, 360; imaginatively constructed, 360; imagined, 361; of nonexistence, 379; relative, 361; superficial, 361; three types of, 193; ultimate, 361; -imaginations, 361; -notions, 302; -status, types of, 125; -unreality, 194. *See also* two realities
realityless causality, 315
realitylessness, 124, 205, 215, 224, 230, 254, 280, 342, 345, 347, 360-61; advocate of, 212; integrated with great compassion, 259; of externals, 274; system of, 385. *See also* unreality
realization: of intrinsic unreality, 309; of relativity, 346; of selflessness, 309
Realization of Vairocana, 70
reason, 45, 168, 171, 272, 319, 330, 332, 343, 376, 378-79; as experiential, 116; discarded mystically, 150; ground for ethics, 151; non-perception of related fact, 286; of philosophers, 383; of relativity, 104, 137, 146, 163, 286, 324, 342, 365-66; personified, 12; proving probandum, 327; relationship with enlightenment, 166; sacrifice of, 13; ultimacy-analytic, 283; varieties of, 272; /concentration, 126; /faith-complementarity, 74
reasoning, 324; absence of unity/multiplicity, 286; analytic of ultimacy, 285, 386; diamond smithereens, 286; determining reality, 364; negating four-alternative production, 286; negating four-extreme-production, 364-65; negating personal self, 366; negating production from existent or nonexistent, 286; negating reification, three, 237
rebirth, 77, 302
Rebuttal of Objections (VV), 26, 155, 260, 320, 329n, 331, 335n, 381
Red-mda-ba, 59, 69, 74, 77, 80, 85
reference, scriptural, 258, 346
referent, 291, 293; and identity, 295; of conventional designations, 369; of conventional expressions, 297, 307, 372; of designation, 268; -investigation (by Wittgenstein), 94
referential bases, 358-59
refutand, *see* negatee
refutation: of literalness, 248-49, 349-50; of private dogmaticism, 323; of ultimate production, 287; of world-creator, 346
reification, 153, 214, 217, 231, 242, 277, 279, 375; absolutistic, 125; defined, 210-11; negation of, 231-42; of identity-reality, 234; of intrinsic reality, 124, 309; of objective self, 244; of real absolute, 153; twofold (conscious/unconscious), 231
reificatory view, absolutist, 146
relative (nature, reality), 79, 117, 118, 126, 195, 200, 212, 216-18, 245-46, 269, 278, 299n, 345, 356, 359-62; as empty of intrinsic reality, 270; as having intrinsically real status, 227; concern, 172; defined, 202; identifiable, 199; non-produced by self, 225; production, 366; the empty (*stong gzhi*), 247; twofold (per Idealists), 218-23; ultimate-unreality, 195-96
relativistic absolutism of wisdom, 160
relativistic interpretation of central way, 95, 165
relativistic origination, *see* relativity
relativity, 7, 10-11, 108, 171, 177-78, 180-81, 260-64, 308, 310, 324, 342, 352, 361, 373, 375n; as all there is, 153; central way, 158; eight properties of, 258; inner and outer, 288; of logic, 102; royal reason of, 365; -unreality-equivalence, 256
reliances, four, 113, 115, 255
repudiation, 125, 198, 210-14, 217, 231, 250-51, 264, 266, 277-78; defined, 210-11; how to abandon, 264; nihilistic, 125, 214
repudiative: nihilism, 199; view, 146
retentiveness (of fundamental), 315
RG, *see Ocean of Reason*
rGyal-tshab Dar-ma Rin-chen, 73

Rin-chen bZang-po, 54
Rin-chen rDo-rje, 69
rJe Rin-po-che, *see* Tsong Khapa
rMa-bya Byang-chub brTson-'grus, 326n
rNgog-lo-tsva-ba, 50, 54-56, 80, 147
roar of emptiness, 180
root-consciousness, 239
rope as the empty (relative), 245
rope-snake simile, 213, 245-46, 267-68, 361
royal reason of relativity, 137, 365ff.
Reugg, D. S., 188n, 244n
Rva-greng monastery, 88

Sacred: Discourse, 187; Doctrine, 112
Sahajavajra, 277
Sakya Pandita, 50, 57-59
salutations, 10-12
samadhi, 13, 18, 383
Samantabhadra, 384
Samkhya, 16-17, 45
samsara-is-Nirvana-view (absolutist error), 150
Saraha, 83
Sarasvati, 83
Saunders and Henze, 90-91n, 106, 110n
Savior (*Natha*), 22, 177-79; Manjughosha, 188; Nagarjuna, 253, 276, 287
science, 58, 70
scriptural, authority, 112, 304, 313; reference, 379
scripture, 341, 345, 347, 352, 382
Scripture on Ultimate Emptiness, 222
Scripture Ornament, see MSA
Scripture Synthesis (SS), 75, 258, 346, 349, 354
scriptures: discriminating identity and identitylessness, 204; of definitive meaning, 254; teaching identitylessness, 204; teaching identity, 204; three types, 203
SDV, *see Analysis of Two Realities*
SDVV, *see Analysis of Two Realities Subcommentary*
second: consequence, 164; key, 140; renaissance, 111; wheel, 280, 352
Secret Biography, 78-81
Secret Biography Invocation, 82
self, 85, 140, 253, 257, 300, 302-305, 345, 348; and possessions, 307; conventional existence of, 101; defined, 298; intrinsic reality, 299; self-sufficient, 302; -advocate, 91; -conscious, apperceptively, 221; -emptiness (*rang stong*), 263n, 375, 376n; -experience, 320; -habit, intellectual and instinctual, 80, 136, 141, 243-44, 246, 297n, 308, 312; -habits, personal, 244; -production, 333, 368n, 374; -reality, 179; -sufficiency, 138; -sufficient person, 310, 350n; -theories, 350
selflessness, 3, 21, 88, 131, 197, 256-57, 259, 275, 285, 302, 307, 354, 361, 376-77; defined, 298; meaning of, 251; objective, 243; of consciousness, 274; of person, 244, 366; ontic and ethical, 171; pure object ultimate, 220; twofold, 134; -advocate, 91. *See also* objective selflessness; personal selflessness
selflessnesses, two, 267, 283, 288, 298, 312
selves, two, 298, 316. *See also* objective; personal
sensation, 290. *See also* aggregates
sense cognition, undistorted, 296
serenity, 81; meditation, 241. *See also* quiescence
Seven Branch Texts of Validating Cognitions, 73
Seven Hundred, 258
Seven Logical Treatises, 273n
seven modes of establishment of self, 365
sevenfold analysis, 370
Shakyamuni, 9, 19, 20, 32, 50, 151, 183, 260; as philosopher, 33; Buddha, 5; his silence, 129; the vision of, 182
Shambhu, 187. *See also* Shiva
Shankara, 39, 48-49
Shantarakshita, 50-52, 265, 273-75, 281, 286-88, 290, 313n, 323, 336n, 338n; his hermeneutic, 125; his interpretation, 273-87; his philosophic position, 59
Shantideva, 54
Shariputra, 329
Shiva, 8, 13-14, 37
Short Essence of True Eloquence, 175-84
Shramanera sDom-brtson bSod-nams bLogros, 385
Siddhas, 382
sign-habit-orientation, 85
sign-habits, 170, 343

signification process, 222
signlessness, 3, 253, 348, 354, 374
silence: as definitive, 129; critique of dogmatism, 160; golden, 89, 172; of Buddhas, 128, 160; of the sages, 152; referential, 92; various types of, 129; Vimalakirti's, 23, 92; Wittgenstein's, 92; /speech nondual integration, 173
Silver Book, Tsong Khapa's, 130
Simhanada, Tsong Khapa's future Buddha-name, 83
simile of illusion, *see* illusion
Sitabhyudaya, Devasharma's central way commentary, 40
six limits, Tantric hermeneutic scheme, 76
Sixfold Canon of Philosophy, 26
sixth bodhisattva stage, 136, 364
skeptical: nihilism, 68; relativism, 154; relativists in Tibet, 155
skepticism: dialectical, 68; nihilistic, 55; systematic, 166
skill in liberative technique, 112
sKyabs-mchog dPal-bzang Lotsawa Rinpoche, 85
smoke: -in-the-lake example, 379; -fire-example, 272
SN, 231-33, 242-44, 249-52, 256-57, 259, 266-67, 269-70, 273, 275, 278-81, 327, 345, 347, 353, 355-56, 359, 363; explained, 277-81; imagined-negation, 242. *See also Elucidation of Intention*
Snellgrove, D. L., 69
social: communication, 293; conventions, 293-94, 307, 319, 365, 369; conventional existence, 369; conventional reality, 368; reality, 164; superficial, nonanalytic reality, 101
Socrates, 90
solitary sage, 243
sophist, 90
soul, 253, 302, 347; -theories, 208, 347-48
sound, 334, 336, 339
space: as imagined, 241; as noumenon, 146; mere formlessness of, 197; -like perfect reality, 198
spacelike: equipoise, 126; samadhi intuition, 148
speech: golden, 89, 172-73; the supreme Buddha-deed, 183
spirit of enlightenment, 26, 46, 170-71, 343
spiritual teacher, 383
sPyan-snga Rin-po-che of the Phag-mo-gru Kagyu, 69
SS, *see Scripture Synthesis*
ŚS (*Emptiness Seventy*), 309
Stages of Array, 76
Stages of Meditation, 132
Stages of the Path of Enlightenment, 54, 72, 326
Stages of Yoga Practice, 30, 42
states of mind, nine, 132-33
status, table of types, 139
Stcherbatski, T., 46, 57, 104n, 150n, 292n, 294n
Sthiramati, 44, 188, 227, 229, 265, 267
stores, two, 300
stream-winner, 312, 329
Streng, F., 150n
Subhuti, 329
subject, 343; -object dichotomy, 138, 168, 197n, 275, 308; -object-difference, 231, 244; -objects-duality, 226, 239, 290, 362; -unfindability in emptiness, 109
subjective, 313-14, 362
subjectlessness, thesis-fault of, 107, 333
substantial: dichotomy, 241; existence (of person), 302; inexistence of conditioned, 272; non-establishment, 267; otherness, notions of, 320; self, 302; self-sufficiency, 301, 352; subject-object dichotomy, 233, 256, 375; subject-object difference, 259
substantiality, 288, 356, 362
substantially existent, 220, 271
substantive, designations, *see* ascriptive, 234n (*see also* ascriptive and descriptive designation); nature, 201
substantivism, 341n
substantivist, 17, 98
subtle: negatee, 328; objective selflessness, 298n, 353, 375; personal selflessness, 298n, 308; selflessness, 138, 308, 350n, 352; substantivism of Dogmaticist Centrism, 104
Subtle Weaving (VP), 358
subtly discriminative wheel of Dharma, 117
Suchness, 170; absolute transcendent,

149; as intimative superficial, 223; opposite of Thatness, 149n
Sudhana, the bodhisattva, 83
Sugata, 21, 187, 254
Supercommentary, 244, 246-47
superficial, 92, 254, 260, 289, 294; as baseless, 215-16; as duality, 225; cognition, 284, 368n; existence, 214, 219, 221-22, 369, 371; objects, 338; production allowable, 98; reality, 79-80, 118, 123, 253, 261, 274, 277, 290, 295, 325n, 337, 340, 361; sense, 340; three types of, 223; truth, 309; /ultimate, modes of, 123, 193, 219-23
superficiality, 108, 337
Supreme Bliss, 70, 76, 87
supreme bliss, relativity as, 158
Supreme Emanation Body, 9
Supreme Meditation, 75
Supreme Philosopher, 151, 260
Supreme Tantra, see Analysis of Jewel Matrix
Sutra and Tantra, 68
Svātantrikamādhyamika (Dogmaticist Centrism), 40
syllogism, 319, 333, 341, 378
symbolic: awareness, 298; interpretation of figurative speech, 254
Synthesis, see Synthesis of Validating Cognition
Synthesis of Educations, 75
Synthesis of Essence of Intuition, 221
Synthesis of Validating Cognition (PS), 12, 45, 47, 73
system of the Champions, 256

taking life, 354-55
Tantra, 20, 27, 53
Tantric: literature, 17, 77; methodology, 81; Vehicle, 382
Tara, 83
Taranatha, 36, 43
Tathagata (Transcendent Lord), 152-53, 261, 306, 349, 350, 354
Tathāgatagarbhasūtra, 208n
Teacher (as Buddha-name), 11-12, 177-78, 183, 204, 258, 309, 311, 348; of Men and Gods, 113
Teaching, 147, 178, 181, 183, 383
Teaching of Akshayamati Scripture (AMN), 43, 123, 126, 127, 253, 255, 353
teaching of relativity, 183
ten equalities, 364
Ten Stages (DBS), 43, 270, 313, 347, 364
terminated thing, as phenomenon, 315-17
tetralemma, 154, 327n
That Art Thou, 15, 129
That Place, 49, 55, 129, 188, 384
Thatness, 130, 135, 157, 189, 340, 347, 351, 383; absolute immanent, 149; of the Teaching, 89, 149-74, 188; ultimate, 85
therapeutic philosophy, 103
thesislessness, 329n, 331
third wheel of Dharma, 204, 206, 353
Thirty (Trimś.), 42, 44, 193
Thirty Commentary, by Sthiramati, 228
THIS (you do not even see it!), 110
thorough investigations, four, 240, 242n, 243
three: collections, 115; doors of liberation, 348; modes of unreality, 249; natures, 61, 117, 201-203, 299n, 345, 355, 361; perceptual habits, 168, 342; poisons, 310; qualities of intrinsic reality, 285n; realities, 266, 281, 359, 361, 363; reasonings against reification, 356, 358; types of wheels of Dharma, 251; unrealities, 203, 248, 277; ways to determine definitiveness, 252; wheels of Dharma, 32, 204, 352-53; wisdoms, 283; -aspected convention, 323n; -nature theory, 125
Three Bodies of Buddha, 19
Three Principles of the Path, 149, 170
threefold analysis, 340
Tibetan Buddhism, view of early, 52, 54
Tibetan philosophy, development of, 52-55
TJ, *see Blaze of Argument*
tolerance of non-production, 224
Traditionist, 24, 42, 93, 138, 232, 289, 291, 317n; Dogmaticist, 125, 138, 287n, 312n; -Idealist, 319n
Transcendence Vehicle, 69-70, 382
transcendences, 300
transcendent: as a mirage, 153; not unknowable, 147
transcendent experience, 169

transcendent insight, 4, 17, 54, 88, 130, 132-49, 169; five stages of, 134-35; stage one of five, 147; two types, 134
Transcendent Lord, *see* Tathagata
transcendent wisdom, 32, 356, 384n
Transcendent Wisdom, 3, 24, 57, 70, 73, 82, 112, 117, 123, 125, 127, 131, 193, 288, 330n, 349, 363
Transcendent Wisdom 8,000, 119, 229, 252
Transcendent Wisdom 18,000, 119, 252, 355
Transcendent Wisdom 18,000 Commentary, 247
Transcendent Wisdom Heart, 280
Transcendent Wisdom Hundred Thousand, 88, 280
Transcendent Wisdom Instruction, 251-52, 276
transcendental doctrine, 289
Transcendental Praise, 261
transcendentalism, 53
transcendentalist misinterpretation, 150
transformative: experience, 65; precepts, 66, 71, 76
translator, *Lo-tsva-ba* (public eye), 4
transmigration, 154
Treasury Abhidharma (AK), 42
Treatise on Validating Cognition (PV), 47, 73, 229-30
true: eloquence, 383; production, 284; status, 281, 343; unity/plurality, 137
truth, 4; of suffering, 117; of truthlessness, 171; -habit, 146, 170, 213, 285, 303, 309, 311n, 312, 343; -limit, 360; -status, 118, 138-39, 146, 208, 251, 263, 282, 285, 357, 374n, 381
Truth Body, 18, 25, 172
truthlessness, 124, 208, 254, 257, 259, 278, 285, 326, 343, 380-81
Tsong Khapa, 3, 5, 9, 11, 16, 18, 38, 40, 51, 56, 80, 119, 140, 160, 166, 298n, 314n, 316n-17n, 322n-28n, 330n, 335n, 338n, 341n, 346n, 350-51n, 359n, 367n-68n, 370n-71n, 374n-75n, 382n, 384n; absolute provable, 151; appreciating Yuan Tsho, 205n; bLo-bzang Grags-pa, 385; biography, 63-89; enlightenment, 65; hermeneutician, 111-38; his oral lineage, 62-63; on view, 170; parallel to Wittgenstein, 93; predecessors, 49-63; scholarship, 331n
Tsuda, S., 70
Tushita, 28-29, 84, 87
twelve factors (links) of dependent origination, 203, 309-10
twenty emptinesses: golden, 88; silver, 88
Twenty Verses (Vimś.), 42-43, 241, 248
two: extremes, 307; extremisms, 378; great systems, 384; kind of ultimates, 282; kinds of negation, 376; methodologies, 383; methods (Idealist/Centrist), 275; modes of interpretable teaching, 350; obscurations, 221, 308; philosophical Champions, 382; realities, 31, 92, 107, 124, 147, 156, 215, 260, 289-90, 306, 333-34, 337, 340, 368n; self-habits, 80; selflessnesses, 266, 350, 364; stores, 300; ultimates: transcendent, conformative, 282
two-reality-theory, 117, 140
twofold analysis, 340
twofold selflessness, 299, 307

ulterior intention, 277
ultimacy, 337, 374; -analysis, 368n; -analytic rational cognition, 282
ultimate, 56, 197, 218, 254, 260, 277, 289; and superficial, 326; as nonduality, 225; as nonreality, 216; concern, 172; existence, 211, 219-21, 247, 284, 307, 381; eye as, 246; form, 356, 361; five characteristics of, 219; inexistence of conditioned, 272; intention, 373; intrinsic identitylessness (identity-unreality), 268n; intuition, 283; nature, 368; non-establishment, 251; non-existence, 307, 359; non-production, 283, 368n, 380; object (*paramārtha*), 282; particular, 292; production, 251, 284, 290, 333, 374; productionlessness, 381; proof of emptiness, 256; reality, 3, 50, 113, 118, 123, 152, 202, 253, 285, 288, 325n, 338, 349, 360, 362, 372, 373, 376, 382; reality intuitive wisdom, 71; reality knowability, 147; reality of selflessness, 88; reality transcendent, 168; realitylessness, 279-80; refutation of emptiness, 256; sense, 340; status, 139, 281-82, 295-96, 332, 339, 343,

358, 364, 370, 374; truth, 55, 149; two kinds, 282; selflessnesses, 266; ultimate-unreality, defined, 196; unreality, two types, 192, 195-97
Ultimate Contemplation, 70
Umapa, Lama, 77-82
unconscious, futile views, 304, 309; "I"-habits, 304; misknowledge, 309-10; objective self-habit, 285, 310; personal self-habits, 310; reification, 238, 291; self-habit, 80, 284, 297, 304, 371
uncreated, 188; as causal, 267n; noumena, fourfold, 146; -emptiness, 247
unenlightened person, 168, 170
unexcelled yoga insight, 148
Unexcelled Yoga Tantras, 53, 70, 76, 135, 147, 170
universal: characteristics in imagined, 241; compassion, 32, 384n; emptiness, 259; impermanence, 263; nature, 314
Universal Vehicle, 3, 19-20, 24, 26, 30-31, 43, 70, 86, 112, 244, 259, 275, 280, 299-301, 308, 312, 353-54; Canon, 355; path, 147; philosopher, 212; schools, 144; teaching, 117, 210; thought, 50-52
Universal Vehicle Compendium, see MS
universalist, 43, 131; disciples, 120; insight, 134; schools, 139
Universalist Compendium, see MS
universalists, 223, 352
universals, 232n, 325
unlocated Nirvana, 131
unpronounced verdicts, fourteen, 128
unqualified, general subject, 337; phenomenon, 342
unreality, 192, 194, 198, 204, 300, 330; of all things, 367; three types of, 193; ultimate, 113. *See also* realitylessness
unreflective inquiry, 297

vague (superficial) reality, threefold, 223
Vairocana Realization, 75
Vaisheshika, 13-14, 17, 45, 107, 317n, 334, 339, 343
Vajra, 11; Vehicle, 69-70, 86, 384n
Vajrabhairava, 70, 87
Vajradhara, 83
Vajrapani, 84
Vajrasattva, 70
valid reasoning, 67
validated cognizability of relativity, 326
validating cognition, 45, 56, 238, 251, 259, 284, 299, 320, 324, 326, 327n, 328, 331, 334-36, 339-43, 368n, 375; and enlightenment, 73; conceptual and perceptual, 140; unmistaken with regard to intrinsic identity, 107; verified by, 291
validating rational cognition, 372
Vasubandhu, 12, 20, 28, 41-44, 51, 58, 188, 193, 218, 222, 224-25, 227, 229, 244, 247-48, 252, 359
Vedanta, 15-17, 45
verbal, conventions, 372; Dharma (three collections), 115; universals, 232, 246
verbally ascriptive conventional intellect, 296
viability: of causality, 157; of conventional logic, 162; of illusory, 162
Victor, 10, 177, 187, 301, 338, 340, 363, 373, 383-84
view: Dialecticist, 78; of emptiness, 261; of nothingness, 198; of pure information, 242; of self, 303; of the profound, 78, 366; that realizes ultimate reality, 343
Vimalakirti, 23, 39, 127
Vinaya, Tsong Khapa's teaching at rNam-rtse, 85
Vishnu, Damodara, 16
voidness, *see* emptiness
Vows of Samantabhadra, 83
VS, *see Compendium*
VV, *see Rebuttal of Objections*
VY (*Principles of Elucidation*), 222-23, 248-50

way of the Champions, 382
Wayman, A., 70
Wen Tshig (Yuan Tsho), 192n
Western interpreters of the central way, 328n
Wheel of Dharma, 112, 117, 125; of determination of ultimate, 207; of fine discrimination, 207, 244; of four holy truths, 207; of identitylessness, 207
Wheel of Time (Kalachakra) Tantra, 59-61, 70, 76
White Exaltation, 265

will to enlightenment, *see* spirit of enlightenment
wisdom: goodness of, 384; illusion-like aftermath, 137; of relativity, 181; self-annihilative, 57; spacelike equanimous, 137; ultimate reality, 71; -technique, integration of, 145
Wisdom (PM, MMK), 5, 10, 25-26, 34, 39, 54, 88, 116, 128, 131, 136-37n, 142-43, 151-54, 156-58, 161, 169, 177, 257, 260-61, 263-64, 268n, 288, 289, 300-301, 305, 308, 316, 323, 327n, 331, 343, 364, 382n, 383-84; eight main commentaries on the, 265
Wisdom Commentary (RG), *see Ocean of Reason*
Wisdom Lamp, see PrPr
Wisdom Lamp Commentary, see PrPrT
Wisdom-Treasure, Manjushri, 77
wisdoms, three, 283
wishlessness, 3, 253, 348, 354, 374
Wittgenstein, L., 4, 25, 79, 103, 109, 152, 164, 320n, 337n, 340n, 343n; as Manjushri incarnate, 90-111; spontaneous Centrism of, 99
world champion of wisdom, 181
world-creator, 313
World-protectors, 184

Yajna, 297, 305
Yama Dharmaraja, as Dharmapala, 82
Yamantaka, 71
Yoga of the Essence, 90
yoga-method, 302
Yoga Tantras, 70
yogi, 366-67; of wisdom, 90
Yogini Tantras, 70
YS (*Philosophical Sixty*), 26, 260, 262-63, 276, 301, 307
YSV (*Philosophical Sixty Commentary*), 300, 303, 316, 368n
Yuan Tsho, sere Wen Tshig, 204-207
Yuan Wu, 129
Yung Lo, Ming Emperor, 89

Zen, 28, 37, 128, 131, 169; its hermeneutic, 127

Library of Congress Cataloging in Publication Data

Tsoṅ-kha-pa Blo-bzaṅ-grags-pa, 1357-1419.
Tsong Khapa's Speech of gold in the Essence of true eloquence.

(Princeton library of Asian translations)
Translation of: Legs bśad sñiṅ po.
Bibliography: p.   Includes index.
1. Dge-lugs-pa (Sect)—Doctrines—Early works to 1800.
2. Buddhism—China—Tibet—Doctrines—Early works to 1800.
I. Thurman, Robert A. F. II. Title.
III. Title: Speech of gold in the Essence of true eloquence.
IV. Title: Essence of true eloquence. V. Series.
BQ7950.T754L4313 1984   294.3'42   83-43096
ISBN 0-691-07285-X